INSIDERS' GUIDE®

INSIDERS' GUIDE®
NORTH CAROLINA'S SOUTHERN COAST
AND WILMINGTON SEVENTEENTH EDITION

*EMILY GORMAN-FANCY, REBECCA PIERRE,
KATE WALSH & HEATHER D. WILSON*

insiderinfo.us

Published and Marketed by:
By The Sea Publications, Inc.
P.O. Box 4368
Wilmington, NC 28406
(910) 763-8464
www.insiderinfo.us

Insiders' Guide®
is an imprint of
The Globe Pequot Press

SEVENTEENTH EDITION
1st printing

Publications from the Insiders' Guide®
series are available at special dis-
counts for bulk purchases for sales
promotions, premiums or fundrais-
ings. Special editions, including per-
sonalized covers, can be created in
large quantities for special needs. For
more information, please write to:

By The Sea Publications
P.O. Box 4368
Wilmington, NC 28406
or call (910) 763-8464

Cover Photo:
Belinda Keller Photography

Please Recycle

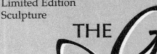

TABLE OF CONTENTS

DIRECTORY OF MAPS

Thank you to our Advertisers...

...for another great year on the Southern Coast!

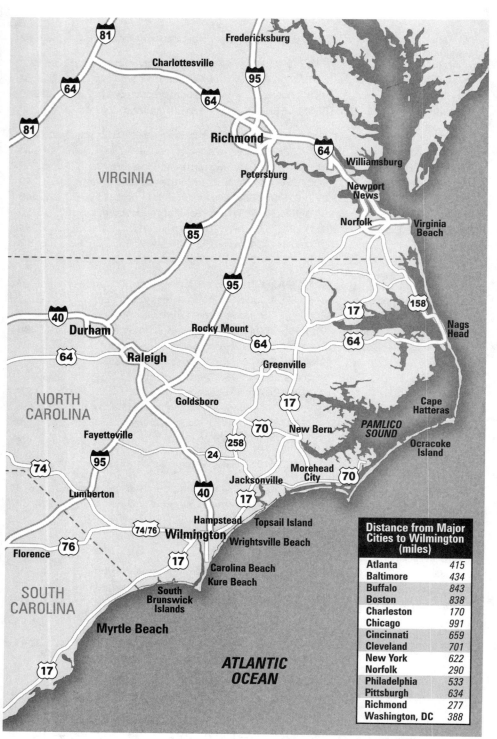

Distance from Major Cities to Wilmington (miles)	
Atlanta	415
Baltimore	434
Buffalo	843
Boston	838
Charleston	170
Chicago	991
Cincinnati	659
Cleveland	701
New York	622
Norfolk	290
Philadelphia	533
Pittsburgh	634
Richmond	277
Washington, DC	388

North Carolina Coast

N

25 mi.
50 km

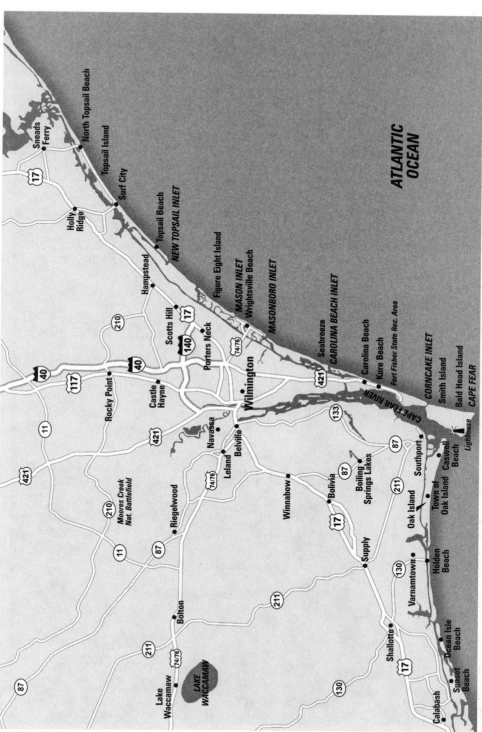

Topsail Island to Calabash

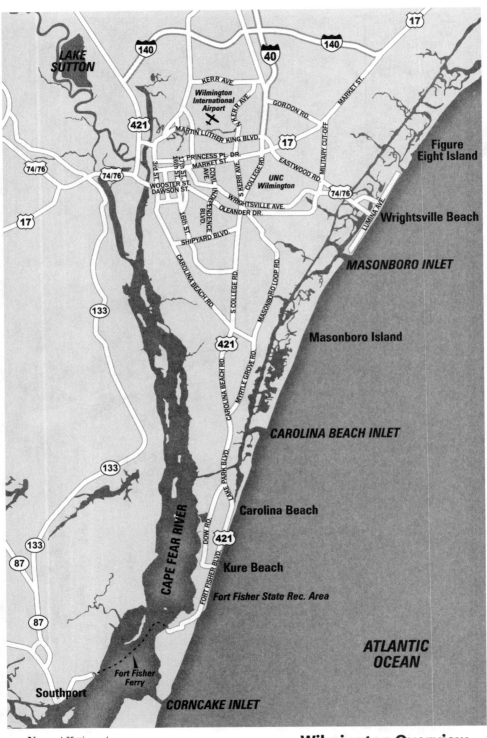

Wilmington Overview

N

25 mi.
50 km

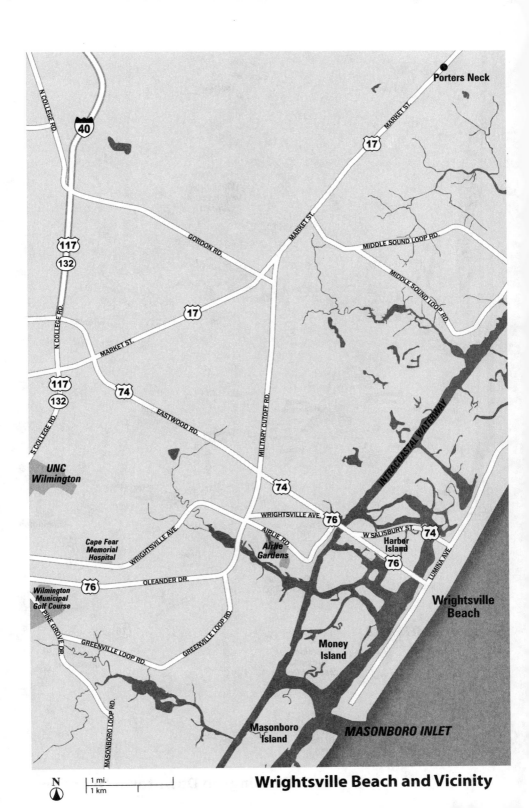

Wrightsville Beach and Vicinity

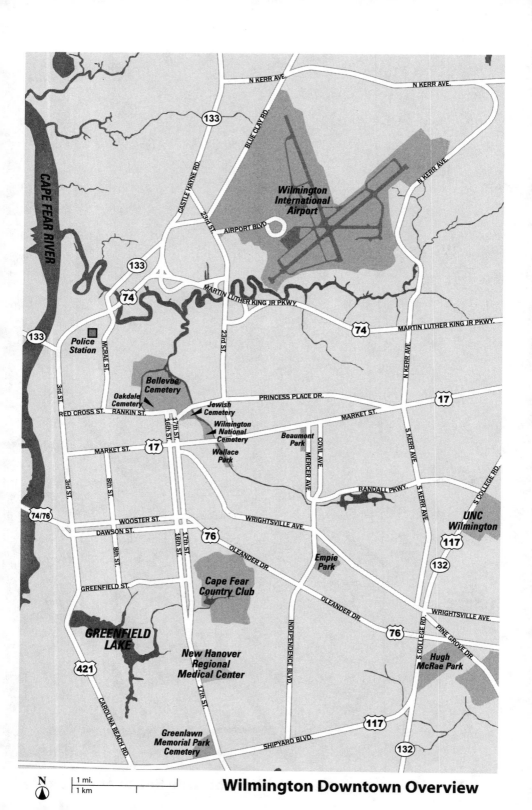

Wilmington Downtown Overview

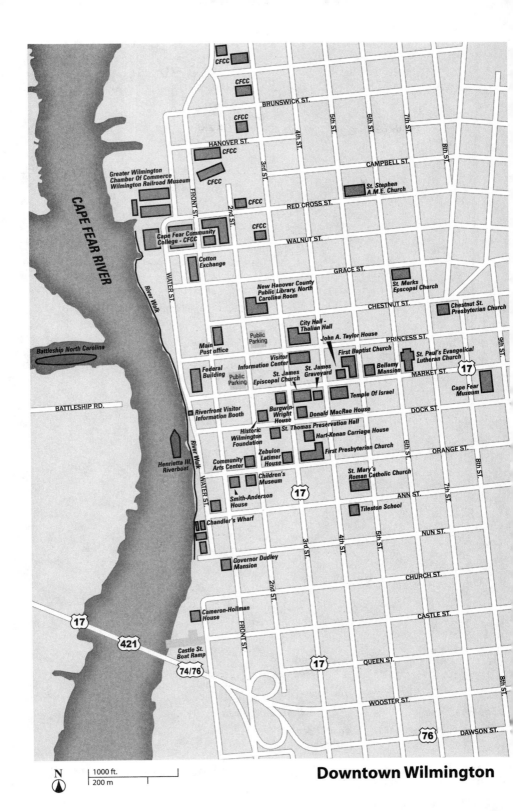

Downtown Wilmington

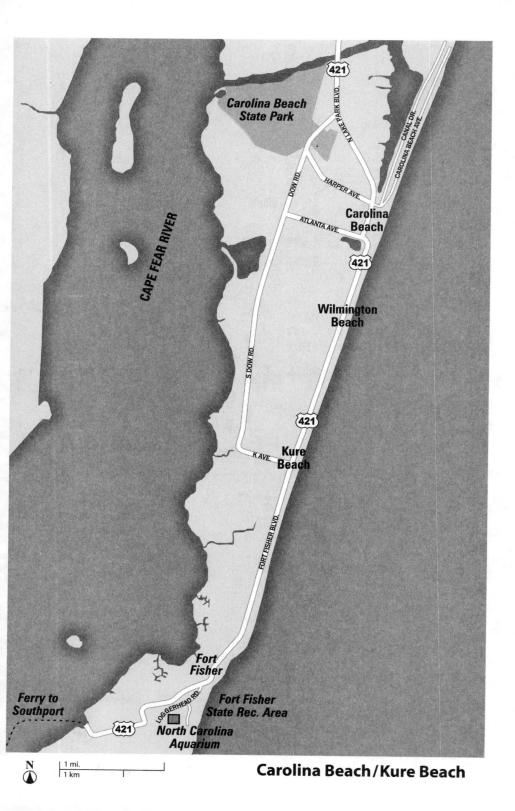

Carolina Beach / Kure Beach

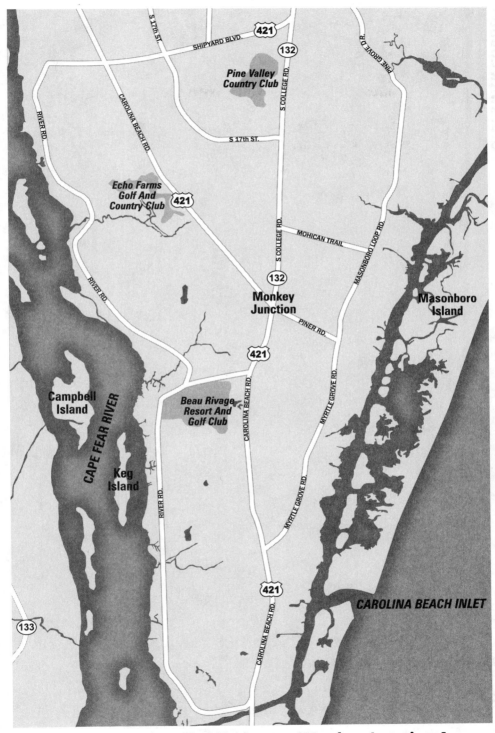

N

| 1 mi. |
| 1 km |

South Wilmington/Monkey Junction Area

Brunswick County

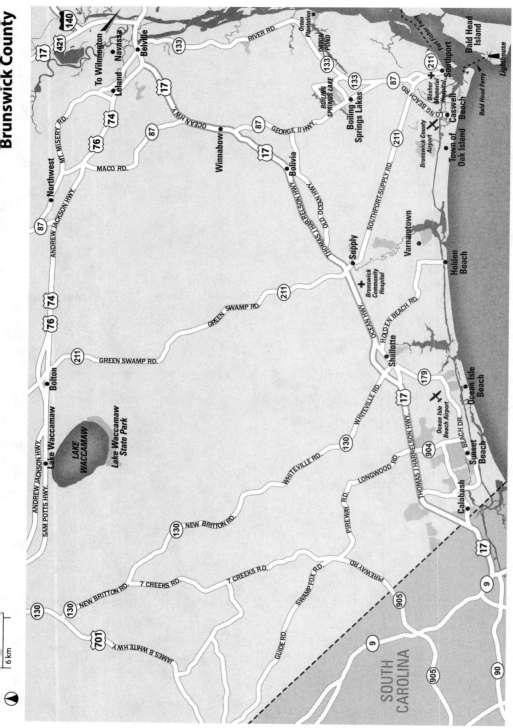

PREFACE

Welcome to the 17th edition of the *Insiders' Guide® to North Carolina's Southern Coast and Wilmington*. We think you'll find this book to be the most reliable and comprehensive collection of information, facts, tips and advice available for the North Carolina's southern coastal region extending from Topsail Island to the South Carolina border.

Inside this book you'll find recommendations on where to hear a symphony, charter a dive boat or shop for antiques. You'll find out where to rent a Jet-Ski, take a yoga class, buy original artwork, avoid traffic snarls, store your boat, locate emergency medical care or repair your bike. You'll also get invaluable information on how to plan an entire wedding on the southern coast.

Those relocating here will find our chapters on Real Estate, Retirement, Healthcare, and Schools and Childcare especially helpful when getting to know their new hometown.

This guide is not merely a checklist of things to do or places to go. Rather, it is designed to give you a sense of the character of the region and its offerings. We've tried to include information that will prove useful not only to short-term visitors, but also to newcomers who plan to stay awhile. Even longtime residents and natives may gain new perspectives about the people, places and events that have shaped this coastal area.

Keep in mind that you'll also find us on the Internet at www.insiderinfo.us. There you can view each and every chapter in this book in its entirety, plus find much more information and chapters that we don't have room for in this book, such Home Services, Photography, Film, Green Pages and Pets. You'll also find pages for neighboring areas and our sister guide, the *Insiders' Guide® to North Carolina's Central Coast and New Bern*.

See this entire guide plus additional content online at insiderinfo.us

ABOUT THE AUTHORS

Emily Gorman-Fancy

Rebecca Pierre

Emily Gorman-Fancy

A love for fiction led Emily Gorman-Fancy to Wilmington for a master of fine arts in creative writing at UNCW. While there she wrote a novel and a collection of short stories, both works in progress. Her background in journalism includes contributing more than 200 articles to national, state and local publications. She has been honored to receive recognition for her writing, including a William Randolph Hearst Award and a Reader's Digest scholarship. Emily also holds a BA in journalism from UNC Chapel Hill. In addition to writing, she has taught creative writing and English classes for a wide range of levels from elementary school to college. Emily lives in the historic Sunset Park neighborhood with her husband, Ben, daughters, Ava and Tessa, and black Lab, Lulu.

Rebecca Pierre

Rebecca Pierre's background in business writing and newspaper journalism led to her second career as a freelance writer. Her work has been published in periodicals and magazines including the *Pelican Post*, the *Independent*, *Focus on the Coast*, *North Brunswick Magazine*, *South Brunswick Magazine* and *Attache Magazine* — the in-flight magazine for US Airways. Her first book of poetry, *A Mystery of Moon*, published in the spring of 2005, was selected to be placed in the NC Historical Archives at UNC-Chapel Hill. In 2009, her poetry and clay art were featured on the website of NC Poet Laureate, Kathryn Stripling Byer. Her experience writing award-winning poetry brings discipline, an economy of words and vivid descriptions to her work. As a resident of Oak Island since 1992, she has her finger on the pulse of Brunswick County.

Kate Walsh

Heather D. Wilson

Kate Walsh

Kate Walsh has a serious case of wanderlust. She lives to travel. Some of her favorite adventures include swimming in the Amazon with pink river dolphins, biking from Paris to the Mediterranean and kayaking North Carolina's coastal waterways. An educational television director for 20 years, Kate has her master of fine arts degree in creative nonfiction and has lived in Surf City for 16 years.

Heather D. Wilson

Heather D. Wilson is a graduate of the University of North Carolina at Chapel Hill, with a degree in English and a minor in creative writing. After working as a manuscript editor for Houghton Mifflin Company in Boston, she moved back down South where she received a master of fine arts in creative writing at the University of North Carolina at Wilmington. A yoga instructor and a grant writer, Heather is happy to live, work and play in this beautiful coastal community. She lives with her husband, stepdaughter and baby boy.

ACKNOWLEDGMENTS

Emily Gorman-Fancy

It is misleading that the book's cover only bears the names of our writing staff, because truly, putting this guidebook together is the product of a tremendous amount of collaboration on the part of everyone who works for By the Sea Publications. I owe a debt of gratitude to all who play a part, especially Molly Harrison, Jay Tervo, Melissa Stanley, Susan Sims, Sam Shelby and my fellow writers. Many of the words in this book were originally and eloquently written by the writers who came before me, and I would be remiss if I failed to acknowledge them, as well. I'd also like to thank my husband for his undying support. Along the journey of researching and writing this book, I've discovered new gems and rediscovered old favorites, giving me a deeper appreciation for this coastal town I call home.

Rebecca Pierre

Having been the Brunswick County writer for the *Insiders' Guide® to North Carolina's Southern Coast and Wilmington* since 2002, I can honestly say that the teamwork is tremendous. The contributions of each person involved in the publication of this book — from the publisher to the editor to the writers to the salespeople to the support staff — are recognized and appreciated. The book itself, in addition to being a guide for residents, prospective residents and vacationers, has proven to be a source of information which has the effect of touching individual lives in delightful and unexpected ways. I am proud to be a part of this effort.

Kate Walsh

Over the years I have held a lot of different jobs — cab driver, short-order cook, longshoreman, TV director and ESL teacher in a men's prison — so I have worked with a lot of different people. The hands-down kindest people I have ever had the privilege to work with are the folks at By The Sea Publications. Writing for the Insiders' Guide® is a dream job, but it is the people I work with who make the process such a pleasure. Thank you.

Heather D. Wilson

I would like to thank all the staff at the Insiders' Guide® for helping me to continue to learn the ropes this year. Thank you for your patience, understanding and generosity. Doing research for this book has allowed me to connect with the community I love, discovering new places, new voices and rediscovering old favorites in the process. I'd also like to thank my family, especially my husband, who makes everything possible.

The Cape Fear River is just steps away from Downtown Wilmington.

GETTING HERE, GETTING AROUND

Both tourists and newcomers to North Carolina's southern coast find it relatively easy to get around. The region consists of four coastal counties: New Hanover, Pender, Brunswick and Onslow, which are tied together by U.S. Highway 17. The city of Wilmington makes up most of New Hanover County, geographically the second smallest but among the fastest growing of North Carolina's 100 counties. Pender County, bordering New Hanover County on the north, includes the southern half of Topsail Island (Surf City and Topsail Beach), Hampstead and Burgaw. Primarily rural, Pender County was founded in 1875 and is the state's fifth largest county in area. The northern half of Topsail Island is in Onslow County, which includes the coastal towns of Swansboro, Holly Ridge and Sneads Ferry. The City of Jacksonville, Camp Lejune Marine Base and Hammocks Beach State Park on Bear Island (accessible only by boat or ferry) are also in Onslow County. Brunswick County, across the Cape Fear River to the west of New Hanover County, is the 29th fastest growing county in the nation. Part of the draw may be its relaxed rural atmosphere and its stunning southward facing beaches. These beaches, on barrier islands between the ocean and the Intracoastal Waterway, stretch from the South Carolina state line to the historic fishing village of Southport. The county's easternmost island, Bald Head Island, lies approximately 4 miles from Southport where the mouth of the Cape Fear River meets the ocean. The island is the home of Old Baldy lighthouse and can only be reached by boat or the Bald Head Island Ferry, which does not transport vehicles.

BY LAND

Roadways

Streets of East Coast colonial-era towns are notorious for being directionally challenging, and Wilmington's streets are no exception. Situated on a tapering peninsula between the Atlantic Ocean and the Cape Fear River, the area's streets, except for downtown, do not follow an orderly grid pattern. As a result, getting around for the tourist or newcomer is best accomplished by following route numbers whenever possible. Because the area lacks a freeway system, city streets must carry all of the traffic flow. Surprisingly, even without freeways, traffic moves fairly well except during rush hours or heavy shopping periods, and even then, only a few streets are involved in the congestion.

Traffic from the west on U.S. Highways 17, 74 and 76 enters Wilmington via the Cape Fear Memorial Bridge, a high, platform-type lift-bridge that allows large ocean-going vessels to navigate up the Cape Fear River to the industrial area north of town. The three routes continue east for several blocks on Dawson Street before splitting at 16th Street. Here U.S. 17 and U.S. 74 turn north to follow 16th Street to Market Street, traditionally the main east-west route to and from downtown. Just east of College Road, Market Street crosses Eastwood Road, which on the north side of Market turns into Martin Luther King Parkway. Follow U.S. 74 south on Eastwood to proceed to Wrightsville Beach. Market Street continues northeast as U.S. 17 N. to access Figure Eight Island and the Topsail Island beaches on its way

For the latest New Hanover County public transportation schedules, go to WAVE Transit Authority's website at www. wavetransit.com.

to Pender and Onslow counties, Jacksonville and Camp Lejeune.

After the split at Dawson and 16th, U.S. 76 meanders on a southerly route toward the ocean on Dawson Street, then on Oleander Drive, a major shopping thoroughfare. At its western end, Oleander crosses Wrightsville Avenue, and then becomes Military Cutoff Road, which then crosses Eastwood and extends north past several shopping plazas, to end at N. Market Street. U.S. 76 leaves Oleander at Wrightsville Avenue and rejoins U.S. 74 at Eastwood Road which continues into Wrightsville Beach. Be aware that delays can occur at the drawbridge on U.S. 74 and 76 going onto Harbor Island. Once there, U.S. 74 heads to the north end of Wrightsville Beach and U.S. 76 goes to the south end.

Market Street, Oleander Drive and College Road are not only the most heavily traveled streets in Wilmington, they also have the greatest concentration of commercial establishments. Restaurants, strip malls and shopping centers proliferate on all three thoroughfares. The largest indoor mall, Independence Mall, is located on Oleander Drive at Independence Boulevard, and the largest shopping plaza is Mayfaire Towncenter off of Military Cutoff Road. Traffic from the north enters Wilmington on Interstate Highway 40, which ends its long journey when I-40 becomes N.C. Highway 132, which is also College Road, the main north-south route through town. College Road crosses Market Street and Oleander, and continues south until it ends at Monkey Junction where it joins with U.S. Highway 421, which is also Carolina Beach Road, coming southeast from downtown. Carolina Beach Road continues south to Pleasure Island, where both Carolina Beach and Kure Beach are located. U.S. 421 ends at the southern tip of Pleasure Island, the location of the state ferry to Southport. Just before College Road crosses Market Street from the north, it crosses Martin Luther King Jr. Parkway, which runs from Eastwood Road to N. Third Street, on the north side of town and is the quickest way to get from one side of town to the other. Just west of Kerr Avenue, it becomes a wide open

six-lane, limited-access highway, but be sure to obey the speed limit. Cars sitting on the side of the road with a police car parked behind them are a common sight. MLK also connects to U.S. Highway 117, which crosses the Isabel Holmes Bridge just north of downtown and goes to U.S. Highway 421 west of the river, where it meets U.S. Highway 17 from the south. The route serves as a bypass for traffic from both the south headed north to I-40, and the north and the west headed for the southern coast beaches.

The beaches of Brunswick County can be accessed either by taking U.S. 17 South from Wilmington and using the various feeder roads, or by taking the ferry from Fort Fisher on Pleasure Island to Southport and using N.C. Highways 133 and 211 until N.C. 211 merges with U.S. 17 South.

DRIVING DISTANCES TO WILMINGTON

Wilmington, one of the few deep-water ports on the southeastern seaboard, is about 50 miles from the South Carolina state line. We've listed a few distances and driving times below to give a feel for how long it takes to here.

Myrtle Beach, SC: 75 mi. — 1 hr.

Raleigh, NC: 127 mi. — 2 hrs.

Charlotte, NC: 197 mi. — 3 hrs.

Asheville, NC: 310 mi. — 6 hrs.

Charleston, SC: 170 mi. — 3 hrs.

Thalian Hall

CENTER FOR THE PERFORMING ARTS, INC.
910-343-3660
310 Chestnut St.
Downtown Wilmington

Thalian Hall Main Attractions and Rainbow Room Series 2010-11 — A Luminous Celebration!

Thalian Hall's illustrious legacy carries the names of noted artists who have made their entrances onto this historic stage for more than 150 years. Since the venue's opening in 1858, a literal "who's who" of national and international artists from every genre of the performing arts have been welcomed to the distinctive Thalian Hall, one of America's most celebrated historic theatres.

Following the just-finished renovation, Thalian Hall's grand auditorium now shines more than ever. And with the 2010-2011 Main Attractions season, we honor the Grand Old Lady with a *"luminous celebration."* Events span the gamut from popular music to outlandish comedy, searing drama to foot-stomping fiddling. Take a trip back to the jitterbugging, big-band music of the 1940s or the squeals of delight of 1960s Beatlemania. Rise in tribute to the newly crowned Queen of R&B and listen to the unforgettable musical journey of an Irishman's remarkable Dublin childhood.

It all happens in one of the most beautiful theatre settings in America. There's no need for giant video screens, no need for binoculars. When your hometown theatre is only 15 rows deep, you can practically reach out and touch the performance, just as the performance touches you.

www.ThalianHall.org

View the renovations through photos on our re-designed website. Access the calendar of events and purchase tickets online, read about our history, become a Friend of Thalian Hall, book a private or group tour, and much more!

2010-11 Touring Artists

John Tesh • John Reep • The Red Clay Ramblers • The Nutcracker Ballet
The Raleigh Ringers Natalie MacMaster • Barbara Bailey Hutchison • Frank Vignola
Mike Wiley • Bettye LaVette Danny Ellis/800 Voices • Susan Werner • "In the Mood"
Galumpha • Cantabile, The London Quartet • Etta Mae's "Dr. Etta, Family Specialist
Yesterday & Today: The Interactive Beatles Experience • Lynn Trefzger • Orquestra GarDel

Columbia, SC: 210 mi. — 4 hrs.

Washington, DC: 375 mi. — 7 hrs.

Atlanta, GA: 416 mi. — 8 hrs.

Nashville, TN: 622 mi. — 9 hrs.

New York, NY: 618 mi. — 9 hrs.

Cleveland, OH: 750 mi. — 14 hrs.

INTERSTATES AND HIGHWAYS

For those wanting to take a really long road trip, Wilmington is linked to Barstow, California, via 2,554 miles of Interstate Highway 40, the longest interstate highway in the nation. The final leg from Raleigh to Wilmington, while scenic, is devoid of towns or distractions. Get some coffee and gas up before you start, because there are few gas stations or service plazas adjacent to the highway. There are a number of towns a few miles off I-40, but they tend to roll up the sidewalks early, so be prepared to run this leg without stopping if you are traveling at night. However, there is one rest area about 55 miles north of Wilmington, where fast food and gas are nearby — Exit 364, Clinton/Warsaw.

From the south, U.S. Highway 17 roughly parallels the Atlantic Ocean shoreline, but is a number of miles inland, so there are no views of the ocean. If you are not stopping in Myrtle Beach, you can avoid the congestion of U.S. 17 by taking the six-lane bypass, S.C. Highway 31. Pick it up west of U.S. 17 at either S.C. Highway 544 or U.S. Highway 501 and breeze through the 25 miles to where it ends at S.C. Highway 9. When you exit, go east, following the signs back to U.S. 17 at Little River, SC. Travel north and you'll cross the state line into North Carolina. Just off U.S. 17 on N.C. 179 is Calabash, famous for its seafood restaurants. Continuing north on U.S. 17 you'll reach Supply. Here you have the option of taking N.C. 211 into Southport, a historic fishing village at the mouth of the Cape Fear River. From Southport, you can take N.C. 133 or N.C. 87 north to rejoin U.S. 17 or take the state ferry to Fort Fisher on Pleasure Island. On U.S. 421 north of the ferry dock are Fort Fisher State Historic Site, Fort Fisher State Recreation Area and the North Carolina Aquarium, the largest of the state aquariums.

From the west, U.S. 74 from Charlotte and Interstate 20, becoming U.S. 76 from Columbia, S.C., merge near Whiteville and continue toward Wilmington. They junction with U.S. 17 just west of the N.C. 133 north exit to the USS NORTH CAROLINA Battleship Memorial. The majority of these roads are easy-to-drive, four-lane highways through gently rolling countryside and coastal plains.

Trolleys

Free Downtown Trolley
WAVE Transit Authority, 1110 Castle St., Wilmington
(910) 343-0106

A fun way to see the riverfront area and some of the city is to take the free downtown trolley. The trolley runs continuously Monday through Friday from 7:30 AM to 9:20 PM, Saturday from 11 AM to 9:20 PM and Sunday from 11 AM to 6 PM. Trolley stops are marked along the route, which goes along Front, Water and Second streets, and you can look for the trolley to stop approximately every 10 minutes on weekdays and 20 minutes on weekends. A route map, schedule and information are available on the website at www.wavetransit.com.

Wilmington Trolley Company
Water St. between Dock and Market sts., GPS # 15 S. Water St., Wilmington
(910) 763-4483

Located near the Henrietta III at the foot of Dock Street, the Wilmington Trolley offers a 45-minute guided tour of historic downtown Wilmington over a course of about 8 miles. Available daily, April through October, the tours leave on the hour from 10 AM to 5 PM. There are some evening tours available during the summer months, with the last tour leaving at 8 PM. Fees are $11 for adults and $5 for children ages 2 to 12. The trolley runs every Saturday year-round. Call ahead for evening and off-season tour availability.

Taxicabs, Shuttle Vans and Limousines

In New Hanover County, taxis, shuttles, sedans and limos abound. Along the rest of the southern coast, these services are available, but are not as plentiful. Some companies provide strictly taxi service, some provide limousine, sedan or shuttle van service, and some companies provide a combination of some or all services. Within the city, taxi fares are uniform. The drop rate is $3 plus 35¢ per one-sixth of a mile. Outside the city limits, fares are a set rate depending on destination; for example, fares from the airport to downtown or the beaches are usually on a flat-fee basis.

Car Rentals

Wilmington is where visitors to southeastern North Carolina rent a car. Along with the national chains and independent car rental services listed here, several new car dealerships also lease cars long-term.

Alamo & National Car Rental
(910) 762-0143
Wilmington International Airport,
(910) 762-8000, (800) 227-7368

Avis Rent-A-Car
Wilmington International Airport
(910) 763-1993, (800) 331-1212

Enterprise Rentals
1930 Castle Hayne Rd., Wilmington
(910) 772-1560
1437 S. College Rd., Wilmington
(910) 397-9110
4911 Market St., Wilmington
(910) 350-0435
5601-B Market St., Wilmington
(910) 799-4042
Reservations,
(800) 736-8222

Hertz
Wilmington International Airport
(910) 762-1010, (800) 654-3131

Thrifty Car Rental
Wilmington International Airport
(910) 343-1411, (800) 847-4389

Triangle Rent A Car
4124 Market St., Wilmington
(910) 251-9812, (800) 643-7368

By Air

AIRPORTS

Wilmington International Airport is the prime entry point for most people flying into the greater Wilmington area. Myrtle Beach International Airport in South Carolina is nearly the same distance from Shallotte as the Wilmington airport (about 40 miles), so visitors traveling by air to or from the Calabash and South Brunswick Islands areas might do well to check flight availability via Myrtle Beach. Those traveling to or from Oak Island, Southport, Pleasure Island or points north will find Wilmington International Airport easier to use. Smaller aircraft destined for Brunswick County can use The Cape Fear Regional Jetport in Oak Island.

Wilmington International Airport
1740 Airport Blvd., Wilmington
(910) 341-4125
www.flyilm.com

Wilmington International Airport is an entirely modern facility, but with Colonial-style architecture and wooden rocking chairs scattered throughout, it has plenty of charm. The recently renovated and expanded airport fronts 23rd Street, 2 miles north of Market Street, and by car is within 10 minutes of downtown Wilmington and about 20 minutes of Wrightsville Beach. Two airlines serve the airport offering non-stop service to Atlanta, New York, Charlotte and Philadelphia: the Delta connection, (800) 282-3424, and USAirways, (800) 428-4322. Wilmington travelers now have additional options for flights to popular Florida destinations, as Allegiant Air began offering nonstop flights from ILM to Orlando and Daytona Beach, Florida, in spring 2008. Short-term parking rates are $1 per half-hour, with a maximum 24-hour charge of $14. Long-term parking is $1 per hour, with a maximum charge of

$8 per day. The first 15 minutes of parking is free in both parking areas.

By Sea

Most boaters coming to the Cape Fear region do so via the magnificent Intracoastal Waterway (ICW), although some use that big puddle offshore, the Atlantic Ocean. Extending 3,000 miles along the Atlantic coast from Boston to Key West, the ICW provides protection from the open sea, along with a multitude of marinas and harbors. In North Carolina, the ICW follows a path behind a nearly continuous string of barrier islands between Virginia to South Carolina. See our information on Marinas and the Intracoastal Waterway for detailed information.

FERRIES

Bald Head Island Ferry
Deep Point Marina, 1301 Ferry Rd., Southport
(910) 457-5003, (800) 234-1666

The ferry between Southport and Bald Head Island is strictly for passengers, luggage and bicycles. Travel on the island is by foot, bicycle or electric cart — no passenger cars are allowed. An individual, round-trip ferry ticket costs $16 for adults and $9 for children ages 3 through 12. Children age 2 and younger ride free. There is an additional cargo charge of $15 for bicycles, kayaks, canoes and other items. It departs on the hour from 8 AM to 10 PM, except at noon, seven days a week. Ferries leave Bald Head Island every hour on the half-hour, except at 11:30 AM. (The winter schedule may be abbreviated, and the summer schedule may be expanded.) The ferry ride takes about 20 minutes and reservations are encouraged. Ferry parking in Southport costs $8 per day. The new ferry terminal features separate arrival and departure areas and an indoor waiting lounge. Prices are subject to change.

Southport-Fort Fisher Ferry
1650 Ferry Rd., Southport
(910) 457-6942, (800) 368-8969

North Carolina's ferry system began in the mid-1920s with a private tug and barge service crossing Oregon Inlet on the Outer Banks. Other private ferries subsequently developed that were subsidized by the state during the 1930s and '40s.

Sand, sea and sky form the beauty of the coast.

photo: Belinda Keller Photography

In the late '40s and '50s, the state began purchasing the private ferry companies, and today the North Carolina ferry system has seven ferry routes, 24 ferries and more than 400 employees. More than 1.1 million vehicles and more than 2.5 million passengers are transported every year over five bodies of water.

The Southport-Fort Fisher ferry service is not only a mode of transportation that saves miles of driving, it's also a wonderful scenic tour. On the approximately 30-minute cruise, the ferry provides a panoramic view of the mouth of the Cape Fear River above Southport. On the Brunswick County side, huge yellow cranes mark the Military Ocean Terminal at Sunny Point, the largest distribution center in the country for military supplies. Other sights include Old Baldy, North Carolina's oldest lighthouse on Bald Head Island; Price's Creek Lighthouse, which guided Confederate blockade runners through New Inlet during the Civil War; and the Oak Island Lighthouse, the nation's brightest. For information on tours and attractions, see our Attractions section for Carolina Beach, Wilmington and Wrightsville Beach.

The Fort Fisher ferry terminal on Pleasure Island is near the southern terminus of U.S. 421 on the right. The Southport terminal is on Ferry Road, just off N.C. 211, about 3 miles north of town. During summer months, plan to get to the terminal at least 30 minutes before departure. The ferry is extremely popular and capacity is limited to about 36 cars.

Departure Times

Winter: Oct. 1 - April 2 and Oct. 2 - Dec. 31
*Summer only: April 3 - Oct. 1

Departs Southport	Departs Fort Fisher
5:30 AM	6:15 AM
7:00 AM	7:45 AM
7:45 AM	8:30 AM
8:30 AM	9:15 AM
9:15 AM	10:00 AM*
10:00 AM*	10:45 AM
10:45 AM	11:30 AM
11:30 AM	12:15 PM
12:15 PM*	1:00 PM*
1:00 PM	1:45 PM
1:45 PM	2:30 PM
2:30 PM	3:15 PM
3:15 PM	4:00 PM
4:00 PM	4:45 PM
4:45 PM	5:30 PM
6:15 PM	7:00 PM

Fares

Pedestrians, $1

Bicycle Riders, $2

Motorcycles, $3

Vehicle and/or combination less than 20 feet, $5

Vehicles and/or combinations in excess of 20 feet up to 40 feet, $10

Vehicles and/or combinations greater than 40 feet to 65 feet maximum, $15

Call in advance if ferrying larger vehicles. Rates and schedules are subject to change. For information about the Southport-Fort Fisher Ferry only, call (910) 457-6942 or (800) 368-8969. For statewide and individual ferry information call (800) BY-FERRY (293-3779) or go to the website www.ncferry.org

AREA OVERVIEW ⌕

It is the confluence of waters — ocean, rivers and sounds — that has shaped the destiny of the Cape Fear coast since its beginning. Explorers, pirates, settlers and traders all found the area to be both compelling and terrifying. Invading armies, even those who occupied the region, were no match for the indomitable spirit of the Cape Fear and its people. The history, culture and economy of North Carolina's southern coast has always depended on the waters and the whim of nature.

While the ocean gets top billing in terms of geographical attractions, it was the existence of the river that gave rise to successful European settlement here. A deep, often fast-moving body of water, the Cape Fear River begins at the confluence of the Haw and Deep rivers near Greensboro, meanders through Fayetteville and empties into the Atlantic Ocean 200 miles south of its source. With a romantic history and dangerous reputation, the Cape Fear River has always been a major influence on the formation and evolution of the coast and particularly the city of Wilmington, some 30 miles upstream of the open ocean.

NEW HANOVER COUNTY

The Cape Fear River

For centuries Native Americans had this area to themselves, until European settlers came. In 1524, when Italian explorer Giovanni da Verrazzano took his French-financed expedition into an unknown river in a wild place, he ushered in a new historical period that would slowly lead to European development of the area.

Verrazzano wrote glowingly of the area in his journal: "The open country rising in height above the sandy shore with many faire fields and plaines, full of mightie great woods, some very thicke and some thinne, replenished with divers sorts of trees, as pleasant and delectable to behold, as if possible to imagine." Despite the explorer's enthusiastic description, very little happened in terms of development at that time.

Initially Queen Elizabeth I had paved the way for colonization of the area by decreeing that the British had a right to conquer and occupy land not actually possessed by any Christian prince or people. Later, in 1629, Sir Robert Heath, attorney general for King of England Charles I, was granted a large area of what is today named Carolina. Neither Heath nor his heirs did anything to develop the area, so in 1663, Charles II granted the area as a reward to eight men who were called the Lords Proprietors.

Members of the Massachusetts Bay Colony, led by William Hilton, attempted to colonize the Cape Fear region in 1663. Their effort failed, and the following year, a new settlement ventured into the region. A group of English settlers from Barbados, led by John Vassal, established a settlement in 1664. By 1667, that settlement was abandoned because of a disagreement with the Lords Proprietors who backed another settlement, Charles Town, farther south on the west bank of the river. That effort failed in 1667 because of hostile coastal Indians, pirates, weak supply lines, mosquitoes and other problems that drove the residents south, where they founded Charles Town Landing, later to become the City of Charleston in South Carolina. Perhaps one of the greatest reasons for failure was, ironically, the very river that had sparked the initial interest in settlement.

In 1879 settler George Davis in James Sprunt's Chronicles of the Cape Fear River vividly described part of the problem with settlement caused by the river:

"Looking to the cape for the idea and reason of its name, we find that it is the southernmost point of Smith's Island — a naked, bleak elbow of sand, jutting far out into the ocean. Immediately in front of it are the Frying Pan Shoals, pushing out still farther, twenty miles, to sea. Together, they stand for warning and for woe; and together they catch the long majestic roll of the Atlantic as it sweeps through a thousand miles of grandeur and power from the Arctic toward the Gulf. It is the playground of billows and tempests, the kingdom of silence and awe, disturbed by no sound save the sea gull's shriek and the breakers' roar. Its whole aspect is suggestive, not of repose and beauty, but of desolation and terror. Imagination can not adorn it. Romance cannot hallow it. Local pride cannot soften it."

In a reverse of the abandonment of Charles Town, the Town of Brunswick was founded by disgruntled English settlers from South Carolina in 1726. Located on the west bank of the river, it soon withered away as more strategically located Wilmington, on the high east bank, began to prosper. There river rafters would stop to trade at a place called the Dram Tree.

Establishing Wilmington says a lot about the tenacity of the successful settlers who managed to tame what was apparently a very wild place. They understood, as do their descendants, that the river presented more opportunities than obstacles and whatever it took to settle the area was worth it. Positioning the City of Wilmington on a bluff created a port relatively safe from storms. Later, it also proved to be a protective barrier against invaders from England during the Revolutionary War and Union troops during the Civil War.

The Cape Fear River was a profitable area for trading goods such as tar, turpentine and pitch, but sailors disliked coming here. The waters were dangerous to navigate and the residents viewed sailors as unsavory. In fact, by statute of the time, tavern keepers, retailers of liquor or keepers of public houses were not permitted to give credit to seamen, and seamen were not permitted to be kept, entertained or harbored by any resident longer than six hours. In addition, Wilmington did not and would not have sewage or drainage systems for years to come. As a result, diseases prevailed, such as small pox and malaria, and there were few doctors, the first of whom, Armande de Rossett, did not arrive until 1735. It was with trepidation and dread that seamen sailed into the river's waters, and that is how it came to be known as the "Cape of Fear."

Wilmington: The Port City

Previously called New Liverpool, New Carthage, New Town and Newton, Wilmington was settled in 1729. That same year, St James Parish was founded and still exists today as St. James Episcopal Church at the corner of Third and Market streets. The name of the city was finally decided when Governor Gabriel Johnston took office. He was so excited and thankful for the prestigious appointment that he named the city after the man who gave him the job — Spencer Compton, Earl of Wilmington.

The City of Wilmington was incorporated in 1740 and continued to grow and prosper. During part of the 1700s, Wilmington also functioned six times as the seat of government for North Carolina, because at that time the Colonial Assembly moved about and was usually located where the governor lived or where the legislators met.

In keeping with its English heritage, many streets in Wilmington, such as Red Cross, Castle, Walnut, Chestnut, Princess, Market, Dock, Orange, Ann, Nunn, Queen and Church streets, are named after streets in Liverpool, England.

Wilmington flourished as a major port, shipbuilding center and producer of pine forest products. Tar, turpentine and pitch were central to the economy, and lumber from the pine forests was a lucrative economic resource. At one time, Wilmington was the site of the largest cotton exchange in the world. The waterfront

bustled with steam ships crowding together to pick up or unload precious cargo.

Involvement in the American Revolutionary movement began for Wilmington in 1765, when the British Parliament passed the Stamp Act. Reaction and vigorous resistance were immediate and colorful, with much of the activity taking place at night and emanating from the taverns. Eventually, the local Stamp Officer was intimidated into composing a letter of resignation, whereupon the residents gave him three cheers, carried him about the town on a chair and treated him to the finest liquors. Subsequently, the colonists refused to receive the stamps from the British and forced officials to abandon the use of stamps. In 1775, Wilmington residents signed a pledge supporting the Continental Congress.

The city became involved in the Revolutionary War when Loyalists battled the Patriots some 20 miles north of the city at Moore's Creek on February 27, 1776. Although outnumbered, the Patriots won this battle, but in 1781 British forces captured the city and held it under the command of Major James Henry Craig. Later that year, Craig was joined by General Charles Cornwallis, who stayed in the Burgwin-Wright House at the corner of Third and Market streets. Across the street, the British Cavalry occupied St. James Church, using it as a riding school. The British troops were later withdrawn from Wilmington when Cornwallis surrendered at Yorktown on October 19, 1781.

Following the Revolutionary War, Wilmington prospered greatly, both socially and as an important trading center. Numerous estates and plantations flourished on the outskirts, and many fine homes were built in the city. However, during the early 1800s the city floundered because of poor roads, few bridges, swamps surrounding the city, inadequate medical and sanitation facilities and navigation problems on the Cape Fear River. With the advent of steam power, railroads and navigational improvements to the river, however, Wilmington again began to prosper, and by 1840 was the largest city in the state. Thalian Hall, which currently houses the oldest continuously operating little theater company in the United States, was built in 1855 and has since been restored.

During the Civil War, Wilmington was the Confederacy's most important port. Fort Fisher and the Cape Fear River were home to many blockade runners who brought materials in from England and the Caribbean islands. Built in 1861, Fort Fisher was the last fort to fall to the Union army.

After the war, cotton, rice, peanuts, lumber and naval stores helped Wilmington regain its trading force. A sizable African-American middle class developed, and Wilmington soon became home to the state's first African-American lawyer and African-American physician. In 1866 the town officially became a city. However, by 1910 Wilmington lost its identity as the state's largest city when inland cities grew due to the development of the tobacco and textile industries.

During World War I, a thriving shipbuilding industry developed and cotton exports peaked. The Great Depression of the 1930s hit Wilmington hard and once again the city declined. However, World War II brought a rebirth of local shipbuilding, and 243 ships were built. In 1945 the North Carolina Legislature created the State Port Authority, which enabled the transformation of the shipyards into a modern port facility. In 1947 Wilmington College was established, later becoming the University of North Carolina Wilmington.

Over the years, much of Wilmington's growth was facilitated by a strong railroad industry, which eventually consolidated into the Atlantic Coast Line Railroad, a major employer in the city. Unfortunately, in 1955 the Atlantic Coast Line closed their offices and moved to Jacksonville, Florida, dealing a severe blow to Wilmington. A major effort was undertaken to bring diversified industry to the area, and by 1966 Wilmington had begun to rebound and was designated an "All American City."

After a statewide campaign to save her from the scrap heap, the famous World War II battleship, NORTH CAROLINA, was brought to the city in 1961 and berthed on the west side of the river across from downtown. Today the ship provides a magnificent backdrop for Wilmington's

Riverfront area. During the 1970s, a strong revitalization effort began to reclaim the deteriorating downtown area, which, coupled with an intense preservation effort in the large historic district, resulted in a renewed and exciting central city.

In the 1980s the city saw another upswing as major companies such as Corning Inc. and General Electric moved in, encouraging other diverse companies, including Applied Analytical Industry and Takeda Chemical Products, to call Wilmington home. Pharmaceutical Product Development, now PPD, became a homegrown Wilmington success story. A major film studio grew here, currently known as Screen Gems Studios, and many movies have been made in the area, earning Wilmington the nickname "Wilmywood."

The downtown revitalization effort in the mid-1980s did much to bring Wilmington into prominence. The successes of Chandler's Wharf Shops, The Cotton Exchange and The Coastline Convention Center encouraged other establishments to set up shop. Restaurants, clothing stores, art galleries and antiques shops soon lined the streets. The flourishing nightlife adds a trendy setting to Wilmington, and the streets in the downtown area are quite safe. Throngs of tourists and residents alike stroll about until late in the evening.

Downtown Wilmington remains the historical core of the community and is still in many ways the neighborhood that defines the region. Suburbs may flourish, but there is something fascinating about the historic homes and buildings downtown, with their intimate proximity to the river. Both visitors and residents are affected by a sense of lingering ghosts. Important events happened here, in places that are still standing — places that have not been obscured by modern architecture or lost in the trends of a constantly changing American culture.

Home to the county's seat of government for more than 250 years, this urban area has been on the forefront of historic changes. The best perspective on Wilmington's rich and colorful history can be found at the Cape Fear Museum, 814 Market Street, (910) 798-4350, where the unique format allows visitors to walk through time in chronological order (see our Attractions section).

NEW HANOVER COUNTY

Greater Wilmington

As the second smallest of the state's 100 counties, New Hanover County encompasses only 199 square miles, most of which is the City of Wilmington. The county's 2008 population of 192,000 reflected a growth of 35 percent since 1990. Wilmington alone saw its population increase to nearly 100,000 in 2007, making it the larger of the two major Wilmingtons (the other one is in Delaware).

Over the last few years, the city of Wilmington and New Hanover County have experienced a tremendous building boom that has affected all aspects of life and culture throughout the area. However, with excellent shopping, outstanding restaurants, antiques to be discovered and a view of the river wherever you go, downtown Wilmington's booming tourist industry vies for visitor attention with the nearby beaches, and remains the focal point of the county.

Perhaps the best thing about downtown Wilmington — and something that separates it from the rest of the city and nearby communities — is its pleasant walkability. Streets lined with shops and restaurants are easily traversed, and the Riverwalk is a great place to stroll, grab a hot dog from a street vendor, listen to free music and watch the river traffic. Nearly a mile long, the Riverwalk stretches from the Greater Wilmington Chamber of Commerce building just north of the Coast Line Conference and Events Center to south of Chandlers Wharf. Complete with wide, patio-style areas and pocket parks with benches, the Riverwalk offers spectacular views of the river, especially at night.

During the day, downtown Wilmington is quaint and charming, but at night it comes alive in a whole new way. Dance clubs, jazz bars, local and touring musicals, venues for rock 'n' roll, rhythm and blues and more can be found in the 55-block

area of the downtown commercial district (see our Nightlife section).

Going east, away from the river, Wilmington's demeanor starts to change. Besides spreading across the peninsula and absorbing much of northern New Hanover County, Wilmington is now the geographic coastal center for shopping. In numerous malls and plazas, the area boasts national chains such as Target, Barnes & Noble, Walmart, Lowe's, Dillard's, Belk's, Sears, JC Penney, Kohl's, Home Depot and many others, in addition to upscale and specialty stores, all of which have enhanced the region's shopping choices considerably (see our Shopping section).

With all this new growth and the continuing popularity of the area, real estate is a lively business. "Plantations," the new name for gated communities and neighborhoods, are developed so quickly that natives have been heard to say they occasionally get lost on once-familiar streets because of the changing landscape (see our Homes & Real Estate section). Housing choices are as diverse as a golf course

condo to a house on the Intracoastal Waterway to Wilmington's extensive Historic District, which is made up of approximately 230 city blocks and has many full-time residents. A stroll through the Historic District, by the way, reveals beautifully restored homes and commercial buildings, many of them antebellum, lining the shaded streets. A number of buildings feature plaques indicating their age: red for 75 to 100 years and black if the structure is more than 100 years old. As more of the city's older homes are restored, and condominiums and townhouses are added, both the Historic District and the downtown population will continue to grow.

Wilmington has always been the educational hub of the southeastern North Carolina coast, with the University of North Carolina Wilmington and Cape Fear Community College within its boundaries. Miller-Motte Technical College and a branch of Mount Olive College are also in Wilmington.

The city also holds the distinction of being the cultural center for the whole southeast coast. Performances by touring and home-based theater, dance and music companies enliven the local stages of Thalian Hall Center for the Performing Arts, the oldest community theater tradition in the United States, and Kenan Auditorium, the Cultural Arts Building and Trask Coliseum on the campus of UNCW. Writers, artists and musicians are evident in abundance. Private galleries abound and, in addition, the Louise Wells Cameron Museum of Art offers a showcase of regional and international artists (see our Arts section). The Community Arts Center is constantly enhancing the arts scene by offering classes and sponsoring productions for adults and children, and numerous theater groups are active throughout the year. Museums, such as the Cape Fear Museum and the Wilmington Children's Museum (see our Attractions and Arts sections) add to the mix.

The film industry lends an exciting opportunity for spotting the occasional celebrity or just watching the process of making movies. For many years, filmmaking accounted for a significant portion of the local economy and it still has the potential for growth because of Wilmington's well-established film industry infrastructure. The cornerstone of the local film industry, EUE/Screen Gems Studios, is complemented by a seasoned crew base, an active regional film commission and a large talent pool. Since the first movie filmed here in 1983 (Dino DeLaurentiis' Firestarter), Wilmington has been home to more than 300 movies and seven television series, including Matlock, Dawson's Creek and One Tree Hill. Stars spotted over the years have included, among others, Bruce Willis, Richard Gere, Katherine Hepburn, Alec Baldwin, Kim Basinger, Patrick Swayze, Julie Harris, John Travolta and Anthony Hopkins. Linda Lavin, Broadway star and a woman known affectionately as "Alice" from the '70s TV series, lives downtown and runs the Red Barn Studio Theatre.

Another major economic influence lies just south of the city on the river. It is North Carolina's principal deep-water port, the North Carolina State Port at Wilmington. The port and some of the industrial complexes north of downtown host hundreds of ships and barges from many nations every year. The river recently has been dredged and deepened so that larger cargo ships and some of the cruise ships can now dock in Wilmington.

Wrightsville Beach

Residential in character, Wrightsville Beach is not your typical beach resort town. There is no carnival atmosphere — no Ferris wheels, no arcade, no mini golf or bumper boats, and only a few gaudy displays of beach merchandise. Instead, Wrightsville Beach is primarily an affluent residential community that has its roots in Wilmington. For more than a century, the 5-mile-long island has been a retreat from the summer heat for Wilmington residents whose families have maintained ownership of beach homes there for generations.

At first, only a few people had access to the island and built houses there. The first large structure, built in 1856, was the Carolina Yacht Club, which today is the second oldest in the country, after the New York Yacht Club. In 1899 Wrightsville Beach was incorporated as a resort community, and the Tidewater Power Company, which owned the island at that time, built a trolley system from downtown Wilmington to the beach. The trolley provided the only land access to the island until 1935.

Interested in development, the company built the Hotel Tarrymore in 1905 to attract visitors and revenue. Later named The Oceanic, this grand hotel burned down in 1934, along with most structures on the northern half of the island. The Tidewater Power Company also built Lumina, a beach pavilion that became a Wrightsville Beach standard. Lumina was located on the site of the current Oceanic Restaurant at the south end of the beach, and offered a festive place where locals gathered for swimming, outdoor movies, and to attend the dances that were held there. Sadly, it too is gone, but many locals still have fond memories of the place and it lingers in the names of area shops, businesses, even the local newspaper.

Development of the beach continued steadily until 1954 when Hurricane Hazel, a monster storm, came ashore and wreaked devastation on the island's homes and buildings. Hazel also shoaled the channel between Wrightsville Beach and adjacent Shell Island. Developers, seeing an opportunity for expansion, filled in the remaining water and joined the islands together.

Today, the area is the site of the Shell Island Resort Hotel, numerous condominiums and large homes. In the aftermath of two hurricanes in 1996, the resort hotel found itself precariously close to an advancing inlet. Sand was brought in to replenish the beach and Shell Island's condominium owners wanted to erect a seawall to save their property from the encroaching sea. However, North Carolina has very strict laws regarding seawalls because of their negative impact on the rest of a beach and the state denied them permission to do so. In 2002, the inlet was dredged and moved north toward Figure Eight Island, thereby, for the time being, reducing the threat to Shell Island.

Today, Wrightsville Beach is a very busy and prosperous place. Because of its popularity with both residents and tourists, there is almost no available land for sale. The area is still a stronghold of long-term residents who summer in family homes built to catch the ocean breeze. The permanent residential population is about 3,000, but that figure swells considerably in the summer.

With a land mass of nearly a square mile, this island manages to maintain its charm despite the surrounding growth. Surprisingly, brisk commercial development in the form of marinas, restaurants, hotels, and other services has not seriously changed the residential orientation of the island and its very clean beaches.

Lifeguards oversee the safety of swimmers in the summer season, and the beach patrol keeps an eye on the area to make sure laws are obeyed. Alcohol and glass containers are not allowed on the beach. If you have questions, just ask one of the friendly lifeguards.

Boaters, sun worshipers, swimmers, surfers and anglers will find much to appreciate and enjoy about the setting. Public beach access points, liberally sprinkled along the shoreline, make a day in the sun a free experience for daytrippers — with the notable exception of parking.

Insiders know the island is extremely crowded during peak summer weekends and are inclined to leave those times for visitors. On in-season weekends, visitors are wise to arrive before 9:30 AM and bring plenty of quarters for the parking meters. Meter rates are $1.50 per hour, or you can try your luck at finding a rare non-metered spot. Free parking is available at Town Hall, 321 Causeway Drive, the boat ramp lot beside the drawbridge, and at the Intracoastal Waterway along Old Causeway Drive. The Town of Wrightsville Beach also uses "pay stations" at some public parking locations. The stations accept credit cards (VISA and MasterCard only), bills ($1, $5, and $10) and coins, and they give change.

Park-By-Phone allows you use your cell phone to pay for parking. Sign up at www.Park-By-Phone.com for an annual membership of $5.95, then you can pay for parking each time by calling (888) 310-PARK and entering the lot or meter number, which are visibly marked on bright yellow signs.

Parking is hourly (and enforced) from 9 AM to 6 PM, but there is no charge before or after these times. Winter visitors enjoy free parking from November through February. It's tempting, but don't make the mistake of parking at business locations or at private homes. Parking lots at area restaurants and hotels are vigilantly guarded, and residents are not inclined to allow unknown cars to occupy their driveways. Towing is very strictly enforced in no-parking zones.

Opportunities for water-related sports and entertainment are plentiful on Wrightsville Beach. Some of the most luxurious marinas along the North Carolina coast are clustered around the bridge at the Intracoastal Waterway and offer a full range of services (see our Marinas section). Charter boats, both power and sail, are available in abundance. Diving, Jet Ski rentals, windsurfing, Parasailing, kayaking and sailing lessons are there for the asking (see Boating & Watersports). Bait, tackle, piers and more than enough advice on the best way to fish are all easy to find (see Fishing). Visitors who bring their own boats will appreciate the free boat ramp just north of the first bridge onto Harbour Island, the island between the mainland and Wrightsville Beach.

A visit to Wrightsville Beach, whether for a day or for a vacation, is bound to be a pleasant experience that will be repeated time after time. The island is wonderfully walkable, and you can find everything you need for a comfortable and memorable vacation almost any time of the year.

Figure Eight Island

Figure Eight Island, just north of Wrightsville Beach, is a private, very exclusive, oceanfront resort community. This highly restricted residential island of 441 expensive homes is accessible only by a bridge over the Intracoastal Waterway. Indeed, it is so private and secluded that a guard will let you onto the island only if you've called ahead to someone on the island, such as a friend or a real estate agent, and are on the list at the gate.

While active visitors will discover an endless array of things to do, such as watersports, biking and tennis, most people are drawn to Figure Eight Island because of what you won't find here. There are no commercial enterprises on the island, which means no hotels, shopping centers or traffic. What you will find is five miles of pure beautiful beaches for the vacationer looking for some R&R and peace and quiet for a noncommercialized retreat.

It's a favorite hideaway for celebrities and political bigwigs who want privacy when they're visiting the area. Former Vice President Al Gore and family, for example, have enjoyed vacationing here since 1997. But the celebrity orientation of the island does not mean regular folk can't rent homes and enjoy a private vacation. In fact, the island is very hospitable to vacationers and welcomes guests to its uncrowded shores. To contact real estate companies on or near Figure Eight Island for rental information (some of the larger Wilmington real estate companies may also handle properties on this exclusive island) see our section on Vacation Rentals.

Masonboro Island

South of Wrightsville Beach and north of Carolina Beach you'll find Masonboro Island. Barren of any development, Masonboro Island is the last and largest pristine barrier island remaining on the southern North Carolina coast. This 8-mile-long island, with an Atlantic Ocean beach on its eastern shore and marshes on its western shore facing the Intracoastal Waterway, is accessible only by boat.

If you are fortunate enough to have a shallow-draft boat, just look for a spot to approach among the reeds — probably alongside other boats — and tie a meaningful line to the shore with your anchor because, as in all areas of the Cape Fear region, the tides have wide fluctuation. If you tie up at high tide, you may have a tough job getting off the sand if you try to leave at low tide.

The island, consisting of about 5,000 acres, has about 4,300 acres of tidal salt marshes and mud flats and only about 600 acres of beach. Although parts of the island belong to private landowners, no development is allowed. Masonboro is a component of the North Carolina Coastal Reserve and the National Estuarine Research Reserve. The island is home to gray foxes, cotton rats, a variety of birds, river otters and several species of aquatic life; it is an important nesting site for the beautiful and famous loggerhead sea turtles.

You can spot the island by the large number of pleasure craft clustered on the Masonboro Sound side. If you want to be alone, pass by this gathering and look for small passages farther south on the island. Access is only limited by the draft of your boat and how easily you can push it off when you run aground. Gather your gear and hike a short way to the ocean side, where it's a special pleasure to take a picnic and relax on the uncrowded beach. There are no facilities so be prepared to rough it. If you make the trip in the fall, be sure to take along insect repellent because the yellow flies can be extremely annoying.

For more information on Masonboro Island, see the following sections: Attractions and Camping.

Monkey Junction

At the southern end of College Road (N.C. Highway 132) where it joins with Carolina Beach Road (U.S. Highway 421), you'll find an area that, in recent years, has experienced enormous growth, both commercially and residentially. Officially it's called Myrtle Grove, but for years locals have called the area Monkey Junction. The name Monkey Junction dates back to the 1920s when the bus to Carolina Beach stopped at this intersection. An enterprising gas station owner, so the story goes, featured live monkeys as an attraction to draw customers from the bus. When the driver stopped, he announced, "Monkey Junction," and that's how it has been known ever since.

Carolina Beach

Carolina Beach, just 30 minutes from downtown Wilmington by car, is on a narrow slip of land between the Cape Fear River and the Atlantic Ocean. Separated from the mainland by the Intracoastal Waterway (Snow's Cut), the island is called Pleasure Island. Established in 1857, when Joseph Winner planned the streets and lots for the 50 acres of beach property he had purchased, the island's only access then was by water. In 1866 a steamship began carrying vacationers down the Cape Fear River to Snow's Cut and a small railroad took them the rest of the way into Carolina Beach. In later years, a high-rise bridge was built over Snow's Cut connecting the island with the mainland.

A drive through Carolina Beach reveals a pleasant 1950s-style beach town of modest cottages, increasingly more upscale single-family dwellings and an abundance of three- and four-story condominiums. The town also has a movie complex, grocery stores, drugstores, beach shops and boutiques, numerous restaurants, both upscale and simple, hardware and variety stores, an ABC store and even bait shops. The beachfront motels, including several vintage motor courts, offer a welcome blast from the past. If you were a kid during the '50s and your parents took you on vacation to the beach, this was the kind of place you probably remember. Some of the best beachfront lodging values are offered here. The nostalgia is free.

Carolina Beach underwent a dramatic transformation during the 1990s. Once considered a wild party spot, it is currently evolving into a heavily residential community dedicated to creating a wholesome family environment. Recent years have seen the cultivation of improved services, pleasant landscaping, attention to zoning and tangible citizen action to make Carolina Beach an attractive visitor destination.

The main business district is centered around an active yacht basin containing a large number of charter fishing boats and large excursion boats. The nearby Boardwalk area is undergoing revitalization and rebuilding in conjunction with the oceanfront Courtyard by Marriott Resort Hotel and several mixed-use condo/retail projects.

Anglers love Carolina Beach. The surf promises wonderful bounty all year long, and there are plenty of tackle shops and piers as well as the opportunity to experience deep-sea fishing from the sterns of a number of charter boats berthed in the municipal yacht basin. Several annual fishing tournaments are based on the abundance of king mackerel, and you can pay a nominal entry fee for a chance to reap as much as $50,000 for the winning fish.

Carolina Beach also offers one of the few state parks in the region. For a modest fee, you can camp and enjoy the wonders of coastal nature. The Venus's flytrap, a carnivorous plant that eats insects, is abundant in the park. This plant, a relic from pre-human existence, grows naturally within a 60-mile radius of Wilmington.

Away from the seasonal bustle at the center of the city, Carolina Beach is a quiet community of about 5,000 year-round residents. That number jumps three to five times at the peak of the vacation season. The community is growing in appeal to both locals from Wilmington and newcomers from other areas for two big reasons: It isn't crowded yet and it's affordable. Many a Wilmingtonian has given Wrightsville Beach over to visitors for the summer in the past few years and turned to Carolina Beach for a quiet spot on the sand.

Kure Beach

To the south, Carolina Beach merges into the town of Kure Beach (pronounced "CURE-ee"). Development here began in the 1870s when Hans Andersen Kure moved from Denmark and bought large tracts of land in the middle of the island. Apparently, things moved slowly because Kure Beach wasn't incorporated until 1947.

Today Kure Beach is overwhelmingly residential, dotted with modest cottages, new upscale houses and a number of beach motels. Several condominium buildings cluster together in one area, but there are few tall buildings. In fact, new structures may not be built taller than 35 feet. At the center of town, a popular fishing pier extends 712 feet out over the ocean and there are several restaurants. A charming boardwalk with benches extends north along the beach and is lighted at night.

Once upon a time, some of the best real estate deals could be found in Kure Beach, but today this sleepy beach town is fast growing in popularity and price, although it's still possible to find a bargain. What you won't find is a lot of amusement park–style entertainment here, although there is an arcade, and there is very little in the way of shopping.

A permanent population of about 1,500 residents makes for a very close community, but Kure Beach's small size should not lead visitors to think they're out in the boondocks. The town maintains its own municipal services and fire protection, and a local planner describes the community as being "like any big city, only smaller."

Kure Beach will remain small because it is completely surrounded. The Fort Fisher State Recreation Area and Historic Site are on the south side, and the U.S. Government owns the west side as part of a buffer zone for the military terminal at Sunny Point across the Cape Fear River. Carolina Beach borders the town on the north, and, of course, the Atlantic Ocean forms the east border.

Fort Fisher

To the south of Kure Beach are the Fort Fisher State Historic Site and Fort Fisher State Recreation Area. The Historic Site, amidst twisted live oaks on the west side of U.S. Highway 421, was the largest of the Confederacy's earthwork fortifications during the Civil War. It fell to Union forces in 1865, cutting off the last of the Confederate supply lines from the sea. During World War II, as an arm of Camp Davis to the north, it became an important training site for anti-aircraft and coastal artillery defenses and a large airstrip was located there. An extensive visitors center offers an historical perspective and guided tours. The Recreation Area on the east side of U.S. 421 has 4 miles of wide, unspoiled beach, a visitors' center with a bath house, a snack bar and restrooms

Also located here is the North Carolina Aquarium at Fort Fisher. The state's largest aquarium, it offers many dramatic exhibits and features a huge shark tank and a half-acre freshwater conservatory. See our Attractions section for more things to do.

At the southern end of U.S. 421 is the Fort Fisher–Southport Ferry, possibly the best $5 cruise in the world. More information about the ferry is in our Getting Here, Getting Around section. Across the road is a public boat launch area that is popular for windsurfing, Parasailing, kiteboarding, kayaking and fishing. All in all, these southernmost beaches of New Hanover County from Carolina Beach to the southern tip of Pleasure Island offer 7.5 miles of enjoyable vacationing and relaxed beach living.

BRUNSWICK COUNTY

Before the U.S. Army Corps of Engineers dredged the Intracoastal Waterway in the 1930s, the only body of water separating Oak Island, Holden Beach, Ocean Isle Beach and Sunset Beach from the mainland was the Elizabeth River. These beach waters were mainly used by local residents for fishing excursions. Today, though tourism is the main industry, more and more people are making their permanent homes here. The weather, the natural beauty of the area and the abundance of recreational opportunities continue to draw vacationers and permanent residents to the area.

Bald Head Island

Though easily identifiable in the distance by its unique lighthouse, Bald Head Island is 4 miles off the coast of Southport at the mouth of the Cape Fear River where it meets the sea. The lighthouse, built in 1817 and retired in 1935, is cataloged as the oldest lighthouse in North Carolina.

Once a favorite hiding spot for pirates such as Blackbeard and Stede Bonnet, Bald Head Island is now an affluent residential and resort community with about 220 year-round residents. It can only be reached by the island's private ferry or by personal boat. No cars are allowed on the island — transportation is by golf cart, bicycle or walking. The island is graciously open to the public, and the summer population can reach 8,000, with visitors renting vacation homes and playing golf (see our Golf section for course information).

It is probably safe to say this is one of the most unspoiled beach and maritime forest areas on the North Carolina coast. The island's natural beauty is protected, despite residential development as well as a few commercial amenities such as a restaurant, bed and breakfast inns, general store with deli, marina, golf course, specialty store, and golf cart and bike rental business.

The island has dunes, creeks, forests and 14 miles of beaches. The 2,000 acres of high land are surrounded by 12,000 acres of salt marshes, maritime forest preserve and tidal creeks. The owners have deeded nearby Middle Island and Bluff Island to the state and The Nature Conservancy. The Bald Head Island Conservancy, a nonprofit organization, was formed to ensure that the unique natural resources of the island are maintained and preserved.

Turtle nesting on Bald Head Island historically accounts for 50 percent of all sea turtle eggs laid in North Carolina. The Sea Turtle Program protects and monitors these wonderful creatures. There is an Adopt-a-Nest Program that pairs concerned humans with turtle nests in an effort to protect the nests and encourage the hatchlings toward the sea. Studies in which female turtles were tagged have revealed that pregnant turtles return to the same site to lay eggs every other year. Due to the many species of birds found on the island, the Audubon Society conducts an annual count here as part of its national program.

A day visitor can take the private ferry from Deep Point, off Moore Street in Southport — an adventure in itself. The cost is $16 round trip for adults and $9 for children ags 3 through 12. Day parking is $8. Prices are subject to change. For a longer stay, there are many rental accommodations on the island. The cost, compared to rentals on much of the mainland, is on the upper end, but so is the experience for the visitor who wants to really get away from it all in quiet style.

Southport

In 1754, Fort Johnston, North Carolina's first fort, was established and a small community of river pilots, fishermen and trades people grew up around it. In 1792 the town of Smithville was created and became the county seat of Brunswick County in 1808. For the remainder of the century, the town made plans to link rail service with the existing river traffic to make the community a major Southern port, and the city was renamed Southport.

Southport was one of the first areas in the state to celebrate the Fourth of July and is widely regarded as the Fourth of July Capital of North Carolina. History records that in 1795, citizens gathered at Fort Johnston and observed a 13-gun military salute to the original 13 states. In 1813, a Russian warship anchored in the harbor fired a 13-gun salute, and it was on this Fourth of July that fireworks were used for the first time to close the celebration. In 1972, the Fourth of July Festival was chartered and incorporated as the official North Carolina Fourth of July Festival, and it has become a tremendously popular four-day event for residents and visitors alike.

Southport, a quaint, historic seaport, is situated at the confluence of the Intracoastal Waterway and the Cape Fear River where it flows out to meet the Atlantic Ocean. The town makes for an interesting daytrip. Leave the car — parking is free — and just walk around as you discover shops, restaurants and pleasing views. It's an extremely casual community that invites visitors to pause and savor a slow pace of life that is fast disappearing in nearby areas. A lovely, leisurely stroll, Riverwalk, begins at Waterfront Park and winds along the riverfront, through the Old Yacht Basin and on to the Southport Marina.

The town is listed on the National Register of Historic Places, and history buffs will especially appreciate a visit for its beautiful old homes and historic cemeteries. The Captain Thompson Home, for example, offers a glimpse into the life of a Civil War Blockade Runner. The literary set will enjoy a visit to the Adkins-Ruark House, where author Robert Ruark lived as a young boy with his grandparents. Ruark's novels, including The Old Man and the Boy, give readers insight into Southport life years ago.

Once known as the best kept secret in North Carolina, this lovely little village with its live oak–lined streets is now being discovered. New shops, restaurants and hotels are springing up in the area as well as in the town, affording residents better choices without the necessity of traveling out of town. New housing developments abound. The Southport Marina has been completely redone, and serious talks and meetings are being held concerning the possible installation of an international port here.

Dosher Memorial Hospital has recently expanded its space and services, and the Southport Area Senior Center is now located in a new 13,000-square-foot space. This space is centrally located and allows for expansion of fitness, educational and nutrition programs with an added benefit of being located close to medical offices and a gym. In addition, year-round golf,

boating and fishing create an enormously pleasant environment, making this a popular place for retirement.

This is the place for people who genuinely want to kick back and enjoy beautiful coastal scenery. With a year-round population of more than 2,900, there's still plenty of elbow room. If you fall head over heels for Southport and decide to make a permanent move, keep in mind that its charm also means that the town includes some of the area's priciest real estate and most exclusive homes.

Southport can be accessed by both ferry and scenic highway. From Wilmington, Southport is reached by N.C. Highway 133 or N.C. Highway 87, although the N.C. 133 route is very beautiful and offers attractions, including Brunswick Town and the Progress Energy Nuclear Plant with its Brunswick Plant Energy Center. For information on the ferry route and schedule, see Getting Here, Getting Around.

Oak Island

Just across the water from Bald Head Island and Southport is Oak Island, a narrow strip of land that includes Caswell Beach and the Town of Oak Island.

Caswell Beach is the site of Fort Caswell, a military stronghold that dates from 1827. Located on the eastern tip of the island at the mouth of the Cape Fear River, Fort Caswell is now owned by the North Carolina Baptist Assembly, which welcomes visitors of all denominations each year. The community has some summer homes, but the area has mostly permanent residences. The year-round population is nearly 500, but up to 3,500 people can be staying on this part of Oak Island in the summer. You will find a golf club, which is open to the public year round. There is no business district on this portion of the island but it is convenient to the Town of Oak Island and Southport on the mainland.

The US Coast Guard station, in operation at this site since the 1930s, is located in Caswell Beach as well. Be sure to visit the Oak Island Lighthouse, which guided seafarers beginning in 1958. In 2003 it was formally declared surplus by the Gen-

Picture Perfect in Any Season!

Southport - Oak Island Area Chamber of Commerce

Caswell Beach • Oak Island • Bald Head Island
Southport • Boiling Spring Lakes • St. James

Welcome Center

4841 Long Beach Road
Southport, NC 28461

8:30 - 5:00 Monday-Friday (Year Round)

Chamber of
Commerce

SOUTHPORT • OAK ISLAND AREA

Call
800-457-6964
for our new
Vacation & Residents Guide

www.southport-oakisland.com

eral Services Administration of the U.S. Government and was deeded to the town. Friends of the Oak Island Lighthouse (FOIL) has been formed with the purpose of preserving and caring for the lighthouse and the 5 acres of beach-front property that was deeded along with it. This organization provides tours of the historic structure on a regular basis during the season and by reservation during the rest of the year.

As the name implies, the Town of Oak Island is famous for its beautiful live oak trees. An unusual feature is the east to west positioning of the island which means the 10 miles of beaches face south providing for gorgeous sunsets and sunrises. On the north side of the island, separating it from the mainland, you will find the Intracoastal Waterway. A third water feature is Davis Creek, which wends its way through the island.

Recreational opportunities include a golf course on the mainland portion of the town, 65 beach-access points, three public parks, a skate park, a recreation center, tennis courts, miniature golf and two fishing piers, as well as opportunities for surf fishing. There are a number of motels, and the business district now includes a Food Lion grocery store along with the many small shops and restaurants. Though Oak Island is being discovered along with Southport (with a year-round population of nearly 9,000 in the Town of Oak Island), it still offers a quiet respite for a peaceful vacation. For the most part, a visitor will enjoy renting a house for an extended vacation. In fact, vacation rental is the liveliest business here, with more than a dozen vacation rental companies operating on Oak Island (see our Vacation Rentals information). Recent growth in the area has led to the development of additional condominium units, but they remain in the minority as far as housing units go.

In recent years the town expanded its limits to include the commercial district along N.C. 133 approaching the Oak Island Bridge. The second bridge to Oak Island is under construction at Middleton Avenue from which a connecting road will intersect with N.C. 211 at Midway Road in Bolivia. As a result the town floated a pro-

posal to expand its limits farther onto the mainland. In October of 2008, the town purchased the former Yaupon Beach Pier which it manages along with an adjoining restaurant. Grant restrictions require the town, though allowed to lease the pier, to retain ownership. They also require the town to maintain it for public recreation use for at least 25 years and to dedicate the land as a recreation site in perpetuity.

Holden Beach

In 1756 Benjamin Holden bought 400 acres of mainland along the Lockwood Folly river as well as the then 100 acre island situated between Lockwood Folly Inlet and Bacon Inlet. He purchased the land by applying for a land patent as was the process at that time. The land was then surveyed by authorization of the Royal Governor, William Tryon, and Benjamin Holden was given 18 months in which to pay the price of 50 shillings per 100 acres. Once this was paid, he was given a permanent grant of the land from the governor. This land was handed down through the Holden family and for generations his family farmed and fished here. In the 1920s they began development of the resort community that thrives today on the enlarged island which is a man made barrier island formed by the construction of the Intracoastal Waterway between 1930 and 1940.

A remarkable bridge that connects the mainland to Holden Beach rises 65 feet above the Intracoastal Waterway, providing a stunning view of the ocean and a sweeping entry to the island. The beach and the sea are the central attractions in this town, which prides itself on a serene quality of life. With 9 miles of oceanfront, Holden Beach is the longest and the largest of the three islands in the group known as the South Brunswick Islands, which are all manmade barrier islands formed when the North Carolina section of the Intracoastal Waterway was constructed. The island is a jogger's paradise and, as of this writing, the town is applying for funds from the N.C. Department of Transportation to prepare a plan for bicycling in town. Approximately 930 year-round residents call Holden Beach home, and though the population swells to more than 10,000 during the season, visitors find a host of opportunities for assimilating themselves into this exceedingly quiet community. Boating, surf fishing and hiking the island are very popular activities. There is a fishing pier, and the island is a sea turtle habitat as well.

While there are limited commercial establishments on the island, the causeway leading to the island is lined with specialty stores and shops and a Food Lion grocery store. The Town of Shallotte, just 10 minutes, away has several shopping centers, which include grocery stores and national chain department stores. A little more than 30 minutes away you will find Wilmington and Myrtle Beach, and there are numerous golf courses nearby.

The Town of Holden Beach was listed in the 2007 AAA Beach Vacation Travel Journal as one of the top 30 beaches in the country. It made the list of the 38 Best American Beaches in the July/August 2007 edition of National Geographic Smart Traveler magazine, and has officially received National Healthy Beach status through the National Healthy Beaches Campaign.

Ocean Isle Beach

Ocean Isle Beach is the center island in the string of three known as the South Brunswick Islands, which are manmade barrier islands formed when the North Carolina section of the Intracoastal Waterway was constructed between 1930 and 1940. This coastal barrier island was incorporated as the Town of Ocean Isle Beach in 1959. The island is approximately 7 miles long and is home to 535 full-time residents with a seasonal population of 25,000. This beach has the only high-rise hotel on the South Brunswick Islands. It provides a family beach environment with a total resort experience: restaurants, specialty shops, public tennis courts, a fishing pier, access to all watersports, a water slide, miniature golf and a museum (see our Attractions chapter). The American Shore and Beach Preservation Association named Ocean Isle Beach a winner of the 2008 Best Restored Beach Awards. The Ocean Isle Beach Community Center is open March through November. Planned activities for adults are held in the spring and fall with children's activities scheduled during the months of June, July and August.

The Town of Ocean Isle Beach has recently purchased approximately 2 acres of land for the construction of a new Town Hall complex. In the mainland portion of the town you will find an airport that makes Ocean Isle accessible by air, but don't expect to see commercial jets at this small facility.

At this writing, a 300-seat amphitheater, eight tennis courts, a parking area, restrooms, a picnic shelter and a playground area have been completed on the 5-acre area designed to accommodate the annual Oyster Festival. Plans are also in the works for two high school and four junior soccer fields, two baseball fields with concession stand and a dog park or disc golf course.

The Ocean Isle Beach Land Conservancy, an independent nonprofit group, was formed in 2003 to preserve open space for conservation and public recreation and to educate the public about the importance of conserving coastal land. Old Ferry Landing Park is a project in which this group is involved jointly with the town. Here you will find a gazebo, a walkway, parking, a fishing pier and a kayak/canoe launch site.

Sunset Beach

The southernmost of the three barrier islands referred to as the South Brunswick Islands, which are manmade barrier islands formed when the North Carolina section of the Intracoastal Waterway was constructed between 1930 and 1940, Sunset Beach is only 3 miles long. The Township of Sunset Beach, however, is comprised of several square miles of mainland as well. At this writing, a new high-rise bridge that is being built to replace the swing bridge that has historically connected mainland and island is scheduled for completion in 2010. Despite its size this island has a current year-round population of more than 2,000 residents.

Although the island is residential in character, it is a great choice for a vacation. Some of the best bargains in vacation rentals are here, and the visitor who wants a quiet coastal place will do very well to book a house on this beach (see our Vacation Rentals chapter). The island boasts a white sandy beach and undisturbed sand dunes, a natural habitat and nesting ground for the abundant coastal wildlife, including the endangered loggerhead sea turtle. There is a full-service fishing pier on this island, and the mainland portion of the town offers shopping centers, grocery stores, small boutiques, dining, golf and the Ingram Planetarium (see our Attractions chapter). Due to the population growth in Brunswick County, condos and a mixed-use development are springing up on the mainland, especially around the planetarium.

Sunset Beach also offers a special delight — a walk to Bird Island. Once a separate island accessible only by walking through shallow Mad Inlet at low tide, Bird Island today is connected to Sunset Beach since the inlet has closed naturally. However, it is completely untouched by development as its nearly 1,300 acres of beach, marsh and wetlands were dedicated in 2002 as a North Carolina Coastal Reserve after 10 years of work by the Bird Island Preservation Society to protect it. This designation protects habitat used by several threatened or endangered species, including sea beach amaranth, Kemp's Ridley and loggerhead sea turtles, piping plover, wood stork and black skimmer. During the summer months early morning bird walks are conducted by persons affiliated with the North Carolina Coastal Land Trust. There are also frequent informal guided tours, announced by posters attached to street markers on the beach, so it's easy to hook up with locals who are pleased to share their knowledge of Bird island. The environment is purely natural and deeply comforting, where people of the twenty-first century can experience life as it was before the development of the land. A unique feature to be found on the island is a mailbox where "kindred spirits" can leave inspired messages.

Calabash

Calabash is a part of a 48,000-acre grant made to Landgrave Thomas Smith in 1691. Prior to 1750, The Boundary House was built as a place of rendezvous for travelers. During the late 1700s, the Altson family owned most of present-day Calabash at Little River Neck. In the late 1800s the area was called Pea Landing because of the growing and shipping of peanuts to Wilmington. Around 1890, Samuel Thomas purchased Hickory Hall Plantation and his descendants live in Calabash to this day. Calabash became known for its seafood restaurants in the late 1940s and, subsequently, as the "Seafood Capital of the World." Calabash was incorporated in 1973.

According to local lore, in the 1930s fishermen brought in their catch and were met by the locals to make their purchases. Calabash quickly became known for its fine quality of fresh shrimp and fish. The fishing crews were fed under the trees, and the aromatic smell of fresh fish cooking in big pots prompted residents to buy any leftover cooked seafood. "Calabash style" seafood was born when Clinton Morse, a local businessman, began serving up tubs of the deep-fried seafood that had been dipped in a light seasoned batter, cooked golden brown and served very hot. These open-air picnics were the beginning of the many original family seafood restaurants that are now run by descendants of the founders. Rumor has it that Jimmy Durante's signature sign-off, "Good-night, Mrs. Calabash, wherever you are," was aimed at the owner of a particular restaurant here.

Calabash sits on the banks of the Intracoastal Waterway and retains much of its original fishing-village atmosphere. Restaurants abound, and deep-sea fishing boats are docked in town waiting to take you on the adventure of your life. Golf courses are nearby and there are many small boutiques and art shops as well as one very large store full of souvenirs, Christmas decorations and more. Though small, with 1,794 year-round residents, Calabash is abutted on the west by the town of Carolina Shores, a residential community with a shopping center that includes a chain grocery store within its limits and is located on U.S. 17 South. Its location at the North Carolina/South Carolina border makes Calabash only a hop, skip and a jump from Myrtle Beach's shopping and entertainment.

Inland

The inland areas of Brunswick County, mostly rural in nature, appeal to those who prefer a quiet lifestyle and peaceful surroundings. The 1,050 square miles that comprise the county include 195 square miles of water where recreational boating and fishing are favorite pastimes. Some of the most serene areas can be found by boating the waters of the Lockwood Folly River. The more than 50 lakes in the Boiling Spring Lakes area, and the 5-mile by 7-mile Lake Waccamaw, which spans the borders of Brunswick and Columbus counties, are favorite sites for swimming, fishing and other water activities. Boiling Spring Lakes includes a nature preserve where The Nature Conservancy has provided walking trails and where the endangered red-cockaded woodpeckers make their homes. Walking trails can be found on the site of the Brunswick Community College in Supply as well.

Two of the 45 official N.C. scenic byways are located in Brunswick County. The 3-mile Brunswick Town Road Byway —Plantation Road (SR 1529) and Tryon Palace Road (SR 1533) off NC 133 — begins near Orton Plantation. This road parallels the Cape Fear River and ends at Brunswick Town State Historic Site. The area, covered by longleaf pine forests, provides opportunities for observing nature including fox squirrels, deer, waterfowl and alligators. Brunswick Town State Historic Site/ Fort Anderson is a Civil War–era battleground containing some of the most extensive surviving earthworks. There is a visitor center containing artifacts and staffed by history experts. You will find the ruins of Russellborough, the residence of two previous governors. Scenic walking paths meander along the river and among the ruins of the town.

The 53-mile Green Swamp Byway (N.C. 211 from Supply through Bolton in Colum-bus County) ends at Bladenboro in Bladen County. The Green Swamp is a 150-square-mile mix of uplands and wetlands that include Royal Oak Swamp, a tributary of the Lockwood Folly River. You can take a side trip to Little Macedonia, a crossroads community that leads to Crusoe Island, an isolated community on the Waccammaw River. Located along this byway is The Nature Conservancy Green Swamp Ecological Preserve. You can stop at a small parking area from which you can walk to a pond. Along the way you will find endangered species like the carnivorous Venus flytrap, pitcher plants and sundew. In the forest area you may spot the nesting cavities of red-cockaded woodpeckers.

Shallotte

The earliest reference to the river and the town of Shallotte dates back to 1734, though records of settlement of the area are dated around 1750. The Town of Shallotte was incorporated on March 6, 1899, and according to some accounts it took its name from a traveler who crossed the river by ferry and referred to it as the Charlotte River. The Charlotte River later became known as the Shallotte River and the town was referred to by the same name. In the early years agriculture, fishing and a river waterfront full of small watercraft used to transport goods to and from the area, were the means by which residents earned a living .

The town of Shallotte now serves as the hub for services for Brunswick County's beach communities. Because of its mainland location and island proximity, Shallotte offers residents and visitors the convenience of larger-town living and services. Here you will find shopping malls with grocery stores and national chain department stores, and a 10-screen movie theater. The Brunswick County Chamber of Commerce is headquartered in Shallotte, as is the office of the Department of Transportation and the North Carolina Welcome Center. With a year-round population of more than 1,900, Shallotte is still considered a small town though it has many of the amenities that larger cities provide. Shallotte is centered almost directly between Wilmington and Myrtle Beach, with the commute to either city being roughly 30 to 40 minutes. It is approximately 10 minutes from Holden Beach, Ocean Isle Beach and Sunset Beach.

Leland

The Leland area was initially settled at the same time that the earliest plantations along the Cape Fear and Brunswick rivers came into existence. Early activity revolved around the post office, the school, two grocery stores, the railroad station, Leland Baptist Church and Leland Methodist Church. For many years Leland was one of numerous small unincorporated communities throughout Brunswick County that served as minor centers of trade throughout the early twentieth century. Due to its location adjacent to the Brunswick River, Leland served as a transportation center, though by modern standards the early roads were primitive. Ferries were in use as the means of crossing the Brunswick and the Cape Fear rivers for travelers going north and south. A bridge was built over the Brunswick River in 1890 before one was built over the Cape Fear River.

The natural boundaries of the Town of Leland include the Brunswick River to the east and Sturgeon Creek to the south, siting it just five minutes west of Wilmington. Leland has emerged as one of the fastest growing communities in southeastern North Carolina and is the centerpiece of northern Brunswick County's continuing economic expansion. Its strategic location offers convenient access to Wilmington, Myrtle Beach, the coastal town of Southport, and the New Hanover and Brunswick County beaches.

Leland was first incorporated in 1989 with a population of approximately 1,800. Steady growth over the years has brought the population close to 13,000, which surpasses that of Oak Island, the longtime forerunner in population in the county. Expansion includes the development of retail centers that house national chain stores as well as mixed use developments along U.S. Highway 17 South, requiring

the reconfiguration of the highway in the area and the addition of a string of traffic lights. Leland is poised for even greater growth in the years to come. In late 2004 the town doubled its geographic size by completing the voluntary annexation of a 4,900-acre tract commonly known as Brunswick Forest. The build-out of this property should result in an additional 10,000 residential units. When a planned U.S. 17 bypass is completed, Leland will be directly accessible from I-40 without the current inconvenience of passing through Wilmington.

In the spring of 2008 the Town of Leland opened its first public water access site, the first of four potentially planned sites. This site provides access to Eagles Island, which groups have been working to designate and protect as a natural conservation area. Twelve endangered species exist within Sturgeon Creek and Eagles Island. A second site being developed was made possible by a grant from the N.C. Department of Environmental and Natural Resources' Division of Coastal Management water access program. Plans for this site include public parking and boat ramps as well as the conversion of an existing building into an environmental education and recreation center.

Navassa

Though located only 5 miles west of Wilmington, Navassa is in Brunswick County and sits at the confluence of the Brunswick and the Northwest Cape Fear rivers. Incorporated in 1977, Navassa takes its name from Navassa Island in the West Indies and the Navassa Guano Factory that was built in Brunswick County in 1869. This factory provided employment in northern Brunswick County for more than 100 years. With a population of just less than 2,000, Navassa continues to grow, along with the rest of Brunswick County. Its convenient location offers easy access to New Hanover and Brunswick County beaches, shopping areas and entertainment. Community parks include Navassa Ball Park with two gazebos, a grilling area, a basketball court and two tennis courts; the park and picnic area located next to

The quiet,
comfortable
coast

A short meander off the beaten path, the Brunswick Islands offer an uncomplicated, small-town lifestyle. Our beaches, golfing, boating and fishing are waiting to restore your mind and spirit. Little wonder vacationers often decide to settle here, making the Islands a premier place to live, work and play.

NORTH CAROLINA'S
brunswick
islands

Click BrunswickCountyChamber.org or call 800-426-6644.
THE BRUNSWICK COUNTY CHAMBER OF COMMERCE

the town hall; and Davis Creek Park with a walkway, piers, docks, a concrete boat ramp and a gazebo. In 2009, thanks to a matching grant from the N.C. Department of Natural Resources' Division of Coastal Management, improvements, including enhancements to the boat ramp and parking area, have been made in this park.

In 2006 the Town of Navassa received a low-interest loan in the amount of $1.2 million, which will be used in combination with a previous grant of $250,000 to construct a community center. Plans for the 16,000-square-foot center include a senior citizen center, a medical/health clinic, a youth center, a recreation room, multipurpose rooms and a cultural center or library. It will serve as an emergency shelter as well. In addition, an $850,000 Community Block Grant is being used to rehabilitate homes and infrastructure in neighborhoods where the need exists. Because the direction of growth in the town includes the influx of new industries, the town hired its first town manager in 2007 to oversee and plan for the expansion with positive results for the community.

Boiling Spring Lakes

Legend has it that long ago Indians camped around "Bouncing Log Spring" on their annual trek to the Atlantic Ocean to harvest fish, oysters and game. They held council meetings at the site and always drank from the spring, believing this would guarantee their return. In 1961 the developers of Boiling Spring Lakes happened upon a gushing spring concealed in a wooded ravine. Wishing to beautify the area, they built a 4-foot high wall to encompass this natural phenomenon. Almost before the masons had completed their work, the spring suddenly stopped running. Within a few hours, it burst out in a free full flow some 15 feet outside the wall. Eventually the wall broke and the spring returned to its original location where it boils today, discharging approximately 43 million gallons of water each day which feeds the lakes. You can visit the spring if you choose, just be prepared as it is located in a wooded area near the dam at the head of Big Lake and is unmarked. You can either stop at the Boiling Spring Lakes City Hall or call (910) 845-2614 for directions to the spot.

The 150-acre Big Lake, the city's centerpiece and one of more than 50 natural and man-made lakes in the city, is fed by five springs and Allen Creek. It is 2.5 miles long with 10 miles of shoreline. Around the shores of these lakes and scattered throughout the pines, oaks and sweet gums of the 16,000-acre area are the homes of the more than 4,200 residents that make up the City of Boiling Spring Lakes. Though rural by the very nature of the landscape, the City of Boiling Spring Lakes provides the services expected from any city, including its own police department and a community center with scheduled activities and a fitness room. A new city hall was completed in 2008. There is a golf club as well, which is open to the public. The proximity of the community to Southport and the Oak Island beaches provides opportunities to participate in a resort lifestyle while living close to nature.

Located within the incorporated limits of the town that is its namesake, the Boiling Spring Lakes Preserve encompasses half of the incorporated area of the town. The establishment of the Boiling Spring Lakes Preserve is the result of a collaborative partnership between the North Carolina Department of Agriculture and Consumer Services' Plant Conservation Program, The Nature Conservancy, the City of Boiling Spring Lakes and the North Carolina Natural Heritage Program. The land is owned by the Plant Conservation Program and is managed by The Nature Conservancy. This preserve contains a fascinating cross section of the Cape Fear region's natural communities. Though the area's dense vegetation may look foreboding, the preserve offers a rare glimpse of a vanishing landscape. This natural area contains a mosaic of unusual geologic features. A series of parallel ridges and swales are the remnants of an ancient dune system. A large concentration of Carolina bays (elliptical wetland depressions) studs the landscape. Fire-dependent natural communities, including high and low pocosins (evergreen shrub bogs) and longleaf pine savannas and flatwoods on the ridges and bay rims, form an intricate mosaic of habitats. Conservancy land stewards are actively working to restore the Boiling Spring Lakes Preserve to its natural condition by conducting prescribed burns in longleaf and pocosin communities and replanting longleaf pines.

In an average natural area, there are 8 to 10 species of plants growing in one square meter, but in the wetlands of Boiling Spring Lakes there are several times that number! A bounty of rare flora and fauna is found in this landscape, including the federally endangered red-cockaded woodpecker, a variety of carnivorous plants, rough-leaf loosestrife and a variety of orchids. The preserve contains more than 400 vascular plant species, including carnivorous plants such as the rare Venus flytrap. Completed in 2004, the Boiling Spring Lakes Nature Trail allows visitors to walk through a portion of the more than 6,000 fragile acres that make up the preserve.

PENDER AND ONSLOW COUNTIES

Topsail Island Area

A single main road runs parallel to the ocean along the length of this narrow 26-mile-long barrier island. In a few instances on the wider parts of the island, you will find an additional smaller street or two running parallel to the ocean, but there is still only one traffic light on the entire island strand. The 3,500 year-round residents here enjoy a relatively quiet lifestyle on the beach, that is until summer rolls around and Topsail's summer population swells to 35,000.

The island is located in both Onslow and Pender counties approximately 45 minutes north of Wilmington. Two bridges allow access to the island — an old fashioned swing bridge in Surf City and a modern high-rise bridge that connects Sneads Ferry to North Topsail Beach. There are three towns on the island: North Topsail Beach, Surf City and Topsail Beach. The two mainland towns of Sneads Ferry

and Holly Ridge complete the section known as the Greater Topsail Area.

North Topsail Beach, the northernmost town, is a residential community with oceanfront resort condominium complexes and rental cottages. With only two restaurants, North Topsail Beach visitors depend on Sneads Ferry or Surf City for most of their shopping and entertainment.

Surf City, located on both the island and mainland, is in the center of the island. It is the commercial hub with a number of restaurants and retail establishments. A variety of vacation rental homes, condominiums and motels are also found here, along with the most year-round residents.

Topsail Beach, on the southern end of the island, is accessible only through Surf City. It is a quieter area with year-round homes, rental cottages, motels and condominiums complementing a small downtown shopping area.

On the mainland, **Sneads Ferry**, near North Topsail Beach, is a small village where shrimping and fishing are a way of life. In recent years, however, the area has grown and is now developing into a community of upscale housing developments. **Holly Ridge**, near Surf City, had an explosive population boom during World War II when Camp Davis was established as an Army coastal artillery and anti-aircraft training base. The town is once again on the move with several new communities being built in the area.

Local residents are protective of their environment. This is particularly evident in the Topsail Turtle Project and the Karen Beasley Sea Turtle Rescue and Rehabilitation Center, both run solely by volunteers. Many of the volunteers locate and monitor loggerhead turtle nests until the young turtles hatch and make their way to the sea, while others maintain the center and care for sick and injured sea turtles until they have been rehabilitated and returned to the ocean. Still others take responsibility for the Turtle Talks, where participants can learn about the turtles and how they can help protect them. A visit to the Turtle Hospital, as it is affectionately known, is a real highlight of a Topsail Island vacation (see our Attractions section for more about the Turtle Hospital).

Surf City

Surf City is the center of the island both geographically and commercially. Here you will find restaurants, gift shops, grocery stores, churches, a fishing pier, tackle shops, surf shops and kayak outfitters — everything you need to enjoy a trip to the beach. The city has an oceanfront welcome center, bike paths, a community recreation center that offers a variety of classes from ballroom dancing to boating. Soundside Park at the swing-bridge is a perfect place to picnic and watch the boats go by.

Hampstead

Hampstead, once a small fishing village and a whistle stop alongside the Atlantic Coast Line Railroad, is now one of the fastest growing areas in the region. Many neighborhoods front the waterway, more are along the numerous creeks and even more line the area's four golf courses. Hampstead is seeing growth and change come quickly, and farmlands once used for blueberries and tobacco are growing houses and neighborhoods as development of the area increases.

Topsail Beach

The Town of Topsail Beach, situated at the southern end of Topsail Island, is the smallest of the three island communities. Though there are more than 1,300 homes, there are only around 500 year-round residents. The seasonal influx of tourists helps sustain the town's motels, restaurants, gift shops, book store, fishing pier and other businesses. Topsail Beach is also home to the Karen Beasley Sea Turtle Rescue and Rehabilitation Center and the Missiles and More Museum.

Holly Ridge

Holly Ridge was incorporated in 1941 when 28 people lived in town. Two years later Camp Davis, an anti-aircraft, artillery training base, came to town and the population soared to 110,000. Today, with 1,180 full-time residents Holly Ridge is once again on the grow. New neighborhoods of single-family homes and condominium communities seem to appear every day. Located halfway between Wilmington and Jacksonville, Holly Ridge is both convenient and close to the beach.

North Topsail Beach

North Topsail Beach stretches from Surf City to the northern point of the island, where the New River Inlet joins the Atlantic. While predominantly a community of full-time residents and rental cottages, there are also large and luxurious oceanfront resort condominium complexes. With only a few restaurants, North Topsail Beach's visitors and residents depend on Surf City or Sneads Ferry for their shopping and entertainment.

Sneads Ferry

The village of Sneads Ferry is a working fishing village located on the New River near the northern tip of Topsail Island off N.C. Highway 172. Here the river joins the Intracoastal Waterway and access to the Atlantic Ocean is easy. Sneads Ferry takes in more fish than any other Onslow County port — more than 385 tons of shrimp, 25 tons of flounder and approximately 493 tons of other delicious seafood like clams, scallops, oysters, mullet, spot, grouper, sea bass, soft-shell and hard-shell crabs per year.

AREA CHAMBERS OF COMMERCE

Chambers of commerce are great resources for gaining an understanding of a community's business, educational, cultural, entertainment and institutional offerings. Although these organizations are not generally in the tourism business, they usually have brochure racks filled with information of interest to visitors, newcomers and even the longtime residents who want to know more about their community. Staff members are always courteous and interested in providing help and information.

Hampstead, our quaint and wonderful little place on the map, is quickly becoming a destination community for those who seek the simpler, quieter lifestyle that our gracious Southern coastal area has to offer.

GREATER HAMPSTEAD CHAMBER OF COMMERCE
Visit our website: www.hampsteadchamber.com
Phone: 910-270-9642 • 800-833-2483
Email: hampsteadcoc1@bellsouth.net

Brunswick County
Chamber of Commerce
4948 Main St., Shallotte
(910) 754-6644, (800) 426-6644
www.brunswickcountychamber.org

Greater Hampstead
Chamber Of Commerce
Hampstead Village Ctr., U.S. Hwy. 17,
Bldg. 24J, Ste. 1, Hampstead
(910) 270-9642
www.hampsteadchamber.com

Greater Topsail Area
Chamber of Commerce
Treasure Coast Landing, 13775 N.C. Hwy. 50,
Ste. 101, Surf City
(910) 329-4446

Greater Wilmington
Chamber of Commerce
1 Estell Lee Pl., Wilmington
(910) 762-2611
www.wilmingtonchamber.org

North Brunswick
Chamber of Commerce
51 Poole Rd., Ste. 3, Leland
(910) 383-0553 x28451, (888) 383-0553

Pleasure Island Chamber of Commerce
1121 N. Lake Park Blvd., Carolina Beach
(910) 458-8434
Southeastern Welcome Center, Inc.
394 Whiteville Rd., Shallotte
(910) 754-2505

Southport-Oak Island Area
Chamber of Commerce
4841 Long Beach Rd. SE, Southport
(910) 457-6964, (800) 457-6964
www.southport-oakisland.com

Town of Surf City
102 North Shore Dr., Surf City
(910) 328-2716

Wrightsville Beach
Chamber of Commerce
315 Salisbury St., Wrightsville Beach
(910) 256-8116, (800) 232-2469

HOTELS AND MOTELS

With all of the growth in commerce and population we're currently experiencing on the southern coast, it's sometimes hard to remember we're also a major vacation destination. Visitors arrive on our sunny shores to relax and enjoy the area's beaches, attractions and festivals, as well as for weddings, family reunions, business meetings and corporate retreats. Fortunately we have a thriving and varied hospitality industry ready to accommodate them.

For those desiring top-of-the-line accommodations, full-service resort and business hotels are located on the beaches and along Wilmington's riverfront. In smaller towns such as Surf City and Oak Island, oceanfront motels are more common, some hearkening back to the bygone days of beach vacations. In Wilmington, the "motel strip" is primarily on Market Street west of College Road, and College Road itself, south of Market Street. You can find motels of every price range, from the budget Motel 6 to the pricier Hilton Riverside. In addition to a major oceanfront hotel and numerous in-town motels, Carolina Beach teems with cozy family-run motels concentrated along Carolina Beach Avenue North within a half-mile of Harper Avenue. Kure Beach offers a similar strip of pleasant motels along U.S. Highway 421 in the center of town. There are no hotels or motels on Figure Eight Island or Bald Head Island. On Bald Head Island, daily accommodations are limited to two large bed and breakfast inns. There are also some rental homes available for stays as short as a weekend.

No matter what type of accommodations you desire — plush or plain, city or beach, large or small — you'll be able to find a motel or hotel to satisfy your needs. This chapter deals only with traditional hotel and motel accommodations. For other accommodation options, see our Bed and Breakfasts and Small Inns, Vacation Rentals and Camping chapters.

PRICE CODE

Since prices are subject to change without notice, we provide only price guidelines based on double-occupancy, per-night rates during the summer (high season). Our codes do not reflect the 7 percent state/county and 1 to 6 percent room occupancy taxes (taxes may vary by county or municipality). Most establishments offer lower rates during the off-season. Always confirm rates and necessary amenities before reserving. It may also be beneficial to inquire about corporate, senior citizen, AAA or long-term discounts even when such discounts are not mentioned in our descriptions. Most establishments accept major credit cards, and some accept personal checks when payment is made well in advance.

$	Less than $90
$$	$90 to $150
$$$	$151 to $200
$$$$	More than $200

Wilmington

Ameri-Stay Inn & Suites   **$-$$$**
5600 Carolina Beach Rd., Wilmington
(910) 796-0770
www.ameristay.net

Centrally located on U.S. Highway 421 S. in the Monkey Junction area, this 65-unit, three-story Ameri-Stay Inn & Suites is just a few miles from the beaches of Pleasure Island, Fort Fisher State Historic Site, Carolina Beach State Park and the North Carolina Aquarium. Family-friendly, this hotel is a great place to put down temporary roots while visiting area attractions or playing a round or two of golf at one of the many nearby courses. Only 7 miles

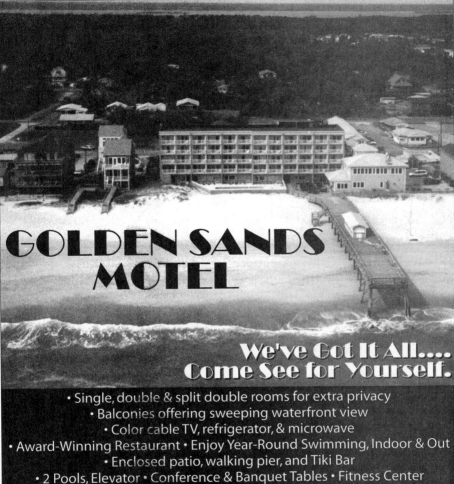

from UNCW and 8 miles from historic downtown Wilmington, this inn rates high on convenience. Ameri-Stay Inn & Suites is within walking distance of restaurants and shopping, too. Guests can choose from standard king, double-bed and whirlpool suites, all featuring free cable TV with HBO, free local calls and free high-speed Internet access. Other in-room amenities include a coffeemaker, an iron and ironing board, a hairdryer and a safe. Some rooms have a wet bar, micro-fridge or recliner. A complimentary continental breakfast is served every morning. After touring, shopping or a day of watersports, enjoy a swim in the large indoor pool and hot tub or lounge around it while watching the kids. A meeting room that accommodates up to 70 people is also available.

Baymont Inn $-$$
306 College Rd., Wilmington
(910) 392-6767

Whether you're coming to Wilmington on business or for a family vacation, Baymont Inn & Suites offers travelers top-quality accommodations and Southern hospitality at reasonable rates. With a AAA 2 diamond rating and backed by a 100-percent customer satisfaction guarantee, your stay is sure to be relaxed and enjoyable at this family-owned and operated inn. The 134 guest rooms feature many amenities, including coffeemaker, alarm

clock, iron and ironing board, hairdryer, pillow-top mattresses and in-room movies on-command. Start the morning with a complimentary deluxe continental breakfast of eggs, yogurt, fruits, cereal, assorted breads and muffins, hot waffles, juice, milk and fresh coffee. All day long you can enjoy complimentary fruit, hot beverages and fresh-baked cookies. Take advantage of free wireless high-speed Internet access and concierge service. Baymont Inn & Suites is adjacent to Outback Steakhouse and located right across the street from the recently opened Carolina Ale House. Baymont Inn is also convenient to Corning Glass, DuPont, General Electric and UNCW and is within walking distance of several popular restaurants and two shopping centers.

Comfort Inn Executive Center $-$$
151 S. College Rd., Wilmington
(910) 791-4841, (800) 221-2222

For a comfortable stay in a business-friendly — and family-friendly — environment, try the Comfort Inn Executive Center. The recently renovated hotel offers rooms with single, double and king-sized beds. Business travelers will enjoy free wireless Internet with copy and fax machines available as well as close proximity to car rental services. Families will appreciate the seasonal outdoor pool and free deluxe continental breakfast. The hotel is

centrally located on College Road, one of Wilmington's major thoroughfares, within walking distance to the university and shopping centers and a short drive from Downtown Wilmington and the beaches. Rooms with refrigerators and microwaves are available, and pets are allowed with a small fee.

Comfort Suites of Wilmington $-$$$
4721 Market St., Wilmington
(910) 793-9300

Comfort Suites of Wilmington is conveniently located between scenic Wrightsville Beach and Wilmington's downtown historic district. This smoke-free hotel offers 73 deluxe suites, each with an iron and ironing board, hairdryer, coffeemaker, microwave, refrigerator, cable television and high-speed wireless Internet. In addition, you get free local phone calls on two-line telephones with voicemail and dataports. Suites have either two double beds or one king-sized bed and a sleeper sofa. The hotel has an indoor fitness facility, an outdoor pool, a business center and

a laundry facility available for guest use. A complimentary deluxe continental breakfast is served daily, and guests receive a free USA Today Monday through Friday.

Fairfield Inn & Suites Wilmington/
Wrightsville Beach $$
303 Eastwood Rd., Wilmington
(910) 791-8082
www.fairfieldwilmington.com

The Fairfield Inn & Suites Wilmington/ Wrightsville Beach offers the convenience of being close to major attractions and a luxurious, comfortable environment at a great value. The hotel's location on Eastwood Road suits both leisure and business travelers, as it's only a short drive from Wrightsville Beach, historic downtown Wilmington and the UNCW campus as well as near many corporate offices, including Corning, PPD and Progress Energy. The hotel offers a complimentary deluxe continental breakfast, business services, an exercise room and an on-site laundry facility, and in-room amenities include wired and wireless Internet, a 32-

inch TV with stereo and CD system, mini refrigerators and microwaves.

Hampton Inn Medical Park $$-$$$
2320 S. 17th St., Wilmington
(910) 796-8881
www.medicalpark.hamptoninn.com

Hampton Inn Medical Park is located just minutes from historic downtown Wilmington, area beaches and local attractions, yet it's nestled within the Medical District (a hospital shuttle is available). In 2005 Hampton Inn Medical Park was awarded the Lighthouse Award recognizing its placement in the top 2 percent of all Hampton Hotels. It was ranked 29th out of 1,200 Hampton Inns nationwide. The hotel features 120 all-interior corridor rooms, including the addition of 35 new spacious king rooms added in spring 2007. The 2007 renovations also include a new meeting facility with more than 2,200 square feet for corporate meetings. Amenities include an outdoor swimming pool in a well-landscaped setting, a fitness center on the property as well as a free full membership to nearby Wilmington Athletic Club. All rooms have brand new 36-inch flat-screen TVs, on-demand movies, refrigerators and wet bars, coffeemakers, hairdryers, irons and ironing boards. Each room also provides free high-speed wireless Internet access and voicemail. In addition, the hotel offers a complimentary

hot deluxe breakfast, a business center and outstanding customer service.

Hampton Inn University Area/ Smith Creek Station $$$-$$$$
124 Old Eastwood Rd., Wilmington
(910) 791-9899
www.wilmingtonuniversityarea.hamptoninn.com

One of Wilmington's newest hotels, the Hampton Inn at Smith Creek Station is in the university area and located just minutes from Wrightsville Beach and only a short drive to Historic Downtown Wilmington. The hotel's 125 guest rooms and suites offer LCD TVs, free high-speed Internet, mini-fridges, microwaves, sleeper sofas and more.

Make yourself at home while enjoying a glass of wine in the hotel's contemporary, inviting lobby or relaxing outside on the terrace. The hotel is 100-percent nonsmoking and offers a complimentary, hot breakfast buffet, a state-of-the-art fitness center, a 24-hour business center and a convenience store. With an array of modern conveniences and all the comforts of home, the hotel is proud to say that service is their ultimate amenity.

Hilton Wilmington Riverside $$$-$$$$
301 N. Water St., Wilmington
(910) 763-5900, (888) 324-8170

The Hilton Wilmington Riverside, located on the Riverwalk overlooking the

Cape Fear River, promises you will discover just as much to love at the hotel as you will find while exploring Wilmington's charming downtown. Each of the hotel's 272 modern guest rooms were renovated in 2008 to maximize guest comfort and complement Wilmington's tranquil milieu. Guest rooms feature complimentary high-speed Internet access, expanded work areas, plush bed amenities and beautiful views of the riverfront or thriving downtown scape. Fit in a workout at the new state-of-the-art Precor® Fitness Center, take care of business at the 24-hour business center, or soak in the sun by the outdoor pool. Once you have worked up an appetite, you can dine in-house at Ruth's Chris Steak House, Current's Riverside Cafe — Proudly Brewing Starbucks or Innovations Restaurant. With more than 20,000 square feet of meeting and banquet facilities, the hotel offers 19 meeting rooms, including the Grand Ballroom, accommodating up to 600 people with food service. The Hilton is only 3 miles from Wilmington International Airport and for added convenience, an airport shuttle is complimentary.

Holiday Inn - Wilmington $-$$
5032 Market St., Wilmington
(910) 392-1101

Just minutes from both I-40 and Wilmington International Airport, in the heart of the southern coastal area, you'll find the peace and quiet of the Holiday Inn – Wilmington. Whether you're traveling on business or pleasure, alone or with your family, Holiday Inn – Wilmington is centrally located and a great place for sampling the area's history, arts, beaches and outdoor fun. This hotel offers a variety of packages that include a complete wedding package, golf on some of the area's finest courses, and corporate retreats. Holiday Inn – Wilmington is a contemporary, full-service hotel with 124 standard guest rooms and studio and two-room suites. Amenities include a microwave and refrigerator in the executive rooms and suites, high-speed wireless Internet, cable TV, coffeemaker, iron and ironing board, hairdryer and a large desk with a two-line speaker phone. There are meeting and event rooms and a 24-hour business center as well. After touring, shopping or sitting in business meetings, take a dip in the heated indoor pool, relax in the whirlpool spa or work out in the fitness center. For dinner, visit the Savoy Grill, enjoy a cocktail in the casual lounge or kick off your shoes and order room service. When they say full-service hotel, they mean just that. You'll find everything you need for a great stay is right at your fingertips.

Holiday Inn Express $$
160 Van Campen Blvd., Wilmington
(910) 392-3227, (800) HOLIDAY

Customer-focused, well-maintained and tastefully decorated, this hotel pro-

vides a wide range of services and amenities. For a modest price, you can have top-notch lodging, from king and double-bed rooms to two-room executive or whirlpool suites. All rooms include ironing equipment, coffeemakers, voicemail telephones, dataports, free high-speed Internet access and cable TV with premium networks, HBO, Pay-Per-View movies and Nintendo. Enjoy your complimentary deluxe continental breakfast by the fireplace in the cozy, living room–style lounge or while relaxing next to the outdoor pool. Hotel amenities also include an exercise room, a coin-operated laundry, an airport shuttle and a complimentary daily newspaper. The hotel boasts a comfortably furnished executive boardroom and several meeting rooms suitable for up to 150 people. Audiovisual equipment is available for rental, and catering can be arranged. Centrally located, the 131-room Holiday Inn Express Hotel & Suites is convenient to Wilmington's business districts, downtown and Wrightsville Beach. Within walking distance are major restaurants, a Walmart Supercenter and several shopping plazas.

Homewood Suites by Hilton Wilmington/Mayfaire $$$
**6732 Swan Mill Rd., Wilmington
(910) 791-7272
www.homewoodsuitesmayfaire.com**

Homewood Suites by Hilton Wilmington/Mayfaire offers spacious studio one-bedroom and two-bedroom suites with separate living and sleeping areas. Each has a fully equipped kitchen with full-size refrigerator, microwave, two-burner stove and dishwasher plus many other comforts of home, such as two TVs, complimentary high-speed Internet access and two phones with voicemail. Homewood Suites features a wealth of amenities to make your stay comfortable and enjoyable, including an outdoor pool, hot tub, kids' pool, business center, 24-hour convenience market and fitness room. Start your day with their complimentary hot breakfast buffet and end it with their evening manager's reception. With its location near Mayfaire Town Center, Homewood Suites is a short driving distance from Wrightsville Beach, UNCW and many major employers.

Hotel Tarrymore $$-$$$
**102 S. Second St., Wilmington
(910) 763-3806
www.hoteltarrymore.com**

Located in the heart of downtown Wilmington, Hotel Tarrymore is a newly renovated boutique hotel featuring spacious one- and two-bedroom suites with classic Southern charm and all the comforts of home. Each suite boasts a fully appointed professional kitchen including granite counter tops. Of course, you may choose to take breakfast, lunch or dinner at Press 102, the Euro-American bistro centered on the first floor of the hotel. There is nothing better than a fresh fruity cocktail out on the patio before you venture out for the evening to stroll quiet tree-lined streets or the lively downtown scene. Hotel Tarrymore also can accommodate up to 200 guests for private parties and dining in the beautiful Veranda Ballroom. Hotel Tarrymore is the perfect place for your classic Carolina experience.

Howard Johnson Express Inn $-$$
**3901 Market St., Wilmington
(910) 343-1727**

This one-story, 80-unit motel offers a variety of comfortable smoking, non-smoking and handicapped-accessible rooms to meet the needs of most travel-

ers. Choose from standard rooms with one king or two double beds or home office rooms with upgraded amenities. All have a private bath, a color TV with cable, a telephone and voicemail, free WIFI, a dataport and a coffeemaker. Many rooms also come with a microwave and small refrigerator. There's no charge for local phone calls, and a complimentary continental breakfast is served from 6 to 9 AM daily. Long-term rates are available. The Howard Johnson Express Inn is located 3 miles from downtown Wilmington, 7 miles from Wrightsville Beach and 3.5 miles from Wilmington International Airport.

MainStay Suites $-$$$
5229 Market St., Wilmington
(910) 392-1741
www.mainstaywilmingtonnc.com

This newly renovated, Platinum Hospitality Award–winning MainStay Suites is a well-thought-out, comfortable, attractive alternative to traditional hotel lodging. Whether you're in town on business or vacation, you can call this your home away from home for as long as you like. Accommodations available to meet your needs include king suites, two-room double queen suites and many choices in between. Thoroughly modern, every suite features its own central heating and air-conditioning system and complete kitchen facilities, including a full-size refrigerator with icemaker, two-burner electric

stove, microwave, toaster, coffeemaker, dishwasher, dishes, utensils, pots, even dishtowels and potholders. If you don't feel like cooking, take advantage of their deluxe complimentary breakfast offering hot and cold cereal, bagels, fruit and muffins. Other in-room amenities include cable TV, phones, high-speed Internet access, ironing equipment, hairdryer and shower organizer. A guest laundry is available, as are a fitness room and a business center with high-speed Internet access. Wireless Internet access is also available in the lobby. A seasonal outdoor pool offers guests a spot to relax, and an enclosed courtyard comes complete with grills for guest use. Convenient to shopping and restaurants, MainStay Suites is only minutes from area beaches, historic downtown and Wilmington International Airport.

Ramada Conference Center $-$$
5001 Market St., Wilmington
(910) 799-1730

Ramada Conference Center's newly renovated double and king rooms are sure to make your stay in Wilmington comfortable. The hotel is centrally located within a short distance of the airport, Wrightsville Beach and historic downtown Wilmington. Consider the Ramada's conference/meeting rooms and ballroom, which can accommodate up to 300 people, for your next special event or business meeting. Hotel amenities include a large outdoor

Plan your wedding in coastal North Carolina.

photo: Tracy Turpen

pool and patio area, daily complimentary deluxe continental breakfast, wireless high-speed Internet access, and in-room microwaves and refrigerators.

Red Roof Inn $-$$
5107 Market St., Wilmington
(910) 799-1730, (800) REDROOF

Red Roof Inn has 118 tastefully appointed rooms, each featuring wireless high-speed Internet, a dataport, an iron and ironing board, a hairdryer, cable TV with HBO and a micro-fridge. Guests can choose from single, double or king rooms. The hotel offers an outdoor pool open from May through September. They serve a delicious continental breakfast daily from 6 to 10 AM. Handicapped-accessible rooms are available, and pets are welcome. Centrally located between Wrightsville Beach and Wilmington's historic downtown, and less than a mile from UNCW, Red Roof Inn is within walking distance of several popular restaurants and shopping venues.

Riverview Suites at
Water Street Center $$$
106 N. Water St., Wilmington
(910) 772-9988

Riverview Suites at Water Street Center provides a great home away from home. Situated overlooking downtown Wilmington and the Cape Fear River, the hotel's 80 well-appointed suites provide a comfortable stay in charming surroundings. Each one-bedroom suite boasts a walk-out balcony with a picturesque view of the riverfront, washer/dryer, separate living room with pull-out sofa, cable television, and full kitchen with stove, full-sized refrigerator and coffeemaker. Perfect for business travelers or longer visits, the Riverview Suites is equipped for every traveler's wants and needs.

Sleep Inn $-$$
5225 Market St., Wilmington
(910) 392-1741, (866) SLEEP99
www.sleepinnwilmingtonnc.com

This eight-time Gold Hospitality Award–winning hotel, with renovation completed in all guest rooms in April 2009, is located less than a half-mile west of the Market Street I-40 overpass, 2.5 miles from Wilmington International Airport, and is convenient to shopping and a variety of restaurants. Sleep Inn offers 104 inside-corridor rooms with either one queen-sized bed or two double beds. Each room comes complete with an oversized shower, key-card security lock, cable TV, high-speed Internet access, a coffeemaker, an iron and ironing board, and a combination micro/fridge. To make your stay more comfortable and pleasurable, Sleep Inn offers a fitness room, business center, guest laundry and seasonal outdoor pool. A copier, fax machine and meeting room are available for guest use, and there is wireless Internet access throughout the hotel. A complimentary morning medley breakfast is offered daily, with hot beverages available free all day in the lobby lounge.

Suburban Extended Stay Hotel $-$$
245 Eastwood Rd., Wilmington
(910) 793-1920

Ideally situated between I-40 and Wrightsville Beach, this 107-room establishment is just 5 miles from the beach and 10 minutes from downtown Wilmington. Since each room features a kitchen, the Suburban Extended Stay Hotel is a great choice for nightly or long-term visits and other special needs. Other amenities include free high-speed Internet access, dataport hookup, cable TV (including

HBO), free local calls and voicemail. The hotel features a conference room, a copier and a fax machine that guests can use, plus an outdoor pool and barbecue grills. Handicapped-accessible rooms also are available.

TownePlace Suites by Marriott $$$-$$$$
305 Eastwood Rd., Wilmington
(910) 332-3326

Enjoy your stay at Wilmington's newest hotel, TownePlace Suites by Marriott. TownePlace Suites offers three comfortable, spacious floor plans, each with a separate living space, sleeping area and full kitchen. The hotel is equipped with an indoor pool, business center and state-of-the-art fitness room with free weights. While staying at TownePlace Suites, you'll also enjoy a complimentary breakfast, evening receptions and the "In a Pinch" 24-hour market. Several top attractions are within a short distance of the hotel, including golf courses, three major beaches, many outdoor recreation facilities and major shopping centers.

Wilmington Quality Inn $-$$
4926 Market St., Wilmington
(910) 791-8850

Newly renovated and centrally located to attractions, beaches, UNCW, the airport and the historic downtown area, Wilmington Quality Inn offers travelers both comfort and affordability. Each of the 120 spacious guest rooms has a coffeemaker, an iron and ironing board, a hairdryer, cable TV, a telephone with free local calls, a microwave, a mini refrigerator and free wireless high-speed Internet access. The hotel is within walking distance of several restaurants and serves a free deluxe continental breakfast every morning. A refreshing dip in the seasonal outdoor pool will revive you after a day of shopping or beach combing, and you can enjoy your complimentary USA Today newspaper while you sip coffee that's always available in the lounge. Guests are also welcome to use the hotel's new grill and outdoor patio. The Wilmington Quality Inn is a pet-friendly hotel.

The Wilmingtonian $$-$$$$
101 S. Second St., Wilmington
(910) 343-1800, (800) 525-0909

The Wilmingtonian comprises three buildings with 26 unique non-smoking suites, plus a small conference room. The buildings, dating from 1904 to 1994, are surrounded by extensive gardens and ponds with courtyards and balconies. This is the perfect spot for business or leisure travelers or wedding guests looking to stay long or short term. Amenities for all suites include a kitchen or wet bar, refrigerator, coffeemaker, microwave, toaster, VCR and DVD. Complimentary high-

speed Internet is available throughout the hotel. The Wilmingtonian's dining room is located near the private City Club and is accessible to guests of the inn. The hotel is just two blocks from the Cape Fear River and within walking distance of area restaurants, galleries, antiques stores and shopping. The beaches are just a short drive away.

Wingate by Wyndham   **$$-$$$**
5126 Market St., Wilmington
(910) 395-7011
www.wingateinns.com

"Built for Business" is Wingate by Wyndham's slogan, but vacationers say it was also built for leisure. This outstanding, smoke-free hotel has the amenities, facilities and service every traveler requires, backed by a 100-percent satisfaction guarantee. Conveniently located near area attractions, beaches, golf, airport, shopping and historic downtown, the hotel is just minutes from Wilmington International Airport and offers a complimentary airport shuttle service. Wingate by Wyndham's over-sized guest rooms are all on interior corridors, and each offers separate areas for sleep and work, free high-speed wireless and T1 Internet access, refrigerator, microwave, hairdryer, iron, ironing board, coffeemaker and electronic safe. The desk phone has two lines, a speaker and conference-call capabilities. The hotel also has a complete business center with free

copies and faxes for guests and meeting rooms available. The 25-inch color TV offers more than 65 free cable channels, including HBO. You can also order a first-rate movie, play Nintendo 64 video games or go online with Web TV from your room. For relaxation you can lounge by the outdoor pool or take advantage of the well-equipped fitness center and spa, read your complimentary USA Today newspaper or watch the news on their 62-inch big-screen TV while enjoying a nutritious complimentary breakfast from the deluxe buffet. The hotel hosts a guest appreciation reception Monday through Thursday evenings, with complimentary wine, beer, soft drinks and snacks.

Wrightsville Beach and Vicinity

Blockade Runner Beach Resort   **$$-$$$$**
275 Waynick Blvd., Wrightsville Beach
(910) 256-2251

Located in the heart of this beautiful barrier island, Blockade Runner Beach Resort is one of the premier oceanfront resort hotels in Wrightsville Beach. Everything you need for a perfect vacation can be found within minutes of your room. At the harborside water center, you'll find complete services for sailing, fishing, kayaking, surfing, diving and eco-tours.

Several championship golf courses also are nearby, and a shuttle service to tennis courts is available.

Families with children ages 4 to 12 will appreciate Sandcamper's, a supervised children's program that includes indoor crafts and games, plus beach, pool and island excursions and evening activities. You'll find a complete fitness center including a whirlpool and dry sauna. Looking for a massage after a long day? The hotel will schedule one for you. During the warm months, they offer oceanfront yoga.

The Blockade Runner's outdoor patio bar provides casual dining with a spectacular view overlooking manicured gardens and the waters of the Atlantic Ocean. Enjoy an unforgettable dining experience and feel the ocean breeze on the dinner deck of the award-winning East Restaurant. There are nightly features including a sushi bar, wine tastings and fresh local seafood and lobster. The popular Sunday Jazz Brunch includes a variety of local favorites and entertainment.

All rooms are either oceanfront or harbor-front with queen or king bedding. The Terrace, the newly renovated oceanfront balcony section, offers additional amenities such as high-thread-count linens, plasma TVs and bathrooms with marble, granite counter tops and rain forest showers, all with a magnificent view of the oceanfront gardens.

Standard in each room is a refrigerator, coffeemaker, hairdryer, ironing equipment and luxurious bathrobes. Other amenities include room service, complimentary breakfast, the Sundry Shop, safe-deposit boxes and a shuttle service around the island. For the business traveler, the Blockade Runner's Executive Club offers discounted room rates, free local calls, incoming fax service and high-powered wireless Internet connections. Conference and banquet facilities are available. Corporate rates are offered year-round.

Carolina Temple Apartments Island Inn $-$$
550 Waynick Blvd., Wrightsville Beach (910) 256-2773

Built by the Temple family in the early 1900s, Carolina Temple Apartments is the oldest business in continuous operation on Wrightsville Beach. Now operated by the Wrights, it has been in the same family since 1952. Located facing the sound on the south end of the island, it is set back from the road like a well-kept secret, yet only a few steps from the beach. The Inn was once Station 6 along the Wrightsville Beach trolley line. The pride with which the place is run is evident everywhere. The building is a good example of early coastal North Carolina architecture with central hallways, spacious, breezy, wrap-around porches furnished with large rockers and the occasional well-placed hammock.

Louvered outer doors to each of the eight apartments gives a Caribbean feel. The apartments are not large but they are beautifully maintained, and are either one- or two-room air-conditioned suites with private baths, ceiling fans and fully equipped kitchenettes. The apartments are perfect for couples or small families. The decor is tropical, with luminous beach colors and Caribbean-style folk art. Rentals are from late March to mid-October. Summer rentals mostly require one week's stay. The Inn closes in winter. Extras include a sound-side pier, a beach and a picnic area with grills. A laundry facility is also available. This is an excellent bargain relative to the area.

Hampton Inn & Suites Wilmington/ Wrightsville Beach- Landfall Park $$-$$$$
1989 Eastwood Rd., Wilmington
(910) 256-9600
www.landfallparkhotel.com

The moment you walk into the lobby of the Hampton Inn & Suites Wilmington/ Wrightsville Beach-Landfall Park, you sense the unique ambiance and quality. The free-standing fireplace is surrounded by decor reflecting a coastal casual elegance. And with 90 traditional rooms and 30 apartment-style suites, the inn provides the ultimate in service.

The hotel is less than one-half mile from the drawbridge and one mile from the beach and just minutes from excellent shopping in Mayfaire Towncenter and The Forum. The Landfall Park Hampton Inn and Suites has many dining options within walking distance, including the popular Port City Chop House.

All suites feature a full kitchen with microwave, stove, dishwasher and refrigerator. Several suites feature a variety of different amenities such as a double-sided fireplace, entertainment center and two-person whirlpool bath.

Executive one and two-bedroom suites are also available and excellent for long term stays. Standard amenities include complimentary high-speed Internet access, "Hot on the House" breakfast daily, a fitness center, a 24-hour business center and a convenience store. Modern meeting facilities accommodating up to 80 people with full catering service are available. The large kidney-shaped pool is surrounded by tropical landscaping and is accompanied by a seasonal gazebo bar serving snacks and frozen beverages.

Harbor Inn $$-$$$$
701 Causeway Dr., Wrightsville Beach
(910) 256-9402, (888) 507-9402
www.harborinnwb.com

Situated where Banks Channel meets the Causeway Bridge, the newly renovated Harbor Inn offers something for everyone. Private balconies overlooking the harbor are just the place to relax with your morning coffee to plan a day on the water or at the beach. Except for the handicapped-accessible suite, which sleeps four, each tastefully appointed suite sleeps up to six people and features a fully equipped kitchenette with microwave, convectional ovens, dishwasher, mini-fridge, coffee-maker and stove. The living room area has a dining table and comfortable furniture enhanced by a picture-perfect water view. Other in-room amenities include telephone, hairdryer, toiletries, individually controlled heat and air conditioning, daily maid service, linens, kitchen utensils, pots and pans, and a wall-mounted flat screen 42-inch cable LCD/HDTV. All of the rooms are non-smoking, however smokers

may use their private balcony to smoke at any time. Harbor Inn has a dock that can accommodate boats up to 25 feet, which makes this a very popular spot for boaters to vacation (reservations required for dockage). It also has laundry facilities and wireless high speed Internet available to all guests. Add to all this a beautiful outdoor swimming pool, and you have the recipe for a great experience. Weekly rates are available.

Holiday Inn Resort $$-$$$$
1706 N. Lumina Ave., Wrightsville Beach
(910) 256-2231, (877) 330-5050
www.wrightsville.holidayinnresorts.com

This full-service resort is the proud recipient of the 2009 IHG Torchbearer Award provided to only a few select properties that demonstrate a consistent level of service excellence and outstanding guest satisfaction scores. The oceanfront hotel has an elegant yet casual Caribbean-like atmosphere that makes you feel relaxed and comfortable, whether you are visiting for fun, on business or attending a convention. As you enter the oceanfront lobby, you are greeted by two blue and gold macaw parrots, one of the hotel's main attractions. The oceanfront Verandah Cafe Restaurant serves breakfast, lunch and dinner with both indoor and outdoor dining options. Gabby's Lounge, offering live entertainment, is ideal for that pre-dinner cocktail and appetizer or late-evening

nightcap. In season Lazy Daze Pool Bar and Grill provides tropical drinks and good eats without leaving the comfort of your lounge chair. A market/gift shop is available for those forgotten items, and there's an ATM on site as well. The resort offers a complimentary, supervised children's program for ages 4 to 12. The KidSpree Vacation Club is a dedicated children's activity room complete with games, toys, Nintendo and videos. A video arcade, beach playground, volleyball court and fitness center with state-of-the-art equipment give you lots of ways to exercise and have fun. Five recreational pools, including one in the indoor atrium, two whirlpools, a kiddie pool and a poolside bar and grill offer total enjoyment whatever the weather.

Most of the 184 guest rooms have large balconies with views of either the ocean or the sound and the Intracoastal Waterway. Whirlpool suites or rooms are also available. All rooms have a microwave, refrigerator and high-speed wireless Internet access is complimentary to all guests. Guest parking is complimentary and the hotel offers a free shuttle service to area restaurants, shopping and the airport. The hotel's conference center, with 8,500 square feet of meeting/conference space, features the 4,100-square-foot Lumina Ballroom. An executive boardroom, smaller oceanfront meeting rooms and a business center make the hotel an ideal

a signature suite with a fireplace and a garden-style whirlpool tub for ultimate relaxation. A great option for families, the Residence Inn by Marriott is located just minutes from the beach and in the heart of Wilmington's east-side shopping and dining meccas of Mayfaire Towncenter and The Forum Shops on Military Cutoff Road.

Enjoy a full, hot breakfast each morning before heading to the beach or to one of the many attractions in the area. Relax in the outdoor pool and hot tub (open April through October), have a cookout on one of the two gas grills available for guest use, or play a pick-up basketball or volleyball game on the hotel's sports court. The fitness room is open 24 hours and there's even a putting green to get your game in shape for one the area's magnificent golf courses. Business travelers will appreciate complimentary in-room high-speed Internet connection and the free Business Center and WiFi in the lobby. On Monday through Thursday nights, an evening social includes complimentary beer, wine and appetizers or a light meal. Kick back in a rocking chair on the veranda overlooking the beautifully landscaped grounds. Residence Inn's unique complimentary grocery shopping service is a great help for both busy vacationers and business travelers. Like all Marriotts, the Residence Inn is a smoke-free environment. The hotel is pet friendly, but pet registration is required.

choice for business meetings, conventions and the corporate traveler.

One South Lumina Suites $-$$$$
1 South Lumina, Wrightsville Beach
(910) 256-9100, (800) 421-3255

A stay at One South Lumina places you right in the heart of Wrightsville Beach, within walking distance of the town's restaurants, stores and, of course, the beach itself. All of the oceanfront suites are one-bedroom condos, which can sleep four to six people. Each condo includes a master bedroom with a queen-sized bed, living room, dining area, full kitchen, washer/dryer and two adult bunk beds. When you're not at the beach, you can relax in the outdoor oceanside pool. The hotel also offers 24-hour security, free wireless Internet and on-site parking.

Residence Inn by Marriott, Wrightsville Landfall $$-$$$$
1200 Culbreth Dr., Wilmington
(910) 256-0098
www.residenceinnwilmingtonlandfall.com

Whether you're here for R&R or to take care of business, this all-suite property offers 90 large, comfortable rooms to help you feel at home for one night or an entire month. Each suite has a fully equipped kitchen with full-size appliances, and you can choose from studio, one-bedroom and two-bedroom styles. There is even

Sandpeddler Motel & Suites $$-$$$$
15 Nathan St., Wrightsville Beach
(910) 256-2028
www.thesandpeddler.com

The Sandpeddler Motel & Suites, located across the street from the Oceanic Pier & Restaurant, offers contemporary one-bedroom, one-bath, condominium-style suites with a kitchenette. Each suite features a private balcony with a great ocean view. All units sleep up to four people with one queen bed in the bedroom and a queen sleeper sofa in the living room. The Sandpeddler also has an outdoor swimming pool, laundry facilities, daily linen and maid service, high-speed WiFi and a fax machine for guest use.

Shell Island Resort $-$$$$
2700 N. Lumina Ave., Wrightsville Beach
(910) 256-8696

Overlooking 3,000 feet of pristine white sand beaches in Wrightsville Beach, this family-friendly resort hotel offers 160 oceanfront suites, each with a magnificent view of the Atlantic Ocean. Each beautifully decorated suite can sleep from four to six people and includes a bedroom, one and a half bathrooms and a combination living room/dining room/kitchenette. The kitchenette includes refrigerator, microwave, stove top, coffeemaker and blender. You will love having morning coffee or afternoon cocktails on your own private balcony. Hotel amenities include the oceanfront North End Bistro, an outdoor pool, an indoor heated pool, a hot tub, a playground, a fitness room, bicycle rentals, a sand volleyball court, a gift shop, a 24-hour business center and laundry facilities. Plenty of parking is available under the covered deck. Also ideal for meetings, conventions, weddings and social gatherings, Shell Island has more than 6,000 square feet of meeting space with an ocean-view ballroom. The beach is just a few steps away. You'll find Shell Island Oceanfront Suites where Lumina ends and the beach begins.

Silver Gull Motel $-$$$$
20 E. Salisbury St., Wrightsville Beach
(910) 256-3728, (800) 842-8894

An ideal beach location and family-friendly service await you at the Silver Gull Motel. Fishing enthusiasts will enjoy the motel's location across the street from Johnnie Mercer's Pier. Each floor provides easy access to the beach, which is only a few steps away, or you can view the ocean from the comfort of your room's balcony. The rooms provide sleeping accommodations for up to four people, and adjoined rooms are available for families or groups. The lobby and all exterior entrances are locked securely at night. All rooms are equipped with remodeled kitchens featuring full-size refrigerators, microwaves and basic kitchenwares. Other room amenities include wireless Internet, irons and ironing boards, cable TV and coffeemakers. This is a popular destination for corporate travelers, and group discount rates are available.

On weekends, a two-night minimum stay is required; on holidays a three-night minimum stay is required. The office is open from 7 AM to 11 PM, seven days a week.

Summer Sands Suites $$$-$$$$
104 S. Lumina Ave., Wrightsville Beach
(910) 256-4175, (800) 336-4849
www.summersandswb.com

This comfortable, 32-suite efficiency motel sits in the heart of Wrightsville Beach within a short walk of restaurants, shopping and the strand. Rooms are ideal for two adults and two kids. Suites feature sleeping accommodations for up to four people, with a queen-sized bed in the bedroom and queen-sized murphy bed in the living room. In addition, the suites offer a kitchen, a dining area and a private balcony with spectacular views of the harbor and ocean. The outdoor pool is open in the spring, summer and fall, weather permitting. Two handicapped-accessible suites also are available as well as on-site laundry facilities and free wireless Internet.

Surf Suites $$-$$$$
711 S. Lumina Ave., Wrightsville Beach
(910) 256-2275, (877) 625-9307
www.thesurfsuites.com

Surf Suites is a beach treasure the whole family will enjoy. You can swim and beach comb all you want just steps away from your room, then relax in the gazebo and enjoy the panoramic ocean view after

a refreshing dip in the pool. Surf Suites offers all-oceanfront suites and complete kitchen amenities, including full-sized refrigerators, microwave ovens and dishwashers, and comfortable living spaces. These spacious suites can accommodate up to four people with a king-size bed and queen sleeper sofa in each room. You'll especially enjoy having your own balcony or patio at the ocean's edge. All suites are non-smoking and are equipped with a 32-inch cable LCD/HD TV, telephone, hairdryer and ironing equipment. High-speed wireless Internet is also available to all guests.

Carolina Beach and Kure Beach

Atlantic Towers $-$$$
1615 S. Lake Park Blvd., Carolina Beach
(910) 458.8313, (800) BEACH-40
www.atlantic-towers.com

This 11-story, oceanfront high rise offers fully furnished one- and two-bedroom condominium suites with separate bedrooms and full kitchens. Each suite includes a private balcony and can accommodate up to six people. All 120 condos are oceanfront, and amenities include an indoor heated pool, an oceanfront outdoor pool, a game room, a gazebo/sundeck,

a grilling area and a club room area with wireless Internet. High-speed Internet also is accessible in each suite for no additional charge. Nightly, weekly and monthly rentals are available.

Beachside Inn $-$$
616 S. Lake Park Blvd., Carolina Beach
(910) 458-5598

For families, Beachside Inn is just the ticket. Homey, comfortable and cheerful, each room is furnished differently, with a variety of arrangements available. Choose from single, double, king-size and combinations to meet your needs. Each unit includes a microwave, refrigerator and 27-inch color TV with cable. Guests can stroll a short distance to the beach or lake or enjoy cooling off in the inviting pool located adjacent to the lovely flower-filled courtyard. Four separate cottage-style buildings house 18 rooms, both smoking and non-smoking. Beachside Inn is one of the best values on Pleasure Island.

Courtyard by Marriott - Carolina Beach $$-$$$$
100 Charlotte Ave., Carolina Beach
(910) 458-2030, (800) 321-2211

The 10-story Courtyard by Marriott at Carolina Beach boasts 144 oceanfront rooms with private balconies. In each beautifully decorated room, amenities include complimentary high-speed wireless Internet access, a coffee station, a mini refrigerator, a hairdryer and a desk with a chair and dataport. Suites also include a separate living area with a wet bar and microwave. A luxurious focal point of the hotel is a custom-designed oceanfront outdoor pool and tropical plaza featuring a sunbathing deck with direct beach access, and staff to deliver cool beverages poolside. The heated indoor pool and hot tub are open year round, and an exercise room and guest laundry facility is also available.

The recently renovated hotel now offers several new amenities, such as a 32-inch flat-screen TV in every guest room, and new carpet, wallpaper and art throughout the hotel, including their 3,300 square feet of banquet rooms. The fitness

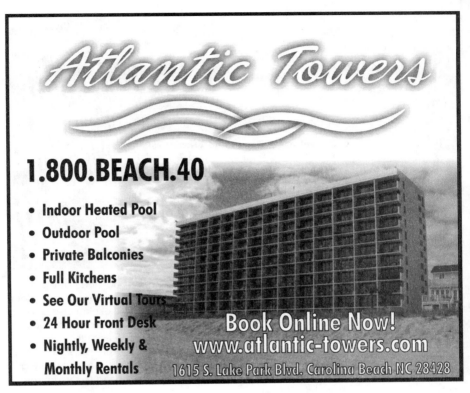

center features all new state-of-the-art equipment with private TVs. Even the outside of the building has been completely painted.

The contemporary hotel lobby design is spacious, bright and attractive, providing a great place to meet with family, friends or business associates. The lobby now has a touch-screen information board, along with media stations and a new business library. The hotel has added the Courtyard Bistro to the restaurant, proudly serving the only Starbucks beverages on Pleasure Island. The new Bistro serves quality breakfast, sandwiches, salads, soups and snacks, with many healthy grab-and-go options. With outlets for your laptop or cell phone, WiFi and plenty of seating areas to work alone or with company, the new Courtyard lobby and restaurant is the perfect place to enjoy your time in Carolina Beach. The Market, which has added many new products, snacks and drinks, is open 24 hours for when you need something in a pinch.

Dry Dock Family Motel   **$-$$**
300 S. Lake Park Blvd., Carolina Beach
(910) 458-8346

Enjoy visiting family or friends or create your own peaceful retreat at Dry Dock Family Motel. The motel is ideally located within a few hundred yards of the Atlantic Ocean and within walking distance of Carolina Beach Park's lake. Stroll to the beach, walk around the lake or enjoy a dip in one of the motel's two pools. All rooms include a refrigerator, a microwave and complimentary coffee, and a coin laundry facility is available. Their affordable prices will leave you with funds to explore the area's attractions.

Golden Sands Motel   **$$-$$$**
1211 S. Lake Park Blvd., Carolina Beach
(910) 458-8334
www.goldensandscarolinabeach.com

You couldn't ask for more — immaculate, comfortable, spacious and attractive accommodations with a fantastic oceanfront location. Each of the 115 tastefully decorated rooms is air conditioned and

has a refrigerator, microwave, telephone, coffeemaker, iron, sofa and cable TV. Some of Golden Sands' rooms feature a convenient split design: two queen beds separated by a half wall, which is perfect for families with children or two couples staying together. Hotel guests can choose from queen, king or efficiency-style rooms. Most face the ocean, and all have private balconies or porches. On site is a popular seafood restaurant with tables out on the pier, where you'll also find a tiki bar featuring live music during the summer season. Golden Sands has a sparkling-blue outdoor pool, a year-round indoor pool and a great gift shop. Complimentary coffee is served in the lobby every morning starting at 6:30 AM. The motel now offers a new exercise facility so you don't have to miss your workout while you're on vacation. There is also a meeting room available.

Kure Keys Motel $-$$
310 N. Fort Fisher Blvd., Kure Beach
(910) 458-5277

No matter which of the ten comfortable rooms you choose, you're only a few steps away from the beach at Kure Keys Motel. Regular rooms include two extra-long double beds and a small refrigerator. The efficiency rooms have complete kitchens with microwave, stove, refrigerator, coffeemaker and all tableware. All rooms have phones and, of course, cable TV complete with HBO and remote. Amenities include an outdoor pool and hot tub, on-site coin laundry, a picnic area, an outdoor fireplace, even a fish-cleaning area and a grill on which to cook your catch. Located in the heart of Kure Beach close to the pier and restaurants, Kure Keys Motel is a great place for a family vacation. During winter months, call ahead to ensure the hotel will remain open.

Sea Ranch Motel $$
1123 S. Lake Park Blvd., Carolina Beach
(910) 458-8681, (800) 849-8977
www.visitsearanch.com

One of the most popular oceanfront motels on the beach, Sea Ranch offers both standard sleeping rooms and efficiencies. While most rooms have two full-sized beds, some singles with one full bed are available, as are some oceanfront efficiencies with queen beds. Every room has a refrigerator, television, telephone and air conditioning. Efficiency units have full kitchens that include a stove, microwave, coffeemaker, pots, dishes and silverware. Whether poolside or overlooking the ocean, these accommodations are clean, comfortable and inviting. An outstanding feature of the Sea Ranch Motel is its large heated pool and adjacent over-sized Jacuzzi, which has room for 20 people. Both are located within a windowed brick enclosure. An oceanfront pool with a slide is great for small children as its depth ranges from just 2 to 6 feet. Guests may also enjoy a poolside gazebo. A relaxing retreat, the Sea Ranch has a wide sandy beach with a private access walk. The motel also plans to offer rental cottages in the near future; interested guests should inquire about availability.

Seven Seas Inn   **$$-$$$$**
130 N. Fort Fisher Blvd., Kure Beach
(910) 458-8122, (866) 773-2746
www.sevenseasinn.com

Family-owned and operated since 1992, Seven Seas Inn is centrally located on the oceanfront in Kure Beach about 30 minutes south of Wilmington. Seven Seas Inn features 32 rooms and efficiencies available in a variety of configurations, including two-room suites, interconnecting units and ground-level rooms. The inn's accommodations offer limited handicapped accessibility as well as standard kitchen and non-kitchen rooms, and all units are non-smoking. In-room amenities include telephone, refrigerator, coffeemaker, 32-inch plasma TV and available WiFi. On the well-kept grounds are an oceanfront pool, gazebos with picnic areas, outdoor grills and guest laundry. Small children, seniors and non-swimmers will appreciate a second 3-foot-deep pool with surround seating. Restaurants, shops and the popular Kure Beach Fishing Pier are within a short walk of the inn. When entering Kure Beach by the main road from the north (U.S. 421), look for Seven Seas Inn on the left with its many beautiful agave plants.

a refrigerator and a coffeemaker. Wireless Internet is available as well. Various patios and sun decks provide a fine sunset view. No pets are allowed. The marina rents floating docks and boat slips with a water depth of 5 feet at mean low tide. (See our Marinas and the Intracoastal Waterway section.) City-owned boat ramps adjoining the marina are available to use for free. The adjoining Fish House Restaurant and lounge is open from February 14 to November 26; call (910) 278-6012 after 5 PM for questions about the restaurant. You will also find a ship's store, a tackle shop and kayak rentals and personal watercraft rentals. Deep-sea fishing is available on two charter boats, and no fishing license is required.

Southport and Oak Island

Blue Water Point Marina Resort   **$-$$**
5710 57th Pl. W and W. Beach Dr.,
Oak Island
(910) 278-1230, (888) 634-9005

Located on the west end of Oak Island, this small, comfortable 28-room motel is especially convenient to boaters, while just across W. Beach Drive is a boardwalk to the beach strand. The motel offers all smoke-free rooms with waterway views, two double beds, a shower, a TV and telephone, cable with HBO, a microwave,

Captain's Cove Motel   **$-$$**
6401 E. Oak Island Dr., Oak Island
(910) 278-6026
www.realpages.com/captainscove

Captain's Cove, family owned and operated for more than 30 years, is located on the main street in Oak Island. Rooms open out onto the central parking court and are surrounded by beautiful oak trees. All rooms contain refrigerators, microwaves, coffeemakers and wireless Internet service. Efficiency apartments are available in addition to the standard rooms. The great things about Captain's Cove are the quiet family atmosphere, the beach access, a pool in a sunny location and the

fact that restaurants and shopping are within walking distance. Captain's Cove allows small pets.

Hampton Inn Southport $-$$$
5181 Southport Supply Rd., Southport
(910) 454-0016, (800) 426-7688
www.southport.hamptoninn.com

A Circle of Excellence Award winner, Hampton Inn Southport, which opened in June 2000, has been rated in the top 10 percent of almost 1,300 Hampton Inns by Hampton Inn guests. It is conveniently located near two shopping centers, halfway between downtown Southport and Oak Island and less than a 10-minute drive from the Brunswick County Airport. Eighty home-like guest rooms are available, containing king or queen-size beds, A/C and heat, TV, coffeemakers, hairdryers, wireless Internet access and voicemail. Some rooms contain a microwave and refrigerator as well. Available upon request are cribs, rollaway beds and refrigerators. Nonsmoking and handicapped-accessible rooms are available. Continental breakfast is provided in the well-appointed dining area. The inn offers an outdoor pool, a fitness center and a business center with free high-speed Internet access. Group rates are available, and the meeting room seats up to 40. No pets are allowed.

Ocean Crest Motel $$
1417 E. Beach Dr., Oak Island
(910) 278-3333

The owners and staff of the Ocean Crest Motel will make you feel welcome from the moment you arrive, and repeat guests just keep coming back. The location is unique to Oak Island because Ocean Crest is located right on the beach, not across the street. The motel offers a swimming pool, guest laundry and an affordable gift shop. This 62-room motel is situated adjacent to a fishing pier and a restaurant, making it an ideal spot for vacation accommodations. Especially attractive is the "Stay for 7 - Pay for 5" special weekly rate available year round. Ocean Crest Motel offers a room choice of oceanfront with or without a private balcony, as well as standard rooms, which are not oceanfront. Regardless of the room you choose, you are literally steps away from the beach. The most requested rooms are oceanfront rooms so be sure to make your reservation early. All rooms are tastefully decorated to remind you of the tropics and are clean and well-maintained (both very important to the owners). Please note the motel does not allow pets, boats, RVs or trailers on the property.

Riverside Motel $$
103 W. Bay St., Southport
(910) 457-6986

This small, eight-room establishment situated on the waterfront between the Cape Fear Restaurant and the Cape Fear Pilot Tower commands a breathtaking view of Southport's harbor where the river meets the sea. Both Old Baldy and the Oak Island Lighthouse can be seen from this spot. The motel was totally renovated in 2002. The cozy double-occupancy rooms are equipped with either two double beds or one queen-sized bed, AC, ceiling fans, microwave ovens, cable TV, refrigerators, coffeemakers and telephones (local calls are free). The location of the Riverside in the historic district is conducive to strolls through the scenic town for meals, shopping or sightseeing.

Ocean Isle Beach

The Islander Inn $$-$$$
57 W. First St., Ocean Isle Beach
(910) 575-7000, (888) 325-4753

The Islander Inn is an oceanfront family hotel that offers 70 beautifully appointed, recently renovated guest rooms. Each oceanfront room has a newly installed 50-inch plasma screen TV as well as a private balcony. Rooms include your choice of two queen beds or one king-sized bed with sofa. All rooms offer a wet bar and refrigerator, a microwave and in-room coffee service, HBO, a telephone with voicemail and complimentary wireless high-speed Internet access. The Islander Inn offers an expanded continental breakfast daily in the pool-side breakfast room. Guests can enjoy the outdoor oceanfront pool with a sun deck and an indoor heated pool with Jacuzzi, as well as an exercise room. The Islander Inn also offers handicapped-accessible rooms. Inquire about AAA and AARP discounts and off-season rates. If you are planning an oceanfront wedding, check out the gorgeous options offered by The Islander Inn and The Isles Restaurant.

The Winds Resort Beach Club $-$$$
310 E. First St., Ocean Isle Beach
(910) 579-6275, (800) 334-3581
www.thewinds.com

A tropical escape closer than you think, The Winds Resort Beach Club is proudly rated the AAA highest rating (3 Diamond). Studios, mini-suites, deluxe rooms, one- and two-bedroom suites, and resort cottages with four, five or six bedrooms are all richly appointed. Some of the resort cottages have private, outdoor Jacuzzis; many accommodations have indoor whirlpools and kitchen facilities. The grounds are beautifully landscaped with 11 varieties of palm trees, banana trees and lush flowering plants nestled among meandering boardwalks and decks. A wide expanse of beach provides for such activities as sunning, castle building or searching for seashells. The Winds has a heated pool indoors, two outdoor pools, several outdoor Jacuzzis, an exercise

room, beach bocce, shuffleboard, volleyball and bike rentals. The Garden Bar Restaurant and oceanfront, poolside Tiki Bar serve a light menu featuring salads, sandwiches, wraps and fresh-baked pizza as well as mixed beverages, including margaritas and daiquiris. A complimentary hot Southern breakfast buffet is served daily. Honeymoon and golf packages are easily arranged. In addition, from June through August, free summer golf programs are available at more than two dozen courses. The Winds has an elevator, and some rooms are handicapped accessible. Ask about special off-season packages.

Sunset Beach

The Sunset Inn $$-$$$$
9 N. Shore Dr., Sunset Beach
(910) 575-1000, (888) 575-1001

The Sunset Inn opened its doors to the beauty of the saltwater marsh and island life in June 2000. The honey-colored hardwood floors in the entrance and living area shine softly in the light that filters through the large windows. Here, continental breakfast is served on a lace-covered table every morning from 8:15 until 10 AM, or you can choose to have your morning meal in the living room or in the privacy of your own room. There are 14 rooms, each with a different theme and decor. All rooms have a king-sized bed, wet bar, refrigerator, love seat and private screened porch with rockers. The four grand rooms each have a Jacuzzi plus a shower in their private baths, and the 10 standard rooms have showers. One handicapped-accessible room and two connecting rooms are available. Special rates are available off season and on weekdays.

Shallotte

Shallotte Microtel Inn & Suites   **$$-$$$**
4646 East Coast Ln., Shallotte
(910) 755-6444, (888) 771-7171

Strategically located in Shallotte, this 62-room hotel provides a haven for business and vacation travelers alike. Beaches are 5 to 8 miles away, six top golf courses are within 5 miles, historic Wilmington is a short 25-mile drive away, and Myrtle Beach is 15 minutes to the south. Room amenities include high-speed wireless Internet access, free local and long distance calls, HBO channels, ESPN and hairdryers. Non-smoking rooms are available. The hotel offers coffee and tea service in the lobby and copy and fax service. Guests can plan their side trips over the free continental breakfast or by the outdoor pool. No pets are allowed in this facility.

Leland

Comfort Suites Magnolia Greens
1020 Grandiflora Dr., Leland
(910) 383-3300

Situated within the popular golf plantation Magnolia Greens is Leland's newest hotel, the Comfort Suites Magnolia Greens. As the name suggests, the hotel was built with comfort in mind, as evidenced by the queen-size bed in all double rooms and the widened king rooms, and the fact that all suites come with sleeper sofas. The hotel offers a free continental breakfast, a 24-hour fitness center, an indoor heated pool and sun deck. Business travelers will appreciate the hotel's library equipped with computers, printers and complimentary high-speed Internet (which is also available in the rooms). The Comfort

Suites Magnolia Greens is a pet-friendly hotel with a designated pet room, walking area and waste station. The hotel is only a short drive from the numerous attractions of Wilmington and the Brunswick and New Hanover County beaches.

Topsail Island Area

Island Inn   **$$**
302 N. Shore Dr., Surf City
(910) 328-2341, (800) 573-2566

The Island Inn is located directly across from the beach in the heart of Surf City's shopping and dining district. Their 21 smoke-free motel rooms vary in size and include ceramic tile floors, a refrigerator, microwave, coffeemaker, cable TV and free Internet access. Children 12 and younger stay free when sharing their parents' room. The pool has plenty of big umbrellas for shade lovers. It's open April through October.

Jolly Roger Inn   **$$**
803 Ocean Blvd., Topsail Beach
(910) 328-4616, (800) 633-3196

Jolly Roger Inn is on the oceanfront, on the same premises as the Jolly Roger Fishing Pier and centrally located in downtown Topsail Beach. Jolly Roger Inn has 65 rooms that include bedrooms, efficiencies and suites; some are equipped with a kitchen. Ten nonsmoking rooms are available. Open year-round, the inn offers daily, weekly and seasonal rates.

Sea Coast Suites   **$$-$$$**
305 N. Topsail Dr., Surf City
(910) 328-0364, (866) 713-7067

Sea Coast Suites offers 27 units for nightly, weekly or monthly rental. Each of the privately owned two-bedroom, one-bath units offers wireless Internet access, a full kitchen and a living area. Elevator access is available in this three-story building, and three units are handicapped accessible. Sea Coast Suites offers direct beach access, and it is close to dining, shopping and the Surf City Fishing Pier.

Oceanfront Ocean Isle Beach

A small, intimate resort ideal for beach vacations, romantic get-aways, beach weddings and golf outings. Relax oceanfront overlooking palm trees, lush subtropical gardens and our breathtaking island beach.

Rooms, 1, 2 and 3 bedroom suites (with kitchens & livingrooms) and 4, 5 and 6 bedroom Resort Houses. Free hot breakfast buffet, daily housekeeping, three pools (one indoor), hot tubs, exercise room, shuffleboard, bikes and more. Our oceanfront, poolside TikiBar/Restaurant features light dining, frozen tropical drinks as well as beer and wine. Golf packages on over 100 coastal Carolinas' courses. Ask about our Free Summer Golf!

Highest Rated (AAA) Accommodations on Ocean Isle Beach!

800-334-3581

RESORT BEACH CLUB

Info@TheWinds.com   www.TheWinds.com

Sea Vista Motel $$
1521 Ocean Blvd., Topsail Beach
(910) 328-2171

This oceanfront motel features apartments and efficiencies with full kitchens and all the amenities. They also have mini-efficiencies that have a small cooking unit, and the standard rooms have a small refrigerator, microwave, toaster and coffeemaker. This motel closes in December and re-opens March 1.

St. Regis Resort $$-$$$$
2000 New River Inlet Rd.,
North Topsail Beach
(910) 328-4975, (800) 682-4882

This vacation resort offers oceanfront and ocean-view condominium units with one to three bedrooms, all with two full baths. Each unit is smoke free, individually owned and tastefully furnished. You'll find a fitness center, sauna, steam showers, tennis courts and indoor and outdoor pools with a Jacuzzi. During the summer units are rented weekly, and in the off-season there is a two-night minimum stay required. St. Regis is open year round.

Tiffany's Motel $-$$$$
1502 N. New River Dr., Surf City
(910) 328-1397, (800) 758-3818

Tiffany's Motel offers lodging by the night, by the week or by the month. The one- and two-bedroom suites, efficiencies and handicapped-accessible units can accommodate two to eight guests and have refrigerators, coffeemakers, hairdryers, color cable TV and wireless Internet. Many of the units have been recently remodeled and there are 12 new condos at the complex. Amenities include two pools, a large sun deck and an elevator. Rental rates include departure cleaning and daily maid service. Small pets less than 25 pounds are allowed in some units. Special group rates are offered for weddings, reunions and sports clubs.

Topsail Island Holiday Inn Express Hotel & Suites $$
1565 N.C. Hwy. 210, Sneads Ferry
(910) 327-8282

This hotel has a large outdoor pool and a great room with scenic views of North Shore Golf Course Country Club and the Intracoastal Waterway. In-room amenities include refrigerators, free high-speed Internet access, coffeemakers, irons and ironing boards, hair dryers, two-line speaker phones with dataports, and color televisions. Out of a total of 68 rooms, there are 15 suites with king-size beds, pull-out sofas and microwave ovens. Some rooms have whirlpool tubs. Guests can enjoy a complimentary hot breakfast bar. Seasonal rates apply. AAA and AARP discounts and government rates are available, as are wedding and golf packages and group rates. The hotel has an elevator, is ADA compliant and is open year round.

Villa Capriani Resort $$$$
790 New River Inlet Rd.,
North Topsail Beach
(910) 328-1900, (800) 934-2400

This exclusive oceanfront resort is bathed in warm terra cotta colors and draped with balconies and is more reminiscent of an old world châteaux than a modern seaside resort. Amenities include three oceanfront swimming pools, two hot tubs, sun decks, two tennis courts, spectacular ocean views and an on-site restaurant and lounge. Villas include one, two or three bedrooms, either oceanfront or ocean-view. Each unit is furnished and offers a fully equipped kitchen and washer and dryer. The Villa Capriani Resort is open year round, and rentals are handled by Treasure Realty at the numbers above. There is a seven-day minimum stay in high season.

BED & BREAKFASTS AND SMALL INNS

The tradition of bed and breakfasts and small inns, strong in Europe and England for many years, began to catch on in this country with Americans' desire to experience romance and escapism in historic homes. Because of Wilmington's small-town charm and vibrant history, the area offers outstanding bed and breakfasts plus a number of wonderful small inns. Most feature fabulous antiques and have unique, fascinating histories, decor and gardens. Some are as casual as a pajama party, while others are steeped in Victorian elegance.

Several beach bed and breakfasts invite you to enjoy the ocean breezes, dine overlooking the sea, wade in the surf and stroll on the sand. You'll find quite a different character at the beaches, a character that is definitely easy-going and informal.

As a point of information, bed and breakfasts differ from small inns when it comes to serving food to guests. If you like a full, cooked breakfast served at a given time usually in a common dining area, a bed and breakfast is for you. On the other hand, an inn usually provides only a continental breakfast, if any at all. Some inns have kitchenette facilities so that guests may prepare their own morning meal; some have variations on the breakfast offering, but inns do not serve a formal meal at an appointed hour. Another difference between an inn and a bed and breakfast is the location. An inn is almost always "in town" and may be associated with a pub, restaurant or have a bar on the premises. Not so with a bed and breakfast, though some offer a self-service refrigerator for wine and beer or soft drinks.

Wherever you choose to stay, your hosts surely will be knowledgeable about the area and can assist you with directions and in making reservations for shows, meals, charters and golf packages. Bed and breakfasts and inns typically do not allow pets, smoking indoors or very young children unless by prior arrangement. Many charge a fee for cancellations, so be sure to ask about the policy. Also note that often they require a full weekend booking, especially during the Azalea Festival in April and Riverfest in October (see our Annual Events chapter for information on these events).

PRICE CODE

Since prices are subject to change without notice, we provide only price guidelines based on per-night rates during the summer (high season). Guidelines do not reflect the 7 percent state/county tax and 1 to 6 percent room occupancy tax (taxes may vary by municipality or county). Some establishments offer lower rates during the off-season. Always confirm rates and necessary amenities before reserving. It may behoove you to inquire about corporate discounts even if they are not mentioned in our descriptions.

$	Less than $90
$$	$90 to $150
$$$	$151 to $200
$$$$	More than $200

Wilmington

Blue Heaven
Bed and Breakfast   **$$-$$$**
517 Orange St., Wilmington
(910) 772-9929

In the heart of historic downtown Wilmington lies Blue Heaven Bed and Breakfast, a beautifully restored Queen Anne–style home built in 1897 by Frederick and Minnie Hashagan. The Hashagans made their residence there until 1922, and the bed and breakfast maintains many of the original details, including seven

fireplaces with their original mantelpieces, plus original moldings and stained-glass windows. The home has been restored almost to its original layout, which features a beautiful hand-carved staircase and foyer, North Carolina heart-pine floors, 10-foot ceilings, and wainscoting and trim. The ambiance is augmented with unique accoutrement and artwork found in local galleries and antiques stores.

Each of the three suites has its own character and appeal. The Key West Room presents a relaxing milieu with decorative, hand-painted pastel walls, while the Newport Room's blue and green decor feels bright and airy. The recently renovated Sanibel Suite is spacious and open and may be rented as a large two-bedroom suite or as two private rooms. Blue Heaven is within a short stroll of downtown's amenities, including museums and attractions, the Riverwalk, shopping and dining. The bed and breakfast is kid friendly, but there is an additional charge for having more than two people per room. Call for rates, which include a hearty Southern breakfast.

C.W. Worth House
Bed and Breakfast   **$$-$$$**
412 S. Third St., Wilmington
(910) 762-8562, (800) 340-8559
www.worthhouse.com

The hosts at C. W. Worth House Bed and Breakfast guarantee to provide you a relaxing atmosphere for a memorable

getaway. Here you can enjoy peace and tranquility and have plenty of space to do, or not do, whatever you choose.

Built in 1893, C. W. Worth House is a unique example of nineteenth-century English Queen Anne style and sixteenth-century French chateaux. This turreted house features a wide front veranda and elegant interior, which includes the original paneled foyer, antiques, a formal parlor with a Victorian-era pump organ and a comfortable study. A television/DVD/VCR is available in the study and in the third-floor sitting room. The seven guest rooms are spacious, and beds include four-poster king and antique queen-size. Each guest room has a private bath, sitting area, ceiling fan, desk and telephone. Ask about the Azalea Room with its separate sitting room or the Hibiscus Room with its whirlpool bath and sitting area nestled in the corner turret. The entire house has central air conditioning and free high-speed wireless Internet access.

A full gourmet breakfast, served in the formal dining room, includes organic coffee, tea, juice, muffins and fresh fruit as a first course. The entree may be eggs Florentine, artichoke/mushroom quiche or a baked banana-pecan pancake. A convenience for guests is a refrigerator on each floor, stocked with beverages and snacks. Outside, beautiful gardens highlighted with shade trees and brick walkways, a goldfish pond and a relaxing waterfall

invite guests to linger a while. C. W. Worth House is a nonsmoking inn. Children age 12 and older are welcome. Gift certificates, specials and packages are available.

Business travelers visiting Wilmington will find all the conveniences needed at C. W. Worth House Bed and Breakfast and a safe, quiet environment as well. Corporate rates are available Sunday through Thursday. Fax and copier services are offered in addition to free high-speed wireless Internet access throughout the inn. A desktop computer with Internet access, located in the third-floor sitting room, is available for guest use.

Camellia Cottage
Bed & Breakfast $$$-$$$$
118 S. Fourth St., Wilmington
(910) 763-9171

Standing on a brick-paved street four blocks from the river, Camellia Cottage is a richly appointed, high-peaked Queen Anne shingle home built in 1889. Once the home of prominent Wilmington artist Henry J. MacMillan, it still houses some of his work. In fact, artwork abounds throughout Camellia Cottage, from murals on the wrap-around piazza to hand-painted fireplace tiles. Camellia Cottage offers three spacious guest rooms and one suite, each with its own character. Queen-size, antique-style beds, private baths, high-speed wireless Internet and gas-fired hearths are standard. Morning coffee is provided.

A sumptuous three-course breakfast is served from 8 to 9:30 AM. The parlor is always available to guests. This charming bed and breakfast is within walking distance of many fine restaurants and shops. A short drive will take you to the beaches, Battleship NORTH CAROLINA, Cameron Art Museum and North Carolina Aquarium. Discounts for long-term stays apply.

Clarendon Inn $$$-$$$$
117 S. Second St., Wilmington
(910) 343-1990, (888) 343-1992

Originally built in 1950, Clarendon Inn was once the site of St. Thomas Catholic School and then St. Thomas Catholic Preschool. A few years ago it was transformed into a quaint bed and breakfast in the heart of downtown Wilmington, and it has recently come under new ownership. Each of the inn's 11 guest rooms has its own personality, but all fit within the same boutique inn feeling. The atmosphere is friendly and comfortable while remaining unpretentious. Two rooms have king-size beds, while the others have queens, and some rooms come equipped with extra sleep facilities, including a trundle bed and a sofa sleeper. Many rooms have jet tubs, and handicapped bathrooms are available in some rooms. All standard rooms are equipped with separate heating and air controls, mini refrigerators, microwaves, DVD players, cable TV, coffeemakers, ironing equipment and hairdryers. Business

travelers will enjoy WiFi throughout the inn and a business center complete with computer, a conference table, a fax machine, a copier and a printer.

A continental breakfast may be enjoyed in the lobby or in your room; or on a nice day, enjoy your breakfast outside on the front or back porches. The lush patio garden and front veranda provide a quiet outdoor retreat complete with two porch swings, two seating areas and garden fountains. Situated in the middle of Wilmington's Historic District, this quaint inn is within walking distance to all downtown restaurants, nightclubs and shopping. If you prefer peace and quiet, the Clarendon Inn's veranda is the perfect location for people-watching or relaxing in a beautiful location.

Front Street Inn $$$-$$$$
215 S. Front St., Wilmington
(910) 762-6442, (800) 336-8184
www.frontstreetinn.com

Front Street Inn greets guests with a natural, understated ambiance and Bohemian charm. The inn features original art, hand-painted 14-foot high walls, maple floors and exposed brick. The 12 rooms and suites are named and decorated according to their inspirations, such as Claude Monet, Pearl S. Buck, Rudyard Kipling and Georgia O'Keeffe. They are beautifully appointed with every amenity a traveler would love, including private

baths, waffle-weave robes, hand-milled soaps, fresh flowers, wet bars, TVs, CD/DVD players, dataports and wireless high-speed Internet access. Some suites have large spa tubs, multi-jet showers and fireplaces; the Hemingway Suite also has a private balcony.

The European breakfast, served buffet-style all morning, offers a variety of healthful (or sinful) selections. Always you'll find coffee, fresh fruit, cold cuts, cheese, croissants, biscotti and muffins. Room service is available. The Sol y Sombra Bar, with its famous handmade cork bar, offers juices, waters, sodas, beer, wine, champagne and snacks. The game room and fitness area in the lower level are wonderful for small groups, family gatherings or informal business meetings.

Polly and Richard Salinetti, along with their staff, will assist you with anything from restaurant reservations to special requests (how about hand-dipped chocolate strawberries, in-house massage, flowers or champagne?). They also offer spa and romance packages. The inn occupies the renovated Salvation Army building, the first in the Carolinas, built in 1923. It is up the hill from Chandler's Wharf and the Riverwalk with picturesque views from the second-floor balconies. Convenient off-street parking is provided. Children 13 years and older are welcome, and pets are accommodated on a very limited basis.

Graystone Inn   **$$$-$$$$**
100 S. Third St., Wilmington
(910) 763-2000, (888) 763-4773
www.graystoneinn.com

This stately historic landmark, recently named by *Our State* magazine as one of 21 perfect places to stay in North Carolina, is one of the city's most prestigious inns. Its rich, spacious interior invites guests to enjoy an ambiance of relaxed elegance. Built in 1905-06, Graystone Inn was originally known as The Bridgers Mansion. Extensive renovations restored the home's turn-of-the-century magnificence and added modern-day conveniences. The vast ground floor includes an incredible library paneled in Honduran mahogany furnished with comfortable chairs, a sofa and a game table. Here you can relax in front of the fireplace and enjoy your morning coffee or evening glass of wine. A full cooked breakfast is served each morning in the beautiful formal dining room featuring mahogany dining tables, English floral wallpaper, a fireplace and period antiques. From the great entrance hall, a grand Renaissance-style staircase made of hand-carved oak rises three stories, culminating in the ballroom.

Nine guest rooms offer the visitor varied luxury, including private en suite baths (several with claw-foot tubs), period antiques, fine pima cotton linens, towels and robes, telephone, WiFi and cable TV. Seven of the guest rooms have decorative fireplaces. Five rooms have king-sized beds and the rest offer queens. Room rates include a full gourmet breakfast, beverage service throughout the day, and evening wine. Outdoors, the garden and terraces are exquisite. Frequently used as a set for motion pictures and television, Graystone Inn is unquestionably one of the most impressive structures in Wilmington. The inn's location is ideal for walking to all downtown attractions and is convenient to the Riverwalk with its popular restaurants and shops. Graystone Inn makes a prestigious venue for weddings, receptions, reunions, birthdays, meetings and other events for up to 150 people. The Graystone Inn is a AAA 4 Diamond property and a member of the prestigious Select Registry, Distinguished Inns of North America.

welcome to the
HOGE - WOOD HOUSE
bed & breakfast
407 SOUTH THIRD STREET
WILMINGTON, NC 28401
910-762-5299

WWW.HOGEWOODHOUSE.COM

Hoge-Wood House
Bed and Breakfast   **$$$-$$$$**
407 S. Third St., Wilmington
(910) 762-5299
www.hogewoodhouse.com.

The Hoge-Wood House offers three upstairs guest rooms with private bathrooms. Each room has cable TV, DVD players, iPod docking stations and wireless Internet. The inn also has refrigerators in each guest room filled with complimentary beverages. The Hoge-Wood House is casual, comfortable and relaxed. You'll find fresh flowers and art throughout, and the downstairs parlor is cozy and inviting. The library has a large selection of books, DVDs, CDs, LP records, reel-to-reel tapes, puzzles and games for you to enjoy. The inn's proprietors, Page & Larry Tootoo (pronounced toe-toe), emphasize flexibility in their service. Page is a Registered Nurse who can easily accommodate special dietary needs. Full breakfasts are beautifully served on a 12 foot chestnut table. Tip: Larry makes great pecan waffles, shrimp & grits, and eggs anyway you like. Page makes homemade syrups, jams and breads. Coffee lovers will appreciate the Kona coffee brewed daily. Guest rooms are named for the Tootoos' children. Katherine's room offers a king-size iron bed, and the bath has a large walk-in shower. Leilani's octagon-shaped room features a king-size cherry sleigh bed, and the bath has a Jacuzzi tub with shower.

Walk along a pier for a unique perspective of the local beaches.

photo: Meagan Dietz

Gabriel and Joshua's room offers a queen-size oak mission bed and a bath with tub and shower. Bicycles, fishing poles and a six-person, deck-side hot tub are available for guest use. The Hoge-Wood House is within walking distance of the Riverwalk and downtown attractions, and it is one of the few bed and breakfasts in Wilmington that offers off-street parking.

Rosehill Inn $$-$$$$
114 S. Third St., Wilmington
(910) 815-0250

At the elegant Rosehill Inn, you can step into the past while still enjoying all of today's modern amenities. Located in the heart of Wilmington's downtown Historic District, this faithfully restored classic Greek Revival home, built in 1848, provides a luxurious yet comfortable getaway. The inn is tastefully adorned with oriental rugs, beautiful fireplaces with hand-detailed mantles and period antiques. It features a magnificent pulpit staircase with quarter-sawn white oak banisters, original inlaid oak floors, and egg and dart moldings. While appearing quite formal, this first-class bed and breakfast inn is genuinely warm and welcoming, as are its hosts, Tricia, Bob and Sean.

Each of the six quiet guest rooms has a private en suite bath, fireplace (non-working), period writing desk, cable TV, wireless Internet and spa bathrobes. Decorated in deep, rich colors, these rooms provide an unforgettable visual experience. The Heritage Room boasts a New Orleans–style iron gate bed. The spacious Wedgwood Room, with its country setting and king-sized bed, is bright and cheery, decorated in a yellow and blue color scheme. The Regency Room features an elaborate iron bed and bathroom with inviting whirlpool tub. The Carolina and Tea Rose rooms have bay windows with cozy sitting areas.

Early morning coffee and tea service start your day, followed by a full breakfast served in the spacious dining room, which boasts an impressive 17-foot dining table and crystal chandelier. Breakfast includes such delights as baked apple-peach French toast, banana-pecan pancakes, "Governor's" egg casserole, country sausages and a colorful fresh fruit plate. The home's large wraparound porch is ideal for reading or relaxing. The Rosehill Inn's convenient location, only three blocks from the Cape Fear River, is a short romantic stroll to popular gourmet restaurants, charming shops and the Riverwalk.

According to *Southern Living* magazine, "This is no ordinary B&B; a stay at the Rosehill Inn is an experience not soon to be forgotten."

The Verandas $$$$
202 Nun St., Wilmington
(910) 251-2212

A nine-time AAA Four Diamond award-winning bed and breakfast, The Verandas is magnificently appointed with antiques and high-quality American, French and English reproduction furniture, original artwork and creative lighting. Owners Chuck Pennington and Dennis Madsen worked magic to restore the burned-out mansion, which was built in 1854 by shipbuilder Benjamin Beery, and the result is a stunning inn with the look and feel of a luxurious European boutique hotel.

The 8,500-square-foot home has a fascinating history as well. At various times it was a military hospital, apartment house, hotel, lodge hall, a refuge for vagrants, boarding house, warehouse and a convent. Four large verandas give guests choice views of the charming gardens, historic neighborhood, downtown Wilmington and tree-lined streets. Spacious, tastefully decorated common areas invite guests to linger over complimentary wine in the evening, perhaps while listening to music played on a restored melodeon, or reading one of the intriguing coffee-table books. With a nod to modern travelers' needs, wireless Internet access is available throughout.

Each of the eight large corner guest rooms is different in character, and every one has a top-of-the-line mattress, hand-ironed sheets and cases, luxurious robes, candies and many extra special touches. Private, marble-floored bathrooms have soaking tubs, showers, custom-made soaps, lotions and shampoo. TVs with cable are discreetly hidden. Rooms also have telephones, individual climate controls and writing areas. In the morning, French-pressed coffee and the same tea served at the White House accompany a homemade, four-course gourmet breakfast, which is served in the formal dining room with its exquisite crystal chandelier.

After 13 years of hosting celebrities and the public, The Verandas continues to receive awards and accolades. Besides the AAA Four Diamond, they were recently awarded the People's Choice Award and "The Best Place to Get on With Your Life!" by *Travellady Magazine*. The Verandas is also a member of the exclusive Select Registry.

The Verandas stands within walking distance of the Riverwalk, Chandler's Wharf, fine restaurants and theaters, so don't think it's a place just for out-of-town visitors, tourists and corporate travelers. The Verandas is a place to consider when you're planning a special celebration, or when you just want to escape from the world for a couple of days. They also offer an attractive corporate program for single business travelers. Chuck and Dennis are gracious, accommodating hosts who will do everything possible to ensure a relaxing, enjoyable retreat.

Carolina Beach and Kure Beach

Beacon House Inn
Bed & Breakfast $$-$$$$
715 Carolina Beach Ave. N, Carolina Beach
(910) 458-6244, (877) 232-2666

Originally a 1950s boarding house, Beacon House Inn Bed and Breakfast is a reminder of a simpler life in days gone by. The decor features pine tongue-in-groove paneled walls, vintage photographs and memorabilia blended with modern amenities. Everything about the place says "relax and make yourself comfortable." Air-conditioned guest rooms are decorated in different motifs and all have queen beds and private baths. There are multiple room options, including a two-person whirlpool tub suite, a two-room suite complete with its own living room, and cottages for families traveling with pets or small children. The Beacon House also has on-site massage services to truly help you unwind.

Full Southern breakfasts are served daily. Two cozy, clean cottages decorated in Caribbean themes are available for rent as well, offering two- and three-bedroom accommodations with fully equipped

kitchens, linens, starter essential kits, satellite TVs and porches. The cottages are pet friendly, and children are always welcome. Custom packages are available, should you choose to rent the entire inn or the inn and cottages for a larger group, wedding or reunion. Private catering is also available on-site should you desire it. In addition, there are spa packages and romance packages for that special occasion, and even an on-site massage therapist. Beacon House Inn is located in Carolina Beach, across the street from the ocean, close to the Boardwalk and near a popular fishing pier. Endless outdoor activities can be found nearby. Golf opportunities are plentiful, and historic downtown Wilmington, the North Carolina Aquarium at Fort Fisher and two great state parks are just minutes away.

Darlings By the Sea $$-$$$$
329 Atlantic Ave., Kure Beach
(910) 458-1429, (800) 383-8111
www.darlingsbythesea.com

If you would like to get away, Darlings by the Sea is the perfect place for rest and relaxation. This small boutique hotel offers five fabulously appointed oceanfront whirlpool suites, just steps away from the beach. Each suite offers oceanfront views, a king-sized bed with Egyptian cotton triple sheets and Siberian goose down comforters, and top-quality interiors with Natuzzi leather seating from Italy.

Baths offer a mirrored whirlpool for two with thick towels imported from Scotland, and custom soaps and bubble bath. Each morning you'll enjoy a breakfast of fruit, pastries, juice and coffee served in your suite, and each evening you'll want to watch the sun set from your private balcony. All suites are non-smoking.

Hidden Treasure Inn $$
113 S. Fourth Ave., Kure Beach
(910) 458-3216

This delightful small inn, nestled under large shade trees, has a comfortable, down-home feel the minute you step through the gate into the garden. Each of the four non-smoking units is like your own little apartment. Take advantage of the gas grill, picnic table and patio for a casual cookout. Sun by the immaculate blue pool. Relax on the porch and enjoy gentle breezes, or take a short stroll over to the beach. Hidden Treasure Inn's atmosphere of warmth and hospitality makes it a great getaway from the business of life. Host Nancy Bryant is cordial and welcoming and makes each of her guests feel like a long-time friend. All units have air conditioning, free WiFi, cable TV, a refrigerator, a microwave and a coffeemaker, and the three efficiency kitchens are fully equipped. Linens, towels and daily maid service are included. Daily and weekly rentals are available.

Bald Head Island

Marsh Harbour Inn $$-$$$$
21 Keelson Row, Harbour Village,
Bald Head Island
(910) 457-1702, (800) 680-8322

The Marsh Harbour Inn overlooks the Bald Head Island Marina with stunning views from every guest room or suite. A third-floor renovation in 2008 offers guests luxurious, newly furnished suites that accommodate four to seven people. These three premier suites include flat-panel televisions with DVD/CD players, sleeper sofas mini-kitchenettes, and decks with views over the harbor to the Atlantic Ocean. (Suites are also available for fractional ownership.) Individual guest rooms in a simple Shaker-style decor include one or two queen beds, televisions and private baths. A handicapped-accessible room is also available. Included in your stay are generous continental breakfast buffets, use of an electric golf cart, Internet and fax services, golf bag storage and temporary membership in the exclusive Bald Head Island Club. This temporary membership offers use of the dining room, pool, tennis court and 18-hole Championship golf course (not including greens fees). Both children and groups are welcome for weeks at a time or just one night. For groups, Marsh Harbour Inn also offers a meeting room with seating for up to 25. It's a delightful place to enjoy a corporate retreat or a wedding party (see our Wedding Planning information).

Southport

The Brunswick Inn $$$
301 E. Bay St., Southport
(910) 457-5278

Since 1800 when it was built as the summer residence of Benjamin Smith, founder of Smithville (Southport) and tenth governor of North Carolina, this Federal-style mansion has looked out over the mouth of the Cape Fear River, the Intracoastal Waterway and the Atlantic Ocean. It served as summer residence for Governor Dudley as well. In 1856 the top two floors were rebuilt by Thomas Meares, owner of Orton Plantation around the time of the Civil War.

In 1997 Jim and Judy Clary purchased the building and went to work restoring it to its previous grandeur, including preserving the original heart-pine floors, the plaster ceiling moldings, the cathedral shaped pocket doors, the Southport bows over the door and window casings, and the nine working fireplaces. Judy chose rich, vibrant colors that set off the spacious rooms and play up the interesting architecture. In the middle of the dining room stands a huge antique table, handmade in the mountains, above which hangs a crystal chandelier dropping from the second-floor ceiling, through the rotunda. This is where the full, home-cooked, gourmet breakfasts, including homemade pastries,

are normally served. Some mornings, though, breakfast is served in the cozy working kitchen in front of the fireplace.

Each beautifully decorated guest room has a private bath and contains a working fireplace for which the proprietors provide a Duraflame log. A well-stocked library, a parlor and an observatory, including telescope, are all available to guests. Afternoon hors d'oeuvre and wine are served, and guests are encouraged to spend some time on the veranda watching the passing scene.

You will be welcomed by Lizzie Lou, the Sunshine Girl (the resident cat). Don't be spooked by Tony, the whimsical resident ghost who sometimes makes his presence known. Tony was a harpist who played at the inn when balls were common occurrences. He drowned in a boating accident off Bald Head Island in 1882 and has made the inn his home since! More recently, Charles Bronson slept here. The Brunswick Inn was used in the making of several movies, including Summer Catch with Freddie Printz, Jr., The Wedding with Halle Berry and Pirate Kids.

Lois Jane's Riverview Inn $$ - $$$
106 W. Bay St., Southport
(910) 457-6701, (800) 457-1152

Owned and operated by fourth-generation descendants of the original owner, this beautifully restored 1892 home is near the old harbor pilot's tower and overlooks the mouth of the Cape Fear River. It is a quiet getaway within easy walking distance of Southport's restaurants, river walk, shops and museums. Porches on the river side of the building are ideal for rocking away the time. Two rooms with private baths and two with a shared bath have queen-size, four-poster beds and period furnishings that have been part of the home for years. Rooms to the front of the inn have expansive river views and access to the second floor balcony. Every morning hot coffee is placed in the upstairs hallway followed by a full Southern-style breakfast in the dining room. Afternoon wine and cheese is a nice way to end the day. Special breakfast arrangements can be made with advance notice. Those interested in a bit more privacy might inquire about the Queen Deluxe Suite. Cancellations require a 72-hour notice for refunds.

Robert Ruark Inn
Bed & Breakfast $$$$
119 N. Lord St., Southport
(910) 363-4169

In 2008 the Robert Ruark Inn opened its doors in the very house where the author spent a good bit of his childhood — his maternal grandfather's home. This elegant, Victorian-style inn offers four rooms, all with private baths and flat-screen TVs. The Captain Adkins Room features seafaring decor and a private balcony. The Robert Ruark Room is decorated to reflect his adventures in Africa. In Charlotte's Room you will find an original stained-glass lancet window. The first-floor Virginia's Room contains a four-poster bed and a gas fireplace. Breakfast may be served in the dining room or on the garden veranda. Located in downtown Southport, the inn is within walking distance of shopping and dining and is surrounded by the natural beauty of the area.

Calabash

The Rose Bed and Breakfast $$
545 Hickman Rd. NW, Calabash
(910) 575-2880

If you are looking for a quiet country retreat close to the beaches and the Little River casino boats, The Rose is a good bet. After a full cooked breakfast, homemade to order, relax on the wraparound porch enjoying nature before setting out for the beach, golf or shopping. When you return after your busy day, the great room awaits you. Catch up with the world with the surround-sound TV, watch a movie on DVD or VHS, play a board game or the piano. On a warm clear evening you can star-gaze from the back deck using the telescope, or if it's cool, you can relax in front of the fire. When you retire to your

suite you will be glad you chose The Rose. Pets and children are not permitted.

Topsail Island Area

Bed & Breakfast at Mallard Bay $$
960 Mallard Bay Rd., Hampstead
(910) 270-3363

This bed and breakfast is unique in that it only has one private suite of rooms. Guests have the entire upstairs, which includes a bedroom with a four-poster, queen-sized bed, a living room with a queen-sized sofa bed, a TV and VCR/DVD and a private bath. Guests also have use of the deck, hammock and gardens. For a relaxing paddle, launch a kayak or canoe from the new floating dock, or, if that's too ambitious, lounge with a good book in the sun room and enjoy the water views. A full country breakfast is served on the weekends, and continental breakfast is offered on weekdays. Fresh local fruit, vegetarian or meat dishes, and blueberry muffins made with locally picked blueberries are some of the house specialties. The Bed and Breakfast at Mallard Bay is within walking distance of Harbour Village Marina, close to local golf courses and only a few minutes' drive from the beach, restaurants and shopping.

The Pink Palace of Topsail $$-$$$
1222 S. Shore Dr., Surf City
(910) 328-5114

Treat yourself like royalty and stay at The Pink Palace, Topsail Island's only oceanfront bed and breakfast. This is a great vacation spot for families, as each large suite can accommodate up to 10 people. All suites have access to a screened porch, three open-air decks and a hot tub. Sip your morning coffee and watch the sun rise from a relaxing rocker, hammock or swing. The Palace is open September through June, and weekly rentals are available all summer.

VACATION RENTALS

There's just something about a visit to the coast that increases your overall feeling of well-being and recharges your batteries. The serene and scenic beaches surrounding the Wilmington area coax guests back year after year to refresh their relaxation skills and rejuvenate their energy levels. Fortunately for visitors from all over the world, the beaches of southeastern North Carolina feature a wide variety of agencies well equipped to connect visitors with a rental property to suit their needs.

Ranging from the remote and picturesque locales on Topsail Island to the quiet seaside hamlets of the South Brunswick Islands, there are condominiums, townhouses, multi-bedroom homes and other lodgings designed to accommodate the vacationing couple, the business excursion or the family reunion.

If you're planning on spending more than just a couple of days on the southern coast, doing your research can result in getting your hands on the perfect spot and maybe even saving a few dollars. While the responsibilities may increase with renting a house, if your party is a big one, the advantages are numerous. The choice is yours. Do you want room service or would you rather be able to sleep late and make your own bed? A long-term rental becomes your sanctuary during your stay at the beach, and the difference in comfort is fairly obvious. Who wouldn't prefer a living room with cable and stereo if you're bringing the entire family on vacation? Also, having a kitchen makes for a more communal atmosphere around mealtime, with guests being able to take advantage of fresh local produce and seafood.

RENTAL AGENCIES

This listing of rental agencies is a sampling of the many fine companies from which you may choose. We don't have room in this chapter to include all of the local rental companies; if you would like to find others contact the chamber of commerce for your area of interest (see our Area Overviews chapter for a list of local chambers of commerce).

Wilmington

Network Real Estate
106 N. Water St., Wilmington
(910) 772-1622, (877) 882-1622

Network's historic downtown Wilmington office offers both long-term and short-term corporate rentals. Network Real Estate also offers a large, ever-expanding selection of premium vacation rentals in Carolina and Kure beaches, including oceanfront cottages and condominiums in a variety of price ranges. Amenities for most beach rentals include central air, major appliances, cable, outdoor decks and easy beach access.

Riverview Suites at Water Street Center
106 N. Water St., Wilmington
(910) 772-9988

Riverview Suites at Water Street Center, located across the street from and operated by the Hilton, offers 40 well-appointed suites overlooking the Cape Fear River. Riverview Suites is the only property on the Cape Fear River that offers walk-out balconies, kitchenettes, Tempurpedic beds and washer/dryers. Riverview Suites is perfect for vacation and long-term corporate rentals. This property has one of the best views in town.

Wrightsville Beach and Vicinity

Bryant Real Estate
1001 N. Lumina Ave., Wrightsville Beach
(910) 256-3764, (800) 322-3764
www.bryantre.com

Offering vacation rental homes, condos and town homes with locations from the ocean to the sound, Bryant Real Estate has been providing quality sales, rentals and property management services in the Wilmington, Carolina Beach, Kure Beach and Wrightsville Beach areas for more than 50 years. For year-round rentals, call (910) 799-2700. Daily, weekly and monthly rates are available in Wrightsville Beach, Carolina Beach and Kure Beach. Bryant also has offices in Wilmington and Carolina Beach/Kure Beach.

Holliday Vacations
2002 Eastwood Rd., Ste. 106, Wilmington
(910) 256-2911, (888) 256-2911
www.hollidayvacations.com

The friendly staff at Holliday Vacations specializes in Wrightsville Beach vacation properties. They offer condominiums, some with a pool and tennis facilities, and distinctive single-family homes. Ask about their free brochure for weekly, weekend and monthly rentals. Holliday Vacations also offers long-term rental properties in both Wilmington and Wrightsville Beach.

Intracoastal Realty Vacation Rentals
605 Causeway Dr., Wrightsville Beach
(910) 256-3780, (800) 346-2463

Whether you choose Wrightsville Beach or one of the Pleasure Island beaches, Intracoastal Realty Vacation Rentals offers hundreds of fabulous vacation homes for your perfect vacation. Choose from oceanfront, ocean-side, ocean-view, soundfront or sound-view homes that range from the small and budget-friendly

to the palatial with all of the amenities. Either way, you can enjoy golf courses, boating facilities, fine dining, shopping and historical sites all within 20 minutes of your exclusive vacation property. Intra-coastal also handles long-term rentals in Wilmington and Wrightsville Beach; visit their website for a complete list.

Figure Eight Island

Bachman Realty - Figure 8 Rentals
2411 Middle Sound Loop, Wilmington
(910) 686-4099, (800) 470-4099

Figure Eight Island offers an exclusive escape from the crowds, plus pristine beaches and luxurious accommodations. Whether you're planning a weekend getaway for the entire family or a month-long summer retreat, Bunnie Bachman will help you find the perfect accommodation that best suits your needs. No one knows Figure Eight Island real estate better than Bachman — she's been a full-time island resident for the last 28 years. She has years of experience in island home sales and rentals. If you decide to purchase a vacation home or make Figure Eight your home, Bachman's experience will be invaluable in helping you find your place in paradise.

Figure 8 Realty
15 Bridge Rd., Figure Eight Island
(910) 686-4400, (800) 279-6085

Figure 8 Realty boasts the largest vacation rental inventory on this exclu-sive, private island. They offer numerous homes on the ocean, sound, interior and salt marsh for those seeking a tranquil and private getaway. Located only minutes away from beautiful downtown Wilming-ton, Figure Eight Island offers vacationers both privacy and convenience. Should you decide to make the island your home or home away from home, Figure 8 Realty offers an experienced sales staff that will assist you with the purchase of island property.

Carolina Beach and Kure Beach

Atlantic Towers
1615 S. Lake Park Blvd., Carolina Beach
(910) 458-8313, (800) BEACH-40
www.atlantic-towers.com

Located on the beautiful sands of Carolina Beach, Atlantic Towers features fully furnished one-bedroom and two-bedroom oceanfront condominiums with private oceanfront balconies. The facility includes both an oceanfront outdoor pool and a heated indoor pool. Free wireless Internet is available in the Club Room area. Atlantic Towers' friendly staff is available 24 hours a day to accommodate your res-ervation needs, whether you're interested in nightly, weekly or monthly rentals. Visit their website for more details and to view virtual tours.

Blue Water Realty
1000 S. Lake Park Blvd., Carolina Beach
(910) 458-3001, (866) 458-3001
www.bluewaterrealtyinc.com

Centrally located on Pleasure Island, Blue Water Realty specializes in water-front homes in Carolina and Kure beaches. Customer satisfaction is important to Blue Water Realty and their staff is dedicated to making your vacation a pleasurable and memorable experience. Now offering

online booking, Blue Water Realty is open seven days a week in season to serve your vacation needs.

Bryant Real Estate
1401 N. Lake Park Blvd., Carolina Beach
(910) 458-5658, (800) 994-5222
www.bryantre.com

Offering vacation rental homes, condos and townhomes with locations from the ocean to the sound, Bryant Real Estate has been providing quality sales, rentals and property-management service in the Wilmington, Carolina Beach, Kure Beach and Wrightsville Beach areas for more than 50 years. For year-round rentals, call (910) 799-2700. Daily, weekly and monthly rentals are available in Wrightsville Beach, Carolina Beach and Kure Beach. Bryant also has offices in Wilmington and Wrightsville Beach.

Bullard Realty
1404 S. Lake Park Blvd., Carolina Beach
(910) 458-4028

Bullard Realty takes pride in offering quality vacation accommodations available at Carolina and Kure beaches. They offer more than 80 oceanfront, ocean-view and second-row accommodations. Amenities include indoor and outdoor pools, spas, saunas; tennis courts, recreation centers, elevators and some pet-friendly homes. Whether you want a one-bedroom condo or a six-bedroom,

ocean-view home that sleeps 16, Bullard Realty would enjoy making your vacation dream a reality.

Cabana
222 Carolina Beach Ave. N, Carolina Beach
(910) 458-4456, (800) 333-8499

Cabana offers a Mediterranean flavor in the heart of Carolina Beach. The oceanfront complex consists of individually owned condos situated on a wide beach covered with white sand. There is a two-night minimum rental in the off season and a weekly minimum during the summer. All units have a fully stocked kitchen.

Carolina Beach Realty
1009 N. Lake Blvd., Ste. B3, Carolina Beach
(910) 458-4444

Whether your interest is in buying or selling a home, booking a vacation or long-term rental, or property management, the professionals at Carolina Beach Realty are ready to assist you. This family-owned and operated real estate firm has been working in the Pleasure Island real estate market for more than 44 years, and they have extensive knowledge of the area's real estate trends. The rental division offers a wide selection of vacation and long-term rentals and includes oceanfront and ocean-view houses and condos. Some properties have private pools and are pet friendly. Long-term rentals include single-family homes, townhomes and condos in Carolina Beach, Kure Beach and Wilmington.

Intracoastal Realty Vacation Rentals
1206 N. Lake Park Blvd., Carolina Beach
(910) 509-7655, (800) 533-1840

Whether you choose Wrightsville Beach or one of the Pleasure Island beaches, Intracoastal Realty Vacation Rentals offers hundreds of fabulous vacation homes for your perfect vacation. Choose from oceanfront, ocean-side, ocean-view, soundfront or sound-view homes that range from the small and budget-friendly to the palatial with all of the amenities. Either way, you can enjoy golf courses, boating facilities, fine dining, shopping and historical sites all within 20 minutes of your exclusive vacation property. A virtual tour of Intracoastal Realty's vacation rentals is available on their website. Intracoastal also handles long-term rentals in Wilmington and Wrightsville Beach; call (910) 509-9700 or (800) 826-4428 for long-term rental information or visit their website for a complete list.

Island Beach Rentals by Walker Realty
501 N. Lake Park Blvd., Carolina Beach
(910) 458-3388

Island Beach Rentals offers a wide variety of condos, townhomes and beach houses, whether your party includes two people or a dozen. With fantastic dining only a short trip from every location and plenty of activities for the entire family, Carolina and Kure beaches have become a popular alternative to the Wrightsville Beach madness. Tour the Fort Fisher historic site or take the kids to the aquarium for an afternoon of ocean discovery.

Joy Lee Apartments
317 Carolina Beach Ave. N, Carolina Beach
(910) 458-8361

This seasonal spot features four efficiency spaces for renters. Operating for more than 60 years, Joy Lee is on the National Register of Historic Places for its unique art deco/mission/prairie style design that hearkens back to a simpler day and time. Look for the funky cement pelicans and the turquoise sign adorned

with a seahorse. Situated across from the ocean as well as across from the harbor, Joy Lee has a lovely pool area with stunning views.

Network Real Estate
1029 N. Lake Park Blvd., Ste. 1,
Carolina Beach
(910) 458-8881

Network Real Estate offers a large, ever-expanding selection of premium vacation rentals in Carolina and Kure beaches, including oceanfront cottages and condominiums in a variety of price ranges. Amenities for most rentals include central air, major appliances, cable, outdoor decks and easy beach access. Additionally, Network's Historic Downtown Wilmington office offers new vacation rentals on the Cape Fear River across from the Battleship North Carolina in addition to long- and short-term corporate rentals.

Palm Air Vacation Rentals
133 N. Fort Fisher Blvd., Kure Beach
(910) 458-5269
www.palmairrealty.com

From small to large, cottages to condos, Palm Air Vacation Rentals offers options for a weekend or week-long stay. With one, two or three-bedroom options, Palm Air is ideal for couples or families. Located on Pleasure Island, the individual private cottages are nestled around a swimming pool and the oceanfront condos offer spectacular views from sunrise to sunset. Guests will find the units completely equipped and fully furnished. Comfortable and convenient, Palm Air Vacation Rentals recently garnered a 5-star rating from the online travel site Trip Advisor. Online voters were especially pleased with the high standard of cleanliness and great value. Palm Air Vacation Rentals is a short drive from historic downtown Wilmington, a stone's throw from Fort Fisher and the N.C. Aquarium and close to shopping and dining. Hiking trails, fishing and boating opportunities abound. Palm Air Vacation Rentals is eco-friendly and offers free wireless in many units.

Prudential Laney Real Estate - Carolina Beach
123 Harper Ave., Carolina Beach
(910) 458-3739, (800) 235-9068

Prudential Laney Real Estate Vacation Rentals brings years of experience as a customer-oriented business to the Carolina Beach and Kure Beach area. Their goal is to deliver personal service to each client and provide them with the best options for their vacation needs. Rental properties are beautifully decorated and well maintained. Their website offers online reservations 24/7 as well as virtual tours of all rentals and a listing of activities, restaurants and shopping opportunities available during your visit to this wonderful beach.

Southern Retreats Managed Properites
904 S. College Rd., Wilmington
(910) 202-1430, (877) 454-0056

This property management company offers a variety long-term and vacation rentals. Whether you're staying for a while or merely a week, Southern Retreats has the ideal rental property for you. The service area includes downtown Wilmington, Leland and local beaches. Properties range from comfortable single-family homes to nicely decorated condominiums, as well as beach-access cottages, and they're all within easy reach of all of the Cape Fear region's wonderful amenities. Visit their website for more information.

United Beach Vacations
1001 N. Lake Park Blvd., Carolina Beach
(910) 458-9073, (866) 730 -7030
www.capefearholiday.com

From a one-bedroom condo to a large, well appointed home perfect for family reunions, this established company manages fully furnished rental condominiums, beach cottages, duplexes, town homes and single-family homes on Carolina Beach, Kure Beach and Fort Fisher. Rentals are oceanfront, ocean-view and second-row and may be rented for either short term or long term. Some properties are pet-friendly and offer amenities that include pools and tennis courts; many are in close proximity to the North Carolina Aquarium at Fort Fisher.

Victory Beach Vacations
206-A Fayetteville Ave., Carolina Beach
(910) 458-0868, (888) 256-4804

Choose from a variety of first-class, smoke-free accommodations for your hard-earned vacation, weekend getaway or off-season stay. Victory Beach Vacations is committed to excellence, with a friendly, patient staff that will help you select the perfect unit and arrange for all of your rental needs. Condos and houses are available with a wide variety of amenities —oceanfront, pools and harbor-front with private piers and boat slips. They also offer beautiful, pet-friendly units from efficiencies to 10-bedroom oceanfront properties.

Bald Head Island

Bald Head Island Limited
5079 Southport-Supply Rd., Southport
(910) 457-7400, (800) 432-7368

This well-established company on pristine Bald Head Island has 100 rental properties, primarily single-family homes, distributed throughout seven island environments: maritime forest, marsh and creek, Harbour Village, golf course, West Beach, East Beach and South Beach. Each rental includes round-trip ferry passage and the use of at least one four-passenger electric golf cart for transportation around the island (cars are not permitted on Bald Head Island). Guests renting through Bald Head Island Limited receive use of the business center located in the Chandler Building at Harbour Village. This company specializes in corporate retreats, weddings, family reunions and social gatherings for up to 200 people. Accommodations are available on a nightly and weekly basis.

Bald Head Island Rentals, LCC
308 W. Moore St., Southport
(910) 457-1702, (800) 680-8322

Bald Head Island Rentals offers a large selection of luxury resort homes, cottages, villas and suites, including The Marsh Harbour Inn on Bald Head Island. Aiming to ensure a dream vacation on the island, their unique Five Star Guest Services program includes accommodation and reservation services, concierge service, valet parking and guest departure services.

Bald Head Island Vacations
Bald Head Island
(910) 367-7091, (888) 367-7091

With Bald Head's 14 miles of unspoiled beaches, there are numerous oceanfront spots perfect for vacationing families or couples. In addition, there are many secluded getaways located throughout the island's lush interior. Dann and Gail Jackson and the entire staff at Bald Head Island Vacations are attuned to every corner of this quiet, secluded haven. Let them help you find the perfect spot for your family retreat, romantic island escape or luxurious second home.

Mary Munroe Realty
Bald Head Vacation and Sales Inc.
2 Killegray Ridge, Bald Head Island
(910) 470-2253

Mary Munroe Realty Bald Head Vacation and Sales offers homes, villas and condos with two to five bedrooms in all areas on Bald Head Island from the creek to the oceanfront, golf course and maritime forest. Each fully furnished and well-equipped rental unit comes with a guest club membership, one or more golf carts, bikes, grills, beach chairs, linens and towels. Some units are pet friendly. Mary can help you plan your family reunion,

wedding, conference or any large gathering.

Southport and Oak Island

Better Beach Rentals
8601 E. Oak Island Dr., Oak Island
(910) 278-1147, (877) 441-0009

Whether you're looking for a large home for your family vacation or a romantic oceanfront condo for a weekend getaway, Better Beach Rentals has just the space for you. They can even find a property with up to 12 bedrooms for large parties. With access to some of the finest properties on Oak Island as well as a super-simple online reservation process, setting up your beach excursion is as easy as clicking a mouse. Find the property that's perfect for your needs, including rentals with dock access, elevators, swimming pools, ocean views and more. Discount golf packages are available, with numerous courses a short jaunt away.

Coastal Vacation Resorts Oak Island
4434 Long Beach Rd., Oak Island
(910) 457-9409, (888) 703-5469
www.coastalvacationresortsoakisland.com

The folks at Coastal Vacation Resorts take great pride in providing guests with the utmost in professional and personal-

ized service. It is very important to them that your stay be a comfortable and enjoyable one. Here you will find a wide variety of rental options, whether you are searching for a long-term rental in a residential area or an oceanfront or waterway location for your special vacation. You will be sincerely welcomed to this family-oriented island and treated like family. Coastal Vacation Resorts is located just before the bridge on the left. Call for a free copy of their vacation guide or visit the website and book online.

Oak Island Accommodations
8901 E. Oak Island Dr., Oak Island
(800) 243-8132
www.oakislandholiday.com

Whether your interest is in deep-sea fishing, golf, kayaking or just kicking back and enjoying the 14 miles of white sand and ocean waves, the staff at Oak Island Accommodations will make planning your vacation a breeze. Their collection of more than 700 all-inclusive oceanfront to sound-side cottages and condos offers you a wide variety of basic to luxury accommodations, some with pet-friendly options. Visit their full-service website to make your choice online or call for a personal touch. Oak Island Accommodations offers linen and beach equipment rentals, wedding and concierge services, and golf discounts for your convenience and pleasure.

Holden Beach

Alan Holden Vacations
128 Ocean Blvd. W, Holden Beach
(910) 842-6061, (800) 720-2200

The Holden family has provided rental properties on Holden Beach for more than 70 years. This busy agency, the largest in the area, manages more than 300 rental properties on Holden Beach, from beach cottages and condominiums to luxury homes with private pools. Locations include oceanfront, canal and waterway, second-row and dune homes. Alan Holden will tell you "nobody knows the beach better than a Holden."

Brunswickland Realty
123 Ocean Blvd. W, Holden Beach
(800) 842-6949, (800) 842-6949

In business since the 1970s, Brunswick-land Realty manages single-family cottages and larger homes. Accommodations are available on the oceanfront, second row, canal side, dunes and Intracoastal Waterway.

Coastal Vacation Resorts Holden Beach
131 Ocean Blvd. W, Holden Beach
(910) 842-8000, (800) 252-7000

This company, located on Holden Beach, specializes in premier vacation accommodations and offers rentals to fit every lifestyle and budget. Oceanfront, second row, waterway canal and dune locations are available. Many homes offer amenities such as swimming pools, cabanas, tennis courts and an Intracoastal Waterway marina. Some have private pools. Bookings are available online, where you can view interior photos of the properties. Call for a free color brochure.

Hobbs Realty
114 Ocean Blvd. W, Holden Beach
(910) 842-2002, (800) 655-3367

Family owned and operated, Hobbs Realty manages approximately 300 rental properties with expertise gained from more than 30 years in the business. Rentals are offered from the ocean to the waterway and everywhere in between. Just cross the bridge to the island, take the first left and you will find Hobbs Realty in the second office on the left. Their website offers both interior and exterior views and online bookings.

Ocean Isle Beach

Cooke Realtors
One Causeway Dr., Ocean Isle Beach
(910) 579-3535 x216, (800) 622-3224

This well-established island realty company on a family-oriented beach offers more than 500 rental homes, cottages and condominiums from one to 12 bedrooms. Choose from oceanfront, second- and third-row, canal-side, West End and Island Park locations. Cooke is currently the exclusive agent for The Resort and The Peninsula developments.

Island Realty
109-2 Causeway Dr., Ocean Isle Beach
(800) 589-3599

Island Realty is a family-owned company, and their staff takes a special interest in making sure that your vacation will be one to remember. The company has beach cottages, condominiums and villas available for rent. Whether on the oceanfront, waterfront or canal, there is a perfect location for everyone.

R. H. McClure Realty Inc.
24 Causeway Dr., Ocean Isle Beach
(910) 579-3586, (800) 332-5476

R. H. McClure Realty is a full-service realty brokerage that has been established on Ocean Isle Beach for more than 20 years. The large rental inventory includes oceanfront homes and condos, mid-island cottages and deep-water canal homes with individual private docks. Spring and fall discounts are available. Virtual tour and on-line bookings are available. Call for a free color vacation brochure.

Sloane Realty Vacations
16 Causeway Dr., Ocean Isle Beach
(910) 579-6216, (800) 843-6044

Sloane Realty Vacations of Ocean Isle Beach and Sunset Beach provides vacationers with accommodations in privately owned homes and condos on Ocean Isle Beach, Sunset Beach and the mainland golf courses. Whether a one-bedroom condo or a nine-bedroom home meets

Before committing to a rental property, familiarize yourself with the location, especially with regard to your personal needs and preferences. Read pertinent chapters in this book, contact the local chamber of commerce or visitor information bureau, and chat with people at the agencies about which area of the southern coast will be suit your needs.

Anglers may want to find a place to stay close to the pier.

photo: Belinda Keller Photography

your needs, Sloane Realty Vacations has a premier selection to choose from. Call for a free brochure or book online. Winter rentals are also available.

Sunset Properties
102 Causeway Dr., Ocean Isle Beach
(910) 575-8603, (800) 445-0218

This family-owned company, founded in 1988, handles the rental of more than 450 vacation homes, duplexes and condos on Sunset Beach and Ocean Isle Beach. Most rentals run from Saturday to Saturday during the season. There are several pet-friendly homes among the properties. A minimum stay of two nights is required in the off-season. Bookings are available online.

Williamson Realty
119 Causeway Dr. SW, Ocean Isle Beach
(910) 579-2373, (800) 727-9222

mong the area's largest vacation rental companies, Williamson Realty, Inc. offers a wide range of individually owned cottages and condos from oceanfront to soundfront. Well established since 1975, this company with its friendly professional staff will help you find that perfect beach rental for you and your family. For photos and more information, check out their website.

Sunset Beach

Carolina Golf & Beach Resorts
818 Colony Pl., Sunset Beach
(800) 222-1524, (800) 222-1524

Carolina Golf and Beach Resorts provides nightly and weekly golf and accommodations packages. Accommodations include one-, two- and three-bedroom condominiums on the Oyster Bay Golf Links and beach rentals on Sunset Beach.

Sea Trail Golf Resort & Convention Center
211 Clubhouse Rd., Sunset Beach
(800) 624-6601

Sea Trail Golf Resort & Convention Center, in Sunset Beach, NC, is an excellent choice for your vacation, be it for a week or more than a month. Accommodation offerings include a guest room, a mini-suite efficiency or a spacious fairway villa. When you decide on a villa, you have your choice of the Royal Poste, River Creek I and II, or Club Villa neighborhoods along the Dan Maples golf course. Also available are The Champions mini-suites and villas on the Willard Byrd golf course, with one or two bedrooms and elevator access. Sea Trail offers three signature golf courses designed by different architects with varying styles of play for a great compliment of golf. See our Golf section for more information. Amenities at the on-site Village Activity Center include an outdoor pool and whirlpool, tiki bar in-season, an indoor pool and whirlpool, a weight room and cardiovascular theater with fitness classes and yoga and a spa with massage, manicures and pedicures. The staff can arrange for bicycling, deep-sea fishing, jet skiing, horseback riding or adventure cruises. Nearby communities offer a variety of entertainment at movie theaters, shopping within walking distance, restaurants, dinner theaters and live shows. Sea Trail also provides a complimentary shuttle service to take you to nearby Sunset Beach and throughout the golf resort.

Sunset Properties
419 S. Sunset Blvd., Sunset Beach
(910) 579-9000, (800) 338-9058

This family-owned company, founded in 1988, handles the rental of more than 450 vacation homes, duplexes and condos on Sunset Beach and Ocean Isle Beach. Most rentals run from Saturday to Saturday during the season. There are several

If you are staying in an oceanfront house during the months of July through October, turn all of the outdoor lights off when possible. This is the turtle-hatching season and newborn loggerhead turtles usually hatch in the dunes at night. They make their way to the sea by following light reflected on the water. Lights on the houses can confuse them and cause them to go in the wrong direction with disastrous results. Sea turtles dig the dark.

pet-friendly homes among the properties. A minimum stay of two nights is required in the off-season. Bookings are available online.

Sunset Vacations - Sunset Realty
401 S. Sunset Blvd., Sunset Beach
(910) 579-9000

Sunset Vacations offers a wide assortment of attractive, single-family homes for rent throughout Sunset Beach, including oceanfront, canal, bay-front and inlet locations. They have beach homes to fit every style, location and budget, and you can book directly online. This is an experienced

company with an extreme commitment to making your vacation just right.

Topsail Island

A Beach Place Realty
203 S. Topsail Dr., Surf City
(910) 328-2522

A Beach Place Realty offers a wide selection of vacation rentals on Topsail Island, including condominiums, townhomes, cottages and large single-family homes. Check it out before you check-in with A Beach Place Realty's online virtual tours of all their rental properties. Your only surprise will be the gift bags waiting for you with information about the island. In addition to this special touch, you can be assured of friendly, efficient service for all your rental needs.

Access Realty
13480 N.C. Hwy. 50/210, Surf City
(910) 329-9800

Access Realty is a full-service brokerage company that offers a variety of accommodations on Topsail Island. Properties include oceanfront, soundfront, mainland homes and condominiums. Some locations offer pool facilities, fitness centers, game rooms or tennis courts. Call or visit their website for more details.

Bryson and Associates, Inc.
809 Roland Ave., Surf City
(910) 328-2468, (800) 326-0747

Bryson and Associates have been serving the Topsail Island area for more than 20 years with a commitment to customer service. Prime rental properties are available on the oceanfront, second row, soundfront and on the canals. Condominium or individual beach home, there is something for every budget.

Century 21 Action, Inc.
518 Roland Ave., Surf City
(888) 826-0563
www.century21topsail.com

With one of the best selections of properties across the entire Topsail Island

area, Century 21 Action can help you find the perfect vacation experience. Choose from an array of luxury homes, cottages, condos or town homes, including many pet-friendly properties. Oceanfront paradise to island hide-away, they have what you're looking for. Visit their award-winning website for an extensive selection of videos, property maps and photos for each vacation property. You also can call their 24-hour, toll-free reservation line. Ready for a longer stay? Visit their real estate sales or long-term rental divisions.

Coldwell Banker-Coastline Realty
965 Old Folkstone Rd., Ste. 108, Sneads Ferry
(910) 327-7711, (800) 497-5463
www.cbcoastline.com

Looking for the perfect spot for your family and friends to enjoy a little summer getaway on the coast? Coastline Realty can help you find the ideal rental for a week, weekend or however long you plan on enjoying the Carolina coast. Offering numerous single-family homes, condos, duplexes, quadplexes and cottages, the team at this Coldwell Banker branch can help you reserve the perfect summer rental.

Intracoastal Realty Vacation Rentals
302 N. New River Rd., Surf City
(910) 256-3780, (800) 346-2463

Whether you choose Wrightsville Beach or one of the Pleasure Island beaches, Intracoastal Realty Vacation Rentals offers hundreds of fabulous vacation homes for your perfect vacation. Choose from oceanfront, ocean-side, ocean-view, soundfront or sound-view homes that range from the small and budget-friendly to the palatial with all of the amenities. Either way, you can enjoy golf courses, boating facilities, fine dining, shopping and historical sites all within 20 minutes of your exclusive vacation property. Intracoastal also handles long-term rentals in Wilmington and Wrightsville Beach; visit their website for a complete list.

Island Real Estate
The Fishing Village, Roland Ave., PO Box 2690, Surf City
(910) 328-2323, (800) 622-6886
www.topsailvacation.com

Cathy Medlin of Island Real Estate has been selling and leasing properties on and around Topsail Island since the 1970s. As a founding member of the Topsail Association of Realtors, she really knows the area's real estate. Cathy specializes in

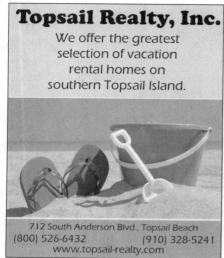
a renter with the right property. Homes or condominiums are offered for weekly, weekend or nightly rentals. This agency is open year round and offers 24-hour telephone service.

Topsail Realty
712 S. Anderson Blvd., Topsail Beach
(910) 328-5241, (800) 526-6432
www.topsail-realty.com

Topsail Realty offers more than 200 Surf City and Topsail Beach vacation homes on the southern end of Topsail Island. Homes range from luxurious to basic and budget friendly, and locations vary from oceanfront to soundfront to Serenity Point townhomes on the southernmost tip of the island. A large number of these homes allow well-behaved adult dogs. Topsail Realty is the only Topsail Island company that specializes exclusively in vacation rentals and property management and provides unsurpassed service for vacationers and homeowners. You can check vacation home availability and place reservation requests online or call their office to reserve the perfect home for your vacation.

residential, resort and commercial properties. Her firm is known to as the "vacation specialist" with 200-plus properties from which to choose for your vacation. Cathy says they specialize in making dreams come true.

Kathy S. Parker Real Estate
1000 N.C. Hwy. 210, Sneads Ferry
(910) 327-2219, (800) 327-2218

This full-service realty office has more than 100 long-term and vacation rental properties, primarily in the North Topsail Beach and Sneads Ferry areas. These rental specialists take pride in matching

Treasure Realty
1950 N.C. Hwy. 174, Ste. P, Sneads Ferry
(910) 327-4444, (800) 762-3961
www.treasurerealty.com

Treasure Realty has specialized in vacation and long-term rentals in North Topsail Beach and Sneads Ferry for more than 18 years. The friendly staff has a combined 90-plus years of experience and holds one of the largest selections of vacation rental properties on Topsail Island, including a large inventory of oceanfront homes and condominiums as well as soundfront and mainland selections. Treasure Realty features several of the largest rental homes on Topsail Island and many of these homes have private pools and hot tubs.

Ward Realty Corp.
116 S. Topsail Dr., Surf City
(910) 328-3221, (800) 782-6216
www.wardrealty.com

Ward Realty has been renting vacation cottages on Topsail Island for more than 50 years and offers more than 250 cottages and condominiums to choose from. Their accommodations range from the luxurious to budget-friendly and from the oceanfront to the sound. With a commitment to service and years of experience they can help you select the perfect vacation spot.

Rental Services

Sweet Dreams Linens
127 J. H. Batts Rd., Surf City
(910) 328-5312

Sweet Dreams Linens provides hospitality-quality bed and bath linen rentals, deluxe baby equipment rentals and quality beach equipment rentals to vacation rental properties, property managers, property owners, guests and tenants and hotels in the Topsail Island Area. Sweet Dreams Linens delivers to Surf City, Topsail Beach and North Topsail Beach.

⛺ CAMPING

With its sandy beaches, barrier islands, tidal estuaries, blackwater rivers and swamp forests, North Carolina's southern coast provides a wealth of settings for all types of campers. The topography of the area has been shaped by the forces of wind, sea and weather and provides a rich experience for outdoor enthusiasts.

If you wear your home on your back and have the use of a small boat, leave the parking lot–style camping behind for the isolation of Masonboro Island, an eight-mile barrier island that stretches between Wrightsville and Carolina beaches. In the off-season, your only neighbors may be pelicans and rabbits.

Campgrounds nearest the beaches are generally RV towns with ample amenities, so if you'd like to take along the kitchen sink, you may as well take your electric bug-zapper too.

Bicycle campers will find campgrounds about a day's ride apart except in the Wilmington vicinity, where campgrounds are less numerous. In any event, camping the southern coast is ideal for visitors on a budget, anglers who want to walk to the water each morning and anyone for whom recreation is re-creation.

Naturally, the highest rates at private campgrounds apply during the summer and on holiday weekends. Tent sites are cheaper than RV sites. At most private grounds, weekly rates often discount the seventh day if payment is made in advance. Rentals by the month or longer are extremely limited from April to August due to the summer crunch. Some campgrounds offer camper or boat storage for a monthly fee.

As the Boy Scouts say, be prepared, especially for blistering sun, sudden electrical storms with heavy downpours, voracious marsh mosquitoes and insidious no-see-ums in summer. Temperatures in the region generally are mild, except for the occasional frost in winter and some scorching days in the midst of summer. Average summer peak temperature is in the 90s, average winter low is 36, and the overall yearly average temperature is 63. April and October tend to have the least rainfall, about 3 inches each, while July can boast some serious showers. However, weather patterns are often unpredictable, so be prepared for rain in any season and for the quick onset of foul weather.

Sunscreen is essential. Hats and eye protection are wise, and insect repellent useful. For tent camping, a waterproof tent fly is a must, and a tarp or dining fly is handy when cooking. Pack longer tent stakes or sand stakes for protection against high winds. Stay abreast of weather reports, especially during hurricane season (June 1 through November 30), and always bring a radio. A lightweight camp stove and cook set will come in handy when restaurants aren't convenient and at the many campgrounds where fires are prohibited.

The primary creature hazards in the area are poisonous snakes and spiders, which are prevalent in forested areas, and ticks, which can carry disease. Beware of poison ivy, poison oak and poison sumac in brushwood and forests. Raccoons and other small nocturnal animals are seldom more than a nuisance, although rabid animals are occasionally reported in rural areas. Normally, the animals posing the greatest threat are human, which is why open fires and alcoholic beverages are restricted in most campgrounds.

For hikers or cyclists carrying packs, there are two noteworthy Wilmington retail outlets for equipment. In business for more than 50 years, Canady's Sport Center, 3220 Wrightsville Avenue, (910) 791-6280, is an excellent outdoor outfitter with a varied inventory. It's closed on Sunday. Another excellent source for equipment and outdoor clothing is Great Outdoor Provision Co. in Hanover Center, 3501 Oleander Drive, Wilmington, (910) 343-1648. It's open seven days a week.

Your other choices for field gear are Dick's Sporting Goods, 816 S. College Road, (910) 793-1904, and the two Walmart Super Centers, one at 5135 Carolina Beach Road, (910) 452-0944, and the other at 5226 Sigmon Road, (910) 392-4034, which are good choices for novices and tailgate campers. In Brunswick County, Walmart Super Centers are located in Southport at 1675 N. Howe Street, (910) 454-9909, in Leland at 1112 New Point Boulevard, (910) 383-1769, and in Shallotte, 4540 Main Street, (910) 754-2880.

In this chapter we've provided a list of the area's nicest, most popular camping destinations.

Wilmington

Wilmington KOA
7415 Market St., Wilmington
(910) 686-7705

Located 5 miles from Wrightsville Beach and 10 miles from downtown Wilmington, the Wilmington KOA is well situated for getting to all of the local attractions. The tree-shaded grounds include a large swimming pool, volleyball court, a children's playground, a soccer field, a giant chess set, a full-service camp store, more than 100 campsites (pull-through and tent sites) and full and partial hookups. This pet-friendly campground has clean restrooms, hot showers, laundry facilities and mail service. If you need a break from seeing the sights around town, the Wilmington KOA features free wireless Internet service and a new RV Wash. Rather than tent camping, why not try the Wilmington KOA's charming heated and air-conditioned Kamping Kabins, Kottages and Lodges? A convenience store and gas station are located at the entrance to the campground. Nightly, weekly and monthly rates are available, and reservations are accepted and recommended in the high

season. The Wilmington KOA is open year round.

Masonboro Island

Accessible only by boat, Masonboro Island is the last and largest undisturbed barrier island remaining on the southern North Carolina coast. It is the fourth component of the North Carolina National Estuarine Research Reserve (see our Higher Education and Research chapter) and deservedly so. This migrating ribbon of sand and uphill terrain, about 8 miles in length, is immediately south of Wrightsville Beach and offers campers a secluded, primitive experience in the most pristine environment on the Cape Fear coast. It is also used by anglers, bird-watchers, artists, the occasional hunter, students and surfers (who prefer the north end). Everything you'll need must be packed in, and everything you produce should be packed out — everything!

Ninety-seven percent of Masonboro Island remains under state ownership and will always be accessible to visitors. Of the reserve's more than 5,000 acres, about 4,400 acres are tidal marsh and mud flats, so most folks land at the extreme north or south ends, on or near the sandy beaches by the inlets. Pitch camp behind the dunes only and use a cook stove; there is little or no firewood so bringing your own is a good idea. While the North Carolina Division of Coastal Management hopes to limit its involvement with the island and preserve its traditional uses, it does prohibit polluting the island and camping on and in front of the dune ridge.

Wildlife is remarkable and fragile. During the warm months, Masonboro Island is one of the most successful nesting areas for loggerhead turtles, a threatened

All North Carolina state parks are wildlife preserves and prohibit the removal of any plants, rocks, animals or artifacts from their sites. Be respectful of these natural sites and leave nothing behind but footprints.

Campgrounds are found nestled in some of the most beautiful regions of the area.

photo: Belinda Keller Photography

species. Piping plovers, also threatened, feed at the island in winter. Keep your eyes open for river otters in the marshes and, at low tide, raccoons. Gray foxes, cotton rats and tiny marsh rabbits all frequent the small maritime forest. The marshes, flats and creeks at low tide are excellent places to observe and photograph great blue and little blue herons, tricolor herons, snowy and great egrets, oyster catchers, clapper rails and many other flamboyant birds. Brown pelicans, various terns and gulls, American ospreys and shear waters all live on Masonboro, if not permanently then at least for some part of their lives. Endangered peregrine falcons are very occasional seasonal visitors.

We recommend plenty of sun protection and insect repellent, perhaps even mosquito netting in the warm months, and trash bags always. Keep in mind that some of the island is still privately owned, not only at the north end, but also throughout the island, and all of it is fragile.

The University of North Carolina at Wilmington's Center for Marine Science Research is conducting an ongoing survey of visitor impact on the island and a continuing study of environmental changes caused by hurricanes and other natural forces. Visitors' behavior and scientific scrutiny together will have some influence on whether Masonboro Island becomes severely restricted, so responsible usage is paramount. For more information about Masonboro Island, see the Islands section in our Attractions.

Carolina Beach

Carolina Beach State Park
1010 State Park Rd., Carolina Beach
(910) 458-8206

Once a campsite for Paleo-Indians, Colonial explorers and Confederate troops, Carolina Beach State Park remains a gem among local camping destinations. Watersports enthusiasts are minutes from the Cape Fear River, Masonboro Sound and the Atlantic Ocean. The park offers a renovated 42-slip marina with gas and diesel fuel and two launching ramps,

which should re-open in 2010. Call (910) 458-7770 for the marina.

Need we mention the great fishing? Home to lizards, deer, snakes, raccoons, opossums, carnivorous plants and occasionally alligators, foxes and river otters, the park is an bird- and animal-watcher's paradise. (All plants and animals are protected within North Carolina State Parks and must not be collected or harassed.)

Six miles of hiking trails wind through several distinct habitats, including coastal fringe evergreen forest, pocosin (low, flat, swampy regions) and savanna. Hikers on the Sugarloaf Trail pass over tidal marsh and dunes and along three lime-sink ponds. Cypress Pond, the most unusual, is dominated by a dwarf cypress swamp forest. Ranger-led interpretive programs deepen visitors' understanding of the region's natural bounty. Bikes are not allowed on any of the trails.

Dense vegetation lends the campsites a fair amount of privacy. Each site has a table and grill, and sites are available on a first-come, first-served basis (at a rate of $18 per site, per day or a senior citizen rate of $13 per day, per site for people 62 years of age and older). Two of the 83 campsites are wheelchair accessible. Drinking water and well-kept restrooms with hot showers are close by the campsites. There is a dump station for RVs, but no hookups. Unleashed pets and possession of alcoholic beverages are prohibited. You may now make reservations for your campsite ahead of time by calling (877) 722-6762 Monday through Friday from 8 AM to 8 PM and Saturday and Sunday from 9 AM to 5 PM. Reservations should be made 48 hours in advance.

The park is 15 miles south of Wilmington, just off U.S. 421. From Wilmington, make a right on to Dow Road at the second stoplight after crossing Snow's Cut bridge. Then turn right on State Park Road. Stop by the Visitors Center at the park entrance for information, trail maps and brochures. You might want to spend some time at the Visitors Center exploring the interactive environmental-education exhibits, which include a computer program that explains prescribed burning, a quiz game on biodiversity, a Venus flytrap puppet and a maze game from the per-spective of an insect trying to maneuver through the park. .

Sunset Beach

KOA Kampground
7200 KOA Dr., Sunset Beach
(910) 579-7562, (888) 562-4240

KOA is a name that everyone recog-nizes as quality when it comes to camp-ing, and this facility provides that familiar camping experience to the Brunswick County beaches area. Only five miles from Sunset Beach and Ocean Isle Beach, the KOA offers RV campsites (including extra-long sites), tent sites, Kamping Kabins and a Kottage/Lodge. Sites include 30-amp or 50-amp service, cable TV and access to a Kamping Kitchen. DSL hook-up and wireless Internet are available, as are a swimming pool, horseshoe pits, a bas-ketball goal, a volleyball net and fishing. Planned activities are offered on holidays and weekends. Amenities available with a small charge include LP gas, firewood and bicycles. Thirty-five golf courses, area attractions and Calabash seafood restau-rants are nearby.

Ocean Aire Camp World, Inc.
2614 Holden Beach Rd. SW (N.C. Hwy. 130), Supply
(910) 842-9072

Open year round and located 2.5 miles from Holden Beach, this 253-site camp-ground offers daily, weekly, monthly and annual rates. Amenities include either 30-amp or 50-amp electricity, water and sewer, modern bathhouses with tiled hot showers, laundry facilities, LP gas,

security lights and a convenience store (open March through October). A large swimming pool, a nine-hole putt-putt golf course, pool tables, video games, volleyball, horseshoes and a children's playground provide recreation options. The campground offers covered and open boat and trailer storage with yearly boat or camper storage rates. Sunday church services are held on-site.

Shallotte

Sea Mist Camping Resort
4616 Devane Rd. SW, Shallotte
(910) 754-8916

Sea Mist's panoramic view of Shallotte Inlet and Ocean Isle Beach is enough to entice any camper, but the view is only one of the appealing amenities. Visitors love Sea Mist's pool, reputedly the largest in Brunswick County, with its shaded deck and picnic area. Volleyball, basketball and horseshoes are among the activities avail-able. Use of the boat ramp carries no extra charge. This Woodall-rated resort is open year round and has 250 spacious RV sites with tables. Most have full hookups. The restrooms, bathhouse and coin-operated laundry facilities are clean. Sea Mist is only 10 minutes from the attractions of Ocean Isle Beach. Leashed pets are permitted. Daily and annual rates are available, as is boat storage for annual guests. Reserve early. Sea Mist is at the Intracoastal Water-way opposite the east end of Ocean Isle Beach. Follow the blue and white camp-ing signs along N.C. Highway 179 to Brick Landing Road and continue to the end of the pavement. Turn left onto Devane Road.

Topsail Island Area

Lanier's Campground
1161 Spot Ln., Surf City
(910) 328-9431

This large and friendly campground is located on the mainland side of the Intra-coastal Waterway in Surf City. Campsites range from full hookups and camper/pop-up sites to tent sites with fire rings and some sites offer shade. Campground ame-nities include free WiFi Internet access, a

---

When packing for your outdoor adventure, remember these small but essential items: Swiss Army knife, twine, lighter, flashlight, insect repellent and basic first aid supplies. A cell phone also can be awfully handy in the event of an emergency, and having a waterproof container for your phone will help keep it functional in foul weather.

swimming pool, boat ramp, fishing pier and fish-cleaning station, dump station, pay phones, picnic tables, limited groceries, a bathhouse, an arcade and a sandwich grill serving hand-dipped ice cream. Horseshoes, beach bingo, a children's playground, holiday activities and interdenominational church services are some of the activities offered in season at the campground. The interior roads are paved, and it is open year round.

Virginia Creek Campground
440 Crooked Creek Tr., Surf City
(910) 329-4648

Virginia Creek Campground is located on a large tract of waterfront land that has been in the King family for more than 200 years. With pull-through sites, full hookups, tent sites and a cute little cabin that sleeps three, there is a spot for every type of camper. Amenities include hot showers, laundry facilities, a nearby boat ramp, fishing and complimentary sunsets on the water. The campground is close to restaurants, shopping and the beach. Virginia Creek Campground is pet friendly, call for details.

🍴 RESTAURANTS

A bounty of mouthwatering, fresh-catch seafood figures prominently almost everywhere you dine along North Carolina's southern coast. These coastal waters yield consistently high-quality seafood, and just about every restaurant offers fresh daily seafood specialties that may include tuna, grouper, mahi-mahi, mackerel, triggerfish and shellfish, to name only a few. Talented local and transplanted chefs vie to create visually appealing entrees and bring innovative flair to seafood preparation. Fresh-catch entrees and specials are often available grilled, baked, broiled, blackened or fried.

The region's restaurants, particularly in the Port City of Wilmington, reflect a rich international community in the choices of cuisine available, including Thai, Chinese (including Szechuan), Greek, Italian, German, Japanese, Mexican, Jamaican, Caribbean and French. Health-food enthusiasts are pleased by exciting vegetarian and organic dishes and products offered at numerous restaurants and markets, including Lovey's Natural Foods and Cafe and Tidal Creek Foods Co-op. Also represented throughout our area are a number of major restaurant chains, both national and regional, as well as the usual fast food options. Well-known pizza franchises offer delivery, and several area restaurants feature gourmet pizzas for the connoisseur.

Favorite Local Foods

Naturally, the traditional regional specialties make up the heart and soul of Southern coastal dining. The famous Calabash-style seafood is ever-present. It gets its name from the Brunswick County town to the south once heralded as the seafood capital of the world for having nearly 30 seafood restaurants within a square mile. Calabash style calls for seasoned cornmeal batter and deep frying and has become synonymous with all-you-can-eat. Calabash restaurants typically serve a huge variety of piping-hot seafood in massive quantities accompanied by creamy cole slaw and uniquely shaped, deep-fried dollops of corn bread called hush puppies.

Low-country steam-offs are buckets filled with a variety of shellfish, potatoes, corn and Old Bay seasoning. When fresh oysters are in season in the fall, oyster roasts abound. Crab meat is popular, and competition is stiff among restaurants boasting the best crab dip. Seafood chowder and chili are two other popular dishes put to the test in local competitions and cook-offs.

New Year's Day dinners may include collards and black-eyed peas, symbolic of paper money and small change, to ensure prosperity in the year to come. Okra, sweet potatoes, grits, turnip greens, mustard greens and kale are also regional favorites. Hoppin' John, based on black-eyed peas and rice, is a hearty dish seen in many variations. Shrimp and grits is another favorite entree appearing in various incarnations from restaurant to restaurant. Boiled peanuts are popular snacks, frequently available at roadside stands, and nowhere does pecan pie taste better. Iced tea flows freely, in most places by the pitcher-full, and locals prefer it sweet.

Many North Carolinians enjoy good barbecue in all its variations — pork or beef, chopped or shredded, sweet or tangy — and the coastal regions are no exception. Several beach communities boast at least one barbecue restaurant hidden among the seafood restaurants, touting the best recipe, of course.

Planning and Pricing

Reservations are generally not required unless your party consists of six persons

Tapas-Style Dining and Wine Bar
910-762-1922
8 N. Front Street
Downtown Wilmington
circa1922.com

Tapas-Style Dining at the Beach
910-256-1887
2025 Eastwood Road
Wilmington
bocabayrestaurant.com

French Brasserie
910-256-2226
Lumina Station
Wilmington
brasseriedusoleil.com

*Wilmington's Best in
Italian Food and Drink*
910-256-7476
1125-K Military Cutoff Rd.
The Forum • Wilmington
osteria-cicchetti.com

OSTERIA
CICCHETTI
RISTORANTE . PIZZERIA . WINE BAR

Kitchen Open Until Midnight
910-256-9133
The Forum
Wilmington
www.grandunionpub.com

LULY'S CUBAN CAFE

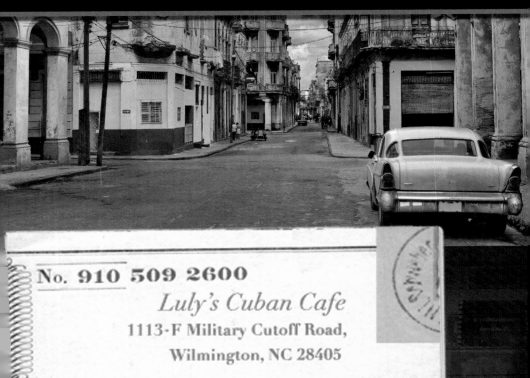

No. **910 509 2600**

Luly's Cuban Cafe

1113-F Military Cutoff Road,
Wilmington, NC 28405

LulysCubanCafe.com f **Become our fan**
on Facebook

Monday to Thursday 10am until 2pm and 6pm until 9
Friday 10am until 2pm and 6pm until 10
Saturday - 10:30am until 10 pm
Closed Sunday

Enjoy the Revolution!

BENTO BOX

SUSHI BAR & ASIAN KITCHEN

The former chef of Echo at the Breakers Resort and Aqua South Beach brings a new level of Southeastern Asian Cuisine to Wilmington.

THINK OUTSIDE THE BOX. THIS IS NO ORDINARY SUSHI BAR

Open 11:30am
Mon - Wed until 9pm
Thu - Fri until 10pm
5 - 10 pm on Saturdays Closed Sundays

Located in The Forum Shops
1121-L Military Cutoff Rd., Wilmington
p (910) 509-0774
f (910) 509-0773

BENTOBOXSUSHI.COM Become our fan on Facebook

Features the best of the land, sea and vine in a casual bistro atmosphere.

Open seven days from 6pm.

Reservations encouraged.

910.256.8847

Jerry Rouse, Owner

7220 Wrightsville Avenue

Wilmington, NC 28405

jerry@jerrysfoodandwine.com

Hotel Tarrymore

102 South Second Street
Wilmington, NC 28401

Phone 910.763.3806
Website www.HotelTarrymore.con
Email ContactUs@HotelTarrymore.c

Hotel Tarrymore is a newly renovated boutique hotel designed in the classic Carolina style with all the comforts of home including...

Professional style kitchen with granite counter tops and full size appliances.

King / Queen sized bedrooms, separate living areas, and a spacious outdoor balcony with rocking chairs.

Each morning, guests are delviered complimentary French pressed coffee from our restaurant Press 102.

Four suites open into an adjoining Atrium with enteratinment center and wet bar.

Flat screen LCD TV's and free WiFi.

Perfectly centered between the exciting downtown nightlife and the quiet, tree-lined streets.

We also offer the Veranda Ball Room that can accommodate 120 - 200 guests.

Nestled in the center of Hotel Tarrymore, Press 102 is a chic, glass-tiled bar and eatery reminiscent of an art deco New York, Rome or Paris where customers meet for breakfast, lunch and fine dining in the evening for...

The finest espresso, cappuccino, and other coffee drinks pressed from locally roasted coffee beans. There is also Free WIFI!

Unique panini sandwiches including the "Tuscan" made with prosciutto, roasted tomatoes, fresh mozzarella, and arugula.

Fresh fruit and herb inspired cocktails including a home-made bread and butter pickle martini and a basil mojito.

The fine dining menu includes a succulent shrimp and grits entrée made with country ham and red-eye gravy!

Enjoy one of the largest wine selections in Wilmington while relaxing outside on the brick patio, surrounded by flowers and passersby.

PRESS 102
ESPRESSO. PANINI. MARTINI

102 South Second Street
Wilmington, NC 28401

Phone 910.399.4438
Website www.Press102.com

Tuesday - Saturday 7am - until
Sunday Brunch 10am - 3pm

or more, and many restaurants throughout the region don't accept reservations at all, especially during peak season. It wasn't very long ago that waiting time at most Wilmington restaurants was negligible. However, with the region's growing year-round visitor season, the wait has changed substantially for many restaurants. At most popular eateries in Wilmington, expect to find waiting lists throughout the summer, during peak dinner time on weekends, during festivals and on most holidays. Some restaurants have call-ahead seating, which allows you to place your name on the waiting list before your arrival. A call to the restaurant regarding their policy is recommended.

Restaurant hours are frequently reduced or curtailed in winter, although some restaurants close entirely for a month or more, especially in the beach communities. Most places serve later on Friday and Saturday nights than on weeknights, so call ahead to verify hours and reservations. You may also want to inquire about early bird specials and senior citizen discounts even if such information isn't included in our listings.

In keeping with the area's resort character and hot summers, dining here is generally very casual. While you might feel out of place wearing shorts at fancier restaurants such as The Pilot House or Caprice, casual dress is commonplace practically everywhere else. Wearing shorts or polo shirts during the summer, even at the better restaurants, may be the only practical way to end a very full day.

Coffeehouses are a welcome addition to the local landscape, particularly in Wilmington, so we've listed a number of the most popular spots at the end of the chapter. Often reflecting the communities in which they thrive, these gathering places exhibit a definite artistic and coastal flair. Local artwork receives pride of place on many cafe walls in this culturally rich region. Warm and courteous friendliness is thrown in for good measure.

PRICE CODE

The following price codes are based on the average price for two dinner entrees only. For restaurants not serving dinner, the codes reflect mid-priced lunch entrees for two. Dual codes indicate that lunch and dinner prices vary significantly. The price codes do not reflect the state/county sales tax or gratuities.

$	Less than $20
$$	$20 to $30
$$$	$31 to $45
$$$$	More than $45

Wilmington

The southern coastal region, especially the Greater Wilmington area, presents an abundance of great places to eat. A complete listing of the region's restaurants and eateries could fill an entire book. This chapter offers a sampling of what's available in each area. If your favorite restaurant isn't listed here, it may be because it's among the many fine restaurants that are impossible to miss because of reputation or location. We've made a special effort to include the more out-of-the-way places that shouldn't be missed, along with some obvious favorites. Please keep in mind that restaurants may frequently change menu items, hours of operation or close after this book goes to press. Call ahead to verify information that is important to you.

HISTORIC DOWNTOWN WILMINGTON

The 55 blocks comprising historic downtown Wilmington are full of some of the area's best and most diverse restaurants. Make the most of your downtown dining experience by choosing a table with a view of the river. After your meal, stroll down the Riverwalk and take in the ambiance of city at night.

Big Authentic Thai Restaurant $-$$
1001 N. Fourth St., Wilmington
(910) 763-3035

Located in the up-and-coming NOFO area, this entry in the Wilmington Thai food clique is tucked away toward the end of Fourth Street. Start your evening with one of their sumptuous appetizers, like the savory Thai dumplings or the coconut flavors of the creamy Tom Kai Gai soup. With many classic traditional Thai dishes, the menu features other contemporary fusions as well (try the pineapple curry with duck). A solid wine and beer selection complements the entree choices nicely, and the staff is accommodating, courteous and knowledgeable. While off the beaten path, this well-priced jewel is worth the effort to find.

Caffe Phoenix $$-$$$
35 S. Front St., Wilmington
(910) 343-1395

This downtown eatery has more than two decades on most other restaurants in the area. Offering the finest in Mediterranean cuisine infused with many other influences, Caffe Phoenix combines delicious food with a casual and comfortable environment. Numerous daily specials highlight the menu, and garlic lovers won't be able to pass up the famous Caesar salad. Rotating art shows feature the finest of Wilmington's creative community, and the renovated space has a fresh, updated feel. With a sidewalk café open in the warmer months for al fresca dining and a reputation as one of Wilmington's best places to be seen, this is one culinary experience you don't want to miss.

Caprice Bistro:
Restaurant & Sofa Bar $$-$$$
10 Market St., Wilmington
(910) 815-0810

The setting is perfect. Historic Downtown Wilmington's riverfront is within view, bricked streets lead to quaint boutiques, and a period horse-drawn carriage passes by regularly. Though lace curtains adorn the windows and white tablecloths drape the tables, Caprice Bistro's atmosphere is one of friendly, casual ease and, for those who have never experienced it, it provides a glimpse of the charm and cuisine of an authentic French bistro. Your choices include a bounty of appetizers, entrees and classic desserts. Prepared with fresh ingredients and innovative style, this cuisine offers a full continental spectrum, from the homemade country pate, French onion soup (offered during winter months only), steak au poivre, duck confit and profiteroles to an array of entrees featuring steak, seafood, poultry and game. The bistro's wine list offers European wines plus a good choice of American labels as well. Caprice Bistro's second floor is an intimate, original sofa bar, perfect for relaxing with a martini or glass of wine. The full menu or simply appetizers and dessert are available in this beautifully appointed bar. Caprice Bistro opens nightly for dinner. The sofa bar remains open until 2 AM.

Circa 1922 $$-$$$
8 N. Front St., Wilmington
(910) 762-1922
www.circa1922.com

Circa has become renowned for serving a tapas-style menu, which allows you and your companions to create your own dining experience by sharing several small plates of specialties from around the world. Or you can order individually by course. Each course is marked by the quality and exceptional service that makes this restaurant stand out from the rest. If you're looking to begin your meal with an appetizer, you may want to consider the Crab and Artichoke Dip. Then it's on to an array of tempting choices for your main course. One excellent choice is the Filet Mignon Porto in Pastry, topped with Gruyere and proscuitto ham and wrapped in a puff pastry served atop a tawny port wine sauce. Save some of your appetite for generously portioned, award-winning desserts. The Bananas Foster will put you in a state of pure bliss, and the creme brulee is heavenly. The greatest part of Circa, aside from their appetizers, desserts and complete wine list, is the authentic 1922 atmosphere. You'll expect F. Scott Fitzgerald to walk in the door before you leave. Circa opens nightly for dinner. Reservations are welcome.

The Copper Penny $-$$
109 Chestnut St., Wilmington
(910) 762-1373

If you're looking for a laid-back pub atmosphere with tastier fare than you'd be likely to find in a pub, you'll flip for The Copper Penny. Based on many of co-owner Christine Cadwallader's family recipes, including her dad's own award-winning chili, the menu has expanded significantly from the restaurant's early sandwich days. Definitely not your ordinary pub grub, The Copper Penny's comfort food pays homage to the old standard neighborhood bar and grill while upping the ante on its menu. The bar features 80 bottled beers, mostly American microbrews. The Penny even offers monthly beer tastings to highlight new selections. Fourteen taps pour a wide variety of brews from ale to stout, and the extensive martini list is a nice way to kick off the night. Utilize The Copper Penny's catering service for your next affair or arrange to have your party thrown on the premises. This stately monument to the pub has a home-style feel that envelops you like a warm wool blanket in winter.

Deluxe $$-$$$
114 Market St., Wilmington
(910) 251-0333
www.deluxe.com

114 market street
historic downtown wilmington

910.251.0333
www.deluxenc.com

Deluxe offers an aesthetically stimulating environment in a lively and casual atmosphere: eclectic decor of art deco, abstract expressionism, architectural formalism, paintings, wood sculpture, glasswork, fresh flowers, high ceilings and clean lines. Featured artwork on exhibit at Deluxe rotates every 10 weeks. It's a sublime and friendly environment for enjoying excellent New American-style cuisine, with the largest selection of fine wines in the region, and one of Wilmington's superior brunches. Dinner is memorable, with innovative offerings including French, Asian, Italian, new Southern and Caribbean dishes that appeal visually while tempting the palate. Try the pan-roasted Atlantic grouper filet with roasted pencil asparagus, jumbo lump crab and fingerling potato hash, Maltaise sauce and Vidalia onion vinaigrette. Or sample the herb-grilled lamb tenderloin with warm cranberry goat cheese polenta and roasted root vegetables drizzled with Tempranillo reduction and Spanish olive oil, studded with grated fresh horseradish.

For brunch, the menu is equally attractive, with selections that include cinnamon pecan swirl French toast; lobster, exotic mushrooms and Brie omelet; or house-smoked salmon served with melted organic white cheddar and two poached eggs and topped with a mustard cream sauce. After dinner, sit back with a vintage port or a chocolate martini and you'll know why this cafe at the very heart of downtown garners a dedicated following. Deluxe is open for dinner every evening and for Sunday brunch from 10:30 AM to 2 PM. Menu selections are prepared with a special emphasis on fresh local ingredients and exquisite plate presentation. Deluxe has achieved a Wine Spectator award of excellence nine years in a row, and the staff is dedicated to re-inventing fine dining styles for today's savvy gourmand.

Elijah's $$-$$$
Chandler's Wharf, 2 Ann St., Wilmington
(910) 343-1448
www.elijahs.com

No one can say they've been to Wilmington until they've tried Elijah's crab dip. Directly on the Cape Fear River, Elijah's offers traditional low-country fare as well as such delights as oysters Rockefeller, the mouthwatering Shrimp and Scallops Elijah, and mahi fettuccine. Elijah's is two restaurants in one — the oyster bar, which includes outdoor deck seating, and the enclosed dining room, with its more formal presentation of seafood, poultry, pasta and choice beef. Nautical artwork recalls the building's former incarnation as a maritime museum. The ambiance is casual, and the western exposure makes it a great place for a sundown toast. Elijah's is open seven days a week year round and serves lunch, dinner and Sunday brunch. Reservations are accepted only for parties of eight or more.

Fat Tony's Italian Pub $-$$
131 N. Front St., Wilmington
(910) 343-8881
wwww.fatpub.com

Founded on the simple joys of a good beer and a hearty Italian meal, Fat Tony's Italian Pub offers plenty of both. They have a selection of 24 draft beers, more than anywhere else downtown, and their menu is filled with generous helpings of fresh and flavorful Italian favorites. Begin your meal with any one of their yummy appetizers, including Pizza Chip Nachos topped with Spinach and Artichoke Hearts or Carolina Crab and Cheese, or try their lightly fried calamari. The huge, made-to-order pizza-dough bread sticks are stuffed with your choice of spinach and cheese, sun-dried tomato and goat cheese, or meatball and cheese. Craving New York–style pizza? Try any one of their specialty pizzas or calzones or select your own toppings. Or how about a pasta dish? Fat Tony's beef lasagna has received rave reviews, and the Pasta Tony (artichoke hearts, mushrooms and ricotta cream sauce baked with angel hair pasta and topped with mozzarella cheese) is another excellent choice. There are also lighter options, such as the Tony's Grilled Chicken Salad, Tortilla Pizza or Grilled Shrimp Caesar Salad. If through some miracle, or careful planning, you still have room for dessert, their homemade tiramisu is utterly divine. You can savor your meal in the comfortable indoor dining area or enjoy the coastal North Carolina breeze on one of the patios. The downtown location, strategically placed in the center of the action for many downtown events, boasts a gorgeous view of the Cape Fear River. Fat Tony's Italian Pub is open Monday through Saturday 11 AM to 2 AM (the late-night menu is served 11 PM to 2 AM) and Sundays noon to midnight. Fat Tony's also has a location at 250 Racine Drive, near Home Depot.

Front Street Brewery $
9 N. Front St., Wilmington
(910) 251-1935
www.frontstreetbrewery.com

Front Street Brewery is a spacious eatery and microbrewery located in historic downtown Wilmington. Every menu item, including reasonably priced appetizers, soups, salads, burgers, sandwiches, entrees and gourmet desserts, is made from scratch with the freshest available ingredients. The building has been completely renovated and features amazing woodwork and beautiful decor, creating an upscale yet cozy environment. Nine hand-crafted beers are made by the restaurant's award-winning brew master, and a number of seasonal brews are switched throughout the year. Whether you're looking for a delicious dinner spot or merely hoping to enjoy some top-notch draft beer, Front Street Brewery should be your first stop.

The George on the Riverwalk $$-$$$
128 S. Water St., Wilmington
(910) 763-2052
www.thegeorgerestaurant.com

The Cape Fear River is a scenic focal point of the Wilmington landscape, and The George is situated right on its eastern bank. You'll delight at the unique and sumptuous selections featured in The George's Southern coastal cuisine. Fresh local seafood, juicy steaks and numerous vegetarian selections round out the menu, and a full bar offers top-shelf cocktails for the discriminating connoisseur. An ideal sunset dining spot in the spring and summer, The George brings you closer to Wilmington's maritime history as well as its seafaring culture. In addition to serving both lunch and dinner, The George's Sunday brunch is a lovely way to spend your last day of the weekend, and the outdoor seating options provide you with a stunning view of the river and, in warmer months, the sunset. With The George's convenient parking, you'll want to start your Riverwalk tour with some tasty treats here.

Hell's Kitchen $
118 Princess St., Wilmington
(910) 763-4133

Formerly a set for the locally filmed Dawson's Creek, Hell's Kitchen has fast become a popular downtown destination for good times among friends. This pub-style setting has a fun atmosphere so when you're feeling devilishly hungry, stop by and try something from their menu of pub sandwiches, wraps, fajitas, nachos, entrees and more. Hell's Kitchen has a full liquor bar and offers a wide variety of draft and microbrew beers as well as select wines. Regular live music from local favorites each weekend turns the spot from a restaurant into a club. Open for lunch and dinner and serving a late night menu, this place is on fire all day long.

The Little Dipper
Fondue on Front $$-$$$
138 S. Front St., Wilmington
(910) 251-0433

For a unique, participatory and fun dining experience, try The Little Dipper

Fondue on Front. The Little Dipper's menu features premium meats, fresh seafood, vegetables, breads and homemade dipping sauces. The full fondue experience starts with the cheese course, followed by salad, then the entree of meats and/or vegetables with dipping sauces, and finally completed with their sublime chocolate fondue desserts. Some favorite choices include filet mignon with a warm au poivre sauce, sashimi tuna dipped in Asian ginger sauce or shrimp with wasabi lime aioli. For dessert, try the classic strawberries dipped in chocolate or bananas with a warm dark chocolate and peanut butter sauce. They feature several nightly specials, including the highly popular Ladies Night on Wednesdays, when ladies can enjoy the cheese and chocolate courses for only $8. Open at 5 PM every day except Mondays, The Little Dipper can accommodate a large group celebration or an intimate dinner for two.

Nikki's Fresh Gourmet $-$$
16 S. Front St., Wilmington
(910) 772-9151

Nikki's is one of the hippest eateries in the downtown area. Featuring numerous organic and vegetarian dishes, Nikki's appeals to anyone with a taste for unique and delicious cuisine. And if you're a sushi fan, this Front Street spot is not to be missed. Try their succulent Angel Hair Roll or any of their dynamic sushi or sashimi

RESTAURANTS

treats. Nikki's serves beer and wine, and the view from their bar seating at the front of the restaurant is great for people-watching, especially during tourist season when Front Street is busy. Nikki's also has a location at Independence Mall, perfect for a pre- or post-shopping meal. Convenient to the University and central Wilmington is the Nikki's at Racine Commons, which has the same menu as the other locations plus a full bar. Nikki's Hibachi Steak House, across the street from Mayfaire on Military Cutoff, offers a hibachi dining experience along with the sushi that has made Nikki's famous.

Paddy's Hollow Restaurant & Pub $-$$
The Cotton Exchange, 10 Walnut St., Wilmington
(910) 762-4354
www.paddyshollow.com

Tucked away in the middle courtyard of The Cotton Exchange buildings, this narrow, intimate restaurant transports you back to friendly neighborhood pubs with an Irish flavor. Seating consists of high-backed wooden booths, tables and chairs or stools at the bar, where you can have a brew and a bite while catching up with the news, both televised and local. The lunch menu offers tasty appetizers, a soup du jour and grilled seafood, chicken or steak

salads. Sandwich selections, featuring seafood, shrimp, prime rib and corned beef, are hearty and include a deli pickle slice and a choice of French fries, potato salad, pasta salad or garlic mashed potatoes. In the mood for a burger? Paddy's 6 oz. Pub-burgers, cooked to order and accompanied by a pickle and fries, are a real treat. In the intimacy of the high-backed booths and the subdued lighting, dinner at Paddy's can be a romantic affair. The dinner menu features the fresh-catch seafood prevalent in the Cape Fear area in addition to tasty beef entrees, specifically prime rib and New York strip, chicken and barbecued baby-back ribs. Check the board or ask your server for the daily lunch and dinner specials. Need some diversion? Check out Paddy's game room. Paddy's has all ABC permits, 16 tap handles for draft beer, and bottled beer and wine. Cigar and pipe smoking are not permitted. It's open for lunch and dinner Monday through Saturday and for lunch on Sunday.

The Pilot House $$-$$$
Chandler's Wharf, 2 Ann St., Wilmington
(910) 343-0200
www.pilothouserest.com

The Pilot House is among the preeminent dining establishments downtown. Overlooking the Cape Fear River at

Chandler's Wharf, the restaurant occupies the historic Craig House (c. 1870) and strives for innovations with high-quality Southern regional cooking. The wide-ranging dinner menu features sautéed and char-grilled seafood, beef and chicken, pan-seared duck, pasta and a delectable roster of appetizers. Daily lunch and dinner specials are equally tempting. Lunch selections include generous traditional and seafood salads, innovative sandwiches and entrees. You will see guests dressed in everything from Bermuda shorts to a shirt and tie. Lunch is more casual than dinner. The wine list is carefully chosen and well-rounded. The Pilot House features additional outdoor seating, weather permitting, and serves lunch and dinner seven days a week, year round, with brunch offered on Sunday. The addition of a newly renovated riverfront bar provides spectacular views of the Cape Fear River to go along with that cocktail. A children's menu is available. Reservations are recommended.

Press 102 $-$$
102 S. Second St., Wilmington
(910) 399-4438
www.press102.com

New to Wilmington's restaurant scene, Press 102 serves breakfast, lunch and dinner in a light, airy and welcoming environment. The "press" in their name is a nod to the item featured most prominently on the menu, paninis. For breakfast or lunch, try the Cape Fear Panini (shaved house-smoked pork, pickled onions and melted American cheese) or the Tuscan Panini (sliced prosciutto, roasted tomatoes, fresh mozzarella, aged white and dark balsamic reductions and baby arugula). Pair your meal with an espresso for a pick-me-up, or relax on their outdoor patio with a glass of wine or a martini. All of their menu items are made from the freshest ingredients from neighboring purveyors to help sustain the local economy, and they use recycled products where possible.

Riverboat Landing $$-$$$
2 Market St., Wilmington
(910) 763-7227

Enjoy a panoramic sunset over the Battleship NORTH CAROLINA from one of the nine intimate two-seater balconies that overlook the Cape Fear River at Riverboat Landing. This downtown landmark restaurant is located at the foot of Market and Water streets, nestled in a building that dates to the 1800s. A newly renovated interior decor complements the modern cuisine, which features numerous amazing dishes. Dinner is served every night. Begin your evening with one of the unforgettable appetizers, including some tasty shellfish, and a cocktail from the bar. Oenophiles will enjoy numerous selections

from the extensive wine list, and the menu offers everything from sandwiches to pastas and even a knockout filet mignon. Do not leave without sampling some legendary desserts. A children's menu is available upon request.

Trolly Stop $
121 N. Front St., Wilmington
(910) 343-2999

Centrally located in historic downtown Wilmington, Trolly Stop serves a specially produced Smithfield all-meat dog, all-beef Sabrett dogs, no-carb veggie dogs and low fat/no-carb turkey dogs in a variety of combinations. Local favorites include the American (chili, mustard and onion), the Cape Fear (melted cheese and mayonnaise) and, naturally, the North Carolina (chili, mustard and cole slaw). Vegetarian and fat-free hot dogs are also available. Additional menu offerings are sweet Italian sausage, their unique Burger dog, and nachos with toppings. Enjoy Hershey's ice cream at this location, which is open year-round.

Wilmington Tea Room $$
224 S. Water St. #6, Wilmington
(910) 343-1832

Enjoy a delicious lunch or a pot of tea and a scone at the delightful Wilmington Tea Room in historic downtown Wilmington. Tea connoisseurs and novices alike will appreciate their selection of high-quality imported teas. A popular menu option is the Full Tea, which includes choice of soup or salad, assorted tea sandwiches, scones and pastries. The Tea Room boasts one of downtown's best outdoor decks with a beautiful Riverfront view, perfect for an outdoor meal on a nice day. The Wilmington Tea Room also hosts special events, such as intimate wedding receptions, bridal or baby showers, rehearsal dinners or anniversary parties. They open for lunch from 11 AM to 3 PM Tuesday through Sunday, and reservations are encouraged (though not required).

OLEANDER, INDEPENDENCE AND BRADLEY CREEK AREA

Flaming Amy's Burrito Barn $
4002 Oleander Dr., Wilmington
(910) 799-2919

Looking for a delicious meal that will fill you up but won't empty your wallet? Flaming Amy's provides amazingly quick service and delicious, reasonably priced burritos, quesadillas and salads in a fun and lively setting. Their salsa bar will give you plenty of unique flavors to try, including a pineapple-jalapeno salsa. And if you're feeling daring, there's always the Wall of Flame, which offers a wide variety of hot, hotter and super-hot sauces for you to sample (read the warning labels carefully before putting these sauces on your food as some are extremely potent). The burritos go way beyond beans and rice, to tasty combos such as The Big Jerk, a tortilla stuffed with rice, beans, cheese, Jamaican jerk chicken, roasted red peppers, sour cream and pineapple-jalapeno salsa. You can also customize your burrito with their selection of meats, tofu, veggies and toppings. For folks who want to hang out for a while, there are video games and a pool table in the back. Flaming Amy's is open daily for lunch and dinner.

FLAT Eddie's $
5400 Oleander Dr., Wilmington
(910) 799-7000

Looking for flat-out good times and great food in Wilmington? FLAT Eddie's modern, upbeat atmosphere and New American menu will satisfy. Flatbreads are the main feature of their menu; think pizza – but better! They have a thin, homemade crust and are loaded with flavorful toppings like house-roasted tomatoes, grilled shrimp, luxurious cheeses and roasted chicken. FLAT Eddie's also serves wonderful salads chock full of ingredients like mixed greens, dried cranberries and candied pecans. All sandwiches and burgers are less than $9 and their entrée selections are unique and bold. In addition, FLAT Eddie's bar is a popular local hang out. Complete with flat screen TVs and a $2 and $3 beer special every day, the bar stays busy and sometimes hosts live music.

Henry's Restaurant & Bar $$
Barclay Commons, 2508 Independence Blvd., Wilmington
(910) 793-2929

Henry's offers an excellent atmosphere and wonderful scratch-made food in midtown Wilmington. Henry's dining room is open for lunch and dinner. Lunch possibilities range from generous salad selections (the grilled tuna and fresh spinach salad is a good choice) to wonderfully huge deli sandwiches. Popular entrees include the best Shrimp & Grits in Wilmington and the very popular Hank's Mom's Meatloaf. Come in for dinner and treat yourself to Henry's Crate to Plate menu, featuring blackboard specials that incorporate local seafood and produce. You can also order from their regular dinner menu, which includes specialties like seafood fettuccine, Parmesan encrusted chicken

and bourbon marinated sirloin. End the evening with one of Henry's mini desserts, the perfect small bite sweet treat. Henry's gorgeous bar offers all ABC permits with premium-pour liquors, eight draft beers and comfortable, upholstered banquettes for lounging. Outdoor dining is available.

Nicola's ~ Italian with a Twist $$-$$$
5704 Oleander Dr., Wilmington
(910) 798-2205

If there's one thing Nick Pittari knows, it's Italian cuisine. Pittari made his reputation in Wilmington as the owner of downtown's Pizza Bistro and then moved on to own Incredible Pizza, perhaps the best pie in the southeast part of the state. Now Nick has turned his efforts to fine dining and his latest enterprise will knock your socks off. Nicola's features only fresh ingredients and authentic recipes, often coming from the cookbook of Nick's Sicilian mother, Nonna. The kitchen prepares five types of pasta every day, and the difference between this sublime ingredient and the boxed version is palatable. They also use only the freshest fish, beef, shellfish and vegetables and make each dish to order.

An amazing selection of fine wines is available, and your server will be more than happy to assist you in pairing the perfect wine with your dish. The interior of Nicola's is chic and unique, boasting vibrant colors and a metropolitan flair. You can even have the kitchen cater your own special dinner to be served at the location of your choice. Let's face it: Italian doesn't get any more authentic than the masterpieces coming out of Pittari's kitchen. Join him for a slice of the Cape Fear region's la dolce vita.

Olympia Restaurant $-$$
Bradley Square, 5629 Oleander Dr., Wilmington
(910) 796-9636

This Greek legend is renowned for its unique approach to traditional Mediterranean cuisine. Lunch offers succulent sandwiches that vary from stout hero-style creations to juicy pita specialties. Olympia's salads are light and crafted from the freshest vegetables and a variety of cheeses that will leave your mouth watering for more. Dinner finds unique house specials such as moussaka, kabobs and tantalizing seafood dishes. The Athenian-style flounder will whisk you away to a crystal blue waterfront cafe on the island of Santorini. For connoisseurs of Greek culture and cuisine, this dining experience would satisfy Zeus himself.

Tidal Creek Cooperative
Food Market and Deli $-$$
5329 Oleander Dr., Ste. 100, Wilmington
(910) 799-2667
www.tidalcreek.coop

In addition to being one of the best spots in Wilmington for natural and or-ganic groceries, Tidal Creek also features a delicious food bar with all sorts of tan-talizing, healthy dishes sold by the pound. Along with the vegetarian and vegan of-ferings, they also offer sandwiches, wraps, salads and a wide assortment of unique beverages. From the sweet broccoli salad to the curry chicken salad and the sumptuous baked goods and gluten-free specialties, you'll want to make this clean, green grocery a regular stop for your fam-ily's healthy lifestyle.

UNC-WILMINGTON AREA

Catering largely to the college popula-tion, in the University area you'll find a variety of restaurants that are budget-friendly and open late.

Break Time Grille & Ten Pin Alley $-$$
127 S. College Rd., Wilmington
(910) 395-6658
www.breaktimetenpin.com

There's more to this dining spot than bowling and billiards. The Break Time Grille serves made-to-order dishes created with fresh ingredients, including pizza dough created fresh each day. A great spot to catch lunch as well as televised sporting events, Break Time has become the loca-tion for local Pittsburgh Steelers and Penn State fans to watch their beloved teams and chow down on a burger or two. With one menu served from 11 AM until mid-night and a late-night menu served from midnight until 2 AM, you can choose from salads, sandwiches and wraps, entrees and deli selections, among other items. Also,

you can reserve the space for a private function or a large group, choosing items off the regular menu or creating your own. For food with fun distractions, you'll have a ball at Break Time.

Fat Tony's Italian Pub $-$$
250 Racine Dr., Wilmington
(910) 452-9000
www.fatpub.com

Founded on the simple joys of a good beer and a hearty Italian meal, Fat Tony's Italian Pub offers plenty of both. They have a selection of 24 draft beers and their menu is filled with generous helpings of fresh and flavorful homemade Italian favorites. Begin your meal with any one of their yummy appetizers, including Pizza Chip Nachos topped with Spinach and Artichoke Hearts or Carolina Crab and Cheese, or try their lightly fried calamari. The huge, made-to-order pizza-dough breadsticks are stuffed with your choice of spinach and cheese, sun-dried tomato and goat cheese, or meatball and cheese. Craving New York–style pizza? Try any one of their specialty pizzas or calzones or select your own toppings. Or how about a pasta dish? Fat Tony's beef lasagna has received rave reviews, and the Pasta Tony (artichoke hearts, mushrooms and ricotta cream sauce baked with angel hair pasta and topped with mozzarella cheese) is another excellent choice. There are also lighter options, such as the Tony's Grilled Chicken Salad, Tortilla Pizza or Grilled Shrimp Caesar Salad. If through some miracle, or careful planning, you still have room for dessert, their homemade tiramisu is utterly divine. You can savor your meal in the comfortable indoor dining area or enjoy the coastal North Carolina breeze on the expansive patio. Fat Tony's Italian Pub is open Monday through Saturday from 11 AM to 2 AM (the late-night menu is served 11 PM to 2 AM) and Sundays noon to mid-night. Delivery is available to the general vicinity and Wrightsville Beach.

Giorgio's Italian Restaurant $-$$
5226 S. College Rd., Wilmington
(910) 790-9954

Tucked away in a small shopping center near the Monkey Junction area of

S. College Road, this family-friendly Italian restaurant is a huge hit with Insiders, who suggest that you come hungry (even the lunch portions are huge). The atmosphere is cozy, with a friendly wait staff focused on making your dining experience a pleasure. Naturally, the food is the centerpiece, with a bountiful selection of salads, zuppas (that's soup for the uninitiated), appetizers and hearty pasta entrees with chicken, seafood, veal or sweet Italian sausage. Locals argue over their favorite dishes, but all are excellent choices. If you prefer something off the grill, try the Kansas rib eye. The lunch menu offers slightly smaller versions of some dinner items plus a selection of create-your-own pasta dishes, a gourmet's choice of calzones and pizzas. Must-try sandwiches include the Italian sausage sub, Rueben, Giorgio's muffaletta and the eggplant Parmigiana sub. The restaurant's small lounge area with full bar service is a cozy place to wait when the dining room is full, and large parties of up to 70 can be accommodated in a private dining area. Giorgio's opens daily for lunch and dinner. While the portions are hearty, the price is very reasonable, as indicated by the dual price code listed above. Take-out services, catering and party platters are available.

Jackson's Big Oak Barbecue $
920 S. Kerr Ave., Wilmington
(910) 799-1581

A repeated winner of local magazine polls for the area's best barbecue since it opened in 1984, Jackson's is a family-run business fully deserving of the praise. The eastern North Carolina–style pork barbecue is moist and tangy, the hush puppies superior, and the friendly, knowledgeable staff is as hard-working as all get-out. The fried corn sticks are a specialty that should be a given with every meal, and if you're a fan of Brunswick stew, barbecue ribs and chicken, you won't be disappointed. The dining room is rustic and familiar, a good place to greet and meet. Jackson's is open for lunch and dinner Monday through Saturday. Contact the restaurant for large take-out orders (for up 200 people).

Krazy's Pizza and Subs $
417 S. College Rd., Wilmington
(910) 791-0598

Krazy's Pizza and Subs has been family-owned and operated since 1986. With a loyal customer following, it offers a variety of Italian delights in a casual atmosphere with prices that won't strain your wallet. Best known for its "kreate your own" pizza, Krazy's has a wide range of toppings sure to please any palate. Or you can choose from their nine specialty pizzas. Krazy's also serves up wonderful salads, including a Greek dinner salad. Don't miss their own tasty homemade Italian dressing. Not in the mood for pizza? Try the delicious homemade lasagna, veal Parmigiana or baked ziti with meat sauce, either as an entree or a la carte. Appetizers, stromboli, calzones and a large selection of subs round out the menu at Krazy's. A children's menu is available.

P.T.'s Olde Fashioned Grille $
4544 Fountain Dr., Wilmington
(910) 392-2293

When you want a freshly grilled burger or chicken sandwich, forget the fast-food mills. Consistently voted Best Burger by *Encore* magazine's annual poll, P.T.'s can't be beat. Every menu item is a package deal that includes a sandwich (whopping half-pound Angus beef burgers, tender chicken breast, hot dogs, fresh roast beef, turkey and more), fresh-cut, spiced, skin-on French fries (or substitute a side salad) and a soft drink, refill included. Prices are low, and quality is high. You place your order by filling in an idiot-proof order form and dropping it through the window if you're eating on the outdoor deck. Order at the counter if you're eating inside. Your meal is prepared to order and ready in about 10 minutes. This is fast food that doesn't taste like fast food. P.T.'s also offers an alternative to beef with the lower calorie, low-fat Gardenburger. P.T.'s is west of S. College Road across from the south end of the UNCW campus. Or try their locations at the Progress Point Center on Military Cutoff Road, across from the hospital on S. 17th Street, in the Harris Teeter shopping center south of Monkey

THE BENTO BOX

SUSHI BAR & ASIAN KITCHEN

弁当

1121-L Military Cutoff Rd.
Wilmington, NC 28405

Open 11:30am
Mon.-Wed. until 9pm
Thurs.-Fri. until 10pm
5-10pm on Saturdays
Closed Sundays

910-509-0774

WWW.BENTOBOXSUSHI.COM

Junction, on Market Street in Porters Neck or at the entrance to Magnolia Greens in Leland. Take-out orders are welcome and may be habit-forming.

Two Guys Grille   **$**
7110 Wrightsville Ave., C-12, Wilmington
(910) 256-3339

When it comes to tasty sandwiches, burgers and fries, why go for fast food when you can sample the succulent fare at Two Guys Grille? The burgers are sumptuous and come in several varieties, including a black bean burger. And while you're at it, try the knockout Philly cheese steak (also with a black bean option). In addition to several chicken, cheese and corned beef sandwiches, there are also a number of fish sandwiches on the menu, including the saucy grilled Cajun catfish. Toss in eight different salad choices and a heaping helping of good ole banana puddin', and you've got one of Wilmington's best quick stops for lunch or dinner. Two Guys Grille has several locations in the greater Wilmington area, including College Road and Wrightsville Avenue, Porters Neck, Independence Mall and the Shops at Waterford in Leland.

WRIGHTSVILLE BEACH, LANDFALL AND MAYFAIRE AREA

The Bento Box Sushi Bar
and Asian Kitchen   **$$-$$$**
1121-L Military Cutoff Rd.,
The Forum Shops, Wilmington
(910) 509-0774
www.bentoboxsushi.com

The Bento Box, located in The Forum, offers some of the freshest, highest-quality sushi around. Chef Lee Grossman earned his stripes under the watchful eye of a master sushi chef and has cultivated his knowledge of the art of sushi over numerous years in the restaurant business. Today he maintains close relationships with some of the finest fish vendors the world over, acquiring amazing cuts of choice fish from Scotland, Japan and many other sought-after fishing grounds. With traditional and contemporary choices, diners will find themselves awash in a sea of delicacies from the cutting board of Chef Lee. In addition to sushi, they also serve entrees from China, Thailand and Vietnam in small-plate format reminiscent of tapas. The full-service lounge has all ABC permits and an extensive wine list. Sit at the sushi bar, in the lounge or enjoy your meal on the patio with soothing sounds of the waterfalls. The Bento Box is open Monday through Wednesday from 11:30 AM until 9 PM and Thursday and Friday from 11:30 AM until 10 PM, and open on Saturdays from 5 to 10 PM. Reservations are available for private parties Monday through Wednesday after 6:30 PM.

Boca Bay   **$$$**
2025 Eastwood Rd., Wilmington
(910) 256-1887
www.bocabayrestaurant.com

Located between Wrightsville Beach and Wilmington, Boca Bay's covered outdoor patio, fountain and palm trees provide a relaxed, upbeat atmosphere. When you're hungry but not quite sure what you're in the mood for, this is the place to go. Boca Bay specializes in some of the freshest seafood in town, including three types of oysters and a variety of fish served grilled, sauteed or fried. For a lighter meal, try their delicious soups, salads, appetizers or sushi rolls. Of course, you'll want to complete your meal with one of Boca Bay's delectable desserts. Boca Bay is open every day for dinner and for Sunday brunch as well. Reservations are welcome.

Brasserie du Soleil $$$
Lumina Station, 1908 Eastwood Rd., Wilmington
(910) 256-2226
www.brasseriedusoleil.com

Loosely translated as "Eatery of the Sun," the latest jewel in restaurateur Ash Aziz's crown is nestled in the heart of Lumina Station and continues his tradition of fine dining establishments. Featuring a delightful assortment of appetizers as well as a make-your-own salad option, the starters on the menu are top notch. Follow these with one of the sumptuous fish or steak entrees for a perfectly cooked main course. If you have any room left, the dessert list is superb. With a distinctive interior design, outstanding service and all the right peripheral touches (including a fantastic selection of wines, beers and cocktails), this spot lights up diners' palates year round.

Grand Union Pub $$
1125 Military Cutoff Rd., Wilmington
(910) 256-9133
www.grandunionpub.com

The newest in restaurateur Ash Aziz's group of Wilmington hot spots, Grand Union Pub Grand Union specializes in burgers served 11 different ways, from the Big Easy (blackened with blue cheese and creole mayo) to the Rodeo Clown (Guinness BBQ, onion straws and cheddar). If you're not in the mood for a burger, try one of their sandwiches, wraps, salads or entrees. Grand Union's prominent circular bar invites guests to relax with a libation or two while watching sports from one of their wide screen TVs. Daily food and drink specials keep the tabs low, and their regular live entertainment always draws a crowd.

Hiro Japanese Steak & Sushi House $$-$$$
222 Old Eastwood Rd., Wilmington
(910) 794-1570

Featuring a diverse and delicious variety of cuisine, Hiro is one of Wilmington's busiest restaurants and caters to large parties such as business meetings, birthdays and other events. Centrally located, Hiro is perfect for fans of sushi as well as those in the mood for a little showmanship with their dinner. The hibachi preparation features top-notch chefs who display their remarkable cooking skills while putting on a dazzling display of dexterity, juggling their implements and your food at the same time. With numerous chicken, beef, seafood and vegetarian options available, you'll undoubtedly be able to find something to your liking. Start off your meal with a custom cocktail or martini from their extensive list.

Lovey's Natural Foods and Cafe, Inc. $-$$
Landfall Shopping Center, Eastwood Rd., Wilmington
(910) 509-0331
www.loveysmarket.com

If you're looking for a healthy meal made with entirely fresh ingredients, Lovey's is the perfect spot for a sit-down lunch or a quick take-out snack. This natural foods spot features an organic hot and cold bar that offers copious salad options

options as well as daily specialty items. Try a delicious organic hot dog or hamburger from their menu. Lovey's has an extensive organic cafe menu with daily specials for both vegetarians and non-vegetarians alike. With a variety of warm soups and beverages for the health conscious, Lovey's is ideal for those watching their diets. In addition to offering carrot and wheatgrass juice at the Juice Bar, they also have an extensive selection of smoothies, made on the spot with only the freshest organic fruits. Vegans and vegetarians, this is the place for you! If you're near the beach and have the urge for something that tastes great and is good for you, give Lovey's a try.

Luly's Cuban Cafe $-$$
1113-F Military Cutoff Rd., Wilmington
(910) 509-2600
www.lulyscubancafe.com

Luly's Cuban Cafe brings the vibrant culture, tastes and milieu of Cuba to Wilmington. The recipes are straight from the owner's family kitchen, prepared with cultural pride. Their menu includes classic Cuban sandwiches such as the appropriately named Cuban (ham, roast beef, Swiss cheese, pickles and mustard on pressed Cuban bread), and the Vaca Frita (shredded beef seasoned with onion, peppers, garlic and sour orange marinade and then grilled). Central to the Luly's experience is cafecito, a Cuban coffee, which Cubans typically enjoy around the clock, especially as a social activity with family and friends. Finish your meal with a cafecito and a pastelito. Luly's welcomes you to enjoy a game of dominoes, a Cuban pastime, around one of their tables, and they host salsa dancing on Friday and Saturday nights.

Mama Fu's Asian House $-$$
Mayfaire Town Center,
941 International Dr., Wilmington
(910) 256-2620

Mama Fu's offers delicious Pan-Asian dishes using the freshest ingredients. Enjoy a stir-fry or noodle bowl freshly prepared in an individual wok with no MSG or trans fats. Mama Fu's also features fantastic appetizers like potstickers, lettuce wraps and sushi grade ahi. Try one of

their tasty salads and indulge in entrees like grouper, pork and steak for traditional American fare. Mama's has kid-friendly menu items like chicken tenders, mac & cheese and Ninja Noodles. Domestic and Asian beers, a fine selection of wines and Sake-tinis round out the restaurant's beverage selections. Enjoy dining inside or on the patio. Reservations are accepted. A terrific choice for take out, Mama can arrange delivery for large orders. Mama Fu's will also bring the party to you with their outstanding catering service. Daily specials include half-price wine and beer on Thursdays. Kids eat free on Monday all day long with the purchase of an adult meal. Kids who dine at Mama Fu's also receive reduced admission passes for Monkey Joe's.

NOFO Cafe and Market $
The Forum, 1125 Military Cutoff Rd., Wilmington
(910) 256-5565

Whether you're dining in for lunch, enjoying a late-afternoon snack or ordering from the deli case, NOFO Cafe & Market is a delicious choice in a casual setting. Luncheon choices include two daily specials and two homemade soups in addition to the regular menu of hearty deli sandwiches, meal-size salads and homemade desserts. Can't find a sandwich to your liking? Try it "your way" from a list of deli meats and salads, cheeses, breads, condiments and side items. If you're on the go for lunch, fax your order and they'll have it waiting for you. NOFO also offers an appetizing alternative menu for special diets, corporate lunch boxes, a take-out deli counter and catering. NOFO To Go features a daily menu of supper specials that are cooked and ready to pick up. Also check out the frozen food case for meal solutions. Sunday Brunch adds egg and breakfast entrees to the cafe's regular menu. NOFO is open for dinner, Wednesday through Saturday, with all ABC permits. A colorful and appealing array of specialty foods awaits you in the market area attached to the deli. You'll find shelves of gourmet foods, condiments and sauces as well as mouth-watering imported chocolates, specialty teas, coffee beans, imported and domestic wine and much more. Gift baskets are a popular feature of the market. NOFO Cafe & Market opens at 10 AM seven days a week.

Osteria Cicchetti $$-$$$
The Forum, 1125-K Military Cutoff Rd., Wilmington
(910) 256-7476
www.osteria-cicchetti.com

Enjoy a slice of Tuscany when you dine at this exquisite restaurant located in The Forum. Featuring brick-oven–baked pizzas, succulent antipasto selections with traditional items, and knockout house specialties, the restaurant offers an experience that's similar to enjoying the Tuscan countryside. With a fabulous selection of wines to pair with your meal, you'll enjoy all the elements of a typical Italian meal served in an warm atmosphere with elegant interior design. Osteria Cicchetti is open for lunch and dinner.

Port Land Grille $$$
1908 Eastwood Rd., Ste. 111, Wilmington
(910) 256-6056
www.portlandgrille.com

This five-star restaurant alone is worth a trip to the coast. Port Land Grille knows the art of fine dining. The ambiance, indoors and out, offers an appealing sense of style with oversized tables draped with white tablecloths, black and white photographs of Old Wrightsville Beach, comfortable rooms with a view, exquisite service and, weather permitting, picturesque dining on the patio overlooking a landscaped pond at Lumina Station. Though the restaurant is reminiscent of the classy supper clubs of bygone eras, the food is its key to success. Chef Shawn Wellersdick is renowned for his ability to transform quality ingredients into a meal of layered flavors and for his side dishes that rival the entree in taste and creativity. An excellent example is his version of mashed sweet potatoes (the secret involves scented vanilla beans).

The menu includes meal-sized appetizers, especially when coupled with one of Port Land Grille's salads. A favorite is the crab cake nestled on a bed of buttered baby lima beans and served with an applewood-smoked bacon vinaigrette. A popular salad choice is characterized as a simple Southern salad — a chilled iceberg lettuce wedge with crisp bacon and bleu cheese dressing. Entrees feature fresh seafood ("from the sea") and organically raised meats ("from the farm") such as lamb, duck and bison. Dessert is memorable, especially Port Land Grille's signature coconut cake. This wonderful confection is seven layers of cake with a lemony filling, topped with a pistachio anglaise. The restaurant's award-winning wine list is almost exclusively American selections, especially small-production boutique wines.

A popular spot for drinks and dining is the beautiful, well-stocked granite bar. Seating here overlooks the action in the open theater-style kitchen. The restaurant is completely nonsmoking, and in addition to the main dining room it offers two private dining areas that seat 20 and 65 people, either of which is perfect for parties and corporate events. Open year-round, Port Land Grille serves dinner Tuesday through Saturday. Reservations are recommended, particularly on weekends, but walk-in guests are graciously accommodated.

Rafaella Restaurant $$
6722 Wrightsville Ave., Wilmington
(910) 256-0702

Just a short jaunt from the beach, Rafaella offers top-notch Italian food in a comfortable, elegant setting. Featuring a fantastic wine list and a selection of martinis, you'll want to start (or end) your evening at their full bar. Using the freshest ingredients, the kitchen creates entrees from ravioli and risotto to perfectly cooked ribeyes and New York strips. With an impeccable assortment of garden-fresh salads and a complement of pasta dishes that would make anyone give up their "no carbs" pledge, Rafaella offers a nice variety of choices.

Terrazzo Pizzeria/Trattoria $$
Landfall Center, 1319 Military Cutoff Rd., Wilmington
(910) 509-9400

For a taste of authentic Italian cuisine, New York–style, Terrazzo is a must-visit. A cozy indoor atmosphere, outdoor patio seating, friendly service and a generous menu make dining here a pleasure. Terrazzo's delicious pizza menu offers a wide selection of toppings, including vegetarian, chicken, surf and turf choices, a white pizza and Terrazzo specialty pizzas. For a light snack, anything from the large selection of tasty appetizers is a good choice. Lunch options include a daily special or generously portioned salads that make a great meal when coupled with the homemade soup of the day. Terrazzo's subs come hot or cold and are truly awesome. The Italian Delight entree choices feature homemade pasta dishes with fresh vegetables, meats and cheeses in delicious sauces and served with Ciabatta bread. Nightly dinner specials often include fresh local seafood. The restaurant serves beer and a huge selection of imported and domestic wines and a full bar. Enjoy an after-work or post-dinner drink in their Euro Lounge sofa bar. Terrazzo is open Monday through Saturday for lunch and dinner. Come early: This is a popular spot in the Wilmington-Wrightsville Beach area.

Texas Roadhouse $$
230 Eastwood Rd., Wilmington
(910) 798-1770

The Texas Roadhouse story is simple: legendary food with legendary service inspired by legendary folks! Everything here is made from scratch. Steaks cut by hand, award-winning ribs, grilled salmon, fried catfish, fresh-baked bread and delightful sides are all made from scratch with only the highest-quality ingredients. Leave room for dessert, including Granny's Apple Classic, strawberry cheesecake and a Big Ol' Brownie. Every Tuesday night is Kids' Night, when kids get to enjoy games, crafts and lots of fun while you relax and enjoy your meal. Texas Roadhouse is open for dinner every night and serves lunch Friday through Sunday only.

MARKET STREET AND KERR AVENUE AREA

A listing of every restaurant on Market Street could fill its own book, but here are a few of our top recommendations.

Brooklyn Pizza Co. $-$$
6932 Market St., Wilmington
(910) 395-5558

Craving real New York pizza? You'll find it at Brooklyn Pizza Co. The owner's father ran a pizza parlor in Brooklyn for decades, and the secret to delicious New York pizza has apparently been passed down from father to son. Besides the ultimate in NY pizza and a complete selection of tasty heroes, Brooklyn Pizza's menu also includes several pasta dishes, including the ever-popular Penne with Vodka Sauce, which includes penne pasta with diced tomatoes, heavy cream, scallions and a dash of vodka. Chicken Marsala with grilled zucchini, Chicken Francese with steamed broccoli, and fried calamari are just a few of their most popular entrees. Brooklyn Pizza is open for lunch and dinner Monday through Saturday from 11 AM to 10 PM and Sundays from 1 PM to 9 PM.

Elizabeth's Pizza $-$$
4304 Market St., Wilmington
(910) 251-1005

Elizabeth's Pizza is locally owned and operated since 1987. Their friendly staff and great pizza make them one of Wilmington's most popular lunch or dinner spots. Their pizza with its hand-tossed crust and all your favorite toppings is huge and always fresh. Sicilian style is also available. Elizabeth's also has an extensive menu of sandwiches, pastas, stromboli and calzones. They are open every day for lunch and late dinner, until midnight.

Genki Japanese Restaurant $$-$$$
4724 New Centre Dr., #5, Wilmington
(910) 796-8687

The key to this authentic Japanese restaurant, owned and operated by Masauki and Reiko Augiura, is that every item is served fresh. The original flavors are tasted in every bite and aren't masked with heavy sauces or preservatives. Choose from tuna, eel, shrimp and California rolls and more, knowing that it's all low in calories and good for your health. You may watch Masauki make the rolls at the authentic sushi bar or sit in the aesthetically appealing dining room with a group of friends. Genki is open for lunch Tuesday through Friday and for dinner Tuesday through Sunday. Reservations are recommended.

Indochine: A Far East Cafe, Thai & Vietnamese $-$$
7 Wayne Dr., Market St. at Forest Hills, Wilmington
(910) 251-9229

You don't have to travel far to discover an exotic paradise. Just take a drive along Market Street and soon you will discover Indochine: A Far East Cafe, serving Thai and Vietnamese specialties. The interior has a quiet, romantic ambiance, and in the outdoor dining area you'll find a serene garden setting with a Lotus Pond and soothing waterfall. The lunch menu offers a variety of Thai and Vietnamese rice and noodle dishes, soups, stews and salads. The dinner menu is filled with traditional Indonesian cuisine as well as house specialties, including the savory Grilled Salmon in Lemon Grass with Mango Salsa. All of Indochine's delectable and generously portioned dinner entrees may be paired with a suggested wine from their extensive list. Banquet facilities for parties of up to 60 people are also available. And for those seeking a hipster cocktail spot, try the Saigon Saigon Martini Lounge adjacent to the dining area. Indochine is open for lunch and dinner Tuesday through Saturday and on Sunday and Monday for dinner only.

Old Chicago $-$$
5023 Market St., Wilmington
(910) 796-0644
www.oldchicago.com

Like your neighborhood pub from bygone days, Old Chicago Pizza, Pasta & 110 Brews offers great food, fun and friendship. Whether it's a quick lunch, or dinner with the gang, there's always something happening at Old Chicago. Check out their daily draft and bottle specials. With 110 beers from all over the world, you're sure to find something new. You can even join their World Beer Tour and "travel the world one beer at a time." For 30 years, Old Chicago has been known for the freshest Chicago-style pizza with made-from-scratch dough, but they also have great sandwiches, salads, calzones and burgers. Want your just desserts? Try

their homemade cheesecake or Famous Big Cookie. With a varied menu and great brews, you might want to make it your neighborhood hangout.

Wrightsville Beach

ON THE ISLAND

Bluewater, An American Grill $$
4 Marina St., Wrightsville Beach
(910) 256-8500

Located in Wrightsville Beach overlooking the Intracoastal Waterway, Bluewater is a sprawling two-story restaurant voted the 2010 "Best Outdoor Dining" venue by *Encore* readers. Bluewater is open daily for lunch and dinner year-round and serves American cuisine with a distinctly coastal flair. For lunch, enjoy starters like the Bluewater Sampler, which includes stuffed oysters, crab cakes and coconut shrimp. Or snack on the fresh mozzarella platter with vine ripe tomatoes, fresh basil and roasted bell peppers and drizzled with olive oil and balsamic vinegar. Bluewater also has great salads, sandwiches and generous lunch-size entrées. Bluewater's dinner menu is equally impressive in its choices. From the sea, enjoy tasty dishes like the Island Style Mahi Mahi with a citrus kick or the Crab Stuffed Salmon topped off with a white wine cheese sauce. The restaurant offers wonderful land lover options as well like the Marinated Flat Iron

Steak and the Coconut Chicken with mango salsa. Seating is available indoors or on the newly renovated outdoor patio. Dine to live music on the patio every Sunday from 4 to 8 PM (from April 18 to October 30). Bluewater has all its ABC permits and serves frosty refreshers, excellent wines, and a full range of imported and domestic beers.

Cafe del Mar $
6 N. Lumina Ave., Wrightsville Beach
(910) 256-1001

Connecting directly to Tower 7, Cafe Del Mar is much more than a coffee shop. The Baja-themed cafe invites you to get cozy and relax with serene ocean artwork and a sociable seating. Stop by to enjoy not just an average cup of joe, but one vamped up by any of their multiple flavors. Complement your coffee with such traditional favorites as muffins, bagels and biscuits, or take a step outside of the lines and try one of their delicious breakfast burritos. Escape from the heat with a signature smoothie, and be sure to try their Peanut Butter and Jelly Smoothie for something especially exquisite.

Causeway Cafe $
114 Causeway Dr., Wrightsville Beach
(910) 256-3730

Full of character and friendly service, Causeway Cafe offers possibly the best breakfast in Wrightsville Beach. Traditional made-to-order egg plates are hearty and standard fare. Choose from 15 different omelets, including the Carolina Blue Crab and Beefy Vegetable as well as traditional options, made from three eggs and cheese, served with hash browns or grits. Not in the mood for eggs? The giant specialty Belgian waffles, in nine mouthwatering flavors, malted pancakes and French toast are tasty alternatives. Lunch options include daily blackboard specials, sandwiches and salads dominated by fresh seafood. Subs, burgers, steak and other sandwiches are also good choices. A children's menu is available for children younger than 10. In-season and on weekends off-season, be prepared to wait for a table. It's worth the time spent on the covered front deck, and the folks at Causeway thoughtfully provide complimentary cof-

fee. Open seven days a week for breakfast and lunch, Causeway Cafe is located near the drawbridge beside Redix beach store. They do not accept credit cards.

King Neptune Restaurant $$
11 N. Lumina Ave., Wrightsville Beach
(910) 256-2525

King Neptune has been in business since 1946, outlasting hurricanes and the competition but not its appeal. From soups and chowders to steamers, platters and hearty specialties that include steaks, King Neptune focuses on seafood and does it well. The dining room is large and bright, decorated in Caribbean colors, with local art, beach umbrellas and photographs. The children's menu is unique in that it was selected and decorated by the third, fourth and fifth grades of Wrightsville Beach Elementary School. After dinner, the adjoining lounge provides perhaps the widest selection of rums on the island as well as an international array of beers. King Neptune serves dinner seven days a week and offers senior citizen discounts. Free parking is available in the lot across the street.

Oceanic Restaurant $$-$$$
703 S. Lumina Ave., Wrightsville Beach
(910) 256-5551

Few culinary experiences are as delightful as dining on the pier at the Oceanic. There's nothing better than a pier table in the moonlight. By day, as pelicans and seagulls kite overhead and the surf crashes below, you could be enjoying a chilled beverage, fresh blackened tuna or some of the region's most acclaimed crab dip. Should the weather turn angry, the Oceanic's three floors of indoor seating offer breathtaking panoramic views. The Oceanic's menu is satisfying, delicious and dominated by fresh seafood. From entree salads, seafood platters and land lover specialties like chicken and steaks, the menu is quite varied and includes items for kids. Entrees include a variety of extras ranging from salads and heavenly she-crab soup to hush puppies, slaw, wild rice, sautéed vegetables and celery mashed potatoes. The Super Duper Grouper, just one of the popular selections, is pan-seared in a crust of cashew nuts and sesame seeds served over celery mashed potatoes with roasted red pepper butter. Nightly specials feature fresh-catch seafood that can be grilled, sautéed, blackened or prepared with Cajun spices. Those seeking the perfect cold cocktail should definitely stop here. Full bar service, including domestic and imported beers, is available, and the juices used in mixed drinks are squeezed fresh daily. The Oceanic also offers a generous wine list, with most available by the glass. The maritime decor features replicas of historic newspapers, the aerial photography of Conrad Lowman and a spectacular Andy Cobb sculpture of a huge copper grouper. Lunch and dinner are served daily with brunch served on Sundays. Parking is free for patrons; towing of all other cars is strictly enforced.

Port City Java $
32 North Lumina Ave., Wrightsville Beach
(910) 509-0430

The Wrighstville Beach location of Port City Java can be found within Robert's Grocery and is only one of the 17 Port City Java cafes in the greater Wilmington area. Port City Java has been Wilmington's number one choice for locally roasted coffee since 1995. They import their coffees from all over the world, but they are roasted fresh right here in Wilmington. They offer a wide variety of Fair Trade and organic certified coffees, hot and cold espresso-based beverages, pure fruit smoothies, milkshakes and baked goods prepared daily in their own bakery. Every Port City Java also serves breakfast sandwiches as well as lunch fare in a clean, comfortable, family-friendly environment. Each cafe offers complimentary, unlimited WiFi service and space for local artists to display their work commission-free.

South Beach Grill $$-$$$
100 S. Lumina Ave., Wrightsville Beach
(910) 256-4646

South Beach Grill, a local fixture for 12 years, offers exquisitely prepared fare in an exotic coastal ambiance. The decor is marked by rich colors with warm candlelight at dinner and dark wood tables and armchairs. The location, immediately south of the fixed bridge near the center of the beach, is convenient and overlooks Banks Channel, which is especially nice at sunset from the patio tables outside. Most important, meals are tasty, healthy and creative, emphasizing fresh-catch seafood, poultry and beef, plus burgers, sandwiches, wraps and an array of interesting appetizers, such as crab meat nachos served on flour tortillas or South Beach's original fried pickles served with ranch dressing. All lunches include french fries or homemade potato chips. South Beach Grill has a children's menu and all ABC permits. Takeout orders are welcome. South Beach Grill opens for lunch and dinner daily. Reservations are accepted.

Trolly Stop $
94 S. Lumina Ave., Wrightsville Beach
(910) 256-3421

Trolly Stop, a beach tradition since 1976, offers hot dogs in a surprising array of choices. How about a Surfers Hot Dog with cheese, bacon bits and mustard? Or go Nuclear with mustard, jalapeno peppers and cheese on your dog. Want something more traditional? The North Carolina Hot Dog is as Tarheel as they come with chili, mustard and cole slaw. Trolly Stop offers a specially produced Smithfield all-meat dog, all-beef Sabrett dogs, no-carb veggie dogs and low fat/no-carb turkey dogs. Another popular item is the nachos with cheese. The Wrightsville Beach location is open daily year-round.

OFF THE ISLAND

The Bridge Tender Restaurant $$$
1414 Airlie Rd., Wilmington
(910) 256-4519
www.thebridgetender.com

Located at the foot of the Wrightsville Beach drawbridge on historic Airlie Road, The Bridge Tender Restaurant features the finest steaks and seafood with a spectacular panoramic view of the Intracoastal Waterway. Since 1976, this fine casual-dining establishment has earned its reputation for excellence through careful attention to detail, unparalleled cuisine and impeccable service. The Bridge Tender offers inside and outside dining with unobstructed views of the marinas, boats and waterway. The dinner menu includes a wide variety of appetizers and entrees, several nightly specials, and a delicious new Shellfish Bar featuring oysters, mussels, clams, crab, shrimp and lobster. Served from 11:30 AM Monday through Friday, the lunch menu has everything from salads and sandwiches to fresh seafood entrees. If you're in the mood for something lighter, visit the waterfront bar and deck to sample one of the unique appetizers as well as a selection of specialty cocktails. The Bridge Tender caters large and small events and is the perfect setting for a rehearsal dinner or holiday party. They serve lunch Monday through Friday and dinner nightly. Boaters can glide right up to the adjacent dock and go from sea to seat in a matter of steps, making this one of the truly unique dining locations in the region.

Dockside Restaurant & Marina $$
1308 Airlie Rd., Wrightsville Beach
(910) 256-2752

The view of the Intracoastal Waterway alone is worth a trip to Dockside. But if you're craving delicious and well-prepared local seafood, you'll also find the dining experience to be a mouthwatering adventure. Fresh seafood, not surprisingly, dominates the menu. Broiled or fried (lightly coated with fine cracker meal) combination platters, shrimp and grits and the popular shrimp boil are just a few of the dinner options. Ask your server about the day's fresh catch, and check Dockside's special board for daily soup, sandwich, wrap and chef's specials. The lunch menu, available all day, is a generous listing of soups, salads, sandwiches and house specials, including broiled or fried seafood plates, served with french fries and cole slaw. Be sure to try the homemade Key lime pie. A children's menu is available. Dockside has all ABC permits, wine, and imported, domestic and draft beers. Seating is spectacular anywhere in the restaurant, but you have a choice of indoors with a view, on the outdoor deck along the ICW or under the canopy. Dockside is open daily for lunch and dinner.

Fish House Grill $-$$
1410 Airlie Rd., Wilmington
(910) 256-3693
www.thefishhousegrill.com

Fish House Grill is a throw back to the fun, old-fashioned "fish shacks" of yesteryear, according to owner John McLatchy. Featuring appetizers, salads, sandwiches and burgers along with traditional favorites and a kids menu, Fish House Grill also offers an affordable "Build Your Own Dinner" menu including all-you-can-eat crab legs. The restaurant's casual atmosphere matches the budget-friendly prices with items ranging from $5.99 to $21.99. Enjoy the same breathtaking views of the Intracoastal that have made the location a favorite of locals and visitors for many years, with plenty of outdoor seating along the water. Fish House Grill provides a great value without sacrificing quality, as all food is made daily from scratch. Join them for lunch or dinner, seven days a week.

Jerry's Food, Wine and Spirits $$-$$$
7220 Wrightsville Ave., Wilmington
(910) 256-8847
www.jerrysfoodandwine.com

Located just before the bridge to Wrightsville Beach, Jerry's has been serving the finest in upscale cuisine for the past 16 years. Utilizing the freshest seafood, Jerry's offers gems like the Caribbean grouper, the stuffed flounder and Jerry's favorite, the grilled salmon. In the mood for something on the heartier side? Try the New Zealand rack of lamb or perhaps the mouth-watering Chateaubriand, served with a port wine and shiitake mushroom sauce. Featuring reasonably priced wines from your basic Hess Select Cabernet to high-end labels such as the Latour private reserve from Jerry's exclusive collection, the wine list has something for the novice to the seasoned connoisseur. Executive Chef Steve Powell has honed his skills at other area restaurants. Open for dinner seven days a week, Jerry's ranks among the finest of Wilmington's upscale dining establishments.

Sweet & Savory Cafe and Bake Shop $-$$
1611 Pavilion Pl., Wilmington
(910) 256-0115

One of the area's premier restaurants, wholesalers and retail bakeries, Sweet and Savory is located off of Eastwood Road before the drawbridge to Wrightsville Beach. This local hot spot is open for breakfast, lunch and dinner seven days a week. The newly renovated and expanded restaurant offers a casual but beautiful dining experience. Diners can choose to sit inside or outside on the new patio/covered deck overlooking the beautiful garden and fountain while listening to live music every night of the week. Dining in the cafe (seating is situated within the bakery) provides a unique experience as you can watch an authentic bakery in action. It comes as no surprise that the lunch menu includes sandwiches on a large variety of homemade breads and the dinner menu includes warm dinner rolls. Sweet & Savory offers daily board specials at lunch that include fresh fish sandwiches, quiches, soups (chilled soups are offered in summer), entree salads, burgers, melts and much more. The breakfast menu is extensive with specialty sandwiches, omelets and other early morning delights. Vegetarian sandwiches and healthy, low-fat or low-carb selections are included on the breakfast, lunch and dinner menus. The dinner menu offers a wide selection of delectable entrees from the land or the sea. Shrimp and grits, prime rib, pot roast and the seafood medley are some local favorites. Don't forget to leave room for the mouth-watering desserts that were rolled out of the bakery ovens that morning. Additionally, the nightly dinner and drink specials cannot be beat. Catering is available for any size party. Starting the day at 7 AM every day except Sunday (when it opens at 8 AM), this spot is always open until at least 9 PM Sunday through Thursday and at least 10 PM Friday and Saturday. But if the party's rollin' who knows how late they'll be open?

Wrightsville Grille $$-$$$
The Galleria, 6766 Wrightsville Ave., Ste. J, Wilmington
(910) 509-9839

The Smith family hoped to create a restaurant that would be the type of place they would like to dine, and their flagship establishment fits that bill to a tee. The all-American atmosphere at Wrightsville Grille is just the sort of place that families crave, featuring numerous bits of standard fare inspired with a bit of the Smith family twist. You'll go nuts for their signature crab dip appetizer as well as their seared rare sashimi tuna. The almond chicken salad is delectable, as are the Carolina crab cake sandwich and the sumptuous Tar Heel Blue Burger, a bleu cheese and bacon burger cooked to perfection. For dinner entrees, the Shrimp Fra Diavolo features a spicy marinara over angel hair pasta and the Filet Mignon Tournedos showcases succulent beef medallions served with tangy onion rings. Top off your meal with the chocoholic special, a coma-inducing sweet treat that will have you marking Wrightsville Grille at the top of your beach dining list.

Carolina Beach and Kure Beach

Big Daddy's Seafood Restaurant $$-$$$
202 K Ave., Kure Beach
(910) 458-8622

A Kure Beach institution for three decades, Big Daddy's serves a variety of seafood and combination platters. In addition to seafood, the restaurant offers choice steaks, prime rib and chicken every day in a family-oriented, casual setting. Seafood can be broiled, fried, char-grilled or steamed. Highlights of Big Daddy's menu include an all-you-can-eat salad bar; a large selection of seafood and beef entrees; special plates for seniors and children; and the sizable Surf and Turf (filet mignon and a choice of snow crab legs or char-grilled barbecue shrimp). An after-dinner walk along the nearby beachfront or on the Kure Beach fishing pier (both are a short block away) further adds to Big Daddy's appeal. The restaurant's interior, consisting of several rooms and a total seating capacity of over 400 people, comes as a surprise; it doesn't seem that big from the outside. Rare and unusual maritime memorabilia make for entertaining distractions. Entrance to Big Daddy's is through a colorful gift shop offering novelties and taffy. Patrons frequently make secret wishes and toss coins into the fountain there. Located at the only stoplight in Kure Beach, Big Daddy's has all ABC permits and ample parking in front and across the street. Big Daddy's is closed during the off-season (Thanksgiving through the beginning of March).

Black Horn Bar & Kitchen $-$$
15 Carolina Beach Ave. N., Carolina Beach
(910) 458-5255

The philosophy of Black Horn Bar & Kitchen is simple: "Great food should be served quickly and enjoyed leisurely with friends." The Black Horn's owners envisioned a high-quality, diverse menu offered in a comfortable environment that is welcoming to everyone. Indeed, the menu features salads, cold and hot sandwiches, wings, wraps and entrees with a focus on American classics with a Southwestern twist, appealing to any palate. With 20 plasma TV screens, the Black Horn is a great spot to catch your favorite sports game, and on the weekends, they feature live music. They serve an extensive list of beer, wine and specialty beverages. Located near the boardwalk in Carolina Beach, the Black Horn is open daily from 11 AM to 2 AM.

Havana's Fresh Island Seafood $$-$$$
One North Lake Park Blvd., Carolina Beach
(910) 458-2822

For the freshest seafood with a hint of Caribbean flavor, head to Havana's Fresh Island Seafood. New to the Cape Fear dining scene, Havana's is owned by an experienced local restaurateur with an innovative vision. Try their Cha Cha Salmon, which is blackened on an open flame and topped with a chunky avocado citrus

salsa. The dining room is light and airy with Caribbean-inspired decor to set the mood. On a nice evening, you can dine on their outdoor deck featuring a scenic view of downtown Carolina Beach. Havana's also features the best Sunday brunch on Pleasure Island. Located in the middle of Carolina Beach, Havana's is open for lunch and dinner seven nights a week.

Michael's Seafood Restaurant
& Catering $$
1206 N. Lake Park Blvd., Carolina Beach
(910) 458-7761

Winner of the 2010 International Chowder Cookoff Competition and 2001 Restaurant of the Year Award (Wilmington Chamber of Commerce Small Business Coalition), Michael's remains a popular local choice. Michael's menu is available all day, and fresh seafood, either steamed or broiled, is the specialty here. Nothing is fried. Alternative menu options include a good selection of steak, chicken, pasta and pork chops. Michael's updates its menu seasonally and offers lunch and nightly specials. Lunch features the award-winning Captain M's Seafood Chowder, a homemade soup of the day and a variety of sandwiches. Enjoy the indoor dining area dominated by a 700-gallon aquarium of the staff's "pets," or outdoor dining on the deck with live entertainment on the weekends. The restaurant has all ABC permits and serves imported and domestic beer and wine. Off-site catering services are also available. Michael's is open for lunch and dinner daily year-round, and they offer a children's menu as well.

Rucker Johns Restaurant and More $$
5564 Carolina Beach Rd., Wilmington
(910) 452-1212

Discover Rucker Johns, a local family favorite since 1992. Renowned for high quality and attention to detail, Rucker Johns' theme is casual and the service is serious. The made-from-scratch menu features an array of fresh salads, appetizers, sandwiches, burgers, hand-stretched grilled pizzas and unbeatable homemade soups. Entree choices include grilled chicken dishes, tender baby-back ribs, awesome prime rib, succulent steaks, tasty pastas and fresh seafood. Adjoining the oak-trimmed dining room is a horseshoe-shaped bar, the perfect place to enjoy live jazz on Saturday evenings or to catch the big game. A second dining area is available for business luncheons and private parties. RJ's has all ABC permits and boasts a wine list with fine selections from around the world. Located near the Ameri-Stay Inn & Suites along the Service Road adjacent to Carolina Beach Road, RJ's is open for lunch and dinner seven days a week, closing late on Friday and Saturday.

Trolly Stop $
103-A Cape Fear Blvd., Carolina Beach
(910) 458-7557

Trolly Stop is centrally located in the heart of Carolina Beach and offers Smithfield all-meat hot dogs as well as all-beef Sabrett hot dogs to suit almost any whim. In addition, they offer no-carb vegetarian dogs as well as low fat/no-carb turkey dogs. Try the classic North Carolina dog with chili, mustard and cole slaw, the Snow's Cut (melted cheese and mayo) or the Carolina Beach (special sauce, mustard and onion). Vegetarian and nonfat hot dogs are also available. Trolly Stop's menu includes their signature Burger dog and nachos with toppings. The Carolina Beach location closes during the winter months.

Leland

Antonio's Pizza and Pasta $-$$
1107 New Pointe Blvd., Ste. 9, Leland
(910) 383-0033

The sauces, herbs and rich flavors of delicious Italian cuisine can be found in this authentic piece of the old country. Antonio's has an extensive menu offering all of the traditional fare of Italian dining with an atmosphere to match. Enjoy sautéed classics, signature pizzas and flavorful pastas. Antonio's boasts a considerable wine selection, allowing you to find the perfect pairing for your dish. Their "Best Hot Taste" award at the 2008 Taste of Wilmington Food and Wine Festival speaks to Antonio's quality. It is open for lunch and dinner daily.

Charlie Macgrooders $-$$
117 Village Rd., Ste. G, Leland
(910) 399-7924

Fantastic food and first-class fun are the priorities at Charlie Macgrooders. Step inside to find an ambiance that blends traditional diner seating with a high-end motif and a menu that covers all themes. American, Italian, Mexican and Asian inspired dishes diversify their selection that ranges from anything to sandwiches and fajitas to pastas and traditional entrees. Charlie Macgrooders has a variety of daily food and drink specials, and a late-night menu to compliment its fully stocked bar. Stop in on Wednesday nights at 7:30 PM for Trivia, or strut your stuff at 8 PM on Fridays for Cruisin' Karaoke. It's daily for lunch and dinner and until 1 AM on Friday and Saturday.

Groucho's Deli $-$$
497 Old Waterford Way, Ste. 100, Leland
(910) 371-2006

Brought to life by the original recipes of Harold "Groucho" Miller, this delicious deli prides itself on high-quality products and ingredients. It began in Columbia, S.C., where the shop and its owner became local legend, winning several of the area's "Best Of" awards. Both status and scrumptiousness allotted this deli to branch out to other locations, and it is a great addition to the Leland area. Stop in for such classics as a Reuben, chicken salad and BLTs, or try one of Groucho's unique specialty sandwiches, like the STP Dipper.

P.T.'s Olde Fashioned Grille $
1035 Grandiflora Dr., Leland
(910) 399-6808

When you want a freshly grilled burger or chicken sandwich, forget the fast-food mills. Consistently voted Best Burger by Encore magazine's annual poll, P.T.'s can't be beat. Every menu item is a package deal that includes a sandwich (whopping half-pound Angus beef burgers, tender chicken breast, hot dogs, fresh roast beef, turkey and more), fresh-cut, spiced, skin-on French fries (or substitute a side salad) and a soft drink, refill included. Prices are low, and quality is high. You place your order by filling in an idiot-proof order form and dropping it through the window if you're eating on the outdoor deck. Order at the counter if you're eating inside. Your meal is prepared to order and ready in about 10 minutes. This is fast food that doesn't taste like fast food. P.T.'s also offers an alternative to beef with the lower calorie, low-fat Gardenburger. This location is at the entrance to Magnolia Greens in Leland, but you can try any of their numerous locations in nearby Wilmington as well. Check out the Wilmington site for those listings. Take-out orders are welcome and may be habit-forming. P.T.'s is open daily until 9 PM and does not accept checks.

San Felipe Restaurante Mexicano $
1114 New Pointe Rd., Leland
(910) 371-1188

If your taste buds are set for authentic Mexican cuisine in an awesome array of mouth-watering choices, San Felipe is an excellent choice. They serve lunch and dinner daily in a lively and friendly atmosphere where regulars from as far away as Wilmington or Calabash sometimes partake of both meals in the same day. The decor is tastefully Mexican, and seating might be a cozy table or booths long enough to accommodate the whole family. San Felipe's made-fresh-daily traditional Mexican cuisine can be ordered in combinations or specialty entrees, with beef, chicken and seafood. The lunch-only options number more than 26. Another combination list offers 30 more. The menu boasts an appealing list of appetizers, vegetarian combinations, tasty Mexican desserts and a child's plate menu for children younger than 12. Regulars say that San Felipe has the best margaritas, regular and flavored, in town. The restaurant also has all ABC permits and serves Mexican and domestic beer. Ask about drink and lunch specials. Take out is available.

Two Guys Grille $-$$
Waterford Shopping Center,
2013 Olde Regent Way, Leland
(910) 371-6588

When it comes to tasty sandwiches, burgers and fries, why go for fast food when you can sample the succulent fare at Two Guys Grille? The burgers are sumptuous and come in several varieties, including a black bean burger. And while you're at it, try the knockout Philly cheese steak (also with a black bean option). In addition to several chicken, cheese and corned beef sandwiches, there are also a number of fish sandwiches on the menu, including the saucy grilled Cajun catfish. Toss in eight different salad choices and a heaping helping of good ole banana puddin', and you've got one of Wilmington's best quick stops for lunch or dinner. Two Guys Grille also has several locations in the greater Wilmington area.

Bald Head Island

The Bald Head Island Club $$-$$$
Bald Head Island
(910) 457-7300, (866) 657-7311

Open for lunch and dinner, The Bald Head Island Club offers an array of venues to enjoy marvelous creations sure to please any palate. The executive chef's seasonal menus include a selection of seafood specialties, char-grilled steaks, pasta and delectable desserts. Regional seafood and the freshest vegetables are hallmarks of the restaurant's cuisine. The wine list is extensive and offers premium vintages to complement each meal. On Thursday you can experience the Land and Sea Menu, featuring local seafood and succulent prime rib. Set in a newly renovated building reminiscent of coastal New England, the elegant dining room is accented by an extensive patio with a commanding ocean view. For those desiring a more relaxed atmosphere, The Palms Room offers a full bar, a dance floor and walls of windows enabling diners to continually observe and absorb island life. Completing the dining options is The Grille. Light and airy with walls that are windows to the magnificent views of the island's award-winning golf course, this room is enhanced with a covered terrace for al fresco dining. A temporary membership, which is included in accommodation rates for all properties leased through Bald Head Island Limited, is required for Club dining. Reservations are requested.

Eb & Flo's Steam Bar $$$-$$$$
Keelson Row, Bald Head Island
(910) 457-7217

Eb & Flo's sits squarely on the dock in the harbor at Bald Head Island Marina. This casual coastal eatery has been featured in Coastal Living magazine as a "great dive." You can bask in the sunshine and breezes in the outdoor seating area or choose indoor seating in the Carolina Room, which features teak tables and chairs and a lounge with great views of the marina. The menu offers fresh seafood, including crab legs, clams, fish, shrimp, mussels and oysters. Indulge yourself in a Steamer Pot. You will find a specialty drink menu and eight beers on tap. Enjoy live entertainment on weekends throughout the summer.

The Maritime Market $
Maritime Way, Bald Head Island
(910) 457-7450

A deli and sandwich counter at the Maritime Market grocery store offers well-prepared sandwiches, salads and hot foods. Some offerings include gourmet salads, taco salad, rotisserie chicken, stuffed Cornish game hens, meatloaf and wraps. There's also the Ice Cream Shoppe serving cold treats, including sundaes, cones and shakes. The bright and spacious market is located off Muscadine Wynd in the maritime forest area of the island.

River Pilot Cafe $-$$
Bald Head Island
(910) 457-7390

River Pilot Cafe has the island's finest view of the Cape Fear River and serves breakfast, lunch and dinner in a more casual setting than the Club dining room. The menu emphasizes Southern cuisine in its use of regional seafood, fresh vegetables, meats and daily specials. The variety of offerings guarantees an enjoyable dining experience. Enjoy a late-night menu and your favorite cocktail in the adjoining River Pilot Lounge. In summer, the cafe serves the island's best breakfasts. It's also a superb vantage from which to view stunning sunsets while enjoying a meal or drink. River Pilot Cafe is open seasonally for breakfast, lunch and dinner.

Southport

Bella Cucina Restaurant
& Pizzeria $$$-$$$$
5177 Southport-Supply Rd., Southport
(910) 454-4540

Beautiful Kitchen, indeed! Beautiful dining room, beautiful lounge, beautiful food. At Bella Cucina you will find Tuscan-style food made with recipes handed down in the family and using only the freshest ingredients, including herbs from a local farm, to achieve the subtle flavors. From Antipasto to Dolce, the dinner menu is filled with delicious selections, such as mussels with a spicy red sauce, Caesar salad, Tuscan chicken, veal Parmesan, shrimp Scampi, pasta and daily specials. Enjoy your meal with your choice of red or white wines by the glass or bottle. Dessert is a must-have with selections of homemade tiramisu, homemade cannoli or New York cheesecake. Follow that with espresso, cappuccino, tea or cordials. Bella Cucina offers a children's menu. Looking for the perfect place to celebrate a special occasion? The folks at Bella Cucina will be happy to help you. For great New York–style pizza, calzones, stromboli and hot and cold subs and pasta dishes, visit their Pizzeria next door. It's open from 11 AM until 9 PM daily; call (910) 454-4357.

Dry Street Pub & Pizza $-$$
101 E. Brown St., Southport
(910) 457-5994

Directly across the street from the Southport water tower you will find Dry Street Pub & Pizza. Local art decorates the walls of this cozy restaurant with small tables and a bar. If it's lunch or a light dinner you want, then you have come to the right place. The food is delicious and can be served with beer or wine. You will find traditional and specialty pizzas with many toppings; tomato bread; crab dip; homemade soups; salads including chef, Greek, shrimp and Caesar; and a variety of sandwiches such as ham and cheese, chicken pita wraps and Italian sausage subs. Save room for the homemade desserts. Daily specials are available as well. All this is served by John and Sheila Barbee and their friendly staff. They're open Monday through Saturday for lunch and dinner.

Fishy Fishy Cafe $$-$$$$
106 Yacht Basin Dr., Southport
(910) 457-1881

Don't miss Fishy Fishy Cafe! Whether you arrive by land or by sea, you will thoroughly enjoy the Caribbean flavor of the restaurant and the food. Dine indoors in the main dining room or outdoors either on the deck or at the Outside Patio Bar. Any seat overlooks the Yacht Basin Marina and provides fantastic views of the Intracoastal Waterway. Stop by in the evening for a drink and spectacular sunset views. The menu includes fresh fish, shellfish, pasta, steak, ribs and more. Lunch is served daily until 4 PM and dinner is served every day.

Live Oak Cafe $$$-$$$$
614 N. Howe St., Southport
(910) 454-4360

Live Oak Cafe, nestled under one of Southport's lovely old live oak trees, is housed in one of three historic homes known as "The Three Sisters." Owner/Chef Sean Mundy and his wife, Jennifer Charron, spent seven months refurbishing the house to spectacular results. When you step inside the door, the original heart pine floors, the vibrant colors on the walls, the intimate dining rooms (there are three), the pub tables, beaded-board ceilings and the decor take you back to a simpler time. Friendly staff will greet you and treat you to superior customer service. During the season, you can be served on the screened porch as well and have your wine in the herb garden if you like. American nouveau cuisine using only the freshest ingredients is the basis for Sean's eclectic menu. From starters to entrees, you will be pleased with dishes such as crab dip, Cajun-marinated fried alligator bites, low-country gumbo, shrimp pasta, grilled rib eyes, herb-roasted pork chops and more. In addition, there is an excellent wine list with selections from Australia, California and Argentina, among others. Live Oak Cafe is open Tuesday through Saturday for dinner. Reservations are accepted.

San Felipe Restaurante Mexicano $
Live Oak Village Shopping Ctr.,
4961-9 Long Beach Rd, Southport
(910) 454-0950

If your taste buds are set for authentic Mexican cuisine in an awesome array of mouth-watering choices, San Felipe is an excellent choice. Located in the Live Oak Village Shopping Center, San Felipe serves lunch and dinner daily in a lively and friendly atmosphere where regulars from as far away as Wilmington or Calabash sometimes partake of both meals in the same day. The decor is tastefully Mexican, and seating might be a cozy table or booths long enough to accommodate the whole family. San Felipe's made-fresh-daily traditional Mexican cuisine can be ordered in combinations or specialty entrees, with beef, chicken and seafood. The lunch-only options number more than 26. Another combination list offers 30 more. The menu boasts an appealing list of appetizers, vegetarian combinations, tasty Mexican desserts and a child's plate menu for children younger than 12. Regulars say that San Felipe has the best margaritas, regular and flavored, in town. The restaurant also has all ABC permits and serves Mexican and domestic beer. Ask about drink and lunch specials. Take out is available.

Taylor Cuisine Cafe & Catering, Inc. $-$$
731 N. Howe St., Southport
(910) 454-0088

If you are searching for a Southern eclectic culinary experience at a full-service restaurant, Taylor Cuisine Cafe is tailor made for you. For breakfast, lunch or dinner you will find quality fresh foods creatively prepared and friendly service at affordable prices. For breakfast, try eggs any style, pancakes, waffles, French toast, bagels, biscuits and gravy, Walt's famous home fries and more, all served with Barnies Gourmet Fresh Ground Coffee. Served for lunch are such scrumptious items as fried green tomatoes, sweet potato fries, crab cakes, salads and sandwiches, including those served on a croissant or in a wrap. Dinners include daily specials. Taylor Cuisine also offers a personal chef service and catering. (See our Wedding Planning section).

Trolly Stop $
111 S. Howe St., Southport
(910) 457-7017

Walking through historic Southport can work up an appetite, and Trolly Stop's long list of dogs is sure to appeal. Trolly Stop serves a specially produced Smithfield all-meat dog, all-beef Sabrett dogs, no-carb veggie dogs and low fat/no-carb turkey dogs. Choose from the Southport (topped with special sauce, mustard and onions), the Battleship (tomato salsa, mustard and onions), the Old Baldy (plain, of course!) and everything in between. Vegetarian, all-meat and nonfat hot dogs are additional options. Trolly Stop also serves grilled sandwiches, sweet Italian sausage and nachos with toppings. This location also serves Hershey's ice cream and is open year-round.

Yacht Basin Provision Company $-$$
130 Yacht Basin Dr., Southport
(910) 457-0654

Unless they have been forewarned, first time visitors looking for 'Provisions' (as this restaurant is referred to by the locals) may go right by it thinking they have been given incorrect directions. The only indication that this little shack on the waterfront is a restaurant is the line of people that may be waiting to get inside. Once you do get inside you will find the menu written on a chalkboard. Sandwiches from grilled yellowfin tuna to grouper salad to hamburgers and hotdogs are included, as are salads and sides. You can get the salads with shrimp, tuna or chicken. Conch fritters and steamed shrimp are on the menu, as are daily specials. All seating is outdoors overlooking the Intracoastal Waterway where you can enjoy the natural scenery and the passing boats. Don't miss the sunset from the seats in the Provision Company.

Oak Island

Bar-B-Que House $-$$
5002 E. Oak Island Dr., Oak Island
(910) 201-1001

The Bar-B-Que House offers quality pork, barbecue, ribs and chicken slow-smoked over hickory logs. The smoking is done at the on-site facility daily, guaranteeing the freshness of their product. They have a choice of sauces, including eastern N.C. red sauce, Lexington-style vinegar sauce and South Carolina mustard sauce, as well as their House Sauce. You can choose pork, ribs, chicken or a combination and sides such as slaw, baked beans, fries, hushpuppies and corn nuggets. The Bar-B-Que House also offers full-service or drop-off catering or you can order takeout.

Island Brews Beachside $
200 Country Club Dr., Oak Island
(910) 278-7100

Island Brews offers a special blend of espresso, flavored coffees and cappuccino as well as tea, smoothies, juices, ice cream and more. Breakfast selections range from scones to breakfast wraps. Daily lunch specials include sandwiches, salads and soups. Don't leave without trying their exceptional desserts, or take some with you. Cakes (like sour cream–coconut and seven-layer ultimate chocolate) are homemade locally. Croissants with fruit and cream-cheese filling are baked on the spot. Or try the gourmet tiramisu cheesecake or New York cheesecake. Wireless Internet is available, and private parties can be catered.

Little Bits $
5902 E. Oak Island Dr., Oak Island
(910) 278-6430

In the area since 1975, Little Bits has become somewhat of a tradition on Oak Island. It's the place for a home-style breakfast or a light lunch whipped up before your eyes and served with a smile. The owner, Little Bit, has transformed a small building into an American-style eatery with red and white decor and successfully incorporated the elegant fans and wall hangings from her native Vietnam in the scheme. Breakfast and lunch are served Monday through Saturday.

Oak Island Sub Shop $
5705 E. Oak Island Dr., Oak Island
(910) 278-9040

Fred and Wilma Workman opened Oak Island Sub Shop adjacent to the post office in the summer of 2004. Since then they have become well known by locals and visitors alike for their scrumptious sandwiches, subs, soups and salads. Their renovation at the beginning of 2009 now allows for customers to dine-in or take out. From children's favorites like PB& J or hot dogs, to more grown up choices including Italian or turkey subs, their menu is sure to please everyone. For something unique try their famous homemade shrimp salad, Cubans, Reubens or muffalettas. Wilma guarantees: "If you come hungry, you'll leave very satisfied!"

Russell's Place Restaurant $
5700 E. Oak Island Dr., Oak Island
(910) 278-3070

Among Long Beach residents Russell's Place is one of the most popular diner-style eateries for breakfast and lunch. No matter how crowded it gets, the food is served hot, fast and with a smile and no one will rush you. Table-to-table conversation comes easily as folks dine on large omelets, flaky biscuits, pancakes and Belgian waffles for breakfast then entrees, sandwiches and burgers for lunch. Russell's Place is open daily for breakfast (served all day) and lunch. Take-out orders are welcome.

Turtle Island Restaurant and Catering $$-$$$
6220 E. Oak Island Dr., Oak Island
(910) 278-4944

Turtle Island Restaurant's decor is inviting, casual and tropical, from the coral-colored walls to the jungle-print tablecloths to the tanks of tropical fish. A good variety of wines is available, and the menu is intriguing, including such items as Wings Over Oak Island and hot crab dip for appetizers. In addition to the entree specials, the restaurant serves Calabash-style seafood, pasta and sandwiches, with great flair. Just wait until you see the work of art that is your meal. Visit on Wednesday night, Steam Night, for specials on all steamed seafood items as well as other great meals. Turtle Island is open for dinner only. Come early or take advantage of call-ahead seating (reservations are available only for parties of six or more, excluding Wednesday nights).

Topsail Island Area

The Atlantis Restaurant & Lounge $$$
2000 New River Inlet Rd.,
North Topsail Beach
(910) 328-2002

While the seventh floor dining room's wall-to-wall, floor-to-ceiling windows offer a fantastic view of Topsail Island's northern strand, this restaurant offers more than just a great view. Entrées range from the traditional broiled King Neptune's platter and grilled Atlantis fillet to the Potato Crusted Red Snapper with roasted garlic and thyme cream sauce and the Smoked Apple-wood Shrimp wrapped in bacon served with a Parmesan grits cake. A children's menu is also available. Located at the St. Regis Resort, The Atlantis can easily accommodate large groups and is an ideal location for special events such as reunions, weddings and corporate affairs. The restaurant has full ABC permits, and reservations are recommended. The Atlantis is open every day for dinner during the summer season.

The Beach Shop and Grill $-$$$
701 S. Anderson Blvd., Topsail Beach
(910) 328-6501

The Beach Shop and Grill in Topsail Beach has been an island tradition for several generations. Sit at the counter or slide into a booth to enjoy fresh-squeezed orangeades, omlettes, biscuits, burgers, hot dogs, salads and crab cake sandwiches. The restaurant ramps up its menu in the evening and serves upscale entrees including grilled rib eyes, filets, Asian sesame tuna and grilled and fried seafood. House specialities are shrimp and grits, crab cake platters, and sausage ravioli. Dinner is served only during the summer and entrees range from $15 to $30. Beer and wine are available, and you may eat in or take-out.

Beauchaines 211 $$$
211 S. Topsail Dr., Surf City
(910) 328-1888

The menu at Beauchaines 211 offers a contemporary twist to traditional beach cuisine. Oysters are Cajun fried, the alligator tail is blackened, and the fried calamari is served with a salad of jicama, red and yellow peppers and napa cabbage tossed in sweet chili vinaigrette. That's just the appetizers. The tantalizing menu of entrées includes shrimp and grits, Baked Pistachio Salmon, as well as the NY Strip Caroline, which is topped with a Gorgonzola and green onion compound butter. Beauchaines 211 has all ABC permits, and the upstairs dining room and bar overlook the beautiful Intracoastal Waterway. Homemade desserts and a children's menu are available. Beauchaines 211 is open seven days a week during the summer, and reservations are strongly recommended. They are closed during the winter months but are available for private parties and catering.

Bella Luna Restaurant $$$
790 New River Inlet Rd.,
North Topsail Beach
(910) 328-0504

An upscale oceanfront bistro serving lunch and dinner, Bella Luna serves authentic Italian cuisine. Special menu items include Penne Tuscana, a grilled chicken breast with sun-dried tomatoes, prosciutto and arugula, and the Filet Di Manzo, a grilled Black Angus filet brushed with roasted garlic oil served with a Gorgonzola and chive potato cake. Bella Luna serves a variety of pastas, chicken and veal dishes and steaks. Enjoy a tropical cocktail at their cabana bar or choose a fine bottle of wine with dinner. The restaurant is located at Villa Capriani Resort, one mile north of the high-rise bridge. Bella Luna is family friendly and offers a children's menu.

Capt. Jim's Seafood Restaurant $-$$
316 Fulchers Landing Rd., Sneads Ferry
(910) 327-3516

Located along the beautiful Fulchers Landing waterfront in Sneads Ferry, Capt. Jim's Seafood Restaurant serves fresh, homemade food. With a choice of made-from-scratch biscuits, eggs, omelets or French Toast, it is a great way to start the day. For lunch try their homemade chicken strips, burgers cooked to order or a fresh seafood basket. Because owner Jeremy Edens grew up in a fishing family and worked at his granddad's fish house for more than 12 years, he knows what fresh

local seafood means to customers and he serves the freshest seafood possible. Capt. Jim's is known for its fresh, hand-peeled shrimp baskets and seafood platters that are served with homemade cole slaw, shoestring French fries and homemade, secret recipe hush puppies. Capt. Jim's serves breakfast and lunch seven days a week and is open for dinner from Wednesday through Saturday.

Crab Pot $-$$
508 Roland Ave., Surf City
(910) 328-5001

Southern low-country and Caribbean food is the theme at the Crab Pot. Specialties of the house include jambalaya, chowders, oysters, jerk chicken and ribs smothered in sauce. The screened-in dining room and bar offers great old-time Topsail fun. Food can be packaged to go, and a children's menu is available. Home of the 64-oz Margarita, the Crab Pot has a full bar, plenty of shaker cans and beach music. It is closed from Thanksgiving until March.

Crabby Mike's $$-$$$
121 S. Topsail Dr., Surf City
(910) 328-4331

Bright blue walls, splashes of lime green and beach-themed art create a cool island vibe inside Crabby Mike's. The lunch menu features homemade soups and chowders, Angus burgers, grilled turkey burgers and Crabby BLTs. Steamed shrimp and crab legs are always a popular choice for dinner, as are their homemade crab cakes. In addition to the full menu, Crabby Mike's offers a chalkboard full of seasonal specials, and beer and wine are available at the Tiki Bar. Crabby Mike's is open for lunch and dinner Tuesday through Sunday during the summer. Give them a call for their off-season hours.

Dr. Rootbeer's Hall Of Foam $-$$
288 Fulcher's Landing Rd., Sneads Ferry
(910) 327-7668
www.drrootbeer.com

Dr. Rootbeer's Hall of Foam, located in a vintage 1950s gas station near the waterfront in Sneads Ferry, sells root beer made from Jerome Gundrum's own recipe. Choose between old-fashioned fountain favorites like birch beer, cream soda and lime ricki while listening to their 1953 Seeburg jukebox. With root beer floats, milk shakes and 16 flavors of hand-dipped ice cream, everyone will be happy. Dr. Rootbeer also serves delicious pot roast sandwiches, sassafras barbecue, homemade chicken salad and tuna salad sandwiches and hot dogs.

'Em R Wings $$
1016 Old Folkstone Rd., Sneads Ferry
(910) 327-2848

Pub-style appetizers, side orders, salads and sandwiches complement the specialty of the house — big, bold buffalo wings, served mild, medium or hot. This is a fun and cozy place to enjoy a bite. Meal choices of ribs or steak are also available. 'Em R Wings has a full bar, which is separate from the dining room. Take-out orders are welcome, and the restaurant is open all year.

Green Turtle $$$
310 Fulchers Landing Rd., Sneads Ferry
(910) 327-0262

This cafe on the bay overlooks the picturesque New River and specializes in seafood, steaks and pasta. Green Turtle offers creative entrees such as Shrimp

Diablo, Linguine Pescatore and Cajun Oysters. Family-friendly, Green Turtle offers a children's menu and is open daily. The restaurant has all ABC permits, and reservations are suggested.

Holland's Shelter Creek Restaurant $$
8315 N.C. Hwy. 53 E, Burgaw
(910) 259-5743

Finish off a day exploring the Pender County countryside with a meal at Holland's. Known for its fresh seafood, Holland's offers hearty platters of catfish, scallops, deviled crabs and frog legs. For those who prefer country cooking, the restaurant has some of the area's best barbecue and pork chops. Dine in a rustic atmosphere with a view of the creek and relax with a cup of homemade catfish stew or shrimp Creole. Holland's has beer and wine, seniors' specials and a children's menu. It is open year-round for lunch and dinner.

Holly Ridge Smokehouse $
511-A U.S. Hwy. 17, Holly Ridge
(910) 329-1708

If you are looking for authentic, slow-cooked, eastern North Carolina barbecue, this is the place. Open for breakfast, lunch and dinner, this well-known restaurant offers home-cooked food, and barbecue is the specialty of the house. A children's menu is available. Holly Ridge Smokehouse is open year round, but is closed Mondays.

Home Port Restaurant & Pub $$
718 S. Anderson Blvd., Topsail Beach
(910) 328-7000

Everyone feels right at home in the warm and cozy dining room at Home Port Restaurant & Pub. The theme here is definitely and deliciously Italian. The chicken, meatball or sausage parmigiana sandwiches are lunchtime favorites, along with burgers, great subs and fresh salads. The dinner menu includes steaks, seafood, homemade lasagna, baked ziti, pasta, pizza and calzones. Home Port has all ABC permits, and the lively pub side of the building has pool tables, a wide-screen TV and live entertainment on Saturday nights.

Island Delights $
316 N. New River Dr., Surf City
(910) 328-1868

Return to the 1950s and the days of the soda shop with a trip to Island Delights. The eatery specializes in burgers, sandwiches and fries, as well as fountain-style milk shakes and sundaes. Vacationing families enjoy returning here year after year for their evening ice cream treats. It is closed in the off season.

Just Baked $-$$
205 S. Topsail Dr., Surf City
(910) 328-3150

In addition to their delicious croissants, cupcakes, pies and cakes, the newly expanded Bistro at Just Baked serves a delightful lunch and dinner. The lunch menu has a variety of hearty salads, including a pepper-crusted rib eye steak salad and delicious sandwiches served on their homemade bread. There is also a nice range of evening entrees. The Bistro Mixed Grill and the chipolte shrimp and grits have already become local favorites.

Lo-Re-Lei $
1019 Old Folkstone Rd., Sneads Ferry
(910) 327-0900

If you are hunting for a homemade hamburger and a tall cold one, head to Lo-Re-Lei's behind the Big Shark in Sneads Ferry. Enjoy mid-week Karaoke, pool and dart tournaments, or kick it up a notch on weekends with their live bands and drink specials, including chilled Jägermeister on tap. Daily lunch specials run $5.95 and the evening menu includes steaks and Calabash-style seafood. Now serving breakfast, Lo-Re-Lei's opens at 6 AM Monday through Friday and they also serve a late-night breakfast on Saturday night.

Long Island Pizza $$
610 N. New River Dr., Surf City
(910) 328-3156

The name says all — Long Island Pizza makes great New York–style pizza. It's hard to choose between all of their specialties, including Margherita pizza, calzones, stromboli, eggplant Parmigiana,

manicotti or baked ziti. If tiramisu is on the menu, be sure to order it. Beer and wine are available. You can eat in, take-out or have your meals delivered to your door. It's closed on Sunday and Monday and during the month of January.

Mainsail Restaurant $$$
404 Roland Ave., Surf City
(910) 328-0010

Soft creamy beach colors, warm woods and bamboo cloth wall coverings create a cozy and upbeat atmosphere at the Mainsail Restaurant. Next to traditional menu favorites like Maryland crab cakes and grilled steaks, are exotic Pacific Rim and Southwest flavors combined in unexpected ways to create fabulous flavors. Mainsail has enough room to seat large parties comfortably during the summer and reservations gladly accepted. Mainsail has a full bar, frozen drinks, and an eclectic wine list.

Max's Pizza $-$$
602A Roland Ave., Surf City
(910) 328-2158

This casual and friendly restaurant located just over the swing bridge serves pizza, spaghetti, salads, burgers and fresh hot-oven subs, along with beer and wine. Take-out orders are welcome. It's open year round, but is closed on Wednesday during the off-season.

Mollie's Restaurant $-$$$
107 N. Shore Dr., Surf City
(910) 328-0505

Start your day off right with breakfast at Mollie's. The full breakfast menu includes omelets, pancakes, biscuits and their signature Crab Cake Eggs Benedict. If you're looking for lunch, you'll be thrilled with their salads and sandwiches, including one of the tastiest burgers in Surf City. In addition to the menu, numerous specials are featured each day. The dinner menu offers a wide variety of fried and broiled seafood, from the Captain's Platter with six different kinds of seafood to Caribbean Mahi. Mollie's also serves a variety of pasta, steaks and chicken dishes. For those successful fishing types, Mollie's will clean and cook your catch for a very reasonable fee. Mollie's also has a nice selection of beer and wine.

New York Corner Deli $
206 N. Topsail Dr., Surf City
(910) 328-2808
www.newyorkcornerdeli.com

From da Bronx to da beach, this deli is da real thing. New York Corner Deli serves authentic deli sandwiches piled high with real New York City pastrami, salami and corned beef. Bite into their fresh rye bread, bagels and homemade salads or try a slice of their New York–style cheesecake and you will think you are in the Big Apple. New York Corner Deli also serves the only lox and bagel plate you will find on the island. Diners can eat inside, outside at patio tables or call ahead for quick take-out. New York Corner Deli hosts and caters private parties and prepares take-home decorated deli trays and party-sized hoagies. The restaurant is open Monday through Saturday from 7:30 AM to 7:30 PM and Sundays from 8 AM to 5:30 PM

Quartermasters Restaurant & Tavern $$$
13741 N.C. Hwy. 50, Surf City
(910) 328-3100

Quartermaster's Restaurant & Tavern menu features freshly prepared American cuisine. The chef loves to char-grill chicken, pork loin, filet mignon, rib eye and New York strip steaks and the fresh locally caught seafood is served either fried, broiled or grilled. Favorite menu items are the shrimp and scallops in lobster Boursin cream sauce and the seafood etouffe, which includes shrimp, scallops, craw fish and spicy sausage. The dining room is cozy and smoke-free. The tavern, known for its buffalo wings, light eats and fine spirits, offers five high-def TVs with a variety of sporting events each night. Weekend sports include the Sunday NFL ticket on DirecTV. The Tavern opens at 12:30 PM Saturday and Sunday. Quartermaster's, located on the causeway in Heritage Square, is open nightly at 5 PM Tuesday through Sunday. Reservations are accepted

Riverview Cafe $$
119 Hall Point Rd., Sneads Ferry
(910) 327-2011

The Riverview Cafe has been a locals' favorite for decades. Overlooking Courthouse Bay in Sneads Ferry, diners can watch the shrimp boats come in while feasting on some of the freshest seafood around. Plates are heaped high with fried seafood, hushpuppies, french fries and slaw. Try to save some room though for a slice of their homemade pie. There is a bar, separated from the dining room, that offers beer and wine. It's open year round for lunch and dinner.

Sawmill Grill
15919 U.S. Hwy. 17, Hampstead
(910) 270-0056

"You passed the rest to get the best!" runs the slogan of Sawmill Grill, and with fresh ingredients combined in lots of spices, the dishes can testify. Serving a wide range of country cuisine, this family-owned restaurant prides itself on providing hearty meals and excellent service. They are open for lunch and dinner and feature dinner specials that vary daily.

Sears Landing Grill & Boat Dock $-$$$
806 Roland Ave., Surf City
(910) 329-1312

Drive up or drop anchor at this soundside restaurant and enjoy fresh grilled fish, soft-shell crabs, peel-and-eat shrimp, sandwiches or the chef's famous Beach Dog. Diners can sit inside or laze about on the waterfront porch and enjoy the view. The restaurant has all ABC permits and is open for breakfast, lunch and dinner. Sears Landing has deep-water access with boat slips available for rent by the day, week or month. While there you can also stock your boat with beer, soft drinks, water and ice.

Subway $
998 N.C. Hwy. 210, Sneads Ferry
(910) 327-3222
135000 N.C. Highway 50/210, Surf City
(910) 329-0800

With 45 years of experience and 32,866 restaurants, the folks at Subway know how to make a great sandwich. At Subway you really can have it your way. Want healthy? With 6 grams of fat or less, their Veggie Delite, Turkey Breast and Black Forest Ham, Oven Roasted Chicken and Subway Club subs can't be beat. For those with classic tastes there are Meatball Marinara, Spicy Italian and Cold Cut Combo subs. Try a Chicken and Bacon Ranch or Roast Beef for a signature taste or dive into a premium sub like their Big Philly Cheesesteak or The Feast, the ultimate sandwich. Subway Platters are the perfect way to feed a hungry crowd. Choose wither the Subway Fresh Fit, Classic Combo or Flavor Craver sandwich platter for your next get together. Subway also serves breakfast sandwiches such as Black Forest Ham, Egg and Cheese fresh toasted and topped with your choice of veggies and sauces.

T's Cafe $
2004 N.C. Hwy. 172, Open Water Marine,
Sneads Ferry
(910) 327-3647

T's Café, located inside of Open Water Marine, serves fresh local shrimp and grouper that owner Charles "Matt" Mitchell catches off his two boats, the Theresa Marie and T-Baby. T's Cafe also features combo speçials, burgers, hot dogs, desserts, salads and kids' meals. It is family owned and operated, and take-out is available.

Thai Grille $$
13700 N. N.C. Hwy. 50, Surf City
(910) 329-4424
www.thaigrille.com

Aromatic chilies, fresh lemongrass and vibrant curries flavor the authentic Thai dishes served at Thai Grille. Skewers of satay, handmade spring rolls and Massaman and Panang curries are made from scratch from family recipes. Curries can be spiced to taste and range from mild to atomic. The menu includes Asian barbecue ribs, sushi-grade yellow fin tuna with wasabi vinaigrette and crispy chicken wings with a variety of Asian inspired sauces such as sweet chili and Teriyaki. Traditionalists will enjoy the grilled pork loin with an Asian twist or the Bangkok NY Strip Steak. The desserts include Thai Fried Bananas with Caramel Toffee Ice Cream and Thai Fried Donuts. Thai Grille has a full bar, a wine list and a nice selection of beer on tap. It is open for lunch and dinner Monday through Saturday and is located in the Surf City Gateway Plaza.

COFFEEHOUSES

An interesting offspring of the traditional coffeehouse is the marriage of the cafe atmosphere and bookstores. The larger book superstores in Wilmington — Barnes & Noble, 850 Inspiration Drive in Mayfaire, and Books-A-Million, 3737 Oleander Drive — feature surprisingly cozy cafe settings that host cultural events, meetings and book discussion groups. The Salt Shaker Bookstore and Cafe, 705 S. Kerr Avenue, Wilmington, offers coffee and cafe-style food. A smaller, independent bookstore that features the twin delights of good coffee and good books is Quarter Moon Books & Gifts, 708 S. Anderson Boulevard in Topsail Beach.

Wilmington

Port City Java $
2099 Market St.
Wilmington, NC
(910) 763-1763

Port City Java has been Wilmington's number one choice for locally roasted coffee since 1995. They import their coffees from all over the world, but they are roasted fresh right here in Wilmington. They offer a wide variety of Fair Trade and organic certified coffees, hot and cold espresso-based beverages, pure fruit smoothies, milkshakes and baked goods prepared daily in their own bakery. Every Port City Java also serves breakfast sandwiches as well as lunch fare in a clean, comfortable, family-friendly environment. Each cafe offers complimentary, unlimited WiFi service and space for local artists to display their work commission-free. There are 17 Port City Java cafes in the greater Wilmington area and nine conveniently located drive-through locations to help you keep moving.

Press 102 $-$$
102 S. Second St., Wilmington
(910) 399-4438
www.press102.com

New to Wilmington's restaurant scene, Press 102 serves breakfast, lunch and dinner in a light, airy and welcoming environment. The "press" in their name is a nod to the item featured most prominently on the menu, paninis. For breakfast or lunch, try the Cape Fear Panini (shaved house-smoked pork, pickled onions and melted American cheese) or the Tuscan Panini (sliced prosciutto, roasted tomatoes, fresh mozzarella, aged white and dark balsamic

reductions and baby arugula). Pair your meal with an espresso for a pick-me-up, or relax on their outdoor patio with a glass of wine or a martini. All of their menu items are made from the freshest ingredients from neighboring purveyors to help sustain the local economy, and they use recycled products where possible.

Topsail Island and Vicinity

Sneads Beans $
2121 N.C. Hwy. 172, Sneads Ferry
(910) 327-0070

Sneads Beans brews a variety of coffees, including organic and fair trade blends. Enjoy a regular cup of coffee or a latte, cappuccino or flavored specialty drink. A variety of cool and refreshing smoothies and iced coffees are also available. Want a little something to go with your coffee? Sneads Beans serves assorted pastries and breakfast sandwiches served on a bagel or croissant with your choice of bacon or sausage with an egg and cheese. There is free wireless Internet, a sitting room and an outdoor patio, but If you're in a hurry, a convenient drive-up window is around the back. It's open seven days a week.

The Trading Post Coffee House $
Atlantic Plaza, 1044 N.C. Hwy. 210, Sneads Ferry
(910) 327-6400

While you can just run in and grab a great cup of coffee to-go, chances are you'll sit down and stay awhile because The Trading Post Coffee House is so inviting. The shop's shiny wood floors, comfortable overstuffed leather couches, homemade pastries and free Wi-Fi make The Trading Post Coffee House a relaxing place to lounge and meet friends. In addition to great coffee drinks and pastries, The Trading Post serves a variety of delicious wraps and fresh-grilled Paninis plus shakes, smoothies and ice cream. Hosting a breakfast or lunch? The Trading Post Coffee House also caters. While you're munching on a muffin and sipping espresso, be sure to browse through their gift shop. There you will find local artwork, wedding and baby gifts, candles, beach-themed home decor, Topsail souvenirs and jewelry. The Trading Post Coffee House is open year round.

BAKERIES

If you have a sweet tooth, you won't be disappointed by the array of bakeries in Wilmington. This section represents just a few of the area's premier bakeries known for the freshest ingredients and most mouth-watering treats.

Wilmington

Apple Annie's Bake Shop $
Outlet Mall, S. College Rd., Wilmington
(910) 799-9023

Boasting five generations of baking tradition, this award-winning bakery offers everything from bread to gourmet pastries. The goods are baked fresh daily on-premises with natural ingredients and no additives or preservatives. Long, windowed pastry cases display a wide range of the day's available goodies, including cakes, pies, cheesecakes, French pastries, cookies, biscotti, danish, muffins, assorted breads and rolls, cannolis, brownies and more. Apple Annie's specializes in wedding and special occasion cakes. Holidays are especially festive at Apple Annie's, and they celebrate them all. Whether you want a heart-shaped Valentine's Day cake, spicy pumpkin pies for Thanksgiving or Challah bread at Rosh Hashanah, call the bakery for their holiday specials throughout the year.

Great Harvest Bread Company $
5327 Oleander Dr., Wilmington
(910) 793-2330

Some of the best breads in Wilmington can be found at Great Harvest. Their breads and pastries are baked fresh daily from high-protein whole wheat flour they mill themselves. Selections vary with the season, but they make around 15 breads daily and nearly 35 each week, in addition to muffins, scones, cinnamon rolls, cookies and seasonal pies. Stop by for a seasonal baking schedule that lists daily offerings.

Christmas gift baskets of assorted breads are extremely popular and available from Thanksgiving to Christmas. These are great ideas for out-of-town gift-giving and are shipped from Great Harvest via UPS. At Easter, try the whimsical Honey Bunnies, a loaf of honey wheat bread made into a bunny shape. It's a delicious and fun addition to your Easter dinner menu. Great Harvest sells their wares at both the Riverfront Farmers Market as well as the Poplar Grove Farmers Market. Limited seating is available in the store if you'd like to enjoy coffee and a treat while making your selections. Firmly believing in the traditions of "the village bakery," Great Harvest contributes to the community in generous donations to area churches, nonprofit organizations and local shelters. Great Harvest is open Tuesday through Saturday 6:30 AM until 6 PM.

Sweet & Savory Cafe
and Bake Shop $-$$
1611 Pavilion Pl., Wilmington
(910) 256-0115

Sweet and Savory has a large professional catering and bakery staff headed by their seasoned manager, Chef Brent Williams. They prepare all of the desserts, breads and meals from scratch daily with only the freshest of ingredients. This restaurant also serves as a wholesaler supplying many of the local restaurants with their desserts, breads and homemade sweets. When you walk into the restaurant, you can smell the aroma from the large assortment of cakes, pies, pastries, muffins, cookies, mini-desserts and breads that were prepared that morning. If you are engaged and shopping for wedding cakes, stop by and have a taste from many different cake flavors and numerous icings. All of the wedding cakes are exquisitely decorated to the customers' specifications. Finally, Sweet and Savory can cater any size party.

Carolina Beach

Britt's Donuts $
#11 Boardwalk, Carolina Beach

What you won't find at Britt's Donuts includes cream-filled, cake, powdered or any other variation of doughnut besides glazed. What you will find at Britt's, however, are hot, delicious, glazed doughnuts made from a time-honored recipe. Their famous doughnuts have kept locals and tourists coming back for more since the shop opened in 1939. With its blue-and-white-striped awning, unembellished counter and sweet aroma of doughnuts cooking, Britt's has long served as an icon of the Carolina Beach boardwalk. During the summer, Britt's stays open from 8:30 AM to 10:30 PM seven days a week. But you better get your fill of their doughnuts while you can, because Britt's closes during the off-season.

Topsail Island and Vicinity

Hampstead Bagel Bakery $
16865 U.S. Hwy. 17, Hampstead
(910) 270-9099

It's always time to make the bagels at Hampstead Bagel Bakery. Fresh bagels are available seven days a week because they are made on site every day. Bagel lovers know the drill: poppy seed, sesame, onion, egg and plain, 18 bagel varieties in all. Of course there are also plenty of cream cheese spreads. Breakfast, including eggs, homemade croissants and muffins, is served all day. The Hampstead Bagel Bakery offers a full compliment of Boars Head meats and cheeses served on homemade Kaiser rolls, bread or wraps, and lunch is served all day. For dessert try one of their brownies or turnovers. There is a drive-through window for those in a hurry, and inside seating as well. They are open from 6 AM to 3 PM Monday through Friday and 7 AM to 3 PM on Saturday and Sunday.

Surf City Donuts $
204-A N. New River Dr., Surf City
(910) 541-0064

Not all donuts are created equal and Surf City Donuts has created the perfect donut — light and airy, rich and incredibly flavorful. Glazed, frosted or filled, these big round beauties are made on site, as are their tender muffins and croissants. Savor

the goodness along with a cup of coffee for a great start to your day.

WINE SHOPS AND WINERIES

Wine in North Carolina? Who'd have thought it, but the truth is, North Carolina is not only a wine-producing state, it is the 10th largest wine producing state in the nation. With more than 70 wineries and some 1,300 acres devoted to grape cultivation, North Carolina wine is making a comeback, particularly along the Southern coast.

To understand where the North Carolina wine industry has been and where it is going, we have to go back to the year 1524. The first recorded account of wild grapes growing along the shoreline occurred in the log book of Giovanni de Verrazano, a French explorer and navigator who discovered them in the Cape Fear River Valley. He wrote that he saw "Many vines growing naturally there that without doubt would yield excellent wines." These wild native grapes came to be known as Scuppernongs.

For the next 316 years, the golden Scuppernong grapes and the black Muscadines were largely grown for eating and personal wine-making. Thomas Jefferson was particularly fond of the Scuppernong grape and liked the wine it produced, although even as President, he had difficulty finding enough to buy. During the 1840s some 25 commercial wineries were operating and North Carolina was the leading wine-producing state in the nation. However, by 1865 the industry was virtually destroyed by the War Between the States. A few wineries tried and failed. Locally, the Castle Hayne Vineyard Company operated in the 1870s before going out of business, but it took at least two decades before wine production was again up to speed. Then came Prohibition. By the 1930s the industry was again non-existent.

In 1976 two brothers in Duplin County started a winery in Rose Hill, about 45 miles north of Wilmington. The plan was to create an agri-coop to help area farmers. The farmers grew the grapes, the brothers made the wine and the people liked it. Customers began trekking to Dup-

lin Winery by the bus loads to sample and buy wine. From that tenuous beginning sprang the present-day North Carolina wine industry. In 2002 the Yadkin Valley near Wilkesboro was declared an American Viticultural Area, recognizing the area as a sound and distinct grape-growing region. Since then, the number of wineries in the state has more than doubled.

Along the southern coast, the number of wineries is growing as fast as the native grapes. From Rose Hill to just over the South Carolina state line you'll find ten wineries, each with a distinctly different approach to wine making. In the three coastal counties of Pender, New Hanover and Brunswick and just across the line into Columbus County, you'll find four delightful wineries to visit and enjoy.

the grape & ale
8521 Oak Island Dr., Oak Island
(910) 933-4384

You will find that the grape & ale is a wine shop — and much more. You can purchase wine and beer by the glass and enjoy it with gourmet cheese and crackers at the bar or on a sofa while enjoying the works of featured artists and free entertainment. You can purchase your favorite domestic and imported beer and wine in person or by phone and have it delivered to your home. You can arrange for a fund-raising wine tasting for your favorite charity, join the book club, join the wine club,

attend free weekly wine tastings, purchase gifts or arrange private parties. WiFi is available as well.

Lighthouse Beer & Wine
220 Causeway Dr., Wrightsville Beach
(910) 256-8622

Lighthouse Beer & Wine is Wrightsville Beach's one stop-shop for wine, beer and cigars. Embracing the light-hearted vibe of the beach, this pastel gem lies to the right after crossing the Wrightsville Beach Bridge. They offer more than 400 varieties of beer and microbrews and give you the option to explore them by mix and matching your own six-packs. Boasting one of North Carolina's largest keg selections, Lighthouse typically has 50-plus kegs available at all times, or call and advance order a specialty keg. Each year, Lighthouse Beer & Wine's staff tastes thousands of wines in order to hand-pick the best available from around the world. The shop is open from 10 AM to 10 PM Monday through Thursday and from 10 AM to midnight on Friday and Saturday. Sundays they are open from noon to 9 PM.

Lumina Winery
6620 Gordon Rd., Ste. H, Wilmington
(910) 793-5299

Named for the famous Wrightsville Beach pavilion, Lumina Winery is located in the heart of Wilmington. You won't find vines growing here, but you will find some delightful wines as well as kits to make your own wines and beers at home. Owner and wine maker Dave Hursey has created a winery with a different concept. Using varietal grape juices from all over the world, including North Carolina, Dave produces wines with names that reflect the area, such as Oleander Rosa, Oleander Bianca and Wrightsville Red. His Ice Wine is very popular, as is the Green Apple Riesling, especially on a hot summer's day. The wines are meant to be consumed early so they contain low levels of sulfites. Dave sells wines wholesale to area restaurants and wine shops and offers free wine tastings in his retail tasting room. Hours are Tuesday to Saturday 11 AM to 6 PM.

Noni Bacca
420 Eastwood Rd., Wilmington
(910) 397-7617
www.nbwinery.com

Located just a few miles from Wrightsville Beach and Historic Downtown Wilmington is Noni Bacca's international award-winning winery. This boutique winery offers more than 65 varieties of wine made on site. Noni Bacca's diverse varietals come from the richest grape-growing regions of the world, including Tuscany, Chile, Australia, Washington state and California. Wine is sold by the bottle or glass, and you are welcome to complimentary samples in their Tasting Room. Relax and enjoy a glass of wine in a comfortable atmosphere with good music and friendly staff. The retail store is open seven days a week — Monday to Saturday 10 AM to 9 PM and Sunday 12 PM to 5 PM. You can also find an assortment of gifts and wine accessories. Create your own vacation souvenir with a personalized bottle of wine; just bring in a photo or photo card and the staff at Noni Bacca will create a personalized label for your favorite bottle of wine. Shipping is available.

Silver Coast Winery
6680 Barbeque Rd., Ocean Isle Beach
(910) 287-2800

Down a dirt road, past an old tobacco barn, you'll find an award-winning upscale boutique winery that is just minutes from the beach. Silver Coast Winery is a high-tech commercial winery producing varietal wines. Owners John and Maryann Azzato have created a destination in the middle of Brunswick County, offering winery tours and wine-tasting events. An art gallery exhibits works by local artists, and a large picnic area is available. They offer 14 different wines, including Chardonnay, Seyval Blanc, Merlot, Cabernet Sauvignon, Rose and White Merlot. This is a great location for group functions such as large meetings, family reunions, weddings, rehearsal dinners and more. March through December the hours are Monday through Saturday 11 AM to 6 PM and Sunday noon to 5 PM. Winter hours, January and February, are Wednesday through Sunday noon to 5 PM.

The Wine Rack
102 W. Brown St., Southport
(910) 457-5147

Located in quaint downtown Southport, The Wine Rack offers domestic and international wines including dessert wines and a full line of Champagne. Also offered are imported beers and microbrews. Special events and regularly scheduled wine tastings are held here. Specialty coffees available by the pound include Costa Rica Tarrazu, Columbia Supremo and Organic Guatemalan. Cigars, wine and coffee accessories and gift baskets are available.

NIGHTLIFE 🍸

A long North Carolina's southern coastline, the term "nightlife" may have very different meanings to area natives and to visitors enjoying the sights. Plenty of residents spend summer nights away from the crowds by searching the beaches for loggerhead turtle nests and helping protect the ones they find. Others prefer the nights for offshore fishing. Many youngsters enjoy surprising ghost crabs with their flashlights as the little critters (the crabs) make their nocturnal runs on the beach. Of course, there's nothing more romantic or peaceful than a leisurely stroll on the beach under a Carolina moon.

If going out on the town is more your style, nightlife is primarily concentrated in Wilmington, with its numerous restaurants, nightclubs, bars and theaters. Stroll the Riverwalk along Water Street in downtown Wilmington. There are plenty of places along the way to pause for a toast or to hear live music. A horse-drawn carriage tour of downtown Wilmington is an exciting and informative introduction to the city, too. The last couple of years have brought a local resurgence of interest in jazz, blues and other musical genres, evident in the increasing number of restaurants and bars offering live music in the evenings, typically between Thursday and Sunday. The Rusty Nail and The Soap Box are great spots to hear live blues music. Wilmington's busy theater scene, with Thalian Hall as its crown jewel, offers quality entertainment year round.

Outlying areas, especially the South Brunswick Islands, are famous for their quiet family atmosphere, but hot spots definitely do exist at Wrightsville Beach, Carolina Beach, Surf City and on Oak Island, particularly in summer. In Brunswick County, the Odell Williamson Auditorium provides a venue for live performances and dramatic productions. Fans of classical music take note of area presenters that sponsor evening concert programs year round.

Billiards (see listings in this chapter) and bowling are fun alternatives to the usual bar scene. Browsing our Attractions chapter will reveal more ideas — for instance, evening cruise opportunities on the Cape Fear River. See our Arts chapter for more information on both concerts and theatrical productions.

You will find some private nightclubs throughout the region. In order for an establishment to serve liquor, it must either earn the bulk of its revenue from the sale of food or it must be a private club open only to members and their guests. Membership to most clubs is inexpensive, usually about $5 per year. At some venues, weekend visitors applying for membership should know that a three-day waiting period must elapse before you can become a full member, but it's easy to be signed in as someone's guest at the door.

What follows is a sampling and by no means the last word on the area's nightlife. At the end of the chapter is a section on movie theaters, for those whose nightlife tends toward the cinematic.

NIGHTSPOTS

Wilmington

Bluepost Billiards
15 S. Water St., Wilmington
(910) 343-1141

Tucked away in the Jacobi Warehouse near the historic downtown Wilmington riverfront, this 5,000-square-foot billiards hall features a number of diversions — two 9-foot diamond pool tables, four valley Blackcat tables, air hockey, Skee-Ball, darts, Foosball, video games and a video

projector with a 10-foot screen. Worked up a thirst? They stock a great list of beers, including 14 on tap. Bluepost is open from 3 PM to 2 AM Monday through Friday and 2 PM to 2 AM Saturday and Sunday.

Break Time Grille & Ten Pin Alley
127 S. College Rd., Wilmington
(910) 395-6658
www.breaktimetenpin.com

Wilmington's largest billiards parlor is also a popular bowling alley, sports bar and casual restaurant, serving sandwiches, burgers, soups, salads and more. Break Time possesses all ABC permits and has 29 top-quality pool tables, including coin-operated tables as well as regulation-size tables. It has 19 televisions, 24 lanes of bowling and arcade-style diversions. Neat attire is required; no tank tops. It's open 11 AM until 2 AM, and food service is available until closing.

The Brown Coat Pub & Theatre
111 Grace St., Wilmington
(910) 233-9914

The Brown Coat Pub & Theatre is home to Guerilla Theatre and is the best place in town to see live comedy. Located in downtown Wilmington, this smoke-free establishment is a great place to unwind, have a drink and laugh with friends. The Brown Coat Pub and Theatre hosts regular

improv comedy nights, trivia, karaoke and, of course, quality theatre productions with Guerilla Theatre. The Brown Coat also screens the best in local film Wednesday through Sunday at 8 PM the first week of the month. If poetry's your thing, their Sunday night Open Mic Poetry Night at 8 PM is for you. Call for more details.

Caprice Bistro: Restaurant & Sofa Bar
10 Market St., Wilmington
(910) 815-0810

Caprice Bistro's second floor is an intimate, New York–style sofa bar, perfect for relaxing with a martini or glass of wine. The Caprice martinis are amazing concoctions of the finest liquors and delectable ingredients. Their chocolate martinis will send you to chocolate-lovers' heaven, or try one of their seasonal martini specials, made with fresh fruit ingredients and garnished with locally grown herbs. During the early evening, the setting is romantic, with candlelight and soft music, but after 11 PM the music gets turned up a notch as the crowd gathers. This is the place to go in downtown Wilmington to enjoy an after-theater martini or dessert with friends. The sofa bar is open until 2 AM. Their full dinner menu is served until 10 PM during the week and 11 PM on the weekends, and appetizers and desserts are available until midnight.

Fat Tony's Italian Pub
131 N. Front St., Wilmington
(910) 343-8881
250 Racine Dr., Wilmington
(910) 451-9000
www.fatpub.com

A staple of Wilmington's downtown nightlife, Fat Tony's Italian Pub has a selection of 24 draft beers that are hands down the best in town. One of the stops along the Haunted Pub Crawl, Fat Tony's has a house brew that's called the "Haunted Pub Brew" in honor of the ghosts (former guests of the old Orton Hotel that burned down in the 1940s) who are said to linger here at the site of their old haunt. With Fat Tony's selection of beers on tap, a big-screen TV and plenty of seats and pub tables, you won't want to leave either. Along with your beer, you can enjoy Fat

Tony's late-night menu of Pizza Chip Nachos and New York–style pizza with all the toppings. There's also live music and an outdoor deck with a fabulous view of the river. Fat Tony's Italian Pub is open until 2 AM Monday through Saturday and midnight on Sunday. Fat Tony's has another location on Racine Drive, near UNCW.

Hell's Kitchen
118 Princess St., Wilmington
(910) 763-4133

Formerly a set for the locally filmed TV show Dawson's Creek, Hell's Kitchen has fast become a popular downtown destination for good times among friends. This pub-style setting has a fun atmosphere, so when you're feeling devilishly hungry, stop by and try something from their menu of pub sandwiches, burritos and nachos. Hell's Kitchen has a full liquor bar and offers a wide variety of draft and microbrew beers. Hell's Kitchen is open in the afternoon until closing at 2 AM.

Level 5 at City Stage
21 N. Front St., Wilmington
(910) 342-0272

Located on the top level of downtown's former Masonic temple, Level 5 has the best rooftop view in town. On summer nights locals and tourists alike mingle beneath the bar's massive awning and enjoy cool breezes off the Cape Fear River. Inside, a 250-seat theater boasts a fall through spring theater schedule produced by the owners of the club. The bar features deejays Friday and Saturday evenings and karaoke on Monday evenings. Available for private parties, the theater/bar combination lends itself well to wedding receptions and fund-raising events. The bar opens at 5 PM every day so you can enjoy a sunset cocktail from this lofty downtown perch.

Longstreet's Irish Pub
135 N. Front St., Wilmington
(910) 343-8788

Named after a Civil War general, Longstreet's was once part-owned by actor Tom Berenger, who portrayed General Longstreet in the film Gettysburg. Longstreet's is a cozy basement pub in the Irish tradition, offering several draft and bottled beers, nightly beer specials, mixed drinks, an Internet jukebox, Foosball, a jukebox and live music. The pub is located in what used to be the barbershop of the old Orton Hotel, which was destroyed in a fire in the 1940s (and may still have a few ghostly guests). The Fat Tony's Italian Pub menu is available at Longstreet's, so you can enjoy fabulous homemade Italian food and New York–style pizza along with your pint of Guinness. Longstreet's is open Monday through Saturday until 2 AM and closed on Sundays.

Orton's Pool Room
133 N. Front St., Wilmington
(910) 343-8881

Known as "America's Oldest Pool Room," Orton's is located in what was the basement space of the old Orton Hotel prior to its burning in the 1940s. The space is entirely renovated, and with 17 satellite televisions with NFL Ticket, it's a perfect place for catching a sports event. But it's the pool that keeps people coming to Orton's. Where else can you play on the very table used by the famed Willie Mosconi in 1953 to set a world billiards record of 365 consecutive balls? Take a trip downstairs and into history with a game of pool at Orton's. The pool room has competition Brunswick tables, coin-op tables, a dart alley and an Internet jukebox, and Orton's has all ABC permits.

Rack 'M Pub and Billiards
415 S. College Rd., Wilmington
(910) 792-6000

This club-style parlor is open Monday through Saturday from 3 PM until 2 AM and Sundays from noon until 2 AM. After 10 PM you must be age 21 or older to enter. You'll find it in the rear of the University Landing shopping center near Krazy Pizza & Subs.

Rum Runners: Dueling Piano Bar
21 N. Front St., Wilmington
(910) 815-3846

Rum Runners is one of downtown Wilmington's hottest night spots. With its wildly tropical atmosphere, hanging out at Rum Runners will make you feel as though you're whiling away the hours on a Caribbean island. Then there is the high-energy show — two baby grand pianos played simultaneously (dueling pianos) by entertainers who encourage the audience to sing along with hit tunes from the '50s all the way up to the '90s. Advance reservations are highly recommended for their popular dueling piano show. Rum Runners opens Wednesday through Sunday and the fun continues until 2 AM.

The Rusty Nail at Beatty's Tavern
1310 S. Fifth Ave., Wilmington
(910) 251-1888

Live blues and jazz enthusiasts won't want to miss this downtown Wilmington club's weekly line-up. The Blues Society of the Lower Cape Fear cuts loose on Tuesdays and the first Saturday of each month. Gary Allen's Acoustic Open Mic Night is on Wednesdays. Various local bands play live on Friday and Saturday nights; call for a complete schedule. Benny Hill's Jazz Jam is a Sunday-night tradition. This live-performance venue includes a state-of-the-art digital recording studio designed to capture some of the amazing music performed here. Open daily at 1 PM, Sundays at noon, the club has all ABC permits, serves beer and wine, and offers bar specials. The Rusty Nail is a private club, but non-members can be signed in as guests. New members are welcome, and fees are reasonable, with several membership options available. Call the club for details. Located between Marstellar and Greenfield streets, the club boasts its own parking lot, a rarity in downtown Wilmington.

The Soap Box Laundro-Lounge
255 N. Front St., Wilmington
(910) 251-8500

The Soap Box Laundro-Lounge is downtown Wilmington's great space for laundry, lounging and libations, as well as the best in local, national and international entertainment. Featuring three floors, including downtown's only Laundromat, a venue for live music, a river-view bar and an art gallery called The Art Box, The Soap Box has something for everyone. They're open until 2 AM every night of the week.

Wrightsville Beach

Buddy's Crab House & Oyster Bar
13 E. Salisbury St., Wrightsville Beach
(910) 256-8966

Located a short stroll away from the sands of Wrightsville Beach, Buddy's Crab House & Oyster Bar is a funky reprieve from the heat of the beach. Wanting to follow the philosophy of Jimmy Buffet, the staff has created a lounge for the laidback lifestyle. Large, fold-open windows provide a cooling ocean breeze that complements a frosty beer perfectly. With an ambiance that blends nautical and tropical, it's impossible not to feel at ease. Buddy's full menu boasts Southern coastal classics such as oyster pecks, shrimp baskets and fried oyster po'boy sandwiches. Buddy's is open year round.

King Neptune's Pirate Lounge
11 N. Lumina Ave., Wrightsville Beach
(910) 256-2525

The Pirate Lounge in the King Neptune Restaurant is as lively as its proprietor, Bernard Carroll, who did the research to accurately identify all the pirate flags hanging in the room. It's the kind of decor you might expect of someone who'd rather be sailing, and, as a salt should, Carroll places importance on rum. His "Rum Bar" features some 19 premium rums from around the world, including Gosling's and Appleton Estate Jamaican Rum. Micro-brewed and imported beers are always in stock, and an inexpensive Pub Grub menu offers plenty of quality munchies (avail-

able for take-out). The lounge is open every day and has all ABC permits.

Lagerheads Tavern
35 N. Lumina Ave., Wrightsville Beach
(910) 256-0171

A favorite spot of locals, Lagerheads is located directly on the main drag of Wrightsville Beach. The inside bar offers a laidback, rustic atmosphere with low-lighting and woodwork that gives off the mystique of a pirate-ship's hull. Live music is offered on weekends, and the fully stocked jukebox is loved by classic rock listeners. Grab a cold beer and head outside to the front porch, where pets are welcome and you can engage in an Insiders' favorite pastime of people-watching. Lagerheads is open every day of the week until 2 AM.

The Palm Room
11 E. Salisbury St., Wrightsville Beach
(910) 509-3040

Located a few strolls away from Johnny Mercer's pier, the beach scene mural painted over the front of this building won't let you just pass by. A chilled out local spot to enjoy bands, karaoke, or

Sometimes all you need are a couple of comfy Adirondack chairs and a stunning view.

photo: George Mitchell

some leisurely games of pool and foosball, the inside vibes perfectly correspond with coastal culture. There are different drink specials daily, with Tuesday's offering an all-you-can-drink for $5 - but get there a little early, cause it's an Insiders' favorite and as soon as the kegs are tapped, so is the deal!

Red Dogs
5 N. Lumina Ave., Wrightsville Beach
(910) 256-2776

Since 1975, Red Dogs has been a haven for surfers and skaters alike. Almost shut down by the powers of Wrightsville Beach three times, this spot has made itself a sort of local legend with their dedication to keeping the doors open and commitment to keep it worth it. There are two levels, both wearing a gnarly, surf-themed atmosphere and plenty of room to chill back in a booth or get groovy on a dance floor. Every Thursday night boasts live music matched with an energetic crowd. To really get a taste of local spirit, try one of their famous "Fish Bowl" con-coctions.

Carolina Beach

Black Horn Bar & Kitchen
15 Carolina Beach Ave. N, Carolina Beach
(910) 458-5255

The Black Horn Bar and Kitchen is the best spot on the Boardwalk at Carolina Beach to grab a drink with friends or a leisurely dinner. Their menu mixes typical American classics with innovative twists, including fried green beans and a knife and fork tuna melt with sushi-grade fish. With over 20 hi-definition plasma screens, the Black Horn is also a hot spot for sports fans. The Black Horn also features live music throughout the week.

Southport and Oak Island

Though the Southport-Oak Island area is very much a family-oriented/fishing area, the growing population has engendered more venues for evening entertainment. Some of these are new restaurants that sometimes have live

Whatever cuisine you're craving, you'll find it on the southern coast.

photo: John Golden

music, especially on weekends. Be sure to check out our Restaurants chapter, consult the local newspaper calendars and call the restaurants that interest you. We have listed some places and activities here that are specifically geared to nighttime fun, however, you may want to check out the Attractions and Arts chapters as well. Here you will find such evening events as Ghost Walks, Gallery Walks and theater productions.

49th Street Game Room and Bar
4901 E. Oak Island Dr., Oak Island
(910) 278-9811

If you are looking for a neighborhood bar where you can relax with a drink after work or socialize and play a game or two of pool, the Station is the one. Being a nicely refurbished former gas station, it is small, but large enough to hold the enthusiastic crowd that gathers for karaoke. The Station is also known for spearheading fund drives for persons suffering as as result of catastrophes or loss of income. Be it a cookout, a float in the Christmas Parade or a Poker Run, they help those less fortunate. Hours of operation are noon until 2 AM seven days a week. Don't miss the Friday night DJs.

Bella Cucina Restaurant & Pizzeria
5177 Southport-Supply Rd., Southport
(910) 454-4540

At Bella Cucina you will find Tuscan-style food made with recipes handed down in the family and using only the freshest ingredients. A big-screen TV is available for viewing your favorite sporting events. For great NY-style pizza, calzones, stromboli and hot and cold subs, visit their Pizzeria next door. It is open until 9 PM daily; call (910) 454-4357.

Chasers Sports Bar & Grill
8520 E. Oak Island Dr., Oak Island
(910) 278-1500

Open seven days a week year round, Chasers remains a favorite place for locals to gather. Here they can share an after-work drink, discuss their golf games and compare scores, socialize and get a good meal and drinks at affordable prices. Don't miss the sporting events, which you can

watch on any of the TVs from seating at the bar or any table in the room.

Concerts on the Coast
Free Concert Series
Garrison House, E. Bay St., Southport
(910) 253-2672, (800) 222-4790

Supported by a grant from the Brunswick Arts Council and sponsored by the Brunswick County Parks and Recreation Department and the Southport Parks and Recreation Department, this outdoor summer concert series features a variety of live bands playing at the Garrison House in the heart of historic Southport. This popular event is held June through September on Tuesday evenings from 6:30 until 8 PM. Call for dates and the schedule or check the Brunswick County website in May for more details.

Duffer's Pub & Grille
928 Caswell Beach Rd., Oak Island
(910) 278-9299

Located on the second floor at the Oak Island Golf Club (see our Golf section), Duffer's Pub & Grille offers a spectacular view of the Atlantic Ocean on one side and the golf greens on the other. White linens on the tables in the dining/banquet room along with the flickering of candles set into the fireplace give an understated elegance to your dining experience. Duffer's offers a fully stocked bar featuring premium liquors and cordials, bottled and draft beer and an excellent wine list. You will find entertainment on Tuesday nights and, in warmer months, Deck Parties on the spacious deck overlooking the golf course. A banquet room is available for private parties. The bar is open every day from 11:30 until. Lunch and dinner are served daily.

Slainte
Smithville Crossing, 1513 N. Howe St., Southport
(910) 457-6554

The owners of Slainte worked hard to make it look like an old Irish pub — to excellent results, with a copper-topped bar and dark woodwork everywhere. Music is kept to a minimum so you can enjoy good conversation as you indulge in traditional

Irish fare such as fish and chips, corned beef and cabbage, and shepherd's pie. You can imbibe in Irish whiskey and Guinness as well as other bar concoctions until 2 AM. With five TVs you can enjoy watching NFL, NASCAR, soccer, rugby and Major League Baseball from any seat in the house. Outdoor seating is available as well.

Southport Film Nights
Garrison Lawn, on the Waterfront, Southport
(910) 457-7927, (800) 388-9635

This outdoor film series takes place the second Friday of each month beginning in June and extending through October with a special screening in December. Moviegoers are invited to bring lawn chairs, blankets, picnics, family and friends to enjoy these free screenings. Call the Southport Visitors Center at the number above for details, times and movie titles.

Spectator's Sports Lounge and Grill
8039 River Rd., Southport
(910) 457-9994

Spectator's caters to locals and families. It's definitely a great place for the sports enthusiast with its wide-screen TVs and a seating capacity of 55 at two-tops and four-tops, as well as at the full bar. In addition to drinks, Spectator's serves daily specials and light casual fare, such as mozzarella sticks, fried mushrooms, bloomin' onions, Philly cheese steaks, Reubens, Angus burgers, quesadillas, chicken Parmesan and their specialty, Spectator's Fried House Salad. They also have occasional live entertainment; call for schedule.

Summer Concert Series
Waterford Village Shoppes, U.S. Hwy. 17 S., Leland

This lively concert series, sponsored by Time Warner Cable and WHQR 91.3 FM Radio, is held the first Friday of May, June and July. The concerts start at 7 Pm and last until 10 PM. Bring your lawn chairs and coolers and enjoy these free concerts.

Holden Beach

Concerts on the Coast
Free Concert Series (HB)
Intracoastal Waterway Stage, Jordan Blvd., Holden Beach
(910) 253-2672, (800) 222-4790

Supported by a grant from the Brunswick Arts Council and sponsored by the Brunswick County Parks and Recreation Department and the Greater Holden Beach Merchants Association, this outdoor summer concert series features a variety of live bands. The concerts are held on a new pavilion stage at the Intracoastal Waterway Stage on Jordan Boulevard, located near the base of the Holden Beach bridge, on Sundays from 6:30 until 8 PM May through September. Call for dates and a schedule.

Surf City

The Brass Pelican Tavern
2112 N. New River Dr., Surf City

The Brass Pelican is an old Topsail Island favorite for local residents and returning visitors. Their large outdoor back deck is a great place to spend a summer evening under the stars. The private club's membership fee is $5, and visitors can be signed in by a member. Entertainment is provided on Friday and Saturday nights with karaoke on Thursdays. Menu choices include deli sandwiches, appetizers and steamed seafood in the evening. There are also daily drink and food specials.

ab Pot
8 Roland Ave., Surf City
0) 328-5001

This funky spot is popular with locals and ks who like beach music and shagging, the nce of the beach crowd. The "Shag Shack," it's known, rocks all summer with beach nds, local DJs and shaker cans. Crab Pot has asual screened-in dining room and bar. No e is a stranger here.

lligan's
C. Hwy. 50, Surf City
0) 328-4090

Gilligan's is a private club with a member-p fee of $5, though visitors may be signed by a member for the evening. Gilligan's has a large dance floor and often offers live entertainment during the summer. A shuttle service is always available, and it's open daily year round.

Margarita's Bar & Grill
2111 N. New River Dr., Surf City
(910) 328-3066

Get ready to shag because the DJs here spin beach music on weekends. Feel the urge to belt out a tune? Margarita's hosts karaoke nights every Wednesday and Thursday. If you work up an appetite singing and danc-ing, Margarita's dishes up the only late-night breakfast on the island, serving between 11 PM and 4 AM.

🎁 SHOPPING

If shopping is your passion, North Carolina's southern coast offers abundant opportunities to indulge it. Wilmington and the surrounding areas include a wide range of shopping options, from one-of-a-kind boutiques to national chain mega-stores. Whether your tastes lean toward the traditional, eclectic, funky or old-fashioned, you'll find what you're looking for here.

Shopping centers, both large and small, lure shoppers with aesthetically pleasing architecture, attractive landscaping, sculptured art, plentiful parking and upscale shops that rival those in any major metropolitan area. These multi-use commercial centers also include restaurants, office space and service providers. Lumina Station, Landfall Center, Mayfaire Town Center and The Forum are excellent examples of this type of center and all are described in this chapter.

Primary business and shopping areas for the Port City include downtown Wilmington, the College Road area, Market Street, Oleander Drive, Monkey Junction and the Military Cutoff/Eastwood Road area adjacent to Wrightsville Beach. However, don't hesitate to venture onto side streets, too, where you'll discover a host of shopping treasures and off-the-beaten-path gems.

Wilmington also has the area's greatest concentration of superstores and discount chains, including Walmart, Best Buy, Target, Sears, JCPenney, Home Depot, Petsmart, Sam's Club, Costco, Office Max and Stein Mart, in addition to the upscale Belk and Dillard's department stores.

As you explore the region's shopping options, you will notice that coastal North Carolinians love gourmet foods, wine, imported cheeses, hard-to-find herbs and spices, ethnic cooking and specialty bakeries. Local food markets and chain grocery stores, while not covered in this chapter, also are abundant throughout the area and will stock or order new items at a customer's request.

This chapter contains a mere sampling of available shopping possibilities, including some of the unique as well as the tried-and-true shops. These have been divided into easy-to-read sections of the major areas of Wilmington, the Wrightsville Beach vicinity and the coastal communities of Carolina Beach, Topsail Island, Southport-Oak Island and the South Brunswick beaches. For the off-season visitor traveling to the beach communities, most of the stores and businesses included in this chapter offer year-round hours of operation. However, some reduce or limit these hours in the winter months, so it is wise to call ahead to make sure the store will be open when you plan to visit.

Historic Downtown Wilmington

Browsing the quaint shops and boutiques of downtown Wilmington is a history lesson as well as a shopping experience. Surrounded by the city's beautiful historic homes and museums, brick streets and serene waterfront, the downtown area provides a relaxed and unique shopping locale. Rare are the shoppers who aren't tempted to slow their steps in this tranquil setting. Personal service by business owners and a cozy, small-town atmosphere further add to the shopping experience.

Most of the stores concentrated along the streets of downtown Wilmington are independently owned and reflect the interests and tastes of their owners. You won't encounter rack after rack of the same items. Here you'll find art galleries, antiques shops, fine clothing, funky garb, beachwear, toys, gourmet items, music,

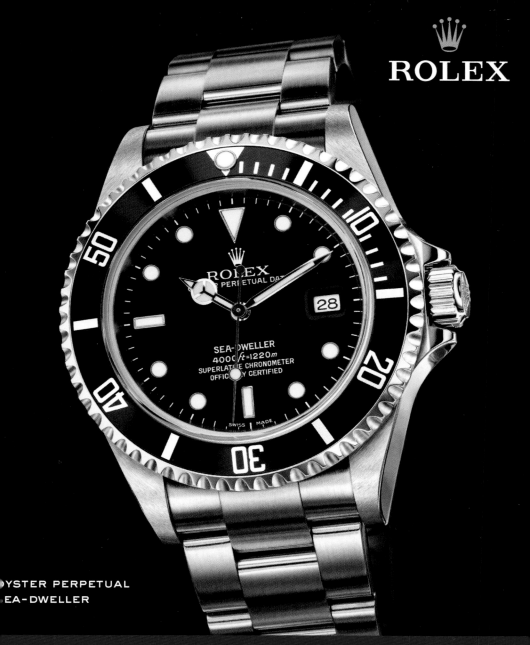

ROLEX

OYSTER PERPETUAL
SEA-DWELLER

KINGOFF'S
JEWELERS
...since 1919

PLATINUM

Portraits · Kids · Families · Pets · Weddings · Senior Class Portraits
Headshots · Composite Cards

PATRICIA ROSEMAN
P H O T O G R A P H Y

East Coast **310.766.6011** West Coast

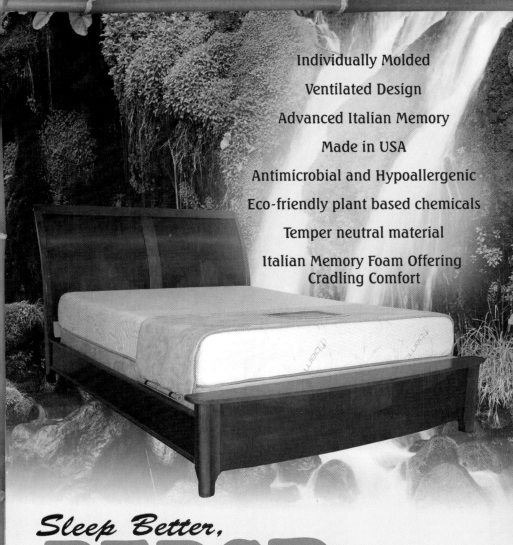

wine, linens, glassware, candies, fine and costume jewelry, collectibles, books, home furnishings, scents, candles and more.

Part of the charm of this shopping district is its compact size and pleasant walkability. Park your car on the street, in one of several parking decks, or, if you're shopping at one of the retail/dining centers, park at no cost in their lots. Downtown is like an open-air mall with an astonishing selection of spots in which to pause and take in the beautiful scenery. Coffee shops, delicatessens, pubs, ice cream parlors, candy shops and full-service restaurants offer constant temptation to shoppers. Many restaurants have outdoor seating right on the sidewalk, a setup guaranteed to lure your weary feet to pause.

Downtown is anchored by two large centers, The Cotton Exchange, a shopping/dining/office complex at the northern end of the riverfront, and Chandler's Wharf, a retail and office center at the southern end. The area between — Water Street, Front Street, Second and Third Streets and their cross streets — includes several busy city blocks lined with restaurants, galleries, banks, services and stores that offer a wide variety of shopping possibilities. Antiques buffs, surrounded by the heady sense of Southern coastal history, will find it impossible to bypass downtown Wilmington's pleasing variety of antiques stores. (See our section on Antiques in this chapter.)

Candles Etc.
Chandler's Wharf, 2 Ann St., Wilmington
(910) 763-1703, (877) 763-1703

The largest Root Candle distributor on the East Coast, Candles Etc. has all 24 colors and 42 fragrances made by this upscale candle company, as well as other high-quality, eco-friendly candles, including The Old Wilmington Candle, produced on-site by their staff. Candles Etc. is the exclusive dealer for Wilmington Historic Prints and Marta Mikey table sculpture. They also carry a wide array of unique home decor items. You'll want to browse for a while, but don't miss the fabulous view of the river from the Cape Fear River Deck, which is available for event rental.

Chandler's Wharf
225 S. Water St., Wilmington
(910) 343-9896

Overlooking the river at the corner of Ann and Water streets, Chandler's Wharf offers many appealing shopping opportunities. Created by Thomas Henry Wright Jr. in the late 1970s, it has evolved over time as a retail/dining complex, but part of it began as a ship's chandler in the nineteenth century. There was a maritime museum here in the 1970s and some marine artifacts are still scattered about the grounds, including an enormous anchor and other reminders of the complex's origins. Cobblestone streets, plank walkways, attractive landscaping and a gorgeous view of the Cape Fear River are a few of the hallmarks that make shopping at Chandler's Wharf such a pleasant experience. The center is flourishing with some of Wilmington's most delightful stores. It also boasts two of the city's most appealing restaurants, The Pilot House and Elijah's (see our Restaurants section). Dining in any one of these is a pleasure heightened by the option of enjoying your meal on outdoor decks overlooking the river.

Some of the shops at Chandler's Wharf include **A Proper Garden**, (910) 763-7177, which has everything and more for the garden and gardener; **A. Scott Rhodes**, (910) 763-6616, a full-service jewelry store specializing in custom design and offering selections in fine diamonds, precious stones, local estate jewelry and designer pieces; and **Candles Etc.**, (910) 763-1703, exclusive distributors of Root Candles and Wilmington Historic Prints.

Chandler's Wharf's remarkable creative gallery scene lures shoppers inside. **Clay Goddess Studio,** a working artisan studio, features clay figurines, fabric and pottery as well as classes and **River to Sea**, (910) 520-2673, exhibits owner Rebecca Duffy's delightfully painted children's pictures and water-related wall hangings, as well as the work of 32 artists of various mediums. **Una Luna**, (910) 772-1777, landed at Chandler's Wharf this year and features African folk art and unique furniture. The gallery also represents local artist legend Ivey Hayes. Don't miss their Friday Full Moon parties with wine tastings. **Artichoke**, (910) 763-

7305, is a unique women's clothing and accessory store that brings a little bit of Soho to downtown Wilmington. **Creations by Justine**, (910) 763-4545, features the clay masterpieces of nationally renowned sculptress Justine Ferreri. **Emily Parker**, (910) 515-0953, makes custom jewelry and demonstrates wax model carving for lost-wax casting. After gallery-hoping enjoy fine coffee, a delicious meal and a great river view at **Barista Bakery and Café**, (910) 409-3440, open for breakfast and lunch daily.

The Cotton Exchange
321 N. Front St., Wilmington
(910) 343-9896

The site of the largest cotton-export-ing company in the world in the nine-teenth century, this collection of eight buildings overlooking the Cape Fear River was converted into a shopping and dining center in the early 1970s. Its renovation marked the beginning of the restoration of downtown Wilmington. Shoppers can enjoy a bit of history as they stroll the mall's tri-level space, where displays of cotton bales, weighing equipment and photographs tell the story of the center's evolution and about many downtown locations. Parking is free in the large lot for visitors of the complex.

The sampling of specialty shops listed here suggests the scope of shopping possibilities at The Cotton Exchange (all stores are within the complex bounded by Water and Front streets). **T. S. Brown Jewelry**, (910) 762-3467, specializes in loose gems, custom settings and hand-crafted pieces. **The Celtic Shop**, (910) 763-1990, features imported Irish and Scottish clothing, Celtic music, jewelry, clan heraldry items, books, authentic Irish breakfast tea and many other gift ideas. **Occasions ... just write!**, (910) 343-9033, features social stationery and invitations, fine writing instruments, sealing wax, journals and desk accessories plus a large selection of cards. **Two Sisters Bookery**, (910) 762-4444, carries a surprisingly wide range of books, including ones of local interest, as well as cards and gifts. **Caravan Beads**, (910) 343-0550, is a bead-lovers paradise offering classes and a venue for birthday parties. **Port City Pottery and Fine Crafts**, (910) 763-7111, features the work of 21 local artists showcasing woodworking, pottery, baskets, metal and weaving. **The Golden Gallery**, (910) 762-4651, exhibits Mary Ellen Golden's watercolor paintings of local scenery. **Pure Life Health Food and Vitamins**, (910) 343-1374, carries a large selection of herbal and loose teas, teapots, and tea accessories. Vitamins, salves, and holistic therapies are only a few items in their inventory.

Some other shops you'll find worth visiting are **Java Dog Coffeehouse**, (910) 343-8890, for specialty coffee drinks and pastries; **Crescent Moon**, (910) 762-4207, for handcrafted stained and blown glass; **Down to Earth**, (910) 251-0041, an aroma-therapy gift shop; **Hummingbird Station/ Candy Store**, (910) 762-3727, for crafts, garden accents, nature-themed gifts, homemade candies, fudge and taffy; and **Cape Fear Footwear**, (910) 763-9945, which carries a large selection of sandals (including Rainbows), handbags and scarves. Don't forget to visit **Top Toad/ Carribean Amphibian**, (910) 343-9245, for Wilmington T-shirts and hats and beach apparel.

Once you have worked up an appetite, try one of The Cotton Exchange's res-taurants, such as **The German Cafe**, (910) 763-5523, which is known for its fresh soups, schnitzels and strudels. If you're more in the mood for a pub atmosphere, stop by **Paddy's Hollow Restaurant & Pub**, (910) 762-4354, which carries a diverse menu of pub favorites. New to The Cotton Exchange is **The Basics**, (910) 343-1050, which has wowed patrons with its "gour-met soul food." Or for just a mid-afternoon treat, get a double dip at **The Scoop**, (910) 763-3566.

Island Passage Elixir
4 Market St., Wilmington
(910) 762-0484

Located near the waterfront at the end of Market Street, this charming bou-tique offers the latest trends in women's clothing fashions as well as a selection of personalized gifts, jewelry and shoes. Visit Island Passage's other Wilmington location, Island Passage at Lumina Station, 1900 Eastwood Road near Wrightsville

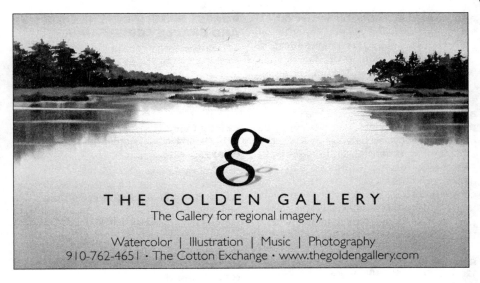

Beach, (910) 256-0407. If you're on Bald Head Island, check out Island Passage's three stores, which include Riverside Adventure Company, (910) 457-4944, your one-stop kayak, bike and golf-cart rental shop for everything you need to enjoy the traffic-free pleasures of the locale; a larger Bald Head Island location on Maritime Way, called Maritime Passage, (910) 454-8420, which has a fabulous selection of clothing, shoes and accessories for men, women and children; and Canopy Outfitters, (910) 454-8248, specializing in comfortable, versatile clothing for the entire family. You won't want to miss the newest shop, Return Passage, 302 N. Front Street, Wilmington, (910) 343-1627, which carries deeply discounted merchandise from all the other Island Passage stores, as well as gently worn items.

The Old Wilmington City Market
119 S. Water St., Wilmington

The Old Wilmington City Market is a riverfront gem. This historic brick and stucco building, built in 1879, stretches a city block in width between Front and Water streets. From its humble origins as a vegetable market, this old world–style arcade with glass skylights throughout is now a shopping haven featuring art galleries and chic specialty shops, including women's boutiques, T-shirts, hats, jewelry, fresh-cut flowers in season, plants, gardening supplies, handmade local soaps, unique exotic woods, imported goods and works by local artists. The market also features a relaxing seating area. It's open year round, but hours vary according to season.

Return Passage
302 N. Front St., Wilmington
(910) 343-1627

On N. Front Street, just a few blocks from Island Passage Elixir, is the latest Island Passage shop. Return Passage has deeply discounted merchandise from all of the other Island Passage locations, as well as gently worn items. They carry the hottest name brands and styles of once-worn clothing, and their inventory changes constantly. At Return Passage, you can trade in your gently worn clothing for cash or store credit that can be used at any of the Island Passage boutiques.

Revolution 9
The Cotton Exchange, Wilmington
(910) 762-8440

Revolution 9 (formerly A Little Bit Hippy) is a paradise of rock-n-roll paraphernalia. With the tagline "peace, threads and rock-n-roll," the store offers an array of T-shirts, postersand other items featuring bands like the Beatles, the Stones, Pink Floyd, the Allman Brothers, the Grateful Dead, Marley, Hendrix, Janis, Led Zeppelin, the Who and many more. Revolution 9 also stocks patchwork and hemp clothing, purses, hats and jewelry. Prefer to make and wear your own creation? Check out their tie-dye clothing kits. For those who want to make a statement, the store boasts one of the largest local selections of bumper stickers and buttons. You will also find Heirloom Spoons, a line of rings, bracelets, wind chimes, earrings and pens made from recycled flatware by a local artist, among other N.C.–crafted goods. And the store demonstrates a touch of altruism with its recycled phone drive; you can drop off your old, unused cell phones there, and the interior parts will be reused to make calling cards for the military troops overseas.

Rôpa, Etc.
120-B S. Front St., Wilmington
(910) 815-0344

Rôpa, Etc. is the area's exclusive retailer for such lines as Flax, Willow and Cut-Loose. This terrific shop also carries Rico and Pure hand-knit sweaters, TSD and Habitat, offering easy-care fabrics with style and comfort guaranteed. Rôpa, Etc. is also known for its unique collection of hand-wrought American and European jewelry plus great accessories to complement any outfit. Other Rôpa, Etc. stores in the area include their location at The Forum, 1121-D Military Cutoff Road, and their Southport location at 417-C N. Howe Street.

Twice Baked Pottery Painting Studio
6 Market St., Wilmington
(910) 343-8996

You can while away a few hours after a stroll along the riverfront by stopping in the Twice Baked Pottery Painting Studio. Choose from a wide variety of items to create your own unique pottery piece. With more than 50 paint colors, as well as stencils, stamps and idea books, this is a fun place to forget your troubles and just get into a creative mood. The setting is very cozy and creative, with the owner's and other artist's art displayed for inspiration. Hours are seasonal, so be sure to check their website for updates.

FOREST HILLS, INDEPENDENCE AND BRADLEY CREEK AREA

Midtown Wilmington is defined as stretching from Historic Downtown Wilmington to the Wrightsville Beach vicinity. It includes two main Wilmington thoroughfares, College Road and Oleander Drive.

Crabby Chic
3910 Oleander Dr., Wilmington
(910) 799-4216

Crabby Chic is your destination for a vast array of wonderful gifts, coastal home furnishings and decorative accessories. This delightful store specializes in shabby chic furnishings with a coastal inspiration.

DDT Outlet
Independence Mall, Wilmington
(910) 779-4825
www.ddtoutlet.com

Known as "your beach furniture experts," DDT Outlet has expanded its Wilmington retail locations with a new store at Independence Mall. With its selection of nautical home decor and indoor and outdoor furniture,this is not your typical mall store. You can outfit your home with their unique merchandise, find an unusual gift, or commemorate your trip to Wilmington with a high-quality souvenir. If you're on the hunt for new furniture, you can update your living room with their beautiful Flexsteel couches, or enjoy the view from your deck with their low-maintenance Telescope Casual outdoor table sets. While you're there, be sure to check out their fun retro section featuring Elvis and Betty Boop collector's items. The mall store carries a small showcase of DDT's array of indoor and outdoor furniture; for the full selection, visit the large showrooms at their Hampstead and Ogden stores. All DDT locations are open seven days a week.

Hanover Center
3501 Oleander Dr., Wilmington
(910) 343-9739

This lively strip center was Wilmington's original shopping destination. Opened in 1956 before any other strip malls, it has been completely remodeled and remains a popular shopping venue.

Listed below are merchants and businesses currently located in Hanover Center.

AAA Vacations, (910) 763-8446, offers vacation, travel and insurance services, plus it's a AAA Motor Club office. Four full-service banking centers with ATMs are **Bank of America**, (910) 251-5285; **BB&T**, (910) 313-2000; **RBC Centura**, (910) 772-8890; and **Cooperative Bank**, (910) 392-7894. **Wild Bird and Garden**, (910) 343-6001, offers backyard nature products, garden accessories and seed for attracting birds. **Great Clips**, (910) 362-0054, is a moderately priced salon providing haircuts and permanents. **Great Outdoor Provision Company**, (910) 343-1648, carries outdoor clothing, equipment, footwear and accessories for fly fishing, backpacking, climbing and paddle sports. **Omega Sports**, (910) 762-7212, a running specialty store, offers sporting gear, apparel and shoes. **Learning Express Toys**, (910) 251-6636, specializes in unique and educational toys, books and games that capture imaginations.

K & W Cafeteria, (910) 762-7011, serves some of the best food in town. **J. Michael's**

Philly Deli, (910) 763-6466, is a great place for sandwiches and other deli fare for lunch and dinner. For delicious lunch options (soups, salads, sandwiches, quiche), try **Temptations Everyday Gourmet**, (910) 763-6662, which also sells gourmet treats, chocolates and sweets, North Carolina specialty foods, coffee, tea, wine and gourmet gift baskets. **Harris Teeter**, (910) 343-4216, will take care of all your grocery shopping needs. **Rite Aid**, (910) 763-3367, is a convenient and reliable pharmacy drugstore. For a quick, tasty meal, there's **Chick-Fil-A**, (910) 452-9399. **Cafe Brava**, (910) 762-1171, is open daily 7 AM to 5 PM for breakfast, bagels, lattes, salads, and smoothies. It's also the only place in Wilmington to buy imported South American spices, sauces, and cookies. **Hardees**, (910) 791-5457, offers a quick meal any time.

At **Stein Mart**, (910) 772-1533, you'll find upscale merchandise at discount prices, including clothing, shoes, gifts, linens and accessories. **Sterling House**, (910) 763-3656, is a local retail tradition, offering unique gifts, jewelry, collectibles, home accessories, the full line of Vera Bradley luggage and handbags, Hallmark cards, fine stationery, and outstanding customer service. **Kingoff's Jewelers**, (910) 256-4321, has everything you need for that special someone. **Picture This**, (910) 762-2780, offers arts, gifts and home decor items. **SAS Shoes**, (910) 772-9994, sells comfort shoes for men and women and the complete line of San Antonio Shoes, with extended sizes available. **Shoe Shak**, (910) 772-9993, sells fashion footwear for adults in a wide range of sizes. They also carry handbags and jewelry. **Talbots**, (910) 313-1100, sells high-quality, classic clothing for women.

Adjacent to the main block of Hanover Center is another strip of stores, Azalea Plaza, which is home to **Pier 1 Imports**, (910) 392-3151; **Books-A-Million**, (910) 452-1519; and **Office Depot**, (910) 392-9013.

The Herb Shop
Oleander Oaks, 5725 Oleander Dr., Ste. B8, Wilmington
(910) 452-4372

Owned and operated by a registered pharmacist since 1994, The Herb Shop has the right products for you. A broad range of vitamins, supplements, homeopathic remedies and herbal nutritionals are available. Numerous reputable product lines are featured as well as bulk herbs. You can also find a large variety of teas. Be sure to try some of their excellent smoothies and coffees. Qualified health professionals provide free weight-control and health counseling on-site.

Independence Mall
3500 Oleander Dr., Wilmington
(910) 392-1776

Independence Mall, known simply as "the mall" by area residents, has more than 150 stores offering a wealth of shopping opportunities in an attractive and climate-controlled environment. Planning to "shop 'til you drop"? Strategically placed throughout the mall are groups of upholstered chairs (with a few coin-operated "massage chairs"). You'll find a 400-seat food court with plenty of eateries. **Sears**, **JC Penney**, **Belk** and **Dillard's** department stores anchor this complex of trademark stores, independent shop owners and rented kiosk vendors. There are sporting goods shops, jewelry stores, shoe stores, specialty gift stores, fragrance and bath shops, music stores, home furnishing stores, an impressive range of apparel boutiques for the whole family ranging from infant-size to adult plus sizes, full-service salons, nail care, banking services and much more.

Can't decide on the perfect gift? Gift cards, redeemable in any of the mall stores or restaurants where American Express is honored, are a good choice. The mall management office, located near JC Penney, provides Kiddie Kruzzers, wheelchairs, gift cards, faxing and copying services and friendly assistance. Electric wheelchairs are also available for free. A family rest area, adjacent to the food court, offers co-ed children's bathrooms, changing stations, private nursing areas and TV. Independence Mall is open daily.

Kingoff's Jewelers
Hanover Center, 3501 Oleander Dr., Wilmington
(910) 762-5219
www.kingoffs.com

Jewelers since 1919, Kingoff's offers a large selection of fine diamonds and colored stone jewelry in 18K, 14K and platinum. They also offer Tag Heuer watches and gifts by Waterford Crystal. Guaranteed watch and jewelry repairs are done on the premises, and four Guild Gemologists of the Diamond Council of America are available for appraisals. Kingoff's is the exclusive seller of the Old Wilmington Cup created in the early 1800s by Thomas Brown. This pewter cup is a favored gift among Wilmingtonians for a variety of special occasions. Kingoff's moved from their downtown location in November of 2009 to Hanover Shopping Center. Kingoff's also has a second location at 1119-B Military Cutoff Road.

Learning Express Toys
Hanover Ctr., 3501 Oleander Dr. #12, Wilmington
(910) 251-6636
www.learningexpresstoys.com/wilmington

Learning Express Toys is among those rare places that capture kids' imaginations with high-quality alternatives to the run-of-the-mill products. Interactive and entertaining, the stores succeed in

making learning fun for kids from infancy through early adolescence. The staff includes toy experts with broad knowledge of the products, which translates into excellent service. Learning Express Toys is organized in sections geared to particular interests, such as Science & Nature (including electronics and nature projects), Let's Pretend (fantasy dress-up, Playmobil and Webkinz), Great Beginnings (for infants and toddlers) and Transit (including remote control vehicles, Thomas and Darda race tracks). This is the place to find that volcano your child needs for the diorama. You can find Learning Express Toys in three locations: the Hanover Center store on Oleander Drive is a "come out and play" space with an I Spy Cloud Shapes in the Sky ceiling. Their original location on Military Cutoff Road offers a medieval theme with a giant castle mural in the center of the store. There is also a mini-store in the Children's Museum of Wilmington and a new Toy Take-Out Website for local online shopping with in-store pickup (http://learningexpresstoys.com/wilmington/). Learning Express Toys offers free personalizing, free gift wrapping and a popular Birthday Wish Box registry. Both Learning Express stores also feature a Grandparents' Club and daily UPS shipping. Their mission is to help you find the perfect toy.

Perry's Emporium
Barclay Commons,
520 Independence Blvd., Wilmington
(910) 392-6721, (800) 261-5705

Walk through the leaded-glass doors of Perry's Emporium and step back into the 1890s. Twenty-eight antique floor cases hold one of the largest collections of estate pieces in the city, in addition to more contemporary styles of fine jewelry, loose diamonds and silver flatware. An additional nine antique wall-display cases showcase jewelry, art, fine china and crystal. Celebrating more than a decade of service to the area, this 5,300-square-foot store is the largest retail jeweler in Wilmington. Perry's services include three full-service master jewelers, two graduate gemologists, lapidary services, jewelry repair and a bridal service. Appraisals are available for new, used and antique jewelry.

Protocol
3502 Wrightsville Ave., Wilmington
(910) 796-9595

A visit to Protocol is an absolute delight for the senses. Since John Jordan opened this tucked away boutique on Wrightsville Avenue in 2002, it's become one of the most beautiful and talked-about stores in the Southeast. The eye-popping array of gifts and accessories, linens and tableware in this place includes every price range and everything from

paper napkins to baby silver, china and crystal, sheets, bath and body products and ladies' sleepwear — displayed in a showroom that will make you want to go home and redecorate. Locals and those in-the-know turn out in droves for their famous Labor Day sale, a three-hour bargain frenzy that starts at dawn.

REEDS Jewelers
3500 Oleander Dr., Unit E-4, Wilmington
(910) 799 - 6810
www.reeds.com

REEDS Jewelers is a true American success story, having grown from one hometown store in Wilmington to a full-service jewelry retailer with 70 stores in 17 states. Founded in 1946 by Bill and Roberta Zimmer, REEDS Jewelers continues its tradition of excellence at two locations in Wilmington, Independence Mall and Mayfaire Town Center. REEDS Jewelers offers many exclusive lines of fine jewelry, including the exclusive REEDS Diamond. REEDS Jewelers is also an authorized distributor for prestigious designer brands such as Rolex, David Yurman, Tag Heuer, Omega, Chamilia, Mikimoto, Scott Kay and Tacori..

Sambuca Modern Apothecary
3304 Wrightsville Ave., Wilmington
(910) 799-8282

Sambuca is a unique apothecary and day spa. The apothecary includes Sam-

buca's own handcrafted aromatherapy products made on site along with herbal and homeopathic remedies, teas, flower essences, soap, bath salts and soy candles. Sambuca provides holistic spa therapies, including organic facials, body treatments and therapeutic massage. They sell the purest skincare and makeup made with organic, biodynamic and natural ingredients containing no chemicals or synthetic preservatives. With every Sambuca purchase you are making an investment in better living for yourself and your community. All treatments use 100 percent natural, organic and cruelty-free products. They are committed to creating a more sustainable future through relaxation, rejuvenation, beauty and well-being. Sambuca's mission is to provide organic and sustainable products and services, and their hope is to inspire people to think differently about the things they buy and inspire them to believe that every purchase can make a difference.

Tidal Creek Cooperative Food Market & Deli
5329 Oleander Dr., Ste. 100, Wilmington
(910) 799-2667
www.tidalcreek.coop

Since 1982, a commitment to providing the highest quality natural and organic foods, great customer service and ongoing consumer education has been central to the Tidal Creek philosophy.

This community-owned cooperative food market takes pride in offering the most healthful foods and products available at the best possible prices. Their buyers look for organically produced foods from local growers, small farms and companies that share the co-op's high standards. Among the offerings at Tidal Creek, shoppers will find fresh, natural and organic foods, including certified organic produce, hormone-free dairy products, chemical-free and organic meats, local eggs, frozen prepared foods and desserts and a wide variety of packaged grocery items. Also available are organic bulk items (whole grains and flours, cereals, herbal teas, beans and pasta and natural snack foods are a few examples), health and beauty aids (vitamins, supplements, and herbs), aromatherapy oils, organic wines and microbrewery beers. Tidal Creek features a deli and intimate cafe, complete with a natural and organic salad bar, numerous grab-and-go sandwiches and meals, baked goods, coffee, a fresh, organic juice bar and a smoothie bar. More than just a grocery store, the co-op is the place to enjoy a delicious, healthful meal or snack and keep up with the latest in the Wilmington healthy lifestyle community. While Tidal Creek is community-owned and operated, you don't have to be an owner to shop there — everyone is welcome. Tidal Creek is across the street from Flat Eddie's restaurant and bar on Oleander Drive. It is open seven days a week, Monday through Saturday from 8 AM to 8 PM and Sunday 9 AM to 8 PM.

Williams Carpet and Rug Gallery
5422 Oleander Dr., Wilmington
(910) 763-7993
www.williamscarpetoutlet.com

If you're in the market for flooring, check out the area's only discount carpet store, Williams Carpet Factory Outlet. With more than a thousand carpet rolls in stock, you are sure to find something that fits your taste. The outlet carries basic carpet starting at $3 per yard and high-end carpet for only $12 to $16 per yard — a savings of up to 70 percent over retail. Need other types of flooring? They also offer hardwoods, laminates and rugs.

Real. Honest. Food.

TIDAL CREEK
cooperative food market

5329 oleander drive wilmington www.tidalcreek.coop

UNC-WILMINGTON AREA

As the name suggests, the University Area encompasses College Road and the vicinity surrounding the University of North Carolina Wilmington. Many businesses in this part of town cater to college students and visitors.

McAllister & Solomon Books
4402 Wrightsville Ave., Wilmington
(910) 350-0189, (888) 617-7882

People who love vintage, rare or just plain hard-to-find books will relish a browse through McAllister & Solomon Books. They stock used and rare books, as well as a large selection of regional history books, in this well organized and appealing bookstore. Books are bought, sold or traded, with about 25,000 titles in the store at any given time. Store specialties include local and North Carolina history, military history, world history, African Americana, genealogy, mystery fiction and literature.

New Balance Wilmington
29 Van Campen Blvd., Wilmington
(910) 332-2020

This locally owned, nationally known specialty store features a full line of New Balance and Dunham footwear, New Balance performance apparel and sport bags. New Balance offers a unique "fit-form system," which is composed of 13 carefully crafted shoe forms, each of which are engineered to provide a customized fit and size profile for women, men and kids according to their activity and unique foot characteristics. You will find shoe sizes ranging from 5 to 20 and widths from 2A to 6E. The store is located in the Monk's Corner Shops near Cracker Barrel and the Walmart SuperCenter.

Noni Bacca
420 Eastwood Rd., Wilmington
(910) 397-7617
www.nbwinery.com

Located just a few miles from Wrightsville Beach and historic downtown Wilmington is Noni Bacca's international award-winning winery. This boutique winery offers more than 60 varieties of wine made on site. Noni Bacca's diverse varietals come from the richest grape-growing regions of the world, including Tuscany, Chile, Australia, Washington state and California. Wine is sold by the bottle or glass, and you are welcome to complimentary samples in their Tasting Room. Relax and enjoy a glass of wine in a comfortable atmosphere with good music and friendly staff. The retail store is open seven days a week — Monday to Saturday 10 AM to 9 PM and Sunday noon to 5 PM. You can also find an assortment of gifts and wine accessories. Create your own vacation souvenir with a personalized bottle of wine; just bring in a photo or photo card and the staff at Noni Bacca will create a personalized label for your favorite bottles of wine. Shipping is available.

SOUTHERN WILMINGTON, MONKEY JUNCTION AND CAROLINA BEACH AREA

Heading south on College Road toward Carolina Beach, you'll find an array of big-box stores and locally owned businesses serving the residents of southern New Hanover County.

Divine Wines
Masonboro Commons, 6400-7 Carolina Beach Rd., Wilmington
(910) 792-1251

With more than 1,500 wines, 250 of which are priced less than $10 a bottle, Divine Wines features one of the largest and most eclectic selections of wine this side of Raleigh. This friendly shop hosts regular wine tastings, including themed tastings every Friday from 4 to 7 PM. Does all this talk of wine get you in the mood to cook? They also offer a wide selection of cheese and gourmet foods, including pasta, sauces, and relishes.

Island Appliance
5946 Carolina Beach Rd., Wilmington
(910) 790-8580
www.islandappliance.net

The talented professionals at Island Appliance like to think of shopping at their store as an experience in match-making. You can select from Whirlpool, Maytag, Thermador, Viking, KitchenAid and Electrolux as well as 38 other brands. Don't miss the full outdoor kitchen, one of the latest trends in upscale homes, which is on display. Their trained sales staff can help you select just the right appliance for your needs, from sturdy rental property appliances to designer state-of-the-art kitchen selections for true chefs.

Pine Valley Market
3520 S. College Rd., Wilmington
(910) 350-3663

Encore magazine's Reader's Choice Awards named Pine Valley Market the "Best Gourmet Shop in Wilmington" and "Best Catering" for 2009. Pine Valley Market contains a dazzling selection of fine wines from around the world, a full-service butcher shop and a wide array of gourmet delights. They also offer yummy custom-made and grilled sandwiches, burgers (including a low-carb burger) and fresh salads. With their selection of prepared foods, Pine Valley Market is a great place to stop after work to pick up a delicious gourmet meal for the whole family. Pine Valley Market also has catering menus available for breakfast/brunch, corporate breakfast and lunch, dinner and dessert. Gourmet party platters are available to suit any gathering or special event.

Sutton's Rugs and Carpets
3520 S. College Rd., Wilmington
(910) 794-8100

At Sutton Rugs and Carpets, it's all about style. From custom designed and

manufactured area rugs and wall-to-wall carpeting to hardwood and other surfaces, Hobbs and Donna Sutton and their design team can help you with all of your floor covering needs. Locally owned and operated, this full-service carpet and flooring gallery has everything you need to create beautiful floors.

WRIGHTSVILLE BEACH, LANDFALL AND MAYFAIRE AREA

With upscale shopping like Mayfaire Town Center and The Forum at its epicenter, the Military Cutoff Road area boasts some of the swankiest shopping in the Port City. This is where you will find many of the area's high-end retailers.

Alligator Pie
Lumina Station, 1906 Eastwood Rd., Wilmington
(910) 509-1600
www.alligatorpie.com

Alligator Pie is truly a one-of-a-kind children's boutique that's been offering an amazing collection of clothes, toys, gifts, accessories and baby equipment for the past 14 years. Whether your tastes are traditional, trendy or somewhere in between, this unique and fascinating store is likely to have what you want. It offers the best of American and European clothing brands for boys and girls in newborn up to junior sizes, including well-known brands such as Billabong, O'Neill, Baby Lulu, Catimini, KC Parker, Zutano, Room Seven, Eland, Michael Simon, Petunia Pickle Bottom and Kissy Kissy. Their collection includes dressy, casual, swim, sleepwear, outerwear, bags, jewelry, bows and more than 200 styles of shoes from popular lines such as Polo, Robeez, L'Amour, Pazitos, Liva and Luca, See Kai Run, Lelli Kelly and lots more. Pre-teen and junior sizes can be found in the loft, where tweens will find the latest trends in clothes and accessories. Alligator Pie also offers the hottest award-winning toys, including a great selection of wooden and "green-friendly" toys, dolls, arts and crafts, board games, plush, dress-up and beach toys. You'll find well known brands such as Corolle, Plan, Green Toys, Haba, BlaBla, Douglas and Alex.

Baby Swank
7204 Wrightsville Ave., Wilmington
(910) 509-2969

When it comes to furniture, linens, jog strollers and fabulous accessories, Baby Swank has it covered. Located on Wrightsville Avenue just before the drawbridge into Wrightsville Beach, this upscale shop for little folk is lovingly owned and operated by friends and partners Melanie Mann and Jamie Mayo. Melanie and Jamie firmly believe that babies and young children deserve only the finest and most unique items when it comes to places they sleep, play and grow. So when you are expecting and not expecting to spend a lot of money for a swanky nursery, let them work with you...they welcome all budgets! They offer furniture, bedding, linens, artwork, prams, jog strollers and unique gifts by such names as Serena and Lily, Best Chairs, Bloom and BOB Revolution. They are also the area's exclusive distributor for Munire furniture, Treehouse Trading Company, Newport Cottages and Silver Cross prams. Melanie and Jamie will help you create the perfect child's room filled with custom furniture and fine linens for all ages. They even offer an online baby registry for mothers-to-be.

The Forum
1125 Military Cut-off Rd., Wilmington
(910) 256-2211
www.shoptheforum.com

The Forum is characterized by classical architecture and warmly colored Canadian sandstone, accented with arches, columns, pediments and balustrades. The Forum's shops are unique, upscale and carry a tempting selection of goods. Charming boutiques offer a wide array of gifts, jewelry, wines, women's fashions and children's clothing.

Charlotte's, (910) 509-9701, is an extraordinary gift and jewelry shop, with a diverse selection for any occasion. **Ikebana Design**, (910) 509-1383, is an exceptional, full-service florist and gift shop that specializes in the art of Japanese flower arrangement. **The Beauty Bar Boutique**, (910) 256-5757, is a full-service salon offering hair, skin, nail services and custom cosmetics. They have a unique ladies lounge concept perfect for intimate parties. **Face Rx**, (910) 256-3201 is a facial rejuvenation center with a state-of-the-art laser (featured on Dr. 90210) and facial injections, such as Dysport® and Restylane®, all administered by certified RN's. **Ki Spa Salon**, (910) 509-0410 is the perfect place for a relaxing day at the spa- unwind with a massage, facial or get ready for a night on the town with their full salon services. **Eye Care Center**, (910) 509-1711 offers something for all of your eye care needs- from eye exams to glasses and contact lenses.

Great options for lunch and dinner include **The Bento Box**, (910) 509-0774, with a pan-Asian menu including outstanding sushi and a full bar. Or if you are in the mood for Italian, try **Osteria Cicchetti**, (910) 256-7476, and enjoy a family-style selection of wood-fired pizza, terrific salads, delectable pastas and more, including a full bar. For a great pub burger and full bar with great beers on draft, check out **Grand Union Pub** (910) 256-9133; make sure your try the famous tater tots and if you're brave, "The Kitchen Sink"—a dessert with everything imaginable. Or order a great charburger from **Foster's Grille** (910) 256-1266- they also have loaded salads, spicy wings, sandwiches and desserts. **NOFO Cafe and Market**, (910) 256-5565, is a wonderful place for lunch and dinner, offering delectable soups, salads, sandwiches and entrees such as their famous shrimp & grits. Don't miss their retail shop with an eclectic array of gifts, gardening accessories, home furnishings and books. **Luly's Cuban Cafe**, (910) 509-2600 is the perfect location for a game of dominos and the fresh, simple fare of Cuban cuisine. For a special treat after your meal, head over to **Boombalatti's**, (910) 256-8330, known for making their own fabulous ice cream on-site with natural flavors. For a delicious pick me up, grab some coffee or a donut from **Dunkin' Donuts**, (910) 256-4543, or try out their extended menu- from flat breads to bagels.

Peanut Butter & Jelly, (910) 256-4554, focuses on baby and maternity collections, offering gifts, clothing, furnishings and strollers, as well as stylish maternity lines. **Personal Touch**, (910) 256-8888, specializes in designer ladies' apparel and

fine jewelry; they will help you find just the right outfit for any event. **Kingoff's Jewelers**, (910) 256-4321, has been a Wilmington tradition for 90 years. From shopping for your engagement ring to the fiftieth anniversary gift, they cover all your fine jewelry needs. **Rôpa, Etc.**, (910) 256-8733, specializes in natural fiber women's clothing featuring cotton and linens. **Tara Grinna Swimwear**, (910) 509-9999, is a designer swimwear store with everything you need for resort season including mix-and-match sizes. For your next special occasion be sure to visit **Isabella Grape**, (910) 256-0025. Their selection of cocktail dresses, evening, prom and pageant wear is unmatched. **La Bella Forma Fine Lingerie**, (910) 256-1220, has everything you need to wear under these special-event fashions, as well as custom bra fittings and sleepwear. **Tori/Bell** (910) 679-4081 offers a wide variety of styles and price points that will appeal to every woman- everything from beach cover-ups to cocktail dresses.

Looking for exclusive shops filled with art, imported furniture and home accessories? **Spectrum Art & Jewelry**, (910) 256-2323, features the work of more than a hundred select American artists. Their specialty is custom jewelry designs, hand crafted on-site. **Blue Hand Home**, (910) 509-0088, is a great source for unique and eclectic home décor and offers interior design services. **WineStyles**, (910) 256-0911 will help you hone your palette with tastings by the glass and a extensive selection, organized by eight different style categories instead of varietal or region. At the end of your day, you can turn to The **UPS Store**, (910) 509-0520, to help pack and ship your purchases back home. **Merrill Lynch**, (910) 256-7700, also has an office at the Forum, as does **Realty World**, (910) 256-3528, and **Interiors**, (910) 509-9596. **First Federal**, (910) 509-2000, can help meet your banking needs.

Learning Express Toys
Progress Point, 1437 Military Cutoff Rd., Wilmington
(910) 251-6636
www.learningexpresstoys.com/wilmington

Learning Express Toys is among those rare places that capture kids' imaginations with high-quality alternatives to the run-of-the-mill products. Interactive and entertaining, the stores succeed in making learning fun for kids from infancy through early adolescence. The staff includes toy experts with broad knowledge of the products, which translates into excellent service. Learning Express Toys is organized in sections geared to particular interests, such as Science & Nature (including electronics and nature projects), Let's Pretend (fantasy dress-up, Playmobil and Webkinz), Great Beginnings (for infants and toddlers) and Transit (including remote control vehicles, Thomas and Darda race tracks). This is the place to find that volcano your child needs for the diorama. You can find Learning Express Toys in three locations: the Hanover Center store on Oleander Drive is a "come out and play" space with an I Spy Cloud Shapes in the Sky ceiling. Their original location on Military Cutoff Road offers a medieval theme with a giant castle mural in the center of the store. There is also a mini-store in the Children's Museum of Wilmington and a new Toy Take-Out Website for local online shopping with in-store pickup (http://learningexpresstoys.com/wilmington/). Learning Express Toys offers free personalizing, free gift wrapping and a popular Birthday Wish Box registry. Both Learning Express stores also feature a Grandparents' Club and daily UPS shipping. Their mission is to help you find the perfect toy.

Lumina Commons
Intersection of Wrightsville Ave. and Eastwood Rd., Wilmington
(910) 239-5814

Just minutes from the beach, Lumina Commons offers numerous advantages that the former space, the Plaza East Shopping Center, lacked. Newly renovated and reconstructed, Lumina Commons has a Harris Teeter with a high-end gourmet section, eight new shops, video rentals, new restaurants, a full-service day spa and many more fantastic amenities. Whether you're vacationing at Wrightsville or residing in Landfall, Lumina Commons is your best bet for all your shopping needs.

Island Passage
Lumina Station, 1900 Eastwood Rd., Wilmington
(910) 256-0407

Offering a colorful palette of artistically presented attire plus trendy accessories and shoes, Island Passage is one of Wilmington's favorites. Don't miss their other store at 4 Market Street in downtown Wilmington and their three stores on Bald Head Island — **Riverside Adventure Company**, (910) 457-4944, your one-stop kayak, bike and golf-cart rental shop for everything you need to enjoy the traffic-free pleasures of the locale; a larger Bald Head Island location on Maritime Way, called **Maritime Passage**, (910) 454-8420, which has a fabulous selection of clothing, shoes and accessories for men, women and children; and **Canopy Outfitters**, (910) 454-8248, specializing in comfortable, versatile clothing for the entire family. You won't want to miss the newest shop, **Return Passage**, 302 N. Front St., Wilmington, (910) 343-1627, which carries deeply discounted merchandise from all the other Island Passage stores, as well as gently worn items.

Ki Spa and Salon
The Forum, 1125-Q Military Cuttoff Rd., Wilmington
(910) 509-0410
www.kispasalon.com

Voted "Best Spa" by the *Encore* magazine readers' poll three years in a row, "Best Massage" in a 2005 *Star-News* readers' poll, and "Family Favorite Spa" by *Wilmington Parent* magazine's third annual readers poll, this day spa has local approval. They combine organic products, pure aromatherapy and healing techniques to promote total body renewal. Ki, the ancient Japanese word for energy, is incorporated into all spa treatments. Ki Spa is not only a great place to spend a day, it's a great place to shop. You can take many of the products home with you. Their extensive retail shop offers Aveda, Aromafloria and Jurlique brand skin-care products, plus candles, gifts, gift baskets and gift certificates for all occasions. For added convenience, they are now open on Sundays from noon to 6 PM, and you can purchase gift certificates online.

Kingoff's Jewelers
1119 B Military Cutoff Rd., Wilmington
(910) 256-4321
3501 Oleander Dr. , Wilmington
(252) 762-5219
www.kingoffs.com

Jewelers since 1919, Kingoff's offers a large selection of fine diamonds and colored stone jewelry in 18K, 14K and platinum. They also sell gifts by Waterford Crystal. Guaranteed watch and jewelry repairs are done on the premises, and four Guild Gemologists of the Diamond Council of America are available for appraisals. Kingoff's is the exclusive seller of the Old Wilmington Cup created in the early 1800s by Thomas Brown. This pewter cup is a favored gift among Wilmingtonians for a variety of special occasions.

Kitchen Dreams
700 Military Cutoff Rd., Wilmington
(910) 332-5940
www.kitchendreamsofwilmington.com

Kitchen Dreams is Wilmington's destination store for luxury appliance buyers. Kitchen Dreams features a large selection of top national brands like Viking, Thermador, Kitchenaid, Bosh and Jennair. If you're thinking about building a new home, remodeling, creating an outdoor kitchen space, or updating your current kitchen, this is the place for you. Kitchen Dreams makes creating the kitchen of your dreams easy and exciting.

Landfall Center
1319 Military Cutoff Rd., Wilmington

In the heart of Wilmington's shopping mecca, Landfall Center is just minutes from Wrightsville Beach. This retail, dining and service plaza has shops for all your needs from gifts to apparel to home decor. Here are some we recommend.

Coastal Urge, (910) 256-6468, offers an extensive selection of swimsuits, accessories and apparel. **Apple Annie's Bake Shop**, (910) 256-6585, is a local favorite for the finest hand-made and hand-decorated desserts and cakes. **The Sandwich Pail**, (910) 256-8225, is a good place to grab a delicious sandwich or salad. On a warm day, cool down with a gourmet frozen ice pop from **LunaPops**, (910) 256-5088.

Lovey's Natural Foods Market & Café, (910) 509-0331, is a popular natural food store with a good selection of organic produce, a deli, a juice bar and a salad bar.

Learning Express Toys
1437 Military Cutoff Rd., Wilmington
(910) 509-0153
www.learningexpresstoys.com/wilmington

Learning Express Toys is among those rare places that capture kids' imaginations with high-quality alternatives to the run-of-the-mill products. Interactive and entertaining, the stores succeed in making learning fun for kids from infancy through early adolescence. The staff includes toy experts with broad knowledge of the products, which translates into excellent service. Learning Express Toys is organized in sections geared to particular interests, such as Science & Nature (including electronics and nature projects), Let's Pretend (fantasy dress-up, Playmobil and Webkinz), Great Beginnings (for infants and toddlers) and Transit (including remote control vehicles, Thomas and Darda race tracks). This is the place to find that volcano your child needs for the diorama. You can find Learning Express Toys in three locations: the Hanover Center store on Oleander Drive is a "come out and play" space with an I Spy Cloud Shapes in the Sky ceiling. Their original location on Military Cutoff Road offers a medieval theme with a giant castle mural in the center of the store. There is also a mini-store in the Children's Museum of Wilmington and a new Toy Take-Out Website for local online shopping with in-store pickup (http://learningexpresstoys.com/wilmington/). Learning Express Toys offers free personalizing, free gift wrapping and a popular Birthday Wish Box registry. Both Learning Express stores also feature a Grandparents' Club and daily UPS shipping. Their mission is to help you find the perfect toy.

Lovey's Natural Foods and Cafe, Inc.
Landfall Shopping Center, Eastwood Rd., Wilmington
(910) 509-0331
www.loveysmarket.com

Lovey's is the ideal market for the discriminating shopper who prefers natural and organic goods. They have the area's largest selection of homeopathic and herbal supplements, vitamins, health and beauty aids for hair and skin, and organic and natural groceries, including bulk grains, flour, beans, spices and gluten-free products. The vibe at Lovey's is a friendly one. While the grocery section offers delicious produce and meat-free selections for the vegetarian and vegan customers, it also features organic and free-range meats and poultry. Parents will appreciate their selection of baby food and other toxin-free items available for young children. All shoppers will enjoy the extensive hot and cold food bar and cafe menu. Lovey's can even bring their tasty treats to you through their catering service. Lovey's has a full range of organic and natural pet foods, supplements and supplies. Top off your visit with a refreshing smoothie or delicious carrot or wheatgrass juice and you'll realize why Lovey's is such a hit with the locals. They're open Monday through Friday 9 AM to PM, Saturday 9 AM to 6 PM and Sunday 10 AM to 6PM. The cafe is open seven days a week and closes an hour before the store closes.

Mayfaire Town Center
6835 Conservation Way, Wilmington
(910) 256-5131

Mayfaire is a wonderfully innovative place to shop! Designed to emulate the sense of community and friendly commerce found at the center of town, this shopping haven is one of those rare places where you can go with a diverse shopping list and find everything you're looking for in one shopping center. There are more than 80 chain stores, specialty shops, salons and businesses at Mayfaire Town Center, providing a complete range of goods and services.

Some of the newest editions to their shopping options include **hh Gregg, J. Crew, Pottery Barn** and **Try Sports**, and new stores are being built all the time. You'll also find staples like **Ann Taylor, Banana Republic, Barnes & Noble Booksellers, Bath & Body Works, Belk, Chico's, Claire's, Coldwater Creek, Cost Plus World Market, David's Bridal, EB Games, Eddie Bauer, Fresh Market, Francesca's, Glo Medspa, Good News of Wilmington, GNC, Hallmark, J. Jill, Jos. A. Bank, Luxe Home Interiors, Michaels, New York & Company, O2 Fitness, Palm Garden (Lilly Pulitzer), Pier 1 Imports, Portrait Innovations, Rack Room Shoes, Red Bank Wine, REEDS Jewelers, Rug Décor, Select Comfort, Sunglass Hut, Sweet & Sassy, Talbots, Trade Secret, Try Sports, Ulta, Victoria's Secret, White House Black Market, Williams-Sonoma** and much more.

When all of that shopping leaves you with an empty stomach, meet a friend for lunch at one of the tempting restaurants and cafes scattered throughout the center: **Atlanta Bread Company, Brixx Pizza, Chick-Fil-A, Cold Stone Creamery, Five Guys Burgers and Fries, Fox & Hound, Longhorn Steakhouse, Mama Fu's Asian House, On the Border, Panera Bread, Ruby Tuesdays, Rudino's Pizza, Red Robin Gourmet Burgers, Romano's Macaroni Grill, The Melting Pot, Tokyo 101, Starbucks** and **Zoe's**. After the day is done, you can enjoy a flick at **Mayfaire 16 Cinemas**.

Be sure to come out to their Free Summer Concert Series featuring live regional and local bands performing every Friday evening from May through early September.

Oliver
1055 Military Cutoff Rd., Ste. 103, Wilmington
(910) 256-2233

Oliver specializes in premium denim and clothing for men and women. This trendy, upscale boutique carries everything from your favorite pair of jeans to that perfect pair of earrings. Their extensive designer roster includes names like 7 for all Mankind, Citizens of Humanity, True Religion, Rebecca Taylor, James Perse, Susana Monaco and Tom Ford Eyewear. Oliver is located on Military Cutoff Road across from Mayfaire.

Palm Garden- a Lilly Pulitzer Via Shop
Mayfaire Town Center, 6804 Main St., Wilmington
(910) 256-9984

Palm Garden is a paradise of Lilly Pulitzer™ apparel, shoes and accessories. Offerings include dresses, separates and swimwear for ladies, a new and beautiful men's collection and a wonderfully cheerful children's line. The store also now carries Lilly Pulitzer™ sunglasses, fragrance and stationery.

REEDS Jewelers
Mayfaire Town Center, 926 Inspiration Dr., Wilmington
(910) 256-2962

REEDS Jewelers is a true American success story, having grown from one hometown store in Wilmington to a full-service jewelry retailer with 70 stores in 17 states. Founded in 1946 by Bill and Roberta Zimmer, REEDS Jewelers continues its tradition of excellence at two locations in Wilmington, Independence Mall and Mayfaire Town Center. REEDS Jewelers offers many exclusive lines of fine jewelry, including the exclusive REEDS Diamond. REEDS Jewelers is also an authorized distributor for prestigious designer brands such as Rolex, David Yurman, Tag Heuer, Omega, Chamilia, Mikimoto, Scott Kay and Tacori.

Rôpa, Etc.
The Forum, 1121-D Military Cutoff Rd., Wilmington
(910) 256-8733

Experience the pleasure of fine cottons and linens and make dressing comfortable and fun. Rôpa, Etc. is the area's exclusive retailer for such lines as Flax, Willow and Cut-Loose. This terrific shop also carries great makers such as Rico and Pure hand-knit sweaters, TSD and Habitat. Rôpa, Etc.

is also known for its unique collection of hand-wrought American and European jewelry plus great accessories to complement any outfit. They have two area locations at 120-B S. Front Street in downtown Wilmington and 417-C N. Howe Street in Southport.

S. Burke Fine Jewelry & Gifts
Lumina Station, 1900 Eastwood Rd., Ste. 10, Wilmington
(910) 256-3311

Whether you're looking for a one-of-a-kind piece of jewelry or something high end to commemorate a special occasion, S. Burke Fine Jewelry & Gifts offers a unique selection to meet your needs. They carry a range from designer lucite to 18-karat gold and diamond jewelry. Visitors to the area often celebrate their trip to the coast with a beach-themed piece, such as a starfish, sand dollar or nautical-themed items made by local artists. More than just a jewelry store, this Lumina Station shop also offers handbags, picture frames, scarves, jewelry boxes and travel bags.

Uppity Lu's
7220-A Wrightsville Ave., Wilmington
(910) 679-4305

Uppity Lu's features a large selection of women's and men's clothing, shoes, jewelry, purses and accessories. Uppity Lu's carries a host of well-known brands, including Joseph Ribkoff, Christopher Blue, Molly B, Elliot Lauren, Gracia New York and Lilla P, in a wide range of price points. Located in the Atlantic View Shopping Center near Jerry's, Uppity Lu's is open from 10 AM to 6 PM Monday through Saturday.

MARKET STREET AND KERR AVENUE AREA

Also known as Highway 17, Market Street runs through the heart of Wilmington, and it is peppered with strip malls, boutiques and shopping of all types.

The Bargain Box
4213 Princess Pl., Wilmington
(910) 362-0603

The Bargain Box, a resale boutique, is an outreach ministry of Wilmington's

Church of the Servant, Episcopal. They encourage the recycling of pre-owned goods and the creative utilization of pre-loved merchandise. A wide variety of affordable, quality merchandise is offered, including a complete assortment of clothing, furniture and household items, collectibles and records, tapes and CDs, toys and games, jewelry and accessories. Income is redistributed to existing ministries through a grant program. Vouchers are available from specified churches and social service agencies for people with emergency needs. There is also a bin full of free, usable clothing. Volunteers are needed to steam clothing, provide customer service, pick up furniture, deliver bags of clothes to migrant workers, organize the library, do garden and lawn work and perform handyman duties. Volunteer your time and talents, or help by shopping at The Bargain Box or bringing donations. Encourage your friends and family to do likewise. The Bargain Box is open Tuesday through Friday 11 AM to 6 PM and Saturday 10 AM to 5 PM. They are open on Monday from 10 AM to 4 PM for donations only.

Brookelynn Premium Cigars
7134 Market St., Wilmington
(910) 686-2446

Locally owned and operated since 2001, Brookelynn Premium Cigars prides itself in offering the finest quality products and service. They boast a collection of more than 100 brands of fine cigars, yet if what you're looking for isn't there, the friendly staff will find and obtain it for you. Brookelynn's also has a quality selection of blended tobaccos, pipes, humidors, travel cases, flasks and other accessories. Shop online or stop in and enjoy their cozy smoking lounge, which offers free WiFi and NFL, NHL and MLB viewing packages. If your love for cigars goes beyond just puffing, ask about joining their Cigar Club.

The Napping Cat
107 S. 16th St., Wilmington
(910) 341-1958

If you're looking for the perfect treasure, the Napping Cat is the place to go. Located on south 16th Street, this eco-friendly shop offers unusual and unusually affordable gifts and decor items and one-of-a-kind finds for everyone on your shopping list.

Williams Carpet Factory Outlet, LLC
1808 Castle Hayne Rd., Wilmington
(910) 763-7993

If you're in the market for flooring, check out the area's only discount carpet store, Williams Carpet Factory Outlet. With more than a thousand carpet rolls in stock, you are sure to find something that fits your taste. The outlet carries basic carpet starting at $3 per yard and high-end carpet for only $12 to $16 per yard — a savings of up to 70 percent over retail. Need other types of flooring? They also offer hardwoods, laminates and rugs.

Wrightsville Beach Area

ON THE ISLAND

Shopping is limited on largely residential Wrightsville Beach, but retail options are plentiful just over the bridge on the mainland. That's why we have two sections here: On the Island (Wrightsville Beach addresses) and Off the Island (all the stores in this section have a Wilmington address, but they are very close to Wrightsville Beach).

CoolSweats
7208 Wrightsville Ave., Wrightsville Beach
(910) 509-0273

At CoolSweats, you'll find an array of comfortable yet sophisticated clothing for women. Their clothes are known for their classic, timeless appeal, from casual to dressy styles. Most clothes are 100% cotton, and new colors come in every month. CoolSweats carries the popular Beyond Yoga line, which has been recognized as one of Oprah's favorite things. The Wrightsville Beach store is one of two CoolSweats stores in the Carolinas (the other store is in Pinehurst).

Hallelu Boutique
84 Waynick Dr., Wrightsville Beach
(910) 509-0570

Trendy, elegant, chic, timeless and funky. If any of those apply to your style,

then something truly unique is waiting for you at Hallelu Boutique. Located directly off the south end bridge of Wrightsville Beach, this privately owned shop offers an eclectic selection of clothing, shoes, jewelry and other accessories that range from the designer to the distinctly different. It's open from 11 AM to 7 PM Monday through Saturday. The cheerful staff will always be sure to lend a hand or a second opinion.

Surf City Surf Shop
**The Landing, 530 Causeway Dr.,
Wrightsville Beach
(910) 256-2265**

Celebrating 31 years in business, Surf City describes itself as "a shop for surfers by surfers" and carries a large variety of surfboards, body boards, skateboards and other gear. Whether you're into the classic boards — Hobie, Takayama, Yater and Robert August — or the newer shapes — Lost, Merrick, Rusty, Chilli and Resin8 — Surf City has them all, as well as the clothing and accessories you'll need to hit the waves. Skateboarding is another feature of this lively store, with a large selection of skateboard components, including decks and wheels, clothing and accessories. They also have the area's largest selection of sunglasses. Into snowboarding? Surf City offers some of the best snowboarding gear available from Burton Snowboards, including boards, bindings, boots and clothing.

OFF THE ISLAND

Blush
**Lumina Station, 1900 Eastwood Rd., Ste. 24,
Wilmington
(910) 256-1151**

Blush, Wilmington's premier skin care apothecary, features the finest skin care and cosmetic lines. A vast array of products, combined with a professional staff of cosmetic specialists and estheticians, helps Blush offer its clients a unique, personalized health and beauty experience. Blush carries top international cosmetic brands such as Laura Mercier, Paula Dorf and Kiehl's. Their beauty services include makeovers, facials, chemical peels, and waxing. They can turn any bride into a blushing bride with a full bridal makeup package, and they also offer wedding beauty services for the bridesmaids and mother of the bride.

Harbour Club Day Spa and Salon
**1904 Eastwoood Rd., Wilmington
(910) 256-5020**

After all your shopping, why not treat yourself to a rejuvenating massage or pedicure at Harbour Club Day Spa and Salon? Their team of highly trained professionals is dedicated to providing personalized beauty and body treatment programs, such as facials, manicures, depilatory services, therapeutic massages and pedicures. Their Deep Tissue and Hot Stone massages are favorites with locals and visitors alike.

Getting married? Harbour Club offers complete packages for the bride and her wedding party, which includes a consultation to determine hairstyle with headpiece placement and cosmetic application, if desired. To soothe and polish the bride and groom before their big day, they offer an array of facial and body treatments, hair, skin and nail options. Harbour Club can also arrange delivery of catered food and beverages on the day of the booking.

Hook, Line & Paddle Canoe & Kayak Outfitters
435 Eastwood Rd., Wilmington
(910) 792-6945
www.hooklineandpaddle.com

Hook, Line & Paddle Kayak and Paddleboard Outfitters is one of the largest kayak, canoe and stand-up paddleboard dealers in North Carolina. Not only do they sell fishing kayaks, recreational kayaks, touring kayaks, stand-up paddleboards and canoes but also they carry all the latest accessories from top brands like Native Watercraft, Heritage and Wilderness Systems. If you're not ready to take the plunge and purchase your own equipment, you can rent kayaks through the store, at their Wrightsville Beach location (across from the Blockade-Runner Beach Resort) and at the Yacht Club on Figure Eight Island. If after you rent, you get hooked and want to buy, as an added incentive, Hook, Line & Paddle will refund the cost of your rental toward a purchase. Not only can you get the right gear, but you can also book a tour at the shop or receive instruction from one of the store's master teachers. One of their most popular tours is the Dawson's Creek Tour, a three-hour excursion visiting the Wrightsville Beach house featured in the series. They also sell custom kayak fishing outfitting and Yakima roof racks, with free installations with purchase. The store is open every day from 10 AM to 6 PM.

La Bella Forma Fine Lingerie
1125-I Military Cutoff Rd., Wilmington
(910) 256-1220
www.labellaforma.com

La Bella Forma offers Wilmington's finest selection of bras, lingerie, sleepwear and bathrobes in styles from conservative to elegant to ooh-la-la. Catering to every body type, they carry a wide selection of bras in stock, offering band sizes from 32 to 44 (and up), and cup sizes from A to J. They offer personalized bra fittings to ensure you are wearing the correct size and style to complement your shape. They also sell swimwear in bra cup size D and up for great support while you are on the beach or in the pool. The shop prides itself on being all about solutions to your wardrobe dilemmas. Planning to wear a special outfit but don't know what to wear under it so you'll look your best? Bring the dress into La Bella Forma and let their expert staff advise you. They also offer beautiful bridal lingerie for under your wedding dress and honeymoon romance. Visit La Bella Forma Fine Lingerie at The Forum, where they celebrate every woman's beautiful form.

Lumina Station
1900 Eastwood Rd., Ste. 10, Wilmington
(910) 256-0900

If you are shopping for local flavor, you'll find Lumina Station as satisfying as a day at the beach. Inspired by Lumina, the beloved Wrightsville Beach dance pavilion once central to the East Coast social scene, Lumina Station is so true to its historical roots that it won *Coastal Living* magazine's first-ever award for contextual design. Beautiful landscaping, whimsical sculptures and storybook bridges complement the heavily wooded campus, making strolling the Station a very pleasant way to pass the time. Rocking chairs — the center's signature icon — are grouped here and there under deep overhangs, providing a shady place to rest, enjoy a cappuccino or sit back and visit with passersby. Fortunately, the shops, restaurants and business located here are just as unique as the setting. Local merchants own and operate virtually all of the establishments. You'll find some truly special offerings, from jewelry and art to gift items, home accents and clothing for the entire family.

You can pamper yourself in the day spa, work out with a personal trainer and enjoy a fabulous meal in one of the restaurants, all without ever getting into your car.

Lumina Station's cafes and restaurants provide something for everyone, from your morning coffee to fine dining. Start your day with fresh-brewed coffee from **Port City Java**, (910) 256-0993. For a stylish and truly delightful dining experience complete with tapas-style menu, visit **19 Hundred**, (910) 509-2026. Enjoy a relaxing cocktail at **The Dirty Martini**, (910) 256-5514, then go next door to have an exceptional meal at one of the Station's fine restaurants, including The **Port Land Grille**, (910) 256-6056, which features progressive regional American cuisine; and **Brasserie du Soleil**, (910) 256-2226, an extraordinary French bistro. Embodying casual coastal spirit, **Stone Crab Oyster Bar**, (910) 256-5464, is the perfect place to unwind and enjoy mouthwatering local seafood dishes and other diverse menu items.

The following is a listing of the shops and services you'll find at Lumina Station. You'll also find warmth, friendliness and an authentic old Wrightsville Beach atmosphere. Overall, it's an experience you could not possibly have anywhere else. **Airlie Moon**, (910) 256-0655, is an eclectic, unique gift store offering exceptional products for the bed, bath and home. **Alligator Pie**, (910) 509-1600, is an amazing, one-of-a-kind children's boutique. For the best of New York City's high fashion, stop by **Beanie + Cecil**, (910) 509-9197. Not your average furniture store, **Hewitt**, (910) 202-4657, offers everything you need to furnish your home in style including custom design services that can turn any furniture dream into reality. For original art from regional and national artists, stop into **Fountainside Fine Art Gallery**, (910) 256-9956. Discover **Sole Searching**, (910) 256-0727, for fabulously funky affordable shoes, as well as adorable accessories and one-of-a-kind, hand-made jewelry. For an eclectic array of artisan jewelry, handbags, hats and more, visit **Ziabird**, (910) 208-9650, to find that unique piece to express your personal style. Check out **Glenn Har-**

mon (910) 509-2011 for exceptional interior design services and style for your home.

Take a personal day and relax at Harbour **Club Day Spa Salon**, (910) 256-5020. **Intracoastal Realty**, (910) 256-4503, is one of the area's most popular agencies for sales, vacation rentals and mortgage financing services. Clothing, shoes and elixirs are the specialty at **Island Passage**, (910) 256-0407. For a one-stop boutique shopping experience with personalized service, visit **Jennifer's**, (910) 256-6522, and for your best look, you can't miss a visit to **Blush**, (910) 256-0448, offering quality skin care, cosmetic lines and cosmetic dermatology procedures. State-of-the-art equipment and personal training are both available at **Lumina Fitness**, (910) 509-9404. Swing into **Monkee's**, (910) 256-5886, for the perfect shoes, contemporary ladies clothing and accessories. Home furnishings and exceptional interior design service are available at **Paysage**, (910) 256-6050. **S. Burke**, (910) 256-3311, invites you to discover a unique and beautiful selection of fine jewelry, home accessories and imaginative gifts. **Sito Chiropractic**, (910) 256-2655, offers family chiropractic care.

Motts Channel Seafood
120 Short St., Wrightsville Beach
(910) 256-3474

Since 1990 Motts has been providing fresh seafood to folks from its waterfront location at Wrightsville Beach. Whether you arrive by boat or by car, you'll find a large selection of fresh, first-quality seafood. They also offer an extensive selection of sauces and spices to help you prepare a great seafood meal. For anglers, they have live and frozen bait as well as ice for your catch.

Peanut Butter & Jelly
The Forum, 1121-H Military Cutoff Rd.,
Wilmington
(910) 256-4554

"Eat for two. Sleep for two. Why not shop for two? Baby & you" is the motto for this upscale maternity and children's boutique that is really three boutiques in one. They carry the latest maternity fashions by Olian, Maternal America, 2 Chix and many others, as well as children's clothing and gifts. Their expansive showroom also includes nursery collections by Stanley Young America, Ragazzi and Bratt Decor, gliders by Little Castle, and strollers by Peg Perego, Combi, Baby Jogger and Bugaboo, just to name a few. Moms-to-be will love the Baby Shower Registry Savings Program, and shoppers of all ages will find plenty of items for both giving and receiving.

Ziabird
1900 Eastwood Rd., Ste. 9, Wilmington
(910) 208-9650

Ziabird is a jewel in Lumina Station. The name, a combination of "zia," which means "auntie" in Italian, and "bird," the owner's mother's nickname, celebrates women and women's creativity. Ziabird represents small label designers, many whose work can be found nowhere else in Wilmington. Owner Lynn Manock is a jewelry artist herself, with her own line of inspired designs. Open Monday through Saturday, Ziabird is the perfect place to buy unique jewelry, accessories or clothing for yourself or a special woman in your life.

Odgen and Porters Neck

This section of Market Street runs northward to Hampstead, Figure Eight Island and the Topsail Island area.

Poplar Grove's Farmers Market
10200 U.S. Hwy. 17 N, Wilmington
(910) 686-9518 x26

Beginning the first Wednesday in April and continuing every Wednesday through mid-December, Poplar Grove's Farmers' Market offers fresh North Carolina fruit, vegetables, plants, herbs, flowers, eggs, cheeses, meats, seafood and honey. The market's mission is to educate the public on local farm products and practices, promote the use of local products, and serve the community through programming and activities. The market is held on the lovely grounds of Historic Poplar Grove Plantation and is open from 8 AM until 1 PM.

Stone Garden
6955 Market St., Wilmington
(910) 452-1619

Stone Garden, conveniently located at Military Cutoff Road and Market Street, is a great place to shop when planning or beautifying your home or garden. They have the largest selection of stone in eastern North Carolina. You'll see outdoor kitchens, fireplaces, patios, paths, dry-stack walls and ponds, and you'll enjoy the beautiful garden art, with ornaments ranging from the whimsical to the unique. You'll also find statuary, benches, birdbaths, windchimes, sundials, planters and amusing gargoyles. The oriental garden has lanterns, stepping stones, millstones and buddhas. Choose a fountain from the current selection or visit their catalogue room to place a special order. Check out the showroom to see natural and Cultured Stone® displays, color samples and photos. Don't miss the gift shop with its funky collection of natural gifts, including polished stones, glass art, jewelry, gems, geodes and fossils. The Stone Garden is known to locals as a fun place to shop, and you can feel free to bring the kids.

Carolina and Kure Beach

Most of the shopping on Pleasure Island — Carolina Beach and Kure Beach — is concentrated in Carolina Beach. In addition to a number of chain "beach" stores, Carolina Beach boasts a variety of year-round specialty shops, and more are added each year. Keep in mind that winter months mean shortened or limited hours for many retail businesses. Call ahead so you won't be disappointed by a "closed" sign.

The Checkered Church Gift Shop
800 St. Joseph St., Carolina Beach
(910) 458-0211

Bright, tropical-colored checks adorn the outside of this former church that is filled with beach-related home-decor items. You'll find everything from pine furniture, baskets, prints and M. A. Hadley pottery to weather vanes, wind chimes, bird houses and works by local artists. Christmas items, many with a nautical theme, are available year-round, as is a beautiful, 100-percent-cotton afghan that portrays the Pleasure Island coastline and wildlife found in the area. The Checkered Church is truly that little shop off the beaten path you always hope to discover.

Frame Mart & Gallery
Pleasure Island Plaza,
1009 N. Lake Park Blvd., Carolina Beach
(910) 458-6116

Owner Scott Brown offers a full line of custom framing services, including pick up and delivery, in this combination art gallery and frame shop. In addition, Scott offers photo restoration and canvas reproductions. Bring in a treasured piece for framing or select a favorite from the varied range of work from local, regional and national artists. Framed artwork also is available for purchase, and the shop carries the Harbour Lights lighthouses. Frame Mart & Gallery is open year-round Tuesday through Saturday, or by appointment.

The Fudgeboat
107 Carolina Beach Ave. N,
at the Boardwalk, Carolina Beach

Krazy Kones, on the Boardwalk
(next to the Gazebo), Carolina Beach
(910) 458-5823

Imagine a boatload of fudge. Now add rich, butter-cream fudge and the freshest ice cream into that picture and you have The Fudgeboat. Tracee, Duke and Lou are family, and the crew of this confectionery cruise. They create their fudge from the finest and freshest ingredients, including real butter and cream. They make it, display it and cut pieces to your order, all on top of a restored 38-foot wooden cabin cruiser, or at least part of one. With 40 different flavors to choose from, you can see why their motto is "That's a yacht of fudge!" Stop in and see them on the Boardwalk at Carolina Beach, and take home a pound or two to savor for later. Be sure to check out Krazy Kones, their ice cream shop on the Boardwalk near the Gazebo.

Island Colors
1401 N. Lake Park Blvd., Carolina Beach
(910) 458-7736

Island Colors features a huge selection of comfortable, colorful Fresh Produce, I Can Too and Lula B Sportswear. With sizes from toddler to 3X, you're sure to find something for everyone, as well as coordinating jewelry by Calypso Studios, She Shells and Oceania, woman's sandals by Okab, Margaritaville and Sandlaz and accessories. Island Colors also carries Seadog T-shirts and Margaritaville footwear for men. Island Colors gift cards are available, and the store is open year round.

Linda's Fashions
201 N. Lake Park Blvd., Carolina Beach
(910) 458-7116

Linda's, open seven days a week year-round, has a wide assortment of ladies' sportswear, dresses for special evenings on the town, jewelry, scarves and other accessories. You'll find top-quality resort wear made of comfortable, machine-washable material in stylish cuts and colors, all at affordable prices.

Peter Doran Fine Art Photography
740 Fort Fisher Blvd. N, Kure Beach
(910) 458-6893
www.peterdoranphotography.com

Peter Doran's formal background in graphic design and painting explains his skilled eye for capturing and composing coastal North Carolina nature at its finest. With a BFA from the Rochester Institute of Technology in graphic design and a master's degree from SUNY Buffalo in painting, Peter's work is pleasing to view, desirable to own and highly collectible. Peter is a photographer whose passion for photographing nature is formed by his love and concern for the Carolina coast. He seeks to capture not only the essence and the inherent beauty of the coast, but also to show it in a manner that allows the viewer to see it from a fresh or unique perspective. His unique sense of style and use of light transports the viewer into the scene, standing in the photographer's shoes, seeing with his eyes what Peter saw before capturing the scene on film. Peter and his family live in Kure Beach and publish and distribute high-quality consumer products, including postcards, playing cards, posters, note cards, magnets, key chains and signed prints and gallery wraps. From shots of the state's seven lighthouses to the wild horses on the Outer Banks, the fine art photographs of Peter Doran offer a personal and unique perspective of the coastal North Carolina lifestyle.

Primrose Cottage
1018 North Lake Park Blvd., Carolina Beach
(910) 458-0144

Primrose Cottage has a nice selection of beachy and shabby chic furniture and lightly used consignment items items of all kinds for adults and children. They have home and yard decor items, and they really love browsers.

Squigley's Ice Cream & Treats
208 S. Lake Park Blvd., Carolina Beach
(910) 458-8779

Wow, with 4,050 flavors and taste sensations, this ice cream parlor offers something for everyone. They will make any flavor combination you desire — all that's required is imagination and a sweet tooth. A large board lists customers' favorite combinations, such as cashews, Oreo and Butterfinger. You can also choose from 24 toppings like blueberry, raspberry or peanut butter. Squigley's offers dozens of regular flavors for less daring folk. With lots of indoor and outdoor seating, Squigley's is a great choice for a tasty treat during the day or after dinner. It's open seasonally.

Unique Boutique
207 S. Lake Park Blvd., Carolina Beach
(910) 458-4360

Originally built as a guest cottage for a larger home, Unique Boutique carries one-of-a-kind ladies' sample clothing at wholesale prices from boutiques in various cities around the country. Additionally, they feature shoes, hats, jewelry, accessories and swimwear.

The Yankee Trader
1009 N. Lake Park Blvd., A-2,
Carolina Beach
(910) 458-0097

Look for unusual and one-of-a-kind nautical gifts and framed art at The Yan-

kee Trader. Bestsellers are the stoneware oil-lamp lighthouses as well as canvas Maine bags, N.C. lighthouses, authentic model ships, Lefton Lighthouses and more. Known as the island's Christmas shop, the store carries Snowbabies and North Pole Village by Department 56, Margaret Furlong angels, Boyd's Bears, limited-edition Pipka Santas, Willow Tree angels, Newport collection of scrimshaw, Cape Fear throw, Mercury glass ornaments and other limited-edition collectibles.

Bald Head Island

On Bald Head Island you will find a variety of small interesting shops including places to rent bicycles and golf carts to transport yourself around this unique environment. A convenience store, gift shop and restaurants line the marina while the gift shop at the Smith Island Museum can be found within walking distance. Golfers will find a pro shop at the golf course. Staying for a while? Why not take advantage of the option to order your groceries online and have them delivered to your door?

Turtle Central
700 Federal Rd., Bald Head Island
(910) 457-0917

Turtle Central is the Bald Head Island Conservancy Gift Shop and offers a relevant collection of apparel for the entire family, home furnishings, gifts, books, field guides, educational toys, eco-conscious products, jewelry and accessories. Turtle Central is more than an exciting retail destination — 100% of the proceeds from the shop supports the Conservancy's barrier island conservation, preservation and education programs. The shop is located on the Conservancy campus and is open seven days a week in season.

Southport

The quaint charm of Southport and the quiet of Oak Island's small, coastal community belie the area's growth. Recent increases in residential and commercial construction and development, plus the opening of Walmart on N.C. Highway 211 between the two communities, herald a changing era for this region, and the growing number of year-round retail businesses is a reflection of this trend.

Some of the shops listed here are found in Southport's picturesque historic district. Leave the car parked on the street and enjoy a leisurely stroll along the town's waterfront and main thoroughfare, particularly Howe and Moore streets. You'll find gift and jewelry shops, restaurants, art galleries, clothing stores and a maritime museum. But don't stop there. Interesting galleries and small shopping centers may be tucked back into side streets or located further from the downtown. If you're interested in antiques markets, see the Southport listings in the Antiques section at the end of this section.

Angelwing Needle Arts
507 N. Howe St., Southport
(910) 454-9163

Angelwing is a charming needle arts shop with a great big reputation. The shop stocks such a wide range of quality supplies, kits and accessories for needlepoint, counted thread, crewel embroidery, counted cross stitch, knitting, crochet and quilting that customers come from as far away as Raleigh to shop there. Knitting and stitching groups meet in the evenings on a regular basis to receive inspiration and moral support from each other and from the staff. Finishing services are available as well.

Blue Crab Blue
4310 Long Beach Rd., Southport
(910) 454-8888

Wonder where the locals shop? Discover this quaint boat-builder's cottage near the Oak Island Bridge — it's a fun place to shop! You will find it brimming with handcrafted pottery, jewelry, stained glass, metal work, watercolors and other gift ideas. It is a treasure trove of specially commissioned, exclusive and one-of-a-kind arts all at affordable prices. Owner Barbara Donahue supports local and regional artists and selects each piece with an eye for detail and quality of craftsmanship. Pottery pieces, including raku, ceramic and coiled, range from artistic to

utilitarian to whimsical. The hand-crafted jewelry is of excellent quality and design, made of sterling silver, sea glass and genuine stones. There's much more to see and, with year-round hours, this friendly shop is a must-visit. In addition, every purchase leaves the shop carefully and beautifully packaged. Shipping is available. After-hours appointments to see the collection are welcomed.

Books 'n Stuff
Live Oak Village Shopping Ctr.,
4961-11 Long Beach Rd., Southport
(910) 457-9017

In the bookstore business in the Oak Island-Southport area since 1987, Books n' Stuff owner Susan Warren meets the reading needs of residents and visitors alike all year long. Her store carries close to 50,000 previously read paperbacks, a large section of books on tape and CD, and new books at discounted prices as well as collectible books. Not sure what you want? Susan's extensive knowledge of books and authors will ensure that you leave with just the right ones, and she is a certified e-bay trader. When you're finished, trade in for credit and save on the next one. Journals, book accessories and T-shirts are also available.

Cape Fear Jewelers
102 E. Moore St., Southport
(910) 457-5299

Serving as Southport's jeweler since 1985, Cape Fear Jewelers boasts a large selection of nautical jewelry in gold and silver, including the original Bald Head and Oak Island lighthouse charms. There you will find a wide selection of fine diamonds, gemstone jewelry, silver jewelry and brand-name watches. Conveniently located in historic downtown Southport, this full-service store offers watch repair, onsite jewelry repair and appraisals as well.

Howe Street Purveyors
600–602 N. Howe St., Southport

Stopping at this shopping center on the way to downtown Southport or on the way out again is an excellent idea. **papaya island**, (910) 457-0256, offers comfortable clothing for you and your family in colors that will make you happy. **Cat on a Whisk**, (910) 454-4451, is a perfect spot to find food-related gifts — from gadgets to gourmet foods. What's more, N.C. products are featured here. **Loco Jo's Bar & Grill**, (910) 457-9009, serves beer, wine and scrumptious food from fish 'n chips to Vietnamese dishes. **Renee's Fine Jewelry**, (910) 457-7714, is a full-service jewelry store.

Live Oak Nutrition
114 Nash St., Southport
(910) 457-0550

You will find this natural market nestled among the shops on Nash Street. The shelves are well stocked with vitamins and herbs, natural beauty products, sports nutrition products and homeopathic remedies. Organic food is available and includes grains and cereals. The staff is knowledgeable and willing to share their expertise to help you find the right products.

Olde Southport Village Shoppes
1102 N. Howe St., Southport
(910) 457-5337

Olde Village Restaurant, (910) 363-4472, with indoor as well as outdoor seating, anchors this collection of shops made up of refurbished old buildings where you are sure to find something to please. **The Pink Palace Gift Shoppe**, (910) 454-8385, offers vintage linens, teapots, fine teas, cookbooks, kitchen collectibles and accessories as well as tea served in their tearoom. **Debbie's Hair Design Studio**, (910) 454-0224, includes services, such as haircutting, coloring, highlighting and perms. At **Gigi's Consignments & Curiosities**, (910) 612-0088, the name says it all. At **My Aunt Sal**, (910) 457-9677, you will find handmade natural soy wax candles and more. **Artistry**, (910) 457-0811, carries distinctive handcrafts and fine art . At **Karen's Trails of Treasure**, (910) 457-9991, you will find everything from wind chimes to telescopes. **Scotch Bonnet**, (910) 454-4152, offers local art, books by local authors, jewelry, accessories and shells. Don't leave without visiting the **Village General Store**, (770) 596-8938, to stock up on antique usefuls, homemade jellies, dried apples, walking sticks and more.

Rebecca's
416 N. Howe St., Southport
(910) 457-6182

Rebecca's is a one-stop shop for all your decorating needs. You will find furniture and home accessory consignment items, including antique furniture, accessories, pictures, art objects and more — and at reasonable prices. You can offer your own pieces for consignment as well. Furniture and accessory reupholstering is a specialty at Rebecca's and includes custom bedding, frame rebuilding and building new furniture to order. If you like you can choose from the designer drapery and upholstery fabric and trims available in this shop.

Rôpa, Etc.
417-C N. Howe St., Southport
(910) 454-8833

Are you ready for something new and exciting? Then you're invited to experience the pleasure of fine cottons and linens, which make dressing comfortable and fun. Rôpa, Etc. is the area's exclusive retailer for such lines as Liz and Jane, Flax, Willow and Cut-Loose. This terrific shop also carries great makers such as Rico and Pure hand-knit sweaters, TSD, Habitat, CLICK and Kiko. Rôpa, Etc. is known for its unique collection of jewelry from makers around the world plus great accessories to complement any outfit. Sizes range from extra small to extra large and fit a variety of shapes. Rôpa, Etc. has two other locations to serve you: 120-B S. Front Street, Wilmington, (910) 815-0344, and 1121 Military Cutoff Road, Suite D, Wilmington, (910) 256-8733.

Sole Searching
715 N. Howe St., Ste. 2, Southport
(910) 457-0450

Owner Rebekah Page refers to Sole Searching products as "fabulously funky affordable fun footwear and accessories." In her shop you will find unique women's shoes in sizes 5 to 11, each style with its own personality whether because of the design, the cut, the fabrication, the sole, the heel or the color. Rebekah designs most of the one-of-a-kind jewelry in the shop using semiprecious stones like jade, turquoise and mother-of-pearl along with silver and gold. An additional and unusual service provided is after-hour shoe parties for any occasion. These parties include wine and cheese or champagne and dessert with a 10 percent discount for groups of 15 or more.

Waterfront Gifts & Antiques
117 S. Howe St., Southport
(910) 457-6496

When Southport Insiders need to buy a gift, Waterfront Gifts is often their first stop. This shop, near the waterfront at the end of Howe Street, is known for distinctive gifts for all occasions, including jewelry, greeting cards, distinctive accessories, antiques, wall and table-top sculptures, books on local and regional history and a large selection of nautical gifts.

Oak Island

Oak Island is the only one of the four Brunswick barrier islands on which you will find a full shopping district. Included are a Food Lion grocery store, a post office, several banks and a library. When vacationing here, you could conceivably never leave the island until you are headed home. There are restaurants, clothing, souvenir, fishing supplies and gift shops, an art gallery, a jewelery store and a number of beach stores for all you beach needs. Of course, you will find more shopping available in the mainland portion of the town.

Leland

Brookelynn Premium Cigars
2013 Old Regent Way, Leland
(910) 371-0025

Locally owned and operated since 2001, Brookelynn Premium Cigars prides itself in offering the finest quality products and service. They boast a collection of more than 100 brands of fine cigars, yet if what you're looking for isn't there, the friendly staff will find and obtain it for you. Brookelynn's also has a quality selection of blended tobaccos, pipes, humidors, travel cases, flasks and other accessories. Shop online, or stop in and enjoy their cozy smoking lounge, which offers free WiFi

and NFL, NHL and MLB viewing packages. If your love for cigars goes beyond just puffing, ask about joining their Cigar Club.

Bugsy's Cigars
1107 New Pointe Blvd., Unit 12, Leland
(910) 399-2923

Bugsy's is more than just a cigar shop. In addition to carrying a large selection of premium cigars, pipes, tobacco and all related accessories, Bugsy's offers its customers a spacious lounge area. The lounge features comfortable leather couches and a 57" screen TV where you can meet with old friends, or make new friends, while enjoying your favorite cigars, watching all your favorite sports, and even savoring a cold beer. They are located in the Cross Creek Commons, across from Magnolia Greens, and are open Monday through Saturday 10 AM to 9 PM and on Sunday's from noon to 6 PM.

Coastroad Hearth & Patio
4733 Main Street, Shallotte
(910) 755-7611
www.coastroadonline.com

In this family owned shop a trained and certified staff will help you design your special hearth and patio areas. You will find electric, gas, wood, and pellet fireplaces and fireplace inserts as well as mantels and surrounds in beautiful styles from modern to traditional to classic. Fireplace accessories such as gas logs and coals, firescreens, tool sets, wood holders, andirons and even chimney pots are also available. For the patio you will find grills including wood, charcoal, gas lighting, built-in, free standing and more. In addition there are cabanas, umbrellas, furniture, outdoor refrigerators, cabinets, sinks, warming drawers - the possibilities are endless

Gumdrops & Lollipops
2013 Olde Regent Way, Ste. 230, Leland
(910) 371-2495

Step through the doors of Gumdrops & Lollipops and instantly find yourself transported into an enchanting shop straight from the pages of a children's fairy-tale. Vibrant with color and artwork, this children's clothing boutique carries multiple designer brands, including Kissy Kissy, Funtasia Too and Bailey Boys. Their high-end selection ranges from infant to size 10 for girls and size 7 for boys. In addition to chic children's fashion, Gumdrops & Lollipops also has a range of gifts, accessories and educational toys. The boutique is open from 10 AM to 5 PM Monday through Friday and 10 AM to 4 PM on Saturdays.

Murray Art and Frame
497 Waterford Way, Leland
(910) 371-3833

Murray Art and Frame is the spot for custom frames, artwork and printing needs. Owner and pencil artist George Murray, along with his friendly and knowledgeable staff, will help you get exactly what you need, whether it be a wood or metal frame, shadowbox for memorabilia or local artistic creation. They even boast a massive printer, so you can get banners, outdoor signage or cut-out letters any length you like.

RBR Books
511 Olde Waterford Way, Leland
(910) 383-9843

Leland's only bookstore, this shop is truly a gem. It was voted Best Bookstore by the 2009 Brunswick County Readers Choice Awards, as well as the #1 New Business of 2009 by the readers of North Brunswick Magazine. These awards are a testament to the passion for literature held by the staff, and the uniqueness of their services. RBR Books not only has a selection that ranges from the recent to the rare, but also has a buy and trade policy, where your books are accepted for in-store trade credit or cash. RBR publishes a blog, keeping you up to date with happenings not just in their store, but the community as well. The shop is open Tuesday through Saturday from 10 AM to 6 PM.

Sansha USA Inc.
2080 Mercantile Dr., Leland
(910) 371-0101

An internationally renowned company, Sansha USA Inc has all the pieces any dancer could need. Whether it be for the stage or the classroom, all types of dance wear, warm-ups, and accessories are available. Their selection of footwear is most notably extensive and offers many specific options. Ballroom, flamenco, jazz, student, pointe, tap, stage, and more are all offered in different varieties, such as material type, make, and fit.

Topsail Island

Looking for a little variety? Topsail Island visitors can shop for designer resort wear, a tandem kayak, fine local and regional art, a shark's tooth necklace or the latest must-read novel. Almost all of the area shops are locally owned and operated, which means each shop is unique. So whether you're shopping for a new surf board or a complete condominium furniture package, you will find special touches and helpful and friendly customer service.

Beach Furniture Outfitters
520 New River Dr., Surf City
(910) 328-4181

This shop's specialty is fully furnishing and equipping beach homes and condominiums. They do it all — furniture, bedding, carpet and accessories. Whether you're just setting up house or looking for one special accent piece, Beach Furniture Outfitters has choices for every taste and pocketbook. Free set up and delivery are offered on the island.

Bert's Surf Shop
310 N. New River Dr., Surf City
(910) 328-1010

A longtime favorite on the beach, Bert's has a full line of name-brand sportswear and swimwear for the whole family, as well as sunglasses, T-shirts and shoes. Bert's also offers a full line of sports equipment for sale, including skateboards, skimboards, surfboards and surfing gear. It's open seven days a week.

The Bumblebee Market
513 Roland Ave., Surf City
(910) 328-2105

Vera Bradley is in the house! Shop Bumblebee Market's complete line of Vera Bradley signature print travel bags, jewelry keepers and purses, flip flops and umbrellas. This charming shop is filled with great gifts. There is a wonderful selection of Jessie Steele retro-chic aprons and uber-fancy kitchen gloves (as seen on Desperate Housewives and The Oprah Winfrey Show), beach cover ups, fine jewelry and charms. New this year are Tyler Candles, which not only smell great but also have cute names like Diva, High Maintenance and Limelight. They have also just added greeting cards and stationery. The candy counter filled with handmade chocolates is irresistible, and so are the Paula Deen gourmet biscuit mixes, marinades, glazes and salad dressings. Bumblebee Market also carries fun activity kits for kids, Ugly Dolls, adorable lunch boxes and backpacks and a wide variety of conversation-starting games for both kids and adults.

D's Interior Design
834 N.C. Hwy. 210, Sneads Ferry
(910) 327-2166
www.dinteriordesign.net

If you are building or refurbishing your home or business, D's Interior Design can meet all of your design needs with style. Choose between hardwoods, beautiful ceramic tile, vinyl or carpet. D's Interior Design carries classic floor coverings by Mannington, Congoleum, Shaw and Mohawk. They also have a great selection of fabrics for custom window treatments and bed spreads. D's Interior Design offers traditional and resort furniture, custom blinds and plantation shutters, artwork, home accessories and gifts. Their design staff is there to help you furnish and accessorize your complete home or individual rooms. Store hours are Monday through Friday 9 AM to 5 PM and Saturday 10 AM to 4 PM.

East Coast Sports
The Fishing Village, 409 Roland Ave.,
Surf City
(910) 328-1887

East Coast Sports carries a full line of sports clothing, including Columbia, Bimini Bay and Sperry Topsiders. In addition to clothing, you can find everything you could ever want or need for inshore or offshore fishing, including a professional staff to answer all your questions. East Coast Sports is open year round.

The Fishing Village
409 Roland Ave., Surf City
(910) 328-1887

Built in the style of a coastal fishing village and centrally located in Surf City, the Village is home to East Coast Sports and On Shore Surf Shop. The Fishing Village offers one-stop shopping for everything you need to fish or surf at the beach. You'll find cool clothes, boards, a great selection of fishing tackle and pier carts to haul all of your gear. Marine supplies and fishing licenses are also available.

The Gift Basket
702 S. Anderson Blvd., Topsail Beach
(910) 328-7111

The Gift Basket is best known for its 14K and sterling silver jewelry. They also carry an impressive line of tide and nautical clocks and precision weather instruments. The Gift Basket also carries fashion accessories, fine gifts, housewares and wall art. They have a Christmas room and a collegiate corner where you can even find pasta with your favorite N.C. college logo. Visit them on the south end of the island and see why The Gift Basket is one of Topsail Beach's favorite places to shop since 1973.

Island Traders
303 S. Topsail Dr., Surf City
(910) 328-1004

Island Traders carries name-brand and catalog clothing at 40 to 70 percent below retail prices. This is a great place to stock up on casual clothes for the entire family. Look for jeans, golf wear, casual and school clothing with name brands like Lands' End, J. Jill and Eddie Bauer. New shipments arrive all the time so stop by often.

Island Treasures
627 S. Anderson Blvd., Topsail Beach
(910) 328-4487

The treasures in this shop include nautical prints, lamps, flags, windsocks, sunglasses, hats and beach supplies. Island Treasures also carries toys and cuddly over-sized stuffed animals for the kids and "Topsail Time" T-shirts and sweatshirts for the entire family. The shop is open daily from Easter through September, with reduced winter hours.

LunaPops
206 N. Topsail Dr., Surf City
(910) 328-1517

LunaPops sells all-natural, handmade frozen pops. They offer 20 mouth-watering flavors made with real fruit, fresh cream and unique seasonal ingredients. The flavors range from cookies and cream to strawberry pink peppercorn. Even better, a family of four can enjoy these treats for about $10.

Quarter Moon books & gifts
708 S. Anderson Blvd., Topsail Beach
(910) 328-4969, (800) 697-9134
www.quartermoonbooks.com

Enjoy a delicious cappuccino or a cool fruit smoothee from the coffee bar menu while browsing Quarter Moon's great selection of books. Whether you're looking for a breezy beach read, an intriguing biography, the latest release or a nature guide, they offer terrific choices for all interests. What goes along with a good book? Comfy pajamas, of course! Remember: a book lover never goes to bed alone! Find the most comfortable sleepwear, slippers, lounge wear and sandals along with

other enchanting goodies at the Quarter Moon. Step up onto the porch and find an array of stationery, boxed note cards and the best greeting cards in the area. Quarter Moon also has a delightful children's area with books, games, toys and puzzles. Internet access is available. Call for seasonal hours.

Radio Shack
13741 N.C. Hwy. 50, Surf City
(910) 329-5000
1950 U.S. Hwy. 172, Ste. A, Sneads Ferry
(910) 327-1478

Specializing in consumer electronics and computer repairs, these conveniently located Radio Shacks have the parts and pieces you may have forgotten to bring on vacation. Radio Shack carries a good inventory of replacement batteries, battery packs, prepaid phone cards, flashlights and alarm clocks. They are open Monday through Saturday.

Realo Discount Drugs
13460 N.C. Hwy. 50 / 210, Surf City
(910) 329-1134

Vacationing in the Topsail Island area and forgot a prescription at home? Don't panic, Realo Discount Drugs will gladly contact your home pharmacy or physician and fill your prescription right here. The pharmacy also carries a full line of over the counter drugs, including sunscreens and sunburn products. Conveniently located in the Palladium Shopping Center next to Surf City Urgent Care, Realo Discount Drugs accepts most insurance.

Spinnaker Surf Shop
111 N. Shore Dr., Surf City
(910) 328-2311

Spinnaker's is Surf City's location for surf and beach accessories, such as AJW Surfboards, Billabong, Rip Curl, Volcom and Matix. The store also has a large selection of girls' surf-brand apparel, swimsuits and accessories. Check out their selection of designer eye wear, such as Oakley, Electric, VonZipper and Dragon and sandals by DVS, QS/Roxy, Reef and Rainbow. Looking for surfboards to buy or rent? Spinnaker's has a large selection. It's open daily year round (but it's closed Tuesdays in the winter).

Starfish Distinctive Gifts & Treasures
14210 N.C. Hwy. 50, Ste. B, Surf City
(910) 328-5500

Wall-to-wall cute and filled with the irresistible, Starfish Distinctive Gifts & Treasures is a great place to shop for that perfect wedding or hostess gift. There is a nice selection of cake plates and platters, candles, soaps and spa products. Starfish also features paintings by local artists, jewelry and a children's section. The shop offers complimentary gift-wrapping, and shipping is available.

Surf City Shopping Center Gift Shop
Corner of Roland Ave. and Topsail Dr., Surf City
(910) 328-0835

This shop carries everything vacationers need for a stay at the beach: summer dresses, cute cover-ups, bathing suits, casual wear for the whole family, games, beach toys, sunscreen, floaties and flips. If you're looking for a hostess gift or something to brighten up the beach house, check out their gifts and home accessories. And since this store is connected to the IGA grocery store, you can also stock up on snacks before heading to the beach. It's open daily in the summer season and closed Tuesdays in the winter.

Surfside Sportswear and Gifts
314 N. New River Dr., Surf City
(910) 328-4141

A year-round favorite with residents, Surfside offers the most complete line of women's clothing on the island. The racks are always filled with bathing suits, casual wear and party attire in a wide variety of sizes and in styles for the young and not-so-young. In addition to clothing, Surfside has a great shoe selection, an assortment of jewelry, glassware and home-decorating items. It's open daily year round.

The Topsail Island Trading Company
201 New River Dr., Surf City
(910) 328-1905

The Topsail Island Trading Company carries a selection of resort clothing,

including a large variety of Topsail Island T-shirts and sweatshirts. While browsing you may detect a delicious scent in the air — that's their famous homemade fudge made with fresh cream and butter. With more than 100 flavors, there's something for everyone. Fudge makes the perfect gift, and they can even ship some to your family and friends. Books, toys and cards are also available. Take home a gift from The Topsail Island Trading Company and you'll be taking home a piece of Topsail Island.

The Turtle Factory
1982 N.C. Hwy. 172, Ste. H, Sneads Ferry
(910) 327-3244
318 Fulchers Landing, Sneads Ferry
(910) 327-3244

For all things turtle — ottomans and footstools, jewelry, books and puzzles, garden, kitchen and bath decor, lamps, pillows and picture frames — this Sneads Ferry shop has it. The Turtle Factory also has an amazing array of fiberglass, wall-mounted replicas of dolphins, sharks and turtles. The Fulchers Landing location also offers lots of arts and crafts projects for kids.

Hampstead

Sometimes it's difficult to know exactly where Hampstead begins and ends, but most folks agree that the center of town is where the traffic lights are on U.S. 17 near the Food Lion. Once a crossroads marked only by pine trees and a cottage with a yard full of Venus Flytrap plants for sale, this intersection is now the commercial hub of Hampstead. The area's explosive growth in the 1990s brought several new shopping venues to Hampstead. Many new commercial centers have sprouted up along U.S.1 7 bringing new restaurants and shops to the area. Shoppers will find antiques, gifts, jewelry and surf and skate gear.

DDT Outlet
21740 U.S. Highway 17, Hampstead
(910) 329-0160
www.ddtoutlet.com

DDT Outlet is the area's premier store for the coastal lifestyle. They specialize in coastal fabrics, nautical decor and companies that reflect our way of living. With companies like Capris, Palmsprings Rattan, Carlton, Flexsteel and Tickle, you can be confident that you are purchasing long lasting quality furniture. DDT can also transform your deck or patio into a new outdoor living space with CRP, Telescope, Casual Living, NCI or Grosfillex. Stop by seven days a week in Hampstead or in Wilmington, or call Niki or Fara for custom design ideas.

DoubleWide Surf & Skate Shop
14921 U.S. Hwy. 17, Hampstead
(910) 270-3640

DoubleWide Surf & Skate Shop has some of the coolest skateboard and surf gear around town. Skaters have lots of complete skateboards and decks to choose from, and surfers have their pick of long and short boards, skimboards and body boards. The shop also has an impressive selection of hot, brand-name clothes. Their hip hoodies, shorts, tees and fab sunglasses let you style while you play. Protective gear, skate DVDs, board bags, wax and leashes are all available at DoubleWide Surf & Skate Shop.

The Flower Basket of Hampstead
14361 U.S. Hwy. 17 N, Hampstead
(910) 270-4141, (877) 607-7615

If you love having beautiful floral arrangements in your home, this is the place to shop. In addition to fresh flowers, the shop also carries a selection of houseplants, quality candles and a variety of plush animals. A full-service florist, The Flower Basket staff can help with wedding bouquets, special orders and funeral arrangements. The Flower Basket delivers flowers throughout the Hampstead area, including Topsail Island.

Hampstead Furniture
16202 U.S. Hwy. 17, Hampstead
(910) 270-3393

Furniture shopping in Hampstead is a breeze. Whether you're just moving in or upgrading your current abode, Hampstead Furniture has the designers and the variety you're looking for. There are several lines of designer living room, dining room and bedroom furniture available. If you like to have the gang over, they also have entertainment centers, home theaters, bar tables and bar stools. Be sure to check out their closeout items while you're there.

The Hooked Fish
17061 U.S. Hwy. 17 N, Cedar on the Green, Hampstead
(910) 270-5030

Located in an adorable historical cottage at Cedar on the Green, The Hooked Fish is a unique store that combines the talents and dreams of three women. Beverly "The Renovator," Susan "The Decorator," and Melanie "The Artist" mesh their talents to create a charming shop. To these women, the cottage finds, antiques, one-of-a-kind accessories and "historical" works of art that fill every nook and cranny represent more than just decor, they represent potential ... what can be with a little creativity, hard work and grace. When the ordinary is unacceptable, The Hooked Fish may be the solution.

mcnally's gifts
16717 U.S. Hwy. 17, Hampstead
(910) 270-0087

Variety is the theme of this store. With more than 2,500 square feet to shop, it

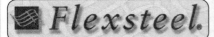

offers something for everyone. To start, the staff makes more than 50 flavors of fudge right in the store. You'll find gifts for wedding, baby and birthday, including Jim Shore and Willow Tree along with Brighton jewelry and accessories and clothing by Fresh Produce, Flax, Pure and many others. For the hostess and home, you'll find N.C. pottery, beautiful oil lamps, cookbooks and Tervis tumblers and an extensive choice of gourmet food items. With great service and free gift wrapping, this is the place to shop for gift giving or just for you.

My Front Porch Gifts & Collectibles
224 Hampstead Village Dr., Hampstead
(910) 270-1177, (888) 302-2955

Located in the heart of Hampstead, this eclectic shop is packed with gifts and treasures. There are garden items, wind chimes and flags, wedding gifts, baby gifts and gifts for pets, golfers and grandparents. Open Monday through Saturday from 10 AM to 5 PM year round, My Front Porch offers complimentary gift wrapping.

Antiques

HISTORIC DOWNTOWN WILMINGTON

If whiling away the hours browsing for antiques is your favorite passtime, you'll love downtown Wilmington and the New Castle Street Art and Antique District. Located between Fifth and Seventh Streets on Castle, the District offers a concentration of many shops featuring art, antiques, flowers, framing, restaurants, home furnishings, nautical items, oriental rugs and expert design services. This once-thriving elite shopping area has come back to life with boutique shops and major local retailers. You can even bring your items and have them appraised.

Start your shopping day with breakfast or take a break for lunch at one of the District's many and varied eateries such as **Hall's Tropicana Restaurant**, a neighborhood favorite since 1920, or **The Jester's Java** for great coffee and snacks. Then shop away at **Michael Moore Antiques, Adams on Castle Antiques, Newcastle Antique Center** (which includes 30 antique

dealers), **Oriental Rugs at Newcastle, Patterson Behn Framing, Wilmington Gallery at Newcastle, The Wine Shop, Time... at Last!, Susie Q's** and **Castle Keep Antiques**.

Front Street also offers a variety of interesting shops, including **Antiques of Old Wilmington** and **Eddie's Antiques & Collectibles**. To guide you through the more than 250,000 square feet of Wilmington's antiques and collectibles stores, pick up a copy of "*A Guide to Greater Wilmington Antique Shops*" leaflet available at any of the antiques stores, the Greater Wilmington Chamber of Commerce and the Cape Fear Convention & Visitors Bureau.

Adams on Castle
545 Castle St., Wilmington
(910) 251-2224

Adams on Castle, part of the New Castle Antiques District, houses a wide range of antiques, including period furniture, nautical artifacts, fine art, china, crystal and silver. Appraisals are available by owner Charles Adams, a veteran appraiser for more than 30 years in Wilmington.

Antiques of Old Wilmington
25 S. Front St., Wilmington
(910) 763-6011

Established in 1982, this store has been in the same location longer than any of the city's antiques shops. Antiques of Old Wilmington specializes in the area's largest line of antique lighting fixtures. They also feature china, silver and glassware.

Eddie's Antiques & Collectibles
127 N. Front St., Wilmington
(910) 342-0026

Eddie's holds an eclectic assortment of furniture, silver, rugs, jewelry, china, crystal and much more. You can browse for hours. It's open Monday through Saturday from 9 AM to 5 PM.

Michael Moore Antiques
539 Castle St., Wilmington
(910) 763-0300

Located in the New Castle Antiques District, this shop features 3,200 square feet of antique furniture, glassware and sterling silver. Michael Moore Antiques is partnered with the Antique Emporium,

Great Accessories
From our Home to yours.

which specializes in lamps, light fixtures and glass shades and offers a large selection of parts for lamps and light fixtures.

Newcastle Antique Center
606 Castle St., Wilmington
(910) 341-7228

If nautical antiques are your passion, you'll find a huge selection in the Newcastle Antique Center. This upscale antiques mall represents about 30 dealers of antique wicker, fine furniture, Heisey glass, porcelain, silver and more. They have recently grown and added a larger variety of antiques, making the mall an even greater treasure trove for antiques hunters. The Newcastle Antique Center is open Monday through Saturday from 10 AM to 5 PM and Sunday 1 to 5 PM.

MIDTOWN WILMINGTON

Ivy Cottage
3030 Market St., Wilmington
(910) 815-0907
www.threecottages.com

The Ivy Cottage is Wilmington's favorite furniture and home accessory consignment shop, consisting of four buildings with more than 25,000 square feet in all. Each of the buildings is filled to overflowing with antiques, classic furniture, china, crystal, silver, oriental carpets and fine jewelry. There are also two large garden areas with outdoor furniture, fountains, planters, fencing, gazebos and wrought-iron decorative pieces. Hundreds of new items arrive daily, so you'll probably never see the same thing twice. Shopping here is like going on a wonderful treasure hunt. Hours are Monday through Friday from 10 AM to 5 PM, Saturday 10 AM to 6 PM and Sunday 1 to 5 PM.

BRUNSWICK COUNTY

Brunswick Antiques
6525 Ocean Highway E., Winnabow
(910) 253-7008

Brunswick Antiques is billed as the largest supplier of English pub tables and vintage linens in the area. They also carry collectibles, china and porcelain, antique furniture, glassware, lamps and pottery, including brown ware, kitchenware and silverware. Consignment items are available, as is shipping.

Fancy Flea Antique Mall
2763 U.S. Hwy. 17, Shallotte
(910) 755-6665

In this shop you will find more than 15,000 square feet of items from the past. Whether you are searching for large or small pieces of furniture, old dolls, bottles or books, vintage fabrics and jewelry, coins,or war memorabilia, you are likely to find it here. There is an indoor auction the first and third Saturday of each month at 6 PM.

Magnolia Gifts & Antiques
301 N. Howe St., Southport
(910) 457-4982

Visitors to this shop will find a large selection of gifts, decorative accessories and jewelry on the first floor. An attractively arranged second floor features antiques, garden gifts and more. Also available are consignment furniture and decorative accessories.

Northrup Antiques Mall
111 E. Moore St., Southport
(910) 457-9569

Antiques shoppers will delight in the many antiques and collectibles dealers housed under one roof in historic downtown Southport. Throughout this one-stop-shopping, two-story building, shoppers will find a variety of unique gifts. The possibilities for found treasures include antique furniture and accessories, sterling silver, Slow Blue, antique toys, glassware, linens, porcelain, books, Civil War artifacts, Byers Choice Carolers and nautical treasures. Don't miss the specialty candles by Root and Tyler Candle Company. Original artwork by local artists is featured and sold exclusively in this shop.

Southport Antiques
105 E. Moore St., Southport
(910) 457-1755

Quality antiques are a specialty of this store. Look for antique furniture, quilts, art, rugs, porcelain, nautical items, glass, folk art, silver, jewelry, linens and more. Need a personal property appraisal for insurance

or estate purposes? This service is available at Southport Antiques.

Furniture

Without a doubt, the best part of a home makeover project is looking for furniture and accent pieces, wall decorations and artwork. While our area has an enormous number of home-furnishing stores with every style imaginable, these are some popular places where you can enjoy leisurely shopping and great service.

UNIVERSITY AREA

Rose Bros. Furniture
421 S. College Rd., Wilmington
(910) 791-1110

Since 1953, family-owned Rose Bros. Furniture has been a Wilmington institution. Here you can find quality home furnishings, fine bedding and accessories at affordable prices, with such name brands as Ashley, Broyhill, Bassett, La-Z Boy, Sealy Posturepedic, Stearns & Foster and Simmons Beautyrest. Hallmarks of Rose Bros.

Furniture are exceptional customer service, knowledgeable staff, flexible financing and professional decorating support.

SOUTH COLLEGE ROAD AND MONKEY JUNCTION AREA

Ashley Furniture Homestore
5309 #3 Carolina Beach Rd., Wilmington
(910) 452-1324
www.ashleyfurniture.com

Established in 1945, Ashley Furniture Industries, Inc. is the largest home-furniture manufacturer in the United States and the number one selling brand of home furniture in North America. At Ashley Furniture Homestore you'll find Ashley Furniture's exclusive lines for bedroom, dining room and casual dining, as well as upholstery, motion upholstery, leather, leather match, occasional tables, entertainment centers, home office, youth bedroom, recliners, curios, mattresses and accessories. You're welcome to come in and browse, and the friendly staff are always happy to answer your questions. What's more, they offer great prices on furniture

as well as flexible payment deals, easy financing, design help and more. Ashley Furniture Homestore is centrally located at the corner of Carolina Beach Road and S. College Road. Store hours are Monday through Friday 10 AM to 7 PM, Saturday 10 AM to 6 PM and Sunday noon to 6 PM.

Beds Plus
5309 Carolina Beach Rd., Wilmington
(910) 799-5559
www.bedsplusstores.com

If you're looking for a good night's sleep, Beds Plus is the place for you. The friendly staff at Beds Plus will help you to find an answer for all your sleep and comfort needs. From high-quality mattresses, to space-saving options for your children's rooms, to the perfect furniture to dress up your bedroom, Beds Plus stocks everything you need to get some rest.

Master Craftsmen Services, Inc.
97 Heathcliff Rd., Wilmington
(910) 793-5945
www.mastercraftsmenservices.com

"Wood and woodworking are a passion for me," admits Ed Mayorga, a longtime resident of Wilmington. Whether the project is reproducing an eighteenth-century piece of furniture, or the restoration of an ornate, carved gilded mirror, Ed uses his intuitive understanding of the power and beauty of wood to coax the desired finished product. The fact that his father was a renowned cabinet maker helped instill his skill of mind and hand. Master Craftsmen Services, Inc. is well known as the place to restore cherished pieces, particularly those damaged by fire or water.

MILITARY CUTOFF ROAD AREA

Luxe Home Interiors
Village at Mayfaire, Wilmington
(910) 256-7919

The design experts at Luxe Home Interiors will help you create custom furniture and decor that suits your personal style.

Redix remains a long-time staple at Wrightsville Beach.

photo: Robert Graves

This family-owned and operated company offers design solutions and custom, upholstered furniture made to your specifications in a range of price points and styles. Their professional design team offers personalized service to furnish your entire home. Luxe caters to every lifestyle, from casual beach cottages to elegantly appointed residences. They'll even come to your house and measure, draw floor plans and help you blend your new furniture and accessories with those you already have. Your furniture will be custom-made to your order and delivered to your home. This trend-setting store is the only one of its kind in Wilmington and well worth a visit.

MARKET STREET AREA

The Furniture Company
7330 Market St., Wilmington
(910) 681-0650

Looking for a place where you can go and browse and not feel pressured? The Furniture Company is that place. Family-owned and operated, it offers a full line of upper-middle to high-end furnishings in a "non-commission sales" atmosphere. With 20,000 square feet of showroom, an on-site warehouse and in-house interior designers, The Furniture Company also offers a large Kincaid Gallery and a Bassett Design Center. From custom upholstery to solid-wood bedrooms and dining rooms, The Furniture Company can help you design and furnish one room or a whole house.

Ivy Cottage
3030 Market St., Wilmington
(910) 815-0907
www.threecottages.com

The Ivy Cottage is Wilmington's favorite furniture and home accessory consignment shop, consisting of four buildings with more than 25,000 square feet in all. Each of the buildings is filled to overflowing with antiques, classic furniture, china, crystal, silver, oriental carpets and fine jewelry. There are also two large garden areas with outdoor furniture, fountains, planters, fencing, gazebos and wrought-iron decorative pieces. Hundreds of new items arrive daily, and you'll probably never see the same thing twice. Hours are Monday through Friday from 10 AM to 5 PM, Saturday 10 AM to 6 PM and Sunday 1 to 5 PM.

The Master's Touch
5517 Building B, Myrtle Grove Rd., Wilmington
(910) 799-4545

Serving the Wilmington area's furniture needs since 1978, The Master's Touch showroom, open Monday through Friday, features fine furniture from original antiques to reproduction and contemporary pieces. They are especially noted for repair and beautiful restoration services of elegant originals to simple sentimental pieces. Winning the title of "Top 125 Craftsmen in North America" by *Fine Woodworking* magazine and featured in the March 2005 issue of *Southern Living* magazine, The Master's Touch is now well known for specialty carving and original designs of American art pieces being considered for the White House. Featured in the Raleigh *News & Observer*, their hand-carved duck, turkey and goose calls are truly works of art and are carved from a variety of hardwoods. They can be custom-designed to feature the image of a hunter's favorite dog or the hunter's initials. Collectible boxes for displaying these unique masterpieces are also available.

SOUTHPORT AND OAK ISLAND

The McNeill Company
4143 Long Beach Rd., Oak Island
(910) 454-8188

Voted the number one furniture store in Brunswick County, The McNeill Company specializes in coastal and nautical designs and colors and is the exclusive carrier of the Marie Osmond Line. They stock sofas, sleepers, arm chairs, outdoor furniture, wall art, metal art, gifts, toys, games, accessories such as rugs, coffee tables, side tables, chests and lamps, and a full line of bedding. The store is open seven days a week. Don't miss the clearance room.

Galleries

HISTORIC DOWNTOWN WILMINGTON

bottega art bar and gallery
208 N. Front St., Wilmington
(910) 763-3737

Wilmington's only art bar, bottega uniquely appeals to everyone from the fine wine connoisseur and art lover to the live music and beer aficionado. The gallery exhibits local, regional and international artwork, including oil, acrylic and watercolor, sculpture, photography, mixed media and printmaking. While you browse their collection of original art you can sip a glass of wine or a beer from a lengthy selection of domestics and imports alongside a superb offering of several organic varieties. Enjoy your libation of choice with an item from their tapas-style cafe menu, and plan to stay for the live entertainment, which includes bluegrass, jazz, folk, experimental and rock performances as well as the occasional literary and film event.

Fidler's Gallery and Framing
The Cotton Exchange, Nutt St., Wilmington
(910) 762-2001

This multi-dimensional gallery houses an eclectic collection of limited-edition pieces, fine-art posters and originals from a wide range of local, regional, national and international artists. These artists include Timberlake, Mangum, Landry, Wyeth, Kunstler and many more. Among the many and varied subjects are florals, wildlife, seascapes and the Civil War. Professional custom framing is also available. Housed within the gallery, Wrigley's Clocks offers a selection of timepieces such as wall, mantel and floor (or grandfather) clocks. Wrigley's services what it sells with authorized factory repairs as well as all other makes of clocks. They even make house calls.

The Golden Gallery
311 N. Front St., Wilmington
(910) 762-4651
www.thegoldengallery.com

A resident of The Cotton Exchange for 32 years, The Golden Gallery is truly a family affair. Artist Mary Ellen Golden's original watercolors and giclée prints depicting Wilmington landmarks and southeastern North Carolina scenery are well-known and sought after among visitors and residents alike. A watercolorist since 1975, Mary Ellen shares her techniques and tips in a DVD, "Watercolor Can Be Easy," created by Mary Ellen and Wilmington artist Eloise Bethell. It's available for sale in the gallery.

Mary Ellen's husband, John Golden, a songwriter and storyteller, is noted for his songs about coastal Carolina's legends, folklore, characters and events. CDs of these ballads and sea songs, including the Civil War-era "The Fall of Fort Fisher" and "Colonial Songs and Scottish Ballads" featuring "The Battle at Moore's Creek", are available at the gallery. His most recent CDs are "Minstrel of the Times," and a storytelling CD, "Stories from the Cape of Fear" featuring local legends and ghost stories.

Fine-art photography and digital illustrations of local landmarks are son John W. Golden's specialty, and many of his black-and-white and color prints are on display. His work has been licensed internationally and is being featured in many national catalogs. The Golden Gallery is home to Wilmington's largest collection of local landmark photography. You can browse for hours.

New Elements Gallery
216 N. Front St., Wilmington
(910) 343-8997

Celebrating 25 years in historic downtown Wilmington, New Elements Gallery has long been regarded an arts destination for visitors and residents alike. This award-winning gallery features a wide range of contemporary and traditional works in oil, watercolor, acrylic and mixed media. Decorative and functional pieces in glass, ceramics, fiber and wood are also featured, as well as handcrafted jewelry. A sampling of the artists at New Elements Gallery include Claude Howell, Dorothy Gillespie, Bruce Bowman, Robert Irwin, Kyle Highsmith, Nancy Tuttle May, Hiroshi Sueyoshi and Dina Wilde-Ramsing. The gallery offers changing exhibitions throughout the year, which coincide with Fourth Friday Gallery Night when downtown galleries and artist studios offer evening hours (6 to 9 PM) to showcase the local art scene.

Wilmington Art Association
616-A Castle St., Wilmington
(910) 343-4370

Operated by the Wilmington Art Association, the Wilmington Gallery at 616 Castle Street houses an eclectic collection of works by local artists at its new space in the Newcastle Antiques District. The gallery represents more than 50 members and features paintings, pottery, fabric art

and jewelry. The gallery is open Tuesday through Saturday from 10 AM to 5 PM and Sundays from 1 to 5 PM.

UNIVERSITY AREA

The Gallery at Racine
203 Racine Dr., Wilmington
(910) 452-2073
www.galleryatracine.com

This g allery is a large yet comfortable place for art enthusiasts of all ages. The Gallery at Racine exhibits one-of-a-kind artwork by local and nationally renowned artists with a delightful collection of artwork in a variety of styles and price ranges. This established venue offers sculpture, oils, watercolor, acrylics, pottery, raku, print making, fine glass, jewelry and more. New works arrive frequently. The Gallery features the work of child prodigy, George Pocheptsov; the unique driftwood and copper sculptures of local artist Shaw Lakey; the limited-edition reproductions of Dr. Seuss; and many more. The Gallery at Racine is an uplifting venue where questions are cheerfully answered and everyone is welcome.

Walls Fine Art Gallery
2173 Wrightsville Ave., Wilmington
(910) 343-1703

Exhibiting fine original oil paintings by nationally known artists, Walls Fine Art Gallery is a 3,000-square-foot haven for art lovers. Owners David Leadman and Nancy Marshall, painters themselves, use their more than 60 years of experience, national renown and extensive connections in the art world to help clients make the best selections. They'll even bring art to your home. Walls offers the finest hand-carved and gilded frames suitable for artwork from contemporary abstract to twelfth-century icon. Gallery hours are Tuesday through Saturday from 10 AM to 6 PM.

MILITARY CUTOFF ROAD AREA

Fountainside Fine Art Gallery
Lumina Station, 1900 Eastwood Rd., Ste. 44, Wilmington
(910) 256-9956

Fountainside Gallery is one of Wilmington's leading destinations for fine art.

Representing local, regional and national artists, Fountainside has a selection of art that will appeal to the serious art collector as well as the casual art lover. The gallery regularly hosts exhibitions, workshops and educational demonstrations, inviting artists from across the nation to capture the beauty of the Cape Fear Coast. Fountainside Gallery specializes in placing art in residental and commercial spaces while partnering with design and corporate clients. Stop by and enjoy their paintings, sculpture, glass and jewelry offerings in the gallery's intimate, relaxed atmosphere.

Spectrum Art & Jewelry
The Forum, 1125-H Military Cutoff Rd., Wilmington
(910) 256-2323
www.spectrumartandjewelry.com

Spectrum Art & Jewelry offers an irresistible collection of dazzling jewelry, colorful contemporary art and select American craft and glass. Spectrum represents more than 100 local, regional and national artists working in all media. Spectrum also offers complete fine jewelry repair and custom jewelry design featuring award-winning designer Star Sosa and master goldsmith Michael Chapman. View the latest collection at Spectrum's monthly Open House and Wine Tasting on the second Friday of each month.

CAROLINA & KURE BEACH

Peter Doran Fine Art Photography
Kure Beach
(910) 458-6893
www.peterdoranphotography.com

Peter Doran's formal background in graphic design and painting explains his skilled eye for capturing and composing coastal North Carolina nature at its finest. With a BFA from the Rochester Institute of Technology in graphic design and a master's degree from SUNY Buffalo in painting, Peter's work is pleasing to view, desirable to own and highly collectible. Peter is a photographer whose passion for photographing nature is formed by his love and concern for the Carolina coast. He seeks to capture not only the essence and the inherent beauty of the coast, but also to show it in a manner that allows the viewer to see it from a fresh or unique perspective. His unique sense of style and use of light transports the viewer into the scene, standing in the photographer's shoes, seeing with his eyes what Peter saw before capturing the scene on film. Peter and his family live in Kure Beach and publish and distribute high-quality consumer products including postcards, playing cards, posters, note cards, magnets, key chains and signed prints and gallery wraps. From shots of the state's seven lighthouses to the wild horses on the Outer Banks, the fine art photographs of Peter Doran offer a personal and unique perspective of the coastal North Carolina lifestyle.

SOUTHPORT AND OAK ISLAND

ArtShak Studio, Gallery and Sculpture Garden
822 N. Howe St., Southport
(910) 457-1757

Thom Seaman, sculptor, and Linda Platt, artist, began their adventure in Southport in 1997 determined to live their dream of making a living doing what they love. The front section of the U-shaped building encompasses the gallery. The ceiling soars to 20 feet with 14 windows lining the top, allowing ambient light to enter. Here you will find original oil paintings, acrylics, prints and custom framing as well as painted glasses and windows from Linda's creative hands. Thom's striking metal sculptures also inhabit this area. These sculptures, ranging from table-top works to outside pieces up to 13 feet in height, are primarily made from aluminum and copper with a wide range of patinas to suit just about anyone's taste. The gallery is home to more than 30 other local artists whose works include pottery, fabric art, silver and pearl jewelry and hand-made beads, oil, acrylic and water color paintings, photography, fused and blown glass and wood-turned art. You will find crystalline pottery from Seagrove as well. The wings of the U are private areas including studios. A sculpture garden is in the center. Thom says they have created an environment, not a business. In addition to the art in the gallery, Thom and Linda accept commissions for custom designs, including murals.

Franklin Square Gallery
130 E. West St., Southport
(910) 457-5450

Since 1979 Franklin Square Gallery has been operated by the nonprofit Associated Artists of Southport. It is housed in an impressive century-old historic building in the heart of Southport directly behind Franklin Square Park. The association is responsible for maintaining and operating the gallery and a pottery studio located on the grounds behind it. The City of Southport provides the buildings and maintains the exteriors. The expectation was that the artists would create and maintain an important cultural center and, indeed, they have. In addition to the workshops, classes and competitions provided by the association, the gallery features paintings and pottery of its members, the annual exhibit of the Oak Island Quilters challenge squares, the annual Brunswick County Photography Contest sponsored by the Brunswick County Parks and Recreation Department, and artwork of the students of the Brunswick County Public School System. All paintings and pottery in the gallery are available for sale to the public.

Lantana's Gallery & Fine Gifts
113 S. Howe St., Southport
(910) 457-0957

Recently moved to a new location, Lantana's carries the same fine quality merchandise you have come to expect from them. You will find MacKenzie-Childs ceramic ware and Claire Murray rugs here as well as work from local artists. The jewelry from Mediterranean Artists Company features sea glass, mother of pearl, gold, sterling silver and precious stones. As the exclusive Southport dealer for M. A. Hadley Stoneware, Lantana's features the handpainted 'Beach" design among others. Metal sculptures, blown glass, Pomegranate Linens, Seagrove Pottery, paintings, prints and more can be found throughout this lovely store.

Ricky Evans Gallery and Southport Picture Framing
211 N. Howe St., Southport
(910) 457-1129

The Ricky Evans Gallery features his lighthouse paintings in addition to a series of paintings of historic Southport landmarks and a coastal waterfront series. Original paintings, watercolors and limited-edition posters are available as well. Throughout the rooms of the gallery you will also find paintings, pottery, stained glass, metal sculptures, handmade jewelry and more — all the work of more than 50 top artists in the area — on display and for sale. Custom picture framing is available, and the gallery is open year round. If you prefer, you can even shop online.

TOPSAIL ISLAND

Mystic Treasures Jewelry
121 S. Topsail Dr., Surf City
(910) 328-6300

This artisan shop carries absolutely gorgeous hand-crafted fine jewelry. Creative pieces are crafted from sterling silver, 14K and 18K gold and platinum. The majority of their designs are hand-crafted on site in their design studio and the balance is by selected guest artists. Mystic Treasures also offers custom designs. They are open Tuesday through Sunday during the summer. Please call for winter hours.

Seacoast Art Gallery
203 Greensboro Ave., Surf City
(910) 328-1112

Just look for the little pink art gallery by the beach and you will find artist in residence Sandy McHugh. Sandy's artwork reflects her love of the beach, and many of her watercolors depict local beach scenes. Stop in and visit with Sandy during the summer months.

Topsail Art Gallery
121 S. Topsail Dr., Surf City
(910) 328-2138

Topsail Art Gallery specializes in American art and crafts. They have a wide variety of originals and reproductions from local, regional and nationally known artists. The gallery offers unique gift items, stained glass, pottery and great hand-crafted metal sculptures. The frame shop can custom-frame any selection. The gallery is open year round. Owners Mike and Judy Hendy pride themselves on their ability to fill customers' special requests. They are closed Mondays.

⏺ ATTRACTIONS

Known for its beautiful beaches and waterways, North Carolina's southern coast also offers a multitude of attractions that have more to do with history than geography. The rich historic legacy of Wilmington and the surrounding communities manifests itself in museums, monuments, churches, grand old residences and other structures that speak eloquently of the past. However, there is little doubt that the proximity to the sea lends a distinct resort quality to this culturally vibrant region.

With the advent of a new trend in vacationing known as heritage tourism, visitors are searching for more than long days on the beach in coastal destinations. What is heritage tourism? This concept addresses the desire of modern visitors to explore sites and attractions that make history come alive and provide the ability to experience life as it was once lived in that area. Historic sites such as the Battleship North Carolina, Thalian Hall, Brunswick Town, Fort Fisher, Penderlea Homestead and Topsail Island's Assembly Building convey specific eras and events as no textbook or commemoration can.

Downtown Wilmington's historic legacy and related attractions are integral to the identity of the Cape Fear region. The historic district has a colorful past and is the most varied single attraction in the area, easily explored on foot, by boat, trolley or horse-drawn carriage.

By 1840 Wilmington was the largest city in North Carolina. Nicknamed the Port City by residents, it was on a par with other great Southern ports such as Charleston, Galveston and New Orleans. But when the Atlantic Coast Line Railroad company pulled out of Wilmington in the 1960s, the city went into such a rapid decline that even its skyline was flattened by the demolition of several buildings and railroad facilities on the north side of town. Downtown was nearly deserted until a core of local entrepreneurs revitalized and restored their hometown. In 1974 downtown Wilmington became the state's largest urban district listed in the National Register of Historic Places. Many of the images of Wilmington's past are preserved in the North Carolina Room at the New Hanover County Public Library's main branch at 201 Chestnut Street, throughout the Cotton Exchange and at Chandler's Wharf in downtown Wilmington. Likewise, the Cape Fear Museum and the Wilmington Railroad Museum interpret the region's history in far-reaching exhibits. Combined with a variety of tour options (listed in this chapter), these places are excellent resources for interpreting what you see today or exploring the rich history preserved here.

This region is so rich in history it would be impossible to list every historical attraction in a book this size. However, preserving and sharing the rich historic bounty is such a point of pride with Insiders that visitors won't fail to notice clearly marked areas of interest as they explore the region. For example, as you travel neighboring Brunswick County to such places as Southport's Old Smithville Burial Ground, stay alert for other sites with similar stories to tell, such as Southport's old Morse Cemetery on W. West Street and the John N. Smith Cemetery on Leonard Street off Herring Drive. Memorials are so abundant you may miss the one at Bonnet's Creek (Moore Street north of downtown Southport), at the mouth of which "Gentleman Pirate" Stede Bonnet used to hide his corsair. (This and many other sites are on the Southport Trail, listed in this chapter.)

Naturally, many attractions are typical of the seashore: excellent fishing, fine seafood dining, the many cruise opportunities. No beach resort would be complete without water slides, go-cart tracks or bat-

ting cages, and we've got plenty of those. These amusements, as well as miniature golf, movies and bowling, are concentrated along our most heavily traveled routes. Just keep your eyes open; you can't miss them. In Wilmington, Oleander Drive east of College Road is the predominant amusement strip, having several more attractions than listed here. North of Ocean Isle Beach, Beach Drive (N.C. Highway 179/904) is another strip with its share of go-carts, miniature golf and curiosities. Around Southport, check out the rapidly expanding Long Beach Road area between Southport and Oak Island. Topsail Beach and Surf City share the limelight as Topsail Island's two centers of attractions. It would be redundant to list every enterprise — they're opening faster than we can list them, and you're bound to stumble across them as you gravitate toward each community's entertainment center.

Reasons to explore Wilmington and the southern coast don't fade with the end of summer heat and sun. The "shoulder" or off-season has gained in vitality since the mid-1990s, except in some of the smaller beach communities. Mild temperatures, reduced rates, the boom in the region's golf courses and year-round activities convince the off-season visitor that southeastern North Carolina is a great place to relax.

It would be difficult to overstate the importance of the region's gardens, for which North Carolina is rightly famous. The fact that the North Carolina Azalea Festival, in which garden tours are focal, is based in Wilmington makes a strong case for the southern coast's horticultural significance. The spectacular 100-year-old Airlie Gardens, containing 67 acres of gardens and 10 acres of lakes, is a must-see for gardening enthusiasts. Annual and perennial plantings are well-supported public works.

In this chapter we describe many of the area's prime attractions, followed by a brief section on the southern coast's islands. Wilmington's attractions are grouped into three subsections: Downtown Wilmington, Around Wilmington and Outside Wilmington. Within each section, attractions are listed alphabetically.

Visitor Information

Information to supplement this guide can be obtained at the following locations. You can also check with the local chambers of commerce for information (see our Area Overview chapter for a list of chamber offices), public libraries and the Visitors Information Booth by the river at the foot of Market Street in Downtown Wilmington.

**Greater Topsail Area
Chamber of Commerce
Treasure Cove Landing, 13775 N.C. Hwy. 50,
Ste. 101, Surf City
(910) 329-4446, (800) 626-2780**

**Southport Visitors Center
113 W. Moore St., Southport
(910) 457-7927, (800) 388-9635**

**Wilmington/Cape Fear Coast
Convention and Visitors Bureau.
24 N. Third St., Wilmington
(910) 341-4030, (877) 406-2356**

Downtown Wilmington

**Battleship NORTH CAROLINA
1 Battleship Rd., Wilmington
(910) 251-5797
www.battleshipnc.com**

Without question, the Battleship NORTH CAROLINA is the centerpiece of the Wilmington Riverfront. A majestic symbol of this country's hard-earned naval victories in World War II, the battleship is a must-see attraction.

Enshrined in a berth on Eagles Island across the Cape Fear River from historic downtown Wilmington, this awesome vessel is the Memorial to the 10,000 North Carolinians of all the armed services who gave their lives during World War II. Commissioned in 1941, the 45,000-ton warship wields nine 16-inch turreted guns and carries nickel-steel hull armor 16 to 18 inches thick. The USS NORTH CAROLINA Battleship survived a direct torpedo hit in 1942, a tribute to the strength of its construction. In fact, the "Immortal Showboat" is known for the relatively small number of casualties it suffered during the war.

The Battleship NORTH CAROLINA came to its present home in 1961. It took a swarm of tugboats to maneuver the 728-foot vessel into its berth, where the Cape Fear river is only 500 feet wide. After much effort and tribulation, the city of Wilmington gained a majestic and ir-replaceable piece of history that continues to provide visitors with an enlightening journey into the past.

You can drive to it easily enough, but using the river taxi is more fun. (See the write-up for Capt. Maffitt Sightseeing Cruise in this section.)

You can absorb all the Battleship NORTH CAROLINA has to offer at your own speed and see what is most interest-ing to you with a self-guided tour that takes you to more than nine decks. In-cluded are the crew's quarters, galley, sick bay, gun turrets and exhibits that reveal the heart of this World War II Battleship, including new visual displays with first-person accounts of daily life aboard the battleship. These individual stories help bring history to life, capturing the imagi-nations of children and adults alike, who may have only read about World War II in textbooks. More features to check out are the engine room, the plotting rooms, radio central, the Admiral's Cabin, the bridge and combat central. Don't miss the Kingfisher float plane, one of the last of its kind to survive, located on the stern of the battleship's main deck.

Plan on taking at least two hours to enjoy the tour. Spend some time in the visitors center, where you can view the fascinating display's related to the Battle-ship NORTH CAROLINA, its place in WWII history, as well as the memorabilia and personal belongings of the people who lived and worked on board. On your way out, don't forget to visit the Ship's Store, a gift shop filled with Battleship NORTH CAROLINA souvenirs and gifts with a nautical or military theme.

Ample parking adjoins the berth, and Battleship Park includes a sheltered picnic area. Please note that only the visitors center and the main deck of the battle-ship are wheelchair accessible. Tours cost

$12 for those ages 12 and older and $6 for children ages 6 through 11. Children 5 and younger get in free. The cost is $10 for seniors 65 and older as well as retired and active-duty military personnel. Guided tours and programs are new at the Battle-ship. Call for reservations and pricing. Be sure to check out the Battleship's website for a calendar of events.

The Battleship is open every day. From Memorial Day weekend to Labor Day, hours are 8 AM to 8 PM. From Labor Day to Memorial Day weekend, hours are 8 AM to 5 PM. Ticket sales end one hour before closing. There is no extra charge for unscheduled appearances by old Charlie, the alligator who makes his home near the battleship at the river's edge.

Bellamy Mansion Museum
503 Market St., Wilmington
(910) 251-3700

Situated at the corner of Fifth and Market Streets in historic Wilmington, the fabulous Bellamy Mansion Museum has been admired by passersby since it's completion in early 1861. The house has stood through urban renewal, fire, vandal-ism, and neglect, only to emerge from the ashes, shake off the dust, and assume its place as a true symbol of the city of Wilmington.

The revival of this great house is the result of a community effort, a community diverse in nature but united in dedication. The house is a result of the fusion of a great Wilmington architect, James F. Post and a planter and physician from South Carolina named John D. Bellamy. The house would not exist, however, with-out the intensive labor of both enslaved and free African American craftsmen. A piece of plasterwork which fell during the fire bears the initials WBG for William B. Gould, a slave who later became a sailor for the Union Navy and kept an extensive diary. The ornate carvings on the front door and elsewhere bear testimony to the skill of the artisans who produced them.

The sheer size of the house is over-whelming. Four full floors and a tiny fifth floor — the belvedere — enclose almost 10,000 square feet of space. The belve-dere is the grand finale of the tour, providing a panoramic view of Wilmington from windows on all four walls.

On the compound (and on the tour) is an incredibly rare building - the urban slave dwelling. This structural masonry building with its 18-inch thick brick walls is a work in progress, but is being sensitively restored. For the historian, it is a must-see.

Bellamy Mansion Museum is open to the public Tuesday to Saturday 10 AM to 5 PM and Sunday 1 to 5 PM. Tours begin at the Carriage House with a brief film on the mansion's history and preservation efforts, and may continue with a docent or an audio headset. Please note that the last tour begins at 4 PM. Admission is $10 for adults and $4 for children ages 5 through 12. Children younger than 5 enter free of charge. Friends of the Bellamy Mansion (only $50 per year), and members of Preservation North Carolina get in free. Call ahead for special group rate information.

Burgwin-Wright House and Garden
224 Market St., Wilmington
(910) 762-0570

When Lord Charles Cornwallis, still in danger of a Rebel pursuit, fled to the coast after the Battle of Guilford Court House in central North Carolina in 1781, he repaired to Wilmington, then a town of 200 houses. He lodged at the gracious Georgian home of John Burgwin, a wealthy planter and politician, and made it his headquarters. The home, completed in 1770, is distinguished by two-story porches on two sides and seven levels of tiered gardens. The massive ballast-stone foundation remains from the previously abandoned town jail. A free-standing outbuilding houses the kitchen and a craft room and is located behind this beautifully preserved Colonial home. A tunnel from the garden area runs down toward the Cape Fear River, and the dungeon, located beneath the cellar, has been opened for viewing. The Burgwin-Wright House, currently owned by the National Society of the Colonial Dames of America in the State of North Carolina, is one of the great restoration/reconstruction achievements in the state, and visitors may peruse the carefully appointed rooms and period furnishings.

Group tours are available by appointment. Call for admission prices. The museum is open Tuesday through Saturday 10 AM to 4 PM, with the last tour at 3 PM on all days. September through December, the schedule may be altered in the morning due to school programs so call for information.

Colonial Christmas is a special event at the house during the second weekend in December. The house is filled with the music of the 1700s and decorated for the holiday season with greenery and fruit, while the art of open-hearth cooking is highlighted. There are performances by dancers in full colonial costume and demonstrations of colonial weaving/tapestry in the craft room, and you can even take a peek in to the old jail's dungeon. And for history buffs, a colonial surgeon demonstrates surgery as it was performed on the battlefield.

Cape Fear Museum
814 Market St., Wilmington
(910) 798-4350
www.capefearmuseum.com

For an overview of the history, science and cultures of the Lower Cape Fear region, from prehistory to the present, Cape Fear Museum stands unsurpassed. Established in 1898, Cape Fear Museum is the oldest history museum in North Carolina. The skeleton of a 20-foot-tall Giant Ground Sloth greets visitors to the museum. A miniature re-creation of the second battle of Fort Fisher and a remarkable scale model of Civil War Wilmington's waterfront are of special interest. Learn all about Wilmington's most famous basketballer before entering the Michael Jordan Discovery Gallery — an interactive science exhibit for the entire family. The Discovery Gallery includes a giant, crawl-through beaver lodge, Pleistocene-era fossils and an entertaining Venus flytrap model you can feed with stuffed "bugs." Children's activities, concerts, special events and acclaimed touring exhibits help make Cape Fear Museum not only one of the primary repositories of local lore, but also a place where learning is fun. The museum is open Tuesday through Saturday 9 AM to 5 PM and Sunday 1 to 5 PM. During the

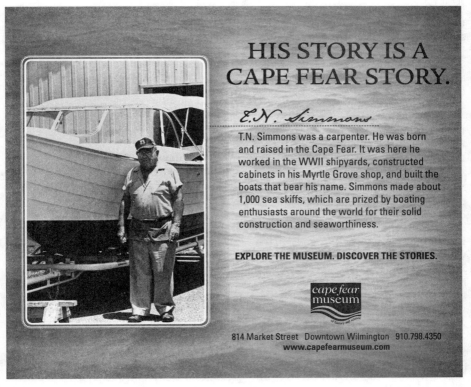
summer season (Memorial Day through Labor Day), the museum is open Mondays from 9 AM to 5 PM. Admission is $6 for adults, $5 for seniors and students with valid ID, $5 special military rate with valid military ID, and $3 for children ages 3 through 17. Children younger than 3 and Cape Fear Museum members are admitted free. Admission is free to all New Hanover County residents on the first Sunday of each month. Groups of 10 or more may be eligible for a discount on admission fees and should contact (910) 798-4362 for details. Cape Fear Museum is handicapped accessible, and it offers an interesting, well-stocked Museum Store for visitors.

Cape Fear Riverboats- Henrietta III
101 S. Water St., Wilmington
(910) 343-1611

This elegant, refurbished riverboat is a large, three-level, paddle-free vessel with a capacity for 600 guests. In fact, the Henrietta III is so spacious that it can accommodate three separate events — wedding parties, dinner cruises, themed cruises, etc. — at once. Cruise the Cape Fear River in style on this beautiful riverboat with a variety of options that include a 90-minute narrated sightseeing cruise, narrated lunch cruise, "Redneck Wedding Comedy" and "Murder Mystery" dinners, dance cruises and more. Most cruises are available from April through December, while others only go out during the summer season. Rates vary according to the type and length of the cruise. Prepaid tickets are required for cruises that include meals. The Henrietta III also offers special events cruises throughout the year. The boat's elevator makes all decks handicapped accessible. The Henrietta III is U.S. Coast Guard–approved.

Cape Fear Segway
106 N. Water St., Unit 108, Wilmington
(910) 251-2572

If you're looking for an innovative and eco-friendly way to tour Wilmington, hop on a Segway. Cape Fear Segway offers one or two-hour guided tours of the historic district and the riverfront. Along the way, you'll learn about Wilmington's storied history, its stately mansions and film and television locations. Cape Fear Segway also offers custom nature tours and Segway and electric bike rentals. For more information, call the number above or stop by their shop on Water Street.

Cape Fear Serpentarium
20 Orange St., Wilmington
(910) 762-1669

Featuring more than 100 species of snakes, most of them deadly, the Serpentarium boasts the largest collection of venomous reptiles in the world. The owner is the major breeder of the spectacular South American bushmaster, the world's longest and deadliest pit viper. The Serpentarium boasts the world's only breeding colony of the nearly extinct blackheaded bushmaster, among other rare finds. The dangerous reptiles of every continent are represented, including king cobras, spitting cobras, Australian taipans, black mambas, Gaboon vipers, gigantic pythons, Gila monsters, Nile crocodiles, 7-foot monitor lizards, and dozens of others, living in lush dynaramas developed for the Serpentarium by the movie industry. The Serpentarium is open daily 11 AM to 5 PM, but in winter months, it is closed on Mondays and Tuesdays. All tickets cost $8. Group tours are available, and school groups are welcome.

CAPT. J.N. MAFFITT Sightseeing Cruise
Riverfront Park, Foot of Market St., Wilmington
(910) 343-1611

Named for Capt. John Newland Maffitt, one of the Confederacy's most successful blockade runners, the Capt. Maffitt is a converted World War II Navy launch affording 45-minute sightseeing cruises with live historical narration along the Cape Fear River. Cruises set out at 11 AM and 3 PM daily from Memorial Day to Labor Day. Off-season weekend cruises are available from May 1 to Memorial Day and from Labor Day to mid-November. Cruise tickets cost $10 for adults and $5 for children ages 2 to 12. The Capt. Maffitt is available for charter throughout the year, and it doubles as the Battleship River Taxi

during the summer. No reservations are necessary, and it runs on the quarter-hour from Wilmington's riverfront to the Battleship NORTH CAROLINA and on the hour and half-hour for the return trip except at 11:30 AM and 3:30 PM during the sightseeing cruise times. River taxi fees are $4 per person and free for children younger than 2.

Chandler's Wharf
225 S. Water St., Wilmington
(910) 343-9896

More than 100 years ago, Chandler's Wharf was crowded with mercantile warehouses, its sheds filled with naval stores, tools, cotton and turpentine and its wharves lined with merchantmen. A disastrous (and suspicious) fire in August 1874 changed the site forever. In the late 1970s, Chandler's Wharf became an Old Wilmington riverfront reconstruction site, a positive turning point for downtown revitalization. Today much of the flavor of the 1870s remains, and Chandler's Wharf is again a business district, or, more accurately, a shopping and dining district. Two historic homes transformed into shops stand on the cobblestone street, beside wooden sidewalks and the rails of the former waterfront railway. The original ship chandler warehouse has been converted into popular boutiques, galleries and a bakery; a pictorial history of Wilmington is displayed there. Elijah's and The Pilot House restaurants overlook the Cape Fear River, and the Riverwalk provides a delightful waterside stroll that connects Chandler's Wharf with the rest of downtown. (See our Restaurants and Shopping sections for more about Chandler's Wharf.)

Chestnut Street United Presbyterian Church
710 N. Sixth St., Wilmington
(910) 762-1074

This tiny church, built in 1858 and originally a mission chapel of First Presbyterian Church, is a remarkable example of Stick Style, or Carpenter Gothic, architecture. Its exterior details include decorative bargeboards with repeating acorn pendants, board-and-batten construction, a louvered bell tower (with carillon) and paired Gothic windows. When the congregation, then slaves, formed in 1858 under the auspices of the mother church, the chapel was surrendered by the mother church to the new, African American congregation, which purchased the building in 1867. The congregation's many distinguished members have included the first African American president of Biddle University (now Johnson C. Smith University), the publisher of Wilmington's first African American newspaper, a member of the original Fisk University Jubilee Singers, the first African American graduate of MIT, and North Carolina's first African American physician.

The Children's Museum of Wilmington
116 Orange St., corner of Second St., Wilmington
(910) 254-3534

This hands-on, learning-through-play museum offers something for children of all ages with all interests. Sail the seas as a pirate in Ahoy, Wilmington!, Climb on the new School Bus, examine your teeth in the ToothaSaurus Pediatric Dental Exhibit, perform examinations as a physician in the Teddy Bear Hospital, experiment in the Science Lab, sing and act in the Star Maker Sound Stage, make a masterpiece in the Art Studio and do much, much more. Art and science programming is offered every day. Toddler Time is on Fridays at 10:30 AM. Their website lists the full calendar of events and programming. For more about the museum, see our Wilmington Kidstuff section.

First Baptist Church
411 Market St., Wilmington
(910) 763-2471

Even having lost its stunning 197-foot, copper-sheathed steeple to Hurricane Fran in 1996, First Baptist was still Wilmington's tallest church. For years this tower, the taller of the church's two steeples, had been known to visibly sway even in an average wind. The steeple's repair was completed in early 1999. Being literally the first Baptist church in the region, this is the mother church of many other Baptist churches in Wilmington. Its congregation dates to 1808, and construction of the red-brick building began in 1859. The church was not completed until 1870 because of

the Civil War, when Confederate and Union forces in turn used the higher steeple as a lookout. Its architecture is Early English Gothic Revival with hints of Richardson Romanesque, as in its varicolored materials and its horizontal mass relieved by the verticality of the spires, with their narrow, gabled vents. Inside, the pews, galleries and ceiling vents are of native heart pine. Sunday School classes occupy an equally interesting building next door on Fifth Street, the Sidbury House, which exhibits such classic Italianate elements as frieze vents and brackets and fluted wooden columns. The church offices are located in the Taylor House next door on Market Street.

First Presbyterian Church
125 S. Third St., Wilmington
(910) 762-6688

Visiting clergymen held services occasionally for Presbyterians in Wilmington in the 1700s, and the First Presbyterian Church was organized here in 1817. This congregation has long had among its members some of the most influential Wilmingtonians, and that is still the case today. The Rev. Joseph R. Wilson was pastor from 1874 until 1885; his son, Thomas Woodrow Wilson, grew up to become slightly more famous in the nation's history.

The church itself, with its finials and soaring stone spire topped with a metal rooster (a symbol of the Protestant Reformation), blends Late Gothic and Renaissance styles and is the congregation's fourth home, the previous three having succumbed to fire. During the Union occupation, the lectern Bible was stolen from the third church, which burned on New Year's Eve 1925. The stolen Bible was returned years later to become all that remains of the sanctuary. Today, intricate tracery distinguishes fine stained-glass windows along the nave as well as the vast west window and the chancel rose. The 1928 E. M. Skinner organ, with its original pneumatic console, is used regularly. Handsomely stenciled beams, arches and trusses support a steep gabled roof. To one side is the Kenan Chapel, with its transverse Romanesque arches. The education building behind the sanctuary is quintessential Tudor, complete with exterior beams set in stucco, wide squared arches, casement windows with diamond panes, interior ceiling beams and eccentric compound chimneys.

Having undergone major renovation in the early 1990s, First Presbyterian is an impressive sight. Its carillon can be heard daily throughout the historic district.

Ghost Walk of Old Wilmington
Riverfront at Market and Water Sts., Wilmington
(910) 794-1866

Visitors and locals alike enjoy this nightly walking tour of downtown Wilmington. The tour meets year round by the Riverfront at the foot of Market Street. From April 1 through October 31, tours are held nightly at 6:30 and 8:30 PM. In November and March tours are held nightly at 6:30 PM. In December, January and February, tours are held Thursday through Saturday at 6:30 PM. Special Halloween times vary, and you're advised to call ahead. Cost is $12 for adults and $10 for seniors, students and military; it's free for children ages 6 and younger. Private tours for groups of 15 people or more can be arranged year round; please call ahead.

Haunted Pub Crawl
Riverfront at Market and Water Sts., Wilmington
(910) 794-1866

Prepare yeself for a party alike no other! Hoist a pint or three in old Wilmington's most actively haunted pubs. Hear tales that will both shiver-ye-timbers and make ye laugh so hard ye'll swab the deck. From the disreputable obsession of the merry wench "Gallus" Meg to the barbarous haunts of a notorious madman, ye'll be beggin' to be keelhauled before it's all over. Reservations are required. The tour begins at 7:30 PM and is only for those age 21 and older. Nights vary; call the number above for the most current schedule. Private group tours for 10 or more adults can be arranged year round. Cost is $15 per adult.

Hollywood Location Walk of Old Wilmington
Riverfront at Market and Water Sts., Wilmington
(910) 794-1866

This 90-minute walking tour of one of America's largest living film sets is a must for all film buffs. The Hollywood Location Walk takes you on a name-dropping tour of downtown Wilmington that will give you a first-hand glimpse of the film industry in the Port City. See real locations and sets for TV shows like *One Tree Hill* and movies like the *Divine Secrets of the Ya-Ya Sisterhood*. Check out where the casts and crews hang out when they're not working. The tour takes place at 2 PM on Tuesday, Thursday, Saturday and Sunday, plus 10 AM on Saturday. Tickets are $12 for adults, $10 for seniors, students or military, and free for children younger than 6.

Horse-Drawn Trolley & Carriage Tours
Market St., between Water and Front Sts., Wilmington
(910) 251-8889

See historic downtown Wilmington the old-fashioned way — by horse-drawn carriage or trolley. This half-hour tour in a fringed-top surrey (open-air trolley) is narrated by a driver wearing nineteenth-century garb. At busy times, such as during Azalea Festival and Riverfest, these horse-drawn tours are especially popular. Don't miss the memorable seasonal events, including the romantic horse-drawn Valentine ride in a French evening coach, an "Easter Bunny"–drawn ride, the Halloween Ghost Trolley ride, the "Thanksgiving Turkey"–drawn ride, or the Caroling by "Reindeer" Christmas ride. Carriage rides are also available for weddings, private parties and other special occasions. Call the number above for reservations and rates. Seating is on a first-come, first-served basis. From April through October, tours operate daily between 10 AM and 10 PM. November to March, the carriages roll Sunday through Thursday from 11 AM to 4 PM and Friday and Saturday between 11 AM and 10 PM. All tours are weather permitting. Expect to pay $12 for adults and $5 for children age 11 and younger; rates are subject to change without notice, however.

Oakdale Cemetery
520 N. 15th St., Wilmington
(910) 762-5682

When Nance Martin died at sea near Cuba in 1857, her body was preserved seated in a chair in a large cask of rum. Six days later, following a quick voyage home, she was interred at Oakdale Cemetery, cask and all. Her monument and many other curious, beautiful and historic markers are to be found within the labyrinth of Oakdale Cemetery, Wilmington's first municipal burial ground, opened in 1855. At the cemetery office, you can pick up a free map detailing some of the more interesting interments, such as the volunteer firefighter buried with the faithful dog that gave its life trying to save his master, and Mrs. Rose O'Neale Greenhow, a Confederate courier who drowned while running the blockade at Fort Fisher in 1864. Amid the profusion of monuments lies a field oddly lacking in markers — the mass grave of hundreds of victims of the 1862 yellow fever epidemic. The architecture of the monuments, the Victorian landscaping and the abundance of dogwood trees make Oakdale beautiful in every season. The cemetery is open from 8 AM to 5 PM daily. Oakdale Cemetery office hours are Monday through Friday 8:30 AM to noon and 1 to 4:30 PM. Admission is free.

The Riverwalk
Riverfront Park along Water St., Wilmington

The heart and soul of downtown Wilmington is its riverfront. Once a bustling, gritty confusion of warehouses, docks and sheds — all suffused with the odor of turpentine — the wharf was the state's most important commercial port. Much has changed today. Now you can experience Wilmington's charm and historical continuity by strolling The Riverwalk. Dining, shopping and lodging establishments line the walk, and live entertainment takes place at the small Riverfront Stage on Saturday and Sunday evenings from June to early August. Check with the Visitors Information Booth at the foot of Market Street for schedules. Every Friday from 6 to 10 PM in the spring and summer months, Riverfront Park is the site of the Downtown Sundown — live music with the Cape Fear River sunset serving as a lovely

Downtown Wilmington offers many attractions.

photo: Chris Tisinger

backdrop for the festivities. Immediately to the north, schooners, pleasure boats and replicas of historic ships frequently visit the municipal docks. Coast Guard cutters and the occasional British naval vessel dock beyond the Federal Court House; some ships allow touring, especially during festivals. Benches, picnic tables, a fountain and snack vendors complete the scene, one of Wilmington's most popular.

St. James Episcopal Church and Burial Ground
25 S. Third St., Wilmington
(910) 763-1628

St. James is the oldest church in continuous use in Wilmington, and it wears its age well. The parish was established in 1729 at Brunswick Town across the river (also see the writeup for St. Philip's Parish). The congregation's original Wilmington church wasn't completed until 1770. It was seized in 1781 by Tarleton's Dragoons under Cornwallis. Tarleton had the pews removed, and the church became a stable. The original church was taken down in 1839, and some of its materials were used to construct the present church, an Early Gothic Revival building with pinnacled square towers, battlements and lancet windows. The architect, Thomas U. Walter, is best known for his 1865 cast-iron dome on the U.S. Capitol. A repeat performance of pew-tossing took place during the Civil

War, when occupying Federal forces used the church as a hospital. A letter written by the pastor asking President Lincoln for reparation still exists. The letter was never delivered, having been completed the day news arrived of Lincoln's assassination. Within the church hangs a celebrated painting of Christ (Ecce Homo) captured from one of the Spanish pirate ships that attacked Brunswick Town in 1748. The sanctuary also boasts a handsome wood-slat ceiling and beam-and-truss construction.

Church offices are in the McRae House, built in 1900 from a design by Henry Bacon, who also designed the Lincoln memorial in Washington, D.C. The cemetery at the corner of Fourth and Market streets was in use from 1745 to 1855 and bears considerable historic importance. Here lies the patriot Cornelius Harnett, remembered for antagonizing the British by reading the Declaration of Independence aloud at the Halifax Courthouse in 1776. He died in a British prison during the war. America's first playwright, Thomas Godfrey, is also memorialized here. The cemetery once occupied grounds over which Market Street now stretches, which explains why utility workers periodically (and inadvertently) unearth human remains outside the present burial ground. Visitors are welcome to take self-guided tours of the church on Monday, Tuesday, Wednesday and Friday between 10 AM and 3 PM when services are not underway.

St. Marks Episcopal Church
600 Grace St., Wilmington
(910) 763-3292

Established in 1869, this was the first Episcopal church for blacks in eastern North Carolina, and it has conducted services uninterrupted since that time. The building (completed in 1875) is a simple Gothic Revival structure with a buttressed nave and octagonal bell tower. All visitors are welcome to attend worship services on Sunday. Please check local Saturday newspapers or call the church at the number listed above for the schedule.

St. Mary's Roman Catholic Church
217 S. Fifth St., Wilmington
(910) 762-5491

Numerous historical writers have referred to this Spanish Baroque edifice (built 1908-11) as a major architectural creation, often pointing out the elaborate tiling, especially inside the dome, which embraces most of this church's cross-vaulted interior space. The plan of the brick building is based on the Greek cross, with enormous semicircular stained-glass windows in the transept vaults, arcade windows in the apse and symmetrical square towers in front. Over the main entrance, in stained glass, is an imitation of Leonardo da Vinci's The Last Supper. A coin given by Maria Anna Jones, the first black Catholic in North Carolina, is placed inside the cornerstone.

St. Paul's Evangelical Lutheran Church
12 N. Sixth St., corner of Sixth and Market Sts., Wilmington
(910) 762-4882

Responding to the growing number of German Lutherans in Wilmington, North Carolina's Lutheran Synod organized St. Paul's in 1858. Services began in 1861 as the Civil War broke. Construction came to a halt when the German artisans working on the building volunteered for the 18th North Carolina Regiment and became the first local unit in active duty. The building was occupied and badly damaged by Union troops after the fall of Fort Fisher in early 1865. Horses were stabled in the building and its wooden furnishings were used as firewood. The completed church was dedicated in 1869, only to burn in 1894. It was promptly rebuilt. There have been several additions and renovations since. Today the building is remarkable for its blend of austere Greek Revival elements outside (such as the entablature, pediments and pilasters) and Gothic Revival (such as the slender spire, clustered interior piers and large lancet windows). Also notable are its color-patterned slate roof and copper finials and the gently arcing pew arrangement. The removal of paneling during renovations in 1995-96 uncovered beautiful stenciling on the ceiling panels and ribs in the vestibule, nave and chancel.

Temple of Israel
**1 S. Fourth St., corner of Fourth and
Market Sts., Wilmington
(910) 762-0000**

The oldest Jewish temple in North
Carolina, this unique Moorish Revival–
style building was erected in 1875–76 for
a Reform congregation that was formed
in 1872. Its two square towers are topped
by small onion domes, and the paired,
diamond-paned windows exhibit a mix of
architrave shapes, including Romanesque,
trefoil and Anglo-Saxon arches. Another
notable feature is a magnificent chandelier,
brought to the United States from Landau,
Germany. Believed to be more than 500
years old, the chandelier was originally
lighted by oil, later by candles and finally
by electricity. The Pilcher-Tracker organ,
constructed in 1901 and restored in 1990,
is one of only three such organs known
to still be in operation. When the Front
Street Methodist Episcopal Church was
destroyed by fire in 1886, the Temple of
Israel congregants offered their building
as a substitute until a new church could
be erected. The offer was accepted and
the Methodists met in the Temple for a
little more than two years. Please call the
Temple office prior to visiting.

Thalian Hall and City Hall
**310 Chestnut St., Wilmington
(910) 343-3664, (800) 523-2820**

Since its renovation and expansion in
the late 1980s, the name has been, more
accurately, Thalian Hall Center for the
Performing Arts. And yes, it does share
the same roof with City Hall. Conceived as
a combined political and cultural center,
Thalian Hall was built between 1855 and
1858. During its first 75 years, the Hall
brought great national performers and
some surprising celebrities to its stage: Lillian Russell, Buffalo Bill Cody, John Philip
Sousa, Oscar Wilde and Tom Thumb, to
name a few. That tradition continues. Full-
scale musicals, light opera and internationally renowned dance companies are
only a portion of Thalian Hall's consistent,
high-quality programming, which includes
more than 250 performances annually.
Today the Center consists of two theaters
— the Main Stage and the Studio Theatre
— plus the Grand Ballroom (which doubles

as the Wilmington City Council Chambers). With its Corinthian columns and
ornate proscenium, it's no wonder Thalian
Hall is on the National Register of Historic
Places. Private and group tours are offered
Tuesday through Friday by appointment
and include the Main Stage, backstage, the
Studio Theatre, the Grand Ballroom, Gallery and City Hall. Contact Thalian Hall's
administrative offices, (910) 343-3660, to
schedule a tour and for tour rates. Visitors can take a self-guided tour Tuesday
through Friday from noon to 6 PM and on
Saturday from 2 to 6 PM. Admission for
the self-guided tour is $1.

Wilmington Adventure Walking Tour
**Riverfront Park, Foot of Market St.,
Wilmington
(910) 763-1785**

For over 25 years, lifelong Cape Fear
resident Bob Jenkins (the man with the
straw hat and walking cane) has been
leading the Wilmington Adventure Walking Tour, speaking passionately and
knowledgeably about his hometown.
Expounding upon architectural details,
family lineage and historic events, Bob
whisks you through 250 years of history
in about two hours. You'll see residences,
churches and public buildings. Tours begin
at the flagpole at the foot of Market Street
at 10 AM daily, weather permitting, April
through October. Cost is $10 for adults
and $5 for children ages 6 to 12. Children
younger than 6 go along for free. Although no reservations are required, it's
best to call ahead, especially in summer.
Off-season (November through March)
group tours are by advance reservation
only.

Wilmington National Cemetery
**2011 Market St., Wilmington
(910) 815-4877**

In 1866-67, immediately after the Civil
War, the United States Congress enacted
legislation to create national cemeteries
to honor and protect the remains of U.S.
soldiers who fell in battle or died of disease. The Wilmington National Cemetery
was established in 1867 on 5 acres of land
about a mile east of downtown. The cemetery originally contained the remains of
more than 2,000 Union soldiers, many of

whom died at Fort Fisher and were later interred here. More than 1,300 are unidentified; many are black, identified as U.S.C.T. (United States Colored Troops) or U.S. Col. Inf. (United States Colored Infantry). Markers with round tops indicate known burials, and stones with flat tops indicate unknowns; nearly all are government issue. Following the Civil War period, the Wilmington National Cemetery received the remains of Americans through the Vietnam conflict. The cemetery no longer has room for additional deceased soldiers; however, spouses and family members of soldiers already interred there may still be buried near their loved one. Visitors interested in finding a specific grave may use the locator at the entrance of the cemetery. Grounds are open daily from 8 AM to 5 PM.

Wilmington Railroad Museum
505 Nutt St., Wilmington
(910) 763-2634

The history and heritage of railroads in Wilmington is clearly borne out by this museum's fine photographs and artifacts. Beyond details of more than 130 years of history, the Railroad Museum is fun for people of all ages fascinated by trains and train culture. For the price of admission, you can climb into a real steam locomotive and clang its bell for as long as your kids will let you. Inside the History Hall, exhibits explain how railroads and the people who worked on them shaped commerce and society. In the museum's "Memories" book, visitors are encouraged to share their favorite train memories; entries include everything from preschoolers' art to nostalgic and touching essays from visitors from around the country and around the world. The museum building was built in 1882 as a freight warehouse and is one of just a few remaining buildings from the golden era of railroading. The boardwalk and Railroad Heritage Square are home to a steam locomotive from 1910, boxcar with hobos, and a caboose to explore. Visitors can run model train on the enormous railroad layout in the Model Hall, which is maintained by the museum's model train committee. A Children's Hall provides lively surroundings for youngest visitors, including Lionel trains with lots of action. Adult program-

ming, children's tours, model train workshops, an Annual Train Show and group discounts are available. The museum also invites you to book your birthday parties on its caboose; the affordable rental fee includes souvenirs and a tour of the museum. April 1 through September 30, the museum is open Monday through Saturday from 10 AM to 5 PM and Sunday from 1 to 5 PM. October 1 to March 30, it's open Monday through Saturday from 10 AM to 4 PM. The museum is closed New Year's Eve, New Year's Day, Easter Sunday, Thanksgiving, Christmas Eve and Christmas Day. Admission fees are only $7 for adults, $6 for military personnel and senior citizens age 60 and older, and $3 for children ages 2 to 12. Children younger than 2 are admitted free.

Wilmington Trolley Company
GPS #15 Water St., Wilmington
(910) 763-4483

Located on Water Street near the Visitor Center Information Booth, the Wilmington Trolley offers a 45-minute guided tour of historic downtown Wilmington over a course of about 8 miles. Available daily, April through October (Friday, Saturday and Sunday tours are available in November and March and on Saturdays year round), the tours leave on the hour from 10 AM to 5 PM. There are some evening tours available during the summer months, with the last tour leaving at 8 PM. Fees are $11 for adults and $5 for children ages 3 to 12. Call ahead for evening and off-season tour availability, as well as rentals for private charters.

Zebulon Latimer House
126. S. Third St., Wilmington
(910) 762-0492

This magnificent Italianate building, built by a prosperous merchant from Connecticut, dates from 1852 and is remarkable for its original furnishings and artwork. The house boasts fine architectural details such as window cornices and wreaths in the frieze openings, all made of cast iron, and a piazza with intricate, wrought-iron tracery. Behind the building stands a rare (and possibly Wilmington's oldest) example of urban slave quarters, now a private residence. What sets the

Latimer House apart from most other museums is the fact that it was continuously lived in for more than a century, until it became home to the Lower Cape Fear Historical Society in 1963. It has the look of a home where the family has just stepped out. The Historical Society is one of the primary sources for local genealogical and historical research. For information on membership, write to 126 S. Third Street, Wilmington, NC 28401. The society's archives are housed at the Latimer House and are available to the public Monday through Friday from 10 AM to 4 PM. The Latimer House is open Monday through Friday from 10 AM to 4 PM and Saturday noon to 5 PM. The last guided tour is at 3:15 PM. Admission is $10 for adults and $5 for students. Walk & Talk Tours, which require reservations, encompass about 12 blocks of the historic district and last two hours. The tours are given every Wednesday and Saturday at 10 AM and cost $10.

Around Wilmington

Airlie Gardens
300 Airlie Rd., Wilmington
(910) 798-7700

Enjoy the pleasures nature has to offer — smell the roses, admire the azaleas, gaze at the camellias and stand in the shade of the 466-year-old Airlie Oak while visiting this quintessential Southern garden. Wander at your leisure along curving paths and walkways in this lush natural setting while admiring the majesty of the maritime forest of trees native to the region — live oaks, cedars, pines and wax myrtles. Need a rest? Sit and enjoy the beauty of the overlook and pier while gazing out on shimmering Bradley Creek.

In the early 1900s Airlie Gardens was designed to showcase plants for all four seasons — azaleas in spring, magnolias and live oaks in summer and camellias in the fall and winter. Statuary, pergolas and fountains grace the gardens. Bordered by Bradley Creek and salt marshes, these beautiful 67 acres support two freshwater lakes that attract swans, ducks, geese, herons, egrets and more. From January 2 through March 19 the gardens are open

Monday through Saturday from 9 AM to 5 PM. From March 20 through the end of the year, the gardens are open seven days a week from 9 AM to 5 PM. Admission is $5 for adults and $3 for children 12 and younger. Admission is free for members. Individual memberships cost $25, with family memberships starting at $50, and each includes free admission to the gardens, the Airlie Concert Series and Enchanted Airlie.

Cameron Art Museum
3201 S. 17th St., Wilmington
(910) 395-5999

The Cameron Art Museum is the only art museum in southeastern North Carolina. The museum presents six to eight special exhibitions annually; monthly family and children's programs (Kids @ CAM); weekly interdisciplinary, public programs (lectures, music, films, dance); and ongoing workshops and classes in ceramics at a unique Clay Studio with a resident master artist and developing artist-in-residence program. The museum also offers weekly yoga and Tai Chi classes. The museum occupies a 40,000-square-foot facility designed in 2002 by the renowned architectural firm of Gwathmey Siegel & Associates (NYC). Cameron Art Museum is sited on a 9.3-acre woodland park known as Pyramid Park, featuring long-leaf pine woodlands, outdoor sculptures, nature trails, a historic Civil War site and The Clay

Studio housed in the Pancoe Art Education Center. The main museum building includes three exhibition areas, the Weyerhaueser lecture and reception hall and a museum gift shop. Parking is free. Admission is free for members, $8 for non-members, $5 for students (with valid ID) and $3 for children ages 2 to 12. Program information is offered on the website.

EUE/Screen Gems Studios Tour
1223 N. 23rd St., Wilmington
(910) 343-3500
www.screengemsstudios.com/nc/tours.html

Movie fans can take a one-hour walking tour of EUE/Screen Gems Studios, the largest full-service production facility east of California. You'll see the actual studio lot and stages where more than 300 film and television projects have been produced, including *Secret Life of Bees*, *Muppets from Space*, *Domestic Disturbance*, *Dawson's Creek*, *Matlock* and the hit CW Network series *One Tree Hill*. Regular highlights of the tour include visits to the sets currently in production, old movie sets and props, video presentation of the studio's history in the screening room and a question-and-answer session. From May through September, tours are offered Saturdays and Sundays at noon and 2 PM. The rest of the year, they're offered only on Saturdays at noon and 2 PM. Call in advance for the current schedule

information. Plan to arrive at least 15 minutes prior to your tour to purchase tickets. Admission is $12 for adults, $10 for students and military with a proper ID, $8 for seniors and $5 for children age 5 to 12. Private group tours for 20 or more people are available by reservation anytime year round. For more information call (910) 343-3433.

Greenfield Lake and Gardens
U.S. Hwy. 421 S (Third St. and Carolina Beach Rd.), Wilmington
(910) 762-5606

In springtime the colors here are simply eye-popping. In summer the algae-covered waters and Spanish moss are reminders of the days when this was an unpopulated cypress swamp. In winter the bare tree trunks rise from the lake with starkness. Herons, egrets and ducks are regular visitors, as are hawks and cardinals. The 5-mile lake-view drive is a pleasure in any season, and there's a paved path suitable for walking, running or cycling around the entire lake. Greenfield Lake is 2 miles south of downtown Wilmington along S. Third Street. Eco-tours of the lake are available for groups of 4 or more at $15 per person upon request through Cape Fear River Watch; call (910) 762-5606 for more information. (See more about Greenfield Lake in our Sports, Fitness and Parks.)

Jungle Rapids Family Fun Park
5320 Oleander Dr., Wilmington
(910) 791-0666

This self-contained amusement magnet includes the only true water park in eastern North Carolina plus more game attractions than a family could exhaust in a week. The quarter-mile-long Grand Prix GoKart track features bridge overpasses, banked turns, timing devices and one- and two-passenger cars. Children less than 56 inches tall, and younger than 12 years of age, must ride with licensed adult drivers. The Waterpark includes seven excellent slides, including the half-pike Sidewinder, the four-tube slide called the Volcanic Express, The Super Bowl and the meandering Lazy River. Lifeguards are always on duty, and there are plenty of lockers, lounges, tables and umbrellas. Private cabanas can be arranged for an additional cost. Also worthwhile are the million-gallon wave pool and the Kiddie Splash Pool (with four kiddie slides). In addition, there's jungle-themed miniature golf, a rock-climbing wall, the adrenaline-pumping Alien Invaders Laser Tag, the high-tech arcade featuring more than 100 games ranging from the classic to state-of-the-art, and the air-conditioned Kids Jungle (Wilmington's largest indoor playground for children ages 8 and younger). Jungle Rapids caters kids' birthday parties on site. They offer on-site catering for meetings and functions (the largest room accommodates 200 people with a minimum of 50). The Big Splash Café and Pizzeria offers an ample menu during park hours. Waterpark opens Memorial Day weekend and is open daily from 11 AM. Dry Park attractions are open at 10 AM. Call for hours.

New Hanover Cooperative Extension Arboretum
6206 Oleander Dr., Wilmington
(910) 798-7660

This 7-acre teaching and learning facility with 33 gardens is the only educational arboretum in southeastern North Carolina. The arboretum was formally opened in 1989 and is still in the midst of development. These gardens rank among the finer theme gardens in the area. Boardwalks and paths wind through a profusion of plants, grasses, flowers, trees, shrubs, herbs and vegetables, and there is plenty of shaded seating. Several sections, such as the Herb Garden with its variety of medicinal, culinary, fragrance and tea species, are sponsored by local garden clubs. Other themed gardens include the Rose Garden's Heritage roses, a hands-on Children's Garden and the Aquatic & Bog Gardens, some of the largest in the state. The arboretum also has an Ability Garden, which helps physically and/or mentally challenged individuals learn about and experience the joys of gardening.

Working in cooperation with the N.C. State University Cooperative Extension, the arboretum also offers community services and educational programs on a variety of skill levels up to Master Gardener courses. The arboretum assists commercial and private horticultural enterprises and helps residents create attractive home landscapes. This last mission is served by their plant clinic and the Garden Hotline, (910) 798-7680, where volunteer Master Gardeners field questions about horticulture from 10 AM to 4 PM.

Need a special gift for a gardener? Don't miss the delightful variety of gifts and gardening books (their specialty) available at The Potting Shed gift shop, (910) 452-3470, in the Hutaff Visitors Center. The shop is open from 10 AM to 4 PM Monday through Friday. Admission to the arboretum is free. Donations are welcome and much needed. Funding is primarily by individual and corporate sponsors, volunteers, fund-raising events and local garden clubs. Volunteer docents lead tours on request during extension office hours Monday through Friday from 8 AM to 5 PM. Self-guided tours are permitted daily from dawn to dusk. (The gates are closed but not locked during this time.) Enter the grounds from Oleander Drive (U.S. Highway 76) immediately east of Greenville Loop Road and west of the Bradley Creek bridge. And, yes, the arboretum is available for weddings.

Tregembo Animal Park
5811 Carolina Beach Rd., Wilmington
(910) 392-3604
www.tregemboanimalpark.com

Tregembo Animal Park will delight and amaze kids of all ages. Carrying on a family tradition that goes back more than 50 years, the Tregembos have expanded and updated the zoo to create habitats for their animals from around the world. There are some of the familiar zoo favorites, like Jashan the white tiger, a lion named Simba and Ben the bear, along with some exotic new additions, including a giraffe, a zebra and a group of ring-tailed lemurs that reside on their very own Lemur Island. Kids will have a great time exploring the park, feeding the ducks and goats, and watching the amusing antics of the mon-

keys. Tregembo Animal Park is a fun place to spend an afternoon with kids. Their large gift shop is filled with educational animal-related toys, T-shirts, plush items and nautical souvenirs. Tregembo Animal Park is open from 10 AM to 5 PM daily and closes during the winter season. Please call for admission prices. Group rates are available for school groups, but please call in advance.

Wilmington Sea Dawgs
Games: Schwartz Center, 610 N. Front St., Wilmington
(910) 791-6523
Office: 430 Eastwood Rd., Ste. 200, Wilmington
(910) 791-6528
www.wilmingtonseadawgs.com

For the past four years, the Wilmington Sea Dawgs have been "unleashing the excitement" of professional basketball in the Port City. Calling Cape Fear Community College's Schwartz Center their home, the Sea Dawgs play an exciting brand of fast-paced hoops that draws substantial crowds and makes fans of first-time attendees. The team participates in many community outreach events and provides discounted or complimentary tickets to most area not-for-profit organizations. Also, each season the team holds open tryouts, making it possible for local hoop stars to have a chance at their dream of pro basketball stardom. Bring the entire family or the neighborhood kids to a Sea Dawgs game and enjoy all the high-flying dunks and sharpshooters this team has to offer.

Outside Wilmington

Cape Fear River Circle Tour
Southport-Fort Fisher Ferry, U.S. Hwy. 421, Southport/Ft. Fisher
(910) 341-4030

A Circle Tour brochure is available at the Southport Visitors Center, 113 W. Moore Street, Southport, (910) 457-7927, (800) 388-9635; the Cape Fear Coast Convention & Visitors Bureau, 24 N. Third Street, Wilmington, (910) 341-4030; and visitor information racks throughout the area. It directs you around a loop that includes a ride on the Fort Fisher/Southport ferry and connects Wilmington, Pleasure Island, Southport and eastern Brunswick County. The Circle Tour will bring you to seven major attractions: Battleship NORTH CAROLINA (fee), Orton Plantation Gardens (fee), Brunswick Town/Fort Anderson (free), Southport Maritime Museum (fee), Progress Energy's Brunswick Nuclear Plant (free), North Carolina Aquarium (fee) and Fort Fisher Civil War Museum (free). Total time for driving is about two hours, which includes about 30 minutes riding the ferry. The brochure provides information on the attractions and ferry schedule.

Moore's Creek National Battlefield
40 Patriots Hall, Currie
(910) 283-5591

This 86-acre National Park Service site commemorates and preserves the land where the Revolutionary War Battle of Moore's Creek was fought in February 1776 between Loyalists and Patriots of North Carolina. A one-mile walking history trail enables you to see much of the battlefield, and there are also exhibits and an audio-visual program in the visitors center. The battle is commemorated annually during the last full weekend in February. The event features living history encampments, weapons demonstrations,

colonial and military music and a wreath-laying ceremony. There is a picnic area with a covered shelter, tables, charcoal grills and restroom facilities. The park is open 9 AM to 5 PM seven days a week and is only closed on Thanksgiving, Christmas and New Year's days. The park is located along N.C. Highway 210 approximately 20 miles northwest of Wilmington. Take I-40 north to Exit 408, then travel west on N.C. Highway 210 for 15 miles.

Poplar Grove Plantation
10200 U.S. Hwy. 17, Wilmington
(910) 686-9518 x26

This 1850 Greek Revival house and plantation is one of the oldest existing peanut plantations in North Carolina. Today, costumed guides lead visitors through this lovingly restored mansion and recount the plantation's history. Skills important to daily nineteenth-century life, such as spinning, weaving, smithery and basketry, are frequently demonstrated, and visitors are invited to walk the estate's grounds and view the plantation's outbuildings, including a tenant house, an outdoor kitchen and more.

The 67-acre Abbey Nature Preserve has a 2.4-mile nature trail winding through woods and crossing over the mill pond. Once the original site of Poplar Grove's

Remember that feeling you felt as a kid when you first saw signs of the beach?

photo: Robert Graves

gristmill, the preserve is now part of the Coastal Land Trust and a wonderful escape from the city. Poplar Grove, dedicated to education, preservation and service to the community, maintains a busy schedule of activities throughout the year. Annual events include a Farmer's Market, a Halloween festival, an Herb and Garden Fair, the Classy Chassis Car Show & Flea Market, and a Christmas Open House.

Listed on the National Register of Historic Places, Poplar Grove Historic Plantation is 9 miles north of Wilmington on U.S. 17 at the Pender County line. Farm animals, a gift shop, a playground and a picnic area, and wedding and party facilities are located on the grounds. Poplar Grove Historic Plantation is open Monday through Saturday 9 AM to 5 PM and Sunday noon to 5 PM. Regularly scheduled tours are Monday through Saturday at 9:30, 10:30 and 11:30 AM and at 1, 2, 3 and 4 PM and Sundays at noon, 1, 2, 3 and 4 PM. Note that the last guided tour of the plantation house is at 4 PM daily. Fees for the guided house tour are $10 for adults ($6 each for groups of 15 or more), $9 for seniors and military, $5 for students ages 6 to 15 and free for children 5 and younger. Admission to craft demonstrations, outbuildings and grounds is $7. Group rates are available. Poplar Grove is closed for Easter, Thanksgiving and from the week of Christmas until the beginning of February. Call for Christmas hours. Parking is plentiful, and access to the estate's grounds is free.

Wrightsville Beach and Vicinity

Wrightsville Beach Museum of History
303 W. Salisbury St., Wrightsville Beach
(910) 256-2569

The Wrightsville Beach Museum is housed in the Myers cottage, one of the oldest cottages on the beach (built in 1909). Opened in May 1995, the museum presents beach history and lifestyles through permanent exhibits featuring a scale model of the historic trolley stops on the beach, a snapshot of 1910 Wrightsville Beach Landmarks, photos, furniture and artifacts. The museum hosts an annual fundraiser called Lumina Daze in August at the Blockade Runner. The museum is open Tuesday through Friday 10 AM to 4 PM, Saturday noon to 5 PM and Sunday 1 to 5 PM. Entrance to the museum and parking are both free. The museum is wheelchair accessible. Upon crossing the drawbridge, bear left at the "Welcome to Wrightsville Beach" sign; the museum is the second right near the volleyball courts beyond the fire station.

Wrightsville Scenic Tours and Taxi
Waynick Blvd. (across from
Blockade Runner), Wrightsville Beach
(910) 200-4002

In the warm season, a cruise aboard a 27-foot motorized catamaran affords breathtaking views of the Intracoastal Waterway. Nature excursions to Masonboro Island are guided by experienced naturalists. Leisurely cruises down the waterway, daytrips to Masonboro Island and shuttles for you and your sea kayaks are other highlights. Inshore fishing charters are also offered. Bait, tackle and guide are provided for only $25 a person. Don't miss their pirate adventure storytelling cruise for kids and adults to the famous Money Island. Call for in-season cruise and excursion schedules and off-season charters and small-group excursions.

Carolina Beach and Kure Beach

Fort Fisher State Historic Site
U.S. Hwy. 421, south of Kure Beach
(910) 458-5538

Fort Fisher was the last major Confederate stronghold to fall to Union forces during the Civil War. It was the linchpin of the Confederate Army's Cape Fear Defense System, which included forts Caswell, Anderson and Johnston and a series of smaller batteries. Largely due to the tenacity of its defenders, the port of Wilmington was never entirely sealed by the Union blockade until January 1865. The Union bombardment of Fort Fisher was the heaviest naval demonstration in history up to that time. During the war, the fort, which stretched for 1.5 miles, was the largest and strongest earthen fort in the Confederacy. Today, the Department of Cultural Resources operates and maintains the remains of Fort Fisher as a State Historic Site.

The property boasts scenic easements of both the Cape Fear River and the Atlantic Ocean. A half-mile tour trail surrounds the archaeological remains of the Confederate fort. Exterior exhibits, a reconstructed palisade fence and a partially restored gun emplacement enhance historic interpretation. The tour trail encircles the Western Bastion, including the partially restored Shepherd's Battery, which boasts a fully functional reproduction of a rifled and banded 32-pounder cannon. This huge gun is the only one in the nation said to be fired on a regular basis. On the north side of the fort, re-created palisades will be of interest to Civil War buffs. Because Fort Fisher is an archaeological site, metal detectors are prohibited. The tour trail is handicapped accessible.

Following your visit to the fort, walk across U.S. Route 421 to The Cove, where you'll find a live oak-lined area overlooking the ocean; it's a great place for a relaxing stroll. Swimming here is discouraged because of dangerous currents and underwater hazards. However, miles of unspoiled beaches are available immediately to the south at Fort Fisher State Recreation Area, complete with bathhouse showers, a visitors center and a concession stand (see our Sports, Fitness and Parks section).

Highlights of the Fort Fisher Historic Site's renovated visitors center include an upgraded theater, an enlarged gift shop, handicapped-accessible restrooms, a free 15-minute audiovisual program chronicling the history of the fort, a museum and a state-of-the-art, 16-foot fiber optic map. An eight-minute narrative accompanying the map narrates the final Battle of Fort Fisher. Civil War enthusiasts will especially enjoy the expanded exhibits, dioramas, artifacts and an informative audio program. The surrounding grounds, including The Cove and earthworks, are open to the public and are available for tours daily. The site, about 19 miles south of

Wilmington, was once commonly known as Federal Point. The ferry from Southport is an excellent and time-saving way to get there from Brunswick County. From April through September, the visitors center is open Monday through Saturday 9 AM to 5 PM and Sunday 1 to 5 PM; winter hours, October through March, are Tuesday through Saturday 9 AM to 5 PM (closed Sunday and Monday). For more information, to schedule a guided tour or to inquire about group tours, call the phone number above or visit www.nchistoricsites.org/fisher. Admission is free, but donations are appreciated.

Fort Fisher-Southport Ferry
U.S. Hwy. 421, South of Kure Beach
(910) 457-6942

More than transportation, this half-hour crossing is a journey into the natural and social history of the Cape Fear River. You'll have excellent views of Federal Point, Zeke's Island and The Rocks from the upper deck. On the Southport side, you'll spot historic Price's Creek Lighthouse at the mouth of the inlet. The crew is knowledgeable, and the cabin is air-conditioned. When traveling between Southport and New Hanover County, timing your trip to the ferry schedule makes getting there half the fun. See our Getting Here, Getting Around section for schedules or call the ferry offices: (910) 457-6942 on the Southport side and (910) 458-3329 on the Fort Fisher side.

One-way fees are $1 for pedestrians, $2 for bicycle and rider, $3 for motorcycles, $5 for vehicles from 20 feet or less, $10 for vehicles 20 to 40 feet, $15 for vehicles 40 to 65 feet.

North Carolina Aquarium at Fort Fisher
900 Loggerhead Rd., Kure Beach
(910) 458-8257
www.ncaquariums.com/fort-fisher

Visitors to the North Carolina Aquarium at Fort Fisher encounter an astounding variety of aquatic life. From inland habitats through coastal waters to aquatic environments beyond the coast, the stunning exhibits showcase a variety of aquatic settings. Located on the ocean, east of U.S. 421 and south of Kure Beach (15 miles south of Wilmington), the facility is one of southeastern North Carolina's most visited attractions. Visitors begin their tour with a huge freshwater conservatory, and then move toward a 235,000 ocean tank. The journey is like a trip down the Cape Fear River, beginning with a Piedmont waterfall, continuing along creeks, swamps, estuaries and beaches, and finishing in the open ocean beyond the river's mouth. Exhibits allow visitors to experience close encounters with a variety of North Carolina wildlife, including sharks, alligators, stingrays, sea turtles, venomous reptiles and the Aquarium's newest residence, a rare albino alligator. The aquarium is open daily 9 AM to 5 PM except Thanksgiving, Christmas, New Year's days. Admission is charged. The aquarium also hosts fun events, classes and programs for all ages.

Wheel Fun Rentals
**107 Carolina Beach Ave. N,
at the Boardwalk, Carolina Beach
(910) 458-4545
Lake Park Blvd. and Atlanta Ave.,
Carolina Beach
(910) 617-9792**

Tired of sunbathing? Try exploring Carolina Beach in a Deuce Coupe, Surrey or Chopper from Wheel Fun Rentals. The Deuce Coupe is a covered bicycle built for two, allowing couples to pedal side-by-side (great idea for a date). Equipped with lights, the four-wheeled covered Surrey can seat up to six adults and two children, making it perfect for a family or group outing. For those who prefer to go it alone, the Chopper offers a sleek and stylish way to pedal along the boardwalk. Don't have any beach gear? Wheel Fun Rentals has everything you could need for a day at the beach, from surfboards and boogie boards to beach umbrellas, chairs and sand toys. Or try their Lake Park location where you can rent paddleboats and kayaks and spend a quiet afternoon paddling on the lake. Wheel Fun Rentals is open every day during the summer from 9 AM to 9 PM (weather permitting) on the Boardwalk and 9 AM to dusk at Lake Park. In the spring and fall they're open weekends and by appointment. Call to book parties or special events.

Brunswick County

BALD HEAD ISLAND

Bald Head Island Historic Tour
**Deep Point Marina, 1303 Ferry Rd.,
Southport
(910) 457-5003**

This guided-tour package may be the most convenient way for a daytripper to get to know Bald Head past and present. Tours are offered Tuesday through Saturday from March 15 until Thanksgiving. Call for tour days after Thanksgiving. The three-hour tour begins with a 10 AM ferry departure and includes visits to Old Baldy Lighthouse, the Smith Island Museum of History and Captain Charlie's Station. Put into service in 1817, Old Baldy is the state's oldest standing lighthouse, the second of three built on the island to guide ships across the Cape Fear Bar and into the river channel. The tour fee ($45 per adult, $40 per child 12 and younger — subject to change) includes the round-trip ferry ride, the island tour, entrance to the museum and lighthouse and a $10 voucher toward the purchase of lunch at Eb and Flow's Steam Bar. Stay and linger; ferries return to Southport at the bottom of every hour. Reservations are required and can be made at the above number. For more information, call (910) 457-7481. You must arrive at the departure site by 9:30 AM for the 10 AM departure. Remember to dress appropriately for the weather and wear comfortable shoes as the tour requires walking.

SOUTHPORT

Brunswick Town/Fort Anderson
**State Historic Site
8884 St. Philips Rd. SE, off N.C. Hwy. 133,
Winnabow
(910) 371-6613**

At this site stood the first successful permanent European settlement between Charleston and New Bern. It was founded in 1726 by Roger and Maurice Moore (who recognized an unprecedented real estate opportunity in the wake of the Tuscarora War, 1711-13), and the site served as port and political center. Russelborough, home of two royal governors, once stood nearby. In 1748 the settlement was attacked by Spanish privateers, who were soundly defeated in a surprise counterattack by the Brunswick settlers. A painting of Christ (Ecce Homo), reputedly 400 years old, was among the Spanish ship's plunder and now hangs in St. James Episcopal Church in Wilmington. At Brunswick Town in 1765, one of the first instances of armed resistance to the British crown occurred in response to the Stamp Act. In time, the upstart, upriver port of Wilmington superseded Brunswick. In 1776 the British burned Brunswick, and in 1862 Fort Anderson was built there to help defend Port Wilmington. The earthworks of Fort Anderson are 100 percent intact and one of the best examples of earthworks that exist today. Occasional church services are still held in the ruins of St. Philip's Church.

Admission to the historic site is free and open to the public all year, Tuesdays through Saturdays from 9 AM until 5 PM. The site is closed on most major holidays. From Wilmington, take N.C. 133 about 18 miles to Plantation Road. Signs will direct you to the site (exit left) that lies close to Orton Plantation. The site's visitors center offers a gift shop, a research library, an exhibit hall, a 14-minute video presentation on the history of Old Brunswick Town and Fort Anderson, staff offices and handicapped accessibility. A new paved ADA walkway has been installed to give visitors a full-circle, handicapped accessible trail to explore the site as well as Russellborough. There is also a handicapped accessible picnic area.

The Chapel of Cross at St. Philip's
E. Moore and Dry Sts., Southport
(910) 457-5643

Southport's oldest church was in continuous use until Easter Sunday 2004, when St. Philip's dedicated a new 350-seat church on property across the street. The new church has the traditional clapboard look on the exterior, a bell tower and carillon. The Chapel of the Cross at St. Philip's is a beautiful clapboard church erected in 1843, partly through the efforts of Colonel Thomas Childs, then commander of Fort

Johnston, one block east. It stands beside Southport City Hall. Within the chapel flies nearly every flag that has flown over the parish since 1741, including Spanish and British. The building exhibits Carpenter-style Greek Revival elements, particularly evident in the pediments and exterior wooden pilasters, as well as English Gothic details. Entrance is made through the small, square tower, with its louvered belfry, simple exterior arcading and colored-glass lancet windows. The church's side windows of diamond-paned clear glass flood the sanctuary with light, illuminating the handsome tongue-and-groove woodwork on the walls and ceiling. It's a beautiful, quiet place that remains open 24 hours a day for meditation, prayer or rest as well as being available for funerals, weddings, healing services and other religious forums. Guidelines are available for those interested in using the chapel for religious purposes.

The Grove
Franklin Square Park, Howe & E. West Sts., Southport
(910) 457-7927, (800) 388-9635

Shaded by centuries-old live oaks and aflame with color in spring, this is a park to savor — a place in which to drink in the spirit of old Smithville. The walls and entrances that embrace The Grove were constructed of ballast stones used in ships more than 100 years ago. Set back among the oaks, stately Franklin Square Gallery was once a schoolhouse and then City Hall and now is an art gallery displaying art in several media. The park is a place to indulge in local legend by taking a drink of well water from the old pump — a sip that is sure to take you back to a simpler time.

Keziah Memorial Park
W. Moore & S. Lord Sts., Southport
(910) 457-7927, (800) 388-9635

A shady little park with a gazebo, benches and a partial view of the waterfront, Keziah Park is notable for its uncannily bent live oak. Estimated to be 800 years old, the tree is called the Indian Trail Tree after the legend that it was curved while a sapling by ancient natives who used it to blaze the approach to their preferred fishing grounds beyond. It later rooted itself a second time, completing an arch.

North Carolina Maritime Museum at Southport
116 N. Howe St., Southport
(910) 457-0003

Read "Gentleman Pirate" Stede Bonnet's plea for clemency, delivered just before he was hanged; view treasures rescued from local shipwrecks; see a 2,000-year-old Indian canoe fragment; inspect the fine details of nearly 100 hand-built ship models; see the military exhibit; learn about hurricanes, sharks' teeth, shrimping nets and much more in one of the region's newest and most ambitious museums. Many of the exhibits are hands-on, and a Jeopardy-style trivia board is a favorite of history buffs of all ages. The museum boasts an extensive maritime research library and video collection and is within walking distance of Southport's restaurants and shopping. Hours are 9 AM to 5 PM Tuesday through Saturday. Admission is free. Ask about periodic special exhibits and lectures. Note: The museum is in the process of raising funds to be used for renovations and construction in anticipation of their move to Fort Johnston on Moore Street at an as yet undetermined date.

Old Brunswick Jail
Corner of Nash and Rhett Sts., Southport
(910) 457-0575

Have you ever considered visiting a jail? Not an enforced visit, of course, but one during which you can leave anytime you want. If the thought intrigues you, consider the Old Brunswick Jail, after all, "It's nothing like Alcatraz, more like Mayberry." Built in 1904 and in service until 1971, this two-story structure contains some of the original accoutrement. The sliding doors to the cells remain, as does the original register of "residents." There is even some left-over graffiti (including caricatures) — mainly from the Nixon era. The jail keeper's quarters contains a coal burning stove and cook oven wth pans and cooking devices as well as pictures of the jailers. You will see original coal burning

pot-belly stoves throughout. Then there are the stories — but you'll have to visit to learn those. The jail opens in April and is open on Wednesdays and Saturdays through October as well as by appointment for groups.

Old Smithville Burial Ground
E. Moore & S. Rhett Sts., Southport
(910) 457-7927, (800) 388-9635

"The Winds and the Sea sing their requiem and shall forever more. ..." Profoundly evocative of the harsh realities endured by Southport's long-gone seafarers, the Old Smithville Burial Ground (1804) is a must-see. Obelisks dedicated to lost river pilots, monuments to entire crews and families who lived and died by the sea, and stoic elegies memorialize Southport's past as no other historic site can. Many of the names immortalized on these stones live on among descendants still living in the area.

Old South Tour and Carriage Company
Whittler's Bench at the Waterfront,
Foot of Howe St., Southport
(910) 713-2072

Dressed in period costume, riding in a surrey pulled by a mule, local historian Katie Stewart offers tours of Historic Southport. She tells tales of the town's history, many with basis in fact. Interesting facts about pirates, blockade-runners and colonial settlers figure prominently in her stories. Also offered are lantern-led Ghost Walks. Dressed in an antebellum mourning gown and carrying an oil lantern, Katie will regale you with local legends of the night while you tour the Old Smithville Burying Grounds and skirt the Old Brunswick Jail. Specialty tours are available upon request, and group rates are available for organizations, clubs, schools and larger family reunions. To inquire about dates and times or to plan a tour, call Old South Tour and Carriage Company at the above number.

Priority Sailing
106 Yacht Basin Dr., Southport
(910) 454-4479

David and Carolyn Pryor, both highly experienced educators and sailors extraordinaire, invite you to participate in their customized adventure cruises aboard the

52-foot cutter, Carolina Gale. With a cockpit that comfortably seats six passengers plus crew, a spacious saloon, three queen cabins, two heads, a galley, a navigation center and a Bimini top for shade, this cruising yacht, luxuriously furnished with original artwork and hand-woven oriental rugs, provides all the comforts you need.

Priority Sailing provides opportunities to sail on the Atlantic Ocean and Cape Fear River. Sailors of various skill levels may participate in the operation of the sailboat, or just sit back and relax. The captains provide information on history, marine life and ecology as well as sailing knowledge and skills. This blue-water cruising sailboat is an excellent choice for birthday and anniversary celebrations, family reunions, a romantic honeymoon or bed and breakfast afloat as well. Morning, afternoon or sunset cruises sail the Atlantic Ocean along Oak Island or Bald Head Island or up the Cape Fear River along Battery Island and the Southport shore.

The Pryors have been involved with the Southport Sail and Power Squadron since its inception (see Watersports section for information about the Southport Sail and Power Squadron). They both have a history of racing and cruising on numerous sailboats, have achieved Senior Navigator status through the U.S. Power Squadrons and are licensed by the U.S. Coast Guard. Interested in sailing instruction? The Pryors also operate a sailing academy affiliated with the American Sailing Association (see our Watersports section for information on the sailing academy).

Progress Energy - Brunswick Plant Energy Center
9520 River Rd., N.C. Hwy. 87, Southport
(910) 457-2418

Have you ever wondered exactly how electricity is produced by nuclear energy? Nuclear power plants are off limits to the general public, but in the Visitors Center you can see a model of the Southport plant, watch it operate and listen to the audio recording explaining the process. Do you know that one million gallons of water per minute flow through the power plant in Southport for cooling? You will find exhibits that show the methods used for keeping sea turtles from entering the intake canal and for screening fish and other sea creatures where the water enters the plant, sending them down the "slide for life" to a holding pond and returning them to their natural environment. Other exhibits include explanations of used fuel storage, a small model of a control room, the fission process, energy and more. The exhibits are open by appointment only, so it's best to call (910) 457-6041 for more information and for a listing of phone numbers. The center is closed on holidays and weekends. Programs, presentations and guided tours are available for school and civic groups with advance arrangements.

S/V Kelly Allen Cruises
Old Yacht Basin, Foot of East West St., Southport
(910) 524-7245

Relax and experience the quiet power of the winds aboard sailing vessel Kelly Allen, a 37-foot O'Day center cockpit sloop. Sail the Atlantic Ocean, the Cape Fear River and the Intracoastal Waterway. Captain Bob Griffith is licensed by the U.S. Coast Guard, and sails are available year round, weather and tide permitting. Give Captain Bob a call to schedule your cruise. There is a minimum of two and a maximum of six passengers.

Skydive Coastal Carolinas
Brunswick County Airport (SKUT), 4019 Long Beach Rd., Southport
(910) 457-1039, (888) 899-5867

Have you ever dreamed of flying? Skydive Coastal Carolinas, a member of the United States Parachute Association, can make that dream come true! There are several options available. A tandem jump allows the first-time jumper to experience freefall from approximately 2 miles in the sky with the use of a parachute harness built for two people. This type of jump, accomplished with a certified tandem instructor, allows you to relax and enjoy the free fall and canopy ride with a minimum of ground training. As a tandem student you will be required to complete a brief ground class, usually 30 minutes. Instruction includes an overview of the jump process, climbing to altitude, exit, opening, canopy control and landing, and proper function and use of sport skydiving gear. There is even a videographer available to record the experience for you. There is skydiving instruction available to train you for Accelerated Free Fall as well. Experienced, qualified jumpers can participate in beach jumps and night jumps.

Smithville Horse-N-Buggy
Southport
(910) 477-2045

Smithville Horse-N-Buggy, a local, family-owned business, offers carriage rides and hay rides by reservation. The carriage is a beautiful Victorian style and is often pulled by a strong but gentle Belgian named Sally Jane. Other members of the family include two Percherons. The carriage ride, the transportation of choice for the First Friday Gallery Walks in Southport, is available for celebrating graduations, birthdays, Valentine's Day or any special occasion — or just because it's a beautiful way to see Southport.

Southport Trail
Southport
(910) 457-7927, (800) 388-9635

This 2-mile-long walking tour links 25 historic landmarks, among them the tiny Old Brunswick County Jail and the Stede Bonnet Memorial. Architectural beauty abounds along the route, revealing Queen Anne gables, Southport arch and bow, and porches trimmed in gingerbread. The free brochure describing this informal, self-guided chain of discoveries can be obtained at the Southport Visitor Center, 113 W. Moore Street (where the tour begins) Monday through Saturday from 9:30 AM to 4:30 PM in summer. Off-season, call for information at (800) 388-9635.

St. Philip's Parish
Old Brunswicktown State Historic Site, 8884 St. Philip's Rd. SE, Winnabow
(910) 371-6613

After St. James Anglican Church left Brunswick Town in favor of the rival port of Wilmington, the Anglican parish of St. Philip formed in 1741. In 1754 it began building a brick church at Brunswick, the seat of royal government in the colony. After struggling with finances and a destructive hurricane, the church was finally completed in 1768, only to be burned by the British in 1776 (the colony's first armed resistance to the Stamp Act occurred nearby at the royal governor's residence). Today, all that remains of St. Philip's church, the only Colonial church in southeastern North Carolina, is a rectangular shell — 25-foot-high walls, 3 feet thick — plus several Colonial-era graves (some of which are resurfacing with time). The ruin's round-arched window ports are intact and suggest Georgian detailing, but little solid evidence exists about the building's original appearance beyond some glazing on the brick. Three entrances exist, in the west, north and south walls, and three, triptych-style windows open the east wall. Services are still held held periodically within the ruins. The body of Royal Governor Arthur Dobbs is interred at St. Philip's, as is that of the infant son of Royal Governor William Tryon, although their graves have not been positively located. St. Philip's Episcopal Church in Southport was named after the Colonial parish to perpetuate its memory.

Trinity United Methodist Church
209 E. Nash St., Southport
(910) 457-6633

Built c. 1890 for a total of $3,300, this church is the third to occupy this site. Today the building features two of the area's best stained-glass windows (at either side of the sanctuary); handsome, diagonally paneled walls; and a beaded ceiling (i.e., finished with narrow, half-round moldings) finished by a 15-year-old carpenter. Emblazoned across the original front-transom window is the abbreviation "M.E.C.S." (Methodist Episcopal Church, South), a remnant of the days when the church was split from its northerly brethren due to the Civil War. The clapboard exterior includes Shingle-style detailing, a cedar-shingled roof and a gabled bell tower. Trinity Church stands at the corner of N. Atlantic Avenue, east of the Fire Department and across the street from the post office.

Waterfront Park
Bay St., at the foot of Howe St., Southport
(910) 457-7927, (800) 388-9635

At the end of Howe Street, you'll come upon this breezy little park and take in the breathtaking scene at the convergence of the Intracoastal Waterway, the Cape Fear River and the Atlantic Ocean. From the swings overlooking the waterfront you can see Old Baldy Lighthouse and Oak Island Lighthouse (the brightest in the nation). Gone are the pirate ships and menhaden boats, but the procession of ferries, freighters, barges and sailboats keeps Southport's maritime tradition alive. Stroll or cycle the Historic Riverwalk trail, an easy 0.7-mile scenic route that meanders from the City Pier, past the fisheries and the small boat harbor, and culminates at a 750-foot boardwalk with benches and handrails over the tidal marsh near Southport Marina. Leave your bike in the rack and walk on to the gazebo for an unbroken view of the Intracoastal Waterway and the ship channel. It's a restful, romantic place where the only sounds you're likely to hear are the cawing of crows and the clank of halyards.

OAK ISLAND

Environmental Overlook Trails
3003 E. Oak Island Dr., Oak Island
(910) 278-5515

If you like wandering and looking for wildlife, these trails are for you. The Butterfly/Hummingbird Garden is located on the trail behind the Recreation Center at 3003 E. Oak Island Drive. There are elevated platforms overlooking the path, which includes indigenous trees and flowers and plants that attract butterflies and hummingbirds. At the east end of 31st Street (next to the Recreation Center) is Tidal Waves Park, where you will find a small picnic shelter near the floating dock, which can be used for launching canoes and kayaks. Canoe/kayak trail maps are available at the center. The Environment Crossover crosses the Davis Canal, giving an elevated view of the canal and the wetlands on either side. The trail winds through the trees to the other side of the island, and a crossover walk leads to the ocean side, giving a closer view of the salt marsh. Wildlife, such as snakes, raccoons, deer and various birds, make their appearances here. The Town of Oak Island also preserves land at the west end of Oak Island. Paths wander through the dunes and stop at overlook points where you may chance to see red fox, black snakes, fiddler crabs, loggerhead sea turtles, raccoons or several species of shorebirds.

Fort Caswell
Caswell Beach Rd., Caswell Beach
(910) 278-9501

Considered one of the strongest forts of its time, Fort Caswell originally encompassed some 2,800 acres at the east end of Oak Island. Completed in 1838, the compound consisted of earthen ramparts enclosing a roughly pentagonal brick-and-masonry fort and citadel. Caswell proved to be so effective a deterrent during the Civil War that it saw little action. Supply lines were cut after Fort Fisher fell to Union forces in January 1865, so before abandoning the fort, the Caswell garrison detonated the powder magazine, heavily damaging the citadel and surrounding earthworks. What remains of the fort is essentially unaltered and is on the grounds of the N.C. Baptist Assembly, which owns the property. A more expansive system of batteries and a sea wall were constructed during the war-wary years from 1885 to 1902. Between the Tuesday after Labor Day and the Friday before Memorial Day, Fort Caswell is open for self-guided visits Monday through Friday 8 AM to 5 PM and Saturday 8 AM to noon. Admission is $3 per person.

Red Sky Aviation
4019 Long Beach Rd., Oak Island
(910) 457-6777

You have taken the walking tours and the carriage rides. For a change of pace and a bird's eye view of the beautiful Brunswick Beaches check out Red Sky Aviation. Their aerial scenic tours are guided by you. They will fly anywhere you like (within 25 miles of the airport) including Wilmington, Wrightsville Beach, Oak Island, Southport and Bald Head Island. You may even be able to spot your house. The length of the flight is up to you as well. Flights can carry one to three passengers so bring along friends and family and enjoy the beauty of the lower Cape Fear area from the air.

OCEAN ISLE BEACH

Museum of Coastal Carolina
21 E. Second St., Ocean Isle Beach
(910) 579-1016

Visit North Carolina's only natural history museum on a barrier island to experience coastal nature for the fun of it!. Standing on the ocean floor would be a wonderful way to experience the marine environment up close. Visitors to this museum can do the next best thing — walk through The Ocean Reef. This seascape diorama is home to life-sized models of sharks, dolphins, game fish, octopus and crustaceans. Explore the shark jaws and Megabites! exhibit. Then touch live sea creatures in the Sea Shore Gallery's touch tank stocked with sea stars, whelks, sea anemones, spider crabs, hermit crabs, an assortment of fish and more. Identify your beach treasures at the Carolina Shells exhibit, an extensive collection of more than 200 shells. Visitors may walk through the dune in the Legacy of the Loggerhead exhibit to watch a video filmed on Ocean Isle Beach about the life cycle of loggerhead turtles. Hands-on exhibits and extensive wildlife dioramas depict the plants and animals that live in the Green Swamp, barrier islands and coastal plain. The lecture series features fascinating topics and field trips. Visit the museum gift shop, Nature's Treasures, where you will find an abundance of educational and entertaining gifts and vacation mementos. Conveniently located beside the playground and a block from the beach and fishing pier, the museum hosts special family programs during the summer and activities throughout the year. Make advance reservations for school groups and tour groups. Family vacation passes, memberships and volunteer opportunities are available. Programs and hours change seasonally.

Planet Fun
349 Whiteville Rd., Shallotte
(910) 755-2386

Planet Fun is a 50,000-square-foot entertainment center that offers an array of activities mostly geared to families. Here you will find Constellation Alley with 32 bowling lanes, Highway 66 Bowling with glow-in-the-dark synthetic lanes, four mini bowling lanes, Ocean Quest Cosmic black light miniature golf, bumper cars, an indoor soft playground, Asteroids Arcade, Space Quest two-level laser tag, a bowling pro shop, Starz Restaurant and private party rooms. Planet fun offers bowling, billiards and laser tag leagues. Customized birthday party packages are available, and you can download invitations from the website.

Silver Coast Winery
6680 Barbeque Rd., Ocean Isle Beach
(910) 287-2800

Who would expect to find a winery just 15 minutes inland from the beach? Not just any winery, mind you, but an upscale, commercial vineyard and production facility situated on 40 acres, surrounded by dense, Carolina woods; a winery that has been winning gold, silver and bronze medals for their wines since opening in May of 2002. The folks at Silver Coast Winery invite you to sample wines in the tasting room, tour the winery and learn about wine making. Their tasting room includes a large selection of award-winning wines and gifts, and the art gallery offers an eclectic display of art from local artists. Plan a private party, corporate event or wedding, or just enjoy a picnic lunch in the breezy gardens. They also host a variety of special events throughout the year, including their annual Purple Feet Festival. During January and February, opening hours are Wednesday through Sunday from noon to 5 PM. March through December hours are Monday through Saturday 11 AM to 6 PM and Sunday from noon until 5 PM.

SUNSET BEACH

Ingram Planetarium
The Village at Sunset Beach,
7625 High Market St., Sunset Beach
(910) 575-0033

Ingram Planetarium is named for Stuart Ingram, a navigator of WWII planes who used the constellations and planets to chart his way. His quest for sharing his learning led to founding both the Ingram

Planetarium and the Museum of Coastal Carolina. New this year, the Planetarium boasts the world's third SciDome HD Digital Sky Theater, a state-of-the-art facility with a 40-foot dome. See the planets up close and in your face. Laser music shows are like rock concerts without the band and they are LOUD! Interactive and entertaining exhibits in the Paul Dennis Science Hall include ViewSpace, an award-winning exhibit featuring a continuous broadcast of the most recent updates directly from NASA. The Galaxy Gift Shop is a veritable storehouse of fun, educational gifts. Make advance reservations for school groups and tour groups. Hours and programs change seasonally. Memberships and volunteer opportunities are available.

CALABASH

The Hurricane Fleet
Deep Sea Fishing Center
Hurricane Fleet Marina, 9975 Nance St., Calabash
(910) 579-3660, (800) 373-2004

The Hurricane Fleet Deep Sea Fishing Center, with more than 30 years experience accommodating passengers, is located in the middle of the "seafood capital of the world," where shrimp are a very large part of the catch. Have you ever wondered just how and where the shrimp are caught? Why not take a cruise on the 90-foot Hurricane II, which engages working shrimp boats while their crews explain shrimping along the Carolinas. You will see dolphin and sharks feed on the by-catch as the nets are pulled only a few feet from the bow of the Hurricane II. Dolphin Eco Tours, narrated by a marine biologist, give you the opportunity to touch and discuss marine life captured in bottom dredges and plankton nets. These tours offer a fun learning experience. Known for their deep-sea fishing experiences, the Hurricane Fleet offers Bottom Fishing Charters, Half-Day Sportfishing Charters, Night Sportfishing and Overnight Gulf Stream Saltwater Fishing.

Topsail Island and Vicinity

Belle of Topsail
111 N. New River Dr., Surf City
(910) 328-1621

Board the *Belle of Topsail*, a 55-foot replica of an 1880s double-decker riverboat, and cruise the scenic waters of the Intracoastal Waterway and Topsail area sounds. The Belle is a completely outfitted party boat with an open-air top deck, two full bars and an air-conditioned formal dining salon. Join Captain David Luther and First Mate Sharon for either a one-hour sightseeing cruise (adults $12, children 12 and younger $8, children 2 and younger free) or the two-hour Sunset Cruise with heaping platters of heavy hors d'oeuvre (adults $25, children 12 and younger $15). Belle of Topsail sails seven days a week, and reservations are recommended. Call for sailing times. This summer, the Belle is also hosting weekend parties on the water every Friday, Saturday and Sunday afternoon ($3). The *Belle* will moor at a local sand bar for the day and guests may dine at umbrella tables on the sand bar, swim or go kite boarding. Boaters can stop by for supplies and those without a boat enjoy a free water taxi to the sand bar.

Buccaneer Cruises
720 Channel Blvd., Topsail Beach
(910) 546-8687

The *Buccaneer* offers sightseeing, sunset and party cruises. Sightseeing cruises provide the opportunity to see dolphins, osprey and other wildlife as you cruise by Blackbeard's old hideout. Sunset cruises offer time to relax and view Topsail's spectacular sunsets. Call Captain Dave for cruise times and rates. To guarantee your space, stop at the Topsail Beach Assembly Building dock to purchase tickets in advance.

Dorothy's Harbor Tours
720 Channel Blvd., Topsail Beach
(910) 545-FISH (3474)

Cruise Topsail Sound and the Intracoastal Waterway in Topsail Island's tour boat, *Dorothy*. With seating for 28 people, this craft offers regularly scheduled daytime and sunset cruises every day from April through September, bringing you a fantastic opportunity to watch dolphins frolicking, ospreys nesting and many other joys of nature. Private charters are available. Call for departure times and rates. No food or drinks are available onboard, but you may bring your own.

Karen Beasley Sea Turtle Rescue and Rehabilitation Center
822 Carolina Blvd., Topsail Beach
(910) 328-3377

While the primary purpose of this all-volunteer facility is the care and rehabilitation of sick and injured sea turtles, the center is open on a limited basis to the public. Visitors can view magnificent loggerhead sea turtles, green sea turtles and perhaps even a rare Kemp's Ridley turtle while learning about the history and the problems each turtle faces. Visitors will also learn about their feeding, treatment and predicted release dates. The center is open during the summer months on Monday, Tuesday, Thursday, Friday and Saturday from 2 to 4 PM. Due to the popularity and the limited size of this facility, it is best to arrive early. No calls for reservations are accepted. The center is not open to the public at other times of the year, and it may close without notice in the summer for emergencies. Donations are appreciated.

Missiles and More Museum
720 Channel Blvd., Topsail Beach
(910) 328-8663

From a beautifully simple Native American dugout canoe to a high-tech Osprey V-22 exhibit, the Missiles and More Museum covers a lot of ground. Kids of all ages will enjoy the pirate exhibit that features the top ten notorious pirates, including the infamous Blackbeard, who once plundered the merchant ships traveling past Topsail Island. Another exhibit is all about Operation Bumblebee, the U.S. Navy's secret guided missile testing program that operated on Topsail Island from 1946 to 1948. Model and original missiles from the project are on display including a full-size Talos guided missile. The Osprey Aircraft exhibit documents the development, design and utilization of the V-22 Osprey Aircraft, the world's first production tilt-rotor aircraft. Since the V-22 is tested at the New River Air Station, they are often seen flying over Topsail. Two audio-visual centers provide tours of the aircraft and provide a history of its development. Visitors will also find a new exhibit on barrier islands. Operated by volunteers, the museum is open Monday through Friday from 2 to 5 PM in the spring and fall and Monday through Saturday from 2 to 5 PM during the summer months. For large groups or off-season visits call the museum to schedule a private showing with a docent.

Sea Turtle Nest Sitting
Surf City

Lucky vacationers walking on the beach between July and October might spot the signs of a turtle nest about to hatch. Turtle project volunteers prepare the nesting area for the emerging turtles by creating smooth runways in the sand and clearing the area of obstacles. At night, trained volunteers sit by these nests and wait for the actual hatching. When visitors and/or residents come upon a roped-off nest that has been prepared with runways, they are welcome to join volunteers in this awe-inspiring experience. However, survival of the baby turtles requires patience and a willingness to follow instructions on the part of the spectators and participants.

Triple J Stables
120 Lake Haven Dr., Sneads Ferry
(910) 327-0577

Triple J Stables offers both trail rides and riding lessons. Guided trail rides are offered by appointment and should be reserved at least one day in advance. The stables are open seven days a week, and a summer day camp is also available.

Turtle Talks
Surf City Recreation Center, 201 Community Center Dr., Surf City

Want to know more about sea turtles? Check out Turtle Talks for an educational and kid-friendly talk on the lifestyle and habits of loggerhead turtles. Learn all about the Topsail Sea Turtle Project and what they do to help this endangered species. Questions are welcomed, and admission is free. No reservations are required. Turtle Talks are held Wednesday afternoons at 3:45 PM between Memorial Day and Labor Day at the Surf City Recreation Center.

Other Islands

MASONBORO ISLAND

Evidence suggests that the first stretch of continental American coastline described by a European explorer may have been the beach now called Masonboro Island. The explorer was Giovanni da Verrazzano, the year, 1524. During the Civil War, Masonboro's beaches were visited by three blockade runners and one Union blockader.

Before 1952 Masonboro was not an island but was attached to the mainland. In that year Carolina Beach Inlet was cut, giving Carolina Beach its boom in the tourist fishing trade and creating the last and largest undisturbed barrier island remaining on the southern North Carolina coast — 8-mile-long Masonboro Island. Made up of 5,046 acres, of which 4,300 acres are tidal salt marshes and mud flats, Masonboro is now the fourth component of the North Carolina National Estuarine Research Reserve, the other three being Zeke's Island, which lies south of Federal Point in the Cape Fear River, Currituck Banks and Rachel Carson Island, the latter two being farther north.

Most impressive is the island's profusion of wildlife, some abundant and some endangered, in an essentially natural state. Endangered loggerhead turtles successfully nest here, as do terns, gulls, ghost crabs and brown pelicans. Their neighbors include gray foxes, marsh rabbits, opossums, raccoons and river otters. Several types of heron, snowy egrets, willets, black skimmers and clapper rails forage in the creeks and mud flats at low tide. The estuarine waters teem with 44 species of fish and a multitude of shellfish, snails, sponges and worms. Masonboro's accessibility to UNCW's marine biology program, among the world's best, makes the island an ideal classroom for the study of human impact on natural habitat. More information on Masonboro Island and barrier island habitats may be obtained through UNCW's Center for Marine Science, (910) 962-2470.

Masonboro Island is a peaceful place where generations of locals have fished, hunted, sunbathed, surfed, camped and sat back to witness nature. Small wonder Masonboro Island has always been close to locals' hearts. Accordingly, the Coastal Management Division of the North Carolina Department of Environment, Health and Natural Resources administers the island with as little intrusion as possible. Camping, hunting and other traditional activities pursued here are allowed to continue, albeit under monitoring intended to determine whether the island can withstand such impact. (See our Camping section for more about staying over.) If you don't own a boat and can't rent one for getting to Masonboro, refer to the listing for Turtle Island Ventures in Rowing and Canoeing in our Watersports section.

ZEKE'S ISLAND

You can walk to this island reserve in the Cape Fear River and you need not walk on water. Simply drive down by the boat ramp at Federal Point (beyond the ferry terminal) and wait for low tide to allow you to walk The Rocks, a breakwater first erected in 1873 that extends beyond Zeke's Island for just more than 3 miles. You can go by boat if keeping your feet on the tricky rocks isn't your idea of fun. This component of the North Carolina National Estuarine Research Reserve consists of Zeke's Island, North Island, No-Name Island and the Basin, the body of water enclosed by the breakwater, totaling 1,160 acres. The varied habitats include salt marshes, beaches, tidal flats and estuarine waters. Bottle-nosed dolphins, red-tailed hawks, ospreys and colonies of fiddler crabs will keep you looking in every direction. Fishing, sunbathing and boating are the primary pursuits here, and hunting within regulations is allowed. Bring everything you need, pack out everything you bring, and don't forget drinking water and sunscreen.

⊛ KIDSTUFF

There's no limit to the wonderful imagination and limitless energy of kids. They want to know everything from "Why is the sky blue?" and "How come Santa's handwriting looks like yours?" to "What's for dinner?" and "What is there to do around here anyway?" Now that's one question you can easily answer.

There really is no better place to visit or to raise a family than along North Carolina's beautiful coast. Being near the ocean means you'll find numerous water activities to engage in. This area cherishes its history and fosters the arts, so there are many exciting educational activities too. Among a parent's greatest area resources for entertaining kids are the various museums, which offer classes and workshops in arts and crafts, and the North Carolina Aquarium at Fort Fisher, which also offers classes and workshops as well as outdoor activities. Opportunities for adolescents to learn boating skills, participate in gymnasium and team sports and take part in many other activities, both physical and cerebral, exist with the various parks and recreation departments throughout the area. To contact these resources, see the listings in our chapters on Watersports and Sports, Fitness and Parks.

Information on child care can be found in our Schools and Child Care chapter. For this Kidstuff chapter, we've tried to ferret out some of the participatory activities that are easily overlooked as well as the bare necessities of kidstuff to balance the ubiquitous consumer-oriented offerings. Keep in mind that many of the activities listed here are not strictly for kids; conversely, many attractions and activities listed in other chapters are not exclusively for adults. Be sure to comb other chapters (especially Attractions) for great kidstuff ideas. Each section in this chapter deals with a type of activity or interest: Amusements (including hobbies and toys), Animals, Arts, Birthday Parties, Eats, Exploring Nature, Farms, Getting Physical, Getting Wet, Going Mental (for inquisitive minds), Go Fish, Holidays and Summer Camps.

Amusements

This section is designed for children who enjoy spending their free time engaging in a favorite hobby. From comics or baseball card collecting, video game playing, airplane building to toy shopping, you've come to the right place.

Break Time Grille & Ten Pin Alley
127 S. College Rd., Wilmington
(910) 395-6658
www.breaktimetenpin.com

This 24-lane bowling alley has plenty of fun opportunities for kids. There's a youth/adult league that bowls every Thursday evening in summer at 7 PM. Ten Pin Alley is filled with arcade games to add to the fun. Call for more information about joining their leagues.

Bullfrog Corner
101 E. Moore St., Southport
(910) 454-9300

Billed as a magical, mystical shopping experience, Bullfrog Corner will delight you and your little ones. You will find this shop filled to bursting with toys, books, candy, videos, stuffed animals, pottery, jewelry and home accessories — not to mention souvenirs of your Southport experience.

Firebird Ceramic Studio
Racine Center for the Arts, 203 Racine Dr., Wilmington
(910) 452-2073

Firebird is a full-service, paint-your-own pottery studio in a delightfully cheerful atmosphere. They provide a large

selection of bisque ware with a wide variety of colors and effects. All you need to provide is your creativity. Studio assistants will glaze and fire your piece for you. Just visiting Wilmington? Firebird will ship the finished pottery to your home. You can also try your hand at mosaics and glass painting with their qualified staff to assist you. This is a great activity for birthday parties, ladies' nights out, couples nights, bridal showers, play dates for children, or just an afternoon out. Come and experience the fun of painting your own pottery. Art supplies and kits are also conveniently available.

Learning Express Toys
1437 Military Cutoff Rd., Wilmington
(910) 509-0153
3501 Oleander Dr., Wilmington
(910) 251-6636
www.learningexpresstoys.com/wilmington

Learning Express Toys is among those rare places that capture kids' imaginations with high-quality alternatives to the run-of-the-mill products. Interactive and entertaining, the stores succeed in making learning fun for kids from infancy through early adolescence. The staff includes toy experts with broad knowledge of the products, which translates into excellent service. Learning Express Toys is organized in sections geared to particular interests, such as Science & Nature (including electronics and nature projects), Let's Pretend (fantasy dress-up, Playmobil and Webkinz), Great Beginnings (for infants and toddlers) and Transit (including remote control vehicles, Thomas and Darda race tracks). This is the place to find that volcano your child needs for the diorama. You can find Learning Express Toys in three locations: the Hanover Center store on Oleander Drive is a "come out and play" space with an I Spy Cloud Shapes in the Sky ceiling. Their original location on Military Cutoff Road offers a medieval theme with a giant castle mural in the center of the store. There is also a mini-store in the Children's Museum of Wilmington and a new Toy Take-Out Website for local online shopping with in-store pickup. Learning Express Toys offers free personalizing, free gift wrapping and a popular Birthday Wish Box registry. Both Learning Express stores also feature a Grandparents' Club and daily UPS shipping. Their mission is to help you find the perfect toy.

Monkey Joe's
4310-101 Shipyard Blvd., Wilmington
(910) 392-5637

This fun-filled indoor playground is a perfect spot for kids up to age 12, rain or shine. Filled with inflatable "moonwalk" type structures, slides and bounce houses, kids can climb, slide and bounce to their heart's content. Guaranteed to burn off excess energy and result in a solid afternoon nap, Monkey Joe's is a safe and healthy way to provide your child with a full day's exercise in an hour or so. Parents can also get in on the fun and get a great workout themselves or relax in a comfortable chair and watch. The adult area has flat-screen TVs, complimentary computer workstations and free WiFi. An ideal place for a play date, a group outing or just some fun with your kids, Monkey Joe's is one place your kid won't forget. Monkey Joe's is not a "drop off" place. Drinks, pizza, popcorn, ice cream and general concessions are available for purchase. No food or drink from outside is allowed. The facility is open 10 AM until 6 PM every day of the week. Fridays they stay open until 8 PM. The cost is $5 plus tax for children 2 and younger. Monday through Friday the cost is $8 plus tax for children older than 2. Saturday and Sunday it's $9 for children older than 2. Adults get in free unless they want to play, in which case it costs $5. Call for information on party packages.

Animals

Despite the growing population of this region, it's not so hard to spot glimpses of nature here and there. In fact, it is not uncommon to witness hawks, ospreys and turkey vultures taking lunch breaks within Wilmington city limits. Deer are frequently sighted in outlying areas at dusk, and watching dolphins cavort mere yards off-shore can be endlessly entertaining. To be

Kids are mesmerized by the nearly 3,000 saltwater and freshwater creatures at the N.C. Aquarium at Fort Fisher.

truly among animals, especially of the petting or feeding-by-hand variety, also check Ashton Farm, listed in the Summer Camps section of this chapter, and Greenfield Lake, listed in our Attractions chapter.

North Carolina Aquarium at Fort Fisher
900 Loggerhead Rd., Kure Beach
(910) 458-8257
www.ncaquariums.com/fort-fisher

The North Carolina Aquarium at Fort Fisher is located on the ocean, along U.S. 421 just south of Kure Beach (about 15 miles south of Wilmington). The aquarium continues to add fascinating exhibits on a regular basis. An Exotic Aquatics gallery includes non-native creatures, such as Hawaiian fishes, lionfish and Pacific coral reef fishes. The aquarium now exhibits four of the state's six venomous snake species: copperheads, cottonmouths, Eastern diamondback and timber rattlers. In 2008, to celebrate International Year of the Frog, the aquarium added a number of exhibits devoted to these reptiles that include colorful poisonous dart frogs native to Central America.

The aquarium's theme, "Waters of the Cape Fear," lets visitors follow the river from the Piedmont to the Atlantic Ocean and see nearly 3,000 freshwater and saltwater creatures. The journey starts in a half-acre freshwater conservatory, which houses the aquarium's newest resident, a rare albino alligator, and culminates in a quarter-million-gallon saltwater tank teeming with sharks and other ocean species. Featured in the Coastal Waters Gallery are seahorses, a loggerhead sea turtle hatchling and an indoor salt marsh.

The aquarium is open daily 9 AM to 5 PM except Christmas, New Year's and Thanksgiving days. All three North Carolina Aquariums offer behind-the-scenes tours and other programs for people of all ages to learn more about aquatic life. The variety at the Fort Fisher facility includes everything from quickie "creature features" to half-day camps and workshops. Many activities require reservations and a nominal fee, but others are free with aquarium admission.

Everyday visitors may encounter impromptu learning opportunities such as "smart-cart" presentations or "creature features" around the touch-pool, the alligator exhibit or the moray eel cave. Videos about everything from sharks to shrimp are shown daily in the auditorium. Divers, using underwater sound equipment inside the Cape Fear Shoals tank, answer questions on a wide range of topics twice a day. At 11 AM at 3 PM daily you can watch aquarium staff feed some of the animals. Educators are on hand to field questions.

Tregembo Animal Park
5811 Carolina Beach Rd., Wilmington
(910) 392-3604
www.tregemboanimalpark.com

Tregembo Animal Park will delight and amaze kids of all ages. Carrying on a family tradition that goes back more than 50 years, the Tregembos have expanded and updated the zoo to create habitats for their animals from around the world. There are some of the familiar zoo favorites, like Jashan the white tiger, a lion named Simba and Ben the bear, along with some exotic new additions, including a giraffe, a zebra and a group of ring-tailed lemurs that reside on their very own Lemur Island. Kids will have a great time exploring the park, feeding the ducks and goats, and watching the amusing antics of the monkeys. Tregembo Animal Park is a fun place to spend an afternoon with kids. Their large gift shop is filled with educational animal-related toys, T-shirts, plush items and nautical souvenirs. Tregembo Animal Park is open from 10 AM to 5 PM daily and closes during the winter season. Call for admission prices. Group rates are available for school groups, but call in advance.

Arts

There's no better way to open a child's eyes to all the hidden beauty of the world than through the arts. Engaging in painting, music, dance and drama is also a terrific way to build a child's self-esteem and sense of community. Facilities hosting such activities are the Community Arts Center, (910) 341-7860, the Cameron Art Museum, (910) 395-5999, the Martin Luther King Jr. Center, (910) 341-7866, and the DREAMS Center for Arts Education, (910) 772-1501. The latter two offer free after-school activities that include arts and crafts. Wilmington also has an abundance of dance schools catering to young children.

The Children's Museum of Wilmington
116 Orange St., corner of Seco, Wilmington
(910) 254-3534

This hands-on, learning-through-play museum offers something for children of all ages with all interests. Sail the seas as a pirate in Ahoy, Wilmington!, Climb on our new School Bus, examine your teeth in our ToothaSaurus Pediatric Dental Exhibit, perform examinations as a physician in the Teddy Bear Hospital, experiment in the Science Lab, sing and act in the Star Maker Sound Stage, make a masterpiece in the Art Studio and much, much more! Art and science programming is offered every day. Toddler Time is on Fridays at 10:30 AM.

Kids-a-lorus at the Cucalorus Film Festival
815 Princess St., Wilmington
(910) 343-5995
www.cucaloris.org

The Cucalorus Film Festival, held each year in November, offers a variety of educational, instructional and fun events for aspiring youth filmmakers during its regular film festival, including the annual Kids-a-lorus! program. Kids-a-lorus is a one day event featuring short films made by children and a host of family oriented and film-infused fun. The 2009 Kids-a-lorus! took place at the Wilmington Children's Museum.

Dance 4 Life
106 SE 58th St., Ste. D, Oak Island
(910) 368-9093

Dance 4 Life Studio provides introductory through avanced dance lessons for all ages. Among the classes offered are tap, jazz, ballet, pointe, hip hop, Irish, Zumba and belly dancing — all taught by professional instructors. Small class sizes allow for individual attention whether you are seeking to increase your fitness or your dancing skills. Ask about the award-winning performance team that competes in two regional competitions and a national competition every year.

DREAMS Center for Arts Education
515 Ann St., Wilmington
(910) 772-1501

The DREAMS Center for Arts Education builds creative, committed citizens — one child at a time — through providing a high-quality, free-of-charge arts education to children in need. DREAMS provides a core after-school program in which participants study visual arts, drama, music, dance, creative writing, photography and film. In addition, the program features a three-week summer arts intensive. DREAMS serves youth ages 8 to 17 at its center in inner-city Wilmington, and the organization offers programming to a wider age range at its outreach sites, which include city recreation centers, public housing sites and schools. Serving more than 600 children each year at more than 20 locations, DREAMS helps kids focus on their creative side and provides a safe environment for self-expression.

The Gallery at Racine
203 Racine Dr., Wilmington
(910) 452-2073
www.galleryatracine.com

A great place to enjoy the arts with your family, the Racine Center welcomes folks of all ages to visit this multi-faceted facility. Classes and camps offer opportunities to learn pottery making, multi-media and other fine arts. All teachers are professional artists who love to teach within this warm, inviting atmosphere. Check out the wonderful galleries full of truly unique pieces at all price levels.

Girls Choir of Wilmington
Wilmington

Formed in 1997, this community-based choral ensemble has approximately 80 girls enrolled. Girls ages 9 and older perform a variety of classical, folk, sacred, secular and popular music. The members learn teamwork, discipline, musicianship and community service through the concerts and activities. Check their website for contact information (www.girlschoirof-wilmington.org).

Inspirations Dance Centre
7969 River Rd., Southport
(910) 612-7441

Inspirations Dance Centre offers quality dance training by a professional, degreed and certified staff who attend conventions, workshops and master classes. Teachers also meet on a regular basis to discuss methods, progress and needs of individual students and to share ideas. Classes are divided by level from young children's classes to intermediate to advanced. After-school programs are available with pick-up at the schools. Two-hour themed birthday parties include a dance class. Summer camps and classes are available, as are Friday Mother's Morning Out classes. Adult classes include clogging, Zumba and Dancercise.

Kids Making It - Woodworking Program
15 S. Water St., Wilmington
(910) 763-6001

Many youth find themselves with too much time on their hands. That's why this nonprofit tries to teach them to use those hands to build things, including a future. Benefiting at-risk youth, this unique program instructs young people in the art of woodworking and carpentry, teaching them new skills and providing them with a sense of pride about their work. Not only do they build handsome items, but they sell them in the Kids Making It shop with the profits going directly to themselves. The shop is open during the school year Monday and Friday 10 AM to 5 PM; Tuesday, Wednesday and Thursday 10 AM to 6 PM; and Saturday and Sunday 1 to 5 PM. In typically selfless fashion, program director Jimmy Pierce also enlists his students in community-oriented projects, instilling the program's "do for others" ethic.

SOLA – School of Learning Arts
216 Pine Grove Rd., Wilmington
(910) 798-1700

SOLA offers something for creative children of all ages and abilities. Over the past ten years SOLA has grown into a busy Morning Preschool, Mid-Day Artsy Preschool and Full After-School Program, all offering arts, crafts, music and academics, in a fun, creative social and developmental growth-oriented atmosphere. SOLA also offers summer camps for children ages 3 to 10. SOLA's environment is alive with energy and nurtures each child's potential.

Thalian Association Children's Theatre
Wilmington
(910) 251-1788

Thalian Association Children's Theater (TACT) produces four fully mounted productions per year, providing hands-on theatrical experience for ages 11 through high school seniors. Three TACT Work-Shops are offered annually for ages 7 to 10 providing training in music, drama and dance. They also offer the Broadway On Second Street Arts Camp for seven weeks each summer, where young people of all ages gain experience in all facets of theatrical production while becoming familiar with the themes, scores and plot lines of well-known Broadway musicals. Campers perform an abbreviated musical at the end of each week's session. If your kid wants to become a star, this is a great place to get them started.

Westermark Voice Studio
620 Cobblestone Dr., Wilmington
(910) 233-1323

Sara Westermark, a classically trained singer with a master's degree in Voice Performance from the University of Missouri-Columbia, offers private voice lessons for all ages. Sara is an active singer in this region and has appeared as a soloist with the Wilmington Symphony Orchestra, American Guild of Organists, Composerworks, Southeastern Oratorio Society, Wilmington Oratorio Society, and sings regularly at St. Paul's Episcopal Church. As a member of the National Association of Teachers' of Singing (NATS), she prepares her students to participate in a variety of venues. Her students have won competitions at statewide, regional and national levels. Many have been selected to attend prestigious summer programs and have been awarded numerous scholarships toward their continued studies in voice. Lessons are recorded on a CD, making practice at home easy. Sara has taught voice lessons for more than 15 years.

The Wilmington School of Ballet and Creative Art Center
3834 Oleander Dr., Wilmington
(910) 794-9590

This is Wilmington's only school dedicated to classical ballet. It emphasizes the fundamental basics of being a disciplined ballerina. Ballet and modern dance classes are available for ages 3 to adult. Their innovative program for preschoolers (ages 0 through 5) utilizes movement, props, music and imagery games to encourage learning the joy of dance; they don't focus on the discipline of ballet until the child is mature enough. Beginning at age 6, training begins to take on more of the academic structure of a ballet class. Levels progress in a planned, sequential manner, each building on the previous level. Pre-professional training offers students the opportunity to study daily, preparing them for professional dance careers. The school offers a Broadway-based tap and jazz program for ages 3 and older. Children from infant to 4 years old can participate in the parent/child music classes, which feature both Kindermusik and music together. Serious students who take four or more dance classes a week can audition for The Wilmington Ballet Company, a nonprofit, in-house youth ballet company, which performs The Nutcracker each holiday season at Thalian Hall. The school recently launched a fine arts preschool. The Wilmington School of Ballet participates in many outreach programs, including scholarships and summer camps for underprivileged youths.

Birthday Parties

Gone are the days of simple birthdays with only presents and cake. Today's kids look forward to gatherings that include numerous physical activities from trampolines and gymnastics to skating and soccer. If you're looking for an extra-special place to give your child a memorable birthday party, look into these venues, offering colorful party rooms and various services. Some include the use of the arcades, games and more. And don't overlook your local bowling center; per-game prices for children younger than 12 are often discounted (see the Bowling section in our chapter on Sports, Fitness and Parks).

Jungle Rapids Family Fun Park
5320 Oleander Dr., Wilmington
(910) 791-0666

Jungle Rapids offers several birthday packages that vary according to age and price. Choose from packages that include go-carts, laser-tag (for older children), a climbing wall, video games or minigolf. Packages feature play time and a party in a private room with a host, pizza and soda.

LunaPops
1319 C Military Cutoff Rd., Wilmington
(910) 256-5088
206 D N. Topsail Dr., Surf City,
(910) 328-1517
5818 Oak Island Dr., Oak Island
(910) 278-6002

LunaPops has been described as "a Willy-Wonka land of icy treats" and now you don't need to find the golden ticket to celebrate a birthday party or other special event at LunaPops. LunaPops offers several party packages depending on the child's age and the size of the group. All parties include a tour of the kitchen to learn how LunaPops are made, an opportunity for the birthday child to invent a special flavor and then an opportunity for the group to make two or more flavors of LunaPops, a craft or game activity, helium balloons, a tower of mini cupcakes to enjoy with a LunaPop during the party, and some of their very own LunaPops creations for all your guests to take home.

Monkey Joe's
4310-101 Shipyard Blvd., Wilmington
(910) 392-5637

This fun-filled indoor playground is a perfect spot for kids up to age 12, rain or shine. Filled with inflatable "moonwalk" type structures, slides and bounce houses, kids can climb, slide and bounce to their heart's content. Guaranteed to burn off excess energy and result in a solid afternoon nap, Monkey Joe's is a safe and healthy way to provide your child with a full day's exercise in an hour or so. Parents can also get in on the fun and get a great workout themselves or relax in a comfortable chair and watch. The adult area has flat-screen TVs, complimentary computer workstations and free WiFi. An ideal place for a play date, a group outing or just some fun with your kids, Monkey Joe's is one place your kid won't forget. Monkey Joe's is not a "drop off" place. Drinks, pizza, popcorn, ice cream and general concessions are available for purchase. No food or drink from outside is allowed. The facility is open 10 AM until 6 PM every day of the week. Friday until 8. The cost is $5 plus tax for children 2 and younger. Monday through Friday the cost is $8 plus tax for children older than 2. Saturday and Sunday it's $9 for children older than 2. Adults get in free unless they want to play, in which case it costs $5. Call for information on party packages.

Ten Pin Alley
Marketplace Mall, 127 S. College Rd., Wilmington
(910) 452-5455

Ten Pin Alley will provide everything you need for a happy bowling birthday party. All you have to bring is the birthday cake, the birthday child and a bunch of their friends (10 person minimum). The cost is $12 per child and includes one hour of bowling (two lanes per 10 kids), bowling shoe rental, four arcade game tokens for each child, your choice of pizza or hot dogs and drinks. Call ahead for further details and to make a reservation.

Wilmington Trolley Company
Water St. btwn Dock and Market, GPS # 15 S. Water St., Wilmington
(910) 763-4483

Located near the Henrietta III at the foot of Dock Street, the Wilmington Trolley offers a 45-minute guided tour of historic downtown Wilmington over a course of about 8 miles. Available daily, April through October, the tours leave on the hour from 10 AM to 5 PM. There are some evening tours available during the summer months, with the last tour leaving at 8 PM. Fees are $11 for adults and $5 for children ages 3 to 12. The trolley runs weekends in November and March and every Saturday year round. The trolley also offers unique transportation for children's outings, including birthday parties and special events. Call ahead for rates for these excursions, as well as evening and off-season tour availability.

Eats and Sweets

No discussion of kidstuff would be complete without mentioning something for the sweet tooth. By sweets we mean not only candy but also baked goods and ice cream. As you travel the coast, you'll be tempted by all manner of strategically placed retailers who will dulcify your day. What follows here are some of the kings and queens of confectionery, the barons of bonbon. Read on at the risk of your waistline. Your kids will love you for it.

TOPSAIL ISLAND AND VICINITY

Dr. Rootbeer's Hall Of Foam
288 Fulcher's Landing Rd., Sneads Ferry
(910) 327-7668
www.drrootbeer.com

Dr. Rootbeer's Hall of Foam, located in a vintage 1950s gas station near the waterfront in Sneads Ferry, sells root beer made from Jerome Gundrum's own recipe. Just one sip of his sweet ambrosia will transport you back to simpler times. Sit back and enjoy the free 1953 Seeburg jukebox, a root beer float, a milk shake or a hand-dipped double scoop of one of his 16 flavors of ice cream. This is more than a soda shop; Dr. Rootbeer's is a museum and a great place to have a birthday party or outing with the kids. The walls are covered with root beer memorabilia that has been carefully collected for 35 years. Dr. Rootbeer also serves delicious pot roast sandwiches, sassafras barbecue and hot dogs.

Sneads Ferry Ice Cream
2121 N.C. Hwy. 172, Sneads Ferry
(910) 327-0070

When junior wants an ice cream cone and grandma wants a malt, head on over to the Sneads Ferry Ice Cream shop (formerly Surf City Ice Cream). This family owned and operated ice cream shop serves floats, sundaes, banana splits, milk shakes and smoothies. With 32 flavors to choose from, the entire family will be happy. Relax on the front porch with a cone or dish and watch the world go by. It's open late every day.

Exploring Nature

The most accessible, most affordable and most attractive sources of fun for kids on the southern coast are the same ones that draw adults in droves: the beaches and nearby waterways. So no matter what your kids' ages, get them down to the water, from Topsail to Calabash. Try a different beach now and then to pique their interest; there's a great difference in character from beach to beach. Combining activities with beach visits may also be worthwhile. Driving a four-wheel-drive vehicle on the beach at the Fort Fisher State Recreation Area is a bouncy jaunt most kids love. The area offers pristine surf, calm tidal waters on the inland side suitable for toddlers, great fishing and, just minutes away, a fine Civil War museum and historic site. North Carolina's southern coast encompasses a wide variety of parks, giving kids plenty of room to run, play and explore. Venerable pine trees surrounded by beautiful flora and interesting fauna make these parks delightful places for families to spend time together.

Buccaneer Cruises
720 Channel Blvd., Topsail Beach
(910) 546-8687

The *Buccaneer* offers great sightseeing cruises that kids love. Cruises provide an opportunity to see dolphins, osprey and other wildlife as you cruise by Blackbeard's old hideout. The cost is $12 per person, with kids 8 and younger paying $8. Reservations are not required, but if you would like to guarantee a space, stop by the dock at the Topsail Beach Assembly Building for advance tickets.

Getting Wet

As if the ocean weren't enough, this area offers plenty of other opportunities for kids to douse themselves, and some of them are downright thrilling, especially the water slides. One of the best is at the Jungle Rapids Family Fun Park, 5320 Oleander Drive, (910) 791-0666, in Wilmington.

Most warm weather attractions are open seven days a week between Memorial and Labor days. Kids can find other places to get wet in our Watersports or our Sports, Fitness and Parks section.

Go Fish
Buccaneer Cruises
720 Channel Blvd., Topsail Beach
(910) 546-8687

Go shrimping like the pros on a Bubba Gump Shrimp Cruise. Learn how commercial shrimp boats operate. Have fun, catch fish and learn about exotic marine life. The cost is $25 per person, and trips depart 9 AM and return at 11 AM. Call for the exact dates this trip is offered.

Going Mental

Cape Fear Astronomical Society
Unitarian Universalist
Fellowship of Wilmington,
4513 Lake Ave., Wilmington
(910) 762-1033

Kids old enough to understand that those bright objects in the night sky are incredibly distant will appreciate the occasional sky observations, using members' telescopes, sponsored by the Astronomical Society to raise interest in membership. Viewing sessions are announced in the calendar of the Wilmington Star-News. The public is also invited to the society's monthly meetings, which feature interesting films and presentations. Meetings take place on the first Sunday of each month (or the second, if delayed by a holiday) and are also announced in the newspaper. The society is open to everyone of any age, regardless of any astronomical knowledge. In addition to the popular public viewing sessions, the society also undertakes periodic school talks and trips to planetariums. Membership has one prerequisite, if you could call it that: a sincere interest in astronomy and in learning more about it. Membership costs $20 per year ($25 for families) and includes the society's monthly newsletter, Cape Fear Skies, and the Astronomical League's quarterly publication, Reflector. Members can also get a reduced subscription rate to Sky and Telescope magazine. Contact

Ronnie Hawes, the club's president, at the society's mailing address, 305 N. 21st Street, Wilmington, NC 28405.

The Children's Museum of Wilmington
116 Orange St., corner of Second St., Wilmington
(910) 254-3534

This hands-on, learning-through-play museum offers something for children of all ages with all interests. Sail the seas as a pirate in Ahoy, Wilmington!, Climb on the new School Bus, examine your teeth in the ToothaSaurus Pediatric Dental Exhibit, perform examinations as a physician in the Teddy Bear Hospital, experiment in the Science Lab, sing and act in the Star Maker Sound Stage, make a masterpiece in the Art Studio and much, much more. Art and science programming is offered every day. Toddler Time is on Fridays at 10:30 AM. The website lists the full calendar of events and programming.

Fort Fisher Aquarium Outreach Program
Assembly Bldg., 720 Channel Blvd., Topsail Beach
(910) 327-2818

The Fort Fisher Aquarium Outreach Program lets kids get up close and personal with a variety of sea creatures. Participants get to touch and learn all about the creatures who live in our ocean waters. This popular program includes a one-hour presentation on invertebrates and is held on Wednesday afternoons from 1 to 2 PM from July 7 to August 11. The Topsail Island Historical Society sponsors this event, and a donation is requested.

Quarter Moon books & gifts
708 S. Anderson Blvd., Topsail Beach
(910) 328-4969, (800) 697-9134
www.quartermoonbooks.com

Quarter Moon has a delightful children's area that offers books, puzzles, toys and games. They focus on beach, sea turtle and pirate related titles, but also feature popular children's characters, including the latest and cutest, Eebee.

Summer Camps

Summer is the main anticipation of almost any school-aged child, but it can be tiring for parents, especially those who work, to invent fun, imaginative activities for their children day after day. Summer camps are a great antidote for this problem. The southern coast offers many different camps for you and your child to choose from. Day camps and sports camps (rather than overnight camps) are the norm in the southern coastal region. For sports camps, children must own basic personal equipment, including protective gear. Team items such as bats and balls are provided. Be sure to review our chapter on Sports, Fitness and Parks as well. Day campers generally need only swim suits, towels, sneakers and a bagged lunch to get the most out of their camp experiences. An extremely useful publication, Summer Alternatives, lists dozens of summer activities for school-age children in our area. It is distributed in late April by the New Hanover County Schools and may be obtained free by calling the Community Schools office at (910) 254-4221, or you can pick one up at your child's school.

Adventures Pathways Summer Camp
302 Willard St., Wilmington
(910) 362-8222

For kids who truly enjoy challenging physical activities and like being on the move, the Adventure Pathways programs are just the ticket. Guaranteed not to be boring, the week-long excursions are held in July. Sessions for boys and girls ages 10 to 13 include exploration, watersports, hiking and climbing. Space is limited. Call the number above for more information.

Ashton Farm Summer Day Camp
5645 U.S. Hwy. 117 S, Burgaw
(910) 259-2431

Ashton Farm, established in 1975, is located on a 72-acre historic plantation about 18 miles north of Wilmington. Owner Sally Martin provides children ages 5 through 12 with down-to-earth fun. Kids participate in farm life, swimming, canoeing, horseback riding, whiffle ball, tennis, hiking, arts and crafts, animal care and archery. One-week sessions from June to August are available (daily with permission). Discounts apply for additional weeks and/or additional children registered. The camp provides round-trip transportation

KIDSTUFF

to Wilmington, camper health insurance and drinks; children should pack their own lunches. Single-day camps have been added to coincide with teacher workdays. In the off season Ashton Farms is open for field trips and can host family reunions and birthday parties.

Bald Head Island Conservancy Camps
7000 Federal Rd., Bald Head Island
(910) 457-0089

The Bald Head Island Conservancy runs summer camps for three age groups. Camp Pollywog, for rising first graders, is billed as..."a great introduction into the world of wild things." Among the activities planned for this half-day morning camp are catching bugs, holding snakes, arts and crafts, reading books and more. Conservancy Camp is geared to kids in the second to sixth grades. Activities included in this camp are shell collecting, nature hikes, kayaking and crabbing as well as hands-on environmental instruction about sea turtles, habitats, plant identification and marsh inhabitants. Summer Eco-Adventure Series is aimed at outdoor-minded youth. Sessions include Fishing 101, Advanced Kayaking, Outdoor Skills and Wildlife Tracking and Nature Crafts. More information can be found on the Bald Head island Conservancy website.

Boiling Spring Lakes Summer Camp
1 Leeds Rd., Boiling Spring Lakes
(910) 845-3693

Open to children 5 years of age, who have completed a full day program, up to 11 years of age, these summer camps run from June through August. Included are crafts, group games, sports and field trips. Registration is in early April. Call (910) 845-7984 for more details.

Brunswick County Parks and Recreation
Parks & Recreation Building, Government Complex, Bolivia
(910) 253-2672, (800) 222-4790

Brunswick County offers a camp co-sponsored with Communities in Schools from June through August. Camp cost is $100 per child per week with a registration fee of $15. All registrations are handled by Communities in Schools and begin in April. Camp hours are from 7 AM until 6

PM. There are four convenient locations to choose from: Southport, Belville, Union and Supply. Each location goes on two field trips a week and participates in various activities such as swimming, ice skating, water parks, miniature golf, skating, bowling and more. Payment is expected at the time of registration.

Camp Seabreeze
N.C. Baptist Assembly, Caswell Beach
(910) 278-9501

Open to children attending kindergarten through fourth grade, this day camp provides activities such as sports, games, crafts, story times and guest speakers. Camp is held 7:30 AM until 5 PM each Monday through Friday from June 11 through August 13. Registration is required and begins March 29.

Cape Fear Museum
814 Market St., Wilmington
(910) 798-4362
www.capefearmuseum.com

A variety of hands-on science and history activities are available for children ages 5 through 10 in half-day camps at the Cape Fear Museum. Different camp themes, such as Young Engineers and Beneath Your Feet, are offered five days a week from June through mid-August. Call weekdays between 9 AM and 5 PM for information and to register. For information on the museum, see our Attractions chapter.

Emma Anderson Memorial Chapel Youth Program
1101 S. Anderson Blvd., Topsail Beach
(910) 328-6371

Some families plan their vacations around this long-running children's program that is sponsored by the Emma Anderson Memorial Chapel. Both daytime and evening activities are offered Monday through Friday during the summer months. A schedule of events is prepared weekly, and activities can include beach volleyball, pier fishing, miniature golf, pizza parties, cookouts, basketball, volleyball, billiards or Ping Pong. The program is open to all children and youth from first through 12th grades, and there is no cost to attend. Participants are welcome to join in the fun for a day or for a week.

Girls Inc. Day Camp
1502 Castle St., Wilmington
(910) 763-6674

Girls Inc. offers full day summer camp in Wilmington starting two weeks after school lets out for summer break and ending two weeks before school resumes. Activities include: sports, crafts, swimming, sewing, field trips, career exploration, science activities and cooking. Guest speakers are brought in to speak with the girls on various topics that concerns today's youth. The Wilmington camp accepts girls ages 6 to 18. Call for information about registration.

Jelly Beans Family Skating Center
5216 Oleander Dr., Wilmington
(910) 791-6000

Jelly Beans' summer day camp for kids ages 5 through 12 is especially convenient (and affordable) because your child can just drop in for a single day at a time. While roller skating is a natural part of regular activities, Jelly Beans concentrates heavily on outdoor and educational field trips.

North Carolina Aquarium at Fort Fisher
900 Loggerhead Rd., Kure Beach
(910) 458-8257
www.ncaquariums.com/fort-fisher

Aquarium summer camps promise learning and fun for youngsters in several age groups — 5 and 6 years old, 7 through 9, 10 through 12, and 13 and 14. Scheduled Monday through Friday from 8:30 AM to 3 PM, sessions are offered in June, July and August. Each group of campers will enjoy age-specific, fun-filled outdoor activities and live animal encounters, including crafts and programs that help kids understand and appreciate aquatic environments.

Pirate Boot Camp
N.C. Maritime Museum at Southport,
116 N. Howe St., Southport
(910) 457-0003

Avast ye parents! To turn your children (ages 6 to 12) into little pirates, send them to Pirate Boot Camp for five days in July — but don't wait to sign up as the camp is limited to 20 participants. The little ones will come home each day with such things names asBloody Tom and Cannonball, eye patches, tin foil and cardboard swords, and skull and crossbones flags. They will learn Pirate-ese along with the history of pirates and Southport. At the end of the week they will hold a Pirate Celebration in Franklin Square Park. Note: The museum is in the process of raising funds to be used for renovations and construction in anticipation of their move to Fort Johnston on Moore Street at an as yet undetermined date.

UNCW Athletic Department
601 S. College Rd., Wilmington
(910) 962-3232

UNCW sponsors day and overnight summer sports camps in baseball, softball, basketball, tennis, swimming, volleyball and soccer. These sessions give younger players a good foundation for the sports and emphasize fundamentals. Call for information early in the season, as these camps tend to be quite popular.

UNCW MarineQuest
601 S. College Rd., Wilmington
(910) 962-2640

The University of North Carolina at Wilmington's Division for Public Service and Continuing Studies invites kids to become part of MarineQuest, one of the most unique marine and environmental education programs in the country. MarineQuest encompasses a wide variety of marine and environmental education programs for ages 5 through 17. They have a total of ten programs that explore everything from exploring marine habitats to animal classification to careers in marine science. Camps include field trips, hands-on activities, water sports, lab experiments and more.

Wilmington Family YMCA
2710 Market St., Wilmington
(910) 251-9622
www.wilmingtonfamilyymca.org

YMCA Summer Day Camps for youth (from rising first graders through age 16) operates June through August on weekdays. The day camps operate from

6:30 AM to 6 PM. Among the many fun things to do are swimming, indoor and outdoor sports, arts and crafts, reading, music, games and character development. There are half-day specialty camps that include but are not limited to sports, service learning, kayaking and more. There are two camp locations, and all camps are inclusive. Financial assistance available. Registrations begin March 15 and spaces are limited. The YMCA operates sports day camps, both half-day and full-day, from June through August, both at the Wilmington Family YMCA and Camp Kirkwood (soccer only) in Pender County. Sports camps include basketball, soccer, softball, volleyball and cheer/dance with the Wilmington Sea Dolls. Register online or at the YMCA front desk.

Wrightsville Beach Parks & Recreation
1 Bob Sawyer Dr., Wrightsville Beach
(910) 256-7925

Art, soccer, lacrosse, tennis and performance arts camp are among the fun offerings for kids sponsored by the Wrightsville Beach Parks & Recreation Department. Call for a brochure and more information on all the activities offered through the Parks & Recreation Department.

Youth Sailing Program
Cape Fear Sailing Academy,
600 W. Brunswick St., Southport
(910) 279-2355

This summer camp runs in three-hour sessions, Monday through Friday. The 9 AM to noon session is for kids age 8 to 11 and the 1 to 4 PM session is for youth age 12 to 15. Training begins with on-shore instruction and a swimming test. On the water, Vanguard Optimist Dinghies are used to teach such things as how to sail figure eights and right a capsized boat as well as points of sail, rigging and docking. Kids will learn sailing concepts and vocabulary and the importance of team work while participating in a fun-filled experience.

ARTS

North Carolina claims a long and rich history in the arts, and the southern coastal region nurtures this heritage through a wide range of cultural opportunities. Wilmington, with its coastal and historical ambiance, competes as a major center for the visual and performing arts. The city's lively downtown area is the hub of arts organizations and activities for the region, and it lures musicians, painters, actors, writers, filmmakers, sculptors and dancers to the coffeehouses and cafes to discuss their crafts.

On any given day year-round the community's calendar overflows with diverse and intriguing cultural events. Residents and visitors to the southern coast find exciting entertainment showcased by the many established institutions devoted to the arts, including the Thalian Hall Center for the Performing Arts, the Cameron Art Museum in Wilmington and the Odell Williamson Auditorium in Brunswick County. These institutions host nationally and internationally renowned artists, as well as local and regional talent.

In addition to a community already rich in theatrical talent, the film industry established a working movie studio in Wilmington in 1985. The studio attracts film-production companies and professional actors to the area on a regular basis. Often, while working on location here, many of these actors — John Travolta, Sandra Bullock and Linda Lavin, to name a few — share their expertise with local actors and thrill audiences with performances on area stages. Some, like Ms. Lavin and acclaimed actor Henry Darrow, choose to stay and become a part of the working arts community.

Cinematique, an ongoing showcase for "classic, foreign and notable films" is jointly sponsored by public radio station WHQR and the Thalian Hall Center for the Performing Arts. The films are shown in Thalian Hall, where the palpable history and opulence add an amazing mood to the screening. On occasion, capacity crowds have held a popular film beyond the normal Wednesday through Sunday night screenings.

Music is another vital part of the regional arts scene. Wilmington has its own symphony orchestra, a vibrant chamber music series, a regular concert series and dozens of ensemble groups ranging from professionals to enthusiastic amateurs. On a daily basis, local clubs and restaurants serve up a stimulating offering of live music from every imaginable genre. Theater companies are plentiful and employ the talents of local writers, musicians and performers. There are several stages in town, including Thalian Hall, Kenan Auditorium and Trask Coliseum at the University of North Carolina at Wilmington, Citystage and the Scottish Rite Temple. Touring companies regularly visit Wilmington, particularly during the Azalea Festival in the spring and Riverfest in the fall.

Over the centuries, Wilmington has hosted such notables as Lillian Russell, Maurice Barrymore, Oscar Wilde and John Philip Sousa. Come closer in time and consider this diverse collection of performers: Al Hirt, Chet Atkins, Frank Sinatra, The Ciompi String Quarter, Judy Collins, Koko Taylor, Itzak Perleman, Roberta Flack, Reba McEntire, Kenny Rogers, Charlie Daniels, the Beach Boys and Ray Charles. In neighboring Brunswick County, audiences at the Odell Williamson Auditorium, located on the campus of Brunswick Community College, have thrilled to an equally impressive roster of performers, including The Tommy Dorsey Orchestra, Doc Watson, The Lettermen, Mike Cross, the Preservation Hall Jazz Band, Lee Greenwood, The Platters and The Glenn Miller Orchestra.

The visual arts occupy a prominent position in the cultural experiences of North Carolina's southern coast. In addition to several commercial art galleries, particularly in the Greater Wilmington area and Southport, the region has the Cameron Art Museum, regarded as one of the finest art museums in the state. The museum's changing exhibitions are sure to enchant and inspire visitors. Local artists exhibit their work in area restaurants, coffeehouses and upscale shopping centers. North Carolina's southern coast region is a rich environment for the arts, offering a variety of opportunities for both creating and enjoying the cultural arts. This chapter lists just a sampling of the arts scene in the region.

Museums, Performance Halls and Organizations

Acme Art Inc.
711 N. Fifth St., Wilmington
(910) 763-8010

An avant-garde renovation of an old warehouse is the perfect home for this artist-owned and operated studio. The working environment zings electric with artists running their drills, welding with their blowtorches and dueling airbrushes on bold mats of color. The gallery space is upgraded with track lighting, and opening exhibits are warm and friendly. A collection of working studios, the organization holds regular advertised events but does not keep business hours for the public.

Associated Artists of Southport
130 E. West St., Southport
(910) 457-5450

Housed in historic Franklin Square Gallery in Southport, this nonprofit organization provides an increasingly rich environment for the growth and development of local visual artists. It is dedicated to the cultural enrichment of the community through education and the promotion of original art. In 2004 the association celebrated the 25th anniversary of its inception and the 100th anniversary of the Franklin Square Gallery building. The gallery houses two floors of painting and pottery exhibit rooms, a sales office and a classroom. There are regularly scheduled workshops in various media by recognized artists as well as judged exhibitions and competitions, all of which are open to the public. A national juried competition and exhibit historically held each July in conjunction with the N.C. Fourth of July Festival will be a regional competition in 2009. Drawing and painting classes are held Monday through Friday in the upstairs studio. Pottery classes are conducted in the pottery studio behind the gallery. Painting and pottery classes for children of the community are conducted yearly and are partially funded by grants from the Brunswick Arts Council. Kids' Day is a community fun day, free to the public, sponsored by the Associated Artists, Brunswick County Parks and Recreation Department and Southport Parks and Recreation Department. Association members serve as instructors, speakers and judges for local schools and organizations. Monthly meetings are held the third Monday of each month. Call for more information or a membership application.

Brunswick Community College
Odell Williamson Auditorium
50 College Rd. NE, Bolivia
(910) 343-0203 x406, (800) 754-1050

Built in 1993 by the citizens of Brunswick County for the educational and cultural enrichment of the community, this 1,500-seat, state-of-the-art facility on the campus of Brunswick Community College offers entertainment opportunities in the heart of Brunswick County. In its short history, this center for the arts has presented the talents of the North Carolina Symphony, the U.S. Marine Band, the Kingston Trio, Jerry Reed, the All American Boys Chorus, the Tommy Dorsey Orchestra, The Lettermen, Lee Greenwood, Pebo Bryson, a presentation of The Odd Couple starring Jamie Farr and William Christopher (Klinger and Father Mulcahey from the TV show M*A*S*H), Kathy Matea, John Berry, Roy Clark, North Carolina Dance Theatre American Masterpieces and various national touring companies performing such classics as Death of a Salesman and Steel

Magnolias. The auditorium and lobby are available for private and public rental. The auditorium has a subscription season each year. Completed in 2008, The Virginia Williamson Event Center is a multipurpose facility connected to the Odell Williamson Auditorium. The Event Center accommodates a wide variety of events including, but not limited to, receptions, banquets, conferences, lectures, dances, small concerts and theatre. A catering kitchen is available. The Odell Williamson Auditorium lobby serves as the entrance for the Event Center. Call (910) 755-7416 for tickets or information about renting the facility.

Brunswick County Arts Council
Supply
(910) 575-0003

Established in 1981, this nonprofit volunteer organization is Brunswick County's primary arts information and funding source. Nonprofit arts funding is channeled to this group from the North Carolina Arts Council. With money received each year, the Brunswick Arts Council provides financial assistance to approximately 18 local nonprofit arts groups through Grassroots Arts Program grants; sponsors community events such as Concert by the Sea; and publishes a directory of Brunswick County artists and art groups as well as sponsoring the Brunswick County Arts Council Art Show. The council also raises funds privately through its annual Miniature Masterpiece Gala. This funding provides assistance to individual artists and arts related groups. Recently, the council partnered with the Brunswick County Board of Education to help introduce arts-integrated programs to all county schools. This valuable resource for local arts information is available through the organization, the Southport-Oak Island Chamber of Commerce, (910) 457-6964, and the Brunswick Chamber of Commerce, (800) 426-6644. Membership in the council is open to all interested citizens. The Brunswick Arts Council offers a range of programs, including cultural symposiums, programs for the classroom, bus trips to regional art venues, and more. Brunswick Arts Council's president, Gary Halberstadt, has recently established a fifth distinct operating division as a means to broaden its footprint throughout Brunswick County. Divisions include the new Multicultural Programs Division, Student Art Education/ Appreciation, Performing Arts, Literary Arts and Visual Arts. Halberstadt invites anyone interested in participating in an operating division to contact him in writing or to attend a council meeting, which is held on the second Monday of every month at 5:30 PM at the Administration Building of Brunswick Community College. Public attendance is invited as well.

Cameron Art Museum
3201 S. 17th St., Wilmington
(910) 395-5999

The Cameron Art Museum is the only art museum in southeastern North Carolina. It presents changing special exhibitions annually; monthly family and children's programs (Kids @ CAM); weekly interdisciplinary, public programs (lectures, music, films, dance); ongoing workshops and classes in ceramics at a unique Clay Studio with a resident master artist and developing artist-in-residence program; and also offers weekly yoga and Tai Chi classes. The museum occupies a 40,000-square-foot facility designed in 2002 by the renowned architectural firm of Gwathmey Siegel & Associates (NYC). Cameron Art Museum is sited on a 9.3-acre woodland park known as Pyramid Park, featuring long-leaf pine woodlands, outdoor sculptures, nature trails, a historic Civil War site and The Clay Studio housed in the Pancoe Art Education Center. The main museum building includes three exhibition areas, the Weyerhaueser lecture and reception hall, a museum gift shop and free parking. Admission is free for members, $8 for non-members, $5 for students (with valid ID), and $3 for children ages 2 to 12.

Chamber Music Wilmington
Wilmington
(910) 343-1079
www.chambermusicwilmington.org

Chamber Music Wilmington (CMW) is a nonprofit organization that brings world-class chamber music concerts to southeastern North Carolina. Now going into its 16th season, Chamber Music Wilmington sponsors a nationally award-winning series of concerts each season. Chamber Music

ARTS

Chamber Music
WILMINGTON

passion
excitement
intimacy

it happens here!

chambermusicwilmington.org

EROL & LOUISE CAGLARCAN IN MEMORY OF THEIR SON GLEN, WITH A JOHNSON & JOHNSON MATCHING GRANT, PRESENT

2010 – 2011 CONCERT SERIES

September 26, 2010

FRENCH IMPRESSIONS
CIOMPI QUARTET & GUESTS

December 5, 2010

BRASS BY CANDLE LIGHT
CAROLINA BRASS QUINTET

January 16, 2011

GAUBERT VIVANT!
NICOLAS DUCHAMP &
BARBARA MCKENZIE

February 13, 2011

DANCE AND ROMANCE
Date Night with the
CAROLINA PIANO TRIO

May 8, 2011

LOVE YOUR MOTHER:
PAST, PRESENT & EARTH
Featuring Special Guest,
MARIA JETTE, *soprano from*
PRAIRIE HOME COMPANION

BECKWITH RECITAL HALL, UNCW   7:30 PM   Kenan Box Office 910-962-3500

Wilmington hires award-winning professional artists from the various cultural institutions across the state, including faculty from Duke, UNC-Chapel Hill, UNC-Greensboro, East Carolina University, the North Carolina School of the Arts plus professionals from the North CarolinaSymphony, Winston-Salem Symphony, Charlotte Symphony and some of the nation's top ensembles. The 2010–11 series presents performances from a wide variety of artists, including the Ciompi Quartet, the Carolina Piano Trio, Nicolas Duchamp, Barbara Mckenzie, Carolina Brass and much more. Tickets for all CMW concerts are available at the UNCW's Kenan Auditorium Box Office by calling (910) 962-3500. The concerts have a reputation of selling out, so reserve your tickets early.

Cucalorus Film Festival
815 Princess St., Wilmington
(910) 343-5995
www.cucalorus.org

For more than 15 years this fearless festival of independent film has brought a wide variety of movies and their makers to the Port City. A non-competitive showcase for the best that creative filmmakers can offer, Cucalorus prides itself on a maverick approach to the festival concept. Organizers group like-minded shorts together in tidy blocks and screen first-run features that often include Q&A with filmmakers and stars alike. Numerous festival-affiliated celebrations and concerts show off the face of the Port City to visiting industry types, and the event's noted reputation has helped make Wilmington a thriving indie film town. Cucalorus offers something for everyone, including family friendly daytime screenings and programs for youth filmmakers. Screening emotional documentaries, naughty short films and hilarious and contemplative features, Cucalorus runs the gamut from experimental to mainstream, always managing to keep its cool.

Jengo's Playhouse
815 Princess St., Wilmington
(910) 343-5995
www.cucalorus.org

Not only does the Cucalorus film festival utilize historic Thalian Hall for its main screenings, it also show films at its headquarters, the magical Jengo's Playhouse. In addition to housing the Cucalorus offices, Jengo's features a 60-seat micro-cinema, technical facilities and an excellent back yard for post-movie chit-chat. Jengo's hosts an odd collection of monthly events from film screenings to poetry readings to performance art gatherings. Resident artists at Jengo's include Adam Alphin, Rob Hill, OTD Hot Glass and others.

Greenfield Lake Amphitheater
1 Amphitheater Dr., Wilmington
(910) 409-5799

Greenfield Lake Amphitheater is a newly renovated, 1,000-seat event venue nestled in the heart of Greenfield Lake Park in downtown Wilmington. A great setting for concerts and theater alike, this amphitheater is home to the Live at the Lake Concert Series. When the weather's fine, come enjoy some of the area's finest music in this great outdoor setting.

The Hannah Block Historic U.S.O./ Community Arts Center
120 S. Second St., Wilmington
(910) 341-7860

The Hannah Block Historic U.S.O./ Community Arts Center is a part of Wilmington's Parks and Recreation Department and is located in the center of historic downtown. Primarily a learning facility where anyone may go to take low-cost lessons in a full range of disciplines, the center also serves as a rehearsal space for most of Wilmington's community theater groups. The Thalian Association community theater manages the building for the city and has offices and rehearsal space within the center. For nominal fees, students of all ages can experience hands-on work under the direction of skilled local artists. In addition to workshops and classes, other programs include performances, concerts and fundraisers, usually staged in the Center's Hannah Block 2nd Street Stage theater area of the facility. This newly renovated building is available for rentals for all occasions; call for details.

Thalian Hall Center for the Performing Arts
310 Chestnut St., Wilmington
(910) 343-3660

Built in 1858, this majestic performance center has gone through several restorations. A tenth renovation was begun in October of 2009 and offers three performance spaces. Housed within are a 675-seat main theater, the 225-seat Wilmington City Council Chamber and a 100-seat studio theater. With a lively local performing arts community and the addition of touring artists and companies, at least one of the spaces is in use each evening or afternoon. More than 35 area arts and civic organizations use the facility, and more than 450 performances and screenings in music, theater, dance and film are presented each year. (See our Attractions section for more information on this facility.) The box office number is (910) 343-3664.

Wilmington Art Association
616-B Castle St., Wilmington
(910) 343-4370

Composed of professional and amateur visual artists and art enthusiasts, Wilmington Art Association (WAA) holds art shows throughout the year and conducts an annual juried exhibition, the Spring Juried Art Show and Sale, held during the Azalea Festival activities in April. The association's Wilmington Art Gallery at 616-B Castle Street is open five to seven days a week depending on the season in the New Castle Art and Antique District and has a wide selection of affordable paintings, photographs, jewelry, cards and other items. The gallery is part of the Fourth Friday Gallery Walk. WAA also holds meetings on topics of interest and sponsors frequent workshops, critiques, educational programs and special projects. Meetings are held monthly September through June on the second Thursday evening of each month at 6:30 PM at the Arboretum on Oleander Drive.

Music

Azalea Coast Chorus of Sweet Adelines
Wilmington
(910) 791-3846

Sweet Adelines, the female counterpart of the Barber Shop Harmony Society (see the writeup for Cape Fear Chordsmen), promotes and preserves the art of singing four-part harmony, barbershop style. The Sweet Adelines meet on Mondays at 7 PM at the Wrightsville Beach Baptist Church. Membership is open to all women who enjoy this original American style of music.

Cape Fear Blues Society
Wilmington
(910) 350-8822

Long a mainstay of Wilmington's music community, the Cape Fear Blues Society has enjoyed exponential growth and expanded membership in the last decade, making it one of the most successful music organizations in eastern North Carolina. The group offers musicians of all skill levels an opportunity to participate in the society's weekly jam sessions and annual events, including an exciting blues talent competition held the first weekend in November. The CFBS also actively participates in state and local arts organizations and programs. Enthusiasts of the genre don't want to miss the annual Cape Fear Blues Festival, the area's premier blues event, held in July. Numerous benefits are available through membership in the society and meetings are held quarterly. Musicians and blues listeners can join the group's long-standing weekly jam session every Tuesday night from 8 PM until midnight (or later). The CFBS provides any professional equipment you may need; just bring your instruments. Call for meeting and jam locations.

The Cape Fear Chorale
Wilmington
(910) 233-2423

The Cape Fear Chorale has been performing in the Wilmington area since the fall of 1998 and presents concerts in the fall and spring of each year. The director, accompanist and more than 50 singers volunteer their time, talents and effort to provide quality choral music to the Cape Fear Region. New singers are welcomed at the beginning of each concert season via audition.

Cape Fear Chordsmen
Wilmington
(910) 799-8455

This group is Wilmington's chapter of the Barber Shop Harmony Society. Members practice male four-part a cappella harmony singing weekly at 7:30 PM on Tuesday evenings at the Winter Park Baptist Church in Wilmington. New members are welcome; call for more information and a concert schedule.

Carolina Vocal Arts Ensemble
Wilmington
(910) 523-2974

Carolina Vocal Arts Ensemble was founded in 2006 and is directed by Stephen Field. The ensemble is a friendly group of people of all ages and backgrounds who love to sing and have fun while approaching classical music with dedication and focus. With a diverse repertoire in multiple languages, including choral masterworks, operatic choruses and spirituals, CVAE offers volunteer singers the opportunity to perform with full orchestra and professional soloists. In 2007 the ensemble initiated a High School Apprentice Singer Program to allow students with an aptitude for singing the opportunity to participate in a performance type not typically available to them at local schools. CVAE rehearses on Tuesday evenings from August through May and is an audition-based group. If you are interested in an audition, the high school program or more information, please call Stephen Field at (910) 523-2974.

Girls Choir of Wilmington
Wilmington

Formed in 1997, this community-based choral ensemble has an enrollment of approximately 80 girls. Girls ages 9 and older perform a variety of classical, folk, sacred, secular and popular music. The members learn teamwork, discipline, musicianship and community service through the con-

certs and activities. See www.girlschoirof-
wilmington.org for information.

Harmony Belles
Wilmington
(910) 799-5850

Formed in 1986, this local women's
group sings four-part harmony a cappella.
Their performances for civic organizations,
churches, nursing homes, conventions,
educational programs in schools and at
local events emphasize their philosophy of
community service. Rehearsals are Tuesday evenings from 6:30 to 9 PM. Harmony
Belles is open to new members; call for
rehearsal location and membership information. The Belle Chords, a female quartet
within the group, performs in a four-part
harmony.

North Carolina Jazz Festival
**Wilmington Hilton Riverside, 301 N. Water
St., Wilmington**
(910) 793-1111

This winter weekend festival, now in its
30th year, is scheduled for the third weekend in February and features traditional
jazz performances by national and international stars. The event is held at the Wilmington Hilton Riverside. This is a hugely
popular festival with fiercely devoted fans,
so don't wait to call for tickets.

North Carolina Symphony
(910) 962-3500

The Cape Fear Series of the North
Carolina Symphony presents six concerts
from September through May at Kenan
Auditorium on the campus of UNC-Wilm-
ington. For tickets, call the Kenan Auditorium Ticket Office at (910) 962-3500 or
(800) 732-3643.

Summer Sundays
**Keziah Memorial Park,
W. Moore & S. Lord Sts., Southport**
(910) 457-7927

Open-air concerts sponsored by the
City of Southport and the Southport
Visitors Center are held in the historic
Keziah Memorial Park from Memorial Day
weekend through Labor Day weekend on
Sundays from 2 until 4 PM. Bring chairs,
blankets, picnic baskets, kids, families
and elders and enjoy music by local art-

ists. Jazz, rhythm and blues, rock 'n' roll,
bluegrass, show tunes, Big Band music
and more assure something for everyone's
taste and enjoyment.

Wilmington Choral Society
Wilmington
(910) 395-6487

This large, well-established chorus
has been a presence in Wilmington since
1950. Attracting singers from Wilmington
and the surrounding areas and from a
cross-section of ages and professions, the
chorus prides itself on high-performance
standards of classic choral selections and
a wide variety of contemporary music. The
group participates in three or four concerts annually. Members rehearse on Tuesdays from 7:25 to 9:30 PM at the Cape
Fear Christian Church in Wilmington, and
the organization is open to all interested
singers. Open rehearsals are in August and
January; please call for details.

Wilmington Concert Association
Wilmington
(910) 791-4137

Established in 1929, the Wilmington
Concert Association brings world-class
music and dance to the Port City, sponsoring several concerts each year at UNCW's
Kenan Auditorium. For tickets call Kenan
Auditorium Box Office at (910) 962-3500
or (800) 732-3643. Membership is open to
everyone.

Wilmington Symphony Orchestra
4608 Cedar Ave., Wilmington
(910) 791-9262

Founded in 1971, the Wilmington
Symphony Orchestra is a cultural jewel in
the Port City's crown, performing a series
of concerts that enrich, entertain and educate thousands of adults and school children throughout the year. The musicians
are local instrumentalists, gifted students
and faculty, all who are selected by audition. The conductor, Dr. Steven Errante, is
Professor of Music at UNCW. The Wilmington Symphony Orchestra also continues
to serve the Cape Fear Region as a leader
in music education through an extensive
educational and outreach program that
includes a Free Family Concert, the Wilmington Symphony Youth Orchestra, Junior

The Cape Fear Playhouse

Home of Big Dawg Productions Theater Company
613 Castle Street in Wilmington

Now in our 16th season, Big Dawg Productions presents a mix of comedy and drama, along with educational programs, including classes, workshops, and our annual Fall Classic. Visit our website for upcoming productions.

www.bigdawgproductions.org • 910-471-0242

Big Dawg is a 501(c)(3) nonprofit corporation committed to producing entertaining, thought-provoking, and socially responsible theater, with an emphasis on education and the promotion of the performing arts.

Strings, an annual Student Concerto Competition and Artist-in-Residence Programs in area schools.

Theater

Wilmington has a rich theatrical tradition that is continually expanding. Wilmington's Thalian Hall Center for the Performing Arts is home to the Thalian Association, the oldest continuous community theater in the country, dating from 1788. The theater hosts professional and amateur productions on an almost nightly basis. Several local theatrical companies present original and popular productions at such area locations as Kenan Auditorium at the University of North Carolina at Wilmington, the Scottish Rite Temple on 17th Street, Citystage Theater and schools and churches.

Big Dawg Productions
613 Castle St., Wilmington
(910) 471-0242
www.bigdawgproductions.org

Now in its 15th year, this nonprofit theater company is dedicated to producing professional theater and cultivating excellence in the arts. It presents a mix of dramas and comedies each year, and other programs developed by the group include

the annual New Play Festival, which showcases talented local youth playwrights and the development of young talent through writing workshops and a technical internship program. One production each season is a classic work, which is offered to local students and teachers at a discount. Past offerings have included Henry V, The Scarlet Letter and Moby Dick-Rehearsed. They recently opened their own theater at 613 Castle Street, where they plan to expand their educational programs and offer classes, additional workshops and other nontraditional theatrical programs.

The Brown Coat Pub & Theatre
111 Grace St., Wilmington
(910) 233-9914

The Brown Coat Pub and Theatre is home to Guerilla Theatre and is the best place in town to see live comedy. Located in downtown Wilmington, this smoke-free establishment is a great place to unwind, have a drink and laugh with friends. The Brown Coat Pub and Theatre hosts regular improv comedy nights, trivia, karaoke and, of course, quality theatre productions with Guerilla Theatre. The Brown Coat also screens the best in local film Wednesday through Sunday at 8 PM the first week of the month, and if poetry's your thing, their Sunday night Open Mic Poetry Night is for you. Call for more details.

Level 5 at City Stage
21 N. Front St., Wilmington
(910) 342-0272

Whether you're in the mood for a serious drama, a musical or comedy, Level 5 at City Stage is the place to go in downtown Wilmington for great theater. Level 5 at City Stage offers an intimate theater setting where there are no bad seats. Adjacent to the theater, Level 5 contains a popular rooftop bar where you can socialize before and after the show. Ticket prices are reasonable, and the performances are Broadway caliber. In its tenth season in 2010-2011, Level 5 at City Stage has already made its mark on the Wilmington theater scene. The Level 5 at City Stage theater group produces its own shows and provides a rental facility for other local theater company performances and independent film screenings. If you need a good laugh, local comedy groups also perform here during the week. Call for schedule and ticket information.

Opera House Theatre
2011 Carolina Beach Rd., Wilmington
(910) 762-4234

A professional theater company presided over by artistic director Lou Criscuolo, this group stages six major productions each season. 2010 is the company's 25th season in the Port City. Guest artists and directors are featured frequently. Auditions are open.

Thalian Association Community Theatre
Wilmington
(910) 251-1788
www.thalian.org

Founded in 1788, Thalian Association is the Official Community Theater of North Carolina. The association presents five full-scale productions annually at historic Thalian Hall, both plays and musicals. They have been honored as Wilmington's Best Theater Company for the past four years by the readers of encore magazine. Thalian Association Children's Theater (TACT) presents four productions annually at the Hannah Block Second Street Stage in the Community Arts Center in downtown Wilmington. Operating under the supervision of a volunteer board of directors, Thalian Association also produces the annual Southern Coast Bluegrass Festival each fall and the Orange Street ArtsFest in downtown Wilmington each Memorial Day weekend. The association welcomes volunteers to take part in all of its activities.

Willis Richardson Players
Wilmington
(910) 763-1889

Established in 1974 as a nonprofit organization specializing in dramas by minority playwrights, the Willis Richardson Players perform several works per season of interest to all audiences. The group strives to promote, involve and educate residents of the Wilmington area in the performing arts through African-American theater and to bridge the cultural gap. The Players perform at Thalian Hall Center for Performing Arts.

Dance

The Wilmington area offers a broad spectrum of dance classes. The following is only a sample.

The Dance Cooperative
118 S. 17th St., Wilmington
(910) 763-4995

The Dance Cooperative is a nonprofit organization consisting of dance professionals who are bound together by one common goal — to nurture the dance community by providing affordable classes, rehearsal space and performance opportunities to those under-served artistically, culturally and economically in the greater Wilmington area. The Dance Cooperative currently has a program of classes for children and adults (drop-ins are welcome), and both an informal and formal performance series. They also host the North Carolina Dance festival and participate in Dance-A-Lorus, part of the Cucalorus Film Festival. Some scholarships are available for children who wish to take these classes. Call (910) 763-4995 for more details and schedule information.

Theatre Dance Workshop
Wilmington
(910) 458-3302

Theatre Dance Workshop is a place where singing, dancing and acting all come together. Classes in the performing arts are available for adults and children ages 7 and older. The students are part of senior and junior companies that perform original choreography, scenes and songs from Broadway shows.

Crafts

Oak Island Senior Center
5918 E. Oak Island Dr., Oak Island
(910) 278-5224

For very reasonable membership dues you can meet others, make friends, be involved in many activities and receive a monthly newsletter through this nonprofit organization. Activities include a monthly covered dish social, van trips for shopping and entertainment, movie nights, brunches, ladies' teas and games, including

Dominoes, Canasta and Pinochle. Classes are available in beginning and advanced watercolor, oil painting, decorative painting, basket weaving including Nantucket baskets, and needlework including knitting and crocheting. They also offer computer classes in beginning computers, word processing, Excel, Quicken, digital PhotoShop and greeting cards. Fees for most classes are $25 for members and $35 for non-members, though some fees are less.

WEDDING PLANNING

What can be more romantic than a beach wedding? Along the southern coast, from church sanctuaries to elegant halls to the surf's edge, the wedding industry is thriving. While couples of all ages still plan a traditional church ceremony, many opt for an outdoor wedding, choosing to tie the knot on one of the local beaches or in an azalea-filled garden. Romantic wedding/reception locations abound, from the Henrietta III Riverboat to the famous Orton Plantation and fabulous Louise Wells Cameron Art Museum.

In this chapter, we help guide you through the intricacies of planning a wedding in the southern coastal area, from applying for a license and choosing a magistrate or minister to hiring a caterer and photographer. We also provide you with information on locations, musicians, florists, formal wear, transportation and rental equipment. If you want someone else to handle all the necessary planning details, we suggest some popular wedding consultants. Be sure to look in our Salons and Day Spas section for some great gift ideas and beauty services for your special day. Planning a wedding can be a thrilling adventure. Our goal is to help you enjoy the experience.

Marriage Licenses

To be married in North Carolina, even on the beach, a North Carolina marriage license is a must. You may get the license in any county, but you must turn it into the Register of Deeds that issued it. This is very helpful for out-of-town couples coming to the beach area to be married, because they can get their license at home (if they live in North Carolina).

Courthouses are open Monday through Friday but are closed on holidays. Hours vary, so phone ahead (Register of Deeds offices are listed below). Both parties must be present when the license is issued. Take with you three forms of identification, including a certified birth certificate, Social Security card and valid driver's license or DMV picture card ID. If one or both parties has been divorced in the last 60 days, you must bring your divorce papers. No blood test, physical exam or waiting period is necessary to obtain a marriage license, which costs $50 and is payable by cash only. In some instances, application forms are available online.

The license is valid for 60 days after being issued. Be sure to bring your marriage license to the wedding. Two witnesses must sign the license following the ceremony. The person who performs the ceremony is responsible for getting the license back to the Register of Deeds in the county in which you were married within 10 days. After you're married, the officiant or magistrate will issue you a marriage certificate.

REGISTER OF DEEDS OFFICES

Brunswick County Register of Deeds
75 Courthouse Dr., Building 1, Bolivia
(910) 253-2690, (877) 625-9310

New Hanover County Register of Deeds
216 N. Second St., Room 2, Wilmington
(910) 798-7758, (910) 798-7754

Onslow County Register of Deeds
109 Old Bridge St., Jacksonville
(910) 347-3451

Pender County Register of Deeds
300 E. Fremont St., Burgaw
(910) 259-1225

Wedding Locations

The southern coast is home to literally hundreds of churches, synagogues, a

Muslim mosque and a Buddhist temple. Houses of worship often require that you have some affiliation if you are planning to use the facilities. Contact the person in charge and he or she will give you the specifics. Prepare to pay a fee for the use of the sanctuary as well as to compensate for services. It is customary to pay between $50 and $300 for ministerial services. See the Yellow Pages or local phone books for a list of houses of worship.

The area's pristine beaches, barrier islands and historic gardens make magnificent backdrops and are a huge draw for couples who are in love with nature as well as each other. Some opt for an informal ceremony on the beach where everyone can go barefoot, while others choose such venues as Airlie Gardens, the New Hanover County Arboretum or Orton Plantation. If an outdoor wedding appeals to you, keep in mind that southern coast weather can be unpredictable, so always have an indoor back-up plan.

You'll have a lot of competition for some locations and services, so be sure to plan well in advance; at least a year out in many cases.

For seaside weddings at Wrightsville Beach, you will need to apply for a special use permit, especially if you want to use the Wrightsville Beach gazebo. There's a fee for the permit based on the number of participants, and some regulations apply. Contact the Wrightsville Beach Parks and Recreation Department, #1 Bob Sawyer Drive, Wrightsville Beach, (910) 256-7925, for information and permits.

Contact the Pleasure Island Chamber of Commerce, 1121 N. Lake Park Boulevard, Carolina Beach, (910) 458-8434, for information regarding the many suitable locations available for weddings in Carolina Beach and Kure Beach. A permit and fee are required for use of the Carolina Beach Lake gazebo or other municipally owned facilities, but none is required for a beach ceremony. Remember, alcohol and glass containers are prohibited on the beach.

WILMINGTON

Airlie Gardens
300 Airlie Rd., Wilmington
(910) 798-7700

A quiet respite in the midst of the urban landscape, historic Airlie Gardens offers 67 acres of azaleas, camellias and some of the world's most exotic plants in a setting that can accommodate up to 300 guests. The Pergola Lawn is the most popular place to conduct ceremonies since it has a natural bridal walk along with a view of the Italian pergola and Airlie Lake. Afterward, many couples choose the famous 467-year-old Airlie Oak as the site for their reception. Airlie Gardens is a one-of-a-kind wedding location, and they are now booking ceremonies and receptions for 2010 and 2011.

Bellamy Mansion Museum
503 Market St., Wilmington
(910) 251-3700

Make your wedding a memorable occasion with an evening event at Wilmington's beautifully restored Bellamy Mansion (1859-1861). This magnificent landmark provides a breathtaking backdrop for ceremonies, receptions, rehearsal dinners and wedding photography. Ornate plaster work, original brass chandeliers, marble and slate mantles and elaborate Victorian-style carpets provide a truly Southern atmosphere. More than 5,000 square feet, including the two main floors of the house, the grounds and the porches, are available for your guests. Your caterer may work on the basement level. Centrally located in the heart of Wilmington's downtown historic district, the mansion enjoys a large on-site parking lot. Bellamy Mansion is an ideal location for a small wedding or larger reception, and your guests will enjoy the comfort and beauty of this antebellum treasure.

Cameron Art Museum
3201 S. 17th St., Wilmington
(910) 395-5999

For a wedding surrounded by fine art, brilliant architecture and beautiful park-like grounds, there's no experience in Wilmington like the Cameron Art Museum. Exchange your vows and hold your reception in your choice of the museum's several indoor and outdoor spaces and semi-enclosed courtyard. Their list of approved caterers includes museum patrons and caterers who have served other museum events. As they say at the museum: "Your event will be a masterpiece."

Cape Fear River Deck
Chandler's Wharf, 2 Ann St., Wilmington
(910) 763-1703, (877) 763-1703

Fantastic views of the river in historic downtown Wilmington create a romantic backdrop for your bridal luncheon, rehearsal dinner, ceremony or reception on the Cape Fear River Deck at Candles Etc. Adjacent to the Riverwalk along the Cape Fear River, the Deck is the perfect location for a Riverfront Wilmington wedding. Owners Michael Lambrix and Howard Brown have more than 25 years of event planning experience and will take care of the details to make your event successful. Since the Cape Fear River Deck is part of Candles Etc., they can provide elegant candle decor for your event if you'd like. Catering is provided by Elijah's restaurant, which is next door to the Cape Fear River Deck. Michael and Howard have excellent referrals for everything from florists and cake bakers to musicians and a horse carriage to provide you with most any service you may need in making your event a special day.

The City Club at de Rossett
101 S. Second St., Wilmington
(910) 343-1880, (800) 525-0909

The City Club at de Rosset epitomizes the architectural style of the old South and combines Southern charm with the very best in gourmet dining and service. The location is perfect whether you're planning a true old-fashioned Southern wedding or a thoroughly modern event. They can even arrange for music, if desired. Weather permitting, plan to have both wedding and reception in the beautiful garden, where up to 200 people can be served, depending on the format. If it's rainy or cold, you'll find a gorgeous setting inside the mansion. All in all, The City Club at de Rosset offers an atmosphere of gracious elegance and refinement for your special day.

Graystone Inn
100 S. Third St., Wilmington
(910) 763-2000
www.graystoneinn.com

The historic Graystone Inn, with its turn-of-the-twentieth-century elegance, frequently hosts wedding receptions and events. The inn's event planner is available to help coordinate your ceremony and/or reception and is present at your event to coordinate all activities. Also, the inn has compiled a recommended list of caterers, florists, musicians and photographers to make your choices as worry-free as possible. The grand, Renaissance-style staircase, with its sweeping curves, provides a feeling of warmth and allows you to make a dramatic entrance to the ceremony. Your guests will have a commanding view of your wedding nuptials from the parlor and grand entrance hall. The beautiful ground floor contains 5,000 square feet of space, accommodating up to 150 guests. The dining room's magnificent 12-foot-long mahogany table is perfect for a catered feast. Along with your wedding festivities, your guests will enjoy taking advantage of all that downtown Wilmington has to offer.

Henrietta III Wedding Cruise
Cape Fear Riverboats, Wilmington
(910) 343-1611

The Henrietta III provides a truly unique wedding and reception location. This antebellum-style riverboat offers a variety of day or evening package plans to suit your nuptial needs. Ceremonies are held on the boat dockside for a peaceful view of the water. After exchanging vows on or off the boat, enjoy a leisurely cruise down the beautiful Cape Fear River with your sweetheart and wedding party. The Henrietta III can host weddings from four to 350 guests, with menus ranging from light hors d'oeuvres to an elegant four-course dinner. Plan ahead and book early.

Holiday Inn - Wilmington
5032 Market St., Wilmington
(910) 392-1101

The Holiday Inn Wilmington's versatile ballroom can be elegantly dressed for an intimate party of 20 or extravagantly outfitted for a grand affair for 225 — and everything in between. The hotel's high-end catering services can meet your culinary desires, from traditional cuisine to specialty, customized menus. Dance floors and custom decorating are also available to create a truly unique wedding reception experience.

Saint Thomas Preservation Hall
208 Dock St., Wilmington
(910) 763-4054

Listed on the National Historic Register, Saint Thomas Preservation Hall is a beautifully restored building that dates back to 1846. Staffed with friendly professionals, the space is designed and fully equipped for rehearsal dinners, weddings, meetings and receptions for up to 250 guests. At Saint Thomas, there are no requirements to use an in-house service. You can choose any band, disc jockey, caterer, bartender or florist you desire, and your providers have all day to set up and decorate at no extra charge. You can also take great satisfaction in knowing that all rental proceeds go to maintain and preserve part of Wilmington's history and support charitable organizations.

CAROLINA AND KURE BEACHES

Atlantic Towers
1615 S. Lake Park Blvd., Carolina Beach
(910) 458-8313, (800) BEACH-40
www.atlantic-towers.com

For an intimate wedding reception, Atlantic Towers provides a wonderful beach-side setting. You can celebrate your special day on their new gazebo and sundeck, an oceanfront space that is perfect for a romantic ceremony. Reception space is available in their Clubroom or on the oceanfront lawn. Group reservations can be made for your family and friends.

Courtyard by Marriott - Carolina Beach
100 Charlotte Ave., Carolina Beach
(910) 458-2030, (800) 321-2211

The Courtyard by Marriott at Carolina Beach, with 144 oceanfront balcony rooms, offers a full range of facilities and services for weddings or other special events. The Cape Ballroom can seat up to 200 guests and has just been renovated along with the entire hotel. With incredible views of the Atlantic Ocean and beach, the Courtyard by Marriott is an ideal setting for a wedding and reception.

North Carolina Aquarium at Fort Fisher
900 Loggerhead Rd., Kure Beach
(910) 458-8257
www.ncaquariums.com/fort-fisher

The aquarium's half-acre freshwater conservatory, 235,000-gallon saltwater tank featuring hundreds of sea creatures, and dramatic exhibit galleries offer exceptional backdrops and romantic photo opportunities for your wedding ceremony. Exchange your vows before a colorful underwater display or amidst ferns and trees in the beautiful Cape Fear River Freshwater Habitat. You may choose the location that's just right for your dream wedding, whether large or small. The North Carolina Aquarium at Fort Fisher can accommodate up to 2,000 guests (strolling), or up to 350 for a seated dinner.

BALD HEAD ISLAND

The Bald Head Island Club
Bald Head Island
(910) 457-7300, (866) 657-7311

The Bald Head Island Club offers a variety of settings with breathtaking ocean views perfect for your special event. The four indoor, air-conditioned site options can beautifully accommodate a relatively intimate rehearsal dinner of 15, an extravaganza reception of 300 and anything in between. If you have always dreamed of celebrating under the stars, an outdoor tent site is available year-round. The attentive, knowledgeable food and beverage staff can help you celebrate the wedding of your dreams.

Marsh Harbour Inn
21 Keelson Row, Harbour Village,
Bald Head Island
(910) 457-1702, (800) 680-8322

If you have always dreamed of a wedding by the sea, Bald Head Island offers an incredible setting that has played host to hundreds of weddings, from the simple to the simply elaborate. The Marsh Harbour Inn provides premier quarters for your special guests, and one of the stunning third floor suites is a perfect place for your honeymoon. The inn offers a daily breakfast buffet, golf carts for guests and temporary memberships to the Bald Head Island Club.

The Village Chapel of Bald Head Island
105 Lighthouse Wynd, Bald Head Island
(910) 457-1183

This exquisite little chapel, nestled among flowers with a panoramic view of the marsh, is a nondenominational church. Services are held every weekend by visiting ministers. It is available for weddings of no more than 110 guests. The visiting minister may be available to officiate or you can provide your own minister. Weddings are limited to one per day, and no weddings are performed during Easter week. Remember that you will need to arrange for ferry transportation and golf cart rental for all guests, as no vehicles are allowed on the island. If you think it would be fun to have a golf cart get you to the church on time, this would be one of the loveliest spots to tie the knot.

SOUTHPORT AND OAK ISLAND

Bald Head Island Limited
5079 Southport-Supply Rd., Southport
(910) 457-7400, (800) 432-7368

Idyllic Bald Head Island is an excellent choice for taking the plunge into the sea of matrimony. You can choose from various locations around the island such as the Shoals Club at East Beach, the Harbourside Pavilion in Harbour Village or the Gazebo at Cape Fear Station located in the picturesque maritime forest. The elegant Shoals Club offers magnificent views of the Atlantic Ocean, while the Gazebo's backdrop includes a lush green lawn and woodland paths. The Harbourside Pavilion's scenery includes an expansive marsh, the Cape Fear River and Old Baldy, which is the oldest lighthouse in North Carolina. Other venues include the Association Center, private homes and, of course, anywhere along the island's 14-miles of pristine beach.

Coastal Vacation Resorts Oak Island
4434 Long Beach Rd., Southport
(910) 457-9409, (888) 703-5469
www.coastalvacationresortsoakisland.com

Why not tie the knot at your favorite vacation location? Coastal Vacation

Resorts Oak Island has some stunning homes available for a perfectly memorable wedding. Copacetic is a soundside home across the street from the ocean. The lighted pier and floating dock provide a backdrop for the outdoor deck. Inside, the great room is an excellent place for a wedding. Tappie Trails and Calm n' Rae's are two more of the many sites available, and the folks at Coastal Vacation Resorts will be happy to offer a group of rental houses for all your guests. They can provide a list of local vendors to help make your occasion the special event it is.

Southport Community Building
223 E. Bay St., Southport
(910) 457-0665

The Southport Community Building, owned and operated by the City of Southport, is available for rental and is a favorite setting for weddings and receptions. It is located at likely the loveliest spot in Southport — on a bluff overlooking the Cape Fear River and surrounded by ancient live oaks. The building offers a huge elegant reception room with honey-colored hardwood flooring, large windows providing panoramic views, a warming kitchen and a private conference room. Wedding ceremonies are held inside or outside on the wooden deck facing the Cape Fear River.

Silver Coast Winery
6680 Barbeque Rd., Ocean Isle Beach
(910) 287-2800

If visions of a wedding in Tuscany fill your dreams, you don't have to travel far for the experience. Say your vows in the vineyard, patio, art gallery or in front of the waterfall in the Barrel Room at Silver Coast Winery. A true vineyard and winery in the heart of Brunswick County, Silver Coast is nestled on 40 acres, surrounded by lush woods and just 15 minutes from the beach. Your guests can enjoy the spacious outdoor setting while sipping award-winning wines. For intimate affairs or larger groups, Silver Coast Winery is a unique setting for your special day. (For more information, see our Attractions chapter).

The Winds Resort Beach Club
310 E. First St., Ocean Isle Beach
(910) 579-6275, (800) 334-3581
www.thewinds.com

The Winds Resort Beach Club offers a captivating beach setting for your wedding event. Creative honeymoon packages and catered receptions are available. The Garden Bar Restaurant and oceanfront, poolside Tiki Bar serve a light menu and mixed beverages, including margaritas and daiquiris. The ceremony, the reception, the catering, the decorating, the flowers and photography — it can all come together in one location. Frolic in the ocean surf, swim in the heated pool, relax in the Jacuzzi spa, explore the island on a bicycle, play tennis or golf, and enjoy romantic dinners for two.

TOPSAIL ISLAND

Assembly Building
720 Channel Blvd., Topsail Beach
(910) 328-4282

Getting married on the beach? The historic Assembly Building in Topsail Beach could be your perfect reception facility. This large, well-equipped building has an on-site kitchen, room for more than 100 people and an area for a band and dancing. Advance reservations are a must; restrictions apply and a donation is expected. Contact Sue Newsome for information and reservations.

Island Real Estate
The Fishing Village, Roland Ave., Surf City
(910) 328-2323, (800) 622-6886
www.topsailvacation.com

Are you dreaming about a wedding at the beach? Destination weddings are all the rage, and there is no better destination than Topsail Island. Whether you are looking for a romantic location for a reception, a 10-bedroom house for the entire wedding party or for a cozy cottage for two, Cathy Medlin and her team of experts at Island Real Estate will help you find the perfect accommodations to make all of your wedding dreams come true.

St. Regis Resort
2000 New River Inlet Rd.,
North Topsail Beach
(910) 328-0739

At this impressive beach resort wedding nuptials can be performed on the beach or in a delightful gazebo. Indoor reception facilities include Onslow Hall, which can accommodate up to 75 guests, and the larger Pender Hall, which can accommodate up to 150 guests. Pender Hall also has two bars and a dance floor. Tables and chairs are provided in both halls. Clients must provide for their own caterer and bartenders.

Reception Facilities and Caterers

The reception facilities in the Wilmington area offer as many choices as the mind can imagine. You can choose a location such as a hotel or restaurant that will provide the food and beverages, or engage a caterer for another setting. Our Restaurants chapter lists a number of excellent establishments that host wedding celebrations — everything from the bachelor's party and bride's luncheon to a rehearsal dinner or a full-blown reception. If you'd prefer to host the reception in Wilmington's Historic District or in a romantic oceanfront house facing one of the many beaches, a caterer can provide all of the services while you enjoy the company of your guests. For a catered function, expect to spend $25 to $50 or more per guest, depending upon your choice of menu and type of bar service.

WILMINGTON

Airlie Gardens
300 Airlie Rd., Wilmington
(910) 798-7700

A quiet respite in the midst of the urban landscape, historic Airlie Gardens offers 67 acres of azaleas, camellias and some of the world's most exotic plants in a setting that can accommodate up to 300 guests. The Pergola Lawn is the most popular place to conduct ceremonies since it has a natural bridal walk along with a view of the Italian pergola and Airlie Lake. Afterward, many couples choose the famous 467-year-old Airlie Oak as the site for their reception. Airlie Gardens is a one-of-a-kind wedding location, and they are now booking ceremonies and receptions for 2010 and 2011.

Beau Rivage Resort & Golf Club
649 Rivage Promenade, Wilmington
(910) 392-9021, (800) 628-7080

An elegant, colonial-style clubhouse offers a formal banquet and corporate meeting facility that can accommodate up to 250 guests. Beau Rivage is the perfect venue for wedding receptions and rehearsal dinners, reunions and banquets. The friendly and professional staff invites you and your guests to have a fun-filled and memorable event, with large and flexible menu selections/styles provided by their in-house caterer, Thyme Savor Catering. For overnight guests, there are 27 comfortable golf villas that can accommodate up to six people. In addition Beau Rivage offers an outdoor swimming pool and tiki bar, tennis courts, free high-speed wireless Internet, complimentary hot breakfast and an 18-hole championship golf course. They also offer a variety of wedding, golf and vacation packages. Whether your group is large or small, Beau Rivage is prepared to meet all your needs.

Caffe Phoenix
9 S. Front St., Wilmington
(910) 343-1395

Conveniently located in the heart of Historic Downtown Wilmington, Caffe Phoenix is only a short stroll from any number of local wedding venues. Their second-floor space is reserved exclusively for private, catered events and can accommodate up to 85 guests. Menus are made to order and showcase the skills of the restaurant's talented kitchen staff, while a full beverage menu can be made available as well. The 150-year-old building's fully renovated space features beautiful heart-pine floors, a fantastic view and parking just across the street. Enjoy your special day in a comfortable and warm environment just steps from the Cape Fear River.

Elijah's
2 Ann St., Wilmington
(910) 343-1448
www.riverenterprisesevents.com

Celebrate your special wedding day at Elijah's restaurant, one of Wilmington's finest riverfront dining destinations. The lounge area comfortably seats 50, and the main dining room approximately 120. Also, in conjunction with the Cape Fear River Deck, (910) 763-1703, Elijah's can provide an outdoor event for up to 100 people. Visit their website for pictures of the dining areas and to look at their menus.

Front Street Brewery
9 N. Front St., Wilmington
(910) 251-1935
www.frontstreetbrewery.com

If Historic Downtown Wilmington is your location for a special event, Front Street Brewery can accommodate you in their recently opened banquet hall located above the restaurant and brewery. You'll find the same fine food, locally brewed beer and attention to detail in a beautiful 3,000-square-foot room that accommodates 100+ people. Catering services available for cocktails, wedding receptions, rehearsals, corporate meetings and dinners, and mixers. With a full range of culinary specialties offered, there is a food and drink menu for every occasion and budget.

Jerry's Food, Wine and Spirits
7220 Wrightsville Ave., Wilmington
(910) 256-8847

Jerry's will coordinate your catering needs for any number of guests. Their knowledgeable staff offers nearly 40 years of professional experience and will happily assist you in selecting the most appropriate menu. Taking any dietary, religious or occasional need into consideration, Jerry's puts together an event for every desire, with nothing left to chance. For your convenience, a complete list of wedding services is offered, such as tent set-up, videography and music, to ensure that your special day is memorable in every way.

Lovey's Natural Foods and Cafe, Inc.
Landfall Shopping Center, Eastwood Rd., Wilmington
(910) 509-0331
www.loveysmarket.com

If you've enjoyed the fresh, healthy, organic, natural foods of Lovey's for lunch, you can bring that experience to your party or wedding menus. Lovey's offers the same delicious fresh fruits, vegetables, salads, soups and beverages in their catering department. Lovey's professional catering staff can create the perfect rehearsal dinner, bridal luncheon or wedding reception. They will help you select just the right menu to complete your perfect day. Need flowers, a photographer or rental items? Lovey's can handle it all. For catering that's delicious and healthy too, call the catering professionals at Lovey's Natural Foods and Cafe.

Nicola's ~ Italian with a Twist
5704 Oleander Dr., Wilmington
(910) 798-2205

Treat your wedding guests to an authentic Italian feast. Nicola's owner Nick Pittari makes only authentic recipes with fresh-made ingredients, including pasta, fish, shellfish and vegetables. Nicola's caters events on site in its chic restaurant or at the location of your choice. The main restaurant holds 80 people seated and 100 people for a cocktail-style party. The banquet room holds 40 people seated. The catering menu includes appetizers, salads, risottos, fresh pastas, Italian entrees, sides and fabulous Italian desserts. Packages are available or the staff will help you customize your menu. Italian doesn't get any more authentic than the masterpieces coming out of Pittari's kitchen. Join him for a slice of the Cape Fear region's la dolce vita.

The Pilot House
Chandler's Wharf, 2 Ann St., Wilmington
(910) 343-0200
www.riverenterprisesevents.com

Enjoy your wedding day, rehearsal dinner, ceremony and reception at one of the most popular Cape Fear riverfront restaurants, located in the historic Craig House in Chandler's Wharf. Serving the finest in both traditional and innovative Southern cuisine for more than 26 years, The Pilot House will serve approximately 150 guests in the casual elegance of the sunny dining room or outdoors on the covered patio, which offers a great view of the river.

Pine Valley Market
3520 S. College Rd., Wilmington
(910) 350-3663

Truly a one-stop shop for off-premise catering, Pine Valley Market will provide everything you need from setting up to cleaning up. From a romantic dinner for two to a full-scale party for 300 people, wine expert Kathy Webb and personal chef Christi Ferretti can handle it. Their specialty is intimate settings with a true gourmet flair. Whether you choose a brunch, dinner or cocktail reception, call this creative team to assist you with an event to remember. You'll love their party platters, accompaniments and entrees. Want vegetarian or low-carb selections? No problem. What they don't do themselves, they can order for you, including specialty items such as wedding cakes and ice sculptures.

Poplar Grove Plantation
10200 U.S. Hwy. 17, Wilmington
(910) 686-9518 x26

If you're looking for someplace truly different to hold your service, reception and rehearsal dinner, Poplar Grove Plantation provides a number of amenities suited to your needs. Couples may rent the Manor House, once the center of this lovely old Southern plantation, or the courtyard, gazebo, cultural arts center and even the entire grounds with its big old shade trees. Conveniently located and an extremely popular destination, Poplar Grove Plantation has a cozy feel for celebrating one's nuptials.

Port Land Grille
Lumina Station, 1908 Eastwood Rd., Ste. 111, Wilmington
(910) 256-6056
www.portlandgrille.com

Your rehearsal dinner, wedding reception or special event cannot go wrong with the exquisite cuisine and elegant ambiance of Port Land Grille. The restaurant offers two private dining rooms for intimate parties of up to 65 people, or if you elect to use both rooms, you can host a group of up to 80. Their experienced staff will create a personalized prix fixe menu that fits any budgetary and dietary preferences. If you envision music at your festivities, Port Land Grille's private space can accommodate a live band. The space is also perfect for business meetings, as the larger room includes audiovisual equipment and a 6-foot TV (but don't worry, it all disappears when not in use).

Ramada Conference Center
5001 Market St., Wilmington
(910) 799-1730

Host your wedding reception at the newly redesigned Ramada Conference Center. The Ramada's spacious banquet room accommodates a wedding reception for up to 300 people. The highly versatile banquet room can be decorated for a casual, intimate affair or dressed up to the nines for a lavish, elegant event. The Ramada is located in the heart of Wilmington, conveniently situated between Historic Downtown and the beaches.

Riverboat Landing
2 Market St., Wilmington
(910) 763-7227

Many marriage proposals have taken place on the nine two-seater balconies of this picturesque restaurant that overlooks the Cape Fear River. Owner Steve Kohlstedt says multiple weddings have resulted from the restaurant's consistently high quality in both food and service. One couple who enjoyed a romantic balcony dinner came back to renew their vows on their 20th wedding anniversary. The next year, they had a reception for one of their daughters and the following year, a rehearsal dinner was held for another family member. In more than 20 years of business, Riverboat Landing has hosted more than 1,000 wedding rehearsal dinners and an equal number of wedding receptions. The restaurant offers in-house catering for up to 110 people in its private banquet room and off-site catering for a maximum of 500. Catering services are fully customized with offerings of the finest seafood and steaks, hors d'oeuvres and buffets.

WRIGHTSVILLE BEACH

The Bridge Tender Restaurant
1414 Airlie Rd., Wilmington
(910) 256-4519
www.thebridgetender.com

If you've enjoyed the exceptional dining at The Bridge Tender Restaurant, why not book Bridge Tender Caterers for your wedding reception, rehearsal dinner or other special event? Located at the foot of the Wrightsville Beach drawbridge on Airlie Road, The Bridge Tender Restaurant hosts private wedding receptions on Saturdays and Sundays between the hours of 9 AM and 3:30 PM. With few places in the area available on the waterfront, The Bridge Tender Restaurant is a great place to have an affordable and elegant waterfront reception with panoramic views of the Intracoastal Waterway. The restaurant offers indoor and outdoor seating for up to 200 guests.

Shell Island Resort
2700 N. Lumina Ave., Wrightsville Beach
(910) 256-8696

If you've always dreamed of being barefoot in the sand when you say "I do," look no further than Shell Island Resort for all of your wedding and reception needs. With a professional catering staff and wedding coordinator dedicated to your event, Shell Island Resort can truly make your wedding day an unforgettable one. Hold your reception there in Wrightsville Beach's only oceanview ballroom, which can accommodate up to 200 people. They offer three wedding packages that can be customized to suit your wedding, including catering, floral arrangements, custom-designed cakes, guest favors and ice sculptures. Among breathtaking scenery on Wrightsville Beach, a wedding at Shell Island Resort is the perfect way to begin your new life together.

CAROLINA BEACH AND VICINITY

Courtyard by Marriott - Carolina Beach
100 Charlotte Ave., Carolina Beach
(910) 458-2030, (800) 321-2211

The Courtyard by Marriott at Carolina Beach, with 144 oceanfront balcony rooms, offers a full range of facilities and services for weddings or other special events. The Cape Ballroom can seat up to 200 guests and has just been renovated along with the entire hotel. With incredible views of the Atlantic Ocean and beach, the Courtyard by Marriott is an ideal setting for the perfect wedding and reception.

North Carolina Aquarium at Fort Fisher
900 Loggerhead Rd., Kure Beach
(910) 458-8257
www.ncaquariums.com/fort-fisher

For your wedding reception, consider the beautiful North Carolina Aquarium at Fort Fisher, situated on the Atlantic Ocean's picturesque shores. Greet your guests in the Cape Fear Conservatory atrium. Dine and dance in the Upper Mezzanine and Lower Cape Fear Shoals in this romantic environment where seahorses gently sway and colorful fishes accent the underwater scenery. The Aquarium can accommodate up to 2,000 people (strolling) and up to 350 for a seated dinner. Contact the Special Events Coordinator, who will work with you to ensure a truly memorable occasion.

BALD HEAD ISLAND

Marsh Harbour Inn
21 Keelson Row, Harbour Village,
Bald Head Island
(910) 457-1702, (800) 680-8322

If you are planning a wedding reception (up to 30 people), Marsh Harbour Inn is an excellent choice. A view of the Harbour, Bald Head Creek and the wide expanse of lovely natural marshland will provide a beautiful backdrop for your special occasion. The dining facility at the inn can be configured in a reception, theater or conference style set-up. Comfortable rooms or suites can be reserved at the inn for each member of your party. In addition there are 40 premier rental homes available through Bald Head Island Rentals.

SOUTHPORT

Taylor Cuisine Cafe & Catering, Inc.
731 N. Howe St., Southport
(910) 454-0088

Taylor Cuisine is ready to cater your wedding reception and/or rehearsal dinner

at the site of your choice or at their own restaurant. Their catering menu includes a variety of items, including breakfast. Some of their specialties include bruschetta, fried-green tomatoes with goat cheese and roasted red pepper sauce, and shrimp and chicken jambalaya with linguine, but there is so much more.

Thyme to Eat Catering
107 River Dr., Southport
(910) 367-1325

Chef Kenneth Egan, owner and operator of Thyme To Eat Catering, is a 1996 Culinary Institute of America graduate. He has performed his culinary magic at some of the finest restaurants, including the Ritz Carlton in Amelia Island, Florida. In North Carolina his catering experience includes a fund-raiser for Elizabeth Dole. In 2008 you may have tasted his fare at the Southport Bridal Expo in the Southport Community Center or at Belk's Bridal Expo at the Independence Mall in Wilmington. Chef Egan offers full wedding packages focusing on affordable fine dining.

OAK ISLAND

Turtle Island Restaurant and Catering
6220 E. Oak Island Dr., Oak Island
(910) 278-4944

The folks at Turtle Island are happy to work with you in planning the menu and in presenting their luscious food in a way that makes it a feast for the eyes. They will cater your wedding reception or rehearsal dinner on-site or off-site to meet your highest expectations. Turtle Island has all ABC catering permits. Contact Kim at Turtle Island for catering information.

OCEAN ISLE BEACH

Silver Coast Winery
6680 Barbeque Rd., Ocean Isle Beach
(910) 287-2800

Your reception can have an old world feel in a true vineyard and winery in the heart of Brunswick County. Silver Coast Winery is nestled on 40 acres, surrounded by lush woods and just 15 minutes from the beach. Your guests can enjoy the spacious outdoor setting while sipping award-winning wines. For indoor accommodations, the barrel room with its indoor waterfalls, or the art gallery exhibiting works by local artists will suit your nuptial needs. For intimate affairs or larger groups, Silver Coast Winery is a unique setting for your special day. (For more information, see our Attractions section.)

TOPSAIL ISLAND AND VICINITY

The Atlantis Restaurant & Lounge
**2000 New River Inlet Rd.,
North Topsail Beach
(910) 328-2002**

More than 8,000 square feet, a stunning seventh-floor view of North Topsail Beach and a dance floor contribute to the atmosphere of this island wedding destination. There's room for a band, 200 guests and plenty of photo opportunities. The Atlantis provides a variety of banquet services. Reservations are accepted year-round.

Dorothy Cruise Boat
**720 Channel Blvd., Topsail Beach
(910) 545-7433**

If you have always wanted to sail into the sunset on your wedding day, the *Dorothy Cruise Boat* is the answer to your dreams. With the gorgeous backdrop of the Intracoastal Waterway, your wedding day is sure to be very special. The *Dorothy* can also be booked for bachelor and bachelorette parties.

Mainsail Restaurant's Commodore Room
**404 Roland Ave., Surf City
(910) 328-0010**

The Mainsail Restaurant has two private reception rooms, the Commodore Room and the Sunset Room, that are available year round. Their largest and completely private room, the Commodore Room, has a dance floor and a gorgeous cherry wood bar and can easily accommodate wedding receptions, anniversary parties and holiday celebrations. The Sunset Room is ideal for rehearsal dinners and more intimate dinner receptions. The Mainsail offers a very nice selection of appetizers, entrees and desserts and has a full bar with all ABC permits. In addition to on-site catering, Mainsail Catering offers full service off-site catering at the location of your choice.

Wedding Cakes

Your wedding is a reflection of your individual style, and you'll want your cake to fit into the theme, satisfying both the eye and the taste buds. The southern coast area has outstanding bakeries and individuals who prepare gorgeous cakes. Since they are too numerous to mention all of them here, we've listed a few of our favorites.

WILMINGTON AND CAROLINA BEACH

Apple Annie's Bake Shop
**Outlet Mall, S. College Rd., Wilmington
(910) 799-9023**

Wedding and anniversary cakes are the specialty of this long-standing Wilmington bakery. Apple Annie's wedding cakes are customized to delight your palate. Each tier is like a torte with four layers of cake and three layers of filling. For your wedding events, Apple Annie's can provide gourmet cakes, cookies, pastries and fine breads. All of their baking is done on the premises, and their cakes are handmade and decorated with loving care. Each is scrumptious and perfect every time.

Island Cakery
**1018 N. Lake Park Blvd. #23, Carolina Beach
(910) 458-5568**

Island Cakery aims to please the discerning palate as well as the discriminating eye. They specialize in custom-made, innovative wedding cakes, cheesecakes and theme cakes designed with an artist's eye and a chef's heart. Island Cakery's staff will work closely with you from the initial consultation to the final presentation. Island Cakery believes that as the centerpiece of your wedding reception, your cake should reflect not only the style and theme of the wedding, but it should be a reflection of you as a couple. To that end, Island Cakery takes the time to make your cake extraordinary.

Sweet & Savory Cafe and Bake Shop
1611 Pavilion Pl., Wilmington
(910) 256-0115

Sweet and Savory has a large professional catering and bakery staff headed by their seasoned manager, Chef Brent Williams. They prepare all of the desserts, breads and meals from scratch daily with only the freshest of ingredients. This restaurant also serves as a wholesaler supplying many of the local restaurants with their desserts, breads and homemade sweets. When you walk into the restaurant, you can smell the aroma from the large assortment of cakes, pies, pastries, muffins, cookies, mini-desserts and breads that were prepared that morning. If you are engaged and shopping for wedding cakes, stop by and have a taste from many different cake flavors and numerous icings. All of the wedding cakes are exquisitely decorated to the customers' specifications. Finally, Sweet and Savory can cater any size party.

SOUTHPORT

Cakes by the Norwoods
208 Yaupon Dr., Southport
(910) 457-5850

Mary and Elmer Norwood, who serve all of Brunswick County as well as Wilmington, have enjoyed working with brides and their special wedding cakes for more than 20 years. The combination of Mary's home economics degree and experience teaching cake decoration along with Elmer's special touch with original artwork is hard to beat. They can bake tower cakes, tier cakes, nautical cakes, whimsical cakes, fondant cakes, satellite cakes for larger groups, specialty cakes decorated from photographs — or any combination of these. Whatever your choice you can be sure your cake will be beautifully decorated, delicious and reasonably priced.

Crazy Cake Chicks
5119 E. Oak Island Dr., Oak Island
(910) 933-4253

Crazy Cake Chicks is billed as "The Sweetest Place on Oak Island" — and how sweet it is. Proprietors Cindy and Micki have combined baking experience of more

than 40 years and are Wilton Method cake decorating instructors. Their standard menu includes such things as After Midnight Cake, Lady in Red Cake, White Rabbit Cake, Sweet Dream Pie, Georgia on my Mind Pie and Black Magic Woman Cheesecake. The names alone are enough to make you want to take a look-see, and when you do you will be sure to require a taste. After that you will be hooked. Specialty cake flavors and fillings are available as well including Amaretto, Mississippi Mud, Blueberry Thrill and more. These can be covered in frostings like whipped chocolate, buttercream and cream cheese. Stop for your morning muffin for a sweet start to your day. Be sure to check them out as bakers of your wedding cake.

PENDER COUNTY

Just Baked
205 S. Topsail Dr., Surf City
(910) 328-3150

From the funky to the classically fabulous, Just Baked's wedding cakes will turn your wildest fantasies into a delicious reality. This family-operated bakery takes great pride in offering fresh, baked-on-the-premises cakes. Since all of their cakes are made-to-order, they are never refrigerated or frozen.

Wedding Officiants

North Carolina law requires that wedding ceremonies be conducted by an ordained minister or a magistrate. A boat captain can't do the trick anymore! The state has replaced its former justice of the peace system with court-appointed magistrates. These officials may perform wedding services, but they are often severely limited as to times and places they can accommodate, and they do charge a fee. If you want to be married by a minister, most major religions are represented in Wilmington. Many denominations require a special counseling period, and some have specific requirements regarding remarrying divorced persons. The following interfaith ministers are among those on the North Carolina coast who can make your wedding ceremony memorable.

A Wedding Minister -
Reverend Penelope Morningstar
4922 Marlin Ct., Wilmington
(910) 232-4839

Reverend Penelope Morningstar is an interfaith minister who has been officiating weddings since 1994. She will help you create a beautiful ceremony and officiate your wedding at the location of your choice. If you are not a member of a local church or are marrying outside your faith, Reverend Morningstar can offer you the blessing and guidance of an ordained minister. Whether you are planning to be married on the beach, on a cruise boat, in the park, at a hotel, in your home or anywhere in the greater Wilmington area, with Reverend Morningstar's help it will be a sacred moment to treasure for a lifetime. Premarital counseling is available but is not required.

Beachpeople Weddings
Sunset Beach
(910) 575-8171

Looking for the real deal in a beach wedding? Beachpeople Weddings is the original conch-shell blowing, barefoot beach wedding business on the southern coast. They specialize in affordable officiant and photography packages for intimate and romantic seacoast weddings that are focused on feelings, love and laughter. Their ceremonies are spiritual, creative and humorous, and their photography and photo-art are, as they say, "uniquely suited to this one magical moment when the power of the sea, the rhythm of the tides and the love of two human hearts join together."

Heartsong Interfaith Ministry
Wilmington
(910) 367-3496
www.heartsonginterfaithministry.com

Creating a special service or wedding ceremony that respects and represents each individual's beliefs is the mission of Minister Barbara McKenzie-Tervo. Working closely with the engaged couple, Reverend Barbara designs wedding ceremonies that reflect the couple's personal faith and commitment. She also offers premarital introductions to creating a healthy marriage.

In addition, she is available to officiate baby blessings, vow renewals, coming-of-age celebrations, house clearings and other ceremonies.

Sea/Side Ceremonies
106 Yacht Basin Dr., Southport
(910) 454-4479

Sea/Side Ceremonies offers wedding ceremonies at a variety of locations around Southport, Oak Island and Bald Head Island, including aboard the 52-foot sailboat, Carolina Gale. Ordained minister Carolyn Pryor, PhD, performs customized services that honor the traditions and beliefs of the couple. Dr. Pryor meets with the couple in advance to design a service that represents their desires. When meeting in person is not possible, she gets acquainted with clients by phone and email. Sea/Side Ceremonies is an outgrowth of charter sailing company Priority Sailing. A unique option for the ceremony is for the bride and groom to actually tie the True Lovers' Knot, creating a symbolic keepsake of ropes joined together. Under way on the Carolina Gale, there is a limit of six guests, due to Coast Guard regulations; for larger weddings, you can "get hitched" on the dock and then sail away to your honeymoon after the reception.

Wonderful Weddings
Barefoot Beach Chapel,
6902 E. Oak Island Dr., Oak Island
(910) 278-9510

Ordained by the Carolina Evangelistic Association of Charlotte, Betty Jo Blackmon has been a minister for more than 30 years. Though she will perform your marriage ceremony almost anywhere you choose, she specializes in beach weddings. One of her special touches is "Sands of Time," a ceremony that includes the bride and groom taking sand from beneath their feet and placing it in a heart-shaped keepsake bottle. Another comes from a Hawaiian custom — the best man blows into a conch shell (bored to make the sound of a trumpet) when the couple is pronounced man and wife. Free vow renewal is offered every year on the 4th of July weekend.

HEARTSONG
Interfaith MINISTRY

Creating celebrations of love, joy & togetherness.

REV. BARBARA MCKENZIE-TERVO
Interfaith Minister, Wilmington, NC
(910) 367 3496 HeartSongInterfaithMinistry.com

Bridal Registries

The Wilmington area offers a wide variety of stores at which the bride and groom may register for gifts. Here are some favorites.

Bed, Bath & Beyond
352 S. College Rd., Wilmington
(910) 784-9707

Independence Mall,
3500 Oleander Dr., Wilmington
(910) 392-1440

Mayfaire Town Center,
940 Inspiration Dr., Wilmington
(910) 256-2115

Cat on a Whisk
Howe Street Purveyors, 600 N. Howe St., Southport
(910) 454-4451

Dillard's
Independence Mall, 3500 Oleander Dr., Wilmington
(910) 796-3300

Fisherman's Wife
1425 Airlie Rd., Wilmington
(910) 256-5505

JCPenney
Independence Mall, 3500 Oleander Dr., Wilmington
(910) 392-1400

Pottery Barn
Mayfaire Town Center, 6815 Main St., Wilmington
(910) 256-6066

Victoria's Ragpatch
10164 Beach Dr. SW, Calabash
(910) 579-2015
117 Causeway Dr., Ocean Isle Beach
(910) 579-3158

Williams-Sonoma
Mayfaire Town Center, 6852 Main St., Wilmington
(910) 256-0266

Florists

What would a wedding be without flowers? They symbolize both romantic and devoted love. The Wilmington area is home to an amazing showcase of artistic florists who will make your most fanciful floral vision come true. Here are just a few big bloomers.

WILMINGTON

A Beautiful Event - Floral Design for Weddings & Events
Wilmington
(910) 327-0877

To make your wedding a truly beautiful event, you need truly beautiful flowers. With 18 years of experience in floral design, Wendy Wright will create the perfect bouquet and floral backdrop for your special day. Wendy's designs are unique in their use of color and texture and she works closely with brides to create custom designs that suit each taste and desire. Wendy designs flowers for elaborate events as well as small intimate affairs. Her floral creations have appeared in weddings, Bar Mitzvahs and corporate gatherings throughout the area.

Ikebana Design and Accessories
The Forum, 1125 Military Cutoff Rd., Ste. S, Wilmington
(910) 509-1383

Master Ikebana specialists Bonnie Burney and Ruth Lees offer the most exotic wedding arrangements we've ever seen. As a full-service florist, they can handle all of your floral needs. For floral excellence, consult with these ladies or any of their professional staff.

Sophia V. West Florist, Inc.
8086 Market St., Wilmington
(910) 686-0496

With 45 years of wedding experience, the experts at Sophia V. West Florist will create any type design that meets the wedding couple's taste. Schedule an appointment for your free, very personal consultation; have your date, time, dress, colors and favorite flowers in mind. It helps to leave the planning a little open-ended for that last-minute flower that might be just perfect for the wedding bouquet. Plant rentals are also available.

CAROLINA BEACH

Island Florals by Roxanne
100 N. Lake Park Blvd., Carolina Beach
(910) 458-5276

Owner Roxanne Thompson relies upon her more than 25 years experience to create personalized, unique floral designs for your wedding. Island Florals by Roxanne is known for its distinctive style combining traditional elements with modern concepts and materials. They cater to any size wedding, from a small, intimate, beach ceremony to a grand affair in historic downtown Wilmington, and everything in between. Wedding consultations are provided at no charge, taking into account the bride's unique vision for her special day. As a full-service florist, Island Florals by Roxanne also creates beautiful floral arrangements for a variety of occasions, including holidays and events. Roxanne has become a sought-after florist throughout Wilmington, Wrightsville Beach, Pleasure Island and Southport. Let her put her fresh, imaginative perspective to work for your wedding or special event.

Marshall Gardens
1230 N. Lake Park Blvd., Carolina Beach
(910) 458-3292

Jan Marshall and her talented floral assistants strive to make your wedding a beautiful floral event. Limited only by the imagination, they can create just about anything you want, from shell bouquets to Hawaiian leis. They have an on-site nursery so live plants, palms and exotic flowers are available to rent, as are gazebos, arches and arbors. Marshall Gardens specializes in weddings held on the beach, on cruise boats or anywhere your heart desires.

BRUNSWICK COUNTY

Brunswick Town Florist
Live Oak Shopping Center, 4161-7 Long Beach Rd., SE, Southport
(910) 457-1144, (877) 230-1144

Brunswick Town Florist offers free consultations for your everyday floral and special events needs. Bridal consultations are by appointment. The owners have extensive experience in weddings throughout Brunswick County, whether in church, on the beach, at Orton Plantation, on Bald Head Island or in Wilmington. They work personally on every wedding serviced through their shop and can accommodate any style of wedding, They are especially especially proud of their unique and organic custom designs.

Sweet Nectar's Florist
503 Olde Waterford Way, Ste. 107, Leland
(910) 371-2224

Sweet Nectar's Florist is a professional FTD florist that delivers flowers and gifts to the Leland and Wilmington areas. Scheduled consultations are available for planning the flowers for your wedding. You are sure to find flowers that add to the beauty of your ceremony. These include altar flowers, floral archways and candelabra flowers. You can choose corsages and boutonnieres for the wedding party and family, flowers to decorate the reception area and even flowers for your cake. No matter the size of your wedding, the staff will work within your budget to make your special day exceptionally memorable.

Wine & Roses
919-D N. Howe St., Southport
(910) 457-4428

With more than 40 years of experience in the florist business, 19 of those years owning Wine & Roses, Steve and Cheryl Dosher have a wealth of experience. In addition to floral decorations for the church and reception hall and the traditional flowers for the members of the wedding party, Wine & Roses offers a variety of invitations. They can refer you to services such as photography, video operators and wedding-cake bakers as well.

TOPSAIL ISLAND AND VICINITY

The Flower Basket of Hampstead
14361 U.S. Hwy. 17 N, Hampstead
(910) 270-4141

A full-service florist, The Flower Basket of Hampstead offers everything from lush houseplants to beautiful mixed bouquets. They maintain an extensive inventory of fresh-cut flowers and offer complete wedding floral services.

Surf City Florist
106 N. Topsail Dr., Surf City
(910) 328-3238

Scheduled or last minute, Surf City Florist is ready to provide beautiful, fresh flowers for your wedding. They offer full wedding services, including rental of candelabras.

Bridal Shops and Formal Wear

Whether you opt for a highly formal church wedding or a casual affair at the beach, the Wilmington area offers an abundance of stores from which to choose your wedding finery. Here are a few that specialize.

WILMINGTON

Beautiful Brides of Wilmington
803-B S. College Rd., Wilmington
(910) 395-0052

This small but complete bridal shop has everything you need to dress the wedding party and more. Offering formal wear for all occasions, owner Sandra Leigh uses her extensive experience and expertise to help you choose bridesmaids' gowns, flower-girl dresses, mother-of-the-bride gowns, even little boys' tuxedos. Select from a wide range of accessories, shoes and jewelry as well as bridal undergarments and bras up to size triple D. Looking for prom gowns and pageant dresses? Beautiful Brides of Wilmington has them, along with tiaras, scepters and pageant pins. For excellent quality formal wear at affordable prices, Beautiful Brides of Wilmington is the little shop you don't want to miss.

Cape Fear Formal Wear
218 N. Third St., Wilmington
(910) 762-8206

Family owned and managed, Cape Fear Formal Wear has been serving the area for more than 40 years. These folks can dress all the men in your wedding party from head to toe. The only business of its kind in southern North Carolina that owns its merchandise, Cape Fear Formal Wear offers the area's largest selection of men's rentals and sales. Cape Fear Formal Wear will handle your special occasion with the utmost care and attention. Same-day service is available.

Photography

Photographs rank high among the most important elements of the wedding. After the cake is cut and the bouquet is tossed, photographs are among the only tangible evidence of the day's events. Preserve your memories with top-quality photos by a professional photographer. The area has many creative photographers who employ the latest techniques. Here are a few suggestions.

Arrow Ross Photography
711-A N. Fifth St., Wilmington
(910) 762-2243

Arrow Ross specializes in photographing people, and weddings offer an opportunity to capture the spirit of the moment in a telling photograph. Using his skills as a photojournalist, Arrow anticipates and captures real moments that hold memories for a lifetime.

Boswell Photography II
1014 W. Dolphin Dr., Oak Island
(910) 278-7957

Mike Boswell has been photographing people and events on the East Coast since 1976. Though his studio is traditional, using classical poses and settings, he intersperses these with candid photos and photojournalism shots for the wedding album. Now 100 percent digital, he posts all weddings and portrait sessions on the website within hours of the shoot. He views his work as recording family history and works with his customers to make that record reflect their part in the history. Any image can be printed in color, black and white or sepia tone. Mike does restoration of old photos as well.

Specializing in weddings, engagement, bridal, couples, maternity, fashion, modeling, children, life-style sessions at your home, family, senior graduation, custom dvd shows, special events, outdoor. Photographer Terry Taylor

910-805-1159 | weddingsbythebeach.net

Eric Von Bargen photography
(910) 264-2666

Eric von Bargen has worked as a photographer in many different arenas both domestically and abroad. Eric's editorial work has been featured in various magazines and TV shows. He uses his unique vision to produce images that are thought-provoking and moving.

Lundie's Photography
4724-8 New Centre Dr., Wilmington
(910) 392-3141

Lundie's Photography specializes in family and children's portraiture, both in the studio and on location, and bridal services. Their beach portraits are especially fun. They also do some commercial photographs by special request.

Matt McGraw Photography
834 Lambrook Dr., Wilmington
(910) 538-6201

Matt's experience in photojournalism and full-service portrait photography allows him to capture the essence of emotion in a single moment. He listens, inquires and adapts to the surroundings of the wedding party, recording the wedding celebration as it happens and telling a story that will last a lifetime.

Naturally Captured Studio, LLC
Wilmington
(910) 520-8283

Naturally Captured Studio, LLC, located in Wilmington, transforms the ordinary charm of everyday life into an art form that captures the natural beauty we often overlook. Naturally Captured can take your most important moments and turn them into visual art that will last a lifetime. The studio offers customized packages to suit clients' individual needs as well as competitive rates for commercial, wedding, portrait and event photography. Naturally Captured also travels out of state for events.

Ocean View Photography
6209 Oleander Dr., Ste. 300, Wilmington
(910) 297-1320

Beach portrait photography has been Denis Lemay's expertise for the past 30 years, making him a natural as a beach wedding photographer. He will work locally or travel the Carolina coast. While beach weddings make up a large percentage of this business, Ocean View also is known for on-location photography of families, large groups and events. This New York Institute–certified, award-winning photographer also specializes in photography at local plantations.

Tom Sapp Photography
3703 Tumbril Ln., Wilmington
(910) 794-9819

A graduate of the prestigious Hallmark Institute of Photography, Tom Sapp has a long list of professional awards and achievements, including the Fuji Masterpiece Award for his expert digital ability. His work has been featured on TLC, TheKnot.com and recognized in *Forbes* and *Business Week* as one of the top eight photographers in the Carolinas. He combines his creative genius and photojournalistic skills to offer contemporary and classical poses and candid images of your wedding. Tom endeavors to put his subjects into situations that display their personalities. His goal is to capture meaningful memories that are so realistic you feel them.

Weddings By The Beach Photography
4210 Wilshire Blvd, Ste 104B, Wilmington
(910) 805-1159
www.weddingsbythebeach.net

Weddings by the Beach specializes in everything to do with your special day. With over 10 years of experience, photographer Terry Taylor knows exactly how important this event is to you and will go the extra mile to capture this day for you. Terry specializes in weddings, engagements, couples, maternity fashion, and modeling. He also offers lifestyles sessions at your home, and services covering family, seniors, graduation, family reunions and special events.

Videography

While photos are wonderful and portable, there's nothing like having a video of your wedding day. Filled with moments and memories you'll treasure forever, a thoughtfully created, artfully edited DVD is your very own masterpiece in motion.

Here are some local videographers you can contact.

Blanchard Productions, Inc.
4922 Northeaster Dr., Wilmington
(910) 392-4211

If you want it done right, Michael Blanchard's upscale videography is for you. Using broadcast-quality digital equipment, he can ensure superior results. His professional background includes news and documentary films aired internationally. Mike will provide DVDs of your wedding reception, if you desire.

Mari Kittredge Video Productions
4930 Pine St., Wilmington
(910) 297-6706

Visually delightful and alive with emotion, a Mari Kittredge wedding video authentically captures the profound love of your wedding celebration. Your laughter, a family's love and all the beautiful details will be secure forever in an engaging cinematic portrait. Mari Kittredge prides herself on capturing life the way the heart sees it.

USC Web Design & Video
Southport
(910) 457-4358

USC Web Design and Video provides a full range of wedding, event video and web design services. They have a variety wedding video packages to fit your individual wedding plans and budget. All packages include a free consultation to discuss your wedding plans and decide on the package that best fits your special day; coordination with your wedding coordinator and photographer; attendance at your rehearsal to determine best camera placement and meet the wedding party and officials; a photo montage set to music; and your finished, professionally edited video delivered with attractive full color packaging and labels. Available enhancements to these packages include your love story, coverage of the rehearsal and rehearsal dinner, additional photos in your photo montage, extra albums and more.

Rental Equipment

L & L Tent & Party Rentals
3703 Wrightsville Ave., Wilmington
(910) 791-4141

L & L will lighten your load by providing all your wedding supplies and equipment, including china, silver, flatware, small and large tents, lights, heaters or fans, dance floors, stages, sound equipment and much more. Local delivery and setup of tents is included in the tent rental cost.

Party Suppliers & Rentals
4013 Oleander Ave., Wilmington
(910) 791-0024, (800) 344-8368

For indoors or out, Party Suppliers & Rentals can provide all of your wedding rental needs. Don't let bad weather spoil your day. They offer a variety of tents, with or without side walls, center poles and French doors. In addition, they have Portofino lights, picket fencing, grills, flooring and staging, tables, chairs, china, linens and silver or polished aluminum serving pieces. You can also choose from their wide selection of candelabra. For more ideas, visit their showroom and talk with the friendly, helpful staff.

Wedding Shows

Bridal expos and fashion shows are held regularly in Wilmington, at various places around town. Belk and Dillard's at Independence Mall have in-house bridal shows, and several other shows, sponsored by consultants and wedding publications, are tremendously popular. Watch for announcements early in January.

Carolina Wedding Guide Bridal Expo
Schwartz Center, Cape Fear Community
College, Wilmington
(910) 259-8323

Each January, area brides get a chance to see the latest in wedding styles and accoutrements at Mike Raab's Carolina Wedding Guide Bridal Expo. The oldest and largest wedding event in coastal North Carolina, the Expo features more than 80 exhibits and displays by most of the area's wedding-related businesses. Door prizes

and special offers are available. In addition, every bride-to-be in attendance receives a copy of The Video Bridal Guide DVD that includes the latest wedding fashions videotaped at the area's top bridal shops, special segments on what to do with weekend guests, and advertisements for various vendors from the show. Check the Carolina Wedding Guide and the local press for date and time.

Southern Cape Fear Bridal Showcase
Southport Community Building,
223 E. Bay St., Southport
(910) 457-6964

The Southport-Oak Island Chamber of Commerce in conjunction with the City of Southport Tourism Division hosts this bridal showcase in the Southport Community Building, one of the loveliest locations available for a wedding. Representatives from caterers, reception venues, entertainment consultants, florists, photographers, jewelers and more are on hand to assist with all your wedding plans.

Wedding Planners

Planning a wedding can be a full-time job in and of itself. The most important thing is to enjoy the process, so if you need help, don't hesitate to ask. The following professionals are happy to assist you, whether you want them to plan the whole event or just help you with some of the details. Many florists also assist with planning and directing both weddings and receptions.

A Carolina Wedding
120 Market St., Wilmington
(910) 762-3312, (888) 762-3312

At A Carolina Wedding, a couture bridal salon in historic downtown Wilmington, you'll find everything you need to create the wedding of your dreams. Tonya Boulware and her talented staff offer full wedding planning services. No matter the size of your wedding, you can design the job description, then let these experienced professionals plan and coordinate packages tailored to fit your needs. Services also are available on an hourly basis. If you're planning a Cape Fear coast wedding, make A Carolina Wedding your first and last stop.

Eventz!
209 Sandybrook Rd., Wilmington
(910) 686-1891

Eventz! coordinator Judy Bradley not only pays attention to detail, she pays attention to you. One couple said that she became their best friend during their wedding preparations. She will help you choose the site, caterer, decorations, linens and anything else you need to make your special day a success.

Music

Music sets the mood of a wedding, adding to the beauty and enjoyment of the ceremony and reception. The southern coast area abounds with musicians to please any ear. Here are a few varied choices for your special day.

DJ Professionals & Video
18 South Water Street, Wilmington
(910) 762-8851

Trust your wedding reception's music and entertainment to DJ Professionals & Video, Wilmington's only full-time deejay company. Making your wedding reception the memorable event you envisioned is their full-time focus, as the team at DJ Professionals & Video do not just moonlight as wedding deejays on the weekend. As the master of ceremonies at your reception, DJ Professionals & Video will set the tone for the event. They customize the musical selection to your taste and event flow, ensuring that the music matches the bride and groom's personalities. Use the convenient Reception Planner function on their website to choose your music. DJ Professionals & Video also offer a full video production department to capture your wedding on video, preserving your occasion forever in digital format. In addition, they offer lighting design for special events. Visit their website to read their long list of testimonials and see for yourself why DJ Professionals & Video is the premier choice for deejay, video production and lighting design services.

Elizabeth MacKay Field, Soprano
3173 Wrightsville Ave., Wilmington
(910) 523-2975

This exceptional, classically trained vocalist is available to add elegance and beautiful music to your wedding ceremony. Elisabeth will work with the organist or music director at your church and will consult with you regarding music selection if you desire.

Gerry White
116 Bradley Creek Point Rd., Wilmington
(910) 256-9880

With more than 30 years in the entertainment field, Gerry delivers professional results utilizing state-of-the-art equipment. With his background as a TV and radio personality, Gerry offers a full program of activities along with winning songs on CDs that are sure to please all ages and tastes.

Key Productions
1027 Captain Adkins Dr., Southport
(910) 457-5243

Jim Minett has been providing wedding music for more than 20 years. His professional music production company will customize music selections to suit your taste. Jim can provide live music, serve as a deejay/master of ceremonies using pre-recorded music, or perform a combination of both for your reception, ceremony, rehearsal dinner or other event. Key Productions presents your favorite music through high-quality Bose professional speakers. Karaoke is also available.

Maura Kropke, Violinist
Wilmington
(910) 612-7348

Maura is a classically trained violinist available for indoor and outdoor weddings throughout the Wilmington area. She attended the School for Strings in New York City as well as Manhattan School of Music and believes that music is one of the most important features of the wedding day. Whether classical, jazz or popular standards, Maura will help you choose music that reflects your personality.

Port City Pipes and Drums
5017 Hewlett's Run, Wilmington
(910) 232-6346

Always dreamed of walking down the aisle to the sound of bagpipes? Port City Pipes and Drums, led by Pipe Major Simpson, specializes in upbeat, happy music with a Highland air. The band prides itself on having fun while they play, and that celebratory, lighthearted attitude transcends to a good time for you and your wedding guests, as well.

Shoresound Productions, LLC
2049 Gilbert Rd. SE, Bolivia
(910) 253-7515

Shoresound Productions LLC provides first class professional entertainment with a personal touch. Their large selection of music, including yesterday's and today's top hits, provides musical entertainment for all types of events. Beach ceremonies are available using a portable, battery-powered system as well as the unique option of a band and DJ combination. A personalized planning service in person and/or online is included with your event. You can relax and rely on more than 30 years of experience at more than 1,000 weddings and other events when Shoresound Productions, LLC provides your entertainment.

SALONS AND DAY SPAS

Beauty is big business on North Carolina's southern coast. Whether you want to look gorgeous in your swimsuit and sandals, wow 'em at a beach party, turn heads at the theater or just treat yourself to a total makeover, there are hundreds of professionals eager to assist you in accomplishing your goal. Besides feeling good about your appearance, you'll enjoy being pampered and fussed over. Choose from a menu of dreamy services at one of the fine day spas. Get a new do at a popular salon. Beat the blahs with a manicure and pedicure. Refresh your skin with a facial or microdermabrasion. Keep your suntan all year. Learn makeup techniques. Get rid of unsightly blemishes or spider veins. Go ahead, pamper yourself! This chapter includes listings of some of the area's favorite day spas and salons. .

Salons

The salon selection in southeastern North Carolina is truly impressive. There is no way to list all of the possibilities or even all of the categories. Instead, we offer some tips for finding your own special places and we'll tell you about a few of our favorites. Area offerings range from high-end designer salons to chains that feature bargain-priced haircuts. You can also support local students and get a great cut at Cape Fear Community College's Cosmetology Department, (910) 362-7352, or Miller-Motte College's Cosmetology program, (910) 392-4660. Both offer a wide range of beauty services at very reasonable prices.

WILMINGTON

La Mirage
5003 Wrightsville Ave., Wilmington
(910) 395-4333

Five licensed, independent operators and a massage therapist occupy this cozy, home-like, full-service hair salon. These friendly, pleasant professionals also offer manicures, pedicures and body waxing. The shop is open Monday through Friday, but hours vary according to the operator. You may call the main shop number or call Joan, (910) 470-9278; Maryann, (910) 392-2862; Phyllis, (910) 470-1778; Eleanor, (910) 392-3553; and Tamekia, (910) 620-8841. Massage therapist Laurie Doody can be reached at (910) 612-2950. Appointments are recommended and take priority, but walk-ins are always welcome.

The Mane Event
University Landing,
419 S. College Rd., Ste. 38, Wilmington
(910) 395-4939

Owner/stylist Krista Rose and the independent operators at The Mane Event are talented, skilled hair professionals. Here you can be assured of high-quality service, a pleasing result and a thoroughly satisfying experience. Offering permanents, color, cuts, styling and careful attention to hair health, The Mane Event is popular with men and women of all ages. They also provide facial waxing.

Panache Hair Salon
530 Causeway Dr., #T5, Wrightsville Beach
(910) 256-6446

The only salon on the island of Wrightsville Beach, Panache Hair Salon offers your hair the reprieve from the sun and salt it deserves. Healthy, beautiful hair is the priority here, with six stylists on staff to provide you with quality hair coloring, styling, cutting and consultations. While

they pride themselves on their specific dedication to hair care, they also offer such pampering necessities as manicures, eyebrow arching and waxing, and facial waxing. On select days, there is a chair masseuse available to ease your tensions. The salon does not have set hours, rather they work their days around the specific needs of their clients and also accept walk-ins, making them a true testament to Southern hospitality, and Wrightsville's easy-going pace!

CAROLINA BEACH

Cut'N Up
913 N. Lake Park Blvd., Carolina Beach
(910) 458-8267

Offering a complete selection of services to meet your individual beauty needs, the experienced Cut'N Up staff prides itself on keeping up with the latest in coloring and cutting trends. On the list of services you'll find perms, cuts, coloring, high and low lighting, waxing, manicures, pedicures and artificial nail enhancement (including the latest in gel applications).

BRUNSWICK COUNTY BEACHES AND VICINITY

Watertown Hair
109 N. Howe St., Southport
(910) 457-4734

This elegant salon has been located in downtown Southport for more than a decade. Owner Marylynn Rehder welcomes all customers with a warm smile. While hair color for women and men is the salon's specialty, the professional staff offers a full menu of hair design and artistry. With excellence as their benchmark and beauty their passion, the staff at Watertown Hair strives to provide total customer satisfaction. They are committed to making your experience the most rewarding it can be. If you are looking for professional tools and hair-care products, this salon can carefully choose the best selection for you.

TOPSAIL ISLAND

A Beautiful New You
322 N. New River Dr., Surf City
(910) 328-2525
1016 Old Folkstone Rd., Sneads Ferry
910-327-1080

A Beautiful New You is a full-service hair, nails and tanning salon. A week of building castles in the sand can wreak havoc with one's nails. Get the gals together and stop by for a manicure and pedicure. Ahhh, that's relaxing at the beach.

Day 7 Salon and Spa
1096 U.S. Hwy. 210, Sneads Ferry
(910) 327-2885

When you're ready for an hour or and afternoon of pampering, Day 7 Salon and Spa offers a full range of salon and spa services. In addition to hair color, cuts and styles, Day 7 Salon offers 30-, 60- and 90-minute massages. Choose between deep-tissue, hot stone or couples massage. For those expecting, a prenatal massage is also available. Skin care, tanning, waxing and men's services are also offered. Bridal services are available and may include makeup, manicure and pedicure, a bridal hairstyle with veil placement and the all-important trial run.

TANNING

Afterglow Tanning Salon
1107 New Pointe Blvd., Ste. 21, Leland
(910) 383-0669

This newly remodeled tanning salon is conveniently located above Antonio's Restaurant in the Walmart Shopping Center in Leland. You will be welcomed by friendly staff and made to feel comfortable in the stylish atmosphere. Afterglow's five high-power beds include four Tan America Pacifica beds with facial lamps and a Tan America Del-/Ray bed, also with a facial lamp. The salon is open seven day a week.

Body Rayz Tanning
5202 Carolina Beach Rd., Wilmington
(910) 392-5000

Exceptionally clean and well maintained, Body Rayz offers a number of tanning options, among them 20-minute custom beds with facials, high-intensity luxury beds, a VHR stand-up booth, and a high-intensity 10-minute leg tanner. These folks are experts in the tanning business and will assure you an informed, comfortable experience. Body Rayz is open seven days a week. They accept appointments, but walk-ins are also welcome.

Tropical Tans
5003 Wrightsville Ave., Wilmington
(910) 392-3311

At Tropical Tans, the friendly, certified staff, clean atmosphere and many amenities make your tanning experience pleasurable. Tropical Tans offers 30-minute and 15-minute beds, plus a standup booth, and a matrix high-pressure bed. Try their Mystic Bed sunless 38-second tanning spray booth, considered the best spray

system in the world. They're open seven days a week and offer a wide variety of pricing and packages.

Skin Care and Cosmetics

Caring for your skin is especially important in this climate. The sun's rays can do serious damage if you don't use protection appropriate for your skin type and exposure level. Local urgent care centers and doctors see a lot of wicked sunburns every summer. Wind, salt spray and sand blasts can be damaging as well. Every drugstore, supermarket, beach shop, sundry and convenience mart carries sunscreen products, though your largest high-end selections will be found in area department stores or salons. And now that you have that perfect tan, your hair is awesome and your nails look like a magazine ad, it's time to get a cosmetic makeover. The area has many Mary Kay, Merle Norman and Avon representatives, so to find one, ask around or just go back to the Yellow Pages. For a freebie, stop by any of the cosmetic counters at a local department store such as Belk or Dillard's. Many hair salons and most day spas offer makeup applications also. For more extensive or medical services, you may want to check out a professional skin-care program.

Blush
1900 Eastwood Rd., Ste. 24, Wilmington
(910) 256-1151

Blush, Wilmington's premier skin care apothecary, features the finest skin care and cosmetic lines. A vast array of products, combined with a professional staff of cosmetic specialists and estheticians, helps Blush offer its clients a unique, personalized health and beauty experience. Blush carries top international cosmetic brands such as Laura Mercier, Paula Dorf and Kiehl's. Their beauty services include makeovers, facials, chemical peels, waxing and eye lash extensions. They can turn any bride into a blushing bride with a full bridal makeup package, and they also offer wedding beauty services for the bridesmaids and mother of the bride.

Book a girls' night out, bachelorette party or other special event at Blush and enjoy a night of pampering.

Sambuca Modern Apothecary
3304 Wrightsville Ave., Wilmington
(910) 799-8282 x28403

Experience the tranquility of Sambuca. Whether it's an organic facial, massage, body treatment, waxing or reflexology, you'll feel pampered and rejuvenated here. With every Sambuca spa treatment, you are making an investment in better living for yourself and your community. Sambuca's treatments use 100% natural, organic and cruelty-free products. Choose from their assortment of facials that include a custom organic facial, the shorter mini-facial, a natural fruit enzyme peel or deep pore cleansing facial. Their selection of massages includes aromatherapy massage, integrative custom massage, reflexology and mom-to-be massage. They also offer Pilates classes and private reformer sessions. Be sure and stop by their apothecary, featuring organic skin-care products, mineral makeup, all-natural soaps, essential oil soy candles and eco-friendly gifts. Sambuca also offers its own line of bath salts, body oils and sprays.

Day Spas

The southern coastal area abounds with many various types of day spa facilities. In some cases, a traditional hair salon has simply added services such as massages, aromatherapy, facials and body wraps to call itself a "spa." However, true day spas are of two kinds. Standard day spas offer body treatments and lifestyle services. Medical spas offer traditional spa services as well as services that must be provided by a licensed medical practitioner, which could be a doctor, nurse, acupuncturist, chiropractor, therapist or other professional. Basic menu offerings ordinarily include body treatments, facials, cosmetic, nail and/or hair services. Depending on your desires (and budget), you can find local day spas as homey as a bed and breakfast or as elaborate as a million-dollar oasis with luxury services to match.

WILMINGTON

Beverly Hills Weight Loss & Wellness
250 Racine Dr., Ste. 8, Wilmington
(910) 793-WRAP (9727)

Who wouldn't want to walk out of a salon looking slimmer than when they walked in? Beverly Hills Weight Loss & Wellness provides chemical-free, physician-recommended body wraps which exchange trace minerals for your body's impurities. With this product they guarantee that you will lose 10 to 30 inches in about an hour. The professionals at Beverly Hills Weight Loss & Wellness work to make sure you feel as comfortable and welcome as possible by engaging you in a fun, interactive environment. Certified Wellness counselors even help establish long-term goals. Beverly Hills Weight Loss & Wellness has been helping people lose weight in a safe and healthy way for over 20 years. Specializing in individual weight-loss programs and counseling makes this program different than others. Other services include infrared sauna therapy, relaxing lay down wraps, ion foot detox and wellness products.

Harbour Club Day Spa and Salon
1904 Eastwoood Rd., Wilmington
(910) 256-5020

A spa where guests can relax and rejuvenate in a haven of tranquility, Harbour Club has a team of highly trained professionals who are dedicated to providing personalized beauty and body treatment programs. On its long list of outstanding services are such specialties as Haute Couture Body Wellness and Advanced Facial Treatments. Also available are facials, therapeutic massages, depilatory services, manicures and pedicures. Harbour Club offers a complete bridal service package for the bride and her wedding party, which includes a consultation to determine hairstyle with headpiece placement and cosmetic application, if desired. Their coordinator can also arrange delivery of catered food and beverages on the day of the booking. To soothe and polish the bride and groom before their big day, the spa offers an array of facial and body treatments as well as hair, skin and nail options.

Head to Toe Day Spa
1970 Eastwood Rd., Wilmington
(910) 256-3370

Serenity and service walk hand in hand at this quality spa where guests enjoy a full range of salon, beauty and therapeutic spa services. The skin-care menu includes facials, chemical peels, microdermabrasion, Vitamin C Renewal Complex Infusion, makeup application and brow/lash tinting. Head to Toe is one of the only salons in the area to offer microcurrent, a nonsurgical facelift-type procedure that reduces signs of aging and tones and lifts facial appearance. Among the hair-care services offered are design, color, straightening, perms, and men's, women's and children's cuts and styling. Manicures, pedicures, body treatments, massages and waxing also are available.

Ki Spa and Salon
The Forum, 1125-Q Military Cuttoff Rd., Wilmington
(910) 509-0410
www.kispasalon.com

Voted Best Spa by the *Encore* magazine readers' poll three years in a row, Best Massage in the most recent Wilmington *Star-News* readers' poll, and Family Favorite Spa by *Wilmington Parent* magazine's third annual readers' poll, this day spa has local approval. They combine natural products, pure aromatherapy and healing techniques to promote total body renewal. Ki, the ancient Japanese word for energy, is incorporated into all spa treatments. Ki Spa offers a tranquil environment that's ideal for specialty and couples massage, body treatments, facials, peels, microdermabrasion, permanent hair removal, waxing, manicures (natural nails) and pedicures. For weddings, relax and rejuvenate your spirit with a package designed especially for you, your bridal party and your guests. Ki Spa 'unlocks the energy of your mind, body and spirit.

Porter's Neck Yoga & Spa
8044 Market St., Wilmington
(910) 686-6440

Escape to wellness and enhance your life at Porters Neck Yoga & Spa, which combines 25 weekly yoga classes with spa services and wellness products. A full-service day spa, complete with a hair and nail salon, Porters Neck Yoga & Spa is the perfect place to spend a morning or afternoon of beauty, relaxation and exercise. The many spa services include a variety of massage therapies, couples massage, customized aromatherapy, reflexology, restorative facials, body scrubs and treatments, all designed to put you in a state of blissful contentment. Looking for the perfect gift? Porters Neck Yoga & Spa has gift certificates and packages available as well.

Prima Day Spa
5101 Dunlea Ct., Ste. 104, Wilmington
(910) 794-8041

Prima Day Spa invites you to "get away from it all, in the center of Wilmington." In an environment of soft light, gentle music and pleasing aromas, expert massage therapists will help you transcend your earthly worries for a well-deserved respite. Perhaps you'd like a facial; choose from an impressive list that includes glycolic peels, photorejuvenation and microdermabrasions. Have a Baby Soft Salt Glow treatment or a Mineral Inchloss Body Wrap. Go home with an awesome spray tan applied by expert technicians. At Prima Day Spa, you can also get a spa manicure and pedicure, cellulite therapy (that really works!), steam-heat therapy and waxing. Permanent cosmetics application by a professionally trained artist is popular with women of all ages. Whatever your choices, at Prima Day Spa, you will leave feeling relaxed, refreshed and recharged.

Sage Salon & Spa
7110 Wrightsville Ave., Wilmington
(910) 679-4377
sagespaandsalon.com

Treat yourself to salon pampering while helping to preserve the environment at Sage Salon & Spa. Wilmington's first and only green certified salon, Sage Salon & Spa specializes in vegan, natural and organic product lines. The salon's design was inspired by mother nature, from environmentally friendly paint to furniture to spa rooms representing the elements of earth, air, fire and water. They offer a full range of hair and color services, manicures and pedicures, facials and massages. If you're looking to truly pamper yourself, try one of their spa packages. Experience dedicated professionalism with their talented team of artists while you escape from your everyday life.

Salon Beyond Basics Day Spa
1124 Floral Pkwy., Wilmington
(910) 452-0072

The team at Salon Beyond Basics and the Anti-Aging Wellness Clinic is equipped to take care of all your hair, skin, nail, body and cosmetic/anti-aging needs. Their comprehensive line of services includes everything a typical salon offers plus the added benefits of their spa, which provides massage therapy, body treatments and facial peels. Want to turn back the effects of time on your body? The Anti-Aging Wellness Clinic offers a program combining hormone optimizing, exercise and nutrition.

BRUNSWICK COUNTY BEACHES AND VICINITY

E Spa & Salon
Live Oak Shopping Center, 4961-4 Long Beach Rd., Southport
(910) 457-0009

Step inside the door to E and let the serenity begin. The new owners invite you to "get Pampered from head to toe." They have enhanced the light, airy atmosphere and included ergonomic shampoo chairs with foot rests to add to your soothing experience. Here you can experience facials, massages, microdermabrasion,body waxing, lypossage, salt scrubs, manicures and pedicures. Top it all off with a new haircut, color, perm or style for the new you. Treat your bridal party to a package of services, including special event hair and make-up, that will have you all floating down the aisle. You can even book the spa for parties of more than five people.

Zen-sation Day Spa & Boutique
1107 New Pointe Blvd., Ste. 6, Leland
(910) 399-7072

Beauty and relaxation are synonymous inside this pampering sanctuary. Zen-sation Day Spa believes that proper skincare goes beyond the surfaceand offers treatments that combine the expertise of

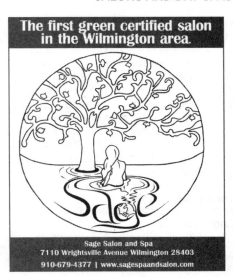

their therapists with professional-strength products and massage therapy in a private, luxurious setting. Each guest receives a consultation by a licensed therapist who evaluates and recommends treatments based on their unique needs. Their serene services include facials, body wraps, nail treatments and many more. Zen-sation is open on Mondays by appointment only, Tuesday through Friday from 10 AM to 7 PM and Saturday from 9 AM to 4 PM.

TOPSAIL ISLAND

Inis Spa
208-J New River Rd., Surf City
(910) 328-3988

Somewhere between the rough-hewn stone wall, the sounds of flutes and fiddles and the scent of citrus oils one enters into another world, a haven of calm and tranquility. This holistic spa believes that the beauty of body and spirit comes from healing and relaxation and their services reflect their philosophy. Inis Spa offers fabulous facials and a variety of massage modalities. Marine and plant based skin products from the Mediterranean Sea are incorporated into all of their facials. The 90-minute Spirit of the Island special includes a soothing one-hour facial, a face, neck, shoulder and scalp massage, a 15-minute foot reflexology session, and an exfoliation treatment for the hands and arms followed by rich hydrating lotion. Treat your face to an Oxygen, Gelatin Verbena or Hydration Facial for a fresh glow. Massage enthusiasts will be thrilled to find a practitioners of Sacred Lomi, an ancient Polynesian-style massage that uses long strokes along, over and under the body. A complete menu of massage types is available and includes deep tissue massage, Swedish and Hot Stone Massage as well as Reiki and Reflexology. Inis Spa is open Monday through Saturday and Sundays by appointment. Gift certificates and packages are available.

The Spa at Topsail
13460 N.C. Hwy. 50/210, Topsail Island
(910) 328-0772

Indulge yourself with extravagant spa treatments and feel the waves of relaxation wash over your entire body. Guests may choose from an extensive menu of soothing spa service options. The Spa at Topsail offers a variety of body treatments and massage, including deep tissue, Swedish, therapeutic full body, sports and Hot Stone. Coupled with the warm towels and choice of soothing aromatherapy oils, guests are guaranteed to feel serene and relaxed. In addition to the 13 different facials offered, The Spa at Topsail also offers a sauna, vichy showers, body wraps, an expanded service menu that includes Botox and Juvederm, skin tightening and laser hair removal. The Spa uses top-of-the-line Obagi skin-care line, which can really make a difference. The Spa at Topsail is located in The Palladium shopping center.

WATERSPORTS ⊛

Whether you're an ardent watersports expert or just an enthusiastic novice, North Carolina's southern coast is the perfect place to hone your skills. With its combination of mild weather, warm water temperatures, good water quality and clean, uncrowded beaches, the region's overall subtropical climate allows watersports aficionados to indulge their particular passions from early spring through late fall. Add the Intracoastal Waterway, sounds, tidal marshes, rivers and their tributaries to a generous Atlantic coastline, and the opportunities for fun in the water are limited only by your sense of adventure.

Please make note of local ordinances and observe safety precautions when near other swimmers, personal watercraft, channel markers, buoys and other water hazards. For example, swimming and surfing are forbidden within 100 feet of most fishing piers. Disturbing or walking on protected dunes is strictly prohibited and carries a fine. Also be careful to not disturb turtle nests.

This chapter is divided into sections dealing with the area's most popular watersports, where to practice them, helpful resources, related businesses and places to find equipment for sale or for rent. Other chapters of this book that address beach and water-related topics include the Fishing and Marinas chapters.

Boating

At times, boating in the lower Cape Fear River involves competition with ocean-going vessels, shallow water or the treacherous shoals that earned the Carolina coast the moniker "Graveyard of the Atlantic." In contrast, the upper Cape Fear, its northeast branch and the winding creeks of the coastal plain offer a genuine taste of the old Southeast to those with small boats, kayaks or canoes. Tannins leached from the cypress trees keep these waters the color of coffee. Many creeks are overhung by trees, moss and, in summer, the occasional snake. Early spring and late autumn are particularly good times to go, since there are fewer bugs. See our Fishing chapter for boat ramp locations.

SAFETY AND RESOURCES

Perhaps the most important thing about boating is preparation. File a float plan; it can be as official or informal as your circumstances require. The point is that you should tell someone where you're going and when you expect to return. You are required to have one life jacket for each person on your boat, and the Coast Guard is within its rights to stop you and see that you have proper equipment. Adults may use their own judgment about wearing a life jacket, but children (and pets) should wear one at all times. Life jackets may not be comfortable or glamorous, but they save lives.

The **U.S. Coast Guard Auxiliary** conducts free vessel safety checks. The exams are not required for boat registration. For information, call the Marine Safety Office at (910) 772-2200. You will be referred to the examining flotilla officer nearest you.

Various flotillas of the local Coast Guard Auxiliary offer **Safe Boating Courses** five times a year (autumn, winter, spring and twice in summer). Locations include the Wrightsville Beach Recreation Center (at Wrightsville Beach Park) and Cape Fear Community College in downtown Wilmington. These courses are strongly recommended for everyone who operates a motor boat. The fee averages $35 and includes all materials. Also inquire about the America's Boating Class, available on CD/ROM, and the Basic Coastal Navigation course. For information call The Coast Guard at (910) 256-4224 or (910)

256-2615; for the greater Wilmington area Coast Guard Auxiliary, call Jim Belluche at (910) 458-9598.

The U.S. Coast Guard website, www. uscg.mil, has excellent information on boating along with links to the Coast Guard Auxiliary and the Power Squadron. Local chapters of the nonprofit U.S. Power Squadrons (USPS), America's largest private boating association, also offer the USPS Boating Course on a regular basis in Wilmington, Southport and Shallotte. The course is free, but there is a fee to cover the cost of the manuals, materials and expenses. The cost varies depending on the squadron location; you need not be a USPS member to participate. For information on the USPS classes closest to you, call (888) FOR-USPS (367-8777).

Carry sufficient non-alcoholic liquids, not only for the humans aboard, but also for any pets you choose to take along. Carry an emergency kit that contains flares, a fire extinguisher, first-aid supplies and various repair items. Make sure that the vessel is well-maintained with the following in good working order: safety equipment, protected and sealed electrical systems, and the inboard or outboard propulsion system. If you're going to be out after dark, turn on your running lights. The ICW is also a highway for commerce, and you want to be sure that barges know you're out there. Understand how to use your ship-to-shore radio and practice in advance of an emergency.

To report emergencies to the **U.S. Coast Guard**, all initial radio calls should be made on channel 16/158.8 MHz. The **Wrightsville Beach Coast Guard Station's** emergency telephone number is (910) 256-3469. Local boating and watersports enthusiasts also report that cellular phone reception is remarkably clear near the shoreline.

Boats under sail always have the right of way over power craft. If power is your chosen method of boating, be aware of the instability your wake can create for sailboats or small boats. If you find yourself in the shipping lanes, give big ships a wide berth. Yielding the right-of-way is often necessary because big ships require at least a mile to stop.

Emergencies happen on the water. The Coast Guard is particular about what constitutes an emergency, and it will not immediately come to your rescue in all situations. Generally, only life-threatening or environment-threatening situations will get its attention. Running aground in the waterway is rarely considered an emergency. A sailboat with a fixed keel is virtually guaranteed to go aground at some point, and it isn't always possible to get loose without a sturdy towboat. If you've got a predicament, **SeaTow**, the largest professional marine assistance provider in the world, will respond 24 hours a day, every day of the year. To receive unlimited free towing plus other benefits, including jump starts, fuel drops, prop disentanglements and navigational assistance, become a member for an annual fee. For information, call SeaTow at (910) 452-3798.

The area's waters are full of shoals, so keep an eye on your depth-sounder. If you don't have one and charts suggest shallow waters, steer clear of questionable areas. The ICW is susceptible to shoaling near inlets, and you can't rely on charts for accuracy because changes occur frequently. The markers entering the Cape Fear River from the ocean were renumbered in 1997, so be alert to the fact that these changes may not appear on older NOAA charts. A very good source of boating information and courses is the **BoatUS Foundation**, (800) 336-2628. The North Carolina Coastal Boating Guide is another excellent resource, compiled by the N.C. Department of Transportation. To obtain a free copy, call (877) 368-4968 or log on to their website at www.ncdot.org/public/publications.

BOAT REGISTRATION

North Carolina requires that motorized craft of any size (including water-jet craft) and sailboats 14 feet and longer at the waterline be registered. The cost is $15 for one year and $40 for three years. Renewal forms are mailed about two months prior to expiration.

Effective January 1, 2007, anyone who purchases or transfers a motorized vessel 14 feet or longer, who owns a personal watercraft (Jet Ski) or who has a lien on a

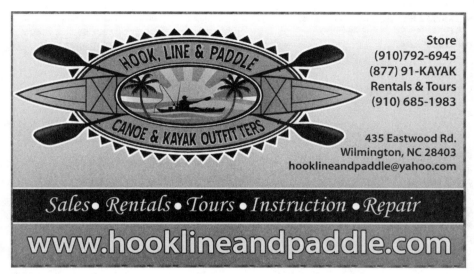

vessel, regardless of size, will be required to title the vessel. The cost of a title is $20 and is effective until the owner sells or transfers the vessel. This mandatory titling requirement affects only new vessel purchases and transfers; existing vessel owners are not required to obtain a title certificate. More information on boating regulations may be obtained from the N.C. Wildlife Resources Commission Boat Registration Section, 1751 Varsity Drive, NCSU Centennial Campus, Raleigh, NC 27606-2576; (800) 628-3773. An extensive list of vessel agents authorized to process North Carolina registration is online at www.nc-wildlife.org. The following area businesses and offices can provide necessary forms and information.

Canady's Sport Center
3220 Wrightsville Ave., Wilmington
(910) 791-6280

Division of Marine Fisheries
Regional Office
127 Cardinal Dr., Wilmington
(910) 796-7267

N.C. Department of Motor Vehicles
License Plates
14687 U.S. Hwy. 17, Hampstead
(910) 270-9010

Shallotte Marine Supplies
4607 Main St., Shallotte
(910) 754-6962

Dockside Watersports
Southwest Corner, Carolina Beach Municipal Docks, Carl Winner Blvd., Carolina Beach
(910) 538-2628

Dockside Watersports offers boat rentals and charters. Dockside rents a 21-foot party barge and a 19-foot center-console outboard any day of the week all year long by reservation. You can also charter a 26-foot cruiser and let the captain chart a course to relaxation. Wakeboard and ski lessons and sessions are also available. Advanced reservations are strongly recommended.

Entropy Boat Rentals
7618 Mason Landing Rd., Wilmington
(910) 686-7677

On the Intracoastal Waterway near Wrightsville Beach, Entropy rents its own line of Sea Mark 17- through 21-foot power boats. Fully equipped center-console vessels are available by the half day, full day or week. For a nominal fee, Entropy also rents water skis and equipment, as well as kayaks. The 12-hour day rate is around $300, and major credit cards are accepted. Entropy is open year-round and serves the lower Cape Fear coast. Call ahead for reservations, location information and off-season rates.

Paradise Landing
318 Fulchers Rd., Sneads Ferry
(910) 327-2114

With Paradise Landing rentals you can either explore the New River on your own in a 20-foot center-console cruiser or charter a six-passenger fishing boat and captain for your party. Reservations are recommended.

Pleasure Island Rentals
2 N. Lake Park Blvd., Carolina Beach
(910) 458-4747

Pleasure Island Rentals has a 17-foot Grady White saltwater fishing boat for rent. This boat, which seats three to four people, is kept at Oceana but rented out of the Lake Park Boulevard location. Pleasure Island Rentals is open daily Memorial Day to Labor Day and weekends during the off-season, weather permitting. After hours and during the off-season, call (910) 228-8103 to make an appointment.

Reliant Marine
Wilmington, Wrightsville Beach,
Carolina Beach, Southport
(910) 256-0638

Reliant Marine offers a variety of services from rentals and charters to fractional ownership and training. They even have a members-only boat club with a dis-counted boat-rental program. Full-day and half-day rentals include names like Grady White, Mako and Sea Pro in sizes from 18 to 37 feet. Reliant Marine is located in Wrightsville Beach at Motts Channel, in Carolina Beach at Mona Black Marina, and in Southport at St. James Plantation Marina. They are open year-round.

Wheel Fun Rentals
107 Carolina Beach Ave. N,
at the Boardwalk, Carolina Beach
(910) 458-4545

Wheel Fun Rentals operates a paddle-boat concession at the Carolina Beach Lake Park. A small kiosk and floating dock are located on the western side near the parking lot. During the summer season, boat rentals are available seven days from 9 AM to dusk. In the off-season, call ahead to make an appointment.

Paddle Sports

This region's paddling season is generally nine months long — March through November — but some experienced paddlers will argue that, due to the mild climate and warm waters, paddle sports can be enjoyed year-round. Along the coast and on inland rivers, the best time to paddle is from August to May, when boat

There's nothing like kayaking at the end of a busy day.

photo: Tracy Turpen

traffic is down, temperatures are lower and humidity is decreased, insects and snakes aren't a nuisance, and the chances of seeing a wider variety of wildlife are greater.

Unlike boating, kayaking and canoeing have few rules and regulations. The one rule that applies is a requirement for one life jacket per passenger aboard a kayak or canoe. Currently, no legislation exists to enforce the issue, but professional kayaking guides strongly recommend wearing a life jacket as a safety precaution.

Perhaps the best aspect of paddling is that you can go almost anywhere. A particularly scenic place to paddle locally is Wrightsville Beach's 14.1-mile kayak and canoe trail. The trail is marked with buoys as it meanders through picturesque marshes and channels. It begins and ends at Wynn Plaza, located at the intersection of Waynick Boulevard and Causeway Drive. For information, contact Wrightsville Beach Parks and Recreation, (910) 256-7925.

KAYAKING

Local guides report that the popularity of kayaking along North Carolina's southern coast has doubled in the last several years. That's not surprising when you consider the bounty of regional waterways and seemingly endless things to see and areas to explore. Tropical sea life, exotic vegetation, a variety of waterfowl, historic landmarks accessible by water, barrier islands and pristine wildlife sanctuaries are just a few of the treasures you'll find. Unique opportunities for guided tours or solo exploration are plentiful due to the abundance of waterways. Explore the coastline, the Intracoastal Waterway, sounds, channels and salt marshes as well as the inland rivers and their tributaries.

Several kayaking businesses, including Salt Marsh Kayak Company, Island Style Adventure Company and Southport's The Adventure Company (see subsequent listings), emphasize ecological responsibility and education and bring paddlers into intimate contact with wildlife and primal silence. All kayaking trips listed in this section are guided by experienced paddlers who bring a love of the sport and dedication to safety on each excursion.

CANOEING

Because the river is a commercial shipping channel, touring the lower Cape Fear River in a canoe isn't recommended for beginners. However, for the experienced canoeist, the lower Cape Fear holds some wonderful surprises. Paddlers who frequent these waters have been known to gather wild rice bequeathed by the vanished rice plantations of the past. The Black River, a protected tributary of the Cape Fear River noted for its old-growth stands of bald cypress, is an excellent scenic canoeing choice, as are several of both rivers' tributaries. A canoe also provides excellent transportation for exploring the tidal marshes and barrier islands all along the southern coast.

In 1997 the Town of Oak Island dedicated some 24 miles of canoe trails known as the Long Beach Canoe Trail System. Four trails make up the system: Lockwood Folly (4.2 miles), Montgomery Slough (7 miles), Howells Point (6.5 miles) and Davis Creek (6 miles). Conditions range from calm, protected waters to rough, exposed waters near inlets, and all are remarkably scenic, quiet and full of wildlife. An additional three floating dock access points on Oak Island include one at NE 52nd Street accessing the Intracoastal Waterway, one at SE 31st Street accessing Davis Canal and the third at 30th Place West. For information visit or call the Oak Island Recreation Department, 3003 E. Oak Island Drive, (910) 278-5518.

Wilmington

Great Outdoor Provision Company
Hanover Center, 3501 Oleander Dr., Wilmington
(910) 343-1648

The Great Outdoor Provision Co. sells a variety of canoes and kayaks as well as paddling accessories, maps, guidebooks, backpacking gear, fly-fishing gear and outdoor clothes. Instructional clinics are available, and the staff at Great Outdoor Provision Co. will be happy to arrange demonstrations of the watercraft or equipment. The store is open seven days a week.

Greenfield Lake and Gardens
**U.S. Hwy. 421, (Third St. and Willard Ave.),
Wilmington**
(910) 762-5606, (910) 341-7868

Pedal-powered paddleboats are available for rent seasonally on the 150-acre Greenfield Lake on U. S. Highway 421 S. in Wilmington. Operated by Cape Fear River Watch Inc., the concession is located near the park's Third Street and Willard Avenue entrance. New this year, they now offer eco-tours featuring birding and alligator watching on an electric boat that seats up to eight passengers. Hours are 11 AM to 6 PM daily from April through September, with special sunset tours from 6 PM to 8 PM by reservation. Off-season (October through April) opening times vary, weather permitting. Call for information and rates.

Hook, Line & Paddle Canoe & Kayak Outfitters
435 Eastwood Rd., Wilmington
(910) 792-6945
www.hooklineandpaddle.com

Hook, Line & Paddle Canoe & Kayak Outfitters carries everything you need for your next kayaking adventure. They specialize in recreational sea kayaks, standup paddle boards and kayak fishing equipment, including a full line of paddles, life jackets, safety gear and accessories. Some of the well-known national brands they carry include Heritage Kayaks, Native Watercraft, Wilderness Systems, Yolo Boards and Mad River canoes. If you're not ready to take the plunge and purchase your own equipment, you can rent kayaks through the store, at their Wrightsville Beach location (across from the Blockade-Runner Beach Resort) and at the Yacht Club on Figure Eight Island. If after you rent, you get hooked and want to buy, as an added incentive, Hook, Line & Paddle will refund the cost of your rental toward a purchase. Not only can you get the right gear, but you can also book a tour at the shop or receive instruction from one of the store's master teachers. One of their most popular tours is the Dawson's Creek Tour, a three-hour excursion visiting the Wrightsville Beach house featured in the

series. They also sell custom kayak fishing outfitting and Yakima roof racks, with free installations with purchase. The store is open every day from 10 AM to 6 PM.

Carolina Beach

Pleasure Island Rentals
2 N. Lake Park Blvd., Carolina Beach
(910) 458-4747

Located in the heart of Carolina Beach, this watersports equipment rental company goes by the slogan, "We rent FUN stuff." Single kayak rentals range from $25 for four hours to $35 for 24 hours and $105 for a week. Tandems run $35 (four hours), $45 (24 hours) and $120 (one week). All rentals include paddles and life jackets. Pleasure Island Rentals is open daily Memorial Day to Labor Day and weekends during the off-season, weather permitting. After hours and during the off-season, call (910) 228-8103 to make an appointment.

Wheel Fun Rentals
**107 Carolina Beach Ave. N,
at the Boardwalk, Carolina Beach**
(910) 458-4545

New to kayaking? A great place to start is at Carolina Beach Lake. Wheel Fun Rentals offers kayaks and paddleboats for rent at a kiosk and floating dock located on the western side of the lake near the parking lot. During the summer season, boat rentals are available seven days from 9 AM to dusk. In the off-season, call ahead to make an appointment.

Bald Head Island

Riverside Adventure Company
Bald Head Island Marina, Bald Head Island
(910) 457-4944

The state's largest expanse of saltwater marshland is found on Bald Head Island. Riverside Adventure Co. provides canoe and kayak trips and rentals on these tidal waterways. Also available are Surf Kayak Rentals. Take a sit-on-top kayak out to the beach to ride the waves or paddle down the shore. New for 2010 are paddleboard lessons and rentals. Call for rental rates and daily schedules. Reservations are suggested.

Southport

The Adventure Company
807-A Howe St., Southport
(910) 464-0607

The Adventure Company specializes in kayak tours, lessons, rentals and coastal environmental education programs as well as kayak and gear sales in the retail shop. Local kayak tours are $45 per person for anyone 13 years of age and older, and group and family discounts are available. Tours include basic kayak instruction, a two-hour guided tour and, of course, the kayak, paddle and life jacket. Bring your own boat and gear and pay only $25 to join a tour. Single kayaks rent for $30 (half day), $45 (full day) and $140 (weekly rentals). Tandems are available for $40 (half day), $55 (full day) and $175 (weekly rental). Owner Emma Thomas, a certified kayak and canoe instructor, has been kayaking for more than 20 years. Also available through The Adventure Company are bicycle tours of historic Southport, bicycle rentals, overnight kayak camping trips and adventure travel to Florida. The Adventure Company is celebrating its 10th anniversary in 2010.

Topsail Island & Vicinity

Herring's Outdoor Sports
701 N. New River Dr., Surf City
(910) 328-3291

Paddle the peaceful Intracoastal Waterway or challenge the waves out in the Atlantic Ocean. Whatever your choice, Herring's has the right kayak available for rent or purchase. There are single and double passenger models and the popular sit-on-top styles. You can rent by the hour, half day, full day or week. The kayaking experts at Herring's will outfit you with all you need for your great adventure. Classes and guided tours are also available. Call for prices and information.

Holland's Shelter Creek
8315 N.C. Hwy. 53 E, Burgaw
(910) 259-5743

Here's your chance to really get away from it all and enjoy a peaceful afternoon on Holly Shelter Creek. Canoes, kayaks and flat-bottom paddleboats are available for the solitary explorer and for families and groups. Boats can be rented by the day. After a long day's paddle, stop in at Holland's restaurant for some great home-style cooking. Camping facilities are also available.

Personal Watercraft

If you have your own personal watercraft, there are access points on Wrightsville Beach that are suitable for beach trailers. One of the easiest is at the foot of Causeway Drive (straight ahead from the fixed bridge), but parking is rarely available there in the high season. Another is the paved access to the left of the Oceanic Restaurant on South Lumina Avenue, provided there are no volleyball tournaments that day. Again, parking is likely to be problematic.

On Topsail Island access points are fewer, largely due to dune erosion. Your best bet would be the crossover near the center of Surf City. Smooth riding is also available in the Northeast Cape Fear River, accessible from the several public boat ramps (listed in our Fishing chapter), but these waters are frequently busy with other boaters, anglers and swimmers in summer. Exercise courtesy and extreme caution.

All the rental craft available in the area launch into the Intracoastal Waterway. Be sure to respect the limitations set by individual rental services, who must operate within the parameters of their permits.

Wrightsville Beach, in cooperation with the local flotilla of the U.S. Coast Guard Auxiliary, offers personal watercraft safety courses at a cost of about $35 in spring, summer, fall and winter. Call Donna Sauer, (910) 270-9830, for more information.

REGULATIONS

If you own your own personal watercraft (PWC), be aware that North Carolina requires that it be registered (see the Boat Registration section in this chapter). Although it is the responsibility of both the boat owner and the operator (including renter) to keep abreast of current PWC regulations, here are some state-wide rules:

No one under 14 years old can operate a personal watercraft. Children ages 14 through 15 may operate personal water-craft if they are riding with a person who is at least 18 years of age, or if the youth has successfully passed a boater's safety education course approved by the state, the Coast Guard Auxiliary or the National Association of State Boating Law Admin-istrators. Two forms of identification must be carried with the 14- to 15-year-olds — a photo ID and the safety course certificate; this is a state of North Carolina regulation. See www.ncwildlife.com and click on Boat-ing/Waterways for complete information.

• No one can operate a PWC on state waters between sunset and sunrise.

• A PWC must have a rear-view mirror or an observer other than the operator on board to legally tow someone on skis or a similar device.

• All PWC riders, passengers and those being towed must wear approved per-sonal flotation devices (PFDs).

Bear in mind that local ordinances may also be in effect regarding the operation of PWCs. For example, the use of personal watercraft in certain New Hanover County waters is restricted to safeguard people, property and the environment. When operating in the Intracoastal Waterway from Carolina Beach Inlet north to Mason Inlet or within the sounds and channels behind Masonboro Island and Wrightsville Beach, watercraft speed is strictly limited to 5 mph within 50 feet of the marsh or shore, an angler, a person in the water, an anchored vessel, a posted waterbird sanc-tuary, piers or docks.

Have fun, but use common sense when operating a PWC. Follow the rules and re-frain from operating at speeds more than 5 mph when in shallow water, especially at low tide. Otherwise, you will most likely contribute to the destruction of oyster beds, plant life and other marsh wildlife.

Canoeing and kayaking are perfect ways to navigate shallow salt marshes, where you'll find tranquility along with many types of birds, such as herons, oystercatchers, egrets and ibis.

Be especially wary of watercraft larger than your own and of water-skiers, since jet craft are more maneuverable. Finally, respect the privacy of waterfront property.

RENTALS

Paradise Landing
318 Fulchers Rd., Sneads Ferry
(910) 327-2114

With Paradise Landing's rentals, you can explore the natural wonders of New River in a kayak or canoe. If you are look-ing for a bit more speed, Waverunners and a 22-foot john boat are also for rent. Reservations are recommended. Call for prices.

Pleasure Island Rentals
2 N. Lake Park Blvd., Carolina Beach
(910) 458-4747

Pleasure Island rents single, double and three-person Jet Skis. Pleasure Island Rentals is open daily Memorial Day to Labor Day and weekends during the off-season, weather permitting. After hours and during the off-season, call (910) 228-8103 to make an appointment.

Sailing

Anchorage in Banks Channel at Wrightsville Beach is free. The limit is 30 days every 180 days. Find complete information on area anchorage and marina services in our chapter on Marinas and the Intracoastal Waterway.

Wrightsville Beach Ocean Racing Association
Wrightsville Beach
(910) 232-3676

The Wrightsville Beach Ocean Racing Association (WBORA) was founded in 1967 to promote local keelboat ocean rac-ing and cruising. While WBORA folks love a relaxing day sail, they are invigorated by the way racing stretches your sailing skills, pumps the adrenalin and tests your mettle against the forces of the sea. Competition is friendly, and sailors can find casual or more serious competition within the fleet. Crew spots are often available; check the website www.wbora.org. The WBORA spinnaker fleet typically races standard buoy courses, while the non-spinnaker (cruising) fleet usually sails a modified triangle course using government markers. While WBORA hosts a standard point race series for members during the summer season, several invitational races are open to non-members for those who'd like to give racing a try. WBORA also coordinates cruises to out-of-town regattas or just for fun. WBORA has coordinated cruises to Southport, Beaufort, Mile Hammock Bay, Long Bay and downtown Wilmington. Cruises to regattas offer an event to attend when you arrive. For more information about WBORA, contact Mary Harrison, WBORA Commodore, at marypharrison@msn.com.

SAILING AND BOATING SUPPLIES, ACCESSORIES AND REPAIR

There are many area businesses that provide service for marine supplies and repairs. For additional listings, see the our Marinas chapter.

Blackbarry Marine
4701 Long Beach Rd., Southport
(910) 457-0667

Blackbarry Marine carries a full line of G-3 Aluminun Jon Boats from 10 to 20 feet and Tidewater Center Console, Bay and Skiffs. Used and consignment boats of all sizes are available as well. The warehouse is stocked with Yamaha Outboard Engines from 2.5 to 300Hp. The mechanics are Certified Yamaha Technicians and special services are available for customers who are unable to bring their boats to the facility. The Parts Department is stocked with products for your boats, trailers and outboard motors and the Retail Outfitting Store has everything for your fishing needs including bait, rods, reels, clothing, electronics and sunglasses.

Masonboro Yacht Club
609 Trails End Rd., Wilmington
(910) 791-1893

Located at ICW mile 288 on Whiskey Creek (5 miles south of Wrightsville Beach), the Masonboro Yacht Club is a private facility that offers dockage (for sale or rent) for boats up to 60 feet, and dry-rack storage for boats up to 28 feet.

A three-story clubhouse includes four private showers, a full kitchen, laundry facilities, a club room and a glorious unobstructed view of the water and unspoiled Masonboro Island. You're guaranteed to find some interesting conversation among the residents.

SAILING INSTRUCTION, SALES AND RENTALS

Cape Fear Yacht Works
111 Bryan Rd., Wilmington
(910) 395-0189

As the largest manufacturer of custom sailboats in the Carolinas, Cape Fear Yacht Works prides itself on producing high quality boats. In addition to innovative design and construction of new boats, they have an excellent reputation for repairs and refurbishments and promoting safety in the workplace and in their products. Insiders say that designer Bruce Marek couldn't design a slow boat if he tried, and that has proved true with their CF38 Regatta version, currently racing in major regattas and in use by college sailing teams. All CFYW boats are built by hand by North Carolina craftsmen in the United States to meet or exceed ORC Category 1 and ABYC Compliance Standards.

Southport Sail and Power Squadron
Southport
(910) 201-1712

The Southport Sail & Power Squadron (SSPS), the local chapter of the U.S. Power Squadrons, was chartered in January of 2002. The SSPS offers educational programs for safe boating as well as civic service and social activities for its nearly 100 members. Members range from individuals new to boating to those with extensive experience, with some of them possessing captain's licenses that are issued by the U.S. Coast Guard. Introductory level courses taught by squadron members include: Introduction to Sailing, GPS, Boat Smart, Chart Smart and Skipper Saver. In-depth courses now open to the public include: Celestial Navigation, Cruise Planning, Seamanship Sailing, Piloting, Weather, Marine Electronics and Engine Maintenance. The SSPS holds monthly programs and free vessel safety inspections for the public.

For information call Bob Salemme at (910) 201-1712.

Scuba Diving and Snorkeling

Diving the southern coastal waters offers rewarding experiences to collectors, nature-watchers and wreck divers, despite there being no true coral reefs in these latitudes. A surprising variety of tropical fish species inhabit these waters, including blue angelfish, damselfish and moray eels as well as several varieties of sea fans, some as large as 3 feet in height. Spiny oysters, deer cowries, helmet shells, trumpet tritons and queen conchs can be found here.

Among the easiest places to find tropical aquatic life is 23 Mile Rock, part of a 12-mile-long ledge running roughly perpendicular to the coast. Another 15 miles out, the Lobster Ledge, a low-lying formation 120 feet deep, is a collectors' target. There are several smaller ledges close to shore in shallower water better suited for less-experienced divers.

Visibility at offshore sites averages 60 feet and often approaches 100 feet, but inshore visibility is seldom better than 20 feet. The coastal waters can be dived all year long, since their temperatures range from the upper 50s in winter and low 80s in summer. However, many local charters typically end their diving season in early fall. Some charters organize destination trips after that.

Good snorkeling in the region is a matter of knowing when and where to go. Near-shore bottoms are mostly packed sand devoid of the rugged features that make for good viewing and collecting, but a good guide can lead you to rewarding areas. When the wind is right and the tide is rising, places such as the Wrightsville Beach jetty offer good viewing and visibility. The many creeks and estuaries support an abundance of life, and the shorter visibility, averaging 15 to 20 feet, is no obstacle in water so shallow. The waters around piers in Banks Channel at Wrightsville Beach are fair but often murky, and currents are strong. Only experienced snorkelers should attempt these waters or those in local inlets, which are treacherous, and then only at stopped tides. It is neither safe nor legal to swim beneath oceanside fishing piers. When in doubt, contact a local dive shop for information.

This region of the Graveyard of the Atlantic offers unparalleled opportunities for wreck divers. From Tubbs Inlet (near Sunset Beach) to New River Inlet (North Topsail Beach), 20 of the dozens of known shipwrecks resting here are accessible and safe. Most are Confederate blockade runners, one is a tanker torpedoed by the Nazi sub U-158, and several were sunk as part of North Carolina's artificial reef program (see our Fishing chapter for more on artificial reefs). These and higher-risk wrecks can be located with the assistance of dive shops.

Wreck diving is an advanced skill best undertaken by professionals. Research prior to a dive is essential in terms of the target, techniques and potential dangers, which in this region include live ammunition and explosives that may be found on World War II wrecks. If you observe anything suspicious while you're diving, leave it alone! Under state law, all wrecks and underwater artifacts within three miles of shore that remain unclaimed for more than 10 years are declared state property.

Charter boats can be arranged for dive trips through all the dive shops listed here, but there are others. Also check the Fishing chapter for fishing charter boats that accommodate dive trips. Many charter boats are primarily fishing boats, so if you need custom diving craft, be sure to inquire. Most dive shops can lead you to a certification class if they don't offer one themselves. Also, proof of diver's certification is required by shops or dive masters when renting equipment, booking charters or purchasing air fills.

Aquatic Safaris & Divers Emporium
**The Galleria,
6800 Wrightsville Ave., Ste. 1A, Wilmington
(910) 392-4386**

This PADI training facility is Wilmington's largest full-service SCUBA charter service and dive shop. The Emporium offers instruction, air fills (including Nitrox and trimix) and a full range of equipment for sale and rental. Dive trips on their USCG–certified 48-foot and 30-foot custom dive boats are available, and both are equipped with a hang bar system, which allows divers to drop down the descent line at the back of the boat and swim to the anchor line, eliminating tiring surface swims. The shop is certified by major manufacturers to perform repairs on most life-support equipment and most other equipment as well. It's open seven days a week all year.

Scuba South Diving Company
222 S. River Dr., Southport
(910) 457-5201

Among the most respected diving experts in the Southport area is Wayne Strickland, who specializes in dive charters to some of the less-frequented targets off the Cape plus such well-known sites as the City of Houston, a passenger freighter that sank in 1878 and which Strickland salvaged for the North Carolina Maritime Museum at Southport (artifacts are on display). Strickland will arrange dives to any site along the southern coast. A recent find is called Megalodon Reef, where you can find fossilized shark's teeth from Megalodon Sharks along with whale bone fossils. Trips are aboard his custom 52-foot boat, Scuba South II. Scuba South sells and rents a full store of equipment, including wet and dry suits, and provides air fills. Nitrox is available.

Surfing

California surfers who come to the southern coast of North Carolina agree: The surf may be less spectacular than on the West Coast, but the water is warmer and the season is longer here. Conditions were considered good enough for the U.S. Amateur Surfing Championships Mid-Atlantic Regionals that were held at Wrightsville Beach in 1997. The East Coast Wahine Championships were held in Kure Beach in 2001 and 2002. The Championships moved to Wrightsville Beach in 2003 and have been held there every year since. Indeed, Wrightsville Beach's prominence

as a surfing destination led *Surfer* magazine to recently name it one of the top ten surf towns in the United States.

In recent years, many surfers from this area have been achieving awards and recognition worldwide. With surfing now part of the pantheon of Olympic events, local surfing has naturally gained further status. Surf shops throughout the region can provide information on surfing competitions.

The beaches running north to south, from Topsail Island down to Fort Fisher, experience consistently better surf than the Brunswick beaches, with their east-west orientation. However, the Brunswick beaches are fine for bodyboarding. A favored surfing spot is Masonboro Island's north end near the jetty. However, it's not an easy place to reach, since Masonboro Inlet is an active boat channel with dangerous currents. Crossing over from the soundside (the Intracoastal Waterway) and hiking to the beach is a good idea.

The northernmost point of the Wrightsville Beach, off Shell Island Resort, is the preferred long-board break because it has a consistent lined-up, sand-point–style wave. More aggressive waves are at the middle of the island, near Columbia Street, an area favored by the more progressive, younger surfers.

Wrightsville Beach has stringent rules governing surfing. Surfing within 500 feet of any commercial fishing piers or the Masonboro Inlet jetty is prohibited year-round. Leash laws are in effect all the time. Surfing is forbidden in front of lifeguard stands, extending to around 100 feet on either side of these stands from 10 AM until 5 PM. Otherwise, the beach is pretty much wide open during morning "dawn patrols" and the evening glass off. Surfing restrictions will not be in effect when red flags are posted. Call Wrightsville Beach Parks and Recreation, (910) 256-7925, for surfing regulations.

For Wrightsville Beach surfing information, tide table, daily surf report and rotating zones, go to www.townofwrightsvillebeach.com/surfing.htm. The Local section of the *Star-News* also carries a tide schedule and surf forecast each day.

SURFING LESSONS

WB Surf Camp, Inc.
530 Causeway Dr., Ste. B-1,
Wrightsville Beach
(910) 256-7873, (866) 844-7873

WB Surf Camp offers professional daily surfing lessons and weekly surf camps for kids, teens and adults with well-trained, certified and fully insured professional instructors. Founder Rick Civelli brings a passion for surfing to all his instructional programs, along with a strong background in marine science education and ocean safety. All programs include high-quality, beginner equipment. Classes range from a two-hour lesson to a full week of Surf Camp where a 3:1 student to instructor ratio is provided. Spots are limited and sell out each summer at this popular camp, so call early.

Wrightsville Beach Parks & Recreation
1 Bob Sawyer Dr., Wrightsville Beach
(910) 256-7925

Beginner surfing lessons are conducted weekly from June through August. The three-day classes are for advanced ocean swimmers age 10 to adult and are limited to six students per session. The course covers surfing etiquette, paddling, wave-catching, maneuvers and basic surfing principles. Pre-registration is required, fees are charged, and you must provide your own surfboard. Call for more information and a schedule.

SURFING GEAR AND SUPPLIES

Many shops in our area offer a complete selection of surf gear, apparel and accessories, including wet suits and videos. You can buy a new or used board, rent one by the day or week and get yours repaired. Shops can lead you to local people who build customized boards, too. The following businesses rent surfboards by the hour, day or week. Most area shops are open seven days a week in season. Call ahead in the off-season.

Aussie Island Surf Shop
5101 Dunlea Ct., Wilmington
(910) 256-5454

Bert's Surf Shop
5740 Oleander Dr., Wilmington
(910) 392-4501

Surf's up!

photo: George Mitchell

Bert's Surf Shop
310 N. New River Dr., Surf City
(910) 328-1010

DoubleWide Surf & Skate Shop
14921 U.S. Hwy. 17, Hampstead
(910) 270-3640

Hot Wax Surf Shop
4510 Hoggard Dr., Wilmington
(910) 791-9283

Local Call Surf Shop
8417 E. Oak Island Dr., Oak Island
(910) 278-3306

On Shore Surf Shop
409 Roland Ave., Surf City
(910) 328-2232

Pleasure Island Rentals
2 N. Lake Park Blvd., Carolina Beach
(910) 458-4747

Side Arm Surf & Skate
8258 Market St., Wilmington
(910) 686-2969

Spinnaker Surf Shop
111 N. Shore Dr., Surf City
(910) 328-2311

Surf City Surf Shop
The Landing, 530 Causeway Dr.,
Wrightsville Beach
(910) 256-2265

Sweetwater Surf Shop
10 N. Lumina Ave., Wrightsville Beach
(910) 256-3821

Wheel Fun Rentals
107 Carolina Beach Ave. N,
at the Boardwalk, Carolina Beach
(910) 458-4545

Stand-up Paddle Surfing

A relatively new surfing variation, stand-up paddle surfing entails standing on a large longboard and propelling yourself with a paddle that is similar to a canoe paddle. While it gained popularity in recent years, the sport can be traced back to the 1960s, when Waikiki surfers would stand on their longboards and paddle with outrigger paddles. Surfing legend Laird Hamilton is credited with being an early practitioner of this water sport, helping to bolster its resurgence.

Here's a basic description of how it works: throw your board in the water, get out past the shorebreak with your paddle tucked under you, and pop to your feet with your paddle in hand. Standing with your feet parallel, you can then balance on the board and begin paddling around. Once you get the feel of it, try propelling yourself into the waves.

To properly practice the sport, you can't just jump on your regular longboard and grab a canoe paddle. Stand-up paddle surfing requires a special surf board and paddle. The board is approximately 10 to 12 feet long, 27 to 31 inches wide and four to five inches thick, and the paddle should be about six inches taller than you.

Part of stand-up paddle surfing's appeal lies in its outstanding fitness benefits, including a strong core body workout, upper body strength and cross training. The sport also challenges one's balance as it requires you to use your leg muscles and core to maintain your board position.

The sport's enthusiasts are also drawn to the way the standing position allows surfers to have a clearer view of incoming waves, enabling them to catch waves earlier. Beginners usually practice the sport in flat water first before braving the ocean current. This can be done on any lake, river, sound or other waterway, similar to the waters commonly canoed or kayaked. Sometimes even more skilled surfers choose to perfect their sport in flat waters.

Swimming

The southern coast is blessed with clean, relatively clear, refreshing waters and a long outdoor season. The ocean water temperature becomes comfortable usually no later than the middle of spring, generally hovering in the 75- to 85-degree range by summer. Most area beaches consist of fine, clean sand. Together with the shores of the central coast and the Outer Banks farther to the north, the southern coast gives evidence that North Carolina does indeed have the finest beaches in the east.

Except for the threat of rip currents, the surf is generally moderate. Several beach communities employ lifeguards during the summer, but the beaches are not staffed otherwise. Swimming in a few areas is hazardous, such as at the extreme east end of Ocean Isle Beach and along the Fort Fisher Historic Site, because of either strong currents or underwater debris. All hazardous areas are well-marked. If pool swimming is more to your liking, check the facilities listed below .

City of Wilmington Parks, Recreation and Downtown Services
302 Willard St., Office/Parks, Wilmington
(910) 341-7855

The City of Wilmington maintains three public swimming pools: Southside/Shipp Pool at 2131 Carolina Beach Road (beside Legion Stadium), (910) 341-7863; Northside/Jackson Pool at 750

Bess Street, (910) 341-7865; and Robert Strange/Murphy Pool at 410 S. 10th Street, (910) 341-7864. All pools are handicapped accessible and are equipped with bathhouses and lifeguard staff on duty at all times. Pools are open Monday through Saturday each summer from Memorial Day weekend through mid-August; daily hours at each pool vary. Pool admission is $1 per child and $2 for adults.

Wilmington Athletic Club
2026 S. 16th St., Wilmington
(910) 343-5950

When the beach is cold and windy, you can still enjoy a refreshing swim at Wilmington Athletic Club. Their competition-size outdoor pool is heated for year-round swim lessons, aqua aerobics classes and fun. Here you'll find a full range of group, semi-private and private lessons for infants to adults as well as exercise classes offered throughout the day. For serious lap swimming, lanes are always available.

Wilmington Family YMCA
2710 Market St., Wilmington
(910) 251-9622

Come on in, the water's fine.

photo: Tracy Turpen

www.wilmingtonfamilyymca.org

The YMCA boasts two indoor pools to accommodate its many members year round. Water fitness, swim lessons, swim team, triathlon clubs and life-guarding classes as well as CPR and First Aid classes are among its many offerings. Membership is required to enjoy general use of these facilities, which are open seven days a week. Some classes are open to the community with discounted fees for members. Call the YMCA for current individual or family rates.

YWCA of the Lower Cape Fear
2815 S. College Rd., Wilmington
(910) 799-6820

The YWCA offers therapeutic and fitness programs for all ages and levels, including water aerobics, swim lessons (private and group), pool rentals, swim team (winter and summer), lap swim, recreational swim and a triathalon club. The facilities have chair lift and ramp accessibility. Red Cross Lifeguard and CPR/PR Certification and Recertification classes are offered. The pool is open year-round, seven days a week.

Water-Skiing

In the greater Wilmington area, the protected waters of the lower Cape Fear River, from Carolina Beach south, are the most popular for water-skiing. These waters are convenient to public boat ramps in Carolina Beach, including those at the marina at Carolina Beach State Park and at Federal Point. Throughout most of the region, the wider channels of the Intracoastal Waterway and adjoining sounds offer water-skiing opportunities, but be alert to other boat traffic. The relatively hushed surf along the Brunswick Islands is well-suited to skiing, yielding about 22 miles of shoreline from Ocean Isle Beach to Sunset Beach. Big Lake, in the community of Boiling Spring Lakes, 8 miles northwest of Southport on N.C. 87, is a long, narrow body of water that's excellent for water-skiing. There is a free public boat ramp off Alton Lennon Drive. Check with the rental services listed in the Motorboat Rentals section above if you need to rent

a towing craft. Many, if not most, services and some boating supply shops also rent skis and equipment.

Windsurfing and Kiteboarding

One of the best and most popular windsurfing and kiteboarding areas is The Basin, the partially protected body of water off Federal Point at the southern end of Pleasure Island (Carolina and Kure beaches). Accessible from a public boat ramp down the road from the ferry terminal, The Basin is enclosed by The Rocks, a 3.3-mile breakwater that extends to Zeke's Island and beyond. Motts Channel and Banks Channel on the sound side of Wrightsville Beach are popular spots, but you'll have to contend with the boat traffic. Advanced windsurfers prefer the oceanside of the jetty at the south end of Wrightsville Beach, where action is fairly guaranteed.

Around Topsail Island, the choices are the Intracoastal Waterway and the ocean. The inlets north and south of the island are not well-suited to uninterrupted runs. Along Oak Island and the South Brunswick Islands, the ocean is your best bet, although limited stretches of the ICW are OK for beginners (near the Ocean Isle Beach bridge when it's not busy, for example). Shallotte Inlet and River are narrow but worth a shot.

Operating a boat while under the influence of alcohol or drugs is illegal in every state. The U.S. Coast Guard also enforces a federal law that prohibits BUI (boating under the influence). The laws pertain to ALL boats, from canoes to large ships. Keep in mind that consuming alcohol is even more dangerous on the water than on land because motion, vibration, sun, wind and engine noise accelerate a drinker's impairment. For your safety as well as the safety of others, don't drink while boating.

Kiteboarding is one of the hottest, up-and-coming watersports. Similar to wakeboarding, kiteboarding uses a large kite to pull you instead of a boat. It requires less wind than windsurfing, the gear packs up much smaller than windsurfing gear, and you don't need a boat to do it. Riders can jump 10 to 40 feet in the air while performing amazing tricks. Since they need less wind to have fun, kiteboarders get more good days in the Cape Fear area than windsurfers do.

The sport uses the principles of sailing in that you tack against the wind and can travel upwind or downwind. The boards are specially designed for the sport, and the kites can re-launch you if you crash in the water. Different-sized kites are available for different wind conditions and different weight riders. You can kiteboard in flat water and waves. The most popular spots to kiteboard around here are the south end of Wrightsville Beach, the Fort Fisher Basin and the north end of Carolina Beach. Riders go where the wind conditions suit them. Kiteboarding is a thrilling sport, but like any extreme sport, it can be dangerous. Participants are strongly urged to seek expert advice or take lessons.

FISHING

The southern coast of North Carolina is an angler's paradise where fishing can be enjoyed 12 months of the year, minus a few uncooperative winter days. The estuaries, brackish swamps and mud flats of these shallow, coastal waters are excellent nurseries for shrimp, crabs, oysters and fin fish, making it a veritable seafood gumbo.

With ocean temperatures ranging from the 70s in the Gulf Stream to the 50s near shore in the winter months, king mackerel, sea bass and tuna can be caught in the ocean, while striped bass can be caught in the rivers. During the spring, summer and fall months, tarpon, red drum, Spanish mackerel, flounder, sea bass, blue marlin, sailfish, shark, wahoo, dolphin and many others are plentiful.

The **North Carolina Division of Marine Fisheries** (NCDMF) has a wealth of information regarding fishing in North Carolina coastal waters. They offer a free, two-page brochure entitled "The North Carolina Recreational Coastal Waters Guide for Sports Fishermen". They also have information on fishing licenses (including the new North Carolina Saltwater Fishing License, which went into effect in 2007), bag and size limits for various species, fishing reports, and recreational and commercial fishing regulations, as well as a handy Fish Finder for identifying and describing all North Carolina fish by common name, with data and color illustrations of the species. These and many other sources of information on fishing can be found on their website at www.ncdmf.net or you can call them at (252) 726-7021 or (800) 682-2632 (NC only).

Since the early 1970s, the NCDMF has helped create artificial reefs that provide habitats for sea life. These reefs consist of old ships, railroad cars, bridge rubble, concrete and FADs (fish-attracting devices). Using the motto "We sink 'em – you fish

'em," reef architects have built dozens of reefs over the years. Judging by the number of sheepshead and mackerel landed on an average day, the program seems to be paying off. Charts and GPS coordinates to lead you to these sites are available by clicking "Artificial Reef Guide" on the NCDMF website.

The Cape Fear River offers excellent freshwater fishing, with available species including largemouth bass, sunfish, catfish, herring and American and hickory shad. Spring is the peak season for largemouths, which usually range between 1.5 to 3 pounds. Bass can be located near the mouths of the larger tributary creeks, such as Turnbull, Hammonds, Sturgeon, Livingston and the upper reaches of Town Creek. Bluegill are also plentiful and are available during the spring spawning season near locks and dams. Bluegills average one-half to three-quarters of a pound. American and hickory shad can be found in the lower Cape Fear River below Wilmington and can be taken below each of the three locks and dams above Wilmington. The three largest members of the freshwater catfish family — the channel, blue and flathead — can be found in the Cape Fear River from Lillington to the Black River. Catfish are considered non-game fish and therefore have no size or creel restrictions. They can be taken by a variety of fishing methods. April, May, September and October are the best catfish months.

Information on inland water limits and licenses is available from the North Carolina Wildlife Resources Commission, 1751 Varsity Drive, Raleigh, NC 27606 (physical address); 1721 Mail Service Center, Raleigh, NC 27699-1721 (mailing address). They offer the North Carolina Regulations Digest, which contains information on inland fishing, hunting and trapping. Call (919) 707-0391 or (888) 248-6834 for license information or (919) 707-0220 for general fishing information. The entire digest is also online at www.ncwildlife.org.

Note that fishing from most bridges in the area is prohibited because bridges often traverse boating channels. Be sure to check the signs on bridges before casting. Small-boat owners have many fishing opportunities around the mouths of creeks and inlets, especially during incoming tides when the boat and the bait can drift in with the bait fish. Small boats should use caution at ocean inlets during outgoing tides because the currents can be strong. If you're traveling without tackle, rental gear is sometimes available. In addition to the fishing piers listed in this chapter, you can check one of the many tackle shops that abound along the coast.

Fishing Licenses

The N.C. Coastal Recreational Fishing License is required for saltwater rod and reel fishing. The license can be purchased on a 10-day, annual or lifetime basis. An annual saltwater fishing license for state residents costs $15, and an annual nonresident license costs $30. Ten-day licenses are $5 for state residents and $10 for nonresidents. Contact the North Carolina Division of Marine Fisheries for saltwater regulations or for more information, (252) 726-7021, (800) 682-2632, or www.ncdmf.net. Be sure to familiarize yourself with regulations, including size and bag limits, which are posted at most piers and marinas.

Freshwater licenses are issued by the North Carolina Wildlife Resources Commission. Call (888) 248-6834 for credit card purchases or purchase from one of the locations listed below. Nonresident freshwater fishing licenses for 12 months cost $30. Three-day licenses cost $15, a license for one day is $10, and trout fishing is an additional $10. For residents, the annual 12-month fee is $15 with an additional $5 for a comprehensive license that includes trout fishing. A one-day license (not including trout waters) is $5. Licenses may be combined with a hunting license and can be obtained at slightly higher rates. As regulations and fees are complex and subject to change, you're advised to

check the website for complete information at www.ncwildlife.org.

WILMINGTON

Canady's Sport Center
3220 Wrightsville Ave., Wilmington
(910) 791-6280

Dick's Sporting Goods
816 S. College Rd., Wilmington
(910) 793-1904

Division of Marine Fisheries
Regional Office
127 Cardinal Dr., Wilmington
(910) 796-7215

Kmart
815 S. College Rd., Wilmington
(910) 799-5360

BRUNSWICK COUNTY

Blue Water Point Marina Resort
5710 57th Pl. W. and W. Beach Dr.,
Oak Island
(910) 278-1230, (888) 634-9005

CJ's Corner Store
5501 Oak Island Dr., Oak Island
(910) 278-5965

Island Tackle and Gifts
6855 Beach Dr., Ocean Isle Beach
(910) 579-6116

Jackey's Creek Outfitters
6361 Ocean Hwy. E., Winnabow
(910) 253-7771

Oak Island Rentals & Island Fishing Center
5319 E. Oak Island Dr., Oak Island
(910) 201-4002

Oak Island Sporting Goods
8800 E. Oak Island Dr., Oak Island
(910) 278-9872

Fishing Reports

The most up-to-date sources of fishing information are charter captains, fishing piers and tackle shops. Detailed reports also appear frequently in the Sports section of the *Star-News*.

Fishing Piers

Each of the area's piers has its own personality. Some have become bent and bowed after years of battering by the ocean and hurricanes, and some have been rebuilt time and again. Many are festooned with odd novelties and memorabilia and proudly display photographs of trophies reeled up from the sea. On busy days, expect to be rubbing elbows with other pier-fishers, but in the off season, a pier is a peaceful place to be. Almost all piers charge a daily fee for fishing and some charge a nominal fee to stroll out and watch the action. Most piers offer seasonal fishing permits, tackle shops, snack bars, wet cleaning tables, restrooms and a great view.

WILMINGTON

River Road Park
6300 River Rd., Wilmington
(910) 798-7198

River Road Park, south of the State Port and about 10 miles from downtown Wilmington, features a handicapped-accessible fishing pier on the Cape Fear River. The park has a boat ramp and parking, playground equipment, picnic tables, bathroom facilities and a shelter that can be rented for social occasions. Call (910) 798-7181 for reservations. The park is open from 8 AM to dusk.

WRIGHTSVILLE BEACH

Johnnie Mercer's Pier
Foot of E. Salisbury St., Wrightsville Beach
(910) 256-2743

Standing 25 feet above sea level, this magnificent concrete structure represents the latest in storm-resistant technology. It is the first pier in North Carolina able to sustain 200 mph winds, and its windows are built to withstand storm gales up to 150 mph. The light poles consist of spun concrete, and even the trash receptacles are made of stone. The pier is open year round and has a gift shop, arcade and restaurant that serves yummy sunrise breakfasts, lunches and dinners with indoor/outdoor seating. General fishing costs $8 per rod. Walk-on admission is $1 for adults and 50¢ for children younger than 12. The

fishing pier has plans to be open 24 hours a day, all year round.

CAROLINA BEACH

Carolina Beach Fishing Pier
1800 Carolina Beach Ave. N, Carolina Beach
(910) 458-5518

Owned and operated by the Phelps family, this 700-foot pier features a snack bar, a game area, a grill with indoor/outdoor seating and an upstairs lounge with ABC permits. The tackle shop offers new equipment for sale as well as rentals and bait. There is a fish-cleaning sink on the pier. The charge for general fishing with one or two rods is $8. King mackerel three-rod fishing costs $13. There is no charge to walk on the pier, and free parking is available for fishing. The pier is open 24 hours a day from April 1 through December 1 and is closed from December through March.

KURE BEACH

Kure Beach Pier
Ave. K, Kure Beach
(910) 458-5524

Built in 1923 by L. C. Kure, this 22-foot-wide, 712-foot-long wooden structure is the oldest continuously operated family-owned pier in North Carolina. Facilities include a 5,800-square-foot building that houses a concession counter with cold sandwiches, drinks and other goodies, a complete tackle shop, a souvenir store and an arcade with four pool tables and video games. Permits are good from midnight to midnight and cost $5 for one rod and reel per person and $12 for a king mackerel permit allowing three rods. The pier is handicapped accessible. No rentals are available, and no alcoholic beverages are permitted. The pier is open 24 hours a day every day from April 1 to December 1.

BRUNSWICK COUNTY

City Pier
Waterfront Park, Bay St., Southport
(800) 388-9635

This small, handicapped-accessible, L-shaped pier is located where the Intra-coastal Waterway, the Cape Fear River and the Atlantic Ocean come together. As a municipal facility its usage is free, and public restrooms are available nearby at the Garrison House. It is adjacent to Waterfront Park, where amenities include a water fountain, park benches, a gazebo, a picnic table and swings. From here you can see the Bald Head Island Lighthouse, the Oak Island Lighthouse, sailboats, fishing boats, the Bald Head Island Ferry and even container ships making their way up the river to the port at Wilmington.

Holden Beach Pier
441 Ocean Blvd. W, Holden Beach
(910) 842-6483

Holden Beach Pier sells daily, seasonal and three-day fishing permits and live bait. A grill and snack counter adjoin a beach gift shop. Holden Beach Pier charges spectators a fee of $1.00 for walking the pier. Handicapped access is available to the pier. The owners prohibit the use of nets and the consumption of alcoholic beverages.

Oak Island Pier
705 Ocean Dr., Oak Island
(910) 278-9400

Known for many years as Yaupon Beach Pier, the Oak Island Pier was purchased by the Town of Oak Island in 2009. Now under new management, the pier is expanding services. No fishing license is required to fish from this 980-foot fishing pier as anglers are covered by the pier's blanket license. Persons confined to wheelchairs fish for free, as do children younger than 10 who are accompanied by an adult. Anglers can rent rods from the bait and tackle shop, which also sells towels, toys, coolers and jewelry as well as a full line of beach needs. The attached restaurant, Upstairs at the Beach, plans to serve three meals a day, year round, with a menu including daily specials, fresh fish, oysters, clams and more. Other activities include music on the beach on weekends and Saturday horseshoe tournaments.

Ocean Crest Pier
1411 E. Beach Dr., Oak Island
(910) 278-6674

This 1,000-foot pier near 14th Place East, voted most popular fishing pier in North Carolina in 2005 and 2006 by Fisherman's Post, has a full tackle shop where special orders are available. You will also find gifts for friends or souvenirs for yourself. The legally disabled fish for free, and the owners provide a community live-bait tank and a shelter at the T-shaped far end that is reserved for king fishers. Season permits are available for bottom fishing and king fishing. An onsite weather station measures wind speed, air temperature, water temperature, wind direction and more. This data is posted online where anyone can retrieve it. All anglers at Ocean Crest Pier are covered under a blanket fishing license. A full-service restaurant and a motel adjoin the pier. Pier Manager Dave Cooper claims this is the premier king mackerel fishing pier.

Ocean Isle Pier
Foot of Causeway Dr., Ocean Isle Beach
(910) 579-3095

The large game room and small grill at this pier are quite popular in summer. Available are ice cream, drinks, ice, supplies, fishing bait, tackle and rods, season passes, and rod and equipment rentals. Fishing fees are $7 per rod. Spectators are charged $1 for adults and 50¢ for children younger than 12.

Sunset Beach Pier
Foot of Sunset Blvd., Sunset Beach
(910) 579-6630

This 900-foot pier has a special area for king fishermen. Amenities at Sunset Beach Pier include a double sink at the cleaning table, a cleaning sink at the king end, a snack bar and grill serving hot sandwiches and pizza by the slice, and an ATM in the air-conditioned pier house. Bait, rods and reels, T-shirts and sweat shirts are for sale at the pier, and rod rentals are available. Three-day, five-day and seasonal fishing passes are available and include parking. The pier is handicapped accessible, and scooter chairs are provided free of charge to handicapped persons. There is a fee of $1 to walk the pier.

TOPSAIL ISLAND

Jolly Roger Pier
803 Ocean Blvd., Topsail Beach
(910) 328-4616

The Jolly Roger is a pier complex with a motel, convenience store and bait and tackle shop with small restaurant facilities. This 850-foot ocean pier, at the southern end of the island, is open from March through November.

Seaview Fishing Pier
124 Fishing Pier Ln., New River Inlet Rd.,
North Topsail Beach
(910) 328-3172

Located on the north end of the island, Seaview is 1,000 feet long. You catch 'em, you clean 'em and they'll cook 'em at the pier's restaurant, or you can just order off the menu. The pier shop has bait and tackle, snack foods and ice. It's open March through November.

Surf City Ocean Pier
112 S. Shore Dr., Surf City
(910) 328-3521

This 937-foot long pier is right in the center of downtown Surf City. Stop by and rent a rod, pick up some bait and try your luck. The grill is open daily during the summer season (sometimes 24 hours a day when the fish are biting), with reduced hours in the fall and spring. If you've had a good day fishing, they will cook your catch on the spot. Spectators are welcome to stroll the pier for a $1 charge for a 24-hour pass. Alcohol is not allowed on this pier, which is open from mid-March until sometime in December.

Surf Fishing

With good access to miles of beaches along our coast, surf fishing is naturally popular. The best time for surf fishing is during high tide with an outgoing tide, but you don't have to fight the sunbathers for space. There are some great out-of-the-way fishing spots in the area.

In Wrightsville Beach, you'll find good fishing behind the jetty at Masonboro Inlet, on the south end of the island. For anglers looking to get away from it all, the Fort Fisher State Recreation Area offers an undeveloped 4-mile stretch of beach and tidal marsh approximately 5 miles south of Carolina Beach that is accessible only by four-wheel-drive vehicles. The entrance to the area is off U.S. Highway 421 before the North Carolina Aquarium (bear left at the fork in the road) and to the right of the beach parking lot. There is also a public beach here with changing rooms, restrooms and shower, a snack bar (open seasonally only) and a ranger contact station. Phone (910) 458-5798 for information about hours, fees and permits. The daily 4WD fee is $10. An annual fee is $40. Otherwise, there are no services, so bring everything you'll need and pack out everything you bring. (See the Beach Driving section in our Sun, Sand and Sea chapter).

If you're looking for something a bit more adventurous, try fishing The Rocks, a 3.3-mile breaker extending from Federal Point, south of the Fort Fisher Ferry terminal. The enclosed water around Zeke's Island is called The Basin, and fishing on both sides of the barrier is excellent. However, The Rocks can be very dangerous, especially at high tide when they're slippery, wet and partly under water, so be sure to enter and leave the area during low tide.

Although surf fishing is popular on all the beaches of Oak Island, a great spot can be found at The Point, at the west end of Oak Island bordering Lockwood Folly

Inlet. You can throw a cast net for bait on the north side of this spot of land then fish either from the south side or the western point. From here you can see the eastern end of Holden Beach and the Holden Beach bridge, but you can't get there from here!

Fly-Fishing and Light Tackle

Although saltwater fly-fishing requires skill, patience and a little luck, it is gaining in popularity on our coast. Those who pursue the sport have a fantastic love for it. Neophytes and aficionados of saltwater fly-fishing can find resources in the Wilmington area and in many tackle shops throughout the region.

Equipment and Supplies

The abundance of fishing equipment suppliers underscores the popularity of the sport in North Carolina's southern region. You'll find full-service stores specializing in everything you need for inshore, offshore and fly fishing. But beyond just gear and bait, these stores offer tips from the experts on the best techniques to catch fish in local waters, so take advantage of their advice.

Greg's Outboard Center
1105 E. Ocean Hwy., Holly Ridge
(910) 329-0040

Greg's Outboard is an authorized dealer of both SeaArk and Blue Wave boats. Known for their durability and versatility, SeaArks and Blue Waves are great for fishing, recreation and traversing the area's shallow waterways. Look for expert boat and motor repairs as well as marine supplies and equipment. Boat storage is also available, and Craig's offers monthly and yearly rates.

Intracoastal Angler
6332 Oleander Dr., Wilmington
(910) 392-3500, (888) 325-4285

Intracoastal Angler is a full-service inshore and offshore tackle shop. Intra-

coastal specializes in custom rigging, destination outfitting and advising anglers on the latest techniques to catch more fish from local waters. You can also book your next guide trip for inshore, offshore and saltwater fishing through the store's network of local captains.

Tex's Tackle & Bait
215 Old Eastwood Rd., Wilmington
(910) 791-1763
www.texstackle.com

The largest independent tackle shop in the region, Tex's Tackle & Bait carries everything you need for a successful fishing adventure, including rods, reels and frozen bait. The store's extensive inventory is impressive, as is its commitment to carrying only the best quality products at competitive prices. The line winding department offers a wide range of monofilament and braided lines, and the frozen baits include ballyhoo, squid, shrimp, cigar minnows and much more. Owner Tex Grissom, a lifelong fisherman, and his knowledgeable staff can answer questions and provide guidance.

Head Boats and Charters

If you want to fish with a group of people, you've come to the right place. From Topsail's Treasure Coast to Calabash, there are fishing vessels aplenty. Choose the large head boats (a.k.a. party boats) accommodating dozens of people or the "six-pack" charters accommodating up to six passengers. Head boats average $40 to $100 per person for full-day excursions, and walk-ons are always welcome. The boats are equipped with full galleys and air-conditioned lounges. Handicapped accessibility to most large head boats tends to be good, but varies from boat to boat and with weather conditions.

Charters offer a variety of trips, half-day or full-day, inshore or offshore, and sometimes overnight. Most are available for tournaments and diving trips, but it's a good idea to reserve early. If you can't find enough friends to chip in to cover the cost, ask about split charters. Many captains book them. Most charter captains prefer reservations but will accept walk-ons when possible. Charters range anywhere from around $300 for half-day excursions up to $1,200 for an entire day of fishing in the Gulf Stream, which from here can be 40 to 70 miles offshore, depending on currents and the marina from which you embark.

Certain provisions are common to all charters and include first mate, on board coolers and ice, all the bait and tackle you'll need for kings, tuna, dolphin, wahoo, billfish and more. With advanced notice, many captains will arrange food packages, and some may even arrange hotel packages. Optional electric reels may be available. Although most six-pack charters are unable to bring wheelchairs aboard, crews are often very accommodating of handicapped passengers, sometimes leaving the wheelchair ashore and providing secure seating on deck, right where the action is. Call the vessel of your choice in advance for details. Remember that no one can guarantee sea conditions. If your captain decides to turn back before you've landed a smoker, rest assured she knows what she's doing. Captains reserve the right to cancel trips if conditions are unsafe for the vessel or passengers.

Carolina Beach is the Gulf Stream fishing hub between Bald Head and Topsail islands. A large number of vessels run out of the Carolina Beach Municipal Docks at Carl Winner Street and Canal Drive. Paid parking is available on the marina's west, south and east sides. There is no central booking office for the charter boats, but since you should know something about what you're chartering in advance, your best bet is to simply walk the docks and eye each one. Signs and brochures there will give you all the booking information you'll need. Ticket booths for the head boats are located at the south end of the marina. Also, check the phone book's Yellow Pages under fishing guides, charters and parties.

Charters in southern Brunswick County are concentrated at the Southport Marina, Blue Water Point Marina on the western end of Oak Island, Holden Beach and Ocean Isle Beach. There are no charters running directly out of Wilmington. Look

instead for charters and head boats running from Wrightsville Beach and Carolina Beach.

Listed in this section are marinas and boats that book fishing charters. The types of vessels available at each location, six-packs or head boats, are indicated.

WRIGHTSVILLE BEACH

Cape Fear Fishing Center
Wrightsville Beach
(252) 671-1684

Cape Fear Fishing Center is host to some of the area's most popular charter companies. No strangers to saltwater fishing, each of CFFC's captains will provide a great experience using the latest techniques and equipment. The company runs its charters out of the 30-foot Grady-White Seaward Action, the 34-foot Yellowfinne Streamweaver and a 41-foot Tiara. These are some of the top tournament fishing boats built with one ultimate goal in mind — fishing. Running at exhilarating speeds of up to 60 miles per hour, their boats will get your lines in the water twice as fast as a traditional fishing charter. At Cape Fear Fishing Center, you'll find a high-quality boat and tackle, knowledgeable captains and affordable prices.

Corona Daze Charters
Wrightsville Beach
(910) 619-8509

Experience a chartered fishing trip in Wrightsville or Topsail Beach aboard the Corona Daze, a TR 22 Triton Sea Hunt with center console. The Corona Daze comes equipped with full electronics, including two GPS systems featuring sonar and radar. Captain Mike Hoffman, a Wilmington native, has been fishing since he was 5 years old and a full-time professional fisherman since 1987. He won numerous awards during his 11 years fishing the Pro Bass Tour. He received his captain's license in 1998 and his master captain's license in 2008. Captain Hoffman ensures that everyone has an enjoyable experience and catches fish. Want to just explore the local waterways without fishing? Captain Hoffman offers guided, scenic tours of local marches, inlets or Figure Eight Island. You don't need a fishing license to fish on the Corona Daze, and children are welcome.

Hieronymus Fishing Charters
Wilmington
(910) 231-6133

Plan your next inshore or offshore fishing adventure through Hieronymus Fishing Charters. They offer a wide variety of inshore fishing, from slight casting for red drum in 2 feet of water to exploring 50 feet of water around near shore reefs for big king mackerel. Other types of fish commonly caught inshore include speckled trout, flounder and Spanish mackerel. For inshore fishing trips, Hieronymus uses the 19' Maycraft equipped with light tackle, GPS navigation and color-scope electronics to fish the creeks, rivers and near-shore areas of southeastern North Carolina. Or go on an offshore fishing trip within the 10- to 30-mile range, where you may catch mahi-mahi, Atlantic sailfish or king mackerel. To cover the offshore area, Captain Cord Hieronymus uses the 42' Stapleton, a twin diesel engine boat with two GPS/chart plotters, two fish-finding color scopes for deep water, radar, air conditioning, a refrigerator and a tuna green stick to attract the best fish. Captain Hieronymus, a native of Wrightsville Beach, offers more than 25 years of fishing and navigation experience ranging from local creeks to beyond the Gulf Stream. Children are welcome on Hieronymus fishing expeditions. Call or check their website for pricing.

Hook, Line & Paddle Canoe & Kayak Outfitters
435 Eastwood Rd., Wilmington
(910) 792-6945
www.hooklineandpaddle.com

Hook, Line & Paddle Canoe & Kayak Outfitters is one of the largest kayak fishing and paddleboard fishing dealers in North Carolina. As the sport of paddle fishing grows in popularity, so does the store's large stock of fishing kayaks, fishing stand up paddleboards and tons of paddle fishing accessories. Join the store's professional guides for a five-hour guided paddle fishing charter in the marshes and inlets of Wrightsville Beach, where you're bound to catch red fish, flounder, trout, blue fish and Spanish mackerel. In addition to kayak fishing gear, the store also sells recreational kayaks, canoes and stand-up paddle boards and all the latest accessories from top brands like Native Watercraft, Heritage, Wilderness Systems and Yolo Boards. If you're not ready to take the plunge and purchase your own equipment, you can rent kayaks through the store, at their Wrightsville Beach location (across from the Blockade-Runner Beach Resort) and at the Yacht Club on Figure Eight Island. If after you rent, you get hooked and want to buy, as an added incentive, Hook, Line & Paddle will refund the cost of your rental toward a purchase. Not only can you get the right gear, but you can also book a tour at the shop or receive instruction from one of the store's master teachers. One of their most popular tours is the Dawson's Creek Tour, a three-hour excursion visiting the Wrightsville Beach house featured in the series. They also sell custom kayak fishing outfitting and Yakima roof racks, with free installations with purchase. The store is open every day from 10 AM to 6 PM.

No Excuses Fishing Charters
Wilmington
(910) 352-2715

No Excuses Fishing Charters specializes in custom, light-tackle saltwater fishing trips around Topsail Island, Wrightsville Beach, Carolina Beach and the Cape Fear River. You won't find a cookie-cutter charter here; indeed, they offer only personalized fishing experiences, taking into consideration your interests, skill level, weather conditions and the fish that are running to design a fishing experience tailored to you. No Excuses provides charters on its 22-foot tournament edition Pathfinder with a Yamaha 150 4-stroke engine. The boat's versatility allows for in-shore, near-shore and off-shore fishing charters. Fishing is truly a passion for Captain Mike Pedersen, who holds a USCG Masters license and has more than 30 years of experience. Through his other business, Riley Rods, Captain Pedersen designs and builds custom fishing rods, which he uses for all No Excuses fishing expeditions.

Seahawk Inshore Fishing Charters
5419 Peden Point Rd., Wilmington
(910) 619-9580
www.seahawkinshorefishingcharters.com

With Seahawk Inshore Fishing Charters you'll find a variety of boats perfect for fishing the calm waters of the Cape Fear waterways. Seahawk Inshore Fishing Charters provides fishing experiences for inshore, near-shore and the backwaters of Carolina Beach, Kure Beach, Wrightsville Beach, Southport and Bald Head Island. From sight-casting for redfish in Buzzard's Bay to live-bait fishing for large flounder in Snow's Cut, Captain Jeff Wolfe will give you the fishing experience you desire. Seahawk Inshore Fishing Charters offers a unique service, the Waterman's Way Seafood Charter, for those looking to catch a variety of seafood such as clams, crabs and various types of popular fish. Wolfe is a USCG–licensed, insured captain with 30 years of fishing experience. He specializes in local fishing trips that are fun and affordable for the entire family. Participants, especially children, enjoy using the different types of fishing gear. Seahawk Inshore Fishing Charters is open year-round.

Fortune Hunter Charters, Wilmington, Custom Charters, (910) 791-6414

On My Way Charters, Wrightsville Beach Custom Charters, (910) 798-6093

Rod-Man Charters, Wilmington, Inshore, near-shore custom charters and tours for 1 to 4 people, (910) 799-6120

Wrightsville Fishing Charters, Wrightsville Beach, (910) 617-4160

CAROLINA AND KURE BEACH

Blue Marlin Charters, Carolina Beach, Six-packs, (910) 458-6136, (866) 420-6136

Captain John's Fishing Charters, Carolina Beach, Custom charters, (910) 458-9111

Class Action Charters, Carolina Beach, Custom charters for 1 to 6 anglers; offshore/inshore, (910) 458-3348

Fish Dance Charters, Carolina Beach, Six-packs, (910) 367-0884

Fish Witch Charters, Carolina Beach, Six-packs, (910) 458-5855

Hooker Fishing Charters, Carolina Beach, Six-packs, (910) 313-2828, (800) 946-1616

Hot Ticket Fishing Charters, Carolina Beach, Six-packs, (910) 791-0443

Large Time Charters, Carolina Beach, Six-packs, (910) 458-3362, (800) 582-5524

Lookout Charters, Carolina Beach, Inshore, offshore, 1 to 6 anglers, (910) 619-0928

Musicman Charters, Inc., Carolina Beach, Six-packs, (910) 796-FISH (3474)

Winner Gulf Stream Fishing & Cruise Boats, Carolina Beach, Head boats, (910) 458-FISH (3474)

BALD HEAD ISLAND

Cool Runnings Charters, Bald Head Island, Four-packs, (910) 278-7006

Fish Whistle Charters, Bald Head Island, Six-packs, (910) 201-1645

Impulsive Charters, Bald Head Island, Six-packs, (910) 457-5331

SOUTHPORT

Bulfighter Charters, Southport, Six-packs, (910) 713-2130

Cool Runnings Charters, Southport, Four-packs, (910) 278-7006

Fish Whistle Charters, Southport, Six-packs, (910) 201-1645, (910) 470-1995

Get Reel Charters Gulf Stream Fishing, Oak Island, Six-packs, (910) 294-2005/2004

Holden Charters, Southport, Four-packs, (757) 510-3346

Impulsive Charters, Southport, Six-packs, (910) 457-5331

Salty Dog Charter Boat, Southport, Six-packs, (910) 278-9834

Yeah Right Spotfishing Charters, Southport, (910) 845-2004, (336) 239-5429

OAK ISLAND

Affordable Fishing Charters, Oak Island, Four-packs, (910) 448-2277

Amber Lady Charters, Oak Island, Four-packs, (910) 278-6707, (910) 471-0157

BlueWater Princess, Oak Island, Inshore, near-shore custom charters and tours for 1 to 4 people, (910) 278-1230, (888) 634-9005

Cool Runnings Charters, Oak Island, Four-packs, (910) 278-7006

Fish Whistle Charters, Oak Island, Six-packs, (910) 201-1645

Fishbuster Charters, Oak Island, Four-packs, (910) 278-7015

Fugitive Charter Boat, Oak Island, Six-packs, (910) 933-4242

Get Reel Charters Gulf Stream Fishing, Oak Island, Six-packs, (910) 294-2005/2004

Impulsive Charters, Oak Island, Six-packs, (910) 457-5331

My Way Charters, Oak Island, Three-packs, (910) 619-1274

HOLDEN BEACH

Holden Beach Charters, Holden Beach, Sixpacks, (910) 842-9055, (910) 233-1215

Intimidator Fishing Charters, Holden Beach, Ten-Packs, (910) 842-6200

Sea Hawk III, Holden Beach, Six-packs, (910) 754-6169

OCEAN ISLE BEACH

Captain Brandt's Fishing Charters, Ocean Isle Beach, Three, four and six-packs, (910) 575-3474

Follow Me Charters, Ocean Isle Beach, Six-packs, (910) 575-5738

Sea Bear Fishing Charters, Ocean Ise Beach, Four-packs, (910) 575-4736, (828) 403-1204

CALABASH

The Hurricane Fleet Deep Sea Fishing Center, Calabash. Head Boats, ten-packs and up to 40 passengers, (910) 579-3660, (800) 373-2004

Voyager Fishing Charters, Calabash, Six-packs and head boat, (910) 575-5978, (843) 626-4900

TOPSAIL ISLAND

East Coast Sports
The Fishing Village, 409 Roland Ave., Surf City
(910) 328-1887

If you are looking for a charter, let Captain Chris Medlin arrange one for you. The friendly, professional staff at East Coast Sports also can help you select the best bait and tackle for either inshore or offshore fishing. East Coast has a full line of sports clothing, including Columbia, Sperry, Topsiders and many other name brands. East Coast is open year round.

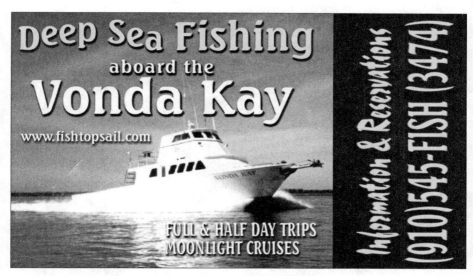

Paradise Landing
318 Fulchers Rd., Sneads Ferry
(910) 327-2114

Private charters for up to six people are available at Paradise Landing. Whether you want to fish the Gulf Stream or nearby waters, Paradise Landing can plan the perfect trip. Paradise Landing also offers boat, personal watercraft, kayak and canoe rentals.

Vonda Kay
743 Cockle St., Surf City
(910) 545-FISH
www.fishtopsail.com

If you're ready to catch the big one, climb aboard the Vonda Kay and head out to the Gulf Stream for a great day of fishing. Fish for black sea bass, snapper, grouper, triggerfish, mahi mahi, amberjack, mackerel and cobia. The Vonda Kay carries 76 passengers and has all of the latest electronics and safety equipment. Bait, tackle and instruction are provided. Private charters are available. Walk-ups are welcome, but reservations are recommended. The on-board galley serves deli sandwiches, burgers, snacks, soft drinks and beer. Fish-cleaning services and half-day trips are available.

The Bald Head Island Lighthouse is known as Old Baldy.

MARINAS AND THE INTRACOASTAL⊿ WATERWAY

Southeastern North Carolina is a boater's paradise. The entire length of the four-county coastal region is fronted by the Atlantic Intracoastal Waterway (AIWW, or simply the Intracoastal Waterway, ICW), a series of barrier islands, numerous sounds and a variety of rivers and streams, all connecting with the Atlantic Ocean.

Authorized by Congress in the Rivers & Harbors Act of 1938, the AIWW was originally developed for commercial water traffic. Over the years, it evolved into a route that is now used more by pleasure craft than by commercial vessels. The total waterway is about 3,000 miles in length and ranges from Boston to Key West on the Atlantic coast, and from Apalachee Bay in northwest Florida to Brownsville, Texas, and the Rio Grande River on the Gulf of Mexico coast.

The toll-free waterway is maintained by the Army Corps of Engineers to a minimum depth of 12 feet for most of its length, although 7- and 9-foot minimum depths will be found in some areas. Because of shoaling, depths as little as 5 or 6 feet can also be encountered, so be sure to check current information, either with the Army Corps of Engineers or at the Atlantic Intracoastal Waterway Association (online at www.atlintracoastal.org) before setting sail.

The Cape Fear segment of the AIWW is a great place for nature and wildlife lovers because so much of it traverses the sounds and marshes between the barrier islands and the mainland. Some of these areas are protected and accessible only by boat. In addition, because of the mild climate in the southern coastal region coupled with the warming effect of the Gulf Stream, boating enthusiasts can enjoy a nearly year-long season on the waterway.

In addition to numerous private and residential community boating facilities, there are more than 40 marinas and boat yards in operation, providing a full spectrum of services and supplies for the boating public. Detailed information about facilities, along with a wealth of other boating information and a searchable database, is available online at www.NC-Waterways.com. A valuable resource for the boater is the North Carolina Coastal Boating Guide, which can be ordered there online or by calling (877) 368-4968. Another valuable source of information about the towns and facilities along the southeastern coast can be found online at www.icw-net.com. Follow the links to the various coastal communities. Further information and photos of many of the marinas can be found by clicking Marinas North Carolina at www.cruisingguide.com.

Marinas

A number of marinas and boatyards dot the Cape Fear Coast. The vast majority of these are located along or adjacent to the Intracoastal Waterway, or on rivers and streams connecting to the waterway. The following list, although not complete, is representative of facilities available for boaters and ranges from north to south. Facilities that are for the exclusive use of a private community or its guests are not listed. In a few instances, the address shown reflects a mailing address rather than a physical location. For maps and detailed, candid information on all these marinas, pick up a copy of native North Carolinian Claiborne Young's Cruising Guide to Coastal North Carolina. Most of the marinas are listed and pinpointed on the North Carolina Coastal Boating Guide map available on the Southport-Fort Fisher Ferry, at local boating stores and by calling (877) 368-4968.

NEW HANOVER COUNTY

Canaday's Yacht Basin
7624 Mason Landing Rd., Wilmington
(910) 686-9116

Canaday's Yacht Basin includes supplies, restrooms and 72 wet slips.

Inlet Watch Yacht Club
801 Paoli Ct., Wilmington
(910) 392-7106

Just north of Snow's Cut is an exceptionally clean, well-maintained marina that offers a ship's store, parts and a full assortment of repair services. Inlet Watch is a private yacht club with 123 wet slips up to 45 feet and 420 dry storage units up to 30 feet. Slips can be rented on a six-month or yearly basis or can be purchased as an investment. Direct ocean access and first-rate service coupled with a picturesque setting and quiet, relaxing environment make Inlet Watch Yacht Club one of the area's best marine facilities. Enjoy the club's pool and tennis court, have a picnic on the point, then watch the moon rise over the sea while sipping a cool drink in your deck chair. To get there by land from Wilmington, take College Road south. Inlet Watch Yacht Club is on the left just before crossing the bridge over Snow's Cut into Carolina Beach.

Masonboro Yacht Club & Marina
609 Trails End Rd., Wilmington
(910) 791-1893

Drive through the neighborhood to where the land meets the ICW to find this private facility offering slips to rent or purchase. A three-story clubhouse includes four private showers, laundry facilities, a club room and a glorious unobstructed view of the water and unspoiled Masonboro Island. You're guaranteed to find some interesting conversation among the residents. To get there by land, take Piner Road from Monkey Junction (junction of U.S. 421 and N.C. 132) for about a mile east to where the road forks. Veer left onto Masonboro Loop Road and go about two miles to Trails End Road on your right just south of the bridge over Whiskey Creek. Turn right at the blue sign to Masonboro

Yacht Club & Marina. By water, the marina is located near mile marker 288 on the Intracoastal Waterway at Whiskey Creek between Wrightsville Beach and Carolina Beach.

Pages Creek Marine
7000 Market St., Wilmington
(866) 686-0659

Located on Market Street near Military Cutoff, Pages Creek Marine offers a variety of services, storage, new boat and brokerage sales, and full Yamaha service.

WILMINGTON

Coming from Carolina Beach by boat, it's a 15-mile ride from Snows Cut across the Cape Fear River into Southport and the more protected Intracoastal Waterway. This is a major shipping lane to the State Port at Wilmington, as well as the route for the Southport-Fort Fisher Ferry, so do keep a watchful eye. Before crossing over, take a sidetrip up the Cape Fear River from Snows Cut, unless you have a sailboat with a mast taller than 65 feet. The Cape Fear Memorial Bridge, just south of downtown Wilmington, is a bascule bridge with a clearance of just 65 feet. If you can get under, head north up the river for one of the most memorable trips on your cruise. You'll find increasingly improved opportunities to dock, and you can take advantage of visiting Wilmington's Historic District.

"Those who miss the many attractions of this seagoing community will be less for the omission," wrote Claiborne Young in his Cruising Guide to Coastal North Carolina. After stopping to enjoy the city's downtown and Riverwalk, head up the Northeast Cape Fear River. You'll pass under the Isabelle Holmes Bridge, which opens at 10 AM and 2 PM and on demand from 6 PM to 6 AM (the bridge tender monitors channels 13 and 18A), and you'll soon find yourself in the midst of spectacular scenery. Continue upriver and you'll see the ruins of antebellum rice plantations from 200 years ago, with endless creeks to explore. You can cruise for miles in complete tranquility with breathtaking scenery all around.

Bennett Brothers Yachts
Cape Fear Marina
1701 J. E. L. Wade Dr., Wilmington
(910) 772-9277

Just beyond the Isabel Holmes Bridge on the Northeast Cape Fear River is Bennett Brothers Yachts and the Cape Fear Marina. It serves as a great place to tie up for the night or the season in one of the most protected marinas along the East Coast. Bennett Brothers Yachts is celebrating 22 years as a family-owned business offering a full-service boat yard, custom builds and yacht brokerage. With a 70-ton Marine Travel Lift, they can haul out just about anything. Twenty-five skilled craftsmen in all disciplines are on board to serve you. Their location at the Cape Fear Marina offers 77 slips, each with power, water, telephone and pump-out. The dock house has immaculate bathrooms, showers, laundry facilities and free ice. WiFi is available at no charge throughout the marina. You can buy or lease a slip, which can accommodate yachts up to 176 feet with very deep draft. The marina is built on a site discovered in 1663 by William Hilton, who chose the spot for its superb natural protection from hurricanes. It remains a safe haven today for boats from all over the world.

Wilmington Marine Center
3410 River Rd., Wilmington
(910) 395-5055
www.wilmingtonmarine.com

Wilmington Marine Center, an N.C.-certified clean marina located at marker 59 on the Cape Fear River between Snows Cut and downtown Wilmington, offers a 102-slip, enclosed-basin marina with floating docks and 110/220V electricity for yachts ranging from 20 to 120 feet. The center sells diesel and unleaded gasoline seven days a week and has on-site bath facilities. Here, too, you'll find a yacht service company with mobile and railway haul-out capacity to 400 tons, a chart and ship supply company, fabricators and welders, boat builders, dock manufacturers, diesel mechanics, and two yacht sales and brokerage companies that handle power boats from 20 to 80 feet.

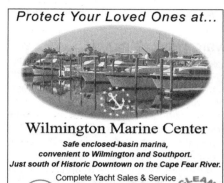
WILMINGTON'S DOWNTOWN WATERFRONT

Cruising the downtown Wilmington waterfront offers a wonderful alternative to the hectic pace of the Intracoastal Waterway. Step off your boat onto one of the docks along the Riverwalk and wander into some of the appealing shops or dine in one of downtown's great restaurants. You'll be within walking distance of museums, historic residences, visitor information centers and theaters.

City of Wilmington Municipal Docks
Downtown Riverfront, Wilmington
(910) 520-6875

Approximately 15 miles from the ICW on the scenic Cape Fear River, you'll find transient, short-term and limited long-term docking facilities in historic downtown Wilmington. The city offers a total of 1,200 feet of floating dock space with multiple floating face docks and can accommodate vessels up to 100 feet. Power (30 and 50 amp) and water are available. The fee for docking is $1.25 per foot/per day or $3 per foot/per day for 30 amp service and $5 per foot/per day for 50 amp service. Part day dockage at $5 for up to six hours is also available. The docks are within walking distance of area attractions, hotels, shopping, dining, theater, nightlife, laundry facilities, the post office, a bank and supplies. Dockage is available by reservation only. The dock master monitors channel 16 on VHF.

WRIGHTSVILLE BEACH

Boaters love Wrightsville Beach's many accommodating marinas, terrific seafood restaurants and relaxed ambiance. Whatever your marine needs, they can be met here. Facilities are available for everything from repairs to fishing gear. However, if you require groceries or want to do major shopping, you'll have to go to the mainland. By sea, Wrightsville Beach is approximately at mile marker 283. For the exact location, check your marine charts. Several marinas are located on Airlie Road, just before the drawbridge leading to Wrightsville Beach. Others are across the bridge on Harbour Island. For those with trailerable craft, there's a free Wildlife Access Ramp just to the north of the drawbridge on Harbour Island.

Atlantic Marine
101 Keel St., Wrightsville Beach
(910) 256-9911

Located on Harbour Island at Motts Channel and open seven days a week, this marina offers repair services and is oriented to serving locals with its dry-docked, small-craft facilities. Gasoline is the only service for transients.

Bradley Creek Marina
6338 Oleander Dr., Wilmington
(910) 350-0029

Just south of the Bradley Creek bridge on Oleander Drive and on the western shore of the ICW, this private membership marine facility serves the local community, but no transients. Wet slips can accommodate watercraft up to 65 feet, and dry storage is available for boats up to 24 feet. Slips are leased by the year or they may be purchased. Fuel is available nearby. Bradley Creek Marina is close to Masonboro Inlet, which allows access to the Atlantic Ocean.

The Bridge Tender Marina
1414 Airlie Rd., Wilmington
(910) 256-6550
www.thebridgetender.com

On Airlie Road at the Wrightsville Beach drawbridge is a marina with a bonus: a great local seafood and steak restaurant. The marina offers all amenities, including gas and diesel fuel. All docks were rebuilt in 2005. One word of caution, however: The current is very swift here, so mind your slippage on entering and be ready with a boat hook to fend off any craft docked nearby.

Dockside Restaurant & Marina
1308 Airlie Rd., Wilmington
(910) 256-3579

Dockside Restaurant & Marina is located just south of the Wrightsville Beach drawbridge at about mile marker 283 on the ICW. You'll find 180 feet of transient dockage, fuel and 30, 50 and 100 amp power, as well as an excellent, casual seafood restaurant. This marina is a great location for an overnight stay. Amenities include a full-service bar. Call ahead for dockage reservations.

Seapath Yacht Club
330 Causeway Dr., Wrightsville Beach
(910) 256-3747

On Motts Channel, just off the ICW, this well-appointed facility has some transient dockage with power, water, fuel, waste pump-out, wireless Internet and cable TV connections. A store provides many essential supplies. Seapath is very close to Banks Channel and is the nearest approach to the Atlantic Ocean. You can't miss Seapath because it adjoins a high-rise condominium building that clearly marks the spot for miles.

Wrightsville Beach Marina
6 Marina St., Wrightsville Beach
(910) 256-6666

On the eastern shore of the ICW, just south of the Wrightsville Beach drawbridge, lies a luxurious place to dock for the night. Wrightsville Beach Marina offers power, water, cable TV, WiFi Internet connection, a swimming pool and fuel. Mechanical repairs can be arranged. For dining, the Bluewater Grill overlooks the docks, welcoming famished boaters to enjoy prime rib and seafood.

CAROLINA BEACH

Below Masonboro Sound you will find a stretch of water with no marinas. The shoreline becomes residential in character, and there is not another port until you get close to Carolina Beach.

Carolina Beach Municipal Marina
300 Canal Dr., Carolina Beach
(910) 458-2540

This city marina, located off the ICW at the southern end of the channel in Carolina Beach, is dedicated to fishing charter and party boats. Day docking is now available for boats 25 feet and under to dock at the marina for convenient access to local restaurants and stores, and the marina also features a pump-out station. Contact the Harbor Master at this number for information.

Carolina Beach State Park Marina
Carolina Beach State Park, Carolina Beach
(910) 458-7770

At the west end of Snow's Cut, which connects the Cape Fear River with the ICW, is Carolina Beach State Park. On land, just go over the Snow's Cut Bridge on U.S. 421 S., take the first right at the second traffic light, which is Dow Road, then after about 0.2 mile, take another right onto State Park Road. The park marina offers a ramp, fuel, a modified ship's store and ample overnight dockage. If you're weary of being on a boat, you can pitch a tent and roast marshmallows over a campfire in the park, or you can take advantage of some of the park's five great trails. The Fly Trap Trail is one of the favorites. Along the trail you can look at the hungry plants known as Venus Flytraps, but don't touch! The Sugarloaf Trail follows along the Cape Fear River, providing beautiful water views as you explore nature.

BRUNSWICK COUNTY BEACHES AND VICINITY

The coastline of Brunswick County is comprised of a string of islands separated from the mainland by the Intracoastal Waterway. Because of this configuration and the fact that the waterway is the north/south route of boaters who follow the seasons like the geese, you will find a number of marinas available to the public. At present, most of these marinas are located in the Bald Head Island and Southport areas but growth in the county is an indicator

that more marinas are likely to be built in the near future.

BALD HEAD ISLAND

Bald Head Island Marina
Harbour Village, Bald Head Island
(910) 457-7380

Located two miles east of ICW marker #307, the Bald Head Island Marina offers slips, cable TV service, wireless Internet, gas and diesel fuel, and a bathhouse with showers, restrooms and a laundry. A convenience store, restaurants, a gift shop and inn line the marina as well. The marina is not reachable by road, the only way you're going to get there is by boat. Odds are you're not going to take the ferry if the marina is your destination for boating; you'll just boat right in and be delighted you did. This marina primarily serves a private, residential community where many of the homes are also vacation rentals, but it has the welcome mat out for visitors.

SOUTHPORT AND OAK ISLAND

Blue Water Point Marina Resort
5710 57th Pl. W and W. Beach Dr., Oak Island
(910) 278-1230, (888) 634-9005

Located at Intracoastal Waterway marker 33, Blue Water Point Marina offers floating docks, a courtesy dock, gas and diesel fuel, boat slip rentals, rod and reel rentals, kayak and Jet Ski rentals, a fully stocked ships store, bait, tackle and ice. Deep-sea fishing is available on two charter boats: a 60-foot head boat that carries up to 59 passengers and a 34-foot sport-fisher six-pack. Both boats have the latest electronics and equipment to fulfill your fishing needs. Party cruises are available. See our Hotels and Motels section for more about the resort.

Deep Point Marina
1301 Ferry Rd., Southport
(910) 269-2380

Transient dockage can be found at this marina located next to the Bald Head Island Ferry terminal across from Cape Fear River buoy #20. Boats of 102 feet in length can dock here where you will find 30, 50 and 100 amp electric hookups, gas, diesel fuel, marine pump-out, cable TV and WiFi.

The terminal houses a snack bar, which is open seasonally and where you can purchase food, coffee, soft drinks, beer and wine. Restrooms are available. The marina is convenient to restaurants, shopping and the historic district in Southport.

South Harbour Village Transient Dock
Fish Factory Rd., Southport
(910) 454-7486

At 1,000 feet in length, this is the longest transient dock in North Carolina. It's a floating dock in 15 feet of water at low tide and sits at a perfect parallel to the channel, making it an easy-in, easy-out dock. In addition to the transient dock, there are 155 slips. Amenities include 30, 50 and 100 amp power, cable TV, water, gas, diesel, two pump-out stations, a courtesy phone, wireless Internet access, a completely remodeled facility containing laundry, showers and restrooms, a hair salon, three full-service restaurants, a deli and an 18-hole golf course on site. Taxi service is available, as are two rental car services who deliver their cars and are located within a half-mile of the docks. The facility is located at Mile Marker 311, Green Channel Marker 9, one mile south of the Cape Fear River Inlet.

Southport Marina
606 W. West St., Southport
(910) 457-9900 x6

Conveniently located on the Intracoastal Waterway at mile 309, marker 2A at the entrance to the Cape Fear River, Southport Marina is roughly halfway between Wrightsville Beach and Myrtle Beach. A multi-million-dollar renovation of the marina began in 2006 and completed renovations include: more than 200 wet slips with Brazilian hardwood docks and new dock boxes, wireless Internet, cable TV, water and metered electricity, more than 700 feet of transient dockage with high-speed gas and diesel pumps, a new pump-out system, a new recreational dock, two new public boat ramps and a new dock office/ship's store. The basin has been dredged to allow a minimum 6-foot depth at low tide. Waterfront renovations include a two-story office building with

rental space available and a renovated live oak park with benches and picnic tables for all to enjoy as well as an events deck for private rentals. All 132 open dry storage racks have been renovated and Phase I of a new dry storage building for 128 boats has begun with expected completion of July2010. Gregory Poole Marine is the marina's designated service provider in the newly renovated boat yard, which includes a 75-ton travel lift. MarineMax operates two sales offices selling new and used boats at the marina.

PENDER COUNTY

Because the Intracoastal Waterway serpentines along the shores of eastern Pender County, marinas old and new dot the coastal landscape. While some marinas have state-of-the-art facilities with sprawling docks, a clubhouse, laundry rooms and spacious showers, others are small and have limited amenities. So whether you're piloting a 60-foot yacht or just want to launch your john boat, you can find the perfect marina in Pender County.

Harbour Village Marina
101 Harbour Village Dr., Hampstead
(910) 270-4017

Just off U.S. Highway 17 in Hampstead, turn into Belvedere Plantation and follow the road and signs to the marina. From the water, this beautiful and serene marina is to the north of flashing day marker #96 and south of red marker #94. The marina has all the amenities a boater could want, including a boaters' lounge area, clean showers and delivery from area restaurants. A limited number of transient boat slips are available, and boaters must call in advance for a reservation.

Open Water Marine
2004 N.C. Hwy. 172, Sneads Ferry
(910) 327-9208

Open Water Marine has a great selection of boats, boat parts and boating and fishing supplies. Look for classic Sneads Ferry sneakers and life jackets plus fishing tackle, tow ropes, marine supplies and boat service.

Scott's Hill Marina
2570 Scott's Hill Loop Rd., Wilmington
(910) 686-0896

This full-service public marina and yacht club offers its members and guests wet/dry slips, supplies, bait, tackle and groceries. The clubhouse, which offers a panoramic view of the inlet, barrier islands and the Atlantic ocean in the background, may be rented for private events. Located north of Ogden, Scott's Hill Marina can accommodate boats up to 38 feet. There is also a boat ramp that is open to the public.

TOPSAIL ISLAND

Beach House Marina
111 N. New River Dr., Surf City
(910) 328-2628

This marina has 192 dry-storage spaces, which can be rented for either six months or a year. There are also some permanent water slips available and limited docking on a daily or weekend basis for transient boaters. Diesel fuel, gasoline and ice are available on site, and boating supplies can be purchased across the street. The marina is located in downtown Surf City and is within easy walking distance of restaurants, shops and the beach.

Swan Point Marina and Boatyard
123 Page St., Sneads Ferry
(910) 327-1081

Located in Sneads Ferry on the New River Inlet, between Mile Marker 2 and 4, is Swan Point Marina and Boatyard. The marina has 450 feet of transient dock space, gas, diesel, free wireless Internet access, showers and restrooms and washers and dryers. Live-aboards are welcomed. The do-it-yourself boatyard has a 40-ton lift, and contract boat repair is available. There is always a pot of coffee brewing at their ship's store that carries marine supplies and parts, as well as popular clothing and accessory lines such as Billabong, Patagonia and Costa del Mar.

SPORTS, FITNESS AND PARKS

Sports are very big on the southern coast. Whether you want to participate or just be a spectator, you'll find almost everything you want right here. In this chapter, we've included information about most of the area's sports and recreational activities, fitness centers and parks. Related businesses and services are described along the way.

Look to our Golf, Fishing and Watersports chapters for information on those sports.

University athletics and professional team sports are popular, as are auto racing (especially NASCAR) and other motor sports. Because we have only a few local teams in this area, you may want to explore what's available in the Raleigh-Durham-Chapel Hill area and the cities of Charlotte and Fayetteville. The area's major phone books provide a surprising amount of useful information, such as how to obtain tickets, driving directions and stadium/arena seating plans. Look in Wilmington's daily paper, the Star-News "Sports" and "Today" pages plus weekly "Play" sections to find announcements about sports clubs and events throughout the region. Many groups and organizations publish information about their activities on the Internet, so check for a website if you're unable to find what you need in this chapter.

Also, be sure to check the Summer Camps section in our Kidstuff chapter for summer sports camps. Parents should note that registration fees for youth league sports are often discounted when registering more than one child in the same league. Frequently, seniors get discounts, too. Be sure to inquire.

Badminton

Wilmington Athletic Club
2026 S. 16th St., Wilmington
(910) 343-5950

The Wilmington Athletic Club (WAC) is the place for a competitive game of badminton. This is not your backyard bunt-it variety, so you'd better come ready for serious play. The badminton club meets every Friday night and Sunday afternoon.

Baseball and Youth Leagues

Somewhere in between youth baseball and semi-pro are the American Legion baseball programs. Area high schools are the feeder system for these high-level amateur teams, which accept outstanding players up to age 19. These games are listed in the Star-News and other local media and are great fun to watch. However, if your little Derek Jeeter is just starting out, the region has several youth baseball leagues. The youth leagues offer divisions from T-ball for toddlers to baseball for teens through age 18, and some offer softball too. Registration generally takes place from early February through mid-March and fees vary. The playing season begins in April. Registrants need to present their birth certificates. Contact one of the organizations below for specifics. The Optimist clubs sponsor many, many teams in our area. Their clubhouse number is listed here, but be advised that you'll seldom get an answer except during the evenings when meetings are held, so watch for fliers at schools, announcements in the newspapers and notices posted in the parks.

Cape Fear Optimist Club
Wilmington
(910) 762-7065

The Cape Fear Optimist Club sponsors spring and fall baseball and softball programs for boys and girls from 6 to 16 years of age and T-ball for 4 to 6 year olds. Teams include Boys Minor League, Boys Major League, Girls 8U, Girls 10U, Girls 12U and Girls 16U. There are also Baseball/Softball Hitting Clinics, a Baseball Pitching Clinic and Speed Classes. For more information, go to www.capefearoptimist.com or call on the first, second and third Tuesdays after 7 PM.

New Hanover County Parks Department
230 Market Place Dr., Ste. 120, Wilmington
(910) 798-7275

Supper Optimist Club
Wilmington

For up-to-the minute baseball and softball schedules and events or to sign up to play, visit the Supper Optimist Club's website, www.supperoptimist.com.

Wilmington Family YMCA
2710 Market St., Wilmington
(910) 251-9622
www.wilmingtonfamilyymca.org

Wilmington Family YMCA offers T-ball for ages 4 through 8. This co-ed instruction program is designed to be non-competitive and focuses on rules and techniques of the game.

Carolina Men's Baseball League
Godwin Stadium, Shipyard & Adams St., Wilmington
(910) 465-0535

The Carolina Men's Baseball League is an adult, wood-bat baseball league for players 18+, 28+ and 48+, dedicated to providing the opportunity for serious amateur baseball players to play in a local league. All ages from 18 and older and all skill levels are welcome. No tryouts, no cuts, just the joy of playing baseball again in a friendly yet competitive environment has long been their policy. You can catch a game almost any weekend from April to November at Godwin Stadium off Shipyard Boulevard. For a complete schedule and more information about the always-free events, visit the website, call (910) 465-0535 or become a fan of the Carolina Men's Baseball League on Facebook.

SPECTATOR BASEBALL

Wilmington Sharks
2149 Carolina Beach Rd., Wilmington
(910) 343-5621

There's only one place in Wilmington where you can enjoy a high-level, high-energy baseball game during the summer — a Wilmington Sharks game. The Wilmington Sharks is one of 14 teams in the Coastal Plain League, a summer baseball league featuring players from top college programs around the country. The level of competition is said to be comparable to that of minor league baseball.

Facing teams from North Carolina, South Carolina and Virginia, the Sharks play 56 regular season games, with 30 being home games and an average 1,650 fans per game. The season starts around Memorial Day and is capped by a best-of-three championship playoff in mid-August.

The games are an exciting blend of fun events and sports entertainment. You can grab hot dogs, pizza and chicken between innings; and there are always great weekly promotions. A great attraction for fans of all ages, you can enjoy the baseball tradition splitting peanuts with your kids or sipping adult beverages with your buddies.

Single-ticket prices range from $5 for kids and seniors to $8 for the best seat in the house. Season tickets cost $140 for general admission and $200 for box seats. A Family Pack includes four general admission tickets, four small sodas, four hot dogs and four bags of popcorn all for the family-friendly price of $25. Whatever you do in Wilmington this summer, be sure to check out the Wilmington Sharks, where baseball is fun.

Basketball

Popular year round, but especially in the cooler months, basketball leagues are available for adults, boys and girls throughout our area. Watch the newspapers for information on registration. The following organizations have programs and most are open to the public. Call for specifics.

Wilmington Athletic Club
2026 S. 16th St., Wilmington
(910) 343-5950

Enjoy a game any time of the year on WAC's climate-controlled championship basketball court. The high-quality, hardwood floor was once used in the NCAA women's final four championships and also belonged to the UNCW basketball team for three winning seasons. Reservations are not required. There are sign-up sheets for pick-up games just inside the gymnasium doors. You will often find a pick-up game at lunchtime, in the evenings or on a Saturday afternoon. The adult WAC Basketball League runs from December to February and games are held Monday through Thursday from 7 to 9 PM.

Wilmington Family YMCA
2710 Market St., Wilmington
(910) 251-9622
www.wilmingtonfamilyymca.org

The Wilmington Family YMCA sponsors basketball programs for kids and adults of all ages. The Youth Basketball season runs from December to March and accepts players from ages 3 to 11, including a post-season tournament for the U-12 Junior Division. Teen Basketball features competition in three divisions and accepts players from ages 12 to 18. Practice and league play goes from March to the end of May. Adult basketball leagues run nearly year-round. Women's 18+ runs September to November. Men's 18+ has a summer June to July season and a fall October to November slate. 35+ Men's Basketball runs in September and October, while Men's 55+ operates from November through February (3 v 3 games). All adult leagues finish with a post-season tournament. Registration begins at least 60 to 90 days

prior to each season, and forms are available on the YMCA website.

Wilmington Sea Dawgs
Schwartz Center, 610 N. Front St., Wilmington
(910) 791-6528
www.wilmingtonseadawgs.com

For the past four years, the Wilmington Sea Dawgs have been "unleashing the excitement" of professional basketball in the Port City. The team's record has awarded them a place in the post-season play-offs every year. Playing in the Continental Basketball League and calling Cape Fear Community College's Schwartz Center their home, the Sea Dawgs play an exciting brand of fast-paced hoops that draws substantial crowds and makes fans of first-time attendees. The team participates in many community outreach events and provides discounted or complimentary tickets to most area not-for-profit organizations. Also, each season the team holds open tryouts, making it possible for local hoop stars to have a chance at their dream of pro basketball stardom. Bring the entire family or the neighborhood kids to a Sea Dawgs game and enjoy all the high-flying dunks and sharpshooters this new league has to offer.

Bicycling

A great way to tour much of North Carolina's southern coastal plain is by bicycle. Even with increasing traffic in the cities, country roads tend to be lightly traveled and flat. Although just a few formal "bike paths" exist in the area, there is a system of well-marked "Share The Road" bike routes, some of which have paved bike lanes on both sides of the road that make trekking fairly easy (see the chapter on Getting Here, Getting Around for information about Bike Routes).

In Wilmington, bike registration is encouraged for your protection as it may help you recover your wheels in the event of theft. Most bikes recovered by the police are never claimed and are auctioned off at year's end. You can register your bikes Monday through Saturday 8 AM to 5 PM at police headquarters located at 615 Bess Street, (910) 343-3600 or 2451 South College Road, Wilmington, (910) 341-0111.

New Hanover County sponsors the Wilmington Metropolitan Planning Organization Pedestrian and Bicycle Committee with members representing law enforcement, transportation, planning, recreation, education, commerce and bicycle user groups. Interested persons may apply and are appointed by local governments for two-year terms. A strong supporter of bicycle advocacy, the committee works with local government groups in planning bicycle routes and developing multi-use trails. This is an active group that works hard to promote bicycle safety and transportation.

As part of the nationwide Bicycle Awareness Month in May, the committee supports Bike to Work Week and the annual 20-mile River to the Sea Ride and the Pleasure Island Pedal. For information, contact the New Hanover County Planning Department at (910) 798-7164 or visit their website at www.hncgov.com for bike route descriptions and maps.

Bicycle clubs can be an excellent way to meet other cyclists and learn about places to ride, upcoming events and current issues. In the Greater Wilmington area, check out the Cape Fear Cyclists. This group is touring-oriented, with rides that often are at a casual or moderate pace. For information, visit their website at www.capefearcyclists.org.

In Brunswick County, the Brunswick County Pedalers welcome interested bicycle enthusiasts to join their free membership organization. The club offers monthly rides, recreational and week-long tour cycling events, bicycling education and advocacy and is involved in the helmet drive. It sponsors short, long, slow, fast and social rides as well as training rides with the racers. The website at www.pedalers.southport.org contains a wealth of information about the club.

Several excellent bicycle specialty shops in our area sell new and used bicycles and provide repair services. Some businesses, particularly in beach communities, offer rentals. Rates are typically around $20 to $30 per day.

Two Wheeler Dealer
4408 Wrightsville Ave., Wilmington
(910) 799-6444

One of the largest bicycle shops around, Two Wheeler Dealer stocks a vast array of bicycles, including some vintage models and secondhand bikes, plus touring equipment, tricycles, bike trailers and infant seats — practically anything that rolls on spoked wheels. They also carry a wide variety of accessories. Professional repair work and proper fitting is done on the premises. If you want to connect with local cycling clubs or are looking for racing information, the Two Wheeler Dealer is the place to visit.

Wheel Fun Rentals
107 Carolina Beach Ave. N,
at the Boardwalk, Carolina Beach
(910) 458-4545

Whether you want to rent a tandem or cruiser, this is the place to find wheels in Carolina Beach. You might even want to try out a Deuce Coupe, Chopper or Surrey. Popular anytime, and equipped with lights, the four-wheeled covered Surreys can seat up to six adults and two children. Owners Duke and Tracee Hagestrom promise you a fun ride, no matter what you choose. Call for more information or reservations.

Bowling

Most bowling centers in our area host not only leagues, but also private parties. Some have even added live music and dancing to their lounge entertainment, and all are family-oriented. Competitive prices average about $3.50 to $4 per game for adults on weekends. Prices on weekdays and for children 11 and younger may be lower.

Cardinal Lanes
3907 Shipyard Blvd., Wilmington
(910) 799-3023

Cardinal Lanes offers a host of opportunities for family fun. There is youth league bowling, pee-wee bowling for those 7 and under, and after school bowling clubs sponsored by various New Hanover County schools. Bowling parties are a fun and inexpensive way to celebrate a special occasion. The two-hour deluxe party package includes bowling, ball and shoe rental, game tokens, soft drinks, pizza and helium balloons. Cardinal Lanes provides a safe and fun place for children to come and bowl. Cardinal Lanes has a snack bar with a variety of menu items including draft beer on tap, a game room and 32 lanes. They are open Monday through Thursday from 9 AM to midnight, Friday from 9 AM to 1 AM and Saturday and Sunday from 10 AM to midnight.

Planet Fun
349 Whiteville Road, Shallotte
(910) 755-2386

Inside Planet Fun you will find the Constellation Bowling Alley with 32 Qubica AMF synthetic lanes and 32-inch flat screen monitors. Leagues for all ages and levels are offered. The facility includes Starz Grille. Thursday from 6 PM to 10PM is family fun night with special rates for families who bowl together.

Break Time Grille & Ten Pin Alley
Marketplace Mall, 127 S. College Rd., Wilmington
(910) 452-5455

Wilmington's popular billiards hall and bowling alley includes a sports bar and casual restaurant. It has 24 lanes of bowling and arcade-style diversions. Families are welcome. Call for information about bowling leagues. Neat attire is required. It's open 11 AM until 2 AM, and food service is available until closing.

Thunder Alley
1224 Magnolia Village Way, Leland
(910) 371-0119

Thunder Alley is a state of the art, digitalized bowling alley. More than that , it is a place for family fun and includes two mini-bowling lanes for those who cannot handle the heavier balls. You will also find four 210-inch satellite screens that drop down at the ends of the lanes, private rooms for relaxing, a corporate meeting room, a room designed for birthday parties, a 2,700-square-foot arcade, and a full-service grille and coffee shop. All this in addition to leagues, clinics and camps.

Boxing

City of Wilmington Boxing and Physical Fitness Center
302 S. 10th St., Wilmington
(910) 341-7872

The City of Wilmington Boxing and Physical Fitness Center offers individuals and families opportunities to participate in traditional health-club activities. Equipped with free weights, weight machines, boxing bags, treadmills, cross trainers, stationary bicycles and stairclimbers, the center offers strength training, prescription exercise and cardiovascular workouts. Classes in aerobics, dance and yoga are also offered. Locker rooms and shower facilities are available. Memberships are among the best bargains in town, just $50 for city residents and $85 for those living outside the city or outside of New Hanover County. Hours are Monday through Wednesday 6 AM to 8:00 PM, Thursdays and Fridays from 6 AM to 7 PM and Saturday 9 AM to 12 PM. The center is closed on Sunday.

Fitness Centers

Many fine fitness centers along the coast offer state-of-the-art equipment and certified instructors. Aerobics, Pilates and yoga classes are standard, as are bikes, treadmills, free weights, elliptical trainers and other equipment. Membership costs usually include a one-time registration fee plus a monthly fee for a required term, but some local centers cater to the short-term visitor by offering daily, weekly and monthly rates. Additional benefits at some clubs are referral rewards, travel passes that allow members to visit affiliated clubs around the country and suspension of membership for medical reasons or extended absences. The larger, more sophisticated clubs offer a variety of amenities that may include a well-stocked pro shop, food bar or cafe serving healthy snacks and drinks, locker room facilities, nutritional supplement sales, tanning beds, spas,

A good rule of thumb: If you packed it in then pack it out. Leave only your footprints behind.

photo: Chris Tisinger

massages, child care and even laundry and dry-cleaning pickup/delivery.

Cape Fear Fitness
1513-14 N. Howe St., Southport
(910) 457-0085

Cape Fear Fitness is a full service fitness center with personal trainers available as well as group classes, a free weight area, a cardio area, a tanning area and a smoothie bar. Group classes include spinning, kick boxing, body sculpt, Karate and yoga and are available for a nominal fee. Yearly, monthly, weekly, daily and seasonal memberships are available.

City of Wilmington Boxing and Physical Fitness Center
302 S. 10th St., Wilmington
(910) 341-7872

The Boxing and Physical Fitness Center provides individuals and families opportunities to participate in traditional health-club activities. Equipped with free weights, weight machines, treadmills, stationary bicycles, cross trainers and stairclimbers, the center offers strength training, prescription exercise and cardiovascular workouts. Classes in modern aerobics/step, yogalates, basic boxing and cardio kickboxing are taught by certified instructors. Locker rooms and shower

facilities are available. Memberships are among the best bargains in town, just $50 for city residents and $85 for those living outside the city or outside of New Hanover County. Hours are Monday through Wednesday 6 AM to 8 PM, Thursday through Friday 6 AM to 7 PM and Saturday 9 AM to 12 PM. The center is closed on Sunday.

The Crest Seaside Fitness Club
6766 Wrightsville Ave., Wrightsville Beach
(910) 509-3044
14653 N. U.S. Hwy. 17, Hampstead
(910) 270-3049

Looking for a hassle-free place to work out? Forget about waiting in lines at The Crest because they have the most equipment per member around. Whether you're interested in circuit training or group classes like Zumba, Pilates or yoga, the fitness professionals at The Crest can guide you through the perfect workout. You will have fun while you tone and tighten, get stronger, lose weight and increase your energy. After a good workout and a relaxing massage at their day spa, enjoy a tall glass of something wonderful at the Phuza Smoothie Juice Bar. With two convenient locations and free child care, The Crest truly is hassle-free. Locally owned and operated since 1984, check out The Crest with a free seven-day membership.

Forever Fit
214 Sneads Ferry Rd., Sneads Ferry
(910) 327-2293

Forever Fit focuses on a balanced approach to fitness and offers yoga, strength training and a full line of cardio equipment plus group training in step, circuit and dance. There is a personal trainer on staff, along with AFAA–certified instructors. Visitors are welcome and can pay either daily or weekly rates. Individual memberships begin as low as $39 per month. Forever Fit is convenient to the northern Topsail Island area.

Gold's Gym
7979 Market St., Porter's Neck, Wilmington
(910) 686-1766
200 Racine Dr., Wilmington
(910) 392-3999
5051 Main St., Shallotte
(910) 754-2270
Longleaf Mall, 4310 Shipyard Blvd., Wilmington
(910) 350-8289

Gold's Gym, a full-service fitness center known for its attentive staff and its array of top-flight equipment and classes, has four locations on the southern coast. Noted for personally designed exercise programs and one-on-one training by certified trainers, all locations offer the newest circuit, cardiovascular and hammer-strength equipment available. They have free child care, locker rooms with showers, and dry saunas. Gold's pro-shops offer sports clothing, smoothie bars and a large selection of supplements and power bars. Group exercise classes vary at each club, ranging from yoga and Pilates to Power Punch, Body Pump, Body Flow and senior classes. The Racine Drive location offers a Women Only area and the Porter's Neck location has a Guppies program for kids. Members of Gold's Gym are entitled to unlimited use of 13 locations in the Carolinas and 650-plus other locations worldwide.

Second Wind Fitness Center
98 Quarter Horse Ln., Hampstead
(910) 270-4044

Perfect for the workout buff or the beginner, Second Wind has treadmills, stationary bikes, a complete line of circuit machines and free weights. Second Wind Fitness Center also has the area's only full-sized heated pool. Surf and turf aerobics are offered in the pool and on the 1,680-square-foot suspended aerobic floor. Personal trainers and certified fitness professionals are on hand to help you design a workout program that fits your needs. Second Wind also has a dry-heat sauna, tanning beds, a juice bar and day care while you're working out. Swimming lessons are available. Day passes and memberships are offered, and Second Wind is open seven days a week.

Wilmington Athletic Club
2026 S. 16th St., Wilmington
(910) 343-5950

Wilmington Athletic Club (WAC), is a great place to work out, play, indulge yourself and improve your health status. Locally owned and operated, this outstanding facility has just about everything you could want or need, from state-of-the-art Pilates and cardiovascular training equipment to a complete day spa. A long list of available activities includes volleyball, basketball, racquetball, squash, badminton, swimming and running. The competition-size outdoor pool is heated for year-round swim lessons, aqua aerobics classes and fun. Personal training, VO2 max assessments, weight management, sport-specific training, senior fitness programs, social events, youth camps and massage therapy are just a few of the special features that make the Wilmington Athletic Club an all-around great place for the entire family. Activity-oriented child care is available while mom or dad work out, and a terrific after-school program is available to keep kids busy and constructively occupied. The Wilmington Athletic Club, open seven days a week to members and their guests, is affiliated with the International Health, Racquet and Sports Club Association (IHRSA) and offers reciprocity privileges through its Passport Program. Members may use affiliated facilities around the world for free or at a discounted rate.

Wilmington Family YMCA
2710 Market St., Wilmington
(910) 251-9622
www.wilmingtonfamilyymca.org

Offering a wide variety of fitness and educational activities, the Wilmington Family YMCA features ample facilities, such as a large gymnasium, two indoor pools, a hot tub, four racquetball courts, a free-weight room, Cybex equipment, cardio theater and even sunbathing decks. Athletic fields, including an outdoor track, are also available and league sports for youth and adults are organized seasonally.

Aerobics (including land and water exercise), Zumba, kettle bells, Physiability and arthritis classes, yoga, Pilates and Spinning are just a few of the Y's vast offerings. The Wilmington Family YMCA also includes and supports persons living with a disability or a chronic medical condition. Exercise programs are individualized to meet the needs and adapted group exercise classes are offered weekly.

The YMCA's new Kids Zone is outfitted with interactive cardio equipment such as Dance Dance Revolution, Game Bikes, Wii and Total Body strength training equipment. Kid Zone classes run each hour between 4:30 PM and 7:30 PM Monday through Friday and between 9 AM and Noon on Saturdays. Kid Zone classes are free with membership.

YWCA of the Lower Cape Fear
2815 S. College Rd., Wilmington
(910) 799-6820

Health and wellness activities at the YWCA include belly dancing, tap, modern jazz dance, and tri-club classes. Especially for youth are La Petite and Thereputic dance, and golf. A full aquatics program offers swim lessons, lifeguard and water safety instructor classes, synchronized swimming, water aerobics, a swim team and pool rentals for parties.

Football

League football beyond the scholastic realm is offered primarily by two organiz-

ing bodies, the Pop Warner program and Brunswick County Parks and Recreation. Look into registration in May or June as most teams start practice early in August.

COASTAL POP WARNER

Pop Warner organizes tackle football and cheerleading teams for boys and girls age 7 through 14 in Pee Wee, Junior Pee Wee, Midget and Mighty Mights divisions. Flag football for 5- and 6-year-olds is offered, too. More than 1,800 youngsters in New Hanover, Pender and Brunswick counties participate in the Pop Warner program each year. Games are played at Ogden Park. For schedule and team information visit their website.

Martial Arts

Whether it's the the open-hand style of karate or the throws and take-downs of Ju-Jitsu that interest you, or it's self-defense, confidence, physical fitness and competition you desire, it's all available in our region. Martial arts schools are proliferating, with many offering family rates and classes.

Cape Fear Martial Arts Center
7134 Market St., Unit 6, Wilmington
(910) 686-2678

Specializing in Hap Ki Do, the Cape Fear Martial Arts Center has been providing martial arts education since 1997. Hap Ki Do is a versatile martial art, emphasizing circular movements and leverage as opposed to physical strength and brute force. For this reason, Hap Ki Do is suitable for every one of all ages. In addition to self defense, some of Hap Ki Do's benefits are self discipline, self confidence, increased concentration and mental strength.

Champion Fitness and Mixed Martial Arts
147 S. College Rd., Ste. 109, Wilmington
(910) 792-1131

As one of the originators of Kickbox Fitness and its concept, owner/instructor John Maynard offers this high-energy, fat-burning, fun work-out at his Wilmington studio. Champion's highly qualified team of instructors can help you achieve your fitness goals through mixed classes for men and women in kickboxing, kickbox fitness and Brazilian Jiu Jitso. They also offer kids' karate.

Shaolin Kempo Martial Arts
4718 Oleander Dr., Wilmington
(910) 793-1161

Stressing physical fitness, flexibility, confidence, coordination and balance, this school uses a well-rounded system with Kempo, Ju-Jitsu, Kung-Fu and weapons. Quality not quantity is the main concern here. Classes are small to enhance the learning process. Head instructor Brian Watkins is a Shihan 5th Degree Black Belt who has had experience in this system since 1982; his wife, Christine, is also an experienced instructor. They invite individuals ages 10 and older to become part of their family in learning. Both day and evening classes are available.

Wilmington Family YMCA
2710 Market St., Wilmington
(910) 251-9622
www.wilmingtonfamilyymca.org

Four evenings a week the Wilmington Family YMCA offers ancient martial arts. There's Karate on Monday and Wednesday from 7:30 to 8:30 PM and Tae Kwon Do on Tuesday and Thursdays from 7 to 8:30 PM. These classes are not just for self defense, they also condition and train the spirit, mind and body for better overall mental and physical health. Call the YMCA at ext 253 for more information.

Racquetball

In addition to these listings, check the Fitness Centers section in this chapter to locate those that have racquetball courts.

Wilmington Athletic Club
2026 S. 16th St., Wilmington
(910) 343-5950

With six championship courts, two of them glass-backed for stadium viewing, the Wilmington Athletic Club is a great place to play racquetball. Daily challenge courts ensure you'll find a game any day of the week. The club also offers instruction, challenge ladders and some of the top competitive events in the region.

Wilmington Family YMCA
2710 Market St., Wilmington
(910) 251-9622
www.wilmingtonfamilyymca.org

Four racquetball courts are available at the Wilmington Family YMCA, and reservations are recommended. They have challenge courts and racquetball games. Use of the facility is free with a Y membership, or guests can purchase a $10 day pass. An annual tournament is offered every fall.

Races

Races are popular in our area, thanks to the gentle terrain and mild weather. Just a few of the regulars are listed here, but if you keep an eye on the Star-News "Sports," "Today" and "Neighbors" sections, you'll likely find more. Some places in Wilmington to pick up event brochures and fliers are **Boseman's Sporting Goods**, 5050 New Centre Drive, Wilmington, (910) 799-5990; **Dick's Sporting Goods**, 816 S. College Road, Wilmington, (910) 793-1904; **Great Outdoor Provision Company**, 3501 Oleander Drive, Wilmington, (910) 343-1648; **Omega Sports**, 3501 Oleander Drive, Wilmington, (910) 762-7212; **Play It Again Sports**, 3530 S. College Road, Wilmington, (910) 791-1572; and **Wilmington Family YMCA**, 2710 Market Street, Wilmington, (910) 251-9622.

NEW HANOVER COUNTY

Battleship NORTH CAROLINA Half-Marathon and Bay Six 5K
Battleship NORTH CAROLINA,
1 Battleship Rd., Wilmington
(910) 251-5797
www.battleshipnc.com

The Carolina Sports Medicine Battleship NORTH CAROLINA Half Marathon (13.1 miles) and Bay Six 5K (3.1 miles) is a challenging race that starts and finishes at the Battleship NORTH CAROLINA. The half-marathon is a USATF–certified course that goes over two bridges, passes through Historic Downtown Wilmington, tours beautiful Greenfield Lake, crosses the Cape Fear Memorial bridge and returns to the battleship. It is the largest half-marathon in the state. A new state record was set on this course in 2009, and

two state records were set on this course in 2007. The 5K is a precisely measured out-and-back course that crosses one bridge, makes a U-turn and returns to the battleship.

This event is presented annually in November by Ed Fore in cooperation with the staff of the Battleship NORTH CARO-LINA Memorial and members of the local running community. The race features chip timing, river taxi and trolley buses to race start, a Saturday Expo/packet pickup at the Battleship Memorial, an awards ceremony overlooking the beautiful Cape Fear River and free beer after the race. Proceeds benefit the Battleship Restoration Fund, The Leukemia and Lymphoma Society TNT, the Cape Fear Literacy Council and several other local charities. The 2010 race date is November 7.

Azalea 5K + TriSpan 10K and 5K
2710 Market St., Wilmington
(910) 251-9622
www.wilmingtonfamilyymca.org

Sponsored by the Wilmington Family YMCA and several area businesses, the Wilmington Orthopedic Azalea 5K Run is held in May and the 28th Annual Maus, Warwick & Matthews Tri-Span 10K and 5K takes place in July. The 10K course crosses three bridges along the Wilmington waterfront, and the 5K goes through historic downtown Wilmington. The YMCA also hosts the largest triathlon from Washington, D.C. to Florida in September. This sprint triathlon held at Wrightsville Beach is sponsored by Maus, Warwick & Matthews. In early November the YMCA hosts its third annual Iron and Half Iron Distance races called Beach 2 Battleship. Sign up for races at the Set Up Events, Inc. website at www.setupevents.com. Money raised from these special events goes to the YMCA We Build People Campaign for after-school programs and scholarship memberships to the YMCA. Call Wendy Lamb at the YMCA for detailed information.

BRUNSWICK COUNTY

N.C. Fourth of July Festival Freedom Run
Southport-Oak Island
Chamber of Commerce,
4841 Long Beach Rd. SE, Southport
(910) 457-6964, (800) 457-6964

The annual 5K Freedom Run in Southport is an integral part of the N.C. Fourth of July Festival activities. The early morning race, which has attracted runners from as far away as Arizona, begins at Waterfront Park, heads west on Bay Street, then winds through the Yacht Basin onto Brunswick, W. West, Atlantic, Leonard, Fodale, Moore and Rhett streets and finishes right where it started. Refreshments and live music await all participants.

Oak Island Lighthouse 10K/5K Run/Walk
4841 Long Beach Rd. SE, Southport
(910) 457-6964, (800) 457-6964

The route of this popular 10K run/walk begins at the Brunswick County Airport, crosses the Oak Island Bridge, turns through tree-lined streets, follows the beachfront and ends just past the Oak Island Lighthouse at the N.C. Baptist Assembly. Awards are given to the three top runners overall and the three top runners in each age group. The 5K run begins at the Caswell Beach Town Hal,l and there is a 1-mile fun run for the children on the grounds of the N.C. Baptist Assembly. Come join the competition!

Soccer

As youth and adult soccer leagues continue to grow in popularity, area fields are constantly busy on weekends. Perhaps the best news for parents and players is that the investment necessary to play soccer is fairly low, generally limited to a one-time registration fee in the neighborhood of $65 to $75 and shin guards that can cost less than $30. Wilmington is home to the United Soccer League's professional team, the Wilmington Hammerheads.

See this entire guide plus additional content online at insiderinfo.us

Cape Fear Soccer Association
314 N. Green Meadows Dr., Unit 100, Wilmington
(910) 392-0306

With more than 200 teams and 2,500 players participating in several divisions, Cape Fear Soccer Association (CFSA) is the leading soccer organization in south-eastern North Carolina and the fourth largest in the state. CFSA provides players (men, women, boys and girls) with the op-portunity to play soccer at their own level of competition. Emphasis is placed on the development of soccer skills, participa-tion, sportsmanship and enjoyment of the game.

Youngsters ages 4 to 8 play non-competitively, while scores and standings are kept for teams 9 years and older. Boys and girls play separately from U7 through U18. Teams are divided into Recreational, Challenge and Classic youth leagues. The Challenge league is comprised of teams from throughout North Carolina's south-eastern counties. The Wilmington-based teams train with professional coaches twice a week in a structured environment on some of the best soccer fields in the state. An Adult League on Sundays and a 7 v 7 league in the evenings is also offered for players over 18 years of age.

Wilmington Family YMCA
2710 Market St., Wilmington
(910) 251-9622
www.wilmingtonfamilyymca.org

Youth coed soccer is offered in the spring and summer. Organized games are played March to May and September to November. The Y now operates youth soccer leagues in both Wilmington and Pender County. This program is offered to youth 3 to 16 years of age. U-12 girls soc-cer is also now available. Most games are on Saturdays. U-12, U-14, U-16 and U-18 age groups are affiliated with North Carolina Youth Soccer. Travel tournament teams are also available for U-16, U-14 and U-12.

Too cold to play? The Wilmington Family YMCA also sponsors youth and adult league futsal, the exciting brand of indoor soccer played on a gymnasium floor — it was actually invented in the 1930s in a YMCA in Uruguay. Recreation and competitive co-ed leagues run from December through February complete with a season-ending tournament.

Tennis

Practically every large park and many smaller neighborhood parks have public tennis courts (see the Parks section at the end of this chapter). The Legion Sports Complex on Carolina Beach Road has four lighted courts that are open until 11 PM seven days a week, no reservation required. For city parks information call (910) 341-7855. Watch the local papers for tournament information.

City of Wilmington Parks, Recreation and Downtown Services
302 Willard St., Wilmington
(910) 341-7855

PeeWee tennis for ages 4 through 8 takes place April through November. Junior and adult clinics also run from April through November. Play is at Empie Park. Call Mike Scott at 794-6702 for more information and registration forms.

Greater Wilmington Tennis Association
8825 Sawmill Creek Ln., Porter's Neck, Wilmington
(910) 686-5457

Over the past few years, tennis has grown by leaps and bounds in the Cape Fear area. To help support and promote the sport, the Greater Wilmington Tennis Association (GWTA) was formed. GWTA is a non-profit, all-volunteer organiza-tion for all tennis activities in the area, with more than 3,500 active players of all ages and skill levels. In affiliation with the North Carolina chapter of the United States Tennis Association (USTA), GWTA sponsors USTA-sanctioned leagues and events for both adults and juniors. The group also sponsors local clinics, social events, fun tournaments, an after-school tennis program for middle-school children, the Wilmington Adult and Junior Ten-nis Ladders, tennis programs for children with disabilities, and USA Team Tennis programs for children of all skill levels.

Adult league teams range in level from 2.5 to 5.0 and include men's and women's singles, doubles, mixed doubles, combo league (mixed levels of play) and Super Seniors ages 60 and 70 years young. One of the organization's main projects is to make tennis available to youth through after-school programs and to make tennis part of the schools' physical education curricula. Through grants, special events and other funding, GWTA has donated more than $25,000 in tennis equipment to schools and youth organizations. Any USTA member or Wilmington Tennis Ladder (WTL) participant residing in New Hanover, Brunswick or Pender counties is automatically a member of GWTA. Check out their website at www.wilmingtontennis.com or call them for more information or to sign up for a league or a ladder.

Tennis with Love
4303 Oleander Dr., Wilmington
(910) 791-3128

If your racket needs repair or you need a new tennis outfit, stop by Tennis with Love in the Landmark Plaza across from Capital Ford. This shop specializes in same-day restringing for tennis and racquetball frames and carries court clothing, shoes and accessories. They're open Monday through Saturday from 10 AM to 6 PM.

Triathlons

Triathlons are very popular in this area. For further opportunities, also check the section on Running and Walking in this chapter.

Azalea Triathlon
Set-Up, Inc., Wilmington
(864) 271-4262

Because this event is so popular, the Azalea Triathlon is held on two consecutive days. This triathlon, sanctioned by USA Triathlon, consists of a 300-yard pool swim, a 10-mile bike race and a 5K run. Except for some of the bike leg, the entire triathlon takes place on the UNCW campus during Spring Break, typically mid-March. Contestants are divided into the nationally standard age and gender

brackets. Registration for the event begins in early January. For registration forms and more information, visit www.setupevents.com.

Kure Beach Double Sprint Triathlon
Set-Up, Inc., Wilmington
(910) 458-0299

Here's an event tailored for overachievers. After you get through the 375-meter ocean swim, the 1.5-mile run and the 10K bike leg, guess what? You get to do the entire thing all over again — in reverse — bike, run and swim. The overall distance is less than half that of an Olympic triathlon, but considering that this USA Triathlon–sanctioned race is in the heat of late June, the challenge is formidable. Contestants are divided into the nationally standard age and gender brackets. Call or visit www.setupevents.com for registration forms and information.

Wilmington Athletic Club
2026 S. 16th St., Wilmington
(910) 343-5950

Whether you're a beginner or an experienced triathlete, you can train for your next triathlon at Wilmington Athletic Club. They offer running clinics, stride analysis and group runs to assist in running training. Regular swims, stroke analysis and underwater photography of your style will help in swim training, while indoor studio training and outdoor group rides focus on cycling. In addition, your training regime includes transition clinics to pull the whole thing together, as well as nutrition counseling. Train for one triathlon or for the whole season. It's a great way to stay fit and satisfy the competitor in you.

Wilmington Family YMCA Triathlon Club
2710 Market St., Wilmington
(910) 251-9622
www.wilmingtonfamilyymca.org

More than 100 members strong, the YMCA Triathlon Club offers a broad range of training opportunities and times as well as informative workshops. Whether you are a newcomer to the sport or training for an Ironman, they can get you on track and be there to cheer you at the finish line. For more information click the Tri Club logo on their website.

Wilmington Family YMCA
Kids Triathlon Club
2710 Market St., Wilmington
(910) 251-9622
www.wilmingtonfamilyymca.org

The YMCA Kids Triathlon Club holds two clubs and two races each year for children ages 5 through 13.The first Kids Tri Club kicks off in March and the first Kids Triathlon is held in mid-May. The second Kids Tri Club kicks off in June and the second Kids Triathlon is scheduled for mid-August. Mileage is adjusted for different age groups, and practice runs prepare youngsters for the competition. In addition, kids learn about bike safety, transitioning, swimming techniques and healthy eating habits. Call the YMCA at extension 253 for details.

Volleyball

If you're not accustomed to playing volleyball in sand, you're in for a real workout, and if you survive, your improved agility and jumping may serve you better on a hard court. As you might expect, competition is fairly stiff, and local players generally take their games seriously. Sand volleyball courts are common in area parks and beaches, and anyone can use them, so enjoy!

Capt'n Bill's Backyard Grill
4240 Market St., Wilmington
(910) 762-0111

The only sand courts within the Wilmington city limits can be found at this popular volleyball-restaurant complex behind the Market Street Plaza. Year round, you can join a pickup game on one of ten courts or register your team in one of Capt'n Bill's leagues, which are for all skill levels. Operated by the husband and wife team of John and Erin Musser, Capt'n Bill's has a friendly staff, hot food, cold drinks, three bars, outside and inside seating and 15 TV sets.

Wilmington Athletic Club
2026 S. 16th St., Wilmington
(910) 343-5950

The region's largest, most complete fitness facility, Wilmington Athletic Club (WAC) offers great volleyball on its "Court of Champions." Call about pick-up games or seasonal league play.

Wilmington Family YMCA
2710 Market St., Wilmington
(910) 251-9622
www.wilmingtonfamilyymca.org

Enjoy indoor volleyball on the Y's two full-sized regulation courts. Adult co-ed play runs from December through early March, concluding with a post-season tournament. A Women's League may also be offered, with the actual season to be determined.

Yoga, Pilates and Tai Chi

In addition to the listings below, some fitness centers also offer yoga, Pilates and Tai Chi classes. To find individual instructors, look for business cards and advertisements in local publications. Frequently, chiropractic offices, coffee shops and health-food stores have yoga, Pilates and Tai Chi information available.

Harmony Yoga
5201 Oleander Dr., Wilmington

Michele Martin, formerly of Seaside Yoga, invites all her friends and yoga enthusiasts to Harmony Yoga. This delightful yoga studio feels like home and offers a wide range of classes for all skills levels.

Offerings
807 N. Howe St., Southport
(910) 616-4391

Offerings is a donations only studio where you can try yoga, Tai Chi and Pilates without making a commitment or signing a contract. In fact, the amount of your donation is up to you. Some people barter services or donate home-grown vegetables. The instructors give their services as well — donations are used to pay the rent

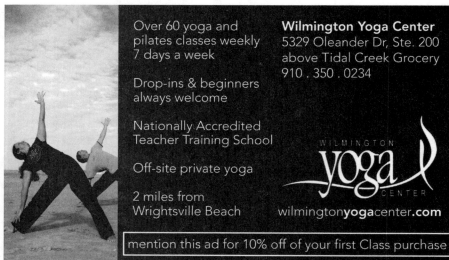

for the building. Class schedules and information are available at the number listed.

Porters Neck Yoga & Spa
8044 Market St., Wilmington
(910) 686-6440

A full-service day spa, acupuncture and yoga studio, Porters Neck Yoga & Spa offers classes and individual instruction in yoga and Pilates. Their schedule includes more than 25 classes with a variety of yoga styles, including Anusara, Beginner & Basic Yoga, Hot Yoga, Ashtanga and Restorative. Porters Neck Yoga & Spa also has yoga cards, gift certificates and gift packages. Hours are Monday through Friday 9 AM to 7 PM, Saturday 9 AM to 5 PM and Sunday 10 AM to 4 PM .

Wilmington Athletic Club
2026 S. 16th St., Wilmington
(910) 343-5950

The Wilmington Athletic Club (WAC) features spacious studios. Classes are held daily in various concentrations of yoga and Pilates and are taught by top instructors. Tai Chi is also available.

Wilmington Family YMCA
2710 Market St., Wilmington
(910) 251-9622
www.wilmingtonfamilyymca.org

The YMCA offers a large variety of yoga and Pilates classes that improve flexibility, posture and balance while strengthening muscles. Allow the experience to unify your mind, body, and spirit. Classes are offered daily and all levels welcome. Belly dancing classes are also available. All classes are free to YMCA members or a day guest pass is available for $10.

Wilmington Yoga Center
5329 Oleander Dr., Ste. 200, Wilmington
(910) 350-0234
www.wilmingtonyogacenter.com

Located above Tidal Creek Health Food Market on Oleander Dr., the Wilmington Yoga Center offers the one of largest variety of yoga & Pilates classes in the Southeast. Open 7-days a week, over 50 classes are offered in their beautiful 3000 sqft space where drop-in students are always welcome. Certified teachers take great care in providing individualized attention while guiding you safely through your practice, no matter if you are a beginner or advanced student. Throughout the year they offer beginner and advanced teacher trainings, private & group-private sessions (on and off site), international retreats, fund-raisers for non-profits and professional trainings in the healing arts.

GOLF

Golfers appreciate the southern coast's relaxed, laid-back feeling. Great weather, beautiful views, majestic long-leaf pines, stately live oaks and flat to gently rolling land are just a few of the reasons golf is popular here. Plus, most of the local courses offer prices that encourage multiple rounds per day.

More new golf courses sprout up along the southern coast than anywhere else in North Carolina. Brunswick County alone boasts dozens of courses, many located in residential golf communities. The area features challenging course designs bearing the signatures of Arnold Palmer, Rees Jones, Tom Fazio, Pete Dye, Jack Nicklaus, Dan Maples, Donald Ross, Hale Irwin, Fred Couples, Tim Cate, George Cobb, Clyde Johnston and Willard Byrd, among others.

Most local courses are semiprivate, which means they're open to the public and club memberships are available. Membership, of course, offers various benefits and privileges, such as lower fees or preferred tee times. Greens fees vary according to season and location. At semiprivate courses, fees range widely, from about $30 to $100 and more, but average between $30 and $50 for 18 holes. Fees are highest at the more exclusive clubs and during the peak seasons (March 1 to mid-May and mid-September to early November). Look for special packages during non-peak times, such as three rounds at drastically reduced prices for either morning or afternoon. Discounts for seniors, corporations and groups are commonplace.

Overall, the region's courses offer an excellent balance between price and playing conditions. Many courses also offer practice ranges and club rentals. Teaching pros are plentiful and eager to help you polish your game. You'll find a proliferation of golf publications at visitors centers, hotels and other touristy locations.

In this chapter we describe some of the area's better courses, judged by overall beauty, location and variety of challenge. We've also included independent driving ranges, retail shops that offer equipment and repairs, information about golf packages and services and a listing of some local annual tournaments. Complete listings of courses can be found at chambers of commerce (see our Area Overviews chapter for a listing of local chambers).

Courses

WILMINGTON

Beau Rivage Resort & Golf Club
649 Rivage Promenade, Wilmington
(910) 392-9021, (800) 628-7080

Elevations up to 72 feet and scads of bunkers (including two waste bunkers) place this course among the more dramatically landscaped in New Hanover County. It is a semiprivate par 72 course in which water hazards come into play on eight holes. Hole 4 (206 yards, par 3) is notable for its island tee box for women and a carry that is entirely over water. The course's greens, made of a genetically engineered form of bermudagrass called ultra dwarf TifEagle, are well maintained and quite pleasing to golfers. Beau Rivage offers a fully stocked golf shop, PGA instruction and club rental. Memberships are available. A bar and grill serving breakfast and lunch provides an attractive setting for post-round analysis. If you need a break from your game, there's a pool and tiki bar and tennis courts. A 32-suite hotel adjoins the clubhouse. Formal banquet facilities accommodating up to 250 guests are popular for weddings, corporate retreats and family reunions.

Country Club of Landfall
800 Sun Runner Pl., Wilmington
(910) 256-8411

Golfing on Landfall's two superlative courses, designed by Jack Nicklaus and Pete Dye and situated along the Intracoastal Waterway, is for members (and their guests) of Country Club of Landfall. The rewards for golfing members include challenges unparalleled on the majority of courses.

The par 72 Nicklaus course has added another nine holes, giving it a total of 27. Overall, the Nicklaus course is perhaps the less forgiving of the two. It looks easier on paper than it really is, thanks largely to the many carries over marshes and water. The "Marsh" 6th hole, for instance, is a tough par 3 playing 191 yards from the back, with little more than marsh all the way to the green. The "Ocean" 8th hole's island green is backed with a bunker with a 5-foot forward lip. Another island green is the signature hole on the Dye course. Completely water-bound, hole 2 slopes away from the sand trap that collars half its perimeter. The Dye course is a par 72. Plenty of uneven lies, marshes and pot bunkers demand that players push the envelope of their game to the utmost.

Members also have access to Landfall's elaborate sports center, which has 14 tennis courts (with grass, clay and hard surfaces) and an Olympic-size pool. In addition, members enjoy a fitness center, aerobics room and spa services, as well as a casual grill, formal dining rooms and lots of exciting social activities.

Echo Farms Golf & Country Club
4114 Echo Farms Blvd., Wilmington
(910) 791-9318

Echo Farms features beautiful stands of moss-draped hardwood and some of the finest TifEagle greens in the area. Links-style course and bunkers make for a challenging game. A former dairy farm (the original farmhouse near the 17th hole is still occupied), it's now a par 72 challenge. Water comes into play on many holes. A driving range, practice greens, grill, bar and snack lounge are open to all. Echo Farms has developed a fine teach-

ing facility that offers clinics and private lessons. The course is 5 miles south of downtown Wilmington off Carolina Beach Road (N.C. Highway 421).

Porters Neck Plantation and Country Club
8204 Fazio Dr., Wilmington
(910) 686-8180
www.porters-neck.com

Porters Neck Plantation is an aficionado's course, aesthetically perfect and strategically challenging. Designed by world renowned golf architect Tom Fazio, this is a par 72 championship course that emphasizes careful club selection. The wide and impeccably maintained fairways undulate in a sometimes deceptive fashion. Distinctive waste mounds planted with native grasses and lakes that span from tee to green (holes 11, 13, 14) add to the course's character. Each hole presents conditions to make the most accurate golfer uncomfortable, yet leave no player unfulfilled. It is no surprise that the 18-hole course was ranked number one on the North Carolina coast by Golf Digest. The course at Porters Neck Plantation and Country Club winds through a private, gated residential development adjacent to the Intracoastal Waterway and just north of Wilmington. Public play is invited but limited. Golfers also have access to a full-service pro shop, PGA–trained staff and a beautiful Federal-style clubhouse. The entrance gate is approximately 1 mile from the property limit on Porters Neck Road. Visit the Porters Neck website for a virtual tour of the course.

Wilmington Golf Course
311 S. Wallace Ave., Wilmington
(910) 791-0558

You'll find this 1926 Donald Ross classic nestled in the heart of Wilmington. Measuring 6,564 yards, the course, known as the "Muni", is challenging yet enjoyable regardless of one's ability. Wilmington Golf Course features the area's most affordable rates and allows golfers the option of walking at any time. Perhaps the most unique design feature of the course is the grass-banked bunkering. Get in the wrong spot and you could be in for an adventure! The course annually hosts the Wilmington City Amateur, attracting top local and state golfers. For tee times book up to one week in advance.

BALD HEAD ISLAND

The Bald Head Island Club
Bald Head Island
(910) 457-7300, (866) 657-7311

If your idea of heaven is an island golf course that can be reached only by boat or ferry, where cars are banned in favor of golf carts and the course extends across an expanse of dunes overlooking the Atlantic Ocean, The Bald Head Island Club is bound to fulfill your fantasy. Much of this George Cobb–designed course follows the natural terrain carved by wind and water, like the first courses in Scotland. Exposed greens on its ocean side contrast sharply with interior holes, where palms, maritime forests and the natural wildlife habitats surround the holes. Awarded 4.5 stars from Golf Digest's Places to Play and extremely demanding, due as much to the ocean wind as to the late George Cobb's brilliant design, this 18-hole, par 72 championship course is among the scenic gems on the East Coast. A complete practice facility and snack bar are available as well.

SOUTHPORT AND OAK ISLAND

Oak Island Golf & Country Club
928 Caswell Beach Rd., Caswell Beach
(910) 278-5275, (800) 278-5275

One of Brunswick County's vintage courses, this George Cobb creation on Oak Island was designed in 1962. It is a forgiving course (6720 yard, par 72 from the back tees) that can be enjoyed by players of varying skills. Its wide bermudagrass fairways are relatively short, lined with live oaks and tall pines and not overly fortified with water hazards. But that ocean wind! The clubhouse is less than 200 yards from the Atlantic, and sea breezes can frustrate even the best players. Hole 9 may send you to Duffers Pub and Grill early. Even so, the TifEagle greens, driving range, putting green and swimming pool make this course quite popular.

South Harbour Golf Links
South Harbor Village, 4188 Vanessa Dr., Oak Island
(910) 454-0905

Operated by the Town of Oak Island, South Harbour Golf Links is an 18-hole executive par three course. This exciting course is woven within South Harbour Village and nestled along the Intracoastal Waterway between historic Southport and the beaches of Oak Island. Designed for a challenging and fun experience, the course has a layout that all levels of golfers can enjoy. Rental clubs and golf carts are available, as are a pro shop, food and beverage, a practice area and a putting green. Soft spikes only please. Memberships are available. Lessons for kids and adults, tournaments and camps are offered.

St. James Plantation - The Members Club
St. James Plantation, U.S. Hwy. 211, Southport
(910) 253-3008, (800) 247-4806

Opened in 1996, this Hale Irwin–designed, par 72 course utilizes the natural lay of the land to good effect, forgoing flashy, amusement-park landscaping. The course has been called user-friendly, although its proximity to the Intracoastal Waterway means winds can be deeply trying. Watch out for the 15th hole, a par 5 with lateral water hazards squeezing the fairway into a bottleneck about 200 yards down and more water in front of the green — potentially an express ticket to bogeyland. Tim Cate designed nine holes that were added to this course. The entire facility has all the amenities of the most exclusive clubs, such as a bar and grill, a pro shop, practice greens and sand traps, a driving range and on-site professionals. The St. James Golf Academy golf school at The Members Club welcomes all ages. Full Stay & Play packages and limited unaccompanied guest play are available. For details, call the golf desk at (800) 247-4806 ext. 8.

St. James Plantation - The Players
St. James Plantation, U.S. Hwy. 211, Southport
(910) 253-3008, (800) 247-4806

Designed by Tim Cate, this 18-hole golf course is both friendly and difficult at the

With so many area golf courses, visitors can play a different course every day.

photo: Erin Whittle

same time. Watch out for the sixth hole, regarded as the most challenging. The course is very aesthetically pleasing, with wild flowers and heather grass in bloom all around. The course is in excellent condition year round. The Players Clubhouse includes a fully stocked golf shop and bar and grill. Private lessons are available. There is also a practice range close by. Full Stay & Play packages and limited unaccompanied guest play are available. For details call the golf desk at (800) 247-4806 ext. 8.

St. James Plantation - The Founders Golf Club
St. James Plantation, N.C. Hwy. 211, Southport
(910) 253-3008, (800) 247-4806

Designer P. B. Dye called this his most challenging course yet. Its many carries over water hazards have been described as heroic, while its multilevel fairways, bulkheads and variety of grasses are stamped with the Dye hallmark. The final three holes play into and over a series of marshes and lakes for a spectacular finish. Five sets of tees present a variety of plays. Most greens are elevated. The Founders Club and its companion courses, The Players Club and The Members Club, are 4 miles outside Southport and offer fine views of the Intracoastal Waterway. A complete practice facility, pro shop and lessons are available. Full Stay & Play packages and limited unaccompanied guest play are available as well. For details, please call the golf desk at (800) 247-4806 ext. 8.

Ocean Isle Beach
Brick Landing Plantation
1882 Goose Creek Rd., Ocean Isle Beach
(910) 754-5545, (800) 438-3006

With 41 sand bunkers and water hazards on 17 out of 18 holes, this handsome waterfront course was rated by Florida Golf Week magazine as among the top 50 distinctive golf courses in the Southeast. The Brick's fairways wind among freshwater lakes and through salt marshes, offering striking visual contrasts and championship challenges. The 18th hole finishes dramatically along the Intracoastal Waterway. The course, recently updated by Dan Maples and Amy Alcott, is 6,586 yards and a par 71. Amenities include practice facilities, a restaurant and a cocktail lounge. Instruction is available, and memberships are recommended for flexible play times. The public is invited but play time reservations are required.

Sea Trail Golf Resort and Convention Center
211 Clubhouse Rd., Sunset Beach
(800) 624-6601, (888) 675-9237

Sea Trail Golf Resort & Convention Center offers three golf courses and a choice of two clubhouses. Each clubhouse has a full-service golf shop. The Jones/Byrd Clubhouse is home to Magnolias Fine Food & Spirits, serving breakfast, lunch and dinner. On the grounds as well are putting greens, a lighted driving range and a PGA–sanctioned Golf Learning Center. More than 58,000 square feet of meeting and function space make it a great place for meetings, reunions or weddings. In fact, Sea Trail Golf Resort and Convention Center is the only North Carolina resort to have been added to the prestigious list of America's Best Resort Courses of Distinction by Golfweek. In 2008 it received the rank of a Top 50 Golf Resort by readers of Golf World Magazine as well as the Reader's Choice Award by readers of the Brunswick Beacon.

Jones Course – This par 72 course opened in 1990 and, being a straightforward course with typical Rees Jones bounding, is a great course for all skill levels. Its wide emerald fairways with large mounds are surrounded by water. In fact, water hazards can be found on 11 holes. The large expanse bunkers make it an interesting and challenging course. Golf Carolina rates this course one of "100 Must-Play Courses of the Carolinas"; Golf Digest rates it 4 stars and "One of the Top 50 Courses in the Myrtle Beach Area"; Golfweek named it "2005 Best Resort Course"; and it was a 2006 U.S. Open Qualifier Round course. The Jones course was also named one of the top ten courses along the North Carolina coast by the North Carolina Golf Panel. The panel's rankings were reported in the April edition of Business North Carolina magazine in a special section spotlighting the state's best 100 courses.

Maples Course – One of Dan Maples finest courses, this par 72 course sits among ancient live oaks and Carolina pines. Five of the holes wind along the Calabash Creek, where nature displays the beauty of southeast coastal wildlife. The course has A1/A4 bentgrass greens and is peppered with waste bunkers, one of which extends the full length of the fairway, adding to the challenge. This course is rated in the top five of the coastal region as "Best Conditioned Course" by North Carolina Magazine; "America's Best Residential Course of Distinction" by Golfweek; and "One of the Top 50 courses in the Myrtle Beach area" by Golf Digest. The Maples Course was also selected by the North Carolina Golf Panel as one of the top 100 courses along the North Carolina coast.

Byrd Course – The Willard Byrd Course, another par 72 course, is built around several very large manmade lakes in a beautiful setting. Strategically placed tee shots and exacting play is necessary with every hole requiring a different approach. The 18th hole is situated between two ponds and finishes at the Jones/Byrd Clubhouse. The Byrd Course is listed as "One of the Top 50 Courses in the Myrtle Beach Area" and is given four stars by Golf Digest.

All three courses ranked among America's best in the 2008-09 edition of Zagat Survey for America's Top Golf Courses Guide.

LELAND

Cape Fear National at Brunswick Forest
1281 Cape Fear National Dr., Leland
(910) 383-3283, (888) 342-3622

The Wilmington area's newest golf course, Cape Fear National at Brunswick Forest features 18 holes of championship golf in a setting of unmatched beauty. This Tim Cate-designed masterpiece was recently named among the "Top 18 Most Significant Course Openings in 2010" by LINKS Magazine and is an absolute "must play". Cape Fear National is also the official host of the 2010 Golfweek Rater Cup. With 5 sets of tees, Cape Fear National

attracts experienced golfers and novices alike, and the layout includes over 1500 linear feet of bridges, 3 waterfalls, beach bunkers and a variety of native grasses/wildflowers. A 7,000 square foot offers locker rooms, a pro shop, indoor and outdoor dining and related amenities. Cape Fear National is conveniently located 5.7 miles south of downtown Wilmington, NC off of US Hwy 17 and is unique to the area in that it is a premium daily fee facility...an exclusive golfing experience open to all.

BOLIVIA

Carolina National Golf Club at Winding River Plantation
1643 Goley Hewett Rd. SE, Bolivia
(910) 755-5200, (888) 200-6455

Carolina National Golf Club is a Fred Couples signature golf facility. It features 27 challenging holes arranged in three nines — Egret, Heron and Ibis — named after the wildlife that inhabits this Audubon Certified Sanctuary Golf Course. Set along the Lockwood Folly River and carved out of low-country marshlands, the course offers an endless variety of playing experiences and stunning natural beauty that will enchant every visitor. Through its innovative design and multiple tee placements, the course will thrill players of every skill level. In addition, Carolina National Golf Club features a 14,000-square-foot putting and chipping green and 320-yard driving range, which provide a great warm-up for the challenges to come. In the clubhouse you will find the pro shop and the Plantation Grille. It's a great place to relax with a drink or a meal after your round of golf. Carolina National Golf Club is located 2.5 miles east of U.S. Highway 17 along N.C. Highway 211 in Winding River Plantation.

TOPSAIL ISLAND AREA

Belvedere Plantation Golf & Country Club
2368 Country Club Dr., Hampstead
(910) 270-2703

Belvedere is a narrow, par 71, 18-hole course with large greens and water hazards. The length is 6370 yards with a slope of 125. Hole 3 stands out for its carry over water to an elevated green. Greens fees range from $25 to $45, depending on the season and time of day. Reservations can be made far in advance, and PGA professional lessons are available. Belvedere has recently renovated its tee boxes and bunkers. There are a small pro shop, a clubhouse and a driving range, and if you work up an appetite, check out The Caddy Shack snack shop or The Sand Wedge restaurant.

Castle Bay Country Club
2516 Hoover Rd., Hampstead
(910) 270-1978

Castle Bay offers authentic Scottish-style links with a rolling terrain and natural indigenous grasses. This par 72 course has lengths ranging from 5466 to 6713. Open to the public year round, seven days a week from sunup to sundown, Castle Bay is about 2 miles off U.S. 17 on Hoover Road in Hampstead. Look for the castle gates at the entrance. Standard rates are $55 for weekend play. Weekday rates for play between 7 AM and 1 PM are $45; tee off after 1 PM and the rate drops to $38. Reservations can be made in advance. There is a practice complex, pro shop and restaurant on the premises.

North Shore Country Club
101 N. Shore Dr., Sneads Ferry
(910) 327-2410, (800) 828-5035

North Shore is among the best-conditioned courses in the Topsail Island area, with a four-star rating from Golf Digest. This course has 6866 yards, a 73.1 rating and a slope of 135, with water coming into play on 10 of the 18 holes. Thick Bermudagrass fairways and well-bunkered bentgrass greens place a premium on accurate shots. This course is quite popular with Raleigh and Triangle-area golfers, who come down to spend a day or two on the coast. The course is built on both sides of N.C. Highway 210, and an underground tunnel connects the two sides of the course. North Shore is lined with homes and tall pine trees. Golfers can sometimes be surprised by alligator sightings in the course waterways. The ninth hole is memorable for its required 250-yard tee

shot — anything less is in the drink. Greens fees, including a cart, range from $40 to $78, and reservations can be made up to a year in advance with a credit card. Professional lessons, a driving range, a putting green, club repairs and custom fitting are available. A clubhouse, bar and restaurant are on the premises. A Holiday Inn Express is next door.

Olde Point Golf and Country Club
U.S. Hwy. 17 N, Hampstead
(910) 270-2403

Olde Point is a mature, traditional course, designed by Jerry Turner. Featuring tree-lined fairways, scenic ponds and lakes, this 18-hole, par 72 course is 6253 yards with a slope of 120. The 11th hole is a long, narrow, 589-yard par 5 with a gradual dogleg that slopes laterally downward to the right into the woods and consistently defies players' depth perception. The course has been recognized by amateurs and professionals alike as one of the toughest in the area. Greens fees include a cart and range from $30 to $50 depending on the season and time of day. A reserved starting time is required. Golf lessons are available and taught by a PGA pro. Olde Point offers a pro shop, clubhouse, driving range, restaurant and snack bar.

Topsail Greens Golf Club
500 Topsail Greens Dr., Hampstead
(910) 270-2883

Topsail Greens is an 18-hole, 6200-yard, par 71 course featuring player-friendly tight fairways, sand bunkers and several holes with water hazards. The 17th hole, a 159-yard with a par 3, is an island green playable only by a small bridge. The greens, similar to those designed by Donald Ross, are cleverly contoured in a way that allows a misplayed shot to roll off the putting surface. Greens fees range from $20 to $40 depending on the time of day and season. There are also special rates for juniors and seniors and for play after 3 PM. Fees include a cart, and reservations are accepted. A pro shop, a snack bar, a driving range, a putting green and a chipping green are on the premises.

Driving Ranges

WILMINGTON

Oleander Golf Center
5026 Oleander Dr., Wilmington
(910) 397-0674

Oleander Golf Center can provide you with all the tee practice you might need. The location features all grass tees. Clinics are held on Saturdays at 9 AM for children and 10:30 AM for adults. Hours are 9 AM until the last person leaves, winter and summer.

Equipment and Repairs

The Golf Shop at Dick's Sporting Goods
816 S. College Rd., Wilmington
(910) 793-1904

One of more than 300 stores nationwide, Dick's has a 10,000-square-foot golf shop with a tremendous selection of golf equipment, clothing, shoes, accessories and gift items. A well-trained staff and two golf pros are available to assist customers at all times. An indoor driving range, with launch monitor, is available for customers to test those new clubs. The store is open seven days a week from 9:30 AM to 9:30 PM.

Pro Golf of Wilmington
323-C Eastwood Rd., Wilmington
(910) 794-8223

Whether you're a novice or professional, Bob and Josh at Pro Golf have the right equipment for you. This complete, 4,200-square-foot golf store is one of more than 140 stores worldwide. A friendly, experienced, knowledgeable staff can fit you with the right clubs for your ability, style and level of play. Besides a full line of equipment, Pro Golf has accessories, gift items and clothing for ladies, men and juniors. It's open Monday through Saturday from 10 AM to 6 PM.

Tee Smith Custom Golf Clubs
323-C Eastwood Rd., Wilmington
(910) 395-4008

Located within the Pro Golf store, Tee Smith has been customizing and repairing clubs commercially since 1975 and has the approval of pro shops throughout the area. Simple repairs often have a one-day turnaround. The shop is open Monday through Saturday year round.

Packages and Services

Coastal Golfaway
023 Wrightsville Ave., Ste. 2, Wilmington
(910) 799-0336, (800) 368-0045

Coastal Golfaway books customized packages in all price ranges from Wilmington to Pawley's Island, South Carolina, including Myrtle Beach and the Brunswick County/Calabash areas.

Comfort Suites Magnolia Greens
1020 Grandiflora Dr., Leland
(910) 383-3300

Located in the sprawling golf plantation of Magnolia Greens, the Comfort Suites Magnolia Greens is the perfect place to stay for your golfing vacation. From beautiful rooms to a complimentary continental breakfast and wireless Internet, the hotel has everything you need for your getaway. Include a 27-hole course and a golf school and practice facility that is just minutes from downtown Wilmington and your stay is complete.

Annual Tournaments

Challenging courses in beautiful settings plus wonderful weather set the stage for competitive golf events throughout the area. Tournaments are popular as fundraising activities, and a number of local organizations sponsor annual events. Many local courses host their own tournaments as well. Local chambers of commerce can provide information (see our Area Overviews chapter for a listing). Major tournaments are announced in the Star-News "Today," "Currents" or "Sports" sections;

some weekly publications, such as Encore, carry details, too.

Wilmington Golf Course, 311 S. Wallace Avenue, Wilmington, (910) 791-0558, sponsors an annual Men's Amateur Championship in September and a Women's Amateur Championship in October. These tournaments are open to golfers of all ages who have an established U.S.G.A. handicap. The fee for this two-day event is $80 per player, which includes lunch both days.

Tournaments, which are held nearly year round in the Southport/Oak Island/South Brunswick Islands, include the following:

In May the **Brunswick County Chamber of Commerce**, (910) 754-6644, (800) 426-6644, hosts the Brunswick County Chamber Golf Tournament and the **Southport-Oak Island Chamber of Commerce**, (910) 457-6964, (800) 457-6964, hosts the Southport-Oak Island Area Golf Classic.

In June the **Brunswick Literacy Council Golf Tournament**, (910) 754-7323, and the **Kiwanis Captain's Choice Golf Tourney,** (910) 253-0731, are held. **The Mayor's Cup Golf Tournament**, (910) 845-2625, is held at The Lakes Country Club in Boiling Spring Lakes; proceeds benefit a different local charity each year.

In August women's golf clubs hold the **Women's Golf Club County Championship**, (910) 754-5726, which benefits Hope Harbor Home.

⌂ REAL ESTATE AND NEIGHBORHOODS

Real estate is big business in the southern coastal region, due in large part to the desirable nature of the Carolina coast. The climate, the amenities of North Carolina's largest coastal city, beaches, a thriving university, extensive shopping and dining options, first-rate medical services, attractions, historical sites, varied recreational opportunities and beautiful coastal scenery lure newcomers and maintain a lifelong hold on residents.

Since the entire region from Topsail Island to Sunset Beach hugs the shore, land is limited to an approximately 180-degree angle. Naturally, the closer a property is to the water, the higher the price. There is also tremendous diversity in terms of neighborhoods, housing styles, scenery and price. The highest level, from $500,000 to beyond $3 million, consists of properties for those interested in waterfront and luxury homes. At the other end of the scale, there are smaller, new homes ranging from $100,000 to $150,000, just right for first-time homeowners and retirees seeking affordable housing.

Because new neighborhoods are continually sprouting in the area, we aren't even going to try describing all that are available. What follows is information about established neighborhoods, average prices (these may fluctuate according to the market) and other general facts. For specific information, contact an area real estate agent (a partial list of agencies is included in this chapter) or visit sales offices in a community that appeals to you.

Note: The real estate prices given in this chapter are intended to serve as a general guideline to area property values. Due to the constant state of flux in the market, prices can change considerably in a very short time. At this writing, the market holds some great deals for buyers.

NEIGHBORHOODS AND DEVELOPMENTS

New Hanover County

DOWNTOWN WILMINGTON

If you are looking for history and charm as well as an energetic and culturally/socially inspirational atmosphere, downtown Wilmington is definitely the place to be. It's lively, warm and relentlessly interesting.

Many of the homes date from the mid-to-late 1800s and the first quarter of the twentieth century. There are stunning examples of Victorian, Italianate, Renaissance, Neoclassical and Revivalist architecture. Homes in the area, small cottages and large mansions alike, feature high ceilings, hardwood floors, fascinating detail, front porches and all of the interesting characteristics one would expect of vintage homes.

The population is as eclectic as the architecture. This vibrant downtown community attracts an interesting mix of lifelong Wilmingtonians and newcomers. What the entire neighborhood seems to have in common is a mutual appreciation for the particular amenities of downtown: easy accessibility to cultural arts opportunities, fine dining, friendly shopping, a beautiful riverfront for strolling, and a strong sense of community identity.

Within the **Historic District** proper, many homes have been restored, but there are still handyman bargains to be had, especially in the areas outside of the district in the **Historic Overlay**. The level of downtown neighborhood restoration is most stable at the river and diminishes as you head east toward the ocean at about Eighth Street.

Although every type of housing style is available, the general downtown real estate market consists of single-family homes. As one local real estate agent put it, there is a range of everything in the way of housing and prices downtown, from larger homes in the district to small cottages, with prices ranging from $150,000 to more than $1 million, depending on the location and condition. Condominiums, often housed in renovated buildings, can range from the low $150,000s and up. There are also a growing number of condominiums and a few duplex developments.

Rental prices in the downtown area range from $800 to $1,200 a month for one-bedroom rentals. If the notion of living over a storefront or in an urban, loft-type space has appeal, ask a Realtor to show you buildings in the downtown commercial district.

Some solidly rediscovered older neighborhoods beyond downtown are the **Mansion District** and nearby **Carolina Heights** and **Carolina Place**. Both flank Market Street beyond 15th Street. These neighborhoods date from the 1920s, and architectural styles vary. In the Mansion District you can certainly purchase a mansion-style home ranging from $450,000 to $1 million, but there are also appealing cottages. Many of the larger homes started out as handyman bargains or fixer-uppers and were returned to their former elegance. Carolina Heights and Carolina Place begin at around 17th Street and continue to 23rd Street.

Carolina Heights is almost exclusively single-family homes with a price range from $250,000 to $550,000. In Carolina Place, the home buyer will find more diversity in architecture and price. Homes start in the $120,000 range and go up into the $300,000s. It is regarded as the new frontier for not only residential investors, but also homeowners, largely thanks to its relatively new status as an Historic Registry District.

WILMINGTON SUBURBS

Forest Hills is, without dispute, a fine address. This large and very stable neighborhood was once a suburb of downtown. Today it is a conveniently located neighborhood of older homes that date from the 1920s. Well-maintained lawns, large setbacks and gorgeous live oaks are the hallmarks of this neighborhood. There are ambling canopied lanes and lots of Southern-style shade. Diversity in square footage and architectural style allows for diversity in price, ranging from $300,000 to $450,000 and up. An attractive feature of this neighborhood is its proximity to shopping and services. It is minutes from the largest mall in the region.

Pine Valley, near South College Road around Longleaf Mall, is about three decades old as a development and still enjoying active home sales. It has attracted many Wilmingtonians to its quiet, pine tree–dotted blocks. A nearby golf course and clubhouse are easily accessible to people who want to live in a stable neighborhood that isn't necessarily exclusive in terms of price. Homes range from the $160,000s to $400,000.

Just off River Road, is **River Pointe**, another high-quality, traditional neighborhood community by the Davy Group. With 45 townhomes situated along the Cape Fear River, each boasting quality construction, a swimming pool with a lovely river view, plenty of boating and beaches nearby, a location that's a one-minute drive from Ashley High School and Murray Middle School, and convenient proximity to Monkey Junction shopping centers, River Pointe promises to become one of Wilmington's most sought-after new neighborhoods. There are two designs to choose from, the Cape Fear and the Cape Hatteras; both plans include a wide front porch and back deck, with all of the charm of traditional, Southern architecture.

Autumn Hall
Eastwood Rd., Wilmington
(910) 344-1010

Autumn Hall and the 236 acres that make up its lush interior is Wilmington's newest mixed-use, master-planned community of new homes and shops. The planned 273 single-family homes, 200 condominiums and 33 town homes are all based on the designs and styles of old

Wilmington's antebellum manors, coastal plantation homes and casual summer cottages.

Residents of Autumn Hall's neighborhoods will enjoy a number of community amenities, such as multi-use trails, the Creek Club, The Autumn Hall Club and the Village Center. Sidewalks and pedestrian paths will crisscross the community, linking homes to parks, lakes, clubs and commercial areas and encouraging residents to leave their cars behind and walk.

Conscientious land planning incorporates live oaks and winding streams throughout the neighborhoods. The Spanish moss–draped live oaks, long-leaf pines and tidal creek headwaters that border the community's natural landscape are true coastal treasures. Autumn Hall's main street leads to an 8-acre lake, where a lakeside amphitheater, along with restaurants, an outdoor plaza, gazebos and decks, are planned.

Demarest Company
6933 Running Brook Terr., Wilmington
(910) 686-4482

The Demarest Company designed and developed the Wilmington communities of Demarest Landing, Demarest Village, The Riptide Swim /Fitness/Day Care Facilities, Tidal Reach and the Calabash Community of Devaun Park. These communities are the area's first neighborhoods to establish the standard for Traditional Neighborhood Design (TND) that is reminiscent of historic Wilmington and Southport, all integrated with beautiful parks and tree-lined streets. The Demarest Company developments of Demarest Landing, Demarest Village and Devaun Park have all been recognized with the "Significant Achievement Award" by the Lower Cape Fear Stewardship Awards Council for precedence in Low Impact Development, preservation of natural resources and extraordinary implementation of land-planning techniques regarding the design and management of stormwater engineering. These neighborhoods are a "must see."

ICW COMMUNITIES

For those that don't want the hassles and extra expense of beach-front property, Wilmington and the surrounding areas offer a unique alternative in Intracoastal Waterway real estate. With plenty of water access and many communities boasting their own marinas, ICW addresses are highly coveted. Most are only a short distance from inlet access to the ocean and many offer amenities like beach clubs so that residents have a home base when enjoying a day on the sand. These areas, many of which continue to be developed, tend to range from $250,000 in some Brunswick County neighborhoods to well over a million for Landfall properties. One major advantage is having a barrier island between you and any approaching storms and avoiding the storm surge that most beach homes must endure during a hurricane. But perhaps the most pleasant aspect is enjoying the sunrise from your dock over a cup of coffee and a newspaper. At any rate, the views and the scenery don't get much better than in these waterfront communities.

NORTH OF WILMINGTON

Demarest Landing, located on the high bluffs of Howe Creek, is a waterfront Middle Sound neighborhood, and it received the "Significant Achievement Award" from the Lower Cape Fear Stewardship Council for 2006. This exceptional community of 46 home sites is accessible to every convenience of suburban living, including area schools. Amenities of this well-planned community were designed to appeal to kids of all ages and include tennis, volleyball, basketball, a swimming pool, a waterfront pier and stocked boathouse, a clubhouse, 1.5 miles of sidewalks, a post office, two fountains, parks and rear service lanes for residents' garages. Endorsed by the Governor's Taskforce for Smart Growth as the "cutting edge" in Traditional Neighborhood Design, Demarest Landing is a community of great neighbors with a child-friendly atmosphere.

Figure Eight Island is a private island of upscale homes and home sites ranging from $475,000 to more than $1 million; single-family home prices range from the $800,000s to nearly $4 million. There is a yacht club and private harbor for members. This lovely island has no commercial development; shopping is available in nearby Ogden and Porters Neck. Call your real estate agent for information.

Porters Neck Plantation and Country Club
8204 Fazio Dr., Wilmington
(910) 686-7400
www.porters-neck.com

Tucked away from main thoroughfares and adjacent to the Intracoastal Waterway, Porters Neck Plantation's classic homes are surrounded by mature landscaping, lush fairways and century-old live oaks in an expanse of green space seldom found in contemporary communities. This private, country club community offers an appealing blend of friendly, old-fashioned neighborhoods and thoroughly modern amenities. Borrowing from the low country sense of tradition and history, there is a handsome eighteenth-century, Federal-style clubhouse and sports center. Porters Neck Plantation and Country Club also has the only 18-hole Tom Fazio golf course in the greater Wilmington region, which has been named the "#1 Coastal Course" in North Carolina by *Golf Digest* magazine. Beautifully landscaped and manicured streets are lined with elegant custom-built homes. Homeowners can select a site with views of the fairways, lakes or marsh and choose from award-winning home designs. Home styles range from traditional Colonial to European-inspired designs, including custom homes, patio homes and townhomes. Porters Neck is north of Wilmington and Wrightsville Beach just off U.S. Highway 17.

SOUTH OF WILMINGTON

The area to the south of Wilmington is currently the fastest growing part of New Hanover county. Along College Road south of Market Street to Shipyard Boulevard, dense commercial growth has been taking place for years. However, with significantly increased residential development farther to the south down to Pleasure Island, commercial development has been following at a rapid pace. This is especially true in the **Monkey Junction/ Myrtle Grove** area at the junction of Carolina Beach Road (U.S. Highway 421) and College Road (N.C. Highway 132), where there is a Lowe's hardware store and a

Wal-Mart Super Center, along with numerous other businesses and restaurants.

South of Monkey Junction along Carolina Beach Road, quite a few residential areas have been developed, ranging from moderately priced to upscale gated communities, interspersed with commercial establishments. The four-lane, divided highway allows easy access to any of these businesses, communities and Pleasure Island.

Just north of the Snow's Cut Bridge on River Road is the growing development of **Cypress Island**. This neighborhood consists of 1,400- to 2,000-square-foot single-family homes and 1,200- to 1,800-square-foot town homes. Homes and lots are offered as a package deal starting around $170,000 to $300,000 for single-family homes and $145,900 and more for town homes. The community has a 14-acre nature preserve with a nature trail, two stocked fishing lakes, a clubhouse, a pool and tennis courts. It has a 9-hole, par 3 golf course.

WRIGHTSVILLE BEACH AND VICINITY

This is a pretty beach town with a year-round population of slightly less than 3,000 residents. It's clean, there is little in the way of garishness, and the local constable does a fine job keeping order in the face of huge crowds of visitors. A person who appreciates small-town living in a beach atmosphere with the convenience of a nearby city will adore this place. There are 5 miles of clean beach on which to jog or simply stroll. On just about any day of the year, you'll see surfers waiting for the big one to roll in.

Wrightsville Beach is densely developed residentially. For the most part, houses are close together, and a person who craves the mythical remote island life is not going to find it here. Development has been largely controlled, thanks to vigilance on the part of local residents and the high cost of land, so the relative density of development is palatable. In 1998 the community put building ordinances into effect that limit the size of new houses based on square footage relative to lot size.

The Wrightsville Beach real estate market is stable. If a property comes onto the market, it will often sell quickly. Many of the existing homes stay in families generation after generation. Quite a few of these properties are used only as summer homes. When homes do go on the market, the price tag is large. Expect to pay between $800,000 and $3 million for any single-family home, and don't be surprised by much higher prices for oceanfront property. Those homes begin at about $1 million.

Since the available land is all but exhausted in terms of development on the island and high-rises are limited to 96 feet, most of the opportunities for purchase are either replacement of older houses with new ones or, more likely, in condominiums. You could easily spend $400,000 to $1.5 million for a two-bedroom condominium on Wrightsville Beach, with those on the lower end of the range far from the beach. Condos built at the present time are typically three-bedroom, two-bath floor plans and range from $600,000 to $950,000. Custom three- to four-bedroom condominiums with 3,000 to 4,000 square feet start at $1,000,000 and up.

There are however, a few residential developments springing up near Wrightsville Beach, and these developments offer patio and single-family homes in an affordable price range.

One of the newest developments near Wrightsville Beach is The Village at Mayfaire, a 31-acre, 208-unit residential development on Military Cutoff Road. Developed by the Charlotte-based State Street Companies, this community offers a fresh, engaging and luxurious condominium experience. Here, homeowners find private estate comforts and strikingly handsome architectural style. Each building in The Village at Mayfaire is selected from a portfolio of six graciously appointed floor plans. Two- and three-bedroom floor plans range in size from 1,260 to 2,037 square feet and include large outdoor terraces, a private garage and assigned courtyard parking.

With prices starting in the upper $300s, The Village at Mayfaire offers the coastal lifestyle for a fraction of what homeowners pay for a comparable condominium at Wrightsville Beach, located 2.5

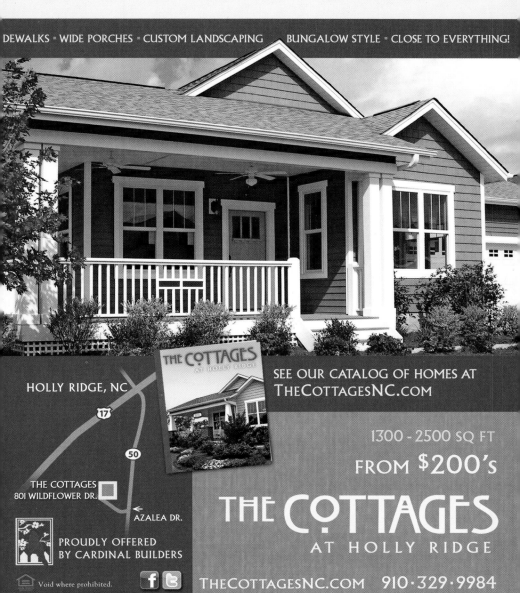

Bungalow living
5 minutes from the ocean
(and less than a half hour to Camp Lejeune's main gate)

Topsail Beach, NC

The Cottages at Holly Ridge is a cozy neighborhood where friendly neighbors enjoy a vibrant coastal North Carolina lifestyle. Our open floorplans make these already spacious bungalows live like much larger homes!

DEWALKS · WIDE PORCHES · CUSTOM LANDSCAPING · BUNGALOW STYLE · CLOSE TO EVERYTHING!

HOLLY RIDGE, NC

17

50

THE COTTAGES
801 WILDFLOWER DR.

AZALEA DR.

PROUDLY OFFERED
BY CARDINAL BUILDERS

SEE OUR CATALOG OF HOMES AT
THECOTTAGESNC.COM

1300 - 2500 SQ FT

FROM $200's

THE COTTAGES
AT HOLLY RIDGE

THECOTTAGESNC.COM   910·329·9984

BELINDA KELLER photography

Custom photography in your home or chosen location.

Belinda Keller Photography serves the Wilmington area creating lasting heirloom photographs your family will treasure for generations.

Schedule a session today
910-622-5122
WWW.BELINDAKELLERPHOTOGRAPHY.COM

miles from the property. Amenities include a 5,525-square-foot clubhouse, 24-hour cardio center and weight-lifting area, 25-seat movie theater and multi-media room, billiards room, conference and gaming room, junior Olympic size pool with 75-foot lap lanes, expansive 18,000-square-foot sunning deck, outdoor heated spa, gas barbecue grill area, lighted tennis courts and residents' picnic pavilion.

Perhaps The Village at Mayfaire's most distinctive amenity is the half-mile link to The Mayfaire Town Center. This inviting "new urbanism" community brings a vital and enchanting mixed-use lifestyle with a great shopping and working environment. Here, residents can walk, browse and shop all day among national and local restaurants and merchants along a traditional "main street," with storefronts facing bustling sidewalks and public squares. For more information about The Village at Mayfaire, contact the sales center at (910) 509-9771.

CAROLINA BEACH AND KURE BEACH

Cross over the bridge on U.S. 421 at Snow's Cut, a U.S. Army Corps of Engineers project that connects the ICW with the Cape Fear River and the Atlantic Ocean, and you come directly into Carolina Beach.

The beach communities of Carolina Beach on the north and Kure Beach to the south are located on the land area known as Pleasure Island. Home to about 10,000 year-round residents, these friendly, family-oriented communities are often mistaken by visitors as one long island beach town referred to as Carolina Beach. This is an understandable error due to the similarities of the towns. Both have clean, wide beaches, an abundance of fishing opportunities, several nice restaurants and a growing sense of community pride that makes living here a charming prospect.

Although Carolina Beach has been a community since 1857, the whole of Pleasure Island has been experiencing substantial residential growth during recent years as an affordable place to locate by or near the ocean. The assortment of ownership opportunities range from condominiums to cottages to upscale homes. There are several high-rises, many multi-story condominium buildings on the northern end, an abundance of small residences and — particularly toward the central and southern parts of the island — quite a few larger homes.

Currently, the island is experiencing considerable commercial growth, and revitalization is underway. Two major chain hotels have recently been opened in the area, increasing the number of visitors to downtown Carolina Beach and the Boardwalk.

Single-family homes along Carolina Beach and Kure Beach range between $250,000 to $500,000 and up, with townhomes and condominiums priced in the upper-$90,000s to the $500,000s. Not surprisingly, oceanfront properties in both markets fall into the upper range of price quotes, $500,000 to $1 million and more. The farther south you go on this island, the more fascinating the scenery becomes. In Fort Fisher, beautiful live oak trees have been sculpted over the centuries by the sea breezes. At the southernmost tip of this strip of land, the Cape Fear River converges with the Atlantic Ocean near Bald Head Island.

In the village of Kure Beach, you'll find **Seawatch**, a residential development with homes on 101 sites ranging from oceanfront to wooded. Single-family, cottage-style homes are from 1,400 to 3,200 square feet in size and are grouped around a community pool, cabana, playground and tennis courts. A private, oceanfront beachwalk features a cabana with showers, restrooms and a covered deck.

Among Pleasure Island's notable residential developments is **Harbour Point**, a traditional waterfront neighborhood and yacht club located on the Intracoastal Waterway at the juncture of Snow's Cut in Carolina Beach. Its 90 townhomes feature tin roofs, white picket fences, pastel exteriors, romantic porches and classic styling. Reminiscent of Charleston, the community has a relaxed ambiance and quiet sophistication. There is a 98-slip marina that can accommodate boats up to 100 feet, a waterfront pool and a clubhouse.

Brunswick County Inland

LELAND

Brunswick County is the 14th fastest growing county in the nation and, with 19 municipalities, has more municipalities than any other North Carolina county.

Leland, just across the Cape Fear River from Wilmington and known as the Gateway to Brunswick County, is one of the fastest growing communities in southeastern North Carolina. In 2004 the town doubled its size by annexing Brunswick Forest, a 4,900-acre tract. A U.S. Highway 17 bypass is planned, which will allow access to the town directly from Interstate 40 without the need to travel through Wilmington. These changes are expected to swell the population from its current 12,623, the largest in the county, to more than 20,000. New developments have provided newcomers with quality housing choices. With the addition of a Wal-Mart and numerous other retail facilities, locals no longer have to journey across the bridge for their shopping needs. This thriving suburb promises to continue expansion, raising land value and creating a "bedroom community" for neighboring Wilmington.

A collaborative effort by town officials and employees, citizens and a professional team of planners and designers have developed a master plan for the town to establish a framework for future land use and development. This plan received an honorable mention outstanding plan award at the N.C. Chapter of the American Planning Association's 51st annual conference held in Raleigh in the fall of 2008. This plan will be used in concert with the Leland Connector Street Plan as well as other efforts including a bicycle master plan, an open space and recreation plan, and the CAMA Land Use Plan Update to maintain a high quality of life for residents as the town continues to grow.

There are several golf courses in the area and shopping can be had at the Waterford Business Center, the Villages at Brunswick Forest and others located along highway 17. Housing developments include Waterford of the Carolinas, Magnolia Greens, The Bluff on the Cape Fear, Palm Cove of the Carolinas, Lanville Trace, Snee Farm, Hunter's Ridge, Rices Creek Estate, Creeks Edge, Brunswick River Estates, Brunswick Forest, Westgate and Wisteria Place, a "green" neighborhood. Single-family homes in the Leland/Belville area may range from $90,000 to over $800,000; lots from $16,000 to $450,000.

The Bluffs on the Cape Fear
1105 New Pointe Blvd., Leland
(866) 725-8337, (866) 725-8337

The Bluffs on the Cape Fear is a dockable, gated community of coastal Carolinian-style homes located just 15 minutes from downtown Wilmington. Home sites and custom homes are available in a variety of different environments — riverfront, lakefront and nature. Amenities include extensive nature trails and parks, a clubhouse, a fitness center, indoor and outdoor swimming pools, lighted HarTrue tennis courts and a private beach club on Oak Island, to name just a few. There is also a waterfront park with transient slips and a boat launch. The Bluffs on the Cape Fear was created to bring both untouched nature and carefully designed recreational amenities to your doorstep. Whether you seek the solitude of a leafy path as it winds through the woods, the stimulation of tennis and swimming, or the convenience of a nearby boat slip, The Bluffs offers the ultimate in outdoor amenities—all in a natural, riverfront setting.

Brunswick Forest
1007 Evangeline Dr., Leland
(910) 383-1425

Across the Cape Fear River just 10 minutes south of historic downtown Wilmington on U.S. Highway 17 is Brunswick Forest, a flourishing new community situated on 4,500 acres of woodlands, creeks, forests and natural areas. After just three years on the market, more than 600 families now call Brunswick Forest home, making it the fastest growing community in the coastal South. Residents at Brunswick Forest can choose from a wide range of prices and lifestyle options, from low-maintenance luxury town homes to home sites and spacious custom homes. Home sites begin at $75,000 and homes are priced from the mid-$200,000s. Secluded neighborhoods, each with its own distinctive character, are found throughout the community. Residents also enjoy a wide variety of amenities in place today, including 18 championship holes of a planned 27-hole golf complex at Cape Fear National, a Fitness and Wellness Center, a Community Commons area, a River Club and more than 100 miles of paths and trails. Most recently, New Hanover Regional Medical Center opened a 40,000-square-foot medical office building at The Villages at Brunswick Forest, a major retail, professional and entertainment center at the community's entrance.

Compass Pointe
8178 Compass Pointe East Wynd, Leland
(888) 71-POINTE

The Compass Pointe community offers a vibrant and active family lifestyle at wonderfully affordable prices. This walkable coastal neighborhood offers residents a true resort-style way of life with tons of fabulous amenities. Imagine living in a community that offers tennis courts, pools, splash parks, fitness centers, a lake beach, a dog park, bike trails, a River Club, 27-holes of championship golf, an 18-hole putting course, putting greens, a sports and wellness center, canoe and kayak launches, and even a soccer field. Located on 2,200 lush acres only ten minutes from Downtown Wilmington, Compass Pointe home sites start in the low $70s, villas from the low $200s and homes from the $200s. Designated as an Audubon International Gold Signature Community, Compass Pointe is a relaxed and casual coastal community, rich in amenities and golf.

Palm Cove of the Carolinas
1000 Olde Waterford Way, Leland, Belville
(800) 383-7535

This exclusive gated neighborhood in Sunset Beach has only a handful of spaces remaining. It is the remarkable nature of these lots that make them so desirable. Extending from the ocean to the sound, these acre-plus lots provide potential homeowners with both beach and boat access. Located within 40 minutes of Myrtle Beach and downtown Wilmington,

Palm Cove homeowners also have access to a wide variety of cultural opportunities and a myriad of golf choices.

Waterford of the Carolinas
1000 Olde Waterford Way, Leland
(910) 383-1011

Just across the Cape Fear River lies Waterford, an exclusive development with reasonably priced homes in a tranquil setting that is filled with amenities. With shopping, golf, water access and many other perks on site or next door, Waterford residents enjoy a prime location tucked right in the heart of this burgeoning area of northern Brunswick County. Choose your home from any of the models available or build your own custom dwelling to suit your needs.

BOLIVIA

Bolivia, located in the heart of Brunswick County, takes its name from burlap bags marked "Bolivia, S. A.", which traveled through the town on railroad flatcars on a regular basis in the nineteenth century. Though small, with a population of 174, Bolivia is the county seat and home of the Brunswick County Courthouse complex. It is home as well to Brunswick County Community College and the state-of-the-art Odell Williamson Auditorium. in tis area. Bolivia has a small commercial district, however, completion of the second bridge to Oak Island will likely contribute to commercial development in this area. Housing developments in the area include older developments like Mary Frances Place, Knotts Landing, Olde South Banks, Marsh Bay and Sandy Bay Retreat. Newer developments include Avalon, The Villages at Goose Creek, Mill Creek Cove, Winding River Plantation and Palmetto Creek of the Carolinas. Real estate prices in Bolivia range from $115,000 to $875,000 for new homes, although small older homes can be had for as little as $40,000.

Mill Creek Cove
1161 Palatka Place, Bolivia

For those seeking an idyllic spot for their new home, Mill Creek Cove offers numerous benefits and amenities, especially for lovers of nature. Located in a secluded marsh-front setting, the home sites at Mill

Creek Cove offer easy access to numerous nature trails and water routes for kayaking or canoeing. With top-notch amenities that include tennis courts, a clubhouse, a pool and more, residents can make the most of their membership in this highly sought-after community. Local beaches are minutes away, as is the Carolina National golf course, making Mill Creek Cove a centrally located neighborhood in north Brunswick County.

Palmetto Creek of the Carolinas
1186 Turnata Dr. SE, Bolivia
(910) 755-6100

For residents of Palmetto Creek of the Carolinas, the natural aesthetic beauty of this Brunswick County neighborhood is a huge bonus. Homeowners have access to lakes, ponds and creeks suitable for fishing or paddling, and nature enthusiasts will find miles of hiking trails perfect for morning strolls. This gated community is surrounded by golf courses and features its own opulent clubhouse, a resort-style pool and a fitness center.

Brunswick County Beaches and Vicinity

BALD HEAD ISLAND

Bald Head Island is a beautiful bit of land where there are no high-rises, no shopping malls, no crowds and no cars. Everyone either walks or travels by electric golf cart or bicycle. To get there you will need you own power boat in order to cross the mouth of the Cape Fear River. Failing that, you can enjoy the exhilarating, 20-minute ride in one of the passenger ferries that depart from the ferry landing at Deep Point Marina in Southport.

In addition to 14 miles of beautiful beaches and 12.000 acres of salt marshes, maritime forest and tidal creeks, you will find Old Baldy, the historic lighthouse as well as the Smith Island Museum and the Bald Head Island Conservancy. Opportunities for fine and casual dining range from the elegant Bald Head Island Club, with its pool, a George Cobb–designed golf course, swimming complex, fitness facility and croquet greensward, to the deli

at the Maritime Market. There are some interesting shops and a marina where you may dock your boat. A resort atmosphere prevails, and the year-round residential population count is quite low, about 220.

Bald Head Island is largely a vacation spot where most of the homes are available for weekly rental. Single-family homes, villas and townhouses dot the island and are connected by paved golf-cart paths. Developments include Keeper's Landing at Cape Fear Station, Harbour Village and The Hammocks. Home sites range from $125,000 to $3,000,000. Home sales begin at $400,000 for an older home and climb upward to above $3 million. Condos and stand-alone town homes range from $322,000 to more than $7000,000, while timeshares/partial or fractional ownership can be purchased anywhere from $35,000 to over $800,000.

SOUTHPORT AND OAK ISLAND

Southport's geographical location on the Cape Fear River near the Atlantic Ocean provides some lovely coastal scenery. But the town's location also made it an ideal location for riverboat captains who settled there and incorporated it in 1805. It is largely a charming town — quaint, quiet and historic, the streets lined with ancient live oaks. Bald Head Island lies just off Southport to the east. Oak Island serves as a barrier to the ocean on the south side. On a clear day you will have an excellent view of Old Baldy, the historic lighthouse on Bald Head Island as well as the Oak Island Lighthouse.

Southport's Victorian homes date from the late 1800s and offer mostly restored, single-family residences. Houses on the waterfront are larger, and a 2,400-square-foot home may run upward from $500,000. Newer homes may cost more. Along River Drive, one can spend more than $1 million. Naturally, the farther back from the water, the lower the price. A nice finished house in Southport will start at $235,000 for 2,300 square feet. Condos start at $200,000.

Subdivision areas are growing rapidly in and near Southport whose population is 2,934. These include Indigo Plantation, Arbor Creek, The Landing at Southport,

Harbor Oaks, Carolina Place, Cades Cove, Marsh Creek, The Cottages at Price's Creek, Mariner's Pointe, Dutchman Village, Rivermist, Smithville Woods, River Run Plantation and St. James Plantation, which is a gated community. These neighborhoods offer a broad range of new homes in attractive settings with some very pleasant amenities.

Oak Island has two beach communities: **Caswell Beach** and the **Town of Oak Island**. Both of these communities have many resort rentals, but they are overwhelmingly occupied by permanent residents with the population in Caswell Beach being nearly 500 and that of the Town of Oak Island being nearly 9,000. And why not? Many people who have been vacationing here for the fishing, swimming, watersports and the natural beauty of the area end up retiring to this family-oriented island. Caswell Beach, which is named for Fort Caswell (c. 1826), is a quiet family town where magnificent views of both the Atlantic Ocean and the Intracoastal Waterway can be had from the second floor of homes on the east end of the island. It is also home to the U.S. Coast Guard Station and the Oak Island Lighthouse, which has the second brightest light in the world. Housing Developments here include the Arboretum and Ocean Greens.

The Town of Oak Island is the largest geographical area on the island. It has recently annexed territory on the mainland side of the mile-long high-rise bridge which connects the two. Included in this territory is South Harbour Village, a PUD. A second bridge to the island is in the process of being built and the town is considering annexing mainland at it entry area on NC 211. You will find restaurants, nightlife, shopping at small boutiques, miniature golf, a recreation center and other attractions on the island. In fact it has the largest commercial district of all the Brunswick County islands. The miles of south-facing beaches afford opportunities for recreational activities, including swimming, surfing, volleyball, dolphin-watching, surf-fishing and more. There are 65 beach accesses and two fishing piers located here, and fishing tournaments abound.

The few small developments on the island include Oceanside at Oak Island, East Beach and Turtle Creek by the Sea. Condominiums include Southern Shore Villas, Savannah Crossing, Long Bay Commons and Yaupon Dunes. At the center of the island, you can expect to pay from $107,000 to over $1,000,000 for a home depending on the style of the house. Oceanside properties from $350,000 to around $1 million, and Intracoastal Waterway properties from $600,000 to $70,000. Condos and own homes on the island and mainland may range from $85,000 to $699,000 and lots from $48,000 to $1.2 million, again depending on location.

Cades Cove
1680 N. Howe St., Southport
(866) 770-COVE, (866) 770-2683

Enjoy life in historic Southport at Cades Cove, a quiet coastal community. This developing neighborhood features traditional homes that blend seamlessly into the fabric of this classic Southern town. Owners have the ability to customize each floor plan to their needs. Developed by Blake Family Properties, this project brings their years of experience to bear, creating a simpler time on a modern street.

Pender County

TOPSAIL ISLAND

Many of the properties on Topsail Island are second homes or investment properties. Properties most in demand are the large oceanfront homes and other waterfront locations. You can expect to pay an average of $800,000 to $1.5 million for a single-family, oceanfront home. Land is limited on this barrier island, and many retirees and new families relocating to the area often choose to live on the mainland, which is still close enough to the beach to feel like they are on a lifelong vacation.

Creeks Edge, a water-oriented community, is located in the quaint fishing village of Sneads Ferry. This upscale planned community offers large waterfront, water-view and interior lots. Located just five minutes from North Shore County Club, this community also has direct access to the Intracoastal Waterway. Its golf course was rated 3 stars by *Golf Digest* magazine. Adding to its old South charm and ambiance is a lovely outdoor gazebo for family gatherings and entertainment. For information call Bud Rivenbark at (910) 327-7711 or (800) 497-5463.

HAMPSTEAD

Hampstead, once a small fishing village and a whistle stop alongside the Atlantic Coast Line RR, is one of the fastest growing areas in the state. Many neighborhoods front the waterway, more are along the numerous creeks and even more line the area's four golf courses. The land side of the sound is officially referred to as Topsail Township and includes many small unincorporated communities and the larger community of Hampstead. There are still quaint fishing shacks on the banks of the Intracoastal Waterway, though most are being replaced by much larger homes as new people move into the area. Hampstead, and in fact all of Pender County, is seeing growth and change come quickly, and farmlands once used for blueberries and tobacco are growing houses and neighborhoods as development of the area increases.

Hampstead is home to two large wholesale-only fresh fish dealers. Every September, J. H. Lea & Sons contributes about 5,000 lbs. of fish to the yearly Spot Festival, the event of the year in the town. There is also a marina, a full-service boat yard and lots of golf courses. History is everywhere, mostly related to marauding pirates. Topsail Inlet was a frequently used entrance to Topsail Sound, a hideout for Blackbeard, Steede Bonnett and Captain Kidd.

HOLLY RIDGE

The Cottages at Holly Ridge
801 Wildflower Dr., Holly Ridge
(910) 329-9984
www.hollyridgenc.com

The Cottages at Holly Ridge is a cozy neighborhood of new bungalow-style homes located just minutes from Topsail Beach and a short drive from Jacksonville. The neighborhood's classic architecture reflects the coastal lifestyle with columns

and wide covered porches that are perfect for sipping a glass of iced tea and catching up with the neighbors or just watching the kids play in the yard. Open and well-designed floor plans feel spacious and range from 1,300 to 2,500 square feet. Built by award-winning Cardinal Builders, these homes exude comfort, casual ease and flexible social spaces for large gatherings or small get togethers with friends.

REAL ESTATE AGENCIES

Any one of the area real estate agencies will be happy to assist you in your search for a new home. The agencies included here represent a fraction of the reputable companies working along the southern coast of North Carolina. Although we've grouped the agencies geographically, many of them sell properties in other communities, and some have offices in several locations throughout the area. Regardless of the office location, choose a Realtor who is knowledgeable about the areas you're interested in and with whom you feel comfortable working.

Wilmington

5 Star Realty
4607 Franklin Ave., Ste. 110, Wilmington
(910) 313-0027

This innovative Wilmington real estate broker offers both buyers and sellers a creative marketing edge. 5 Star assists buyers to find their perfect home while at the same time helping sellers to locate hard-to-find buyers. Utilizing innovative financing strategies and advanced computer technology, 5 Star offers a complete and comprehensive real estate package. Serving the Cape Fear region, including Wilmington, Leland, Brunswick County, Carolina Beach, Kure Beach, Wrightsville Beach and Landfall, 5 Star specializes in waterfront properties. Executive Realtors Joe Pascal, one of only 5 percent of North Carolina Realtors who qualifies as an Accredited Buyer Representative, and David Girardot promise to make the real estate transaction experience positive and hassle-free.

Bachman Realty
2411 Middle Sound Loop, Wilmington
(910) 686-4099, (800) 470-4099

Whether you're an avid golfer or simply want the comfort of luxury beach house, Bunnie Bachman can help you find your slice of paradise. A Figure Eight Island real estate specialist for 28 years, Bachman has a unique perspective on the area and a comprehensive knowledge of what's necessary to purchase a home on this private, secluded island. Bachman's knowledge of water rights, property values and neighborhood regulations allows her clients to make educated choices regarding their purchases. With contacts in the Landfall and Porter's Neck areas as well, Bachman connects discriminating buyers with the kind of properties that most people only dream of. Whether you're looking for an investment property, second home or primary residence, Bunnie Bachman knows where to find the ideal location for you.

The Keith Beatty Team - Intracoastal Realty Corporation
1904 Eastwood Rd., Ste. 202, Wilmington
(910) 509-1924, (800) 533-1840 x 1924

Buying or selling a home is one of the most important decisions of our lives, financially and personally. With so much on the line, why would you trust this decision to anyone but trained professionals who understand their client's needs and desires? Keith Beatty has been a top seller in the Wilmington market for years and, along with his team of highly trained agents, has sold more than 2,400 homes totaling over half a billion dollars in volume. Priding themselves on the belief that all sales are important, big or small, they refrain from limiting their clients by listing and selling properties of all prices ranges.

Bryant Real Estate
501 N. College Rd., Wilmington
(910) 799-2700, (800) 322-3764
www.bryantre.com

Offering vacation rental homes, condos and townhomes with locations from the ocean to the sound, Bryant Real Estate has been providing quality sales, rental and property management service in the Wilmington, Carolina Beach, Kure Beach and Wrightsville Beach areas for more than 50 years. For year-round rentals, call (910) 799-2700. Daily, weekly and monthly rates are available in Wrightsville Beach, Carolina Beach and Kure Beach. Bryant also has offices in Wrightsville Beach and Carolina Beach/Kure Beach.

Century 21 Sweyer & Associates
1630 Military Cutoff Rd., Wilmington
(910) 256-0021, (800) 848-0021

As a locally owned and operated family company since 1987, CENTURY 21 Sweyer & Associates understands the importance of your home to your family and are committed to delivering outstanding service. For the 6th consecutive year they have been ranked the No. 1 CENTURY 21® in North Carolina in closed sales and units (out of 300 plus offices). With over 130 sales agents, they service residential real estate from the Southern tip of Brunswick County to the Northern reaches of Jacksonville in Onslow County. Their Landfall office handles residential sales, commercial sales, residential and investment/rental properties, long-term rental management for tenants and property owners, community-association management, mortgage services and residential maintenance. They also offer training services for new agents, relocation assistance for clients new to the area and a professional in-house marketing department that can help you sell your property. After all these years, their original commitment to customer satisfaction through quality service remains the same.

Coastal Carolina Properties
5911 Oleander Dr., Wilmington
(910) 465-9135
www.coastalcarolinaproperties.com

Coastal Carolina Properties is an exclusive buyer's agent and does not list property for sale, so they're the ideal company for someone wishing to purchase a new home, investment property or lot. A Wilmington real estate agent and licensed Accredited Buyer Representative, Paul Coffman and his team of experts not only possess years of experience and local knowledge, they also offer a comprehensive relocation division for those moving to the area. Also serving the Wrightsville, Carolina/Kure Beach, Topsail and surrounding areas, Coastal Carolina Properties features oceanfront homes as well as properties just a stone's throw from the water. In the past three years alone, Coastal Carolina Properties has saved its clients more than $1.8 million through tough negotiations.

Coldwell Banker Sea Coast
1001 Military Cutoff Rd., Ste. 101,
Wilmington
(910) 799-3435

Coldwell Banker Sea Coast Realty is southeastern North Carolina's largest, top-selling real estate company. It also ranks as one of the nation's top-selling affiliates of Coldwell Banker Real Estate, which J.D. Power & Associates ranked #1 in Home Seller Satisfaction in 2009. Coldwell Banker Sea Coast Realty operates offices in Wilmington, Leland, Jacksonville, Carolina Beach, Topsail Island, Hampstead, Southport, Sneads Ferry, and Oak Island staffed by more than 300 experienced real estate professionals. It represents an impressive list of new home communities and offers expert assistance with all types of residential properties, resort/vacation properties, home sites/land/acreage, as well as commercial properties and relocation services.

Demarest Company
6933 Running Brook Terr., Wilmington
(910) 686-4482

The Demarest Company designed and developed the Wilmington communities of Demarest Landing, Demarest Village, The Village Swim /Fitness/Day Care Facilities, Tidal Reach and the Calabash Community of Devaun Park. These communities are the area's first neighborhoods to establish the standard for Traditional Neighborhood Design (TND) that is reminiscent of historic Wilmington and Southport, all integrated with beautiful parks and tree-lined streets. The Demarest Company developments of Demarest Landing, Demarest Village and Devaun Park has been recognized by the Lower Cape Fear Stewardship Awards Council with the "Significant Achievement Award" for excellence in land planning and environmental stewardship, setting the precedent for mixed-use communities in the southeastern North Carolina. To learn more about The Demarest Company and their communities visit www.demarestcompany.com.

EXIT Coastal Connection Realty
3825 Market St., Ste. 6, Wilmington
(910) 762-1951

EXIT Coastal Connection Realty is a locally owned and operated full-service real estate company in Wilmington. EXIT Realty has grown to 50,000 agents in North America and 1,500 offices. Their experienced Realtors are committed to helping customers buy, sell and invest in real estate.

Intracoastal Realty Sales
Lumina Station, 1900 Eastwood Rd., Ste. 38, Wilmington
(910) 256-4503, (800) 533-1840

Intracoastal Realty is proud of its unparalleled tradition as the area's leading firm for properties of distinction. Built upon a 30-plus year history of expertise, integrity and personalized service, Intracoastal Realty has represented generations of homeowners in the coastal areas of North Carolina, Wilmington and the historic district, Wrightsville Beach, Pleasure Island Beaches, north to Topsail and Surf City, and south to Oak Island. Intracoastal Realty has aligned itself with a select network of world-class industry leaders through their affiliation with Luxury Portfolio. In addition to serving buyers and sellers in all price ranges, the agency's New Homes division represents many new home communities in the area. In addition, their vacation and rental divisions provide vacation rentals as well as long-term property management.

Just For Buyers Realty, Inc.
5 Silva Terra Dr., Wilmington
(910) 202-4813

When it comes to real estate, the savvy buyer chooses an Exclusive Buyers' Agent. Those who've been through the purchasing process know they're more likely to save money, negotiate more repairs, get better financing, do less work and enjoy the process more when they select an Exclusive Buyers' Agent to represent them. They understand the benefits of working with an agent who has no responsibility to the seller. The brokers at Just for Buyers Realty love to answer your questions and there is never a high pressure sales pitch.

Landfall Realty
1816 Mews Dr., Wilmington
(910) 256-6111

Landfall Realty is the exclusive on-site sales office for the fine properties in Landfall, a private gated neighborhood of single-family custom homes, villas, patio homes, town homes, condominiums and home sites. The community boasts numerous amenities, including two championship golf courses, a Jack Nicklaus 27-hole course and the Pete Dye 18-hole course, and the Landfall Sports Center, designed by tennis legend Cliff Drysdale. Two well-appointed clubhouses overlook Landfall's golf courses: the luxurious Landfall Clubhouse near the Nicklaus course and the Dye Clubhouse on Landfall's Pete Dye course.

Network Real Estate
106. N. Water St., Wilmington
(910) 772-1622, (800) 882-1622

Locally owned and operated by lifelong residents Bob and Marilyn McKoy, Network Real Estate has been providing top-notch real estate services in the greater Wilmington area for the past 28 years. Specializing in residential and single-family homes, Network will connect you with its trained staff of more than 60 agents who provide a comprehensive look at all properties available and invite you to utilize the "Internet office" that their well-equipped website provides. In addition, commercial and land properties are another avenue that Network includes in its vast array of services. Network also has offices in Carolina Beach and Brunswick County.

Pointe South Realty
497 Olde Waterford Way, Ste. 201, Belville
(910) 795-4673, (888) 71-POINTE

Pointe South Realty specializes in the sales and marketing of new home communities. Conveniently located at the corner of Market and Front streets in Downtown Wilmington, Pointe South agents are on staff seven days a week for private tours of their communities and model homes.

Port City Properties
219 S. Water St., Wilmington
(910) 251-0615

Established in 1995, Port City Properties represents residential and commercial properties throughout New Hanover, Brunswick and Pender counties. This full-service realty company covers a full geographical and price spectrum, specializing in historic downtown Wilmington and all area beach communities.

Porters Neck Plantation and Country Club
8204 Fazio Dr., Wilmington
(910) 686-7400
www.porters-neck.com

Tucked away from main thoroughfares and adjacent to the Intracoastal Waterway, Porters Neck Plantation's classic homes are surrounded by mature landscaping, lush fairways and century-old live oaks in an expanse of green space seldom found in contemporary communities. This private, country-club community offers an appealing blend of friendly, old-fashioned neighborhoods and thoroughly modern amenities. Borrowing from the low-country sense of tradition and history, there is a handsome eighteenth-century, Federal-style clubhouse and sports center. Porters Neck Plantation and Country Club also has the only 18-hole Tom Fazio golf course in the greater Wilmington region, which has been named the "#1 Coastal Course" in North Carolina by *Golf Digest* magazine. Beautifully landscaped and manicured streets are lined with elegant custom-built homes. Homeowners can select a site with views of the fairways, lakes or marsh and choose from award-winning home designs. Home styles range from traditional Colonial to European-inspired designs, including custom homes, patio homes and town homes. With more than 37 years of real estate experience, agent Bruce Koch will help you find the perfect property in this lovely development.

RE/MAX Coastal Properties
2018 Eastwood Rd., Wilmington
(910) 256-8171

RE/MAX agents lead the industry in on-going education and number of sales per agent, as well as website activity. Being affiliated with the global RE/MAX network provides their agents — and buyers and sellers — with a competitive advantage through national television advertising and their highly rated website. RE/MAX enjoys brand-name recognition worldwide. Their office is open seven days a week; stop in or call for all of your real estate needs.

Realty World Cape Fear
1113-A Military Cutoff Rd., Wilmington
(910) 256-3528

With access to more than 1,500 homes, condos and apartments in the Wilmington area, Harold Chappell and the agents at Realty World-Cape Fear have their finger on the pulse of the surrounding real estate market. Whether you're looking for short-term relocation information or thinking about making a real estate investment, you'll find what you're looking for with Realty World Cape Fear. And if you're interested in selling your property, the agency's vast knowledge of Wilmington's diverse neighborhoods and current price trends will ensure that you get the best value in your sale. A top producer that ranks in the top 1 percent of Realtors locally and nationally, Harold Chappell and his associates will find the ideal place for your needs.

Rockford Partners
2 N. Front St., Wilmington
(910) 763-8895

Development, construction and real estate define Rockford Partners. Driven by a desire for excellence, Rockford Partners provides quality personal service and is perfectly positioned to leverage their talents and abilities, not as a remote third party consultant but as a fully integrated, hands-on partner through every step of the real estate development process. The Rockford Partners Construction Group has a stunning selection of plans that can be customized to meet your needs, or they will work with your architect. Rockford Real Estate, Inc. is dedicated to providing you with quality properties. Their professional staff will filter your criteria and only show you properties that suit your needs.

Tregembo & Associates Realty
5813 Carolina Beach Rd., Wilmington
(910) 799-9234

Sherry Tregembo is a lifelong resident of Wilmington and that experience helps her and her team of agents be "a small company that's big on service." Dedicated to providing comprehensive services to homeowners who would like to sell their properties, Tregembo's team is also skilled in finding the ideal home or vacation property for prospective buyers. Covering the Wilmington area along with all local beach locations, the company also serves Pender and Brunswick counties. Tregembo can provide services tailored to your specific needs.

Wilmington Real Estate 4U
5041 New Centre Drive, Ste 108, Wilmington
(877) 379-2589

Dedicated to providing clients with a level of service beyond their expectations, Sandy and Dick Beals believe that buying or selling a home is an important life transition and they work hard to ensure that it is worry free. With an experienced team of professionals, Wilmington Real Estate 4U guarantees privacy and respect while delivering results. The conveniently located office is fully equipped and has an integrated network of computer and communications systems to facilitate access to all the Multiple Listing Services, public record searches and other tools that agents need in order to better serve clients.

Wrightsville Beach

Bryant Real Estate
1001 N. Lumina Ave., Wrightsville Beach
(910) 256-3764, (800) 322-3764
www.bryantre.com

Offering vacation rental homes, condos and town homes with locations from the ocean to the sound, Bryant Real Estate has been providing quality sales, rentals and property management services in the Wilmington, Carolina Beach, Kure Beach and Wrightsville Beach areas for more than 50 years. For year-round rentals, call (910) 799-2700. Daily, weekly and monthly rates are available in Wrightsville Beach, Carolina Beach and Kure Beach. Bryant also has offices in Wilmington and Carolina Beach.

Intracoastal Realty Sales
535 Causeway Dr., Wrightsville Beach
(910) 256-4503, (800) 533-1840

Intracoastal Realty is proud of its unparalleled tradition as the area's leading firm for properties of distinction. Built upon a 30-plus year history of expertise, integrity and personalized service, Intracoastal Realty has represented generations of homeowners in the coastal areas of North Carolina, Wilmington and the historic district, Wrightsville Beach, Pleasure Island Beaches, north to Topsail and Surf City, and south to Oak Island. Intracoastal Realty has aligned itself with a select network of world-class industry leaders through their affiliations with Luxury Portfolio and Leading Real Estate Companies of the World. In addition to serving buyers and sellers in all price ranges, the agency's New Homes division represents many new home communities in the area and their vacation and rental divisions provide vacation rentals as well as long-term property management.

Michelle Clark Real Estate Team - Intracoastal Real Estate
523 Causeway Dr., Wrightsville Beach
(910) 367.9767
www.wrightsvillebeachagent.com

With nearly 40 years real estate experience, Michelle Clark and her team are Wrightsville Beach real estate specialists. Clark's team of experts will make all of your real estate transactions seem absolutely effortless because Michelle Clark, Linda Woods, Kelly Strickland, Irene Hathaway, Susan Snider and Amy Caliva will handle absolutely everything for you. All you will need to do is relax and let them take care of you. No one knows the community better than the Michelle Clark Team. Actively involved in the community, the Michelle Clark Team is consistently a Top Producer in Wrightsville Beach and Wilmington sales and has been for years. Whether you're buying, selling or investing at Wrightsville Beach, you will receive personalized attention and exceptional service from the Michelle Clark Team.

Figure Eight Island

Figure 8 Realty
15 Bridge Rd., Figure Eight Island
(910) 686-4400, (800) 279-6085

This agency, located on Figure Eight Island, focuses on the island's luxury, single-family homes. Oceanfront, marshfront

and soundfront properties are available. Figure Eight Realty also offers vacation rentals on the island.

Carolina Beach and Kure Beach

Blue Water Realty
1000 S. Lake Park Blvd., Carolina Beach
(910) 458-3001
www.bluewaterrealtyinc.com

Centrally located on Pleasure Island, Blue Water Realty specializes in waterfront homes in Carolina and Kure beaches. Their experience and expertise lead to great customer service and client satisfaction. They truly realize that service after the sale is important. Blue Water Realty offers a full-service vacation division with online booking for their guests. When your first love is your second home, call Blue Water Realty.

Bryant Real Estate
1401 N. Lake Park Blvd., Carolina Beach
(910) 458-4450, (800) 994-5222
www.bryantre.com

Offering vacation rental homes, condos and townhomes with locations from the ocean to the sound, Bryant Real Estate has been providing quality sales, rentals and property management services in the Wilmington, Carolina Beach, Kure Beach and Wrightsville Beach areas for more than 50 years. For year-round rentals,

call (910) 799-2700. Daily, weekly and monthly rates are available in Wrightsville Beach, Carolina Beach and Kure Beach. Bryant also has offices in Wilmington and Wrightsville Beach.

Bullard Realty
1404 S. Lake Park Blvd., Carolina Beach
(910) 458-4028

Established in 1980, Bullard Realty Inc. is a full-service real estate company specializing in sales and rentals on Carolina and Kure beaches. Owner Beth Bullard and her staff can represent buyers and sellers in Wilmington, as well as the beaches. As members of the Wilmington Association of Realtors and the Multiple Listing Service, Bullard Realty can meet all of your real estate needs. Bullard Realty offers the personalized service of a small company with the professionalism and technology of a larger agency.

Coldwell Banker Sea Coast Realty
1001 N. Lake Park Blvd., Carolina Beach
(910) 458-4401, (800) 847-5771

Coldwell Banker Sea Coast Realty is southeastern North Carolina's largest, top-selling real estate company. It also ranks as one of the nation's top-selling affiliates of Coldwell Banker Real Estate, which J.D. Power & Associates ranked #1 in Home Seller Satisfaction in 2009. Coldwell Banker Sea Coast Realty operates offices in Wilmington, Leland, Jacksonville, Carolina Beach, Topsail Island, Hampstead, Southport, Sneads Ferry, and Oak Island staffed by more than 300 experienced real estate professionals. It represents an impressive list of new home communities and offers expert assistance with all types of residential properties, resort/vacation properties, home sites / land / acreage, as well as commercial properties and relocation services.

Intracoastal Realty Corporation
1206 N. Lake Park Blvd., Carolina Beach
(910) 256-4503, (800) 533-1840

Whether you choose Wrightsville Beach or one of the Pleasure Island beaches, Intracoastal Realty Vacation Rentals offers hundreds of fabulous vacation homes for your perfect vacation. Choose from oceanfront, ocean side, ocean view, sound

front or sound view homes that range from the small and budget-friendly to the palatial with all of the amenities. Either way, you can enjoy golf courses, boating facilities, fine dining, shopping and historical sites all within 20 minutes of your exclusive vacation property. A virtual tour of Intracoastal Realty's vacation rentals is available on their website. Intracoastal also handles long-term rentals in Wilmington, Carolina Beach, Kure Beach, Wrightsville Beach and surrounding areas; call (910) 509-9700 for long-term rental information or visit their website for a complete list.

Island Beach Rentals by Walker Realty
501 N. Lake Park Blvd., Carolina Beach
(910) 458-3388

The Carolina Beach and Kure Beach areas are more popular than ever for those seeking a serene and relaxed environment. The team of real estate experts at Walker Realty can help you find and purchase the perfect home for you. Their portfolio of properties includes a wide variety of condos, town homes and beach houses.

Network Real Estate
1029 N. Lake Park Blvd. #1, Carolina Beach
(910) 458-8881

Owners Bob and Marilyn McKoy recognize the popularity that the Carolina Beach, Kure Beach and Fort Fisher areas

have gained each season. You'll be happy you chose a connected real estate company like Network to guide you through your potential property purchase. The company's more than 50 agents have access to each MLS listing in this booming market, and they will make every effort to accommodate your needs and desires in a second vacation home, a primary residence or your dream retirement location. Network also has an office in Wilmington.

Palm Air Realty
133 N. Fort Fisher Blvd., Kure Beach
(910) 458-5269
www.palmairrealty.com

Building on their proven track record and experience, Anne and Ea at Palm Air Vacation Rentals have broadened their business by opening the real estate firm Palm Air Realty. They now offer services for buyers and sellers of real estate and have expanded their vacation rental property management on Pleasure Island. Owners of vacation rental property will feel at ease with Palm Air's property management services since they really do understand what it means to have your own property offered to vacation renters. Their own rental business, Palm Air Cottages, had a 7 percent increase in 2008 rentals over 2007 and recently garnered a 5-star rating from the popular online travel site Trip Advisor. Palm Air Realty is a small local company with a larger community presence.

Bald Head Island

Bald Head Island Limited
Southport
(910) 457-7400, (800) 432-7368

Bald Head Island Limited and The Island Agency sell single-family homes, cottages, condominiums, townhouses and home sites on Bald Head Island as well as at Indigo Plantation & Marina in Southport. Properties are located along the Cape Fear River, the Atlantic Ocean, the Intracoastal Waterway, Bald Head Island creeks and marshes, the 18-hole George Cobb–designed golf course and the pristine maritime forest on the island.

Cape Fear Realty/
Bald Head Island Rentals
308 W. Moore St., Southport
(910) 457-1702, (800) 680-8322

Cape Fear Realty invites you to discover real estate opportunities on Bald Head Island, Middle Island Plantation, Southport, Oak Island, the Intracoastal Waterway, the Cape Fear River, St. James Plantation and the Brunswick County Islands. As a full-service real estate company, Cape Fear Realty works with both buyers and sellers and specializes in new-home construction, resort and recreational home re-sales and investment acquisitions. Cape Fear Realty also offers resort rentals on Bald Head Island. The agency is a member of the Brunswick and New Hanover County Multiple Listing Services. Offices are located in Southport and on Oak Island.

Mary Munroe Realty:
Bald Head Vacations & Sales Inc.
2 Killegray Ridge, Bald Head Island
(910) 470-2253

Involved in sales for more than 16 years, Mary Munroe specializes in resale and rentals of Bald Head Island and Middle Island Plantation properties. Home sites are available overlooking the ocean and high dunes, the golf course, the maritime forest and saltwater creeks. In Middle Island Plantation, a residential-only community at the eastern end of Bald Head

Island, all home sites are more than a half-acre, and amenities include a beach walk, Bald Head Island Club membership, a swimming pool, a tennis court and a floating dock system for boats up to 25 feet.

Southport
and Oak Island

The Carolina Coast Group -
Coldwell Banker Seacoast Realty
4911 Long Beach Rd. SE, Southport
(910) 443-0836, (888) 864-5960

Dennis and Penny Krueger and the Carolina Coast Group with Coldwell Banker Sea Coast Realty take an all-hands-on-deck team approach that guarantees complete customer satisfaction. With an in-house web assistant, their extensive website is updated frequently, which allows customers to shop for their perfect palace from the comfort of their home or office. The Kruegers and Coldwell Banker Sea Coast Realty offer real estate assistance and information for Southport, Oak Island and all of Brunswick County as well as Wilmington and the New Hanover, Pender and Onslow County areas. With more than 30 years experience in banking and real estate, Dennis and Penny Krueger with Coldwell Banker Sea Coast Realty can make your real estate transaction a smooth one.

Century 21 Dorothy Essey Associates Inc.
6102 E. Oak Island Dr., Oak Island
(910) 278-3361, (877) 410-2121

This real estate company serves all of Brunswick County, including Southport and Oak Island as well as Boiling Spring Lakes, Bald Head Island, Caswell Beach and the South Brunswick beaches. It offers general brokerage and services for single-family homes, condominiums, duplexes, lots and commercial properties. The company has a new-home specialist on staff.

Coastal Development & Realty Oak Island
8118 E. Oak Island Dr., Oak Island
(910) 278-6111

A progressive, full-service real estate firm with offices on Oak Island and Holden Beach, Coastal Development & Realty has been representing coastal Brunswick County since 1984. Professionals without a doubt, they can assist you with buying, selling, construction, home design, lots, land and commercial buildings. Their tasteful and attractive Coastal Home Designs are known for easy maintenance and durability and are customized to your specifications. If you like, you can search their listings online or complete the Dream Home Finder application and let them do the searching for you. Whatever process you choose, you will find a commitment to complete customer satisfaction.

Coldwell Banker Sea Coast Realty
4811 Long Beach Rd. SE, Southport
(910) 457-6713, (800) 346-7671
8821 East Oak Island Drive, Ste. 1,
Oak Island
(910) 278-3311, 877-770-3967

Coldwell Banker® Sea Coast Realty is southeastern North Carolina's largest, top-selling real estate company. It also ranks as one of the nation's top-selling affiliates of Coldwell Banker Real Estate, which J.D. Power & Associates ranked #1 in Home Seller Satisfaction in 2009. Coldwell Banker® Sea Coast Realty operates offices in Wilmington, Leland, Jacksonville, Carolina Beach, Topsail Island, Hampstead, Southport, Sneads Ferry, and Oak Island staffed by more than 300 experienced real estate professionals. It represents an impressive list of new home communities and offers expert assistance with all types of residential properties, resort/vacation properties, home sites / land / acreage, as well as commercial properties and relocation services.

Corporate at the Beach, LLC
4983 Glen Cove Dr., Southport
(910) 798-1060, (877) 798-1060

Pat Maloney, owner of Corporate at the Beach, specializes in finding homes in resort areas for corporate use. Each home is well designed and spacious enough to accommodate large groups. Located in or near beach communities, these homes offer a relaxing atmosphere for off-site company meetings, trainings or special events. A week at a resort facility would

Fabulous architecture abounds in Wilmington's historic district.

photo: John Golden

also make a terrific productivity incentive for staff members. Some of the properties lend themselves to weekly resort rentals, particularly in June, July and August. That allows you to earn income on your purchase if you schedule the corporate use for September through May. Professional property management companies are available to handle rentals and maintain your investment in your absence. The Brunswick County Airport is nearby and can accommodate fairly sizable jets. The Myrtle Beach and Wilmington International Airports are available for commercial flights.

Port Realty
1330 N. Howe St., Southport
(910) 457-5226, (800) 767-8735

This full-service realty company specializes in new homes of distinction, featuring a number of thriving developments in Brunswick County, including Cades Cove. Founded by Charles Blake, an experienced homebuilder and broker, Port Realty has the inside track on hundreds of gorgeous properties. Whether you find your ideal abode among the already constructed or decide to create a new house to suit your specifications, Blake's 38-plus years of experience in the business assures you of receiving the best deal for your dollar as well as quality construction, aesthetic appeal and four-star customer service.

RE/MAX at the Beach
6237 E. Oak Island Dr., Oak Island
(910) 278-1950, (866) 350-SOLD

One of four office locations in Brunswick County, this Alan Holden company sells all types of property and is a leader in southeastern North Carolina real estate.

Realty World Cape Fear
4700 Long Beach Rd. SE, Southport
(910) 457-7715, (866) 405-4147

From their offices in historic Southport, Realty World Cape Fear handles real estate sales for a large geographic area. Their knowledgeable agents can help you solve your real estate needs in much of Brunswick County, including Southport, Oak Island and Boiling Spring Lakes. They deal extensively in both residential and commercial properties.

Southport Realty
114 S. Howe St., Southport
(910) 457-7676, (866) 883-4783

The friendly professionals at Southport Realty invite you to "stroll Southport with a local." You can enjoy views of the Cape Fear River while sitting on their porch and discussing options. Whether you are interested in Southport, the beach communities, historic homes, waterfront property, land or even commercial property, the folks at Southport Realty are ready to serve you. For your convenience, offices are located in Southport and Sunset Harbor.

Holden Beach

Brunswickland Realty
123 Ocean Blvd. W, Holden Beach
(910) 842-1300, (800) 842-6949

Brunswickland, a leader in property sales, is a buyer/seller agency. In addition to offering homes for sale in all locations on Holden Beach, Brunswickland offers properties on the mainland. Included are homes and lots in Lockwood Folly Country Club, bounded by the Lockwood

Folly River on the east and the Intracoastal Waterway on the south.

Century 21 Anne Arnold
309 Clubhouse Dr. SW, Holden Beach
(910) 842-5500

Century 21 Anne Arnold, located in Holden Beach, specializes in properties at and around the Brunswick County beaches. Whether it is a little beach cottage getaway or an oceanside castle, Anne and her associates are completely capable and eager to help you find that dream home or home site. The recent market turn has resulted in some incredible opportunities in many amenity rich communities throughout the area.

Coastal Development &
Realty Holden Beach
131 Ocean Blvd. W, Holden Beach
(910) 842-4939

Coastal Development & Realty is a unique company with general brokerage offices located in Holden Beach and Oak Island. Established in 1985 and a leader in Brunswick County real estate, Coastal provides professional services in real estate sales, vacation rentals and custom-designed homes. SeaScape at Holden Plantation, SeaWatch at Sunset Harbor, Ocean Isle Palms, Rivers Edge Golf Club and Plantation and Ocean Ridge Plantation are affiliated specialized residential neighborhoods offering the marvelous Carolina lifestyle.

Hobbs Realty
114 Ocean Blvd. W, Holden Beach
(910) 842-2002, (800) 655-3367

Situated on the island of Holden Beach close to both Wilmington and Myrtle Beach, this family-owned and operated business with more than 30 years of building experience offers resort real estate sales, rentals and new construction from the ocean to the waterway and everywhere in between. The company has an in-house relocation service as well. Check out the website for both interior and exterior views of homes. A drive across beautiful Holden Beach Bridge, a turn to the left and a stop at the second office on the left will bring you to Hobbs Realty.

Martha Lee Realty
3369 Holden Beach Rd., Holden Beach
(910) 846-2402, (866) 696-6232
6934-3 Beach Dr. , Ocean Isle Beach,
(910) 579-2402

Martha Lee Realty, with 35 years of experience, is in the unique position of representing all of Brunswick County. This includes Bald Head Island, Southport, Oak Island, St. James, Sunset Harbor, Lockwood Folly, Holden Beach, Ocean Isle Beach, Sunset Beach, Shallotte, Calabash and Carolina Shores as well as acreage in the interior. Martha Lee Realty specializes in waterfront property, new communities, commercial property and large tracts of land. Real estate showcase tours are offered daily.

RE/MAX at the Beach
128 Ocean Blvd. W, Holden Beach
(910) 842-8686, (800) 360-9770

With locations at Holden Beach, Sunset Beach, Calabash and Oak Island, RE/MAX at the Beach has the Brunswick County coast covered. Selling all types of property, they are leaders in southeastern North Carolina real estate.

Ocean Isle Beach

Coldwell Banker - Sloane Realty Inc.
16 Causeway Dr., Ocean Isle Beach
(910) 579-1144, (800) 237-4609

Serving the region for more than 50 years and owned by the first permanent family to live on Ocean Isle Beach, Sloane Realty Inc. offers a wide range of new-home construction and residential re-sale options, including oceanfront living, deep-water canal homes, golf course communities and the adjacent mainland. Properties include single-family homes, condominiums and home sites. They also have an office in Sunset Beach.

Cooke Realtors
One Causeway Dr., Ocean Isle Beach
(910) 579-3535 x216, (800) 622-3224

This well-established island realty company offers complete real estate sales services for homes, condos, town houses and home sites. They also manage rentals

for 500 rental homes, cottages and condominiums. They offer properties on the oceanfront, second- and third-row, canalside, West End and Island Park, as well as off the island. Mainland sites include golf course and Intracoastal Waterway locations, and they are the exclusive agents for The Resort and The Peninsula developments. Their professional construction division is waiting to assist you with your plans or theirs.

Island Realty, Inc.
109-2 Causeway Dr., Ocean Isle Beach
(800) 589-3599

Island Realty is a family-owned company that specializes in sales and rentals of residential properties on Ocean Isle Beach and the local mainland areas. With more than 20 years experience in the vacation rental and real estate business, they have a select group of private homes in areas from oceanfront to deep-water canal and many condominiums and villas to choose from.

R. H. McClure Realty Inc.
24 Causeway Dr., Ocean Isle Beach
(910) 579-3586, (800) 332-5476

R. H. McClure Realty Inc. is a full-service realty brokerage that has been established on Ocean Isle Beach for more than 20 years. The firm specializes in residential re-sales, property management, long and short-term vacation rentals, and design and construction of new homes. Ralph McClure has been the premier builder on Ocean Isle Beach for many years. Their inventory of homes and home sites include oceanfront, deep-water canal, mid-island, condos, golf course communities and mainland properties. Friendly and knowledgeable agents will provide the individual attention and personal service you deserve.

Sunset Properties
102 Causeway Dr., Ocean Isle Beach
(910) 575-8603, (800) 445-0218

This family-owned company has been in operation since 1988 and is the largest sales and rental agency on the island, with more than 400 cottages and condos to choose from. Single-family homes dominate this quiet residential island that attracts second-home investors, retirees and people who simply appreciate living away from it all.

Sunset Beach

Century 21 Sunset Realty
502 N. Sunset Blvd., Sunset Beach
(910) 579-1000, (800) 451-2102

Serving Brunswick County since 1958, Century 21 Sunset Realty is a leader in the real estate market in both the mainland and beach communities of this lovely area. They strive to provide every real estate service available in this rapidly growing marketplace, and they can assist you in finding that perfect vacation investment property or help you find the perfect home suited to your lifestyle and budget.

RE/MAX at the Beach
6900 Ocean Hwy W, Sunset Beach
(910) 575-SELL, (888) 414-SELL

With four locations (Holden Beach, Sunset Beach, Calabash and Oak Island), all Alan Holden Companies, RE/MAX at the Beach has the Brunswick County coast covered. Selling all types of property, they are a leader in southeastern N.C. real estate.

Simmons Realty Inc.
641 Shoreline Dr. W, Sunset Beach
(910) 579-0192, (888) 683-0550

This real estate company has been working in sales on Sunset Beach since 1990, and Broker Beth Simmons is a lifelong native of the area. The company offers general real estate services on the Brunswick Islands and the adjacent mainland. It handles general brokerage to include commercial, residential and development.

Sunset Properties
419 S. Sunset Blvd., Sunset Beach
(910) 579-9000, (888) 348-9058

This family-owned company has been in operation since 1988 and is the largest sales and rental agency on the island, with more than 400 cottages and condos

to choose from. Single-family homes dominate this quiet residential island that attracts second-home investors, retirees and people who simply appreciate living away from it all.

Sunset Vacations - Sunset Realty
401 S. Sunset Blvd., Sunset Beach
(910) 579-9000

Sunset Vacations offers a wide assortment of attractive, single-family homes for rent throughout Sunset Beach, including oceanfront, canal, bay-front and inlet locations. They have beach homes to fit every style, location and budget, and you can book directly online. This is an experienced company with an extreme commitment to making your vacation just right.

Williamson Realty
119 Causeway Dr. SW, Ocean Isle Beach
(910) 579-2373, (800) 727-9222

Serving the Ocean Isle Beach area since 1975, Williamson Realty specializes in the sale of beach properties, including condominiums, rental cottages, permanent homes and residential construction. The friendly staff has the experience and expertise to help you find the home of your dreams on Ocean Isle Beach.

Surf City

A Beach Place Realty
203 S. Topsail Dr., Surf City
(910) 328-2522

Everyone wants a place at the beach, and the professional Realtors at A Beach Place Realty can help you find your perfect "place" at the coast. Whether you're looking for residential or commercial property on the island or the mainland, A Beach Place Realty can help find the right property for you. Being members of both the Topsail and Wilmington MLS, they have access to hundreds of available properties. Shop for your perfect beach place online with A Beach Place Realty's link to the MLS and view virtual tours of all their listings.

Access Realty
13480 N.C. Hwy. 50/210, Surf City
(910) 329-9800

Access Realty is a full-service broker-age company that offers a variety of options on Topsail Island. Properties include oceanfront, soundfront, mainland homes and condominiums. Some locations offer pool facilities, fitness centers, game rooms or tennis courts. Call or visit their website for more details.

Bryson and Associates, Inc.
809 Roland Ave., Surf City
(910) 328-2468, (800) 326-0747

High-end, oceanfront, single-family homes are the specialty of Bryson & Associates. Committed to quality customer service, Bryson and Associates also handles homeowner association management.

Century 21 Action, Inc.
518 Roland Ave., Surf City
(888) 826-0563
www.century21topsail.com

An established business since 1969, Century 21 Action professionally markets real estate in the entire greater Topsail Island area. With more than 20 agents and two offices, there is always someone ready to assist with a sale or purchase anywhere on Topsail Island or on the mainland from Hampstead to Holly Ridge and Sneads Ferry. Century 21 Action also has a large and well-managed vacation and long-term rental division.

Coldwell Banker Sea Coast Realty
326 New River Dr., Unit B, Surf City
(910) 328-2625, (877) 786-7787

With an office on Topsail Island, mainland offices in Sneads Ferry and Jacksonville and more than 40 real estate sales professionals on staff, Coldwell Banker Sea Coast Realty is one of the largest real estate companies serving the area. The company also has offices in Hampstead, Wilmington, Carolina Beach, Leland, Southport and Oak Island. Coldwell Banker Sea Coast offers single-family oceanfront homes, condominiums, townhouses, soundfront hideaways, mainland property and commercial real estate.

Everyday Dreamers Inc.
1208 N. New River Dr., Surf City
(910) 382-5075, (800) 328-6590

Everyday Dreamers is your one-stop source for real estate services in the Hampstead, Holly Ridge, Sneads Ferry and Topsail Island area. Real estate is one of the most exciting investments one can make, and owner/broker Charles Turner at Everyday Dreamers believes that it should be a fun and rewarding experience. Here you'll find everything you'll need to buy or sell a home as well as learn about the market value of the homes you may own or want to buy in the area. Everyday Dreamers and the Seashore Realty Group offers first-hand local knowledge and unparalleled service.

Island Real Estate
The Fishing Village, Roland Ave., Surf City
(910) 328-2323, (800) 622-6886
www.topsailvacation.com

Cathy Medlin knows real estate. She has been selling and leasing properties on and around Topsail Island since the 1970s and was one of the founders of the Topsail Island Board of Realtors. This company sells beach, waterway and mainland homes and lots, as well as commercial buildings and property. The company also handles more than 200 vacation and long-term rental properties. They specialize in making dreams come true.

Jean Brown Real Estate, Inc.
522 New River Dr., Surf City
(910) 328-1640

Jean Brown Real Estate, Inc. has been a top-producing island real estate firm for more than 26 years. Sales agents offer a wide range of experience in both residential and commercial real estate. This office consistently maintains one of the most diverse listing inventories of properties for sale and is a member of both the Topsail Island and Jacksonville MLS Services.

King Co. Real Estate
202 S. Shore Dr., Surf City
(910) 328-0239

n Onslow County native, Nathan King has been a local builder since 1983. His full-service real estate business consists

of residential and commercial sales and new construction both on Topsail Island and the surrounding areas. He is also a licensed real estate appraiser.

Turner Real Estate
Surf City Shopping Center, Surf City
(910) 328-1313

Specializing in sales from single-family homes and condominiums to commercial property and building lots, Turner Real Estate has been serving all of Topsail Island since 1988. Broker-in-charge Rick Turner really believes in personalized service and even has business calls forwarded to his home after regular business hours.

Ward Realty Corp.
116 S. Topsail Dr., Surf City
(910) 328-3221
www.wardrealty.com

The original developer of Topsail Island, Ward Realty has more than 60 years of dedicated service in sales, home construction and vacation rentals. Broker David Ward continues the family tradition

of commitment to the buyers' interests. The rental and sales departments are strong assets that work hand-in-hand to provide a compatible, full-service real estate program.

Topsail Beach

Intracoastal Realty
804 Carolina Ave., Topsail Beach
(910) 328-3001

Intracoastal Realty is proud of its unparalleled tradition as the area's leading firm for properties of distinction. Built upon a 30-plus year history of expertise, integrity and personalized service, Intracoastal Realty has represented generations of homeowners in the coastal areas of North Carolina, Wilmington and the historic district, Wrightsville Beach, Pleasure Island Beaches, north to Topsail and Surf City, and south to Oak Island. Intracoastal Realty has aligned itself with a select network of world-class industry leaders through their affiliations with Luxury Portfolio and Leading Real Estate Companies of the World. In addition to serving buyers and sellers in all price ranges, the agency's New Homes division represents many new home communities in the area and their vacation and rental divisions provide vacation rentals as well as long-term property management.

Sea Path Realty
920 S. Anderson Blvd., Topsail Beach
(910) 328-4201, (888) 328-4201

Located just south of the Topsail Beach business district in a round, light green house, Sea Path Realty is easy to find. Five agents can assist you with your residential real estate and beach rental needs. Sea Path Realty is a member of Multiple Listing Service (MLS). Office hours are 9 AM to 4 PM, and they are closed on Wednesdays.

Sneads Ferry

Coldwell Banker-Coastline Realty
965 Old Folkstone Rd., Ste. 108,
Sneads Ferry
(910) 327-7711
www.cbcoastline.com

This company, established in 1994 as the original Coldwell Banker affiliate in the Topsail Island area, works primarily with homes and resort properties on Topsail Island and in the Sneads Ferry area. Coastline Realty offers a full range of real estate properties, including single-family homes, townhouses and resort condominiums. Their agents are very knowledgeable about the properties and the area, as they are all long-time residents. This company also handles commercial sales, vacation and long-term rentals and is a member of the Coldwell Banker Relocation Network and the MLS.

Treasure Realty
1950 N.C. Hwy. 174, Ste. P, Sneads Ferry
(910) 327-4444, (800) 762-3961
www.treasurerealty.com

Treasure Realty is proud to have been the top-producing firm in North Topsail Beach and Sneads Ferry for the past 18 years. Waterfront property and condominiums are their specialties. With many

years of experience, Treasure Realty's professional sales staff is ready to serve as a buyer's or seller's agent.

Hampstead

Century 21 Sweyer & Associates
16406 U.S. Hwy. 17, Hampstead
(910) 270-3606, (800) 848-0021

As a locally owned and operated family company since 1987, CENTURY 21 Sweyer & Associates understands the importance of your home to your family and are committed to delivering outstanding service. For the 6th consecutive year they have been ranked the No. 1 CENTURY 21® in North Carolina in closed sales and units (out of 300 plus offices). With over 130 sales agents, they service residential real estate from the Southern tip of Brunswick County to the Northern reaches of Jacksonville in Onslow County. Their Hampstead office handles residential sales, commercial sales, residential and investment/rental properties, long-term rental management for tenants and property owners, community-association management, mortgage services and residential maintenance. They also offer training services for new agents, relocation assistance for clients new to the area and a professional in-house marketing department that can help you sell your property. After all these years, their original commitment to customer satisfaction through quality service remains the same.

Stephanie Gasparovic & Associates
16076 U.S. Hwy. 17, Hampstead
(910) 264-7826

Stephanie Gasparovic understands her role in real estate. For her, it's to provide information, education and guidance to help her clients reach their home-buying, selling or investment goal. As the leader of her own real estate team, Stephanie Gasparovic & Associates, Inc., Stephanie has the experience and knowledge to make your move a smooth transition. Her peers agree; Stephanie was recently named one of the top 30 Realtors nationwide under the age of 30 by REALTOR Magazine.

Town Pro Realty
111 Hampstead Village Dr., Hampstead
(910) 262-7355

Looking for property? As a resident of Hampstead, Lara Beaudoin is your local expert and can help you find just the right home or investment property in Hampstead, nearby Wilmington or the Topsail Island area. Ready to sell? With more than 15 years experience in marketing and advertising and several years as a multi-million-dollar real estate producer, Lara Beaudoin knows how to effectively market your property. Call for a free, no-obligation presentation to see how Lara can help sell your most valuable asset.

Apartments

If you are not ready for the hassles of home ownership or you are saving up for that down payment, renting an apartment is an affordable way to handle your housing needs. Wilmington features a myriad of apartments ranging from low-income, affordable housing to lovely historic spaces downtown. Prices for rentals range from around $600 to more than $1,500 per month, depending on the location and extras. While newer apartment complexes generally offer more modern amenities, apartments in the downtown area often have historic touches such as a wrap-around porch or fireplace. Be prepared to provide a deposit, a month's rent and references in addition to undergoing credit and background checks when renting an apartment. For some suggestions on apartments, see the following list. Or try

Wilmington's grand historic homes are fabulous settings for bed and breakfast inns.

a real estate agency that has a rentals department.

WILMINGTON

Brightmore of Wilmington
2324 41st St., Wilmington
(910) 350-1980, (800) 556-6899
www.brightmoreofwilmington.com

Wilmington's preferred continuum of lifestyle choices, Brightmore offers three distinct communities on one campus. Brightmore - Independent Living attracts independent seniors with a lifestyle featuring one-bedroom and two-bedroom apartment homes and includes many service and amenities, such as housekeeping, delicious meals, fitness programs, frequent activities and scheduled transportation. The Kempton - Assisted Living offers supportive services for individuals who may need assistance with certain everyday activities. The caring staff provides three meals a day, medication administration and medical transportation. The Commons - Personal Care provides around-the-clock care for residents with personal healthcare needs. The Commons also offers Paraklay Way, a secure unit for individuals with Alzheimer's or dementia.

Glenmeade Village
1518 Village Dr., Wilmington
(910) 762-8108

Located in a quiet, secluded setting, Glenmeade Village, an apartment home community designed for those 55 and over, is convenient to shopping, medical facilities, the senior center, the Cameron Art Museum, beaches and the riverfront. With its vintage charm, indoor heated pool, greenhouse, tennis court and clubhouse, along with sociable residents, the atmosphere is warm and friendly.

Still Meadow Village Apartment Homes
4632 Still Meadow Dr., Wilmington
(910) 793-1984

Still Meadow Village offers great apartment homes with spacious floor plans, tons of storage space and numerous amenities. Residents enjoy screened-in porches, and some units offer fireplaces for those chilly winter nights. With one, two and three bedroom configurations, there's an apartment for almost any renter's requirements. Their friendly staff members are certified by the National Apartment Association and look forward to helping you with finding your home.

RETIREMENT

With a mild climate, beautiful beaches, an active arts community and abundant recreational opportunities, the southern coast of North Carolina is attracting younger retirees to its sunny shores in ever-increasing numbers.

THE EARLY YEARS

Naturally, the temperate climate of the area entices transplants from the North who are tired of frigid winters, snow, ice, potholes and gray skies. Winter, such as it is here, is moderated considerably by the warming effect of the Atlantic Ocean and the Gulf Stream. The average summer high temperature is 88 degrees, the average winter low is 36 degrees and the overall average for the year is 64 degrees.

Active retirees will find no shortage of outdoor pursuits to enjoy in the southern coast region. With the Intracoastal Waterway, rivers, sounds and Atlantic Ocean beaches, water figures primarily into the lifestyle of the southern coast. Golf is huge here, especially in Brunswick County, and there are literally hundreds of courses from Topsail Island in the north to Brunswick County in the south; see our Golf chapter for listings. For those who enjoy being in, on or around the water, the southern coast offers water-oriented activities such as boating, sailing, fishing, paddling and surfing. Details can be found in our Marinas, Fishing and Watersports chapters. Our Sports, Fitness and Parks chapter features the many other activities people enjoy in the area, including softball, cycling, racquetball, martial arts, yoga and much more.

For those interested in gardening in their retirement years, the southern coastal area is in USDA growing zone 8, averages 248 or more growing days per year and has an annual rainfall of 54 inches. The heaviest rainfall months are June, July and August, and more often than not, it rains at night and is sunny during the day — Camelot right here in Dixie. Several varieties of flowers bloom all winter, and numerous shrubs and trees retain their foliage all year.

For cultural pursuits, Wilmington is the arts epicenter of the region. No matter where retirees choose to live, the cultural offerings are never too far away. Wilmington has a thriving film industry, a theatrical community much bigger than one would expect of an area this size and performing arts series in a host of fabulous venues. A rich collection of artists are drawn to the southern coast region. See our Arts chapter for more information.

Downtown Wilmington offers many activities for seniors, including horse-drawn carriage, trolley or walking tours of the Historical District, riverboat tours, unusual stores and boutiques, the Riverwalk and a number of antebellum homes open for visiting, to mention just a few (see our Attractions chapter). Any given evening will find both seniors and younger people strolling about, shopping and dining outside. When the grandkids come to visit, there are abundant activities to entertain them (see our Kidstuff chapter), and those who want to volunteer will find a wealth of opportunities.

For those ready to enjoy the good life, the region offers a broad range of dining options (see Restaurants) and the shopping possibilities are seemingly endless, from national chains of every sort to unique boutiques to antiques shops to souvenir shops (see Shopping).

Another aspect of the southern coast area attracting retirees is a considerably expanded healthcare system that is increasingly focused on the needs of seniors. Healthcare on the southern coast

includes a major hospital offering state-of-the-art care, private physicians practicing the full range of specialties, urgent care centers, complementary care practitioners and alternative healthcare practitioners. See our Healthcare chapter.

The housing options for retirees on the southern coast are wide and varied. There is a strong upswing in the development of retirement communities, many of them with golf courses, tennis courts and swimming pools and offering a wide variety of housing choices. Other choices include golf course communities, waterfront estates, beach-community condominiums, low-maintenance town homes, downtown Wilmington loft-style apartments, acreage in the country and more. See our Real Estate and Neighborhoods chapter for a glimpse of what the region offers.

Although progressive and growth-oriented, this area still possesses elements of charm, graciousness and gentility of the South, which, coupled with the cosmopolitan influence of retirees and new residents from all across the nation, results in a delightfully relaxed but upbeat ambiance. Also, partly due to the enormous number of activities available to them, retirees tend to feel more included living in the southern coast communities than they would living in a large urban area.

THE LATER YEARS

When it comes time to slow down, seniors do not have to leave the southern coast. The region has numerous facilities to support seniors as they age and are in need of more care.

As mentioned, the Wilmington area offers outstanding medical facilities and services that are increasingly geared toward the aging population (see our Healthcare chapter).

As people age, their living and care needs sometimes change. Accredited independent and assisted living communities and home-care services are found throughout the area, and we feature some of them in this section.

Deciding Where to Live

For those wishing to retire to this four-county coastal haven, there is a wide variety of home styles and home sites, as well as a range of prices. Oceanfront property

Enjoy beautiful views such as these along the North Carolina coast.

photo: Robert Graves

in older exclusive communities commands the highest price, of course, partially because there is so little of it remaining. Generally speaking, the closer to the water, the more expensive the property. However, the southern coastal region is surrounded by ocean, rivers, creeks and lakes, so the dream of living on or near the water is still within the means of those other than the very wealthy. In addition to these, there are sounds, which are bodies of water between the mainland and the ocean-facing barrier islands, and which in this area, are connected by the Intracoastal Waterway. More reasonably priced housing, especially condominiums, is available on or near these waters. Often a group of homes or a condominium complex is built in conjunction with boat slips or a marina. (See our section on Real Estate and Neighborhoods for more in-depth information about locations and developments.)

Independent and Supported Living Communities

Senior adult or retirement communities are those with congregate housing intended specifically for older occupants. These communities feature single homes and/or apartments providing several services, which may include meals in a central location, housekeeping, a pool, transportation and social activities. They may or may not offer healthcare services. We have listed only some of these communities. For further assistance, contact the chamber of commerce in the area you choose for relocation (see our Area Overview section for a list of chambers) or one of the government agencies listed.

Brightmore of Wilmington
2324 41st St., Wilmington
(910) 350-1980, (800) 556-6899
www.brightmoreofwilmington.com

Brightmore welcomes active retirees who wish to combine independence with a small-town atmosphere. Studio, one-bedroom, one-bedroom deluxe, two-bedroom and two-bedroom deluxe apartments are available for a monthly rental

fee. Each apartment home includes a full kitchen, all utilities (except phone service), 24-hour security and medical emergency call stations, weekly housekeeping and flat linen service, scheduled transportation, daily choice of meals, recreational/exercise programs and an onsite beauty/barber shop. The new Aquatic/Fitness Center features an exercise room and pool with a flume for resistance lap-style swimming and walking. There's also a seated whirlpool area. Brightmore is located midtown between the Cape Fear River and Wrightsville Beach. It is on the same campus with The Kempton (assisted living) and The Commons (personal care). Brightmore residents are priority listed for services at any of the other communities that make up the continuum of lifestyle choices. Call to learn more about the refundable priority deposit program.

Clare Bridge of Wilmington
3501 Converse Dr., Wilmington
(910) 790-8664

Clare Bridge is designed specifically for people with Alzheimer's disease or other memory impairments. Everything is geared to help individuals with memory problems to live the most independent and fulfilling life possible. Clare Bridge's homelike settings are designed to re-create environments people have enjoyed throughout their lives, with interior spaces scaled and decorated like those of a private home. Indoor and enclosed outdoor walking paths give residents the opportunity to explore safely. Clare Bridge also offers its own dining program designed by a team of specialists including a gerontologist, corporate chef and professional dietitian. This unique program preserves residents' ability to enjoy meals with special culinary offerings, personal assistance, consistent seating arrangements, music, centerpieces and fresh linens to heighten the dining experience. Other amenities include 24-hour staff and licensed nurse, assistance with personal care and hygiene, laundry and linen service, mealtime and feeding assistance, housekeeping, medication management, and an audio-security system. Clare Bridge also offers life-enrichment activities, memory-support programs and outings to increase self-esteem and independence.

Carillon Assisted Living
1125 E. Leonard St., Southport
(910) 454-4001

For assisted living, Carillon is an excellent choice. Carillon has wraparound porches with Carolina rockers, parlors with fireplaces, sun rooms, patios, courtyards and dining on linens and china. Carillon has all the comforts of home and more — from lovely furnishings to light and airy private studios, semi-private studios and suites to the spa with a whirlpool bath. The caring, dedicated professionals reinforce self-reliance, dignity and social wellbeing. At the same time, assistance with daily activities, home health and therapy services, daily exercise classes and walking programs, are offered. Carillon has The Garden Place where residents with Alzheimer's live and participate in an activity-programmed environment focused on reducing anxiety, restoring socialization and enhancing life skills. Respite and rehabilitative care are available as well.

Glenmeade Village
1518 Village Dr., Wilmington
(910) 762-8108

This small community for active, mature individuals age 55 or older is located in a quiet, secluded setting, within walking distance of New Hanover Regional Medical Center, physicians' offices and shopping. Glenmeade Village offers 104 apartment homes available in four floor plans. Choose from spacious one-, two- or three-bedroom units on one level, or a two-bedroom townhouse design. All of the tastefully decorated apartments are air-conditioned, energy efficient and fully carpeted, and include ample closet space, large windows, washer/dryer (three-bedroom units only) and fully equipped kitchens. Community amenities include an enclosed heated pool that is open year round, with aqua fitness classes offered two days a week, a clubhouse that's open daily for socializing and card games, a tennis court, a greenhouse and a laundry room. Twenty-four-hour emergency maintenance service is available. Small pets are accepted.

Lake Shore Commons
1402 Hospital Plaza Dr., Wilmington
(910) 251-0067

This outstanding retirement community offers attractive, unfurnished apartment homes with a variety of floor plans. Units are available in studio, one-bedroom or two-bedroom styles at affordable month-to-month rents; a lease or buy-in is never required. Within the main building, each apartment has a kitchenette, carpeting and window treatments; most feature a balcony or porch. Free laundry facilities are located on each floor. There are also many comfortable common areas, a huge fully equipped kitchen for resident use, exercise facilities, a pool table, two libraries and several multi-purpose rooms. In addition to the apartments, eight cottages are available, equipped with full kitchens and washer/dryer. Resident managers are on duty 24 hours every day for assistance. Included in the monthly rent are heating/air conditioning, electricity, water, cable TV, all maintenance and repairs, weekly housekeeping (including linens and towels) and three daily chef-prepared meals with a choice of entrees (main building residents only). Transportation at no charge is available on a scheduled basis for residents who have appointments or shopping to do. In addition, the facility offers numerous organized activities.

Plantation Village
1200 Porters Neck Rd., Wilmington
(910) 686-7181, (800) 334-0240

Plantation Village is a life-care retirement community on 56 acres within Porters Neck Plantation. The campus has a library, bank facilities, an auditorium, a gym, an indoor swimming pool and spa, a woodworking shop, a crafts room and many more amenities in addition to the standard flat laundry, lawn and maintenance, and planned activities services. Plantation Village is a unique retirement community in that it receives people in good health age 62 and older and offers professional, long-term nursing care services from nearby Cornelia Nixon Davis Health Care Center and Champions Assisted Living. Before nursing care is needed, residents have access to a wellness center on the campus, a 24-hour nurse on call and the visit of a doctor each week.

Shallotte Assisted Living
520 Mulberry St., Shallotte
(910) 754-6621

The combination of 80 home-like residential units and a management team of licensed health professionals make Shallotte Assisted Living an excellent choice for those who are in need of assistance with day-to-day living. Residents have access to a community nurse who directs individual plans for care, an in-house physician and psychiatric services. The convenience of home visits by physicians and mental-health professionals adds to the comfort of all residents. Other available services include housekeeping, laundry service, meals and snacks, scheduled activities and transportation.

Spring Arbor Residential Assisted Living
809 John D. Barry Dr., Wilmington
(910) 799-4999

Spring Arbor offers a community that is really more of an extension of your family, with caring professionals that have developed a comfortable, enjoyable lifestyle experience for residents. Spring

Arbor values and nurtures residents' independence while offering privacy, security and comfort. There are many amenities to enjoy at the assisted living center, such as a front porch with rocking chairs, planned regular activities and a sun room. The Wilmington location also includes the Special Care Cottage, designed specifically for Alzheimer's and dementia residents.

The Woods at Holly Tree
4610 Holly Tree Rd., Wilmington
(910) 793-1300

The Woods at Holly Tree provides a caring environment in a secure and gracious surrounding. One all-inclusive monthly rent begins with several styles of apartments and ends with a large list of amenities, including three chef-prepared meals a day served in a well-appointed dining room, weekly housekeeping and flat linen service, all utilities (except telephone), cable TV, free laundry facilities, and social and recreational activities. The Woods at Holly Tree is an affordable residence where attention to detail and personal consideration are paramount. No lease or buy-in fee is ever required. The Woods at Holly Tree has two sets of resident managers on site 24 hours a day. For the convenience of residents, scheduled transportation is available. On the premises are a beauty/barber shop, an exercise/activity room, a billiards and game room, a library, a chapel and a large-screen TV lounge as well as several cozy nooks for visiting or reading.

Keep on Going

UNCW's Osher Lifelong Learning
601 S. College Ave., Wilmington
(910) 962-4034

UNCW's Osher Lifelong Learning (OLLI) program offers a tremendous selection of lectures, concerts, plays, educational courses and activities, many of them geared to the retired population. Keep busy all year long by taking advantage of the extensive offerings. Choose from art, history, music, languages, women's courses, personal growth, travel and professional development programs. A variety of topics are also covered in the breakfast or lunch lecture series and foreign policy discussions. Call for your free copy of the catalogue, Pathways.

Through UNCW's Adult Scholars Leadership Program (ASLP), seasoned adults learn about past and current issues in the region together with possible solutions. Subjects covered in this seven-week program include local history, Southern culture, health and human services, media, government, arts and economic development. Adult Scholars are encouraged to use what they've learned to become more involved in enhancing the community through volunteer and entrepreneurial service. For information about this program, call (910) 962-3699.

Government Agencies

Seniors can learn a lot about North Carolina's many valuable programs by calling the state CARE-LINE, (800) 662-7030, or by visiting the Division of Aging and Adult Services website: www.dhhs.state.nc.us/aging/. County departments of aging offer a variety of services, including congregate and/or home-delivered meals, transportation, minor home repairs, senior center operations, in-home aides, health promotion/disease prevention, and fan/heat relief. If you're age 60 or older, ask about getting a free Senior Tar Heel Card

for discounts at local businesses. Although most businesses offer discounts, especially if you ask, the Senior Tar Heel Card is honored throughout the state and extends the purchasing power of older adults, especially those living on fixed incomes. Participating businesses typically display the Senior Tar Heel Card emblem decal, but seniors are encouraged to ask if the store honors the card even if there is no posted emblem. For more information about the card or other assistance for seniors, contact one of the following agencies.

Brunswick Center at Southport
1513 N. Howe St., Ste. 1, Southport
(910) 454-0583

Cape Fear Council of Governments,
Area Agency on Aging
1480 Harbour Dr., Wilmington
(910) 395-4553, (800) 218-6575

New Hanover County
Department of Aging
2222 S. College Rd., Wilmington
(910) 798-6400

Pender Adult Services, Inc.
901 S. Walker St., Burgaw
(910) 259-9119

SHIIP, Brunswick County
Cooperative Extension
Government Center, Bldg. N, 25
Referendum Dr., Bolivia
(910) 253-2610, (800) 443-9354

HEALTHCARE (H)

The southern coast's excellent healthcare facilities and services — a result of rapid growth, increased development and a booming retirement population in North Carolina's southern coastal region — rival those in larger cities. However, that hasn't always been the case and, as recently as 25 years ago, residents sought advanced medical treatment in larger university medical centers or metropolitan hospitals.

Now, residents and visitors have access to more sophisticated healthcare and state-of-the-art technology and are no longer forced to travel inland for treatment of serious illness or injury. In New Hanover County, more than 500 practicing physicians in a wide range of medical and surgical specialties now utilize some of the most technologically progressive facilities and equipment in the state through New Hanover Regional Medical Center. This network, the primary source of healthcare in the Greater Wilmington area, comprises three formerly independent hospitals — New Hanover Regional Medical Center, Cape Fear Hospital and Pender Memorial Hospital — as well as three hospitals located on the medical center's campus — The Rehabilitation Hospital and The Behavioral Health Hospital. Affiliate agencies include New Hanover Regional Medical Center Emergency Medical Services, NHRMC Home Care, NHRMC Health & Diagnostics, NHRMC Urgent Care, Betty H. Cameron Women's and Children's Hos and the New Hanover Regional Medical Center Foundation. This far-reaching partnership enlarges and enhances the region's overall healthcare capabilities through upgraded and expanded facilities, more options in a range of medical and surgical specialties and improved access to healthcare.

Although smaller in size, Brunswick County's two hospitals — Brunswick Community Hospital and Dosher Memorial Hospital — offer a wide range of services from general medicine and round-the-clock emergency room physicians to medical/surgical specialties and community healthcare affiliates. When necessary, medical care beyond the scope of their services is referred to Wilmington's larger hospitals. Residents and vacationers along the Brunswick beaches will find these smaller hospitals more convenient and an excellent source when medical attention is needed.

Hospitals

WILMINGTON

New Hanover Regional Medical Center
2131 S. 17th St., Wilmington
(910) 343-7000
www.nhrmc.org

For residents throughout the region, New Hanover Regional Medical Center (NHRMC) offers the best features of welcoming, patient-centered care combined with next-generation medicine. While strengthening the legacy of its close ties to the community and region, NHRMC continually pursues the best technology and advances in treatment.

New Hanover Regional Medical Center has inpatient and outpatient locations throughout the area including the main campus on 17th Street and Cape Fear Hospital on Wrightsville Avenue in Wilmington. Pender Memorial Hospital in Burgaw and NHRMC Home Care are also affiliated with NHRMC.

NHRMC's main campus is a teaching hospital and tertiary referral center. Originally built in 1967, the hospital has recently undergone a significant expansion and upgrade with the addition of the new 186,500-square-foot Surgical Pavilion and the 150-bed Betty H. Cameron

Women's & Children's Hospital. Inpatient units throughout NHRMC have also been renovated so patients can expect to find a comfortable, quiet setting with all-new interiors, room for family and access to caregivers who are never far from the room.

Cape Fear Hospital is the primary home of NHRMC's nationally recognized orthopedic program. Cape Fear Hospital also offers a 24-hour emergency department, inpatient and outpatient surgery, respiratory therapy, rehabilitation medicine, radiology services and laboratory services.

New Hanover Regional Medical Center is the ninth-largest healthcare system in the state and the largest employer in the region, with a team of more than 4,700 employees, 540 physicians and 800 volunteers.

Betty H. Cameron Women's & Children's Hospital – Redefining the boundaries of innovation in the field of women's and children's care, the Betty H. Cameron Women's & Children's Hospital's models of care, technology, architecture and interior design all reflect bold new thinking in bringing care for women, newborns and children to the next level. The hospital features all-private rooms with space for the patient and family. The hospital offers obstetrical care for routine and high-risk deliveries and welcomes more than 4,000 new lives each year. In addition, the Neonatal Intensive Care Unit cares for babies born premature or critically ill. The Betty H. Cameron Women's & Children's Hospital also has the only pediatric unit and pediatric intensive care unit in the region. Women admitted to the hospital needing gynecological treatment, including gynecological oncology, are also cared for in the Betty H. Cameron Women's & Children's Hospital.

Heart Center– A key element in NHRMC's role as a preeminent heart center is its open-heart surgery program, the only such program in the region. Advances in both traditional open-heart procedures and less invasive or minimally invasive techniques have revolutionized the treatment of heart disease. NHRMC's cardiovascular physicians stay at the forefront of breakthroughs in surgical techniques

as well as new diagnostic and treatment technologies. The Heart Center houses a 16-bed Coronary Care Unit, a 14-bed Cardiovascular Intensive Care Unit as well as cardiac catheterization, electrophysiology and cardiovascular labs. The Heart Center also includes the Cardiac and Pulmonary Rehabilitation Programs, which offer classes on nutrition and stress management, as well as exercise classes monitored by registered nurses and exercise physiologists.

Orthopedic Center - Ranked in the top 10 percent of all orthopedic facilities nationally, New Hanover Regional Medical Center Orthopedic Center at Cape Fear Hospital offers both inpatient and outpatient surgical services for patients with problems with their muscles, joints, bones, ligaments, tendons and nerves. More than 1,800 hip and knee replacements are performed annually at the NHRMC Orthopedic Center.

Health and Diagnostics- New Hanover Regional Medical Center offers advanced diagnostic radiology services at many locations throughout the region to provide residents with sophisticated diagnosis and treatments close to home. Services include Interventional Radiology, Nuclear Medicine, CT scans, MRI, Digital Mammography, Bone Mineral Density Testing and Ultrasound.

Zimmer Cancer Center– New Hanover Regional Medical Center's cancer program has been nationally designated as a Teaching Hospital Cancer Program by the American College of Surgeon's Commission on Cancer. Its Zimmer Cancer Center includes physician specialists in medical, surgical and gynecologic cancers, an infusion unit for chemotherapy, a radiation oncology department and a Cancer Research Program that offers patients access to new therapies for the treatment and prevention of cancer. Patients with cancer also benefit from an extensive support system that includes nutrition counseling, pharmacy, social care and complementary therapies. Patients also benefit from inpatient treatment areas designed to make long stays more comfortable with private patient rooms and space for family members to stay and provide support.

Caring for Your Life

With primary care, specialties, and nearly 100 providers, Wilmington Health can take care of your entire family's healthcare needs. Visit us at one of our many locations, or learn more about what we have to offer at wilmingtonhealth.com. At Wilmington Health, we are committed to the care and health of our community.

WILMINGTON HEALTH

Everything you
care about is here

Your life, your family, friends, they're all here. And so is your health care, thanks to New Hanover Regional Medical Center. We've brought the best of medicine home. Where your life is, where you live, here.

- The region's only open-heart surgery program and a heart center recognized as a center of excellence
- An orthopedic program that ranks in the top 10% nationally
- A teaching cancer center that offers cutting edge clinical trials
- A new women's and children's hospital featuring neonatal intensive care and the region's first pediatric intensive care unit
- And a Surgical Pavilion that provides the ideal setting for the latest advances in surgery in an easy-to-access facility

For a physician referral call VitaLine: 910.815.5188

**New Hanover
Regional Medical Center**

www.nhrmc.or

Trauma and Emergency Medical Services– New Hanover Regional Medical Center's Emergency Services Department is highly integrated to help ensure patients get the best care possible. It includes the region's only Level II Trauma Center and Emergency Departments at NHRMC, Cape Fear Hospital and Pender Memorial Hospital. It also incorporates New Hanover Regional EMS, which operates the region's paramedic service as well as a critical care transport system with VitaLink mobile intensive care units and AirLink, an air ambulance service. Widely recognized for its outstanding level of care, New Hanover Regional Medical Center EMS was named North Carolina's first model system.

Rehabilitation Services– New Hanover Regional Medical Center Rehabilitation Services includes a CARF–accredited, 60-bed inpatient rehabilitation hospital and outpatient therapies for adults and children. The outpatient locations, which include Independence Rehabilitation, Oleander Rehabilitation and Pender Health & Diagnostics - Rocky Point, provide different services that include therapy for patients with orthopedic, musculoskeletal and neurological conditions, as well as children with developmental delays. Pool therapy is among the therapies used at Oleander Rehabilitation.

Spine Center– From the most common to the most complex, the New Hanover Regional Medical Center Spine Center treats a variety of back, neck and spine disorders. Neurologic and orthopedic surgeons experienced in diagnosing and treating everything from traumatic injuries to chronic disorders work with dedicated healthcare providers to customize both short- and long-term treatment plans. Patients hospitalized for brain and spinal injuries, stroke, multiple sclerosis, ALS, Alzheimer's disease and seizures related to neurological disorders are often cared for in NHRMC's Neuroscience Unit.

Surgery– A wide range of surgical specialists perform inpatient and outpatient surgery at each of NHRMC's hospital campuses. Surgery at New Hanover Regional Medical Center is performed in the Surgical Pavilion, a technologically advanced environment that allows specially trained surgeons to perform minimally invasive surgeries, including using the daVinci Surgical Robotic System.

Behavioral Health Hospital – A psychiatric crisis stabilization hospital, New Hanover Regional Medical Center's Behavioral Health Hospital offers inpatient psychiatric programs for adults with mental health disorders.

NHRMC Home Care- NHRMC Home Care offers services to residents in eight counties in southeastern North Carolina. Services include skilled nursing, physical, occupational and speech therapy, infusion therapy, wound care and diabetes management. The service has been recognized as one of the country's top home-care providers through HomeCare Elite™.

New Hanover Regional Medical Center Foundation – The Foundation exists to generate philanthropic support for special projects, equipment, staff education and patient care that would be difficult, perhaps impossible, to fund from the hospital's operations budget alone. The Foundation works with donors to choose how their gift can have the biggest impact in the area of their choosing. The Foundation also organizes special events to fund programs that support cancer, heart disease and other initiatives that directly affect the lives of the community NHRMC serves.

Physician Referral and Health Information – No matter what time of day, area residents and visitors can get health information, talk to a nurse or find a physician through VitaLine, a free 24-hour-a-day call center. The number is (910) 815-5188.

New Hanover Regional Medical Center's website, www.nhrmc.org, also has extensive health reference guides, an online physician directory and more information about the services available through NHRMC facilities.

BRUNSWICK COUNTY

Brunswick Community Hospital
1 Medical Dr., off U.S. Hwy. 17, Supply
(910) 755-8121

Serving area residents since 1977, Brunswick Community Hospital, centrally located in Supply, is a 60-bed Joint

Commission accredited, not-for-profit, acute care facility offering a wide range of medical and surgical services, including a 24-hour Emergency Center and a Maternity Center. The hospital's comprehensive medical services also include intensive and critical care units, laboratory and radiology services, cardiopulmonary services, inpatient and outpatient physical therapy, speech therapy, and cardiac and pulmonary rehabilitation programs. The hospital is in the process of building a 74-bed replacement facility with all private rooms. This new facility is scheduled to open in 2011 and will be situated approximately 3 miles north of the current hospital location on U.S. Highway 17. For a complete listing of services, visit the website, which offers an extensive health library covering a full range of health topics as well as a complete physician listing, including doctor's credentials. Brunswick Community Hospital also has a location at Sunset Beach called the Sea Trail Medical Center, (910) 575-5100. This outpatient center offers both laboratory and radiology services, including mammography and diagnostic X-rays.

Dosher Memorial Hospital
924 N. Howe St., Southport
(910) 457-3800

Dosher Memorial Hospital is a nonprofit, public hospital with 36 acute care and 64 skilled nursing care beds. Established in 1930, this community hospital serves the southeastern Brunswick County area, attracting patients from Southport, Bald Head Island, Oak Island, St. James, Boiling Spring Lakes, Bolivia, Supply and surrounding areas. Dosher Hospital's scope of services includes a 24-hour emergency department, inpatient and outpatient surgeries, emergency medicine, endoscopy/colonoscopy, acute (inpatient) and skilled nursing care, cardiac rehab, cardiac CT scoring, cardiopulmonary and respiratory therapy, diagnostic imaging with nuclear medicine, fixed-base MRI, CT scanning, osteoporosis screening with a DEXA bone-density scanner, mammography using digital technology, physical, occupational and speech therapies; com-

prehensive lab services; and diabetic and nutrition education. Medical specialties include family practice, internal medicine, gynecology, pediatrics, orthopedics, general surgery, plastic surgery, opthalmology, pulmonology, cardiology, otolaryngology and urology. Dosher Memorial Hospital is accredited by the Joint Commission on Accreditation of Healthcare Organizations. In 2008 the Dosher Medical Plaza was opened on Long Beach Road and includes digital mammography, X-ray, DEXA, MRI, an outpatient laboratory and a specialty center.

PENDER COUNTY

Pender Memorial Hospital
507 Fremont St., Burgaw
(910) 259-5451

Pender Memorial Hospital in Burgaw has been serving Pender County and the surrounding area since 1951. PMH is an accredited 86-bed, not-for-profit, community hospital that is affiliated with New Hanover Regional Medical Center. Pender Memorial Hospital provides a full range of services to the community including a 24-hour emergency department, comprehensive imaging and lab testing, inpatient and outpatient rehabilitation services and respiratory therapy 24-hours a day. The surgery department has large, modernized operating rooms located on the main hospital campus in the Surgery and Endoscopy Center, which opened in June 2008. PMH also has a skilled nursing facility with short-term rehabilitation and long-term care available. Pender Memorial Hospital offers all private rooms and also has a home health agency that covers an eight-county radius.

Immediate and Urgent Care

For non-surgical medical services, Wilmington and the surrounding communities offer an ample number of immediate-care centers, sometimes referred to as urgent-care centers. Vacationers or residents with relatively minor injuries, illnesses or conditions may prefer the convenience of visiting these centers over making an appointment to see a private doctor. Illnesses and injuries beyond the centers' capabilities are referred to area hospitals. These are convenient places to get flu and tetanus shots or to have a limited variety of tests or physicals for school, sports or insurance purposes. Most centers have their own labs and X-ray services, and all are staffed by qualified, licensed physicians and nurses.

Be advised that most of the centers operate on a first-come basis, so don't expect to be able to make an appointment. However, serious illnesses, injuries or conditions will receive first priority. These medical service facilities are not open 24 hours a day. In many cases, they are not open seven days a week. A few medical or family practice centers offer walk-in appointments. If you need attention and choose any of these centers, you're advised to phone ahead.

Visitors to Topsail Island are within a one-hour drive to hospitals and clinics in Wilmington; another public hospital within driving range is Onslow Memorial, (910) 577-2345, in Jacksonville.

For serious injuries and illnesses, the coastal region has ample emergency response services that can be reached by calling 911. The listing here is for your convenience only and does not imply endorsement of any facility.

WILMINGTON

Convenience Care at Porters Neck
8114 Market St. #200, Wilmington
(910) 686-2870

Located behind Porter's Neck Family Practice, this care center is open Monday through Friday from noon to 8 PM and Saturday and Sunday from 8 AM to 8 PM.

The Downtown MedCenter
119 Chestnut St., Wilmington
(910) 762-5588

Founded in 2001, The Downtown Med-Center provides primary care, urgent care and diagnostic services to the residents of New Hanover County, Brunswick County, Pender County and surrounding areas.

Med Care of North Carolina
5245 S. College Rd., Wilmington
(910) 392-7806

Open seven days a week from 8 AM to 8 PM, Med Care is dedicated to providing exceptional healthcare to the Wilmington area.

Medac
4402 Shipyard Blvd., Wilmington
(910) 791-0075
1442 Military Cutoff Rd., Wilmington
910-256-6088
8115 Market St., Wilmington
910-686-1972

Those in need of immediate medical attention will be pleased to know that a facility like MEDAC is there to serve them at a moment's notice. With doctor's appointments difficult to come by and emergency room visits often prohibitively expensive, MEDAC allows patients to receive fast, affordable treatment for most minor ailments and injuries. Staffed by board-certified, local physicians with a solid grasp of urgent-care patients' needs, these centers continue to be a vital source of medical assistance for Wilmington residents.

Next Care Urgent Care Centre
4815 Oleander Dr., Wilmington
(910) 452-1111

NextCare offers convenient walk-in healthcare services. NextCare is a great alternative to the emergency room for non-life-threatening illness or injuries and can be the perfect solution if you are visiting the area and are hit with an unexpected sickness. Their office is open 8 AM to 8 PM Monday through Friday and 8 AM to 4 PM on Saturday and Sunday.

Southeastern Healthcare
2595 S. 17th St., Wilmington
(910) 791-2788

The doctors and chiropractors at Southeastern Healthcare are dedicated to providing patients with immediate care directed toward pain relief and patient recovery.

Southside Medical Center, PA
1925-A Oleander Dr., Wilmington
(910) 251-7715

No appointment needed to visit this family-friendly medical center. Southside Medical Center can help you with your urgent care needs as well as complete physical exams.

NHRMC Urgent Care
1135 Military Cutoff Rd., Ste. 103, Wilmington
(910) 256-6222
www.nhrmc.org

Urgent Care of Wilmington provides quality affordable medical care of non-life threatening illnesses and injuries, diagnostic testing and occupational medicine.

BRUNSWICK COUNTY

Brunswick Urgent Care
509 Olde Waterford Way, Leland
(910) 383-2182

Coastal Immediate Care Center
4654 Long Beach Rd., Southport
(910) 457-9564

North Brunswick Family Medicine
117-H Village Rd., Leland
(910) 371-0404

Oak Island Medical Center
8715 E. Oak Island Dr., Oak Island
(910) 278-3316

Seaside Medical Center
710 Sunset Blvd. N., Ste. A, Sunset Beach
(910) 575-3923

Southeastern Healthcare, Chiropractic and Medical
110-C Village Rd., Leland
(910) 371-1000

WHA Brunswick Forest
1333 S. Dickinson Dr., Ste. 140, Leland
(910) 371-0404

TOPSAIL AREA

Surf City Urgent Care & Family Medicine
13520 N.C. Hwy. 50/210, Surf City
(910) 329-9812

Topsail Family Medicine & Urgent Care
16747 U.S. Hwy. 17, Hampstead
(910) 270-0052

Medical Services

Brunswick Forest Medical Pavilion
1333 S. Dickinson Dr., Ste. 140, Leland
(910) 371-0404

This 40,000-square-foot, state-of-the-art facility, part of the New Hanover Regional Medical Center with main offices located in Wilmington, opened in April 2010. The facility offers family-care physicians for children and adults as well as specialists in the fields of cardiology, dermatology, gastroenterology, neurology, pediatrics, sleep medicine and urology. Laboratory, imaging and diagnostic services, including MRIs, CT Scans, X-rays, bone density scans, ultrasounds and digital mammography, are available on site. Office hours are Monday through Friday 8 AM to 5 PM. Convenient Care services are also available without appointment for patients and non-patients of Wilmington Health physicians. Hours are Monday through Friday noon to 8 PM Saturday and Sunday 8 AM to 8 PM.

C. Clayton Walker III, DDS, PA
4405 Junction Park Dr., Wimington
(910) 350-6944
www.claytonwalkerdentistry.com

C. Clayton Walker II, DDS, PA is a family dental practice that specializes in creating happy, healthy smiles through general and restorative dentistry. Their offices offer a welcoming, comfortable environment combined with the best and latest dental

claytonwalker, dds

Clayton Walker, DDS is a family dental practice that specializes in creating happy, healthy smiles through general and restorative dentistry.

Dr. Walker

Dr. Farmer

4405 Junction Park Dr
Wilmington, NC
(910) 350-6944
www.claytonwalkerdentistry.com

treatments — all to provide you with the optimum dental care available to get the confidence and beautiful smile you desire. Dr. Walker and Dr. Michael C. Farmer, DMD are committed to offering patients the best care. The office is conveniently located in Monkey Junction.

Wilmington Health Associates
1202 Medical Center Dr., Wilmington
(910) 341-3300
www.wilmingtonhealth.com

For more than 35 years, Wilmington Health has been a leader in providing medical care to people of all ages in southeastern North Carolina. Their team of more than 100 providers offers 10 convenient locations in Wilmington and surrounding areas, such as Leland, Porters Neck and Carolina Beach.

Started in 1971, Wilmington Health is Wilmington's first multi-specialty physician's practice and has always been committed to providing the best possible healthcare in the most affordable way. This value-based approach is at the root of its popularity, and it has now expanded to offer full services in a number of medical specialties, including cardiology, pain, podiatry, pulmonology, gastroenterology, infectious diseases and neurology. Primary care services include family medicine, internal medicine and pediatrics at the Children's Clinic.

Surgical services include vascular surgery, general surgery, colorectal surgery, obstetrics and gynecologic services, ear-nose and throat, podiatry, as well as urologic and robotic surgery. Many of the physicians still provide care for their patients in the hospital settings at both New Hanover Regional Medical Center and Cape Fear Hospital. Wilmington Health offers the only private practice in the area with its own specialized team of hospitalist physicians dedicated to care for patients requiring hospitalization.

Wilmington Health provides several easily accessible outpatient facilities covering services such sleep medicine, physical therapy, a travel clinic, pain management, neurodiagnostic testing, radiology and MRI services. Though large in scope, Wilmington Health takes a uniquely patient-focused approach to its delivery of patient services. Their website is a community resource with information regarding important developments in the medical field. Wilmington Health has incorporated an electronic medical record, which further empowers its physicians to care and co-care for patients in a cooperative approach.

Wilmington Health welcomes walk-ins at their primary care locations including their Main Campus (1202 Medical Center Drive), both Convenient Care Locations (Porter's Neck and Brunswick Forest)

and at both Children's Clinic Locations (Silvers Stream off Medical Center Drive and Northchase). You can be seen on your schedule at the Convenient Care Locations between noon and 8 PM weekdays and 8 AM to 8 PM on weekends.

Wilmington Health is committed to utilizing a team approach to provide the highest quality of care and evidenced-based medicine.

Mental Health and Addictions

Numerous organizations and agencies in the area help people struggling with substance abuse. Make sure you inquire about the credentials of any therapist you engage. Accreditation, certification and academic degrees vary according to professional fields and levels of counsel-ing service. While it is always best to get a proper referral from a physician or li-censed professional, you can contact with confidence one of the following organiza-

tions. Additional listings are in area phone books under headings such as "Alcohol & Drugs," "Alcoholism (or Drug Addiction) Information & Treatment Centers" or "Drug Abuse & Addiction."

Alcoholics Anonymous
5901 Wrightsville Ave., Wilmington
(910) 794-1840, (800) 711-6375

Bridge Builders Counseling Center
Arboretum Centre, 5919 Oleander Dr., Ste. 104, Wilmington
(910) 792-9888
www.bridgebuilderscounseling.com

Bridge Builders Counseling Center is an outcome-based therapy practice specializing in a wide range of therapies, including anger management, art therapy, DWI assessment services, chronic mental illness, and marriage and family counsel-ing. Bridge Builders' team of experienced counselors work with children, teens and adults using a compassionate approach that focuses on the individual client, not the problem or the solution. Therapy is

provided in a comfortable, supportive environment to help you realize your goals and bridge the gap from where you are to where you want to be. Conveniently located in the Arboretum Centre on Oleander Drive, Bridge Builders accepts most insurance plans.

Coastal Horizons Center
615 Shipyard Blvd., Wilmington
(910) 790-0187

Southeastern Center for Mental Health, Developmental Disabilities
2023 S. 17th St., Wilmington
(910) 332-6888, (800) 293-6440

Wilmington Treatment Center
2520 Troy Dr., Wilmington
(910) 762-2727

Alternative and Complementary Health Care

ACUPUNCTURE

Acupuncture Alternative
Oleander Oaks, 5725 Oleander Dr.
Ste. E-2, Wilmington
(910) 392-0870

Owner/therapist Karen Vaughn describes Acupuncture Alternative's services as combined therapies to treat physical, mental, emotional and spiritual levels. She incorporates classical Chinese acupuncture, herbal therapy formulas, auricular therapy, Qi Gong, and nutritional and lifestyle counseling. These elements are used to create a treatment plan as unique as the individual client. Sessions are by appointment only Monday through Saturday.

CHIROPRACTIC CARE

Atlantic Coast Chiropractic
6841-D Market St., Wilmington
(910) 798-0101

Atlantic Coast Chiropractic is a state-of-the-art chiropractic facility in Wilmington, dedicated to promoting the health and well being of their patients. Dr. Anthony Giacalone and his staff offer adjustments, corrective and rehabilitative exercises, physiotherapy modalities, nutritional counseling, and postural correction to keep you feeling your best.

Back in Motion Chiropractic
6303 Oleander Dr., Ste.102-A, Wilmington
(910) 313-1322

Back in Motion offers chiropractic care for the entire family. They accept and file more than 800 insurance plans and offer easy payment plans. They're open until 6 PM on Monday, Tuesday, Wednesday and Friday.

Sito Chiropractic
1904 Eastwood Rd., Ste. 103, Wilmington
(910) 256-2655
www.sitochiropractic.com

Why suffer through pain or mask it with prescriptions when you can choose chiropractic to alleviate your physical issues? Featuring three doctors to care for your back, neck and overall health issues, Sito Chiropractic could be the place where your pain ends and renewed vigor begins. The professionals at Sito Chiropractic focus on helping patients achieve their true health potential and peak performance level, all the while keeping each individual's needs in mind. With just a few simple tips for everyday living and expert adjustments of the spine, neck and other neuromuscular regions, you'll go from overloaded to overjoyed with the help of the personable staff at Sito Chiropractic.

MASSAGE THERAPY

The region has an abundance of practitioners of massage therapy for wellness, chronic pain, strain and injuries. Therapists offer various methods that range through Swedish, deep tissue, myofascial release, neuromuscular, craniosacral therapy, trigger point, foot reflexology, polarity, Shiatsu, acupressure, prenatal and sports. Some massage therapists work in their homes, others in offices or fitness clubs, and a few will be happy to come to your own home.

The City of Wilmington has an ordinance that requires licensed massage therapists to have a minimum of 500 hours of training at an accredited school. Therapists are also required to carry liability insurance, and the State of North Carolina now recognizes massage therapy as a licensed profession throughout the state. Miller-Motte Technical College, 5000 Market Street, Wilmington, (910) 254-0995, offers massage-student clinics that are open to the public.

Listed below is a sampling of the massage therapists available in Wilmington for your convenience. We do not endorse any practitioner. Check area phone books for more listings.

Ki Spa and Salon
The Forum, 1125-Q Military Cuttoff Rd., Wilmington
(910) 509-0410
www.kispasalon.com

Voted best massage in the *Star-News* Readers' Poll, the therapists at Ki Spa combine natural organic products, pure aromatherapy and healing techniques to promote total body renewal. Their spa services include facials, massages and wellness packages, as well as unique relaxing treatments like shirodhara, an ancient Ayurvedic therapy that uses warm herb-infused oil poured on the forehead to promote tranquility and mental clarity.

SCHOOLS AND CHILD CARE

Three public school systems serve Wilmington and the southeast coast: New Hanover County Schools, the largest system, which includes Wilmington; Brunswick County Schools to the south of New Hanover County; and Pender County Schools to the north of Wilmington. Additionally, the region offers a growing list of independent (private) schools, both secular and religion-based, that meet a broad range of educational needs. As home schooling has become increasingly popular, we have included some helpful information about state and local resources and requirements.

Unless they are home-schooled, school-age children moving into New Hanover County should be immediately enrolled in a public or independent (private) school. To enroll a child in the public schools, the parent or guardian must bring to the school a certified copy of the child's birth certificate along with the child's Social Security card, completed health assessment, immunization records and proof of residence. Children entering kindergarten must be 5 years old on or before August 31 of that year. Parents of students who were enrolled in a different school should bring the student's last report card and copies of standardized test reports to the new school.

Public Schools

Cape Fear Center for Inquiry
3131 B Randall Pkwy., Wilmington
(910) 362-0000

Cape Fear Center for Inquiry (CFCI) is a public K-8, innovative "school of choice" that does not discriminate in its admission procedures nor charge for enrollment. As a state-funded charter school, CFCI's mission is to promote students' abilities to think and create in personally meaningful ways through an inquiry-based, integrated curriculum in an encouraging, supportive environment. Experienced, licensed teachers strive to ensure that every child develops knowledge in the traditional content areas. Because CFCI considers the teacher/child relationship to be of paramount importance, class sizes are small. Teachers for the elementary grades (K-5) stay with their classes for two school years (looping), and students take Spanish, technology, PE, music and art. Grades 6 through 8 are ability- grouped for language arts and are assigned grade-level math, science and social studies classes. For all middle schoolers, PE and technology are required, and Spanish, band and art are elective classes. All student emphasis is on individualized instruction, utilizing each child's strengths. Parents attend a parent education meeting (beginning in January of every year) to receive an application. A lottery of all those children who applied is held in February. The school teaches the North Carolina Standard Course of Study, complies with the North Carolina ABC's Accountability Program requirements and administers all required state tests.

New Hanover County School System
6410 Carolina Beach Rd., Wilmington
(910) 763-5431

With numerous higher education options, it is only natural that the area has excellent preparatory education as well. New Hanover County Schools serves more than 24,000 pre-kindergarten through 12th grade students in 42 schools in the city of Wilmington and the county, including the beach communities of Figure Eight Island, Wrightsville Beach, Carolina Beach and Kure Beach. The county student population is approximately 36 percent minority enrollment.

Through the ABCs of Public Education, end-of-grade tests measure student achievement in reading and math for grades 3 through 8. High school students take end-of-course tests in 10 subjects. In school year 2008-09, New Hanover County Schools had five Honor Schools of Excellence, which means 90 percent or more of students at grade level met or exceeded growth and also met the federal standard of Adequate Yearly Progress under the No Child Left Behind act; 10 Schools of Distinction (80-89 percent of students at or above grade level, met or exceeded growth) and 12 Schools of Progress (60 - 79 percent of students at or above grade level, met or exceeded growth).

The district's SAT scores average 1039 for math and critical reading and 1530 for math, critical reading and writing combined. The national average for math and critical reading combined is 1016, and the national average for critical reading, math and writing is 1509. North Carolina's average for critical reading and math is 1006 and 1486 for critical reading, math and writing. New Hanover County Schools' average writing score of 491 is above the state's average at 480 and slightly below the national average at 493. Writing is one of the newer components of the SAT, therefore a five-year trend analysis is not yet available.

The system has had the benefit of tremendous support from the business community and community volunteers who contribute in many different ways, including tutoring, working to lower the dropout rate and offering opportunities for students to gain exposure to the corporate realm beyond the classroom. The Greater Wilmington Chamber of Commerce Education Foundation, a community education support organization, provides an estimated $10,000 annually to fund mini-grants to support classroom teachers. Other businesses in the area have shown tremendous support for the school system, including a large grant initiative with the GE Foundation and significant volunteer support from GE staff.

New Hanover County Schools' operating budget for the 2009–10 school year is approximately $211 million, with approximately 57 percent coming from the state, 34 percent from local monies, 9 percent from the federal government and 5 percent from other sources. Per-pupil expenditure is $8,739.

The district consists of elementary schools serving kindergarten through grade 5, middle schools serving grades 6 through 8, and high schools serving grades 9 through 12. New Hanover County Schools have three pre-kindergarten centers, which are a part of Governor Easley's More at Four Program. The school year runs from August until early June, although year-round schooling is now available at Codington Elementary and Eaton Elementary schools. After considerable investigation, the Board of Education found that the advantages of year-round schooling include increased learning, a reduction in stress levels for both students and teachers, greater opportunity for effective enrichment and remediation, and higher motivation.

New Hanover County Schools offer two early college high schools, Isaac Bear Early College High School in partnership with the University of North Carolina Wilmington and Wilmington Early College High School in partnership with Cape Fear Community College. While attending the early college high schools, students have the opportunity to gain college credit hours or work toward completing an associate's degree in art or science.

Three elementary magnet schools — Gregory School of Science, Mathematics and Technology; Rachel Freeman School of Engineering; and Snipes Academy of Art and Design — offer curriculum with specific areas of study integrated throughout all grade levels and subject areas.

There are four traditional high schools in New Hanover County, and seven middle schools that feed into these according to district lines. Mary S. Mosley Performance Learning Center is an academic alternative/school-of-choice for students in grades 10 through 12 who qualify for admittance. More than 250 courses are available to high school students, including social studies, mathematics, computer science, English, foreign languages and the full range of sciences. Students can participate in Army, Navy and Air Force JROTC Honor units as well as a broad range of extracurricular activities and programs. There are approximately 62 challenging, competency-based, Career Technical Education courses, including marine sciences and oceanography. A cultural arts curriculum includes band, orchestra, chorus, drama, art and dance. Middle schools offer a similar, though more limited, curriculum to that of the senior high schools.

Elementary schools emphasize hands-on experience in all disciplines. Elementary school students participate in a curriculum based on the use of manipulatives and inquiry to build a foundation that will support the learning of concepts in the middle grades and high school. A comprehensive program has been designed for exceptional children at all grade levels.

Basketball and football figure largely in interscholastic athletic programs. Other available sport programs are volleyball, baseball, soccer, wrestling, golf, tennis, lacrosse and track. What else would you expect from the sports-minded city that produced such athletes as Michael Jordan, Meadowlark Lemon and Roman Gabriel on its public school courts and fields?

Pender County School System
925 Penderlea Hwy., Burgaw
(910) 259-2187

Pender County Public Schools provide a first-class education for more than 8,000 students. Schools are located in both suburban and rural communities, and serve students in pre-kindergarten through grade 12. There are seven elementary schools, four middle schools, three high schools and one alternative learning center. Each school day 1,200 employees work together to provide an environment that capitalizes on all children's natural curiosity, nurtures their desire to learn, and respects their individual learning style. Pender County Schools' progressive leadership, dedicated professionals and commitment to excellence are consistently reflected in their high-test scores.

Pender County varies greatly from one side of the county to the other. While the western section remains largely rural, the coastal side of the county has experienced explosive growth, which has resulted in a 42 percent increase in population. To accommodate this growing population, the Pender County Board of Education built a new high school in Hampstead. The 224,727-square-foot Topsail High School, which opened in January 2009, accommodates 1,400 students. The facility includes two gymnasiums, a theater/auditorium wing, and a separate shop building for wood, metal and automotive classes. In an effort to reduce dropout rates, Topsail High School has implemented a Freshman Academy as part of the Small Learning Community initiative. Freshmen have core classes exclusively with other freshmen, and most teachers in the academy only teach freshmen. Renovations to turn the old high school building into a new building for Topsail Middle School will begin this year.

Pender County Schools has received a multi-year grant from the U.S. Department of Education for more than $5.7 million to implement programs that combat drugs, violence and other unhealthy behaviors among students. The Safe Schools, Healthy Students grant will assist the district's efforts to provide prevention and intervention services for students. Additionally, the grant will provide after-school programs for middle school students; drama, recreation, and arts programming; after-school transportation for program participants; mental health services; parent workshops; and Rural Entrepreneurship classes for high school students. Partner agencies include the Pender County Sheriff's Department, Communities in Schools of the Cape Fear, Dreams of Wilmington, Coastal Horizons and N.C. Department of Juvenile Justice.

The Roger Bacon Academy
Charter Day School
7055 Bacon's Way, Leland
(910) 655-1214

Serving the counties of Brunswick, New Hanover, Bladen, Columbus and Pender, Charter Day School offers a Direct Instruction curriculum that includes reading with phonics instruction as well as particular attention to penmanship, spelling, grammar and style. More than just the mechanics of education, CDS utilizes numerous classical sources in its mathematics, science, music and art classes. Students find themselves intellectually stimulated and well versed in the aesthetic and moral traditions of western civilization.

CDS received its charter in 2000, at that time enrolling 53 students in grades K through 2. In 2005 CDS was designated an Honor School of Excellence by the State Board of Education and is among the top 25 K through 8 schools in the state for exemplary academic growth. In the 2008-09 school year they served 747 students in grades K through 8. Charter Day School is a public, tuition-free charter school open to all North Carolina children. An independent Board of Trustees oversees the school's management by The Roger Bacon Academy. Each student is expected to embody the four classical qualities of prudence, justice, fortitude and temperance and to practice the virtues of faith, hope and charity. Members of the school community are accountable for ensuring their actions comply with these principles. As a result, CDS students develop the necessary skills to become valuable members of society and leaders in their communities.

Independent (Private) Schools

The southern coast region's private schools offer curricula and activities for children from preschool to high school. While tuition and expenses are the responsibility of the parent or guardian, most of these schools offer financial aid or easy-payment plans. In many cases, having more than one child in a particular school allows a discount on tuition for other children within the same family. All of the area's independent/private schools are not included here, but the following list suggests some alternatives to public education.

WILMINGTON

Cape Fear Academy
3900 S. College Rd., Wilmington
(910) 791-0287
www.capefearacademy.org

Cape Fear Academy is the most prominent secular private school in the region. Established in 1967, this coeducational day school is open to students interested in a traditional, challenging, college-preparatory education. The school places special emphasis on the development of tactical, higher-order thinking skills as well as organizational and study skills.

The academy's mission statement — "To be a learning community sharing a commitment to respect, integrity and academic excellence" — forms the framework for student life at the school as well as fostering a spirit of unity and high ideals. Close relationships with teachers are a hallmark of the academy.

There are approximately 650 students in pre-kindergarten through grade 12. Pre-kindergarten is a half-day program, with after-school care available. The Lower School comprises pre-kindergarten through grade 5. In addition to the traditional subjects, instruction by professional faculty includes art, music, science, foreign language (Spanish), drama, computer science and physical education. A new classroom has been designated as the Lower School "Think Lab," which allows groups of students to explore math and technology by creating robots, using GPS navigation systems, and using interactive computer applications.

The Middle and Upper schools emphasize a college-preparatory curriculum. Students are also involved in an array of extracurricular clubs as well as athletic programs and the performing arts. During the Middle School years, importance is placed on building positive peer relationships, particularly through outdoor-education opportunities that include rock climbing and ropes courses. Community service is a key component of the Middle and Upper school programs. The Upper School student government organization

has an entire branch devoted to community service. Group and individual activities are planned as students work to serve a minimum of 72 hours required for graduation.

One hundred percent of graduates attend four-year college programs, and more than 80 percent of those students are accepted into their first-choice college or university. The five-year average of reading and math SAT scores is 1190, which is about 200 points higher than local, state and national averages. Cape Fear Academy offers Advanced Placement courses in 11 areas and was recently recognized twice by the College Board for having the largest percentage of students who scored in the highest range for a school of their size in the world. A survey of recent alumni produced an extremely high ranking of their experience at Cape Fear Academy, especially related to academic quality and sense of community.

Present facilities include three classroom buildings, a gymnasium and a student activities center as well as a brand-new athletics complex with a synthetic turf field. The Primary Building contains pre-kindergarten and kindergarten classrooms as well as a multi-purpose commons and a teaching kitchen. The Beane Wright Student Center includes a dining hall, music and art classrooms, and a fitness/weight training area. An Upper School building, Cameron Hall, includes drama and media/technology spaces. Along with the Bruce B. Cameron gymnasium, there are three athletic fields (one of which is synthetic turf), six tennis courts and a Lower School playground.

To arrange for a tour, call the Admissions Office at (910) 791-0287 ext. 1015.

The Children's Schoolhouse - Montessori
612 S. College Rd., Wilmington
(910) 799-1531

Wilmington's oldest Montessori School with 25 years of academic excellence, The Children's Schoolhouse offers classes for youngsters ages 3 to 6 years old. A small, warm, home-like, nurturing environment fosters positive growth and development

SCHOOLS AND CHILD CARE

along with solid educational programming. Located within St. Matthew's Lutheran Church, the school includes a state-recognized kindergarten curriculum, high-quality instruction and lots of fun, too. Owner/Director Lucy Hieronymus oversees every facet of the school's operations as well as teaching kindergarten and working with her staff of well-trained, experienced professionals; every classroom has a certified Montessori Directress. Each child gets daily individualized instruction in math and reading mixed with a wide variety of educational activities that include such things as botany, music, art, geography, earth science, history and zoology. During the months of June and July, the school offers a half-day onsite Montessori Marine Science Camp where marine life, provided by Hieronymus Fishing Charter and Guide Service, is brought into the classrooms for the children to enjoy. Although everything the child does at the school is called "work," and reflects a level of responsibility, kids love it. Days and hours of attendance vary according to the child's age, level of development and parents' preferences. Generally, younger children attend from 9 AM to 1 PM; kindergartners may choose to stay until 2:30 PM. Children bring their own snacks and lunches.

Friends School of Wilmington
207 Pine Grove Dr., Wilmington
(910) 791-8221

Friends School of Wilmington is a warm, nurturing, educational community that prepares independent thinkers in the Quaker tradition for a global, knowledge-based future. Continuing a 300-year Quaker educational tradition of fostering intellectual and spiritual integrity while affirming the value of each individual, the school offers a well-rounded program and a developmentally appropriate curriculum. Challenging, relevant, hands-on learning activities, including frequent projects, field trips and personalized growth opportunities, create a dynamic setting for learning that helps students to develop an awareness of the interdependence of life that extends to the world at large and "empowers the next generation for global good." Permeating the entire approach to education is the school's basic philosophy

that young people who are convinced of their own value will, in turn, seek and speak to the good in others. Accordingly, individual differences are honored, cooperation is fostered, responsibility is expected, and personal standards of excellence are developed.

The school has two campuses spanning ages 18 months through 8th grade. Preschool is an established Montessori program, and the elementary school builds on this developmental approach to learning. The teacher-pupil ratio is quite low (1:12). A very active Parent/Teacher Organization and a high rate of family involvement help build community and keep tuition low. The pre/elementary school is located in a 6,000-square-foot building at 207 Pine Grove Drive next to Winter Park Elementary School's playground. Call (910) 791-8221 for admissions information. The middle school is located on a 5-acre campus at 350 Peiffer Avenue off Oleander Drive near Greenville Loop Road. Call (910) 792-1811 for admissions information.

Myrtle Grove Christian School
806 Piner Rd., Wilmington
(910) 392-2067

Biblical principles serve as a framework and spiritual foundation for all that is taught at Myrtle Grove Christian School. Academic excellence combined with strong moral values ensures a sound learning environment for more than 430 students in preschool through 8th grade. A ministry of Myrtle Grove Evangelical Presbyterian Church, the school offers a Christ-centered education that aims at a well-balanced development of mind, spirit and body. The school strives to equip each student with the knowledge necessary to develop a strong Christian character in order to meet the challenges of life and to serve Christ in the world.

An important component of Myrtle Grove Christian School's approach to education is cooperation with home and church. Parents take an active role by helping with school activities as well as assisting their child academically. Regular church attendance is encouraged, and more than 50 churches are represented in the student body.

Enrichment programs in the lower school include computer, art, music, library, Spanish and physical education. Upper school non-core classes are required in physical education and computer, while electives may be selected from drama, art, praise band and Science Olympiad. An extracurricular athletic program for students in grades 7 and 8 includes tennis, basketball, soccer, cheerleading, volleyball, and baseball.

Kindergarten through 8th grade students annually take the Stanford Achievement Test and consistently score in the top 20 to 25 percent in the nation in core subject areas. The school is fully accredited by the Southern Association of Colleges and Schools (SACS) and the Association of Christian Schools International (ACSI).

New Horizons Elementary School
3705 S. College Rd., Wilmington
(910) 392-5209

At New Horizons Elementary School, students in kindergarten through 5th grade learn in a highly creative, positive environment that provides ongoing opportunities for self development as well as academic growth. An unusual, home-like campus, small class size and a stimulating curriculum, coupled with a professional, friendly and nurturing staff, make this school an excellent choice. Founded in 1983 by a group of parents and three current faculty members to provide a quality educational alternative for area children, New Horizons Elementary School's educational program stresses reading, oral and written expression, mathematics, science and social studies. Instruction in critical thinking, problem solving and study skills is integrated throughout the various subject areas. The school's challenging, innovative curriculum is designed to help a child develop internal motivation, self-reliance and self-discipline. The curriculum includes P.E. daily and once-a-week Spanish class and choral music for all grades. In keeping with the school's philosophy and mission, active parental involvement is a required component. This includes monitoring a child's homework, projects, independent reading, returned class work and evaluations. Parents are expected to serve on committees, attend school events, help with fund-raising, chaperone field trips and even assist with building maintenance. Upon enrollment, each family becomes a voting member of New Horizons Elementary School, Inc., a non-profit organization. The governing body is a board of directors made up of parents and teachers. The professional staff oversees day-to-day operations as well as instructional, curricular and academic matters. For more information, contact the school office between the hours of 8:30 AM and 12:30 PM on Mondays, Wednesdays and Thursdays.

St. Mary Catholic School
217 S. Fourth St., Wilmington
(910) 762-5491 x40

Located downtown in the historic district, St. Mary Catholic School serves preschool through 8th grade. The school's mission is to "ensure learning for all our students within the framework of Catholic Christian values, to help our students grow in a manner consistent with their needs, interests and abilities, and to prepare them to live in a changing world as self-directing, caring, God-loving, responsible citizens."

St. Mary School offers a rich core curriculum, including language arts, literature, science, math, social studies, daily religion classes and weekly mass celebrations. Additional classes include physical education, Spanish, library/media and technology instruction. The fine arts program offers weekly art classes, chorus, band, creative music and Suzuki violin.

Middle school students can participate in team sports such as basketball, volleyball, soccer, lacrosse and tennis. Extracurricular activities include chess club, liturgical dance and Science Olympiad (grades 6-8). St. Mary Catholic School's graduates are prepared to enroll in the honors courses offered by area high schools. The school's emphasis is on preparing students to be independent learners who maintain high academic achievements and standards throughout their high school and college years. St. Mary Catholic School, established in 1869, is historically notable as the first Catholic school in North Carolina.

Wilmington Academy of Arts and Sciences
4126 S. College Rd., Wilmington
(910) 392-3139

The Wilmington Academy of Arts and Sciences (WAAS) offers a challenging curriculum with significant enrichment and individualized attention for academically motivated and gifted students in grades 4 through 8. Faculty members have high expectations for their students as they promote academic achievement, personal responsibility, social development and lifelong learning. A traditional core of subjects along with Spanish, music and art are taught at all grade levels. A variety of academic and athletic extra-curricular activities are offered. Weekly tours are available by appointment.

Wilmington Christian Academy
1401 N. College Rd., Wilmington
(910) 791-4248
www.wilmingtonchristian.com

Situated on a large campus at the beginning of I-40, Wilmington Christian Academy is the largest private school in southeastern North Carolina. Celebrating 40 years of success, WCA is a ministry of Grace Baptist Church and serves students in high school, middle school, elementary, kindergarten and preschool. The advanced curriculum is combined with conservative Christian values to produce students who will glorify God with their lives while successfully competing in today's world. Students receive a well-rounded educational experience including academics, athletics, the fine arts, social opportunities and spiritual instruction.

The elementary curriculum strongly emphasizes the basic skills of reading and math augmented with studies in Bible, English, spelling, science, history, handwriting and health. Students learn to read early through phonics-based reading instruction while hands-on learning projects and practice drills enhance math instruction at all grade levels. Elementary students are also taught art, music, physi-cal education, foreign language and library skills. Subject-integrated computer application training begins in kindergarten.

Middle school students enjoy a program designed to solidify and augment basic academic skills in an enjoyable environment that encourages group interaction while developing individual responsibility. Ongoing team competitions build a sense of unity, excitement and teamwork.

High school students may enroll in general, college preparatory or honors programs. Advanced placement and honors courses are available. Resource classes are available for students with mild learning disabilities. Comprehensive computer training is integrated with the academic curriculum through grade 12. Students may also take advantage of formal group training in art, drama, music (choral and instrumental) and journalism. Private instrumental and vocal lessons are also available. Various clubs and student organizations such as student council and honor society encourage student participation, leadership development and community service.

The academy's sports program includes intramural elementary leagues that lead to middle school, junior varsity and varsity team sports in soccer, basketball, baseball, golf, cross country, volleyball, tennis and cheerleading. WCA's teams compete with Christian, public and private schools.

Students score exceptionally well on national achievement tests, and graduates gain acceptance into major Christian, public and private universities across the United States. Students also enjoy the benefits of excellent facilities, including a 25-station computer lab, two well-equipped science labs, a media center, a gymnasium, a mobile laptop lab, a full-service cafeteria and several athletic fields and playgrounds. Parents have 24-hour web access to current grades and assignments. Affordable tuition with multiple-child discounts makes WCA an outstanding educational value. WCA is fully accredited by the North Car-

See this entire guide plus additional content online at insiderinfo.us

olina Christian School Association and the American Association of Christian Schools.

The Wilmington Preschool of Fine Arts
3834 Oleander Dr., Wilmington
(910) 794-9590

The Wilmington Preschool of Fine Arts, the preschool affiliated with the Wilmington School of Ballet and Creative Art Center, has three classrooms for children from 18 months old to 3 years old. Along with the basics of preschool education, including academics, physical education and library time, children receive instruction in art, music and movement.

Special Education

Child Development Center, Inc.
3802 Princess Place Dr., Wilmington
(910) 343-4245

The Child Development Center is a developmental preschool serving both typically developing and special needs children from 2 to 5 years old. The center has a long history of working with children who have developmental delays and disabilities. All children are served in small classes with a highly qualified staff. The center is a United Way partner agency. Operating hours are 7:30 AM to 5:30 PM weekdays. Call for information on enrollment and openings.

Easter Seals UCP
Wilmington Children's Center
500 Military Cutoff Rd., Wilmington
(910) 392-0080

Children from New Hanover and surrounding counties who have physical and/ or other developmental delays can be referred by a parent, physician or community agency to this inclusive preschool. The Easter Seals UCP Developmental Center is a licensed center and is accredited by NAEYC. The center serves children from birth to 5 years of age who have cerebral palsy, motor delays or other developmental concerns. They also accept students without special developmental needs because the agency believes it is beneficial to bring students with and without special needs together in a quality preschool program. Educators and therapists facilitate learning through play and promote development in areas such as gross and fine motor skills, speech and language, social, emotional, cognitive and independence skills. ESUCP also has an outreach program, ECHOES (Enhancing Childhood through Outreach & Educational Services) that serves children in New Hanover and the surrounding counties. They support inclusion of children with, or at risk of, special needs through consultation and technical assistance in community child care or preschool settings.

Child Care

A wide range of child-care facilities, preschools and programs is available in the southern coast area. We encourage parents/guardians to visit facilities they are considering at least once and preferably several times prior to enrolling their youngsters. After-school enrichment and youth development programs are offered by many day-care centers, schools, churches, the Wilmington Family YMCA and YWCA, the Wrightsville Beach Parks & Recreation Department, Girls Inc., Brigade Boys & Girls and other organizations. Check our chapters on Sports, Fitness and Parks and Kidstuff (Summer Camps section, in particular) for more day camp and summer camp information. Again, a visit or two in advance is advisable.

HIGHER EDUCATION AND RESEARCH

Southeastern North Carolina features some of the most outstanding universities and colleges in the state. Dating back to its beginnings, this area was famous not for its tourism but for its prosperous commercial industries. As a result, education and research have played a major role in helping the southern coast grow and expand to meet the needs of local businesses.

Now, as North Carolina's southern coast finds itself thrown in the limelight of popularity, more people are deciding to move here permanently, including many new and exciting industries. Research companies such as PPD, AAI Pharma, and Quintiles have made Wilmington their home, as have major corporations such as Corning and General Electric Company. Higher education, therefore, is working hard to meet the demands of booming industry.

The University of North Carolina at Wilmington focuses its academics to connect student learning across four broad themes: information technology, internationalization, natural environment and regional engagement, so students graduate with a sense of civic responsibility and leadership. Cape Fear Community College and Brunswick Community College have added new buildings to meet the needs of their expanding enrollment.

The research industry also is increasing in importance and size. Not surprisingly, the major emphases of the research performed in the area are in the fields of oceanography, wetland and estuarine studies, marine biomedical and environmental physiology, and marine biotechnology and aquaculture.

Universities and Colleges

Cape Fear Community College
411 N. Front St., Wilmington
(910) 362-7000
www.cfcc.edu

As one of North Carolina's largest and oldest community colleges, Cape Fear Community College (CFCC) provides a wide variety of educational services and job training for students of all ages. Dedicated to providing career training for local people for local jobs, CFCC is a major educational and economic development presence in the area and serves more than 27,000 citizens every year.

CFCC offers classes all over New Hanover and Pender counties. The Wilmington Campus is located in downtown Wilmington and houses health care programs, college transfer and the college's unique Marine Technology department. The North Campus, located on in Castle Hayne, is home to more than a dozen technical, engineering and business programs. The North Campus is also home to a new state-of-the-art safety training center for fire fighters, law enforcement and rescue personnel. CFCC's award-winning cosmetology department relocated to the North Campus in August 2009. A Pender County satellite center is located in Burgaw, about

Adults can continue their education or just have fun by taking courses or attending programs offered by UNCW's Division for Public Service and Continuing Studies. Call for information and request a copy of Pathways, their Lifelong Learning Catalog, (910) 962-4034.

21 miles north of Wilmington, (910) 259-4966. Classes are also held at area schools and community centers. Most recently, CFCC began offering classes at the Surf City Community Center.

The college also offers an increasing number of online and hybrid classes which can be accessed online. CFCC offers more than 60 programs in technical and skilled trades, along with a very popular college transfer program. The college's two-year Associate in Applied Science (A.A.S.) degrees include: accounting, architectural technology, associate degree nursing, automotive systems technology, business administration, chemical technology, computer engineering technology, criminal justice technology, dental hygiene, e-commerce, early childhood associate, electrical/electronics technology (instrumental concentration), environmental science technology, heavy equipment and transport technology (marine systems concentration), hotel and restaurant management, information systems, interior design, landscape gardening, machining technology, marine technology, mechanical engineering technology, mechanical engineering technology (drafting and design concentration), network administration and support occupational therapy assistant, office systems technology, paralegal technology, radiography and surgical technology. Construction management technology and medical office administration began in the fall of 2009.

One-year diploma programs include: air conditioning, heating and refrigeration technology, auto-body repair, boat building, carpentry, cosmetology, dental assisting, early childhood associate, electrical/electronics technology (marine systems concentration), film/video production, industrial maintenance technology, marine propulsion systems, masonry, medical transcription, pharmacy technology, practical nursing and welding technology.

Twenty-two certificate programs range from six weeks to two semesters. They include many of the same areas as the diploma and degree-granting programs, but training is less comprehensive and of shorter duration. Some others are truck driver training, manicuring/nail technology, real estate and real estate appraisal, customer service and licensed practical nurse refresher.

As part of its continuing education program, CFCC offers hundreds of non-credit computer classes, re-certification classes and enrichment courses for life-long learners. CFCC also provides customized workforce training programs for local companies and organizations that are expanding or moving to the area. CFCC's Small Business Center offers dozens of free courses and counseling services for new and existing businesses throughout the year. Through the Gateway Program, CFCC offers college classes to high school students so that they can earn college credit while still in high school. CFCC is home to Early College High School for Pender County and the Wilmington Early College High School in New Hanover County. The college also offers free courses in high-school equivalency (GED), English as a Second Language (ESL) and adult literacy. Many other special programs and seminars are free or very reasonably priced. CFCC's Marine Technology program is the only one of its kind on the East Coast. The college maintains small and large ocean-going vessels for the program, which is enhanced by a deep-water pier on the Cape Fear River at the Wilmington campus. One of these vessels was integral to the recovery of artifacts from the wreck of what is believed to be Blackbeard's flagship, Queen Anne's Revenge.

The college has a growing number of intercollegiate sports teams in men's basketball, men's soccer, golf, women's soccer and women's volleyball. Day and evening classes in semester-long cycles are available at all campuses, and financial aid is available for eligible applicants.

Cape Fear Community College is one of 58 colleges in the North Carolina Community College System and is accredited by the Commission on Colleges of the Southern Association of Colleges and Schools. The public is always welcome to visit the campus to see all that CFCC has to offer.

University of North Carolina Wilmington
601 S. College Rd., Wilmington
(910) 962-3000

From its establishment as Wilmington College in 1947 with 238 students to its 2009 enrollment of nearly 13,000, the University of North Carolina Wilmington has transformed the lives of its students over the past 60 years and has had a major impact on the community it serves.

Consistently recognized by several publications as a top public undergraduate institution, the university continues to soar to even greater heights. In the 2010 edition of "America's Best Colleges" published by U.S.News & World Report, UNCW was ranked the sixth best public regional university in the South. This is the 12th consecutive year UNCW was ranked in the top 10. Among the 121 public and private universities in the South that provide a full range of undergraduate and master's level programs, UNCW maintained its overall ranking of 12th.

UNCW was named among the 2010 "Best in the Southeast" by The Princeton Review, making this the sixth consecutive year the university has been honored with this designation. Colleges were selected based upon student responses to a survey about their respective schools' academics, administration, campus life and student body.

UNCW has received notice from many other top guides to the nation's universities. The prestigious Fiske Guide to Colleges featured UNCW in its 2010 edition. Kiplinger's 2008-09 rankings include it as one of the top five "Best Values" among public universities in the state. UNCW is also one of only four North Carolina public universities included in Peterson's Competitive Colleges 2008: Top Colleges for Top Students. UNCW also ranked among the top 15 percent of colleges, universities and trade schools recognized by G.I. Jobs as "Military Friendly Schools." Southeastern North Carolina has a large and growing military community and the university has made numerous changes to its admissions and advising processes to better assist its military-affiliated students, which include active duty, veterans and dependents of active duty.

The 2009 freshman class has the highest average SAT score (1168) in the university's history, among the highest in the UNC system. The average high school GPA for the class was 3.78.

The university is made up of the College of Arts and Sciences, the Cameron School of Business, the School of Nursing, the Watson School of Education and the Graduate School. It offers bachelor's degrees in 52 majors, 35 master's degrees, a Ph.D. in marine biology and an Ed.D. in educational leadership.

Enrollment for 2009-10 included nearly 11,600 undergraduates and 1,300 graduate students. Estimated cost of attending UNCW for 2009-10 for in-state students living on campus was $15,844 and $26,726 for out-of-state students.

UNCW's strength in the natural sciences, especially biological sciences, chemistry and other disciplines, form the core of its internationally respected niche in the marine sciences. In the area of arts and literature, UNCW's highest profile programs are in film studies and creative writing. The Department of Film Studies has evolved from a few film-related courses in various departments to the fourth-largest major on campus. The Master of Fine Arts in creative writing has become one of the most respected on the East Coast.

Degree programs in the School of Nursing, Watson School of Education and Cameron School of Business are designed specifically to meet professional workforce needs in the region.

UNCW's Randall Library contains more than 960,000 volumes, subscribes to approximately 25,000 periodicals and has 22,000 videos/DVDs, 27,000 e-books and 53,000 audio titles. The library is a selective depository for U.S. government publications and is a full depository for North Carolina documents, which are available to all users. Adult North Carolina residents (older than 18 and out of high school) may purchase a borrower's card, valid for one year, for $15 upon presentation of a valid North Carolina driver's license or military ID. The fee is waived for citizens age 65 years and older. Non-students may obtain checkout privileges for up to four items per visit.

The university has taken a leadership role in the long-term economic, environmental, educational, social and cultural health of southeastern North Carolina. Through the Professional Development System in the Watson School of Education, faculty work closely with nearly 117 area schools and agencies to improve the quality of public education in the region.

The School of Nursing has developed collaborative partnerships with area healthcare providers to improve community health-care services. As Southeastern North Carolina's population expands, the university has taken a lead in providing training and support for the region's health care community. UNCW's School of Nursing has graduated more than 1,500 alumni, the majority of which work in the region. In August 2010 the university will open a state-of-the-art, $30 million home for the School of Nursing.

UNCW's Swain Center for Business and Economics Services, the business research and extension division of the Cameron School of Business, maintains a database to monitor and analyze business and economic trends and conditions in the region. The Small Business and Technology Development Center provides counseling services and training events to area businesses. The Division for Public Service and Continuing Studies carries out the university's strong commitment to adult learners by offering short, non-credit university courses, seminars, lectures, travel excursions and other educational opportunities through the Osher Lifelong Learning Institute. The Adult Scholars Leadership Program provides students with an up-to-date snapshot of the political, economic, educational, law enforcement, historical and cultural forces that drive southeastern North Carolina. Participants identify and respond to critical issues, invest their organizational and entrepreneurial talents to solve problems and volunteer in the community.

Based at the UNCW Center for Marine Science at Myrtle Grove, MarineQuest is a popular youth program that offers marine and environmental education through the

Summer Science-by-the-Sea Day Camp, Coast Trek and OceanLab. It also offers the Odyssey Program for adults. The UNCW Executive Development Center at the New Hanover County Northeast Regional Library offers corporate and community groups a state-of-the-art facility for professional meetings, retreats and small conferences. The center is designed to accommodate groups of various sizes and needs and offers high-speed wireless Internet, video conferencing, an on-site technician, a convenient location and ample parking.

The UNCW Seahawks compete in the Colonial Athletic Association as an NCAA Division I program, fielding 19 varsity teams. In 2009, UNCW's student-athletes captured three CAA championships: men's track and field, men's swimming and diving and men's tennis. Overall the student-athletes have consistently posted one of the highest average GPAs in the UNC system and have the second highest graduation rate in the CAA.

For general university information, call (910) 962-3000. For information on undergraduate admissions call (910) 962-3243; for graduate studies call (910) 962-3135. For information on lifelong learning programs call (910) 962-3195. Contact Randall Library at (910) 962-3760.

Research Facilities

North Carolina National Estuarine Research Reserve
UNCW Center for Marine Science, 5600 Marvin K. Moss Ln., Wilmington
(910) 962-2470

The U.S. Congress created the National Estuarine Research Reserve (NERR) system in 1972 to preserve undisturbed estuarine systems for research into and education about the impact of human activity on barrier beaches, adjacent estuaries and ocean waters. The reserves are outdoor classrooms and laboratories for researchers, students, naturalists and others.

Masonboro Island and Zeke's Island are the southeastern North Carolina components of NCNERR. In the northeast of the state, NCNERR manages the Rachel

Carson Reserve near Beaufort and Currituck Banks. A partnership between the University of North Carolina Wilmington and the N.C. Division of Coastal Management, NCNERR has its headquarters at the UNCW Center for Marine Science Center.

The NCNERR program manages four estuarine reserve sites as natural laboratories, coordinating research and education activities at these sites. Nationally threatened loggerhead sea turtles make their nests at Zeke's Island, Rachel Carson and Masonboro Island. Brown pelicans and ospreys are common to all four points. With more than 5,000 protected acres, Masonboro Island is the last and largest undisturbed barrier island remaining on the southern North Carolina coast and one of the most productive estuarine systems along the coast.

The Zeke's Island component of the reserve consists of three islands — Zeke's, North Island and No-Name Island — that lie immediately south of Fort Fisher and include nearly 2,000 acres. Along with the islands, the Zeke's Island component includes the Basin, a body of water enclosed by the breakwater known locally as the Rocks. NCNERR allows traditional activities, such as fishing and hunting, to continue within regulations on Zeke's and Masonboro Island. (For further information about these islands, see our sections on Attractions; Camping; and Sports, Fitness and Parks.)

The NCNERR sites are also managed as part of the North Carolina Coastal Reserve (NCCR) system. Containing 10 sites in all, the NCCR serves as the state counterpart to the federal NERR system. In our area, two sites are of particular interest. The first of these is Bald Head Woods on Bald Head Island. This site is the best example of an intact maritime forest in the southeastern part of the state. A globally imperiled ecosystem, the maritime forest serves to stabilize barrier islands and provides habitat for coastal species. The other NCCR site of local interest is Bird Island, located just south of Sunset Beach. While many of the barrier islands along the N.C. coast are experiencing beach erosion, Bird Island is one of the few on which the beach is actually growing larger. As such, visitors can observe the stages of succession in coastal ecosystems as the dunes grow and the beach extends seaward. Both sites are free and open to the public during daylight hours.

North Carolina State Horticultural Crops Research Station
3800 Castle Hayne Rd., Castle Hayne
(910) 675-2314

One field of research important to the region is horticulture. The North Carolina Department of Agriculture and North Carolina State University run 18 horticultural research stations around the state. The station in Castle Hayne is the primary local research site. Its varied, ongoing programs concentrate on crops of local economic importance, such as blueberries, strawberries, grapes, ornamentals and cucurbits. Variety trials, breeding, insect and disease control, and herbicide tests are among the studies performed. The station works in limited association with the New Hanover County Extension Service Arboretum, especially regarding soil studies, but primarily serves local horticulturists by making useful publications available to them through the N.C. Cooperative Extension Service.

UNCW Center for Marine Science
5600 Marvin K. Moss Ln., Wilmington
(910) 962-2301

The Center for Marine Science (CMS) at the University of North Carolina Wilmington provides an environment that fosters a multidisciplinary approach to questions in basic and applied research in the fields of oceanography, coastal and wetland studies, marine biomedical and environmental physiology, and marine biotechnology and aquaculture.

Faculty members conducting marine science research in the departments of biology and marine biology, chemistry and biochemistry, geography and geology, and physics and physical oceanography participate in this program. They serve on regional, national and international research and policy advisory groups, thereby contributing to the development of agendas on marine research in the United States and the world. International interactions with labs in Europe, North and South America, Australia, New Zealand, Asia, Africa, Bermuda, the Bahamas and Caribbean and all regions of the coastal United States augment extensive programs addressing North Carolina coastal issues. By integrating these advisory functions with research programs of the highest quality, CMS enhances the educational experience provided by UNCW for both undergraduate and graduate students in marine science.

Located on the Atlantic Intracoastal Waterway just six miles from the main campus, the 100,000-square-foot Center for Marine Science provides easy access to regional marine environments such as tidal marshes/mud flats/sand flats, tidal creeks, barrier islands and tidal inlets, the waterway, near-shore forests and both highly developed and minimally developed estuarine environments. It has a 900-foot pier on the waterway, which can accommodate several coastal research vessels, and maintains specialized equipment for underwater research and 19 research vessels ranging in size from 16 to 70 feet. The facility includes a 150-seat teaching auditorium, fully equipped research laboratories, classrooms, marine science laboratories, a greenhouse with running seawater, a radioisotope lab, computer workrooms, cold rooms, walk-in freezers and temperature-controlled rooms.

Through a $15 million matching grant from the federal government, CMS will construct a marine biotechnology research center in North Carolina. The facility will house the state's marine biotechnology program, creating a center that will focus on one of the latest and most promising areas of biotechnology.

UNCW has broken ground on the new oyster hatchery at CMS. This project, a partnership with the North Carolina Department of Environment and Natural Resources Aquarium Division, will help UNCW continue significant research into the best ways to rebuild the state's oyster population. The project will provide cultural, economic and environmental benefits to the region. A staple of the region's cuisine, oysters provide jobs through the seafood industry and play a huge role in filtering waste from the ocean.

CMS also is a partner in a new cooperative institute funded by a $22.5 million grant from the National Oceanic and Atmospheric Administration. The institute's mission focuses on three areas: development of advanced underwater technologies, exploration and research of frontier regions of the eastern continental shelf and beyond, and improved understanding of deep and shallow coral ecosystems. The center serves as host for the NOAA–sponsored National Undersea Research Center, the Coastal Ocean Research and Monitoring Program, an extension office for N.C. Sea Grant, the Marine Mammal Stranding Network, the N.C. National Estuarine Research Reserve, the Harmful Algal Bloom Laboratories for Analytical Biotechnology and UNCW's MarineQuest Program, an extensive community outreach program for public schools and adult education.

The Bluefish Society supports the center's public outreach efforts, helping to defray operating costs for the popular Planet Ocean Seminar Series and other community enrichment programs. An individual membership is $75 per year; membership for a couple is $150; family membership is $200 per year. Contributors have the opportunity to interact with world-renowned scientists, high-level government officials and other environmental experts featured at Planet Ocean Seminars. They also receive invitations to selected special events at the center, discounts on Odyssey programs and a Bluefish Society lapel pin.

MEDIA

A wealth of print and broadcast media sources keep Wilmington and the surrounding coastal communities well-informed on topics of national, international and local importance. The region's large and well-established business, arts, education and film communities create a talented pool of writers, performers and media professionals. In terms of staying power, the area's dominant newspapers, magazines, radio and television stations are stable sources of information. In the print medium, visitors will also notice an abundance of tourist-oriented publications in street racks. We haven't listed all of them here, but they are generally handy guides to the area's attractions. Some of these periodicals have been around for years, while others seem to drift in one day and out the next. There's a robust business in publications on real estate; in fact, these magazines and booklets are so pervasive you can hardly go anywhere without encountering them.

Choices for radio listening are eclectic, ranging across talk, country music, religious, urban contemporary, Top 40 and the diverse offerings of the city's own National Public Radio affiliate. Television is a somewhat limited medium without cable or satellite services, in which case a whole spectrum of channels becomes available. Public Television, broadcast from Jacksonville by way of Chapel Hill, has a strong signal.

The media resources listed in this chapter have settled into their own niches on what seems to be a permanent basis as a result of their thoroughness of coverage, accuracy, reliability and professionalism. In an ever-changing and expanding industry, these information/entertainment outlets have proved their stamina over time.

Newspapers and Journals

Brunswick Beacon
208 Smith Ave., Shallotte
(910) 754-6890

A weekly community newspaper published on Thursdays, the *Brunswick Beacon* has won dozens of awards during the past decade for advertising and editorial content. It covers and is distributed to all of Brunswick County, with particular emphasis on the southwestern portion of the coast. The Beacon is available through subscription, retail outlets and news racks throughout Brunswick County.

Greater Diversity News
272 N. Front St., Ste. 406, Wilmington
(910) 762-1337, (800) 462-0738

Greater Diversity News is a state-wide diversity-focused publication based in Wilmington, with additional distribution throughout North Carolina. Published weekly on Thursdays, it is a subscription-based periodical and can be purchased at certain news racks.

Greater Wilmington Business Journal
130 N. Front St., Ste. 105, Wilmington
(910) 343-8600

Greater Wilmington Business Journal is the region's best source for local business news and information in New Hanover, Brunswick and Pender counties. Regular areas of coverage include commercial and residential real estate, healthcare, technology, retail, restaurants, banking, hospitality and the local film industry as well as profiles of business leaders and up-and-coming entrepreneurs. The newspaper is published every other Friday and offers free daily e-mail updates.

The Island Gazette
1003 Bennet Ln., Ste. F, Carolina Beach
(910) 458-8156

Published weekly on Wednesdays since 1978, The Island Gazette is a well-established source of local news, sports, features and real estate in southern New Hanover County, with an emphasis on Carolina Beach and Pleasure Island. Copies are available in news racks throughout New Hanover County or by subscription.

Lumina News -
Wrightsville's Weekly Newspaper
Lumina Station II,
1904 Eastwood Rd., Ste. 205,
Wrightsville Beach
(910) 256-6569

Published weekly every Thursday, *Lumina News* reports the news and features the lifestyle of the greater Wrightsville Beach area including Landfall. This award-winning community paper carries everything of interest from government news and school events to sports and fishing. Each issue is information-packed. Available by paid subscription, by purchase at the newsstand and free online at www.luminanews.com.

StarNews
1003 S. 17th St., Wilmington
(910) 343-2000
www.starnewsonline.com

The *StarNews* is the only major daily newspaper along the southern coastal region of North Carolina. Established on September 23, 1867, it is the oldest daily newspaper in continuous publication in North Carolina. Owned by The New York Times, the StarNews covers national, international, state and local news. Most stories may be found first at StarNewsOnline.com. Regular in-print features cover regional politics, community events, arts, sports, weather, real estate, the local film industry, business news and more. Blogs, forums, photo and video communities may be found at StarNewsOnline.com.

Supplements to the daily newspaper include "*Real Estate Showcase*," published every three weeks; "*Health & Medical*," published bi-monthly; and periodic special sections on a range of topics from commercial real estate to hurricane preparedness to a holiday gift guide. Most special sections have an online component as well. The annual Living Here section contains a wealth of intriguing facts, figures and community data of special interest to visitors and newcomers. In addition, the *StarNews* publishes *Wilmington Magazine*, a publication that covers local people and lifestyles in greater depth.

Newspaper subscribers have the option to receive all editions, weekends and holidays or just the Saturday and Sunday editions. Home delivery is available, and the newspaper may be found in news racks and stores throughout New Hanover, Pender and Brunswick counties.

The State Port Pilot
114 E. Moore St., Southport
(910) 457-4568

Covering eastern Brunswick County in the Southport-Oak Island sphere, including Bald Head Island, Boiling Spring Lakes, St. James and Caswell Beach, this award-winning newspaper features regional and community news, special event coverage, local sports, feature articles and more. *The Pilot* is available by subscription in both print and electronic editions or in news racks throughout its coverage area every Wednesday.

Topsail Advertiser
206-A S. Topsail Dr., Surf City
(910) 328-3033

This weekly community newspaper covers all of the island news, local school sports, special events and happenings in the Topsail area. The *Advertiser* is published on Thursdays and is free and available in most area shops.

The Topsail Voice
Hampstead
(910) 270-2944

This weekly newspaper covers Topsail Island and Pender County news, including school sports and special events. *The Topsail Voice* is available by home delivery and it can also be found in news racks throughout the area.

The Wilmington Journal
412 S. Seventh St., Wilmington
(910) 762-5502

Founded in 1927 as *The Cape Fear Journal*, this weekly began as the offspring of R. S. Jervay Printers, founded in 1901, and describes itself as the voice and mirror of the African-American community in New Hanover, Brunswick, Pender, Onslow and Columbus counties. The name changed to The Wilmington Journal in the 1940s. It is available each Thursday at news racks throughout the city or by subscription.

Magazines

The Beat - Wilmington's Music Magazine
616 Silver Grass Ct., Wilmington
(910) 793-3668

The Beat Magazine is Wilmington's only monthly magazine that focuses on the area's unique music, film and theater scene. This publication offers in-depth feature stories, interviews, historical footnotes and stories that capture the spirit, fun and personality of the Cape Fear area. The Beat Magazine is a free publication and can be picked up at many locations throughout New Hanover, Pender and Brunswick counties.

Encore Magazine
210 Old Dairy Rd., Ste. A-2, Wilmington
(910) 791-0688

Hailed as Wilmington's alternative voice for more than 20 years, encore is the prime alternative weekly of the Port City. Featuring everything regarding area arts and entertainment, political commentary and cartoons, fiction writing and an extensive calendar of events, the magazine hails a staff of local writers, with the exception of syndicated columnist Chuck Shepherd, whose "News of the Weird" is only one of many reasons folks reach for the paper every Wednesday. Locals look to encore for the most creative writings on what's happening in dining, theater, music and film. Distributed in racks from Wilmington to Wrightsville Beach, Pleasure Island to Southport, encore always keeps its readers active and culturally engaged.

Focus on the Coast Communications, Inc.
6406 Shinnwood Rd., Wilmington
(910) 799-1638

Focus on Communication, Inc. is a multi-media marketing business that publishes Focus on the Coast magazine and Health Mattersprovider referral directory. Focus on Communication also coordinates the popular "original Wilmington" Girls' Nite Out events, which offer marketing and networking opportunities to local businesses in front of more than 300 women. Focus on the Coastmagazine provides local insight on where to dine, where to shop and where to play at the coast. This upscale, full-color, digest-size magazine is a connection to the arts, entertainment, fashion, dining and culture and contains features, columns, reviews and profiles on people and places in the Cape Fear region. It also serves as a resource with its Shops & Services Listings, Dining Out Guide and Gallery Guide. You can pick up a complimentary copy in more than 400 area locations including Port City Java coffee shops and Harris Teeter. Subscriptions are available.

KIDZink Magazine
Wilmington
(910) 791-0688

A publication about kids, by kids and for kids and their families, KIDZink is a free monthly magazine featuring spotlights on outstanding local kids, community organizations, teachers and schools, as well as showcasing kid-oriented events and happenings that make for ideal outings for the whole family. Artwork and writings abound in the magazine, as local students show off their creativity and imaginations. The magazine always accepts and encourages submissions from the public. Games, puzzles and community news keep readers actively informed on all fronts. Parents, children, educators and regular folks who remember how much fun it was to get covered in mud and take midday naps will have a blast with KIDZink.

Reel Carolina: Journal of Film and Video
301 Beacon Falls Ct., Cary
(910) 233-2926

This bi-monthly magazine is unquestionably the best source of information

about movie making in the Carolinas. "Production Notes," "EUE Screen Gems Studios Clips" and "News & Notes" are regular columns packed with information about what's going on in the area. To get the scoop on film-related groups, meetings, classes, workshops and websites, turn to "Lagniappe," which also has a section on film festival news. Other features include business profiles, reports from regional production facilities, celebrity interviews and film-production feature articles, plus a wide range of industry-related ads. Reel Carolina is available by subscription or free in racks across both Carolinas.

Wilma: Wilmington's magazine for women
130 N. Front St., Ste. 105, Wilmington
(910) 343-8600

Wilma is a monthly magazine devoted to women in Wilmington. The publication includes regular features on staying healthy, building careers, the latest styles, living green, volunteering, finding balance, things to do and much more. Wilma is distributed for free throughout the greater Wilmington area and is available online. The magazine also hosts quarterly Wilma Nights events.

Radio Stations

ADULT ALTERNATIVE
WUIN 106.7 FM

COUNTRY
WWQQ 101.3 FM (contemporary)

NATIONAL PUBLIC RADIO
WHQR 91.3 FM (classical, jazz, blues, news, Radio Latino, National Public Radio and Public Radio International) www.whqr. org

NEWS, TALK, SPORTS
WAAV 980 AM
WMFD 630 AM (ESPN radio)
WLTT 93.7 and 106.3 FM

SURF

WSFM 98.3 FM

WGNI 102.7 FM (classic and current)

WLGD 98.7 FM (Hispanic)

ROCK, CLASSIC ROCK AND OLDIES

WFXZ 103.7 FM

WKXB 99.9 FM (classic rock)

WILT 104.5 FM (classic/ contemporary rock)

WODR 105.3 FM (beach music and oldies)

URBAN CONTEMPORARY

WMNX 97.3 FM (hip hop)

Television Stations

WECT-TV 6
322 Shipyard Blvd., Wilmington
(910) 791-8070

NBC–affiliated WECT is the number one television station in southeastern North Carolina and was the first in the area to broadcast its local news in high definition. WECT is the "go-to" station for severe weather coverage and alerts.

UNC-TV 39, PBS
Research Triangle Park, Raleigh
(800) 906-5050

Life-changing public television programming from PBS and other national sources, and a host of award-winning local programs, is yours on UNC-TV, North Carolina's statewide public television network. Fans of the BBC will find delightful offerings in drama, news and comedy. Southeastern North Carolinians enthusiastically support UNC-TV during on-air pledge drives and with online contributions. In addition to UNC-TV, now availble in high definition, enjoy sister channels UNC-KD, a full-time children's channel, and, as of November 1, 2009, UNC-EX, the Explorer Channel.

WILM-TV 10, CBS
3333-G Wrightsville Ave., Wilmington
(910) 798-0000

CBS 10 WILM is Wilmington's only CBS affiliate, broadcasting in HD over the air on digital channel 10.1, and through every major cable provider (Time Warner, ATMC and Charter) and in SD over satellite services. With news coverage from the state capital by sister station WRAL in Raleigh, WILM offers an extensive selection of regional and state news. WILM also produces BYLINE: Wilmington, a local current affairs program that airs on Sunday mornings.

WSFX 26 Fox TV
322 Shipyard Blvd., Wilmington
(910) 791-8070

This station's strength is its Fox affiliation and syndicated entertainment programming. WSFX FOX 26 features broadcast television's only local prime time television newscast in the market; Fox 26 News at Ten.

WWAY-TV3, ABC
615 N. Front St., Wilmington
(910) 762-8581

ABC–affiliated WWAY NewsChannel 3 is another of Wilmington's major television stations broadcasting throughout the southeastern coastal region. WWAY offers full national and regional news and complete meteorological forecasts.

INDEX

INDEX

INDEX

Z